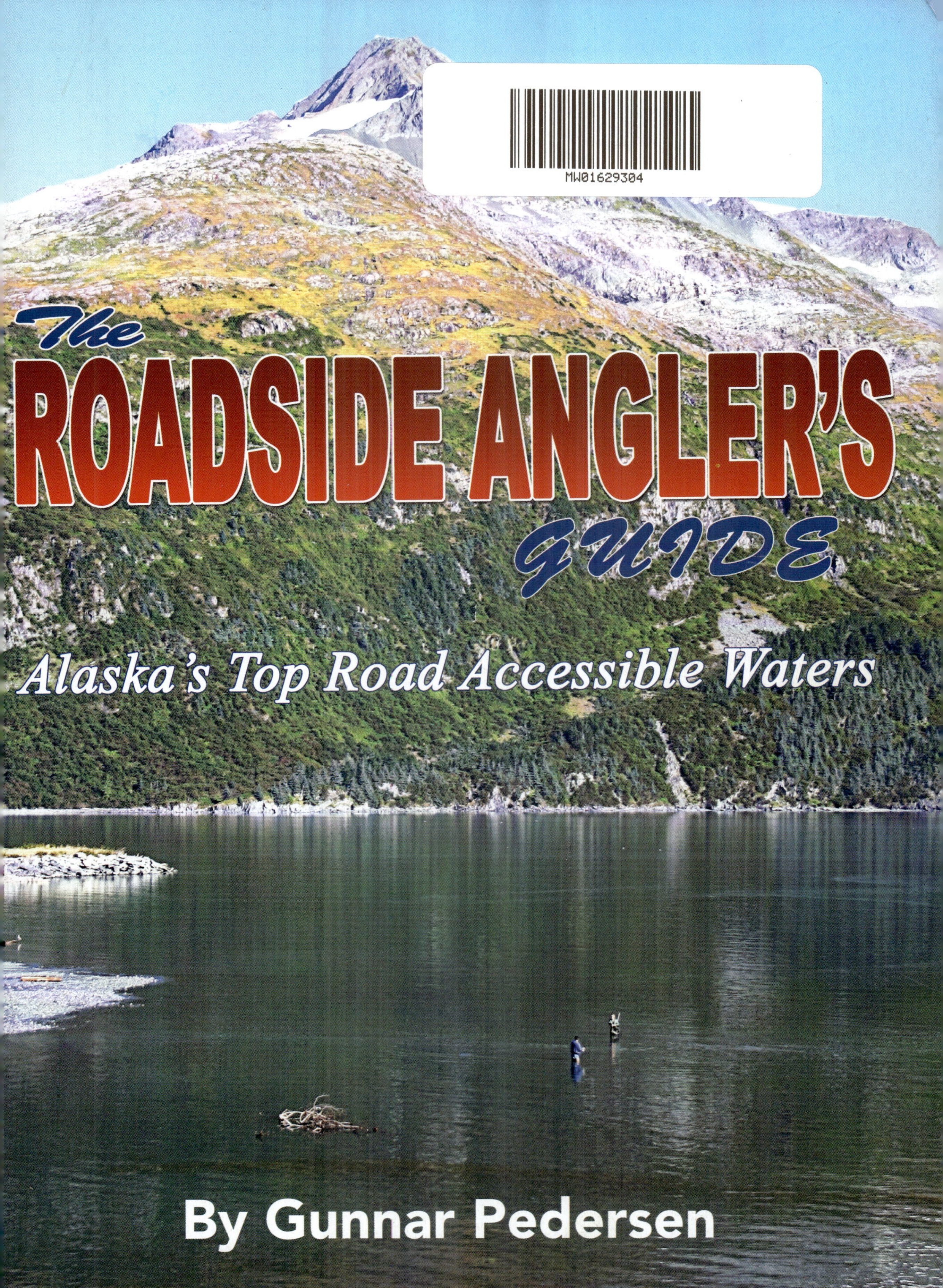
MW01629304
The
ROADSIDE ANGLER'S
GUIDE
Alaska's Top Road Accessible Waters
By Gunnar Pedersen

**The Roadside Angler's Guide**
P. O. Box 90557, Anchorage, AK 99509
www.roadsideanglersguide.com
(907).334.1984

Gunnar Pedersen
Editor/Publisher
editor@roadsideanglersguide.com

Kelsey Gray
Graphics Designer
graphics@roadsideanglersguide.com

**Contributing Photographers**
If interested in contributing photos/images, contact The Roadside Angler's Guide for information:
editor@roadsideanglersguide.com

**Advertising**
For inquires regarding advertising, contact The Roadside Angler's Guide for rates, deadlines, and specifications:
advertising@roadsideanglersguide.com

**Sales**
To purchase copies for retail sale, contact The Roadside Angler's Guide for prices, discounts, and delivery:
sales@roadsideanglersguide.com

**Letters**
The Roadside Angler's Guide welcomes letters to the editor. Please send all correspondence to:
editor@roadsideanglersguide.com

ISBN: 978-0-615-93277-4

Printed in China

# Table of Contents

## Contents Overview

## Fishing Alaska's Road System

## Alaska's Roadside Game Fish

# Contents (continued)

## Alaska's Roadside Destinations

# Contents (continued)

## Appendix & Index

# Fishing the Road System

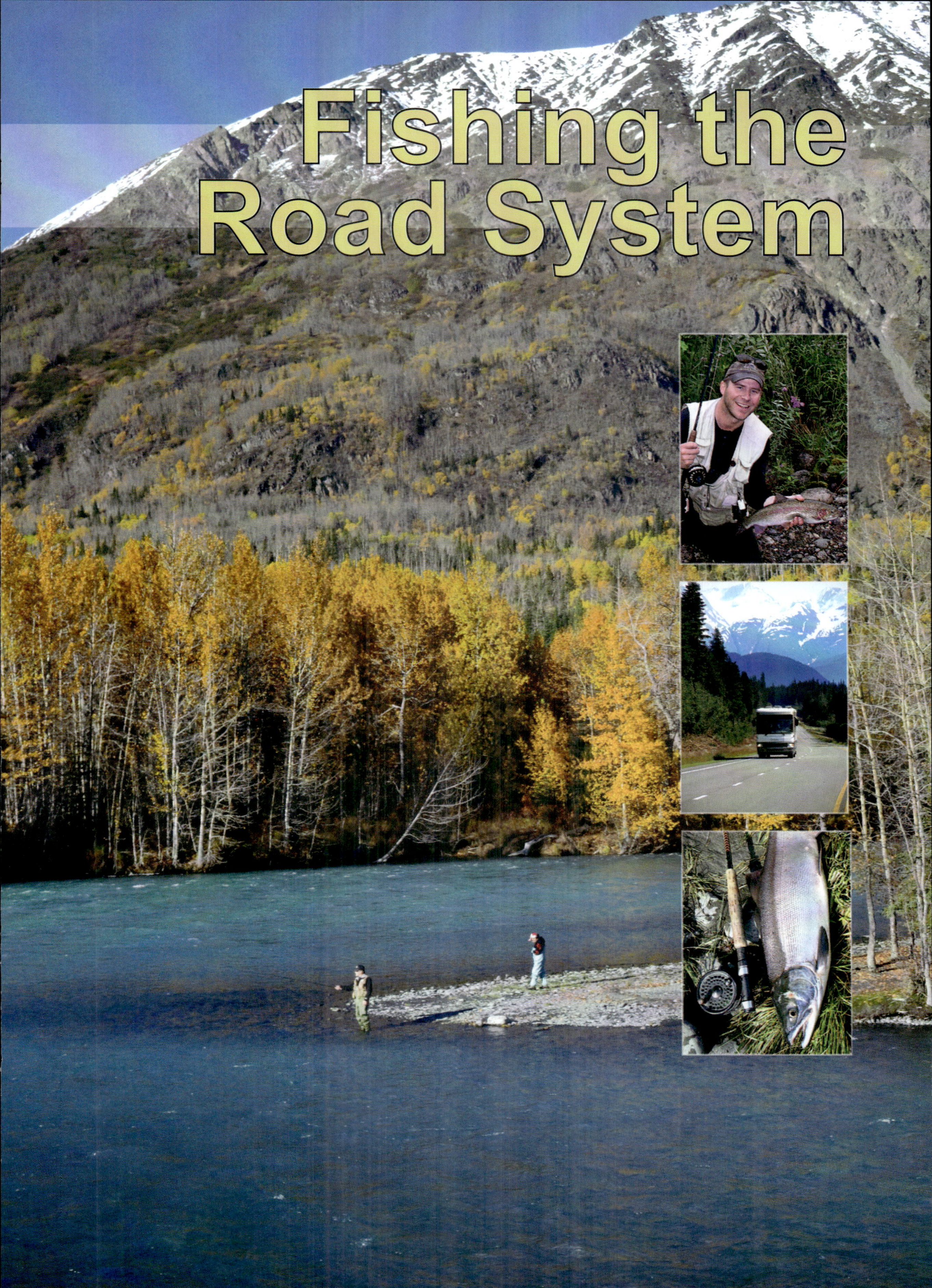

Fairbanks
Delta Junction
Cantwell
Tok
Talkeetna
Glennallen
Wasilla
Palmer
Anchorage
Valdez
Cordova
Kenai
Whittier
Soldotna
COOK INLET
PRINCE WILLIAM SOUND
Homer
Seward
Kenai Peninsula
GULF OF ALASKA
Kodiak Archipelago
Fishing Regions
Kenai Peninsula & Turnagain Arm
Matanuska-Susitna Valleys & Knik Arm
Copper Valley & Valdez Arm

# Introduction

**Putting together a fishing trip to Alaska can be a daunting challenge. There are seemingly an endless number of points to consider, all of them important in seeing the success of catching fish, perhaps bringing home well-earned future meals, and memories sure to last a lifetime. Although it is always recommended to inquire as much as possible regarding types of fish available, rules and regulations, places to go, what to use, and when and how to use it before leaving, this book will provide invaluable information and hopefully answer at least most if not all questions about fishing on the road system.**

The Roadside Angler's Guide deals with the main roadside fisheries of the state, specifically the Southcentral region that includes the ever-popular Kenai Peninsula and the Matanuska, Susitna, and Copper valleys, as well as the Gulf Coast. The vast majority of roadside angling effort in Alaska occurs in these areas and for good reason. Salmon runs are heavy and in great shape in terms of both sport and consumptive purposes. Resident species such as trout and char flourish in the many lakes and streams. Moreover, there exists a multitude of other angling options to take advantage of, like fly-in trips and deep-sea fishing excursions. In addition, for those taking a break in their hectic fishing schedule, wildlife and scenic viewing is unmatched.

Without a doubt, salmon are the number one target for anglers on the road system with resident species following a distant second. Therefore, this book focuses primarily on the opportunities available for salmon but certainly still covers fishing for trout, char, and other valuable game fish to a reasonable extent as well. The main emphasis is on river, stream, and saltwater fishing with all of the "Hot Spot" and additional information reflecting exactly that. Lake fishing is covered to a much lesser degree with only the more popular and productive locations mentioned.

The following segments will introduce how to use this book and deal with the most important aspects of trip planning, including issues such as timing, if having a set schedule to fish, targeting certain kinds of fish, and expected weather conditions.

## How to Use This Book

The Roadside Angler's Guide is logically laid out for ease of use. Divided into two major sections, the first deals with the various game fish species that are present along the road system. Presented are chapter breakdowns of salmon, trout, char, grayling, and others, as well as a chapter on angling strategies. The second section is all about destinations. Here are the very best and most productive waters that are accessible by road, detailed in multiple pages and color images.

## Alaska's Roadside Species

This section is broken up into four chapters. The first three presents groupings or categories of sport fish available to anglers on the road system and highlights topics of interest such as biology, hot spots, timing, common methods and techniques, preferred tackle and gear, and finding right structure for each species. The fourth chapter explains general nuances of fishing in Alaska, including structure and food sources in both fresh- and saltwater.

Select the species of interest, learn the key of how, where, when, and what, and apply this knowledge to the desired location(s) detailed in the section on Areas & Destinations.

## Areas & Destinations

After familiarity has been gained with roadside species in Alaska, anglers need to consult the section describing the places to go. Also here there are categories, one for each area in Southcentral, and includes Kenai Peninsula & Turnagain Arm, Matanuska-Susitna Valleys & Knik Arm, and Copper Valley & Valdez Arm. These areas are represented by color maps, area descriptions, and detailed information on the top fishing locales – or "hot spots." Additionally, secondary angling locations are listed with a summary of fishing conditions.

All of the "hot spots" feature color maps of the drainage, pointing out parking areas, campgrounds, trails, boat launches, and nearby communities or settlements. Furthermore, a description of what to expect in terms of scenery and fishing season follows, with a breakdown of the most common species present. Each species is given an angler rating (one to five stars), when during the season that particular species can be caught, best tackle to use, size range, and some tips that may prove helpful. Color-coded charts are shown for all salmon species (see below), depicting exact timing as well as consumptive quality of fish.

## Fish Availability Chart

This color-coded chart shows average angling success according to weekly periods during the season.

| *Species* | *MAY* | *JUN* | *JUL* |
|---|---|---|---|
| **King Salmon** | Closed | Closed, Closed, Closed, Closed | Moderate, Moderate, High, High |
| **Red Salmon** | Low | Low, Moderate, High, High | High, Moderate, Low, Moderate |
| **Rainbow Trout** | Low, Low, Low, Low | Low, Low, Moderate, Moderate | Moderate, Moderate, Moderate, Moderate |
| **Dolly Varden** | Low, Low, Low, Low | Low, Low, Low, Low | Moderate, Moderate, Moderate, Moderate |
| **Arctic Grayling** | Low, Low, Low, Low | Moderate, Moderate, Moderate, Moderate | Moderate, Moderate, Moderate, Moderate |
| Angling Pressure | | Low, Moderate, High, High | High, Moderate, Moderate, Moderate |

● = *High* This color represents high abundance or activity for the indicated species. In other words, this is the peak for angling success. Anglers usually experience good to excellent fishing during these times.

● = *Moderate* Indicated species is shown to be in moderate abundance or activity level. Anglers can expect fair or mediocre fishing on average but can range from poor to very good depending on skill level.

● = *Low* The marked species are in low abundance or activity level at these times. Typically, fishing tends to be slow or poor; skilled or experienced anglers may do quite well at times.

● = *Closed* Black means that the indicated species is present during these times but fishing is prohibited by regulation.

## Timing/Quality Chart

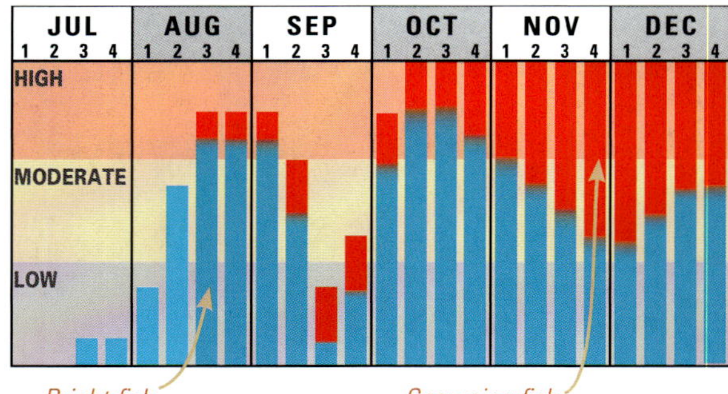


■ **Blue:** This color depicts seasonal timing and abundance of ocean bright to semi-bright fish of the indicated species. Study the peak of the runand plan your trip accordingly to be there when fresh fish are available in greatest numbers.

■ **Red:** This color depicts seasonal timing and abundance of pre-spawning and spawning fish of the indicated species. This helps anglers to figure out the proportionate numbers of colored fish compared to fresh salmon.

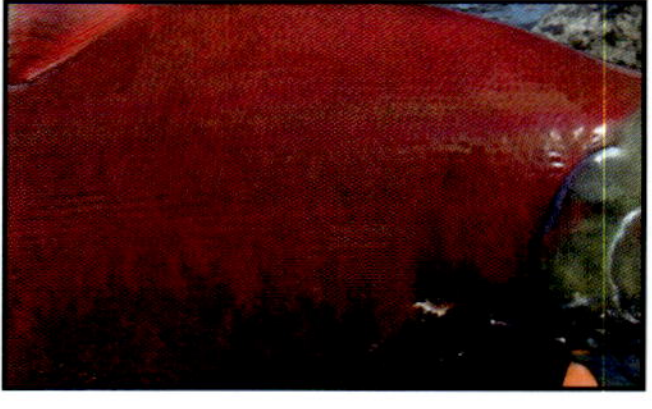

In addition, anglers seeking resident species such as trout and char can use this code to plan correct tackle (egg and flesh imitations).

**Note:** Timing remains for the most part consistent from year to year. In rare cases, however, timing may be off by up to two weeks due to a variety of factors.

## Appendix

This feature presents a few final notes regarding items of interest or consideration, such as wildlife, hiring a guide, dealing with roadside fishing situations, and the field care, shipping, and transportation of fish.

## Resources

A section listing other publications that may be useful in fishing on the road system, including addresses and phone numbers to various agencies, such as the US Forest Service and Bureau of Land Management.

# TRAVEL PLANNER

There are several ways to approach a roadside fishing trip. For those that already live in Alaska, things are obviously much less complicated with an awareness of the fish and fishing conditions probably already in place, thus some parts of this book may not be as helpful. However, for the angler that resides outside of the state or anyone not familiar with the opportunities at hand, The Roadside Angler's Guide will show to be very practical and informative in many ways.

## Destination: Alaska

The first thing to be dealt with is the mode of access and there are a couple of them. That is, how does one fish the road system? Some people arrive by commercial air carriers to one or more main airports, rent a car or motorhome, and proceed to explore the fishing. Others opt to rent or drive their own vehicle to Alaska from the outside. Additionally, someone may see fishing as a one day opportunity only and not the primary reason for being up here, usually coinciding with business or other types of travel.

If flying to the main gateway of Anchorage, which connects with the majority of flights to the continental United States and beyond, reservations should naturally be made months ahead of time for lowest airfares and choice seating. However, Alaska is very much a seasonal market with the months of June through August being peak both in airfare costs and in available fishing opportunities. The shoulder seasons of May and September-October present lower airfares but the fishing is generally less varied (although autumn can be phenomenal fishing for certain species).

*Anglers cast from the shoreline of Port Valdez along Dayville Road in hopes of connecting with silver salmon. Gorgeous vistas and great fishing are often synonymous in Alaska.*

If driving up, the seasonal aspects of fishing is of course the same as for anyone else but weather may be a deciding factor, particularly early and late in the season. Driving very long distances with the potential of encountering snow or ice on the road can be an issue for some. The peak time for RV traffic in Southcentral Alaska is from late May to early September, which typically reflects both favorable fishing and driving conditions.

## Timing is EVERYTHING

Fish are not present in all drainages all of the time; they are seasonally abundant. The main fishing season in Alaska reflects when the various species as a whole are readily available in the majority of areas and locations. The roadside fisheries are in their prime from June through September, the "shoulder" seasons of May and October being quite productive as well. However, realize that each river and stream has its own unique timing for each species of fish. For someone unfamiliar with these timing issues, fishing can be exceedingly complex – even disappointing. As a matter of fact, it is just as easy to get skunked in Alaska as anywhere else in the world. This book focuses heavily on timing in order to ensure optimum opportunity.

Salmon are notoriously precise in their appearance and fishing for them can change drastically from one week to the next. Additionally, some waters produce good action several months out of the season, others for only a few short weeks a year. In certain rivers it can be like turning a faucet on or off. Do not waste valuable time casting into dead water. Be informed. Fish when the faucet is on. Study the chapter on Pacific Salmon (page 27).

Trout and char and other species can be a little more forgiving when it comes to timing. The crucial factors here include broader seasonal migrations and food sources.

Spawning migrations may or may not be as distinct as salmon runs yet it is the availability of food sources that should be of focus to anglers. Salmon and its byproducts and insect activity drive the majority of feed for resident freshwater species. Match the "hatch." The chapters on Trout & Char, Other Game Species, and Angling Strategies (pages 61, 81, and 93 respectively) will explain the details.

On a different scale, learn how weather and water conditions influence fish. To sum it up, cloudy and rainy days are generally better for fishing than bright sunny ones. The twilight hours of dawn and dusk are best. In coastal waters, fish the rising tide. These and many other aspects of timing are covered specifically in the chapter on Angling Strategies (page 93).

## Fish According to Schedule

If on a set schedule, check the general timing chart below to see what species of fish are present during which months. When having established the time of season and species to target, consult the species chapters for more exact information regarding timing issues on various waters. Then refer to the Areas & Destinations section (page 94) for the chapter describing fishing opportunities in the specific areas and waters of interest.

## Target Specific Species

There are 14 kinds of game fish readily available in waters along the road system. Most anglers, resident or visiting, will choose to target one or two species, these

### General Species Availability

Freshwater — ☐ = Present ■ = Peak

| *SPECIES* | *APR* | *MAY* | *JUN* | *JUL* | *AUG* | *SEP* | *OCT* |
|---|---|---|---|---|---|---|---|
| **King Salmon** | Present | Peak | Peak | Peak | Peak | | |
| **Red Salmon** | | Present | Peak | Peak | Peak | Present | |
| **Pink Salmon** | | | Present | Peak | Peak | Present | |
| **Chum Salmon** | | | Present | Peak | Peak | Present | |
| **Silver Salmon** | | | | Present | Peak | Peak | Peak |
| **Steelhead Trout** | Present | Present | | | Present | Peak | Peak |
| **Rainbow Trout** | Present | Peak | Peak | Peak | Peak | Peak | Peak |
| **Lake Trout** | Peak | Peak | Peak | Present | Peak | Peak | Peak |
| **Dolly Varden** | Present | Present | Present | Peak | Peak | Peak | Peak |
| **Northern Pike** | Present | Peak | Peak | Present | Present | Peak | Peak |
| **Arctic Grayling** | Present | Peak | Peak | Peak | Peak | Peak | Present |
| **Whitefish** | Present | Present | Present | Peak | Peak | Peak | Peak |
| **Burbot** | Present | Present | Present | Peak | Peak | Peak | Peak |

Saltwater — ☐ = Present ■ = Peak

| *SPECIES* | *APR* | *MAY* | *JUN* | *JUL* | *AUG* | *SEP* | *OCT* |
|---|---|---|---|---|---|---|---|
| **King Salmon** | Present | Peak | Peak | Peak | Present | Present | Present |
| **Red Salmon** | Present | Present | Peak | Peak | Present | Present | |
| **Pink Salmon** | | | Present | Peak | Peak | Present | |
| **Chum Salmon** | | Present | Present | Peak | Peak | Present | |
| **Silver Salmon** | | | Present | Peak | Peak | Peak | Present |
| **Steelhead Trout** | | | | Present | Present | Present | Present |
| **Dolly Varden** | Present | Peak | Peak | Peak | Peak | Present | Present |
| **Pacific Halibut** | Present | Peak | Peak | Peak | Peak | Peak | Present |
| **Lingcod** | | | | Peak | Peak | Peak | Present |
| **Rockfish** | Present | Peak | Peak | Peak | Peak | Peak | Present |
| **Salmon Shark** | Present | Present | Present | Peak | Peak | Present | Present |
| **Bottomfish** | Present | Peak | Peak | Peak | Peak | Peak | Present |

*This angler came to fish Alaska's road system targeting king salmon for a week and was richly awarded.*

usually being some type of salmon or trout and char. All the other species are more or less peripheral opportunities or added bonuses. For example, an angler wishing to target king salmon on the Kenai Peninsula in mid-June will also be able to find good action for red salmon and rainbow trout in streams and halibut aplenty in the salt along the coast. While king salmon on the peninsula may be the main fishery of interest, the other species and locations become supporting fisheries. Since there can be an endless variety of combinations depending on the exact time of the season an angler decides to go, study this book thoroughly in order to pinpoint the main fishery and all possible supporting fisheries.

Identify species of interest and select the area(s) where to go. The easiest way to accomplish this is by referring to the Alaska Roadside Game Fish section of the book (page 22). This section covers all the sport fish available along the road, when they are present and where, what gear, tackle, and techniques to employ, and so forth. Furthermore, a detailed timing chart is given for each species listing the main areas and various "hot spots" for the calendar season. Pick one or more locations and look them up in the appropriate chapter for all the details, including access, facility, and regulations information as well as a summary description of the fishery as a whole.

## Terminal Gear & Tackle

The Roadside Angler's Guide covers necessary and popular gear and tackle largely in the Species and Angling Strategies chapters, as well as for each individual hot spot in the Areas & Destinations section.

The majority of anglers bring their own personal gear (rod and reel) setup. Study the recommended gear in this book and make the choice whether to acquire suggested equipment prior to the fishing trip or at the time of arrival. Local sporting good stores in Anchorage and other towns and communities have a large assortment of terminal gear available at reasonable prices and seasoned employees at hand to assist in proper selection.

Unless having previous experience with fishing the various areas on the road system in Southcentral Alaska, obtain tackle such as lures, flies, and bait from local sporting good vendors. Mention to one of the staff members at the time of purchase what species and waters will be targeted. These people are highly knowledgeable of the specific river or stream and will offer additional advice on specific choices of tackle such as popular sizes and colors and other information that may prove invaluable.

## Water Type Preference

With many anglers a factor of concern is the type of water that is considered desirable to fish. Some prefer the vast expanses of large rivers or the coastline to satisfy their angling needs while others value being on a small mountain stream or lake as the zenith of a fishing trip. Perhaps a combination of various types of water and species is what is most important. Another point is that although salmon and at least one or two different resident fish species can be found in most any type of water, some species show a distinct particular preference for a certain habitat. It is the mending of these factors that will determine if a trip becomes successful or not in the eye of the angler.

Become familiar with the various areas on the road system and what each has to offer in terms of scenery and structure of the drainages. Refer to the introductory section of each location chapter to harness a greater feel of the particular area and the species present.

## Weather Conditions

Alaska weather can be very unpredictable and notorious for changing drastically not just from day to day but also within a few hours. But there are times during the fishing season and in certain areas that present more stability, as well as instability.

The spring months of April and May can be quite dry with occasional rainfall or even light snow showers. Breakup on most streams occurs in April with lowland lakes completely ice-free by early to mid-May. Expect overnight temperatures to drop below freezing, especially at higher elevations.

Cool weather often prevails into the middle of June before true summer conditions take hold. A few larger mountain or highland lakes have ice persist into June. The period from late June to mid-August is relatively warm with daytime highs in the 60s along the coast and 70s in inland areas, spiking into the 80s time to time. Nights are still cool, however.

Rain is prevalent starting the latter part of July on through September. Below freezing temperatures at night is common in inland areas starting by mid-August but the days can still be quite decent (50s and 60s).

September is a true fall month and the scenery, water conditions, and weather reflects this. Especially the coastal areas frequently experience very inclement conditions, including the possibility of near-torrential rain and high winds, with minor flooding commonplace in more exposed rivers and streams.

Late fall (October) can be mixed with the early part often being dry and cool with temperatures into the 40s during the day and 20s at night. Mountain passes usually receive the first significant snowfall of the year sometime in early October; therefore, traveling with an RV is not recommended beyond the first of the month.

The first hard freeze (teens and low 20s) in lowland and coastal areas generally occurs by mid-October with the first measurable snowfall soon thereafter. The southernmost areas on the Kenai Peninsula, however, may not see any snow until November. Most lakes and flowing waters freeze over in November and are usually solid enough to walk on by December.

## Clothing & Fishing Gear

Layered clothing is always best in the field with most anything wool or comparable synthetics an absolute necessity in Alaska. A warm hat, scarf, gloves, sweater, socks, and long johns are essential, even in the middle of summer. Coastal areas may be cool and windy and if not acclimated to such temperatures a fishing trip can turn very miserable.

Standard winter gear is particularly useful if planning a deep-sea fishing excursion or anywhere along the coast where cooler (and wetter) weather and strong winds prevail.

Rain gear, including rain jacket and pants and rubber boots that reach almost up to the knee, is another worthwhile investment for comfort.

Hip-boots or chest waders are a must if fishing on the road system. They will allow an angler to cross shallow channels in order to approach deeper water and the best fishing holes. In fact, angler success increases substantially when boots or waders are added and in some places (such as high fishing pressure zones) may be seen as required.

Polaroid glasses are another must-have in Alaska fishing. With many rivers and streams running shallow and crystal clear, polaroid glasses will greatly assist in locating schools of migrating salmon by eliminating glare off the water. It is very much possible to target small groups or even individual fish this way. As a matter of fact, sight-fishing is one of the most efficient methods of catching fish. Perhaps even more importantly, polaroid glasses serve as shields from flying sinkers or lures with sharp hooks.

A fishing vest is a tremendous tool for storing glasses, lures and flies, knives, pliers, and other lose items. Also, use a hat with rim or bill for blocking direct sunlight. Like glasses, rims act like a shield from hooks and sinkers.

## Watercraft

For the vast majority of visiting anglers, bringing a canoe, raft, or small boat is highly impractical. These types of watercraft are not necessary or required to fish any of the angling locations discussed in this book. However, if an angler would like to enhance the experience, these items are available for rent in a few locations, such as in Anchorage and larger towns and communities along the road.

The best option for anglers concerned with ease and budget, a float tube may be the right thing. Relatively light and very versatile, float tubes are great on lakes and ponds or anywhere there is still water.

For more information on watercraft, see page 21 in this section.

(Courtesy Gary Sinnhuber)

*Good fishing and nice weather do not always coincide. In spring and fall especially, always dress warmly.*

## ROADSIDE DAY TRIPS

It is entirely possible to experience some excellent fishing in Alaska if only having a day – or even just hours – to do so. There are many roadside waters that produce surprisingly good catches within an hour driving time of Anchorage. Area lakes yield top-notch action for rainbow trout and landlocked salmon while some streams (a few of which are within city limits) offer great opportunities for all five species of salmon. All of the locations mentioned are listed in detail in this book. Check the index for water of interest and page number where it can be found.

### 1- to 1 ½ -Hour Road Trip

Within the city of Anchorage, Ship Creek – only minutes from downtown – has excellent king salmon action during the month of June and likewise for silvers in August. Campbell Creek is another August silver salmon fishery and supports a good population of rainbow trout and Dolly Varden as well. City lakes are stocked with salmon, trout, and char.

South of Anchorage, along Seward Highway in Turnagain Arm, day-trippers can find very good fishing for pink and chum salmon in Bird and Glacier creeks in the latter part of July. In August, look to Bird Creek for some of the best silver salmon action anywhere. Down the road even farther is Resurrection Creek (about 1.5 hours from Anchorage) that supports a huge run of pink salmon in July along with lesser numbers of chum and silver salmon. Nearby Ingram and Sixmile creeks can be worthwhile too.

North of Anchorage, in streams accessed from the Glenn Highway near the towns of Palmer and Wasilla, about 45 minutes to an hour drive, anglers can locate a multitude of lakes and streams harboring salmon and trout. Eklutna Tailrace has excellent king and silver fishing in June and August, respectively. Jim Creek, only a few miles away, support good runs of red salmon in July and August and silver salmon in August and September. Wasilla, Cottonwood, and Fish creeks are small weekend-only fisheries that receive runs of silver salmon in August. The Little Susitna River, off of Knik-Goose Bay Road (1.5 hours from Anchorage), supports runs of all five species of salmon in addition to trout and char.

### 2-Hour Road Trip

Looking beyond the one- to one-and-a-half-hour trip, there is a vast range of possibilities. Whittier and Passage Canal is the nearest marine fishery, and Seward and Resurrection Bay is only two hours away from Anchorage. They both offer surfcasting for king and silver salmon. Russian River and the upper section of Kenai River are both within a two-hour drive of town. Excellent red salmon and trout fishing is the norm in July and August, with late-run silver salmon, rainbow trout, and Dolly Varden plentiful in October (Kenai only). Willow, Sheep, and Montana creeks are three east-side Susitna River tributaries perfect for day trips. All of them are very productive waters for king, pink, chum, and silver salmon, arctic grayling, and rainbow trout. And again, within two hours driving time.

All of the above mentioned waters are discussed in more detail in this book. Use the index in the back to locate chapter and page number.

*One does not need to travel far to go salmon fishing in Alaska. Here, Ship Creek in downtown Anchorage.*

## REMOTE FISHING TRIPS

Anglers that have already spent several days to perhaps a couple of weeks or more fishing on the road system may want to indulge themselves by flying in or boating to some remote location for a day or even half a day. Cost is reasonable, usually in the $250 range per person depending on the specific air taxi/charter, whether a guide is needed or not, distance traveled, species targeted, and number of people traveling. Many outfits also combine fishing with sightseeing or bear viewing, which really adds to the charm of seeing Alaska the way most people are not familiar with, even locals.

### Fly-In Trips

This book highlights many options for fly-in fishing trips from various towns and communities along the road and they are listed under "Additional Opportunities" in the Areas & Destinations section.

Popular fly-in destinations include various tributaries (rivers and lakes) of the Susitna River for all five species of salmon, trout, char, grayling, and pike. There are also several good drainages on the west side of Cook Inlet for salmon and trout. Some carriers offer trips to remote waters of Prince William Sound, including stream and surfcasting opportunities for salmon and trout. A few of them even have secluded floating cabins tucked away in quiet coves or bays at or near salmon streams or halibut holes. Small skiffs may be available for use.

Anglers should, however, be aware of the fact that many streams only accessible by air from Anchorage do receive a fair amount of angling pressure during the height of the respective seasons. Remote does not necessarily translate into meaning a solitary experience; it only implies that the particular water is not on the road system. If strict solitude is what is important, anglers must state this clearly prior to booking a flight so arrangements can be made to satisfy the request.

Another highly attractive option to keep in mind is doing a simple "Drop-Off." That is, the pilot flies a group of anglers and gear out to a prime location and picks them up again at a predetermined time, day, and place. If choosing this option, a mind-set of acceptance of being in the wilds of Alaska far away from emergency facilities and responders is a must. However, the excitement of great fishing and wildlife viewing is absolutely worth it.

Drop-off trips are very popular, with locals as much as visitors, and a great way to go if only for a half- or full-day. To stretch the experience even further, anglers can even opt to bring a raft along and float a particular river or stream on their own. Typically, these trips last from two or three days to a week or more. Inquire with the air service for details.

### Deep-Sea Excursions

Next to the standard roadside salmon fisheries, angler participation is greatest on ocean charters out of one of several ports along the Gulf Coast. Seen as a supporting fishery, many anglers will hire a charter boat for a day to fish for halibut and other bottomfish, including saltwater salmon. While some charters specialize in perhaps one or two specific species of fish, others offer a more rounded trip, targeting several major game fish within a day worth of fishing.

The Kenai Peninsula & Turnagain Arm and Copper Valley & Valdez Arm chapters (pages 109 and 375, respectively) will offer a multitude of marine options listed in the Additional Opportunities sections.

The fishing experience may be very different depending on the size of the boat and the number of people it holds. Typically, charter boats carry around six with some companies offering much larger "party" vessels that may hold up to a dozen or more anglers. All fishing rods, including bait, are furnished and part of the cost. Also, fish cleaning and filleting is included in the price as well.

Travel time to the fishing grounds may vary considerably, around one to two hours one-way being average. Inquire about this as well as species targeted, boat size, fishing gear, weather cancellations, and other information of importance at time of booking.

## TRANSPORTATION & ACCOMMODATIONS

The final segment of trip planning discussed in this chapter covers the options available to anglers when it comes to ground transportation and accommodations.

Rental vehicles are a popular way of experiencing roadside fishing in Alaska. Reservations should be done half a year in advance to ensure best price and availability. Inquire about specials for extended rentals lasting a week or more.

Depending on rental period or season, price range is $75 for an economy car to $190 and up per night for a standard-sized RV.

Anglers will find a vast range of accommodations along the road system, from first-class lodges and hotels to simple cabins and bed & breakfasts. Prices depend on season, service level, and room size but usually run for as little as $75 per night in more affordable motels, bed & breakfasts, and cabins to well over $250 per night in better hotels and lodges.

For accommodations in an area of angling interest, consult the Services & Information section at the back of each location chapter.

### Automobiles

Some anglers opt to use the fuel efficiency of cars to take them to their selected fishing spots. This is a great option for tent camping. Cars allow for more time to book but do not wait more than a few months before departure.

### Vans

For those that do not desire the full comfort RVs offer and still allows the option to sleep inside a vehicle, recreational vans are ideal. Only a few companies rent vans so early booking is necessary.

## Motor Homes

Without a doubt the ideal way to have high levels of comfort on a fishing trip. The majority of roads and highways, including fishing access areas, can be reached by most any size of recreational vehicle.

## Hotels/Motels

Located in abundance throughout the road system, available in most towns and communities. Service levels range from four-star hotels offering meal service and airport shuttle and a series of other more luxury amenities, to motels that typically only offer a room with limited beverage availability. Occasionally associated with a guide outfit.

## Lodges/Resorts

Wide array of accommodations, some being full service and others service, usually located on a river or lake. Many lodges offer guided fishing trips at extra cost and package deals are available. Boat or canoe rentals are a possibility and may be available free or at least a nominal fee.

(Courtesy Roy & Beverley Bailey)

*Many lodges or inns are situated right at the heart of smaller communities close to fishing. This is a glimpse of downtown Talkeetna.*

## Bed & Breakfasts

Southcentral Alaska has an abundance of B&Bs that offer a multitude of service levels and amenities. Often situated close to major fisheries, such as those featured in this book, B&Bs are increasingly popular with visiting anglers. Basics are room (twin beds) and morning meal service, with internet, guide services, and freezer space options available.

## Cabins/Cottages

Basic is sleeping berths and lamp, others fireplace, electric lighting and heating, comfortable beds, and divided rooms with kitchenettes. Cabins are often provided by fishing lodges and guide outfits and located next to a river or lake.

## Public Use Cabins

There are only a small number of these cabins available on the road system. Inquire with the US Forest Service or Alaska State Parks for areas and availability. Reserve early as these are popular. All cabins are accessed by trail from the road and may be furnished with firewood and a small skiff. Very low cost, usually $25 to $45 per night.

*There are considerable options available to anglers wanting the extra comfort of a lodge. This one, virtually a stones throw away from the busy Seward Highway, provides solitude as well as convenience.*

## WATERCRAFT RENTALS

Anglers that have experience using and navigating boats, canoes, and kayaks or other craft may want to consider renting one for a day or more. While fishing on foot can be superb along many roadside waters, at times it is amazing how much of a difference it can make by using a watercraft.

Watercraft have a way of opening up new territory for anglers, be it searching for pike or trout hiding in weed mats on a lake, cruising along a river searching for sloughs containing schools of salmon, or even plying the briny in pursuit of the myriad of bottomfish that may be just out of reach from shore.

Before setting out, however, anglers need to be aware of the characteristics and potential dangers of fishing Alaska's waterways. The water up here is as cold as it is unpredictable -- even in summer -- and the most simple mistake or error may turn deadly if not prepared. This means carrying emergency gear and supplies varying from floatation devices to flares and extra food. Also, a high-caliber gun or rifle should be included on the list, especially if traveling into bear country (which would be the better portion of the state). Keep in mind that cell phone service may not always be available off the road.

### Boats

There are very few outfits that actually rent out boats, with or without covered cabins. Seaworthy craft may be available in local ports for a price ranging from $250 on up per day. River boat rentals are a rather rare commodity unless associated with a commercial outfit such as a lodge.

### Rafts

Anglers will not have much issue finding a facility offering tough and sturdy rafts for rent. Some are located right in Anchorage, others at or near a few of the more popular rivers. Prices are reasonable, ranging from $75 to $160 per day.

### Canoes

A few places rent out canoes, usually in conjunction with cabin rentals, and may be situated in the vicinity of larger recreational areas offering access to lake fisheries. Usually around $30 to $60 per day.

### Kayaks

Increasing in popularity among anglers, kayaks are a great tool for those wanting to travel relatively light. These watercraft rent for $30 to $50 per day and are available in same locations as rafts and canoes.

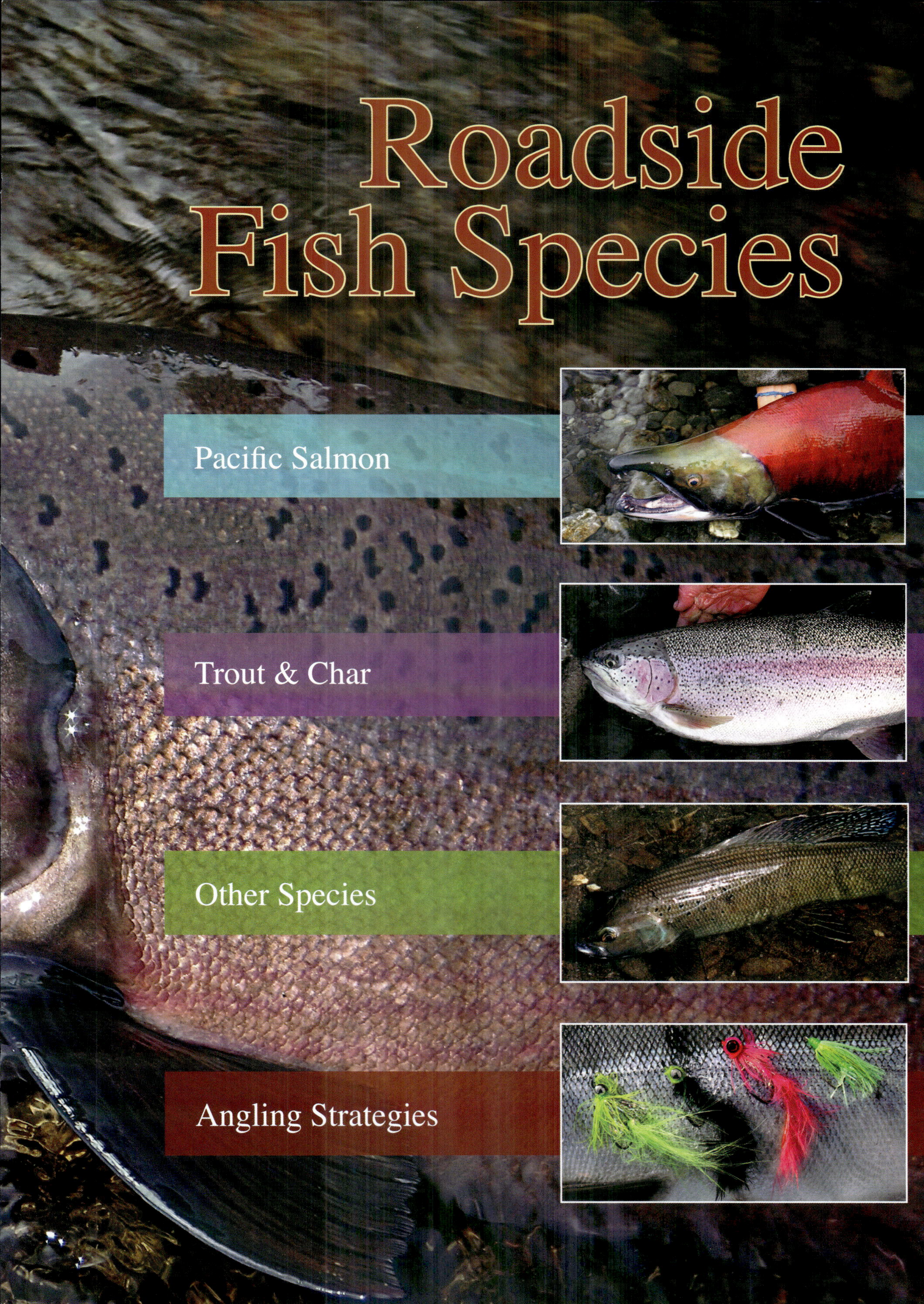
Roadside
Fish Species
Pacific Salmon
Trout & Char
Other Species
Angling Strategies

# Alaska's Fish

**No matter what time of year an angler may decide to cast a line into Alaska's waters, he or she can expect to encounter a varying number of popular game fish. While it is true that each species has its own period – or window – of prime opportunity, it is also correct that depending on the drainage and the specific fish populations present, anglers are more than likely to find good and consistent success for at least two or three different sport species at the same time and place as the presence of one often leads to the survival of others. In other words, it is this interconnectivity between species, coupled with the visual aspects that the state is known for, that virtually guarantees a memorable fishing trip.**

The fish migrations and their relationship to the seasons makes for very dynamic sport fisheries. While waters in more southern latitudes commonly have longer periods of species availability during the year, Alaska's game fish generally see significantly contracted windows of angler opportunity as the ice-free seasons of spring, summer, and fall are very brief (perhaps a few short weeks each). This means that timing is the most crucial element to any angler, followed by other pertinent points such as gear and tackle, and methods and techniques.

It is no secret that salmon help drive a huge component of Alaska's ecosystem. The annual influx of protein-rich nutrition is what sustains many species throughout the year, from decaying flesh of dead adult fish to eggs to juvenile salmon; all contribute as a natural fertilizer that ensures healthy populations of trout, char, grayling, and whitefish among a myriad of other species, both sporting- and non-sporting. While migrating and spawning salmon may be a feast to the senses in several different ways, anglers take it as a good omen in locating a couple of the more popular game quarries, such as rainbows and Dolly Varden.

And in places where salmon are not present, fish display their feeding habits along the lines of other available nutrients, such as insect activity and smaller fishes, each which offer their own unique seasonal patterns. Understanding and applying this intricate cycle of life to the activity of fishing is key in being a successful angler here as anywhere else in the world.

A great many anglers residing in and visiting Alaska each year appreciate and even depend on fish. Yet it is without a doubt that salmon is the leading interest and the engine that drives the financial side of the sport. The state has become synonymous with salmon fishing and perhaps nowhere is this as obvious as it is seeing the number of tackle shops, guide services, charter companies, lodges, and fish processors lining a great many road and highways all over the more populated regions and areas.

Apart from salmon, the bottomfish business is flourishing with the help of a growing appetite for halibut, rockfishes, and lingcod, all of which add by considerable measure to the local angling infrastructure, particularly among the major coastal ports.

The exclusive market for trout and char is holding its own and is especially big in the realm of the fly-fishing crowd. In fact, few species can match the level of determination and infatuation witnessed here, despite being ruled by a mainly catch-and-release state of philosophy.

This section of the book deals with the various fish species available to roadside anglers with particular emphasis on the main ones, like the five kinds of salmon, trout, and char. Also covered in moderate depth are types of fish perhaps not as coveted, in general, as the previously mentioned species, such as grayling and pike. Lastly, there is a fairly broad discussion on the more sought-after saltwater species. Species identification and descriptions of locations and timing are given, as well as listings of top lures and flies, including proper methods and techniques.

## Record & Trophy Fish of Alaska - ADF&G's Trophy Fish Program

| Species | Record Lbs.-Oz. | Location | Year | Angler | Trophy Lbs |
|---|---|---|---|---|---|
| **Pacific Salmon** | | | | | |
| Chum Salmon | 32-0 | Caamano Point (SE) | 1985 | Fredrick Thynes | 15 |
| King Salmon | 97-4 | Kenai River (SC) | 1985 | Lester Anderson | *75/50 |
| Pink Salmon | 12-9 | Moose River (SC) | 1974 | Steven Lee | 8 |
| Red Salmon | 16-0 | Kenai River (SC) | 1974 | Chuck Leach | 12 |
| Silver Salmon | 26-0 | Icy Strait (SE) | 1976 | Andrew Robbins | 20 |
| **Trout & Char** | | | | | |
| Arctic Char/Dolly Varden | 27-6 | Wulik River (NW) | 2002 | Mike Curtiss | 10 |
| Cutthroat Trout | 8-6 | Wilson Lake (SE) | 1977 | Robert Denison | 3 |
| Lake Trout | 47-0 | Clarence Lake (SC) | 1970 | Daniel Thorsness | 20 |
| Rainbow/Steelhead Trout | 42-3 | Bell Island (SE) | 1970 | David White | 15 |
| **Other Freshwater Species** | | | | | |
| Arctic Grayling | 5-1 | Fish River (NW) | 2008 | Peter Cockwill | 3 |
| Burbot | 24-12 | Lake Louise (SC) | 1976 | George Howard | 8 |
| Northern Pike | 38-8 | Innoko River (SW) | 1991 | Jack Wagner | 15 |
| Sheefish | 53-0 | Pah River (NW) | 1986 | Lawrence Hudnall | 30 |
| Whitefish | 9-0 | Tozitna River (IN) | 1989 | Al Mathews | 4 |
| **Saltwater Species** | | | | | |
| Lingcod | 82-6 | Cook Inlet (SC) | 2008 | Robbie Hammond | 55 |
| Pacific Halibut | 459-0 | Unalaska Bay (SW) | 1996 | Jack Tragis | 250 |
| Rockfish | 39-0 | Sitka (SE) | 2013 | Henry Liebman | 18 |

* Trophy weight for the Kenai River is 75 pounds and the rest of the state 50 pounds.

*Regional Abbreviations:*
*(IN) Interior*
*(NW) Northwest*
*(SC) Southcentral*
*(SE) Southeast*
*(SW) Southwest*

*To submit trophy and/or record fish to the ADF&G for recognition, affidavit forms and complete program rules are available at most ADF&G offices and can be downloaded from www.sf.adfg.state.ak.us/statewide/trophy/form.cfm*

# Pacific Salmon

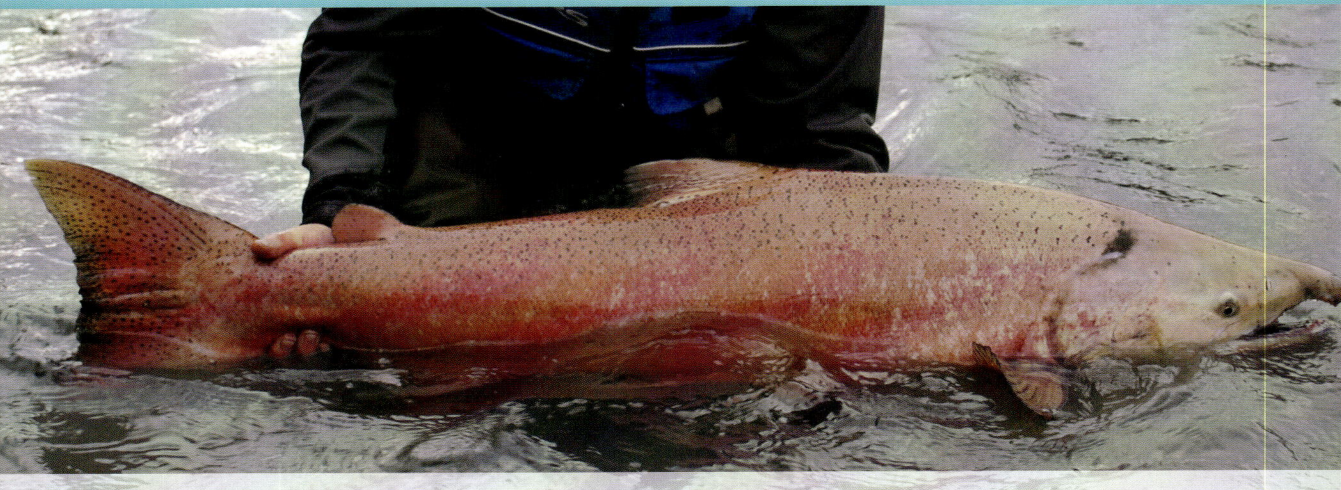

# Introduction

There are five kinds of Pacific salmon in the state of Alaska and along the road system, all of which are present in varying degrees of abundance according to species and location, these being king (chinook), red (sockeye), pink (humpback), chum (dog), and silver (coho) salmon. It is a remarkable family of fish, their numbers sometimes staggering to the mind and distribution no less incredible as they appear in most any type and size of water from shallow coastal streams to glacial rivers and remote headwaters a thousand miles or more from sea.

## Salmon Facts

There is a series of very important points one should consider prior to pursuing salmon, all of them having to do with proper knowledge regarding behavior and appearance that are critical to angling success. Having this fundamental understanding of the life cycle and habits of these fascinating fish will greatly enhance the enjoyment of salmon fishing.

### Life Cycle & Habits

Salmon are usually anadromous; that is, they spend their lives in both freshwater and saltwater, migrating between the two extremes in pursuit of food and to complete the reproductive cycle. The fish begin their journey as eggs on the bottom of a river or stream, the juvenile salmon migrating to sea after a period of a few weeks up to some years, spend at least one year to five years eating and growing in the nutrient-rich marine environment, and then return to the exact place of birth to spawn and die. It is an amazing cycle of life and can be witnessed at least in part by anyone, especially during the summer and fall months when in-migrating, spawning, and dying salmon are present in many roadside waters.

When salmon first begin returning to freshwater all species are very similar in many respects; their bodies are sleek and slender, the skin silvery in appearance. But as these fish spend some time near the spawning grounds, things start to change. Distinct differences surface between the species as coloration and bodies begin to reflect the spawning phase, a process which may take as little as a few weeks to as long as several months depending on environmental and physiological conditions. The end result is a fish that looks nothing like it did when it swam in the sea.

A few salmon populations have adapted to a life cycle limited strictly to freshwater, spending their whole life in or near the area of their birth. It is

*A group of sockeye crowd a pool, waiting to ascend a series of falls. Salmon are very ept at negotiating such barriers.*

almost always red salmon that display this characteristic (popularly coined Kokanee), although occasionally silver salmon and kings are known to exhibit this trait of being non-anadromous.

The reasons for salmon not migrating to sea as their larger brethren can be many but usually entails habitat where the fish are able to find sufficient availability of food and a place to spawn. These "landlocked" populations may be so out of instinctual choice, yet some stocks exist as a result of being planted by state or government agencies in order to expand sport fishing opportunities. The difference, however, is that natural landlocked populations are able to reproduce, human induced fish are not. After breeding, the fish die.

All landlocked salmon are significantly smaller in size than ocean fish, rarely exceeding 20 inches and 3 pounds in Alaskan waters regardless of species. Also, their coloration may be similar to sea-run salmon although often appear slightly darker.

The information presented henceforth reflect conditions associated with sea-run salmon as this is the trait anglers are most interested.

## Runs & Run Timing

Each salmon species is present for a certain period, usually lasting a couple of months depending on the kind of salmon and the drainage. And as all local anglers know and visiting anglers soon come to learn, these yearly migrations are referred to as "runs," hence the popular term "the salmon are running." A run can be defined in several ways but usually described as a population of salmon from a specific drainage as it enters that drainage in concentrated form within a certain window of time.

Runs develop as a result of each population of salmon reflecting unique conditions within a drainage, such as water temperature and flow, which help shape the habits as well as physical attributes of the fish that are present. Larger systems often comprise a multitude of tributary rivers, creeks, and lakes, each with its own character based on various geological and biological factors, hence supporting multiple runs of one or more salmon species.

Timing is the single most important factor concerning salmon fishing. Correct gear and tackle does not matter if the timing is incorrect. The window of appearance in which a run enters a drainage is called run timing and is amazingly predictable every year, often within a few days, and seldom varies more than a week or two in any given year.

*Four salmon fillets. The meat is red and firm, the skin silvery, making for excellent food quality.*

## Salmon as Food

Anglers must target salmon close to saltwater if looking for food quality fish. This is one of the reasons why the rivers and streams of Southcentral Alaska are so popular; all drainages are within a short distance of the ocean meaning salmon found there are prone to be in excellent condition for both sport and consumption. The farther away from sea a fish has to travel, the more body fat it will burn, hence more progressive maturation of the skin and flesh.

Some species retain their silvery coloration and meat quality longer than others. King, red, and silver salmon all have reasonably good quality retention upon entering freshwater, approximately three to five weeks, while pink and chum salmon are known to shed quality in as little as a week. For this very reason, these latter species are not targeted to any degree even along coastal waters, let alone streams that are situated very far inland.

As salmon age, the skin turns color and the flesh deteriorates in condition, being yellowish white or white and the texture soft and mushy with a pungent aroma when cooked. The more exterior coloration a fish displays, the greater the likelihood of that salmon being unpalatable. Therefore, release all pre-spawn or spawning salmon back to the water.

The flesh of a bright king salmon is orange-red in color, the texture firm, and flavor among the best of any fish. Because of diet, king meat is fairly oily, seen by many as a big plus, giving a "juicier" taste compared to other salmon. Kings make for excellent fresh table fare as well as frozen, smoked, and canned food.

Apart from its sporting qualities, the red is a superb eating fish, the meat firm and often ruby red in color. Many anglers prefer this salmon for consumption over any other salmon species. Taking into consideration the abundance

## Identifying Salmon

Since there are strict measures regulating the targeting and/or killing of certain salmon species in many drainages, being able to identify salmon correctly is of critical importance. Do not rely completely on other anglers to establish the identity of a salmon; it is a fact that many anglers – even locals and life-long residents – cannot distinguish key species under certain conditions. Claiming ignorance will not excuse a citation.

The comparison chart below illustrates the various salmon species and gender in the saltwater/ocean phase of their life cycle. For more specific and detailed identification, see the sections for each individual species.

*King Salmon - Male*

*King Salmon - Female*

*Red Salmon - Male*

*Red Salmon - Female*

*Pink Salmon - Male*

*Pink Salmon - Female*

*Chum Salmon - Male*

*Chum Salmon - Female*

*Silver Salmon - Male*

*Silver Salmon - Female*

and ease of catching reds relative to kings, for example, it only makes common sense to stock the freezer with this fine gamester. Fresh, frozen, smoked, or canned, red salmon are perfect.

Pinks are not regarded very favorably in terms of food quality compared to other salmon species, much due to the rapid deterioration of the flesh as the fish nears spawning areas. However, dime bright pinks do make for fine eating when fresh or canned.

Chums are not particularly sought-after as food fish within the angling community in Alaska, much of it due to the abundance of seemingly more "attractive" species such as reds and silvers. Another aspect is that chums deteriorate quickly as the spawning period draws close, rendering few available bright salmon. When sampled dime-bright, however, the meat is firm and orange in color. Fresh is best but also good smoked and canned.

The flesh of a dime bright silver straight out of the sea is firm and of excellent texture and flavor and preferred by many over other salmon species. Like kings, the meat is slightly oily – reflecting the diet of the fish – and makes for perfect food fresh, frozen, smoked, and canned.

## Fishing for Salmon

Anglers in Southcentral Alaska, as well as elsewhere in the state, successfully target salmon in their various stages of the life cycle, from the ocean feeding phase to the annual in-river migrations. Timing of species and location as well as tackle presentation and proper structure is what form the necessary means in the pursuit of salmon.

### Saltwater

As salmon begin arriving in nearshore waters along the Gulf of Alaska they are still feeding heavily and gaining weight but as the season progresses the appetite slows and by the time they nose into the mouths of rivers and streams their hunger has usually abated completely.

(Courtesy Roy & Beverley Bailey)

Salmon, generally, do not eat once having entered freshwater, yet there is sufficient evidence that at least a few species in certain populations do continue to feed in tidal areas of their home waters for up to several days.

Boaters must concentrate on feeding areas such as points and tidal rips, including reefs and other structures that attract baitfish, and thus salmon. Trolling or mooching with bait such as herring is popular as long as the salmon are in the salt, hardware like spoons and spinners also proving to be quite effective.

Shore anglers usually do better focusing on migratory corridors and areas that may temporarily hold fish, such as coves or lagoons. The mouth of clearwater streams act as a magnet for all salmon species, as the fish "taste" the water in search of their own natal stream. Casting hardware or bait or fishing bait with a strike indicator are both excellent methods. Many anglers, particularly at terminal fisheries, choose to snag salmon, a legal harvest method in saltwater.

### Freshwater

In any specific run of salmon, there are a few individual fish that appear in their stream of birth weeks before the vanguard of the population arrives and are known as "scouts". When fish enter drainages at the tail end of a run, they are often referred to as "stragglers". As salmon enter freshwater, they will first mill around the tidal area for a few days before venturing farther upstream, moving in and out with the tides. As they finally commit to the river or stream, the migration may be quite rapid and usually coincide with a rising tide. The tidal zone is a prime spot to intercept salmon casting or drifting a variety of lures, flies, and bait.

*Sea lice cling to the sides of a salmon. A harmless parasite, they soon fall off after salmon enters freshwater, usually within a week. The presence of sea lice is a sign that the fish has been in freshwater for a very short time, usually a good omen for anglers seeking quality meat. When at sea, all salmon carry sea lice.*

### Salmon Fishing Rod & Line Weights

*[ ] = Weight needed for locations with large fish present and/or strong currents*

| *Salmon Species* | Bait Casting & Spinning Rods | Fly Rods |
|---|---|---|
| **King** | Heavy action, 20 - 30 lb. test [40 lb.] | Heavy action, 9 - 11 weight [12 wt.] |
| **Red, Silver, & Chum** | Medium action, 10 - 17 lb. test [20 lb.] | Medium/Heavy action, 7 - 9 weight [10 wt.] |
| **Pink** | Light action, 4 - 10 lb. test [12 lb.] | Light/Medium action, 4 - 6 weight [7 wt.] |

### General Salmon Run Timing: Roadside Waters

*● = Present ◉ = Peak * = Available year round*

| *Species* | | *May* | *June* | *July* | *August* | *September* | *October* |
|---|---|---|---|---|---|---|---|
| **King** (Chinook) | **Saltwater* | ●●◉◉ | ◉◉◉◉ | ◉●●● | ●●●● | ●●●● | ●●●● |
| | *Freshwater* | ●●●◉ | ◉◉◉◉ | ◉◉◉◉ | ◉● | | |
| **Red** (Sockeye) | *Saltwater* | ●●●● | ●●●● | ◉◉◉◉ | ●●●● | ●●●● | |
| | *Freshwater* | ●●● | ●●◉◉ | ◉◉◉◉ | ◉◉◉◉ | ◉●●● | ●●● |
| **Pink** (Humpback) | *Saltwater* | ● | ●●●● | ◉◉◉◉ | ◉◉◉● | ●●●● | |
| | *Freshwater* | | ●● | ●●◉◉ | ◉◉◉◉ | ●●●● | |
| **Chum** (Dog) | *Saltwater* | ●●● | ●●●● | ◉◉◉◉ | ◉◉◉● | ●●●● | |
| | *Freshwater* | | ●● | ●●◉◉ | ◉◉◉● | ●●●● | ● |
| **Silver** (Coho) | *Saltwater* | | ●●● | ●●●◉ | ◉◉◉◉ | ◉◉◉◉ | ●●●● |
| | *Freshwater* | | ● | ●●●◉ | ◉◉◉◉ | ◉◉◉◉ | ◉◉◉◉ |

Moving upstream into their new environment, salmon make frequent stops in areas containing less current, such as holes, runs, and pools. The confluence of large rivers and tributary streams make perfect holding areas. Resting for as little as a few minutes to perhaps as long as a day or more, these places are tops for consistently locating salmon.

As the fish begin closing in on their spawning grounds, their habits relating to how they interact with artificial offerings become less enthusiastic. Bait such as salmon roe is more effective. However, male salmon well into the reproductive phase will often respond with heightened aggression, likely due to territorial impulses. The upside of this fact is that pre-spawn fish, for some reason, have a better rate of survival in catch and release than "brights".

## Rules & Regulations

Not all waters are open to salmon fishing throughout the year. Some drainages, especially the smaller or more popular ones, have seasonal or total closures for salmon or a specific species of salmon, or perhaps tackle and gear restrictions. The ADF&G, through the Board of Fisheries, establish rules and regulations in order to protect salmon at a time when they are vulnerable to angling activity. It is particularly the spawning period that is of concern for most species, most notably king, red, and silver salmon, yet other species such as pink and chum salmon are of lesser importance regulatory speaking due to the huge volume of fish and relatively little angling interest.

The following chapter sections describe all five species of salmon in Alaska and details the process of sport fishing for them, including brief information on biology. There are certain methods and techniques that can be used not just for salmon but other species as well and these are illustrated in the section on Angling Strategies at the end of this chapter in order to eliminate redundancy.

*(Courtesy King of the River)*

*Salmon of the same species may vary considerably in appearance according to age and physical maturation. All three of these anglers are holding a catch of king salmon, caught from the exact same location on the same day. Recognizing these differences within and between species is imperative in fishing for salmon and will keep anglers on the right side of the law. Remember; size of fish, time of season, and coloration are not always good indicators in determining species.*

# King Salmon

**Highlights:** Kings are extremely powerful and aggressive fish, prone to displays of sheer, unrelenting strength and endurance, often sounding deep in a bulldog manner along with long runs. Thrashes on the surface with occasional spectacular leaps.

**Common Name:** Chinook
**Timing:** May into August
**Size:** 15 to 40 pounds, up to 70 pounds

**State/World Record:** 97 pounds, 4 ounces
**Gear:** Heavy rod/reel; 20- to 30-pound test
**Tackle:** Lures, flies, and bait

King salmon – or chinook – is the largest species of the Pacific salmon family, known to attain weights of over 100 pounds. Regularly tipping scales upward of 30 to 40 pounds or more, kings are a very formidable opponent for any angler. It is the king that signals the official start of the fishing season in Alaska.

Springtime is synonymous with the arrival of early-run king salmon in May with most areas producing salmon by June, which is regarded as the best month overall for this species. A few rivers also offer late runs that will extend the season through July. Saltwater aficionados report outstanding catches early in the season (May and June) with year-round opportunities for immature feeder kings.

Despite being the least numerous of all salmon species, kings are regarded as the most sought-after quarry of all anglers. Action can be excellent in many locations, the drainages of Kenai Peninsula, Susitna Valley, and Copper Valley being of particular interest. All three of these areas have something special to offer in terms of king fishing. The peninsula is known for its coastal stream and saltwater opportunities for chrome salmon in the prime of their life, while the Susitna area has, on average, larger fish. Copper Valley is the least utilized by anglers looking for kings but nonetheless has some awesome fishing.

## Biology

**Scientific Name:** *Oncorhynchus tshawytscha*
**Description:** Black irregular cross-markings on back and upper sides. Both lobes of tail fin and top of head are covered with black spots, tongue and gum line on lower jaw is black.
**Size:** Common weight 10 to 50 pounds, averaging 15 to 30 pounds in most waters. Maximum weight generally 60-70 pounds; known to reach well over 125 pounds.
**Habitat/Abundance:** Clear to semi-glacial coastal, inland, and interior drainages. Large or important populations are found in tributaries of the Susitna, and Copper rivers, and in drainages of Matanuska Valley and Kenai Peninsula.

**Ocean Phase:** Greenish blue-black on back; silvery to white on lower sides and belly. Flesh color is orange-red.
**Adult Diet:** Primarily herring, sand lance, squid, and crustaceans.

**Presence:** Year-round offshore, mature kings peaking May and June near shore. Fish enter fresh water from late April to early October, peaking late May to mid-July.
**Spawning:** Rivers and streams from mid-June to late October, most July and August. Females deposit 2,000-14,000 eggs, hatching in late winter or early spring
**Life Span:** One to two years in fresh water, one to six years at sea; up to eight years of age.

**Spawning Phase:** Dark red to copper, brown, occasionally almost black. Males develop a kype, large teeth protrude from jaw, and spine takes on a ridgeback condition. Flesh color is pale pink to white.

## Identification

*Black mouth and gums are distinct for kings. Note large spots on neck, top of head, and upper gill plate.*

*Black "X"-shaped or irregular markings and spots on top of back and dorsal fin.*

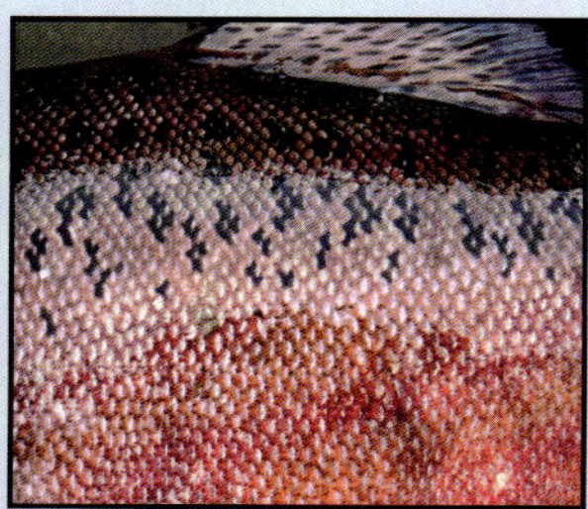

*Markings are very pronounced on the reddish back and sides of pre-spawning and spawning fish.*

*The whole tail fin is covered with black spots, a unique feature for kings.*

## Fishing for King Salmon

(Courtesy Eagle Eye Images)

**Top Areas:** The tidewater streams and larger glacial rivers of Kenai Peninsula have a long record of producing quality sport for dime-bright kings. Great marine fisheries here as well. Look to the small coastal and inland drainages of the Matanuska-Susitna valleys for top-notch excitement of casting to big kings in small waters. Copper Valley only has a few productive waters but they are world-class in producing intense action for potentially trophy-sized specimens.

**Regulatory Season:** Varies greatly according to specific location but often commence on January 1 and conclude sometime during the month of July as the spawning period draws near. With few exceptions, all freshwater fisheries have ended by August 1.

King salmon are voracious predators, this fact clearly showing in their willingness to strike artificial lures and flies. This coupled with the fact that kings grow to significant proportions and display intense fighting abilities sure to test the skills (and stamina) of the most experienced angler. It is sometimes an intimidating challenge to the beginner or anglers not familiar with salmon fishing in general; however, knowledge is the key to overcoming any obstacle and these fish can be enjoyed by young and old alike at any skill level.

The southern Kenai Peninsula streams and the mouth of tributaries draining into the glacial Susitna River are perfect locations for novice king anglers.

### Saltwater

Surfcasting the briny for kings display more of a challenge to roadside anglers. First of all, the number of freshwater locations vastly outnumber available saltwater opportunities. Second, intimate knowledge of habits associated with tidal movements and feeding patterns become a necessity for consistent hook-ups.

For angler's casting from shore, the best king fishing is experienced at or near the mouth of clearwater drainages, this being especially the case in locations experiencing runs of hatchery fish. Incoming tides are often preferred as fish focus in on potential breeding waters, but action is sometimes equally productive – if not even more so – on an outgoing tide as a lot of fish back out into the briny again from the lower reaches of rivers and streams. Spinners are very effective as are clusters of salmon roe or small whole herring drifted with or without a strike indicator.

Some success can also be had casting in areas with a steep drop-off, typically off breakwater and deepwater docks. Mature (spawn-bound) as well as "feeder" (immature) kings are available. Use jigs and large silvery spoons with a touch of blue or green. Whole or cut herring fished deep draw strikes.

Trolling or mooching from a boat is the most predictable way of connecting with salty kings. Spinners and herring are popular but hammered spoons and jigs work well too. Try around kelp beds and pinnacles, looking for signs of baitfish by bird activity and seals.

(Courtesy Jack Rambac)

A tidewater king puts up a valiant fight all the way up to the very end. This is a scene from a cove near Whittier.

### Freshwater

Target kings in moderate to slow moving current, keeping lures and flies near the bottom where fish lie in cover. Unlike most other salmon species, kings often favor the deeper section of river and stream channels, even in some of the swiftest glacial waters, with the biggest specimens occupying the deepest spots. Yet

## King Salmon Hot Spots & Timing

● = High ● = Moderate ● = Low ● = Closed

(Dots transcribed as: H = High, M = Moderate, L = Low, C = Closed)

| Kenai Peninsula | APR | MAY | JUN | JUL | AUG | SEP |
|---|---|---|---|---|---|---|
| Passage Canal | L L L L | L L M M | M M H H | H M M L | L L L L | |
| Resurrection Bay | L L L L | L L L M | M H H H | M M L L | L L L L | L L L L |
| Kenai River (middle) | | L L L M | M H H H | M M H H | C C C C | C C C |
| Kenai River (lower) | L | L L M M | H H H M | M H H H | C C C C | C C C |
| Kasilof River | L | L L M M | H H H M | M M H H | C C C C | C C C |
| Ninilchik River | C | C C C H | H H C C | L L L L | L L | |
| Deep Creek | C | C C C H | H H C C | C C C C | C C | |
| Anchor River | C | C C M H | H H H C | C C C C | C C | |
| Dudiak Lagoon | L | L L M H | H H H M | M L L L | L L | |
| Cook Inlet | L L L L | M M H H | H M M M | H H M M | L L L L | L L L L |
| Kachemak Bay | L L L L | L M M H | H M M L | L L L L | L L L L | L L L L |

| Matanuska-Susitna Valleys | APR | MAY | JUN | JUL | AUG | SEP |
|---|---|---|---|---|---|---|
| Ship Creek | L | L L M M | H H H M | M L C C | C C | |
| Eklutna Tailrace | L | L L M M | M H H M | M L L L | L L | |
| Little Susitna River | L | L L M M | H H H H | M L C C | C C | |
| Willow Creek | | L L L | M M H H | C C C C | C C | |
| Little Willow Creek | | L | L L M H | C C C C | C C | |
| Kashwitna River | | L L | L M H H | C C C C | C C | |
| Caswell Creek | | L L | L M M H | C C C C | C | |
| Sheep Creek | | L L | L M H H | C C C C | C C | |
| Montana Creek | | L L | L M H H | C C C C | C C | |
| Talkeetna River | | L | L L M H | H M C C | C C | |
| Sunshine Creek | | L | L L M H | C C C C | C | |
| Rabideux Creek | | L | L M M H | C C C C | C C | |
| East Fork Chulitna River | | | L L M H | H H C C | C C | |

| Copper Valley & Valdez Arm | APR | MAY | JUN | JUL | AUG | SEP |
|---|---|---|---|---|---|---|
| Gulkana River | | L | L M H H | H M M C | C C | |
| Tazlina River | | L | L M M H | H H M C | C C | |
| Klutina River | | C | C C C C | H M H H | H M C C | C C |
| Tonsina River | | C | C C C C | H M H H | H M C C | C C |
| Port Valdez | L L L L | L L M M | M M M M | M M L L | L L L L | L L L L |

the traditional holding areas for salmon still apply, anglers doing very well focusing on holes and runs, the confluence of large rivers and clearwater tributaries, and estuaries on an incoming or outgoing tide.

Still or stagnant water with little or no current influence are generally not good for hooking into fish on a consistent basis, and fish in such locations often develop a lockjaw condition, frustrating anglers. However, a few kings may still be enticed at dawn, especially, using bait such as roe or herring fished under a strike indicator.

Spoons, spinners, attractors, flies, and bait are preferred tackle for anglers fishing off the bank, while boaters often have the advantage of using plugs as well. Plugs are most often fished stationary or by back trolling, with or without a sardine wrap, and are particularly effective in spring when water is cold and kings tight-lipped. In smaller drainages, flipping a lure or fly to holding areas and letting it drift is a good option. Larger waters may warrant long casts, followed by a drift or slow retrieve.

Lures are ideally medium to large in size; green, blue, and chartreuse are good all-around colors and fish very well early in the season, with orange and red coming into play in murky water, low-light, or warmer water temperatures. Silver, copper, and bronze hues with or without color inserts or combinations are perfect under most conditions, many angler preferring them when sunny and water clear.

Spinners in particular can draw savage strikes, buzzed at an angle through the water column. If water is cold, such as after snowmelt, spinners held in place or slowly backed downstream through a hole containing kings is likely to be slammed. Spoons may have the same effect at times. In contrast, when water is warmer, spinners sliced rapidly downstream through a holding area can be deadly.

Equally with hardware, flies are quite large compared to standard patterns used for other salmon and trout. Bulk and flash often dictate most anglers' choice in king flies but smaller, darker varieties work just as well and, in some cases when the water is clear and skies sunny, even better. Black and metallic purple, blue, and green are tops.

Sleek, eyed streamers imitating baitfish do very well in coastal waters, often eliciting swift, bone-jarring strikes. The gaudier patterns in orange, pink, and red resembling salmon roe are more universal, kings generally mouthing them carefully but firmly.

Where legal, bait can have a phenomenal effect on kings, especially when all else seems to fail. A medium-sized cluster of salmon roe – fished either alone or with an attractor – is proven lethal if allowed to drift with the current. Plug-cut herring can be equally effective, usually when a slow retrieve is applied, allowing the herring to "swim" through a slot.

## Equipment

### Spin- & Bait-Casting

**Rod:** 7 ½- to 8 ½-foot, medium-fast action, heavy salmon rod.

**Reel:** Heavy freshwater or light saltwater spinning- or bait-casting reel.

**Line:** 200 yards of 20- to 30-pound test mono/braided line.

**Advice:** Lighter rod and line (down to 15 lb. test) can be used in slackwater areas or from boat. Line in the 20-25 pound test bracket is good almost universally and ideal when fishing small clearwater streams such as those found on southern Kenai Peninsula where kings are of average size. Bank fishing on large, swift-flowing glacial waters, like the Kenai and Klutina rivers, use at least 30- or 40-pound test, preferably with bait-casting reel. Heavy line and gear recommended in trophy fish locations, in saltwater fisheries, and during crowded condition.

**Best Lures:** Spoons, spinners, plugs, attractors, jigs.

Popular Brands

**Spoons:** Pixee, Krocodile, HotRod, Syclops, Super Duper, Little Cleo (Sizes ½-1 oz.).

**Spinners:** Vibrax, G.I. Spinner, Aglia, Black Fury, Tee Spoon, Flash Glo (Sizes 4-6).

**Plugs:** Kwikfish, Flatfish, Tadpolly, Wiggle Wart, Hot Shot (Sizes 8-15).

**Attractors:** Spin-N-Glo, Cheater, Corkie (Sizes 2-3 in.).

**Jigs:** Krocodile, Buzz Bomb, Kastmaster, Swedish Pimple (Sizes 3-5 in.).

*Pixee*
Orange & Silver 7/8 oz.

*Vibrax*
Blue & Silver #5-6

*Flash Glo*
Orange & Silver #5

*Kwikfish*
Silver & Chart. K-14

*Spin-N-Glo*

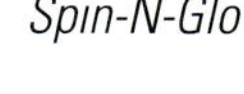

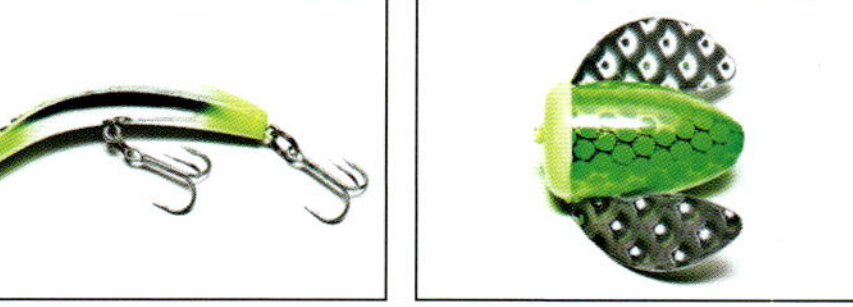

### Fly-Fishing

**Rod:** 9- to 12 weight, 9- to 10-foot, medium-fast action fly rod with fighting butt section.

**Reel:** Large salmon/tarpon class reel; strong and smooth drag system.

**Line:** 150 yards of 30-pound backing, WF full float or sink tip Type III-IV lines or T-series, 300-600 grain lines with heavy steelhead/salmon leader, 15- to 25-pound tippet.

**Advice:** Although rods down to the 8-weight class with matching reel and line can be used successfully on smaller king streams (Anchor, Deep, Ninilchik), anglers usually fare better with 9- and 10-weights in most conditions. In the Susitna and Copper valleys, 10-weight rods or larger may work better due to size of fish. Big waters (Kenai/Klutina) command heavier gear like a 12-weight with fast sinking line and at least 30-pound tippet.

**Best Flies:** Attractors, Egg, Saltwater.

Popular Patterns (Hook size 1/0-3/0)

**Attractors:** Flash Fly, Alaskabou, Bunny Fly, Sparkle Shrimp, Wiggletail, Polar Shrimp, Egg Sucking Leech, Alaska Mary Ann, Popsicle, Everglow, Zonker.

**Egg/Flesh:** King Caviar, King Killer, Fat Freddie, Bunny Bug, Battle Creek.

**Saltwater:** Candlefish, Deceiver, Baitfish, Clouser Minnow, Shrimp, Salmon Treat, Herring Fly.

**Local Favorites:**

*Trailer Trash*
Chart. & Blue #1/0

*Fat Freddie*
Chart. & Orange #4/0

*Stinger Prawn*
Black & Blue #2/0

*Stinger Prawn*
Pink #1/0

*Jumbo Critter*
Pink & Orange #1/0

# Red Salmon

**Highlights:** A superb gamester, reds are known for spectacular aerial jumps multiple feet high. Always going airborne several times in a row, initial runs are lightening fast and powerful, usually keeping near the surface, with plenty of thrashing and rolling when starting to tire.

**Common Name:** Sockeye
**Timing:** June into September
**Size:** 4 to 10 pounds, up to 14 pounds

**State Record:** 16 pounds, 0 ounces
**Gear:** Medium rod/reel; 8- to 17-pound test
**Tackle:** Flies and bait

Red salmon – or sockeye – are reputed to be, pound for pound, the hardest fighting species of salmon. Also, their sheer abundance and exceptional value as a food has helped make the red the most popular salmon in the state.

Generally a summer visitor to Alaska's roadside waters, entering popular fisheries anytime between June and September with most drainages seeing peak returns in July and August. As is the case with other salmon species, some areas experience more than one run of fish during a season. Early runs reach full strength in June while the late runs appear in July and August. A few locations even have salmon available into September.

Anglers targeting reds in rivers and streams report phenomenal catch rates in several of the larger fisheries on the Kenai Peninsula and in the Copper Valley. Overall, the red is not as widely distributed as other species, owing largely to the fact that these fish prefer waters with connecting lakes for reproductive purposes. Runoff streams in general do not have worthwhile fishing for reds. Yet, what these salmon lack in distribution they make up for in numbers. The Kenai River for example, a major red producer on the Kenai Peninsula, may in some years receive in the order of 1 million or more salmon, the fish swarming throughout the drainage resulting in outstanding action.

## Biology

**Scientific Name:** *Oncorhynchus nerka*
**Description:** Very minute black freckles may occasionally be seen on back, usually none at all.
**Size:** Common weight 3 to 10 pounds, averaging 4 to 7 pounds in most waters. Maximum weight generally 12 pounds; known to reach 16 pounds or more.
**Habitat/Abundance:** Clear to semi-glacial coastal and inland drainages associated with lakes. Large or important populations are found in tributaries of the Susitna and Copper rivers, and in drainages of Matanuska Valley and Kenai Peninsula.
**Adult Diet:** Primarily crustaceans (shrimp).

**Ocean Phase:** Dark steel-blue to greenish blue on back; sides are silvery, fading to silvery white on belly. Flesh color is ruby red.

**Presence:** April to October offshore, peaking May to August. Fish enter fresh water from early May to late October, peaking early June to mid-August.
**Spawning:** Lakes, rivers, streams, and springs from mid-June to mid-March, most July to October. Females deposit 2,000-4,500 eggs, hatching in late winter or early spring.
**Life Span:** One to three years in fresh water, one to four years at sea; up to five years of age.

**Spawning Phase:** Brilliant red, also dirty brown, pale red, dark purplish to almost black. Distinct olive green head. Males develop a slight humped back and tooth-filled kype. Flesh color is pale pink to white.

## Identification

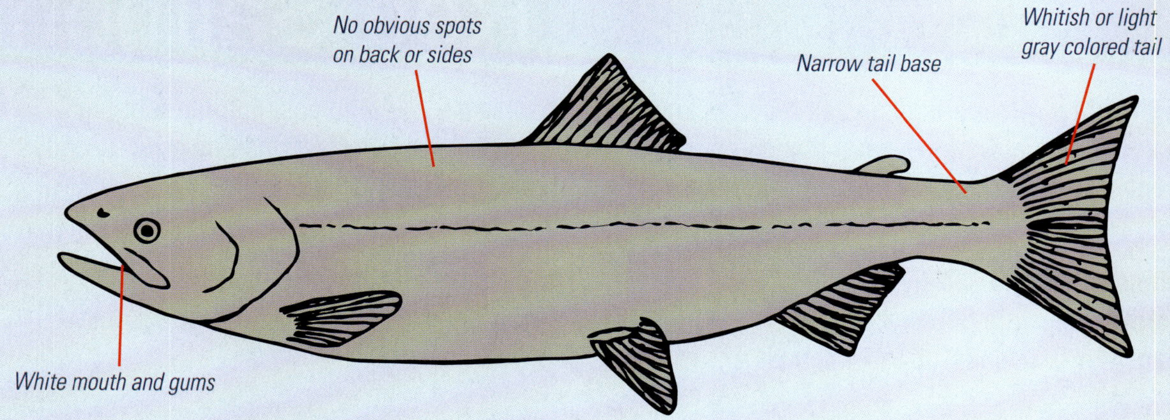

*Mouth and gums are white to light grey, no spots present on head or neck. Distinct green to blue color.*

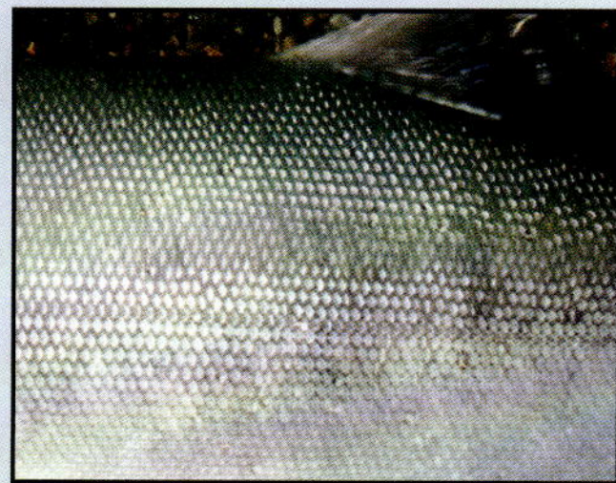

*No spots present on back or dorsal fin, although fish in some stocks may have very faint speckles.*

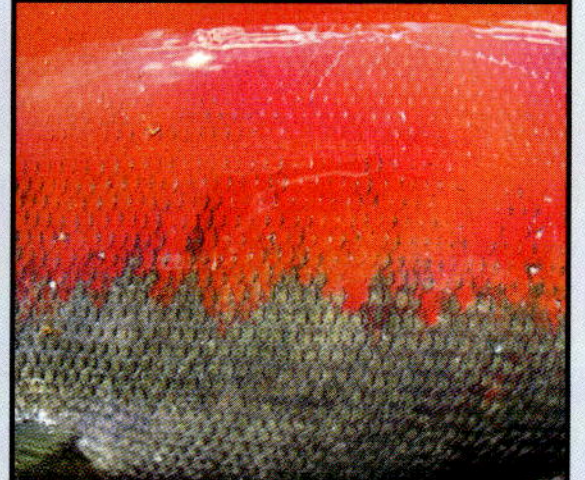

*Bright crimson color with light grey belly on spawning fish, lacking spots on back and sides.*

*Tail is typically light in color, no spots. Kokanee may have spots.*

## Fishing for Red Salmon

**Top Areas:** Although generally not as prolific in distribution as other salmon species, runs tend to be heavy where found. The coastal and inland glacial drainages of Kenai Peninsula are legendary for producing huge numbers of fish and superb action. A few isolated spots in Matanuska-Susitna valleys. Copper Valley rivers can be exceptional.
**Regulatory Season:** Very few species-specific restrictions in place most anywhere red salmon are found.

(Courtesy Eagle Eye Images)

Reds are often quite finicky about striking angler's offerings because these salmon do not have a very developed hunt-and-chase instinct like that of true predators such as kings and silvers. A few aggressive males may at times lash out at hardware yet the vast majority of red salmon are caught on flies. Additionally, as many inexperienced anglers or anglers new to Alaska soon discover, reds holding in still water (such as lakes and sloughs) are infamously tight-lipped.

### Saltwater

Although rivers and streams may be teaming with literally tens of thousands or more of these silvery torpedoes, there is surprisingly little angling taking place in saltwater despite the obvious presence of salmon. This is perhaps for the most part due to the reluctance of reds to strike offerings on a consistent basis because adult salmon feed strictly on small crustaceans and not fish as is the case with other salmon species. Thus, reds do not generally strike lures such as spoons and spinners with any vigor. The few fish that are landed in the ocean are either incidental catches while targeting other species or intentionally snagged when located in schools.

The method of trolling colored single hooks have not caught on in roadside locations around the Kenai Peninsula or Prince William Sound as they have elsewhere in the Pacific northwest, perhaps due to the fact waters having less visibility due to glacial silt. However, fishing for ocean reds is still in its infancy in Alaska and successful methods and techniques could very well develop in the future.

A few snag fisheries targeting saltwater sockeye have developed in recent years and is growing in popularity with anglers more concerned with stocking their freezers than the sporting value of the fish. These fisheries take place in and around the mouth of rivers and streams where fish congregate in preparation to moving upstream, anglers using snag hooks or similar setups for efficient harvest.

The intertidal area of Resurrection River in Seward is a typical example of this type of fishery and a couple of similar, but smaller, harvest locations exist as well.

### Freshwater

Without a doubt, the vast majority of sockeye fishing done in Southcentral Alaska takes place in flowing waters. Although not aggressive strikers, a proven "jawbreaker" is a fly drifted just above the bottom in moderate to swift current. Since reds for the most part follow the shoreline, perhaps six to 15 feet from the bank in two to four feet of water, wading out deep

*Fishing for sockeye is synonymous with summer activity on some of Alaska's most gorgeous rivers and streams.*

## Red Salmon Hot Spots & Timing

🔴 = High 🟠 = Moderate 🟣 = Low ⚫ = Closed

| **Kenai Peninsula** | MAY | JUN | JUL | AUG | SEP | OCT |
|---|---|---|---|---|---|---|
| Kenai River (upper) | ⚫⚫ | ⚫🟠🔴🔴 | 🟠🟣🟠🔴 | 🔴🟠🟠🟣 | 🟣🟣🟣🟣 | 🟣 |
| Russian River | ⚫⚫ | ⚫🟠🔴🔴 | 🔴🟠🟠🔴 | 🔴🔴🟠⚫ | ⚫⚫⚫ | |
| Kenai River (middle) | 🟣🟣🟣 | 🟠🔴🟠🟣 | 🟣🟠🔴🔴 | 🔴🟠🟠🟣 | 🟣🟣🟣🟣 | 🟣 |
| Kenai River (lower) | 🟣🟣🟣 | 🟠🟠🟠🟣 | 🟣🟠🔴🔴 | 🔴🟠🟠🟣 | 🟣🟣🟣 | |
| Kasilof River | 🟣🟣 | 🟣🟠🔴🟠 | 🟠🟠🔴🔴 | 🔴🟠🟠🟣 | 🟣🟣🟣🟣 | |
| Ninilchik River | | ⚫ | 🟣🟠🟠🟠 | 🟣🟣🟣🟣 | | |
| **Matanuska-Susitna Valleys** | **MAY** | **JUN** | **JUL** | **AUG** | **SEP** | **OCT** |
| Jim Creek | | 🟣 | 🟣🟣🟠🔴 | 🔴🟠🟣🟣 | 🟣🟣 | |
| Cottonwood Creek | | 🟣 | 🟣🟣🟠🔴 | 🟠🟣🟣🟣 | | |
| Little Susitna River | 🟣🟣 | 🟣🟠🟠🟠 | 🟣🟣🟠🟠 | 🟠🟠🟣🟣 | 🟣 | |
| Talkeetna River | 🟣 | 🟣🟣🟠🟠 | 🟠🟣🟠🔴 | 🔴🔴🟠🟣 | 🟣🟣 | |
| Byers Creek | | | 🟣🟣🟠 | 🔴🔴🟠🟣 | 🟣🟣 | |
| **Copper Valley & Valdez** | **MAY** | **JUN** | **JUL** | **AUG** | **SEP** | **OCT** |
| Gulkana River | 🟣🟣 | 🟣🟠🔴🔴 | 🔴🟠🟠🟠 | 🟠🔴🔴🔴 | 🔴🟠🟠🟣 | 🟣🟣🟣 |
| Klutina River | 🟣🟣 | 🟣🟠🔴🔴 | 🔴🟠🟠🟠 | 🔴🔴🟠🟠 | 🟣🟣🟣🟣 | 🟣 |
| Tonsina River | 🟣🟣 | 🟣🟣🟠🟠 | 🟣🟣🟠🔴 | 🔴🔴🟠🟠 | 🟣🟣🟣🟣 | |
| Robe River | 🟣🟣🟣 | 🟠🔴🔴🟠 | 🟠🟣🟣🟣 | | | |

and/or making long casts becomes unnecessary, anglers adapting to the conditions by using techniques that reflect the situation.

"Flipping" is a very effective technique when fish are streaming through a channel or narrow area near shore. In large drainages with considerable current, such as the Kenai and Klutina rivers, the majority of salmon swim upstream close to the bank, making for relatively easy targets using the flipping technique. Straight cast-and-retrieve is considered unproductive in most areas, as is most forms of stationary fishing methods.

In some locations, however, a small cluster of salmon roe (about 1 square inch in size) on a single-hook setup, allowed to sit on the bottom in a calm current or quiet pool, will draw consistent strikes, a proven technique in such places as the Kenai and Little Susitna rivers, Jim Creek, and the Eklutna Tailrace, among others. Krill-scented egg cures, in particular, are responsible for limit catches.

Also, a small corkie or bead left hanging in a migratory channel can draw hard, savage strikes. Plugs fished from a boat will also provoke reds to bite on occasion.

Yet it is flies, for various reasons, that are more readily

*A male sockeye in full spawning attire is readied for release. On many inland waterways, be prepared to scuffle with breeding fish.*

accepted by anglers and fish alike, perhaps in part because some patterns mimic natural food sources (shrimp) more precisely. But it must never be discounted that a great many, if not the vast majority, of reds caught on standard flies are simply "lined"; that is, the fly just drifts into the mouth of the fish with the help of the current, the line tightens, and the angler sets the hook–fish on. A simple and highly effective process that works.

Swinging wet flies is absolutely the technique of choice among Alaska anglers. Whether going by the theories of fish being lined or fair strike, the undisputed fact is that reds are caught in massive numbers around Southcentral with the locations on Kenai Peninsula and Copper Valley leading the way.

Fairly small, sparsely-tied patterns in dark or neutral colors or color combinations (black, purple, dark green and blue, white) are generally much more effective in clearwater situations, with larger, gaudy creations in fluorescent orange, pink, and chartreuse often being the ticket in glacial systems. Anglers casting flies do so successfully using spin-/bait-casting rods and fly rods both.

While takes are typically soft and subtle, there are times when hard and heavy strikes can be felt. Fish can also be observed moving a foot or two to intercept a fly, although such instances are not common, except for those occasions when a correct presentation is made to a school of fish.

As anglers pursue the wily sockeye in search of the perfect fly and accompanying technique that will positively result in consistent fair-hooked game, and thus changing the way fishers think and apply their sport, catching these reds remains an unpredictable and fascinating challenge that continues to attract anglers to Alaska.

## Equipment

### Spin- & Bait-Casting

**Rod:** 6 ½- to 8-foot, medium action salmon rod.
**Reel:** High performance freshwater spinning/bait-casting reel.
**Line:** 150 yards of 12- to 17-pound test mono/braided line.
**Advice:** Lighter rod and line (down to 6 lb. test) can be used in slackwater areas or from boat. Line in the 15-pound test bracket is perfect under most conditions. Use up to 20-pound test when bank fishing on large, swift-flowing glacial waters like the Kenai and Klutina rivers. Heavy line and gear is also recommended during crowded conditions.

### Fly-Fishing

**Rod:** 7- to 9-weight, 9- to 10-foot, medium-fast action fly rod.
**Reel:** Salmon class reel; smooth and reliable drag system.
**Line:** 100-150 yards of 20- to 30-pound backing, WF full float or sink tip Type II-IV lines, 200-250 grain lines with salmon leader, 8- to 17-pound tippet.
**Advice:** Smaller streams and in slower moving water, use weight forward floating line. In large, fast-flowing glacial rivers, 9-weight rods with sink tip line and at least 15-pound test tippet are good due to current and battle antics of fish. Kenai and Klutina are typical big-water locations.

**Best Flies:** Attractor, Egg/Flesh, Forage.
*Popular Patterns (Hook size 2–8)*
**Attractor:** Flash Fly, Alaskabou, Sparkle Shrimp, Sockeye Willie, Fall Favorite, Yarn Fly, Polar Shrimp, Egg Sucking Leech, Sockeye Orange, Sportsman Special, Russian River, Alaska Mary Ann, Sockeye Charlie, Popsicle, Everglow, Skykomish Sunrise, Boss, Green Butt Skunk, Mickey Finn, Coho Fly.
**Egg/Flesh:** Battle Creek, Yarn Fly, Babine Special, Two-Egg Sperm Fly, Glo Bug, Marabou Flesh Fly.
**Forage:** Leech.

**Local Favorites:**

*Hot Stone Nymph*
Green #6

*Salmon River MVP*
#4

*Baranof Bomber*
#6

*Green Beret*
#6

*Polar Shrimp AK*
#6

# Pink Salmon

**Highlights:** Typically very aggressive and ideally targeted when chrome and fresh from the ocean. Bulldogging along with short and speedy runs and plenty of surface thrashing are common traits and battle antics of these diminutive salmon. Not much of a jumper but will do so when ocean bright.

**Common Name:** Humpback
**Timing:** July and August
**Size:** 2 to 6 pounds, up to 9 pounds

**State Record:** 12 pounds, 9 ounces
**Gear:** Light rod/reel; 4- to 8-pound test
**Tackle:** Lures, flies, and bait

Pink salmon – or humpback – are the most abundant of all salmon species, often clogging certain coastal streams during the spawning runs, creating the easiest fishing there is with fish-on-every-cast action common. Typically, runs are heaviest on even-numbered years in Southcentral Alaska waters with a few areas being better on odd.

The pink is a summer-run fish throughout the majority of Alaska's roadside rivers and streams, showing up in July and August with peak abundance from mid-July to early August. Probably exhibiting the greatest contraction in run timing of any salmon, appearances are typically fairly brief yet overwhelming. Early runs, peaking in July, are most common throughout Southcentral Alaska with late runs (August peak) only being the norm in certain locations on the Kenai Peninsula and in Prince William Sound.

Superb action await anglers trying their luck at the mouth of clearwater drainages of the Susitna Valley, in the Anchorage area, Matanuska Valley, and most all coastal streams on the Kenai Peninsula. The marine fisheries of Prince William Sound and southern Kenai Peninsula harbor outstanding pink salmon fishing. Largest runs occur at Port Valdez (known as the Pink Salmon Capitol of the World) with fish numbering in the tens of millions, and the Kenai River that also has a run totaling in the millions.

## Biology

**Scientific Name:** *Oncorhynchus gorbuscha*
**Description:** Fait oval-shaped black spots cover back and both lobes of tail fin.
**Size:** Common weight 2 to 6 pounds, averaging 3 to 5 pounds in most waters. Maximum weight generally 7 pounds; known to reach 12 pounds or more.
**Habitat/Abundance:** Clear to semi-glacial coastal and inland drainages. Large or important populations are found in tributaries of the Susitna River and in drainages of Matanuska Valley, the Anchorage area, Prince William Sound, and Kenai Peninsula.
**Adult Diet:** Primarily fish and crustaceans.

**Presence:** May to October offshore, peaking July and August. Fish enter fresh water from mid-June to early October, peaking mid-July to mid-August.
**Spawning:** Rivers, streams, and estuaries from early July to late October, most August and September. Females deposit 800-2,300 eggs, hatching in winter.
**Life Span:** A few weeks in fresh water, 1 ½ years at sea; nearly 2 years of age.

**Ocean Phase:** Steel blue to blue green on back; silver on sides fading to white on belly. Flesh color is orange.

**Spawning Phase:** Dirty brown on back; sides are yellowish green; belly creamy white. Males develop very distinct humped back and elongated, hooked snout. Large, black oval spots are visible on back, dorsal fin, both lobes of tail fin. Flesh color is yellowish white to white.

## Identification

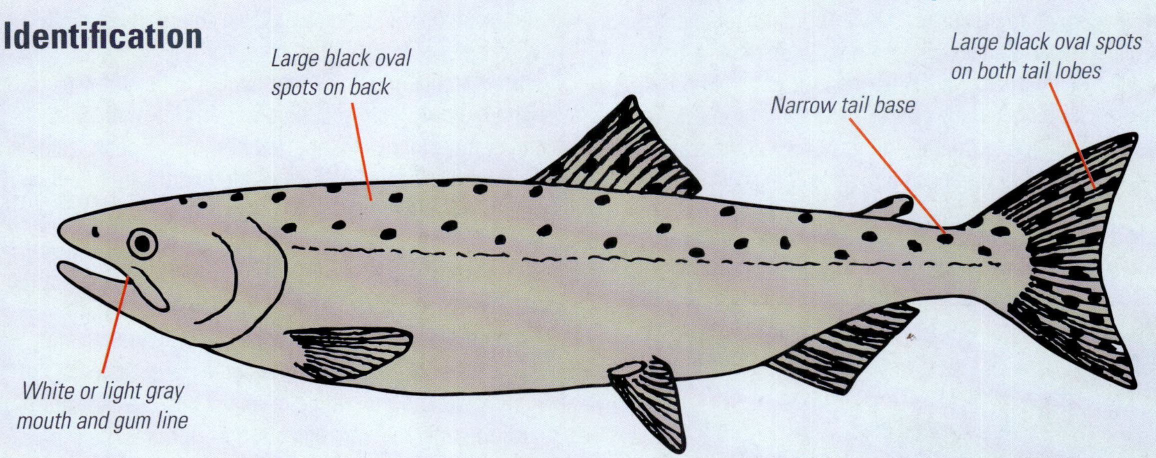

*Large spots on neck, none on gill plates. Mouth and gums are white or light grey.*

*Large oval spots cover back and upper sides, may not be obvious on very chrome specimens.*

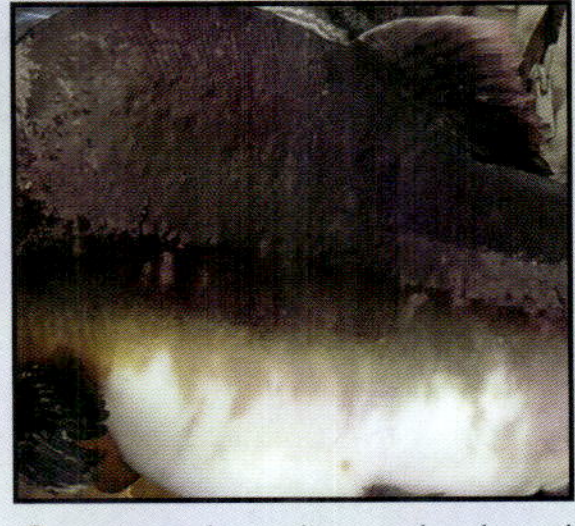

*Spawners have brown back and upper sides, yellowish-green markings on lower sides.*

*Large markings on both tail lobes, bigger than any other salmon species.*

## Fishing for Pink Salmon

**Top Areas:** The marine fisheries all along the coast of Kenai Peninsula and Prince William Sound are prime locations to target pinks. Tidewater and inland rivers and streams of these areas as well as those of Matanuska and Susitna valleys may produce some of the fastest action seen anywhere. As a rule, focus on coastal waters.
**Regulatory Season:** Very few to no species-specific restrictions in place anywhere pink salmon are found.

Pinks are usually not a bit shy about striking a variety of lures and flies, especially when concentrated in big numbers, which is common on many waters. The "fish-on-every-cast" notion is most definitely a case in point with pinks as these very social salmon stage en masse in bays, at the mouth of spawning streams, and in deep holes of coastal and inland drainages. Yet there are times when pinks can be surprisingly reluctant to bite and this is when rules governing fishing in general become important.

One of the reasons why pinks are underrated in many ways is because most anglers do not use proper gear and tackle. More "glamorous" species – such as reds or silvers – may be present, prompting anglers to use heavier line and rod than what would ordinarily be necessary for a fish averaging only a few pounds. Use ultra-light equipment to truly experience the best of these fish. Remember, a fresh pink will often outperform the battle antics of a char of the same size, lending serious credibility to their prowess. The biggest impediment, strangely enough, may actually be the availability of pinks: too much of a good thing.

*On a mid-summer day on one of many coastal and inland rivers and streams, catching dozens or more bright pinks is typical.*

*(Courtesy Eagle Eye Images)*

### Saltwater

Many anglers, when targeting pinks, do so exclusively in saltwater as fish are much more likely to be in top condition for both sport and eating qualities.

Surfcasting is good early in the season in locations along breakwater, points, and steep drop-offs using silvery spoons and weighted flies in blue or green inserts and small or cut pieces of herring. Later on, focus attention in coves, small bays, and exposed beaches near the mouth of spawning streams. Incoming and high tides are usually most productive when fish concentrate in big schools. Spoons, spinners, and flies in neutral hues draw strikes, as will pink, orange, red, and chartreuse colors – especially in glacial or semi-glacial waters.

Boaters frequently encounter huge numbers of fish in offshore areas while scouting for early silver salmon. Trolling or mooching smaller-sized herring or spoons take fish on a regular basis, as does casting hardware and flies directly to schools of fish.

### Freshwater

Ideal water for catching pinks include moderate to fast current. Slack water conditions can be productive at times, particularly if pinks are present in large schools, but can just as well be frustrating to anglers as the fish seem to go off the bite. In rivers and streams with fast current, pinks tend to hug close to the shoreline, successful anglers employing very short casts or, better yet, the flipping technique for efficiency. Conversely, moderate to slow moving water spread fish throughout the main channel, making longer casts more practical.

Adjust the angle of making a cast according to current flow and depth. Usually, casting at a 45-degree angle upstream and follow with a slow retrieve or drift is effective in hooking pinks on a regular basis. Do not retrieve or strip the lure or fly rapidly as one would for a king or silver; let the offering work the water columns.

Pinks in general are fond of small- to medium-sized lures, preferably with a chrome/silver base and a touch of

## Pink Salmon Hot Spots & Timing

● = High ● = Moderate ● = Low ● = Closed

| Kenai Peninsula | MAY | JUN | JUL | AUG | SEP | OCT |
|---|---|---|---|---|---|---|
| Indian Creek | | Low | Low, Moderate, High, High | Moderate, Low, Low, Low | | |
| Bird Creek | | Closed | Closed, Closed, High, High | Moderate, Low, Low, Low | | |
| Glacier Creek | | Low | Low, Moderate, High, High | Moderate, Moderate, Low, Low | Low | |
| Passage Canal | | Low, Low | Moderate, Moderate, High, High | Moderate, Moderate, Low, Low | Low | |
| Ingram Creek | | Low | Low, Moderate, High, High | Moderate, Low, Low, Low | | |
| Sixmile Creek | | Low | Low, Moderate, High, High | Moderate, Moderate, Low, Low | Low | |
| Resurrection Creek | | Low | Low, Moderate, High, High | Moderate, Low, Low, Low | | |
| Resurrection Bay | | Low, Low | Low, Moderate, High, High | High, High, Moderate, Moderate | Low, Low, Low, Low | |
| Kenai River (middle) | | Low | Low, Low, Moderate, Moderate | High, High, High, Moderate | Moderate, Low, Low, Low | |
| Moose River | | Low | Low, Low, Moderate, Moderate | High, High, High, Moderate | Moderate, Low, Low, Low | |
| Kenai River (lower) | | Low, Low | Low, Moderate, Moderate, High | High, High, High, Moderate | Moderate, Low, Low, Low | |
| Kasilof River | | Low | Low, Low, Moderate, Moderate | High, High, Moderate, Moderate | Low, Low, Low | |
| Ninilchik River | | Low | Low, Moderate, Moderate, High | High, Moderate, Moderate, Moderate | Low, Low, Low | |
| Deep Creek | | Low | Low, Moderate, Moderate, High | High, Moderate, Moderate, Moderate | Low, Low, Low | |
| Stariski Creek | | Low | Low, Moderate, Moderate, High | High, Moderate, Moderate, Moderate | Low, Low, Low | |
| Anchor River | | Low | Low, Moderate, Moderate, High | High, Moderate, Moderate, Moderate | Low, Low, Low | |
| Kachemak Bay | | Low, Low, Low | Moderate, High, High, High | Moderate, Moderate, Moderate, Low | Low, Low, Low | |

| Matanuska-Susitna Valleys | MAY | JUN | JUL | AUG | SEP | OCT |
|---|---|---|---|---|---|---|
| Ship Creek | | Low | Low, Moderate, High, High | Moderate, Low, Low, Low | | |
| Little Susitna River | | Low | Low, Moderate, High, High | Moderate, Moderate, Low, Low | | |
| Willow Creek | | Low | Low, Moderate, Moderate, High | High, Moderate, Low, Low | | |
| Little Willow Creek | | | Low, Low, Moderate, High | High, Moderate, Low, Low | | |
| Caswell Creek | | | Low, Low, Moderate, High | Moderate, Moderate, Low, Low | | |
| Sheep Creek | | | Low, Low, Moderate, High | High, Moderate, Low, Low | | |
| Goose Creek | | | Low, Low, Moderate, High | High, Moderate, Low, Low | | |
| Montana Creek | | | Low, Low, Moderate, High | High, Moderate, Low, Low | | |
| Sunshine Creek | | | Low, Low, Moderate, High | Moderate, Moderate, Low, Low | | |
| Rabideux Creek | | | Low, Low, Moderate, High | Moderate, Moderate, Low, Low | | |
| Byers Creek | | | Low, Low, Moderate | High, Moderate, Low, Low | | |

| Copper Valley & Valdez | MAY | JUN | JUL | AUG | SEP | OCT |
|---|---|---|---|---|---|---|
| Robe River | | Low | Low, Moderate, High, High | Moderate, Moderate, Low, Low | | |
| Port Valdez | Low | Low, Low, Moderate, Moderate | High, High, High, Moderate | Moderate, Moderate, Low, Low | Low | |

green or orange depending on the water conditions.

Chartreuse or any fluorescent colors are effective in glacial waters. Spoons and flies with a softer, wobbling action are generally preferred over fast, spinning lures. Blue and metallic green have a way of attracting dime bright pinks in coastal clearwater rivers and streams.

In general, lures or flies with a baitfish appearance are much more likely to get a strike compared to something of bulk and extravagant colors. As for bait, small pieces of cut herring used in a simple cast-and-retrieve fashion work well in tidal waters. Salmon roe, however, does not elicit the same response and most pinks will not mouth eggs at all, a tip that anglers pursuing silvers amidst masses of pinks can capitalize on.

## Equipment

### Spin- & Bait-Casting

**Rod:** 6 ½- to 8-foot, fast action salmon rod.
**Reel:** High performance freshwater spinning/bait-casting reel.
**Line:** 150 yards of 4- to 6-pound test line.
**Advice:** Use at least 8-pound test when bank fishing on large, swift-flowing glacial waters like the Kenai or during crowded conditions.
**Best Lures:** Spoons, spinners, plugs, attractors.
Popular Brands
**Spoons:** Pixee, Krocodile, Syclops, Little Cleo, Fiord Spoon (Sizes ¼-¾ oz.).
**Spinners:** Vibrax, G. I. Spinner, Aglia, Panther Martin, Flash Glo (Sizes 2-4).
**Plugs:** Kwikfish, Flatfish, Wiggle Wart, Hot Shot (Sizes 3-12).
**Attractors:** Spin-N-Glo, Cheater (Sizes 1/2-2 in.).

*Little Cleo*
Green & Silver 2/3 oz.

*Pixee*
Pink & Silver 1/2 oz.

*Flash Glo*
Orange & Silver #3

*Stee-Lee*
Green & Silver 1/4 oz.

*Sy's Jig*
Pink #6

### Fly-Fishing

**Rod:** 5–6 wt., 8–9 ½ ft., medium-fast action fly rod.
**Reel:** Salmon/trout class reel; smooth and reliable drag system.
**Line:** 100-150 yards of 20–30 lb. backing, WF full floating, intermediate, or sink tip Type II-IV lines, 4–8 lb. tippet.
**Advice:** Smaller streams and in slower moving water, use weight forward floating line. In large, fast-flowing glacial rivers and saltwater, 6-weight rods with sink tip line and at least 10-pound test tippet are good due to current or wave activity. Kenai is a typical big-water location.
**Best Flies:** Attractor, Egg, Forage, Saltwater.

Popular Patterns (Hook size 2–10)
**Attractor:** Flash Fly, Alaskabou, Sparkle Shrimp, Polar Shrimp, Egg Sucking Leech, Comet, Russian River, Alaska Mary Ann, Sockeye Charlie, Popsicle, Everglow, Skykomish Sunrise, Boss, Everglow, Krystal Bullet, Mickey Finn, Green Butt Skunk, Coho Fly, Woolly Bugger.
**Egg/Flesh:** Wiggletail, Battle Creek, Marabou Flesh Fly.
**Forage:** Alaska Smolt, Black Nose Dace, Blue Smolt, Leech.
**Saltwater:** Candlefish, Deceiver, Needlefish, Baitfish, Alaska Candlefish, Clouser Minnow, Salmon Trolling Fly, Sandlance, Shrimp, Salmon Treat, Herring Fly, Crazy Charlie.

**Local Favorites:**

*Caberello*
Pink #6

*Loop Leech*
Pink #4

*Baranof Bomber*
Pink #6

*Egg Sucking Leech*
Purple #6

*Egg Sucking Leech*
Pink #6

# Chum Salmon

**Highlights:** A much-underrated species, strong and willing opponent wherever found, known for soft strikes but long and powerful runs, often with a twisting or rolling motion. Very stubborn, sounding deep between surface thrashings, with occasional aerial stunts.

**Common Name:** Dog
**Timing:** July into September
**Size:** 6 to 12 pounds, up to 17 pounds

**State Record:** 32 pounds, 0 ounces
**Gear:** Medium rod/reel; 10- to 17-pound test
**Tackle:** Lures, flies, and bait

Chum salmon – or dog – are more known for their deep-sounding, bulldog-style tug-of-war than aerial antics so common with reds and silvers. They are recognized as the second largest salmon species and known to reach 35 pounds.

Like pinks, chum salmon are typically summer-run fish in Alaska's coastal roadside rivers and streams, showing up during July and August and peaking in numbers at the split. Late-arriving chums are less common with peak abundance the latter part of August. Adjacent marine waters may see fish a little earlier, toward the latter part of June, with most appearing in July and continuing through August and even into September in some locations.

Currently there are no major species-specific fisheries for chums but several locations do offer excellent catch rates, such as in various clearwater drainages in the Susitna Valley. Additionally, good runs of chum salmon may be found in waters of the Matanuska Valley, the Anchorage area, Turnagain Arm, and parts of the Kenai Peninsula. Prince William Sound also support productive populations of these fish.

As with pinks, the lower reach of drainages, including the intertidal sections and mouths, are tops for hitting chrome chums.

## Biology

**Scientific Name:** *Oncorhynchus keta*
**Description:** Iris of eye is large, base of tail thin. Fine dusting of small specks is visible on back and top of head.
**Size:** Common weight 5 to 13 pounds, averaging 6 to 11 pounds in most waters. Maximum weight generally 15 to 18 pounds; known to reach 30 pounds or more.
**Habitat/Abundance:** Clear to semi-glacial coastal and inland drainages. Large or important populations are found foremost in tributaries of the Susitna River but also in drainages of Matanuska Valley, the Anchorage area, Prince William Sound, and Kenai Peninsula.
**Adult Diet:** Primarily fish and crustaceans.

**Ocean Phase:** Dark metallic blue on back, silvery sides, and silver white on belly. Flesh color is light orange.

**Presence:** May to October offshore, peaking July and August. Fish enter fresh water from mid-June to early October, peaking early July to mid-August.
**Spawning:** Rivers, streams, springs, and estuaries from early July to early November, most August and September. Females deposit 2,000-4,000 eggs, hatching in late winter or spring.
**Life Span:** A few months in fresh water, 2 to 5 years at sea; up to 6 years of age.

**Spawning Phase:** Crimson markings cover sides in bright red, black, and dirty yellow. Back is olive green, black, or brown. Pectoral, anal, and pelvic fins have distinctive white tips. Males develop a hooked jaw with protruding canine-like teeth, females a dark horizontal band across sides. Flesh color is yellowish white to white.

## Identification

*No spots on tail*
*Minute freckles on the back*
*Narrow tailbase*
*Large pupil of the eye*
*White or light gray mouth and gum line*
*Creamy white tips*

*Minute spots or freckles on top of head and neck, mouth very light grey, pupil of eye is very large. Head may be golden-silver.*

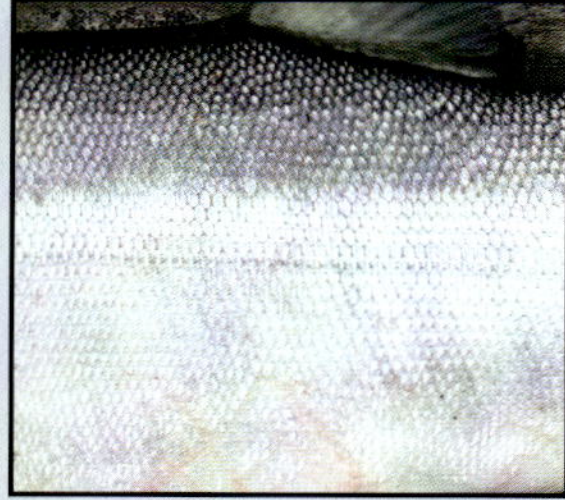

*Abundance of tiny spots cover back, dorsal fin; may be difficult to see on very chrome fish.*

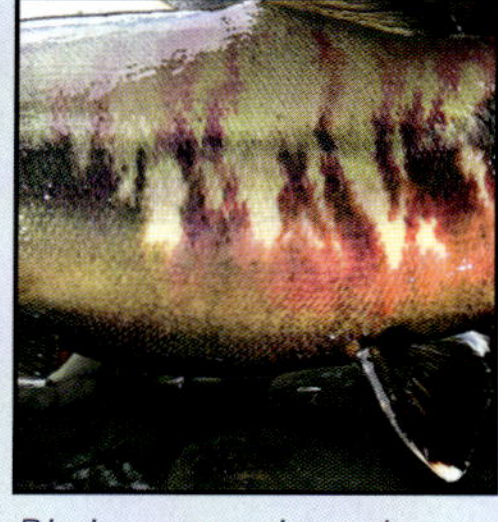

*Distinct spawning colors; reddish-purple, black, and yellow bars on sides.*

*No visible spots/markings, often iridescent silver-purple color on tail fin.*

## Fishing for Chum Salmon

**Top Areas:** Without a doubt, the coastal and inland drainages of the Matanuska and Susitna valleys are the prime locations for this species. The Kenai Peninsula offers only a limited few hot spots, generally smaller tidewater streams; however, there are some quite decent marine opportunities for chums here and in Prince William Sound.
**Regulatory Season:** Very few to no species-specific restrictions in place anywhere chums are found.

(Courtesy Eagle Eye Images)

Chums are very unpredictable at times in their mood for taking angler's enticements. In years past, these salmon were believed to strike lures and flies only occasionally but with increased effort and experience, anglers soon discovered that the secret lies in the type of water fished and lure choice. Still, however, new techniques are being developed to counter the times when these fish do not seem to cooperate. Yet, it must be noted that in some locations, chums are the most aggressive species present.

### Saltwater

Saltwater action for chums is somewhat spotty along the road system with a few of the more promising locations being in the ports of Prince William Sound and the eastern half of Kenai Peninsula. Anglers sometimes do quite well using flashy spoons, spinners, and flies near the mouths of streams on an incoming tide or if a big school of fish happens by but in general expect fishing to be slow unless targeting a specific population of fish at the mouth of its spawning stream. Anglers commonly resort to snagging in order to harvest saltwater chums successfully; however, they can be caught by sporting means just as well.

The key to experiencing good ocean chum action is to locate schools or concentrations of fish in bays, coves, or channels with freshwater influence. Chums often break the surface and anglers need to work medium-sized lures that display a slow, wobbling effect in contrast to faster, spinning hardware that often go ignored.

Fly-fishers can do exceptionally well using fairly large saltwater patterns in green, purple, and chartreuse base colors with white and/or silver. Allow flies to sink towards bottom and do a slow but steady retrieve towards shore.

Anglers of all persuasions should pay attention to tidal currents and work movements accordingly as one would a large, slow-flowing river. Adjust techniques and allow current to work lure or fly through the water layers.

### Freshwater

Focus on clearwater streams with moderate current, letting the lure or fly drift near the bottom or at least work through the mid-column. Spoons or plugs with a slow

*The intertidal region of clearwater drainages are perfect locations to tie into chums fresh from the sea. Expect to do battle with chrome fish at the height of runs.*

wobbling action and pulsating, articulated flies are best. If the current is strong and water deep, cast close to shore, perhaps six to ten feet; flipping is a good technique to employ at such times. Weighted flies are optimum.

The confluences of clearwater streams and glacial rivers are hot spots. Also, check deep, calm holes and runs that concentrate fish. Casting into the mixing zone on a rising tide of a coastal stream can bring fast results. The key is to fish offerings slow and deep.

Anything in silver and green is generally favored with chums but darker shades, such as black and purple, often outfish any other colors by a wide margin, especially in bright sunshine. Some anglers prefer to use bulky egg imitation flies to entice fresh chums.

Small clusters of roe can work exceptionally well in some instances, fished with a strike indicator and drifted slowly along the bottom.

In semi-glacial drainages with a greenish or turquoise tint, use fluorescent colored lures in chartreuse, pink, or orange. Add roe for scent. Attractors in combination with roe can be deadly, as well as big spinners. While chums do strike offerings fished quickly through a hole, anglers

## Chum Salmon Hot Spots & Timing

● = High ● = Moderate ● = Low ● = Closed

| **Kenai Peninsula** | *MAY* | *JUN* | *JUL* | *AUG* | *SEP* | *OCT* |
|---|---|---|---|---|---|---|
| Bird Creek | | Closed | Closed, Closed, High, High | High, Moderate, Moderate, Low | Low | |
| Glacier Creek | | Low | Low, Low, Moderate, High | High, High, Moderate, Low | Low, Low | |
| Passage Canal | Low, Low, Moderate | Moderate, Moderate, Low, Low | Low, Low, Moderate, Moderate | Moderate, Moderate, Low, Low | Low | |
| Sixmile Creek | | Low | Low, Moderate, High, High | High, Moderate, Moderate, Low | Low | |
| Resurrection Creek | | Low | Low, Low, Moderate, High | High, High, Moderate, Low | Low | |
| Resurrection Bay | | Low, Low, Low, Moderate | Moderate, High, High, High | High, Moderate, Moderate, Low | Low, Low | |
| **Matanuska-Susitna Valleys** | *MAY* | *JUN* | *JUL* | *AUG* | *SEP* | *OCT* |
| Ship Creek | | Low | Low, Low, Moderate, High | High, Moderate, Low, Low | Low | |
| Eklutna Tailrace | | Low | Low, Low, Moderate, Moderate | Moderate, Low, Low, Low | Low, Low, Low, Low | Low |
| Jim Creek | | | Low, Low, Moderate, Moderate | High, Moderate, Moderate, Low | Low, Low, Low, Low | Low |
| Little Susitna River | | Low, Low | Low, Moderate, High, High | High, Moderate, Moderate, Low | Low, Low | |
| Willow Creek | | Low | Low, Moderate, Moderate, High | High, High, Moderate, Low | Low, Low | |
| Little Willow Creek | | | Low, Low, Moderate, High | High, Moderate, Low, Low | Low | |
| Kashwitna River | | Low | Low, Low, Moderate, High | High, High, Moderate, Low | Low, Low | |
| Caswell Creek | | Low | Low, Low, Moderate, High | High, Moderate, Low, Low | Low | |
| Sheep Creek | | Low | Low, Low, Moderate, High | High, High, Moderate, Low | Low, Low | |
| Goose Creek | | Low | Low, Low, Moderate, High | High, Moderate, Low, Low | Low | |
| Montana Creek | | Low | Low, Low, Moderate, High | High, High, Moderate, Low | Low, Low | |
| Sunshine Creek | | Low | Low, Low, Moderate, High | High, Moderate, Low, Low | Low | |
| Talkeetna River | | Low | Low, Low, Moderate, High | High, High, Moderate, Moderate | Low, Low, Low, Low | Low |
| Byers Creek | | | Low, Low, Moderate | High, Moderate, Low, Low | Low | |
| **Copper Valley & Valdez** | *MAY* | *JUN* | *JUL* | *AUG* | *SEP* | *OCT* |
| Port Valdez | | Low, Low | Low, Moderate, Moderate, High | High, High, High, Moderate | Moderate, Low, Low, Low | |
| Robe River | | | Low, Low, Low, Moderate | Moderate, Moderate, Low, Low | Low | |

are much more prone to get consistent hits by slowing presentations down to a mere crawl, perhaps even pausing temporarily, simply letting the current do the work. Avoid fishing in heavily silted, glacial, or turbid waters, at least using lures and flies. A few chums, however, may be coaxed into striking a cluster of salmon roe fished stationary on the bottom in a hole with very slow to near still current. Add a medium-sized orange corkie for added effect.

## Equipment

### Spin- & Bait-Casting

**Rod:** 6 ½–8 ft., medium action salmon rod.
**Reel:** High performance freshwater spinning/bait-casting reel.
**Line:** 150 yards of 12–17 lb. test mono or braided line.
**Advice:** Lighter rod and line (down to 6 lb. test) can be used in slackwater areas or from boat. Line in the 15-pound test bracket is ideal for most conditions. Use at least 20-pound test when bank fishing during crowded conditions.
**Best Lures:** Spoons, spinners, plugs, attractors.
Popular Brands
**Spoons:** Pixee, Krocodile, Daredevle, Syclops, Super Duper, Little Cleo, Fiord Spoon (Sizes ½ - ¾ oz.).
**Spinners:** Vibrax, G. I. Spinner, Aglia, Panther Martin, Flash Glo (Sizes 3-4).
**Plugs:** Kwikfish, Flatfish, Wiggle Wart, Hot Shot (Sizes 4-12).
**Attractors:** Spin-N-Glo, Cheater (Sizes 1-3 in.).

*Pixee*
Green & Silver 1/2 oz.

*Little Cleo*
Green & Silver 2/3 oz.

*Flash Glo*
Chart. & Silver #4

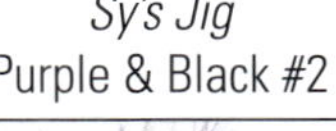

*Sy's Jig*
Purple & Black #2

*Spin-N-Glo*
Green & Chartreuse #

### Fly-Fishing

**Rod:** 7–9 wt., 9–10 ft., medium-fast action fly rod.
**Reel:** Salmon class reel; smooth and reliable drag system.
**Line:** 100-150 yards of 30 lb. backing, WF full float or sink tip Type II-IV lines, 200-400 grain lines with salmon leader, 8–17 lb. tippet.
**Advice:** Smaller streams and in slower moving water, use weight forward floating line. In large, fast-flowing glacial rivers or during crowded conditions, 9-weight rods with sink tip line and at least 15-pound test tippet are good due to current and battle antics of fish.
**Best Flies:** Attractor, Egg/Flesh, Forage, Saltwater.

Popular Patterns (Hook size 2–8)
**Attractor:** Flash Fly, Alaskabou, Sparkle Shrimp, Polar Shrimp, Egg Sucking Leech, Comet, Russian River, Alaska Mary Ann, Sockeye Charlie, Popsicle, Everglow, Skykomish Sunrise, Boss, Everglow, Krystal Bullet, Mickey Finn, Green Butt Skunk, Coho Fly, Woolly Bugger.
**Egg/Flesh:** Wiggletail, Battle Creek, Marabou Flesh Fly, Fat Freddie.
**Forage:** Alaska Smolt, Black Nose Dace, Blue Smolt, Leech.
**Saltwater:** Candlefish, Deceiver, Needlefish, Baitfish, Alaska Candlefish, Clouser Minnow, Salmon Trolling Fly, Sandlance, Shrimp, Salmon Treat, Herring Fly, Crazy Charlie.

**Local Favorites:**

*Flash Fly*
Green & Silver #2/0

*Hareball Leech*
Chart. & Black #1/0

*Hareball Leech*
Orange #1/0

*Dolly Llama*
Pink & Purple #2

*Egg Sucking Leech*
*Purple #3*

Take The Road MOST Traveled
...to Mountain View Sports
YOUR LOCAL FISHING & HUNTING EXPERTS
Mountain View Sports Fly Shop
We Know the How, When and Where to Fly Fish in Alaska
Mountain View Fly Shop
11124 Old Seward Hwy
907-222-6633
mvsports@alaska.net
Alaska's Best for 55 Years!
MtViewSports.com

Catch the BIG ONE?
ENTER NOW!

# Silver Salmon

**Highlights:** Silvers tend to be very aggressive, striking enthusiastically and charging ahead with several long and powerful runs. They are renowned for aerial antics, often leaping several feet into the air with plenty of surface thrashing and rolling.

**Common Name:** Coho
**Timing:** July into October
**Size:** 5 to 12 pounds, up to 18 pounds

**State Record:** 26 pounds, 0 ounces
**Gear:** Medium rod/reel; 10- to 17-pound test
**Tackle:** Lures, flies, and bait

Silver salmon – or coho – is the third largest species of salmon behind kings and chums, although throughout most of the state (and particularly on the road system) it is often second in size. Their tenacity for artificial lures and flies, great abundance and distribution, and long period of availability has earned the silver top marks with anglers and rivals even the mighty king salmon in popularity.

Being the last salmon runs of the brief Alaska open water season, silvers are a late summer and fall fish. The majority of rivers and streams support early runs that peak sometime during the month of August with only a very few locations hosting late runs in September and October.

Saltwater opportunities are typically a mid to late summer affair, anglers experiencing the best of it during July offshore and August inshore.

Distribution and abundance of silver salmon provide anglers with ample opportunities throughout the range, excellent fishing being the norm in many locations. The coastal and central fisheries on the Kenai Peninsula, Susitna Valley drainages, marine hot spots in Prince William Sound, and select streams of Matanuska Valley and the Anchorage area are all known as exceptional silver salmon waters. There are significant fisheries in both salt- and freshwater.

## Biology

**Scientific Name:** *Oncorhynchus kisutch*
**Description:** Moderately small black spots cover top of head, back, and upper lobe only of tail fin. Tail base is thick; gum line is white.
**Size:** Common weight 4 to 13 pounds, averaging 5 to 11 pounds in most waters. Maximum weight generally 14 to 18 pounds; known to reach 25 pounds or more.
**Habitat/Abundance:** Clear to semi-glacial coastal, inland, and interior drainages. Large or important populations are found in tributaries of the Susitna and Copper rivers, and in drainages of Matanuska Valley, the Anchorage Area, and Kenai Peninsula.
**Adult Diet:** Primarily fish (herring) and crustaceans.

**Ocean Phase:** Metallic blue on back, silvery on sides, white on belly. Flesh color is orange-red.

**Presence:** May to December offshore, peaking July to October. Fish enter fresh water from mid-June to early January, peaking early August to early October.
**Spawning:** Rivers, streams, and springs from early August to late April, most September to December. Females deposit 1,400-5,700 eggs, hatching in late winter or spring.
**Life Span:** One to three years in fresh water, one to three years at sea; up to five years of age.

**Spawning Phase:** Brilliant red, also bronze, greenish brown, even almost black. Back is dark olive green to a faded red or copper. Males develop a very distinct hooked snout, prolonged teeth, and a slightly humped back. Flesh color is yellowish-white or white.

## Identification

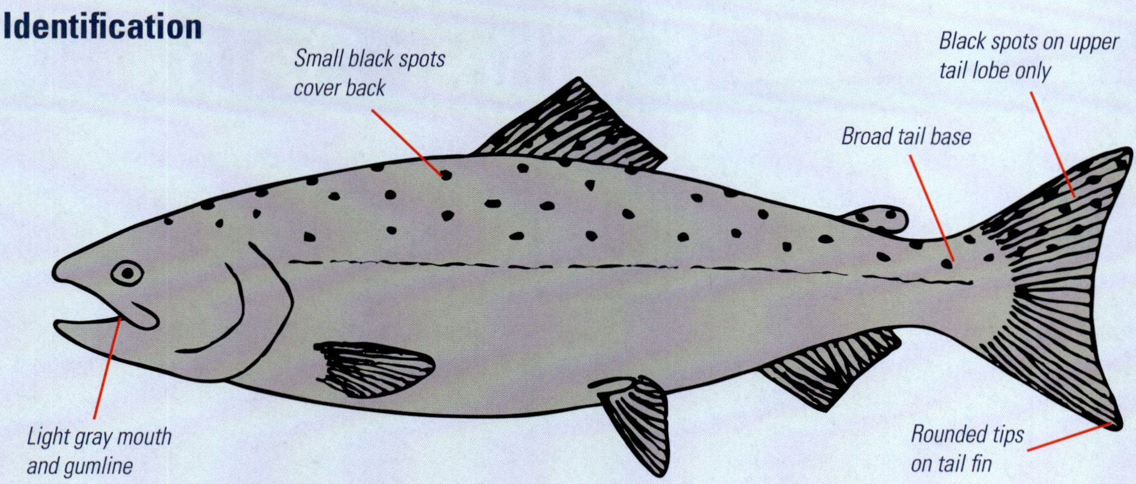

*Small spots cover top of head and neck, mouth and gums are grey; pupil of eye is relatively small.*

*Black spots on back and upper sides, including dorsal fin; markings are quite obvious even on chrome fish.*

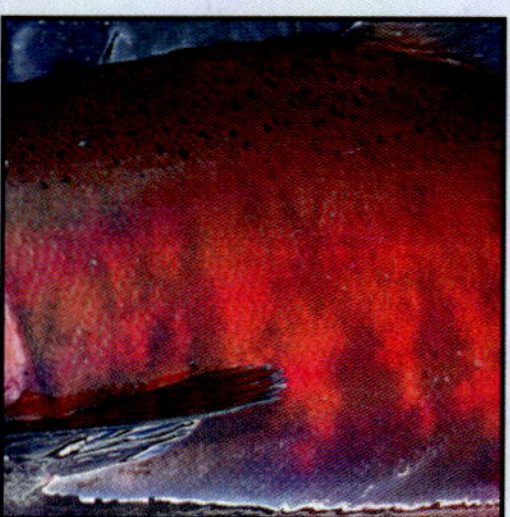

*Spots are accentuated on spawning fish; dark vertical markings on sides.*

*Spots present on upper tail lobe only; may not be clearly visible on some specimens.*

## Fishing for Silver Salmon

**Top Areas:** The marine fisheries of Kenai Peninsula and Prince William Sound offer superb and consistent action, with most of the tidewater and inland rivers and streams producing quality angling as well. Matanuska-Susitna valleys have good runs of this species in most drainages. Very limited opportunities present in the Copper Valley.
**Regulatory Season:** Very few species-specific restrictions anywhere, but some fall closures in effect starting October 1 to protect spawning fish.
Silver salmon are regarded by many as the premier sport fish in Alaska. With propensity for a large assortment of lures, flies, and bait, the silver is, for the most part, not a bit apprehensive of angler's offerings and is often the most aggressive fish in any water where found. Although the silver is an excellent gamester both in taking lures as well as in fighting abilities, there are times when even these fish develop lockjaw and lack the type of performance expected of salmon. More often than not, however, silvers will use a combination of tug-of-war with fast runs, spinning, and acrobatic jumps.

### Saltwater

Boaters undoubtedly have an advantage, yet surfcasters can do exceptionally well if coordinating their efforts with tidal movements along with areas of known fish concentration.

Early on in the season, anglers casting from shore do best focusing on deeper sections of water, often around docks or steep drop-offs. Look for signs of fish jumping clear out of the water, a common trait with silvers. Cast large spoons and spinners – even smaller jigs – in neutral colors such as blue, green, and even black in combination with silver, and let them work the lower water columns. A bait setup, such as herring along with a sinker, is effective. When silvers are found near the surface, use the bait with a strike indicator. Fish the incoming and outgoing tides.

Later in season when the salmon begin zeroing in on the mouths of spawning streams, a multitude of tackle can be used with success. Among the more popular items include spinners, attractor and saltwater flies, and cut pieces of herring and salmon roe fished with a strike indicator. Try from a few hours before high tide to a few hours after.

Anglers fishing from boats frequently troll or mooch for saltwater silvers using spinners, attractors, and plug-cut herring. When fish are situated in more shallow water, casting hardware and flies usually have the desired results. Anglers using jigs can do exceptionally well in some locations or circumstances.

Snagging is a popular harvest method at a few of the terminal fisheries.

### Freshwater

Places that provide moderate to slow current are favored resting spots for silvers. Fish any lure, fly, or bait near the bottom for results, this being especially the case in smaller, clearwater streams. However, as these salmon are

*Late summer angling for coastal coho on Deep Creek.*

highly curious and prone to explore, anglers can hook them at any depth – even off the surface using dry flies. In larger waters with fast and deep current, look for fish along the shoreline; also scout sloughs or quiet channels for schools of silvers, this being especially the case when targeting fish in large bodies of water.

Sight fishing is an exciting possibility in still water. Silvers have a tendency to hold near the surface, the tip of their tail fins often sticking up out of the water, a trait particular to this salmon species. Expect a fast and aggressive response to lures and flies invading their space.

Otherwise, anglers should prospect the mouth of tributaries draining into glacial rivers and the "edge" in estuaries where the slack water of a rising or receding tide meets the faster stream current.

Lures or other attractions can be in a large variety of sizes and colors depending on mood of fish and water conditions. Orange and red have always been choice colors in any drainage, but more neutral shades such as metallic silver in combination with blue or green can certainly be effective at times, particularly when the skies are sunny and the water very clear. In murky or glacial rivers and streams, use pink, orange, or chartreuse hues. Plain chrome can be deadly.

Hardware is very efficient, spinners being perhaps the number one choice and works on a consistent basis in most any location. Spoons and plugs may do the job as well but usually not as well as spinners.

## Silver Salmon Hot Spots & Timing

🔴 = High 🟠 = Moderate 🟣 = Low ⚫ = Closed

| **Kenai Peninsula** | *JUN* | *JUL* | *AUG* | *SEP* | *OCT* | *NOV* |
|---|---|---|---|---|---|---|
| Campbell Creek | | ⚫⚫⚫🟣 | 🟠🟠🔴🔴 | 🔴🟠🟠🟣 | ⚫⚫⚫⚫ | |
| Bird Creek | ⚫ | ⚫⚫🟠🟠 | 🔴🔴🔴🟠 | 🟠🟠🟠🟣 | 🟣🟣🟣 | |
| Glacier Creek | | 🟣🟣🟣🟠 | 🟠🔴🔴🔴 | 🔴🟠🟠🟣 | 🟣🟣🟣🟣 | 🟣 |
| 20-Mile River | | 🟣🟣🟣 | 🟠🟠🔴🔴 | 🔴🟠🟠🟠 | 🟣🟣🟣🟣 | 🟣 |
| Portage Creek | | 🟣🟣 | 🟣🟠🟠🔴 | 🔴🔴🟠🟠 | 🟠🟣🟣🟣 | 🟣🟣 |
| Passage Canal | | 🟣🟣🟣 | 🟠🟠🔴🔴 | 🔴🔴🟠🟠 | 🟠🟣🟣🟣 | |
| Resurrection Creek | 🟣 | 🟣🟣🟣🟣 | 🟠🟠🔴🔴 | 🔴🟠🟠🟣 | 🟣🟣 | |
| Sixmile Creek | 🟣 | 🟣🟣🟣🟠 | 🟠🔴🔴🔴 | 🟠🟠🟣🟣 | 🟣🟣 | |
| Kenai River (upper) | | 🟣🟣 | 🟣🟠🔴🔴 | 🔴🟠🟠🟠 | 🔴🔴🔴🔴 | ⚫⚫⚫⚫ |
| Russian River | | 🟣 | 🟣🟣🟠🔴 | 🔴🔴🟠🟠 | ⚫⚫⚫⚫ | |
| Resurrection Bay | | 🟣🟣🟣🟣 | 🟣🟠🟠🔴 | 🔴🔴🔴🟠 | 🟠🟣🟣🟣 | 🟣🟣 |
| Kenai River (middle) | | 🟣🟣🟣 | 🟠🟠🔴🔴 | 🔴🟠🟠🔴 | 🔴🔴🔴🟠 | 🟠🟠🟠🟠 |
| Kenai River (lower) | | 🟣🟣🟣🟠 | 🟠🔴🔴🔴 | 🟠🔴🔴🔴 | 🟠🟠🟠🟠 | 🟣🟣🟣🟣 |
| Swanson River | | 🟣🟣🟣 | 🟠🟠🔴🔴 | 🔴🟠🟠🟠 | 🟠🟣🟣🟣 | 🟣 |
| Kasilof River | | 🟣🟣🟣 | 🟠🟠🔴🔴 | 🔴🟠🟠🔴 | 🔴🔴🟠🟠 | 🟣🟣🟣🟣 |
| Ninilchik River | | 🟣🟣🟣 | 🟠🟠🔴🔴 | 🔴🟠🟠🟣 | 🟣🟣🟣🟣 | |
| Deep Creek | | 🟣🟣🟣 | 🟠🟠🔴🔴 | 🔴🟠🟠🟣 | 🟣🟣🟣🟣 | |
| Stariski Creek | | 🟣🟣🟣 | 🟠🟠🔴🔴 | 🔴🟠🟠🟣 | 🟣🟣🟣🟣 | |
| Anchor River | | 🟣🟣🟣 | 🟠🟠🔴🔴 | 🔴🟠🟠🟣 | 🟣🟣🟣🟣 | |
| Dudiak Lagoon | 🟣🟣 | 🟣🟠🔴🔴 | 🔴🔴🟠🟠 | 🟠🟣🟣🟣 | | |
| Cook Inlet | 🟣🟣🟣 | 🟣🟣🟠🟠 | 🔴🔴🔴🟠 | 🟠🟠🟠🟠 | 🟣🟣🟣🟣 | 🟣🟣🟣🟣 |
| Kachemak Bay | 🟣🟣🟣 | 🟠🔴🔴🔴 | 🟠🟠🔴🔴 | 🟠🟠🟣🟣 | 🟣🟣🟣 | |

Flies are generally fairly bulky or extravagant, the colorful and pulsating, articulated types producing hookups; however, darker and thinner varieties are often more successful if water conditions are low and clear and/or if silvers easily spook. Black and purple are both shades favored on small clearwater streams during bright sunshine.

Perhaps the all-time favorite offering for freshwater silver salmon is a medium-sized cluster of salmon roe. Drifted with or without a strike indicator through holes and runs, eggs have a uncanny way of dredging up fish when all else seems to fail. Additionally, anglers may want to fish the roe cluster stationary on the bottom, letting the fish catch scent and come to the offering. Small whole or cut herring works extremely well in lower reaches of coastal drainages, such as tidewater holes and pools. Rig herring for a fast spin when retrieved.

## Silver Salmon Hot Spots & Timing

*🔴 = High 🟠 = Moderate 🟣 = Low ⚫ = Closed*

| **Matanuska-Susitna Valleys** | *JUN* | *JUL* | *AUG* | *SEP* | *OCT* | *NOV* |
|---|---|---|---|---|---|---|
| Ship Creek | 🟣 | 🟣🟣🟠🔴 | 🔴🔴🟠🟠 | 🟠🟠🟣🟣 | 🟣🟣🟣🟣 | 🟣 |
| Eklutna Tailrace | 🟣 | 🟣🟣🟠🟠 | 🔴🔴🔴🟠 | 🟠🟠🟠🟣 | 🟣🟣🟣🟣 | |
| Jim Creek | 🟣 | 🟣🟣🟣🟠 | 🟠🔴🔴🔴 | 🟠🟠🟠🟣 | 🟣🟣🟣🟣 | |
| Wasilla Creek | | 🟣🟣🟣🟠 | 🟠🔴🔴🟠 | 🟠🟣🟣🟣 | 🟣 | |
| Cottonwood Creek | | 🟣🟣🟣 | 🟠🔴🔴🔴 | 🟠🟣🟣🟣 | | |
| Fish Creek | | ⚫⚫⚫ | ⚫🔴🔴🔴 | 🟠🟠🟣🟣 | 🟣🟣 | |
| Little Susitna River | 🟣 | 🟣🟣🟠🟠 | 🔴🔴🔴🔴 | 🟠🟠🟣🟣 | 🟣 | |
| Willow Creek | 🟣 | 🟣🟣🟠🟠 | 🔴🔴🔴🟠 | 🟠🟠🟣🟣 | 🟣 | |
| Little Willow Creek | | 🟣🟣🟣🟠 | 🟠🔴🔴🔴 | 🟠🟠🟣🟣 | 🟣 | |
| Kashwitna River | 🟣 | 🟣🟣🟣🟠 | 🟠🔴🔴🔴 | 🟠🟠🟣🟣 | 🟣🟣 | |
| Caswell Creek | | 🟣🟣🟣🟠 | 🟠🔴🔴🔴 | 🟠🟠🟣🟣 | 🟣 | |
| Sheep Creek | | 🟣🟣🟣🟠 | 🟠🔴🔴🔴 | 🟠🟠🟣🟣 | 🟣 | |
| Goose Creek | | 🟣🟣🟣🟠 | 🟠🔴🔴🔴 | 🟠🟠🟣🟣 | 🟣 | |
| Montana Creek | | 🟣🟣🟣🟠 | 🟠🔴🔴🔴 | 🟠🟠🟣🟣 | 🟣 | |
| Talkeetna River | | 🟣🟣🟣🟠 | 🟠🟠🔴🔴 | 🔴🟠🟠🟣 | 🟣 | |
| Sunshine Creek | | 🟣🟣🟣🟣 | 🟠🟠🔴🔴 | 🟠🟠🟣🟣 | 🟣 | |
| Rabideux Creek | | 🟣🟣🟣🟣 | 🟠🟠🔴🔴 | 🔴🟠🟣🟣 | 🟣 | |
| Moose Creek | | 🟣🟣 | 🟣🟠🔴🔴 | 🟠🟠🟣🟣 | 🟣 | |
| Peters Creek | | 🟣🟣 | 🟣🟠🔴🔴 | 🟠🟠🟣🟣 | 🟣 | |
| Byers Creek | | 🟣 | 🟣🟠🔴🔴 | 🟠🟠🟣🟣 | 🟣 | |
| East Fork Chulitna River | | 🟣 | 🟣🟠🔴🔴 | 🟠🟠🟣🟣 | 🟣 | |

| **Copper Valley & Valdez** | *JUN* | *JUL* | *AUG* | *SEP* | *OCT* | *NOV* |
|---|---|---|---|---|---|---|
| Tonsina River | | | 🟣🟣🟣🟠 | 🔴🔴🟠🟠 | 🟣🟣🟣🟣 | |
| Little Tonsina River | | | 🟣🟣🟠 | 🔴🔴🟠🟠 | 🟣🟣🟣🟣 | |
| Robe River | | 🟣 | 🟣🟣🟣🟠 | 🔴🔴🔴🟠 | 🟠🟠🟣🟣 | 🟣🟣 |
| Port Valdez | | 🟣🟣🟣 | 🟠🟠🔴🔴 | 🔴🟠🟠🟣 | 🟣🟣🟣🟣 | 🟣 |

## Equipment

### Spin- & Bait-Casting

**Rod:** 7–8 ½ ft., medium weight/action salmon rod.
**Reel:** High performance medium-heavy freshwater spin-/bait-casting reel.
**Line:** 175 yards of 12–17 lb. test mono or braided line.
**Advice:** Lighter rod and line (down to 8 lb. test) can be used in slackwater areas or from boat. Line in the 15 pound test bracket is perfect for most roadside streams. In saltwater or on rivers with strong current (Kenai), use heavier rod and line (20 lb. test) and bait-casting reel. Stronger gear also recommended during crowded conditions.
**Best Lures:** Spoons, spinners, plugs, attractors, jigs.
Popular Brands
**Spoons:** Pixee, Krocodile, Syclops, Super Duper, Little Cleo, Fiord Spoon (Sizes ¼ - 7/8 oz.).
**Spinners:** Vibrax, G.I. Spinner, Aglia, Black Fury, Panther Martin, Bang Tail, Flash Glo (Sizes 3-5).
**Plugs:** Kwikfish, Tadpolly, Flatfish, Wiggle Wart, Hot Shot (Sizes 4-12).
**Attractors:** Spin-N-Glo, Cheater, Okie Drifter, Corkie (Sizes 1/2-2 in.).
**Jigs:** Krocodile, Buzz Bomb, Kastmaster, Swedish Pimple (Sizes 2 ½ - 4 in.).

*Pixee*
Orange & Silver 1/2 oz.

*Vibrax*
Blue & Silver #4-5

*Flash Glo*
Orange & Silver #4

*Little Cleo*
Green & Silver 2/3 oz.

*Kodiak Custom*
Green & Silver #4-5

### Fly-Fishing

**Rod:** 7–9 wt., 9–10 ft., medium-fast action fly rod.
**Reel:** Medium salmon class reel; smooth and reliable drag system.
**Line:** 100-150 yards of 20–30 lb. backing, WF full float/performance taper floating, Type II-V or 200-300 grain T-series lines, sink tip, 8–17 lb. tippet.
**Advice:** Smaller streams (southern Kenai peninsula/Matanuska Valley, most every where else) and in slower moving water, use weight forward floating line. Fast-flowing glacial rivers command heavier gear such as a 9-weight rod with sink tip line. Kenai River is a typical example of big water as current can be strong and fish larger than average.
**Best Flies:** Attractor, Egg/Flesh, Forage.

Popular Patterns (Hook size 1–6)
**Attractor:** Flash Fly, Alaskabou, Sparkle Shrimp, Sockeye Willie, Woolly Bugger, Fall Favorite, Polar Shrimp, Egg Sucking Leech, Sockeye Orange, Maraflash Fly, Russian River, Alaska Mary Ann, Sockeye Charlie, Popsicle, Everglow, Skykomish Sunrise, Comet, Zonker, Coho Fly.
**Egg/Flesh:** Bunny Leech, Battle Creek, Fat Freddy, Wiggletail, Babine Special, Two-Egg Sperm Fly, Glo Bug, Marabou Flesh Fly.
**Forage:** Leech.
**Saltwater:** Candlefish, Deceiver, Baitfish, Clouser Minnow, Shrimp, Salmon Treat, Herring Fly.
**Specialty:** Pink Pollywog.

**Local Favorites:**

*Hareball Leech*
Pink #1/0

*Hareball Leech*
Pink/Purple #1/0

*Intruder*
Pink #1/0

*Pollywog*
Pink #2/0

*Egg Sucking Leech*
Articulated Black #2

# Trout & Char

(Courtesy of Alaska Wildland Adventures)

# Introduction

**Aside from salmon, there are two other general groupings of fish that are actively targeted in Alaska's roadside waters. These are trout, which include the resident and sea-run forms known as rainbow and steelhead, followed by char, such as Dolly Varden, arctic char, and lake trout. Their numbers and distribution – as well as physical size – are highly variable dependant on location but generally thought of as being abundant throughout the Southcentral region.**

Being predominantly resident freshwater fish, two species do exhibit seasonal migrations to the sea. Steelhead are a true anadromous form of rainbow trout with a life history very similar to that of Pacific salmon; that is, they are born in a river or stream, migrate to sea for a period of several seasons, and return to natal waters to spawn. Dolly Varden, however, only spend a few weeks in the marine environment before returning to freshwater.

As for the other forms or sub-species, they reside in lakes, rivers, and streams year-round but may still commit seasonal migrations for varying degrees and reasons, usually from a lake to a river or stream for the summer months and back again to overwinter.

Identifying trout and char is usually a very simple process. A plethora of small, black spots cover the back, sides, and tail fin of trout and scales are large. Char display large colored markings of varying intensity on back and sides while scales are very small, no spots on tail.

Rainbows are not especially attracted as a food, reason being anglers see these fish as a species of conservation due to fragile populations. The flesh, however, is very flavorful and at its peak in quality from late summer into winter. Search out waters that are stocked with trout if wanting to retain rainbows for food purposes.

## Fishing for Trout & Char

For anglers to target trout and char properly, familiarity with the seasonal migration patterns and local food sources are of primary importance. The following information illustrates the general timing and feeding trends during the calendar season for the various species.

### Spring—Early Summer (April – June)

Fish commence their seasonal migration from over-wintering areas to spring spawning and summer feeding grounds. For trout, the spring months are synonymous with the reproductive cycle and breeding fish will be present in many clearwater rivers and streams. Char, being fall spawners, will begin feeding actively in lakes and

(Courtesy Mystic Waters Fly-fishing)

*Alaska's waters do not just proliferate with salmon; various resident species are often just as abundant and aggressive, sometimes even more so.*

coastal streams, with sea-run Dolly Varden soon present in the marine environment.

The fish are often aggressive and strike a number of lures and flies, such as forage/smolt patterns, as there will be an abundance of juvenile salmon migrating downstream at this time. Insect hatches are peaking and any fly replicating the early stages of this life form will likely draw attention.

### Mid-/Late Summer (July – August)

Coastal rivers and streams begin to see action pick up in earnest by the arrival of salmon, which plays a major role in the health of resident species. As eggs begin to drop, usually sometime between mid-summer and late fall depending on salmon species and timing, predatory fish gather to feast. Insect-related feeding will still be important in many areas, especially in inland or mountainous waters (including landlocked lakes), yet a vast majority of trout and char are increasingly seeking out salmon spawning beds for a high-protein meal.

Flies and attractors/beads simulating single salmon eggs or small clusters of roe are phenomenally effective this time of year. In some locations, flesh flies will also be productive as salmon die off following the spawn, usually starting in August.

### Fall (September – October)

With cooling water temperatures, resident species go on a feeding binge preparing for the winter months ahead. Resident rainbow trout are in prime physical condition throughout their range and steelhead trout runs will peak in coastal waters. All species of char will prepare for spawning and often found in concentration in clearwater streams and lakes.

(Courtesy Robert Laskodi)

*It is well known that with the influx of this rich protein source – salmon eggs, resident fish generally grow larger and are often found in much greater abundance than in waters void of salmon.*

(Courtesy Mystic Waters Fly-Fishing)

*Salmon help feed the ecosystem by nurturing all aquatic life through decomposing flesh to eggs to juvenile fish – all of which sustain trout and char of all age classes. Above, as salmon runs begin to wane and fish are dying off, anglers must change their tactic. Although egg patterns may still work, the flesh fly will draw response as the decomposing bodies of salmon slowly release bits and pieces into the current.*

Although the majority of insect activity ceases this time of year, some fish will aggressively continue to strike larger patterns imitating aquatic life forms. More likely to be noticed, however, are egg and flesh imitation attractors/ beads and flies since spawning and dying salmon will still be the main attraction in most areas. If fish appear finicky, mix it up, trying large forage pattern lures and flies for a change of pace.

### Winter (November – March)

Large, deep rivers and lakes will hold resident species throughout the winter months, with ice fishing being the most productive method this time of year. Open-water stream fishing is very limited. Trout and char are both active through early winter, slowing down in responding to artificial lures and bait come January and February.

## General Techniques

Anglers targeting resident species use light or medium-light spin- or fly-fishing rods, depending largely on water conditions and size of fish. The presentation of lures and flies should be based on the premise of imitating local food sources as much as possible, hence the seasonal descriptions above.

### Stripping

The basic cast-and-retrieve/strip technique employing forage patterns is standard for all waters throughout the

## Trout & Char Availability

● = Present ◉ = Peak Resident species available year round

| Species | | May | June | July | August | September | October |
|---|---|---|---|---|---|---|---|
| **Steelhead Trout** | *Ocean* | ●●●● | | ●● | ●●●● | ●●●● | ●●●● |
| | *Rivers/streams* | ◉◉●● | ●●● | | ●●●● | ●◉◉◉ | ◉◉●● |
| | *Lakes* | ●●●● | ● | | ●● | ●●●● | ●●●● |
| **Rainbow Trout** | *Rivers/streams* | ●●●● | ●●◉◉ | ◉◉◉◉ | ◉◉◉◉ | ◉◉◉◉ | ◉◉●● |
| | *Lakes* | ◉◉◉◉ | ◉◉◉● | ●●●● | ●●◉◉ | ◉◉◉◉ | ◉◉◉◉ |
| **Dolly Varden** | *Ocean* | ◉◉◉◉ | ◉◉◉◉ | ◉◉●● | ●●●● | ●●●● | ●● |
| | *Rivers/streams* | ◉◉●● | ●●◉◉ | ◉◉◉◉ | ◉◉◉◉ | ◉◉◉◉ | ◉◉◉◉ |
| | *Lakes* | ◉◉◉◉ | ◉◉●● | ●●●● | ●●◉◉ | ◉◉◉◉ | ◉◉◉◉ |
| **Lake Trout** | *Lakes* | ●●●◉ | ◉◉◉● | ●●●● | ●●◉◉ | ◉◉◉◉ | ◉◉●● |
| **Arctic Char** | *Lakes* | ●●●◉ | ◉◉◉● | ●●●● | ●●●◉ | ◉◉◉◉ | ◉◉●● |

## Fishing Rod & Line Weights

*[ ] = Weight needed for locations with large fish present and/or strong currents*

| *Resident Species* | **Bait Casting & Spinning Rods** | **Fly Rods** |
|---|---|---|
| **Steelhead Trout, Trophy Trout & Char** | Medium action, 10 -14 pound test [17 lb.] | Med/Hvy action, 7 - 8 weight [9 wt.] |
| **Rainbow & Lake Trout, Dolly Varden, Arctic Char** | Light/Medium action, 6 - 8 pound test | Light/Medium action, 5 - 6 weight |
| **Small trout/char** *(<25 inches)* | Ultra light/Light action, 2 - 4 pound test | Light action, 2 - 4 weight |

open-water period but particularly effective in late spring/early summer and again in fall. The movement simulates baitfish (such as salmon smolts and fry), small rodents, and various forms of aquatic insects. Lakes, including inlets and outlets, calm stretches of rivers and streams, estuaries, and saltwater areas such as bays, coves, creek mouths, and tidal rips are all good locations.

### Dead Drifting

This exceptional technique involves presenting a fly or bead to appear free-floating in a current. The angler keeps control of line by lowering or raising the rod tip properly so the presentation does not create an unnatural drag through the water column. A small strike indicator is often employed for better visual control. Although most any type of offering may be used, dead drifts are mostly known for presenting egg imitations to resident species in areas where salmon are spawning.

### Swing Drifting

A very effective technique not just for salmon but many resident species as well, such as steelhead and rainbow trout and Dolly Varden.

Employed in rivers and streams with at least moderate current, presentations consists of mainly forage imitations yet egg and flesh patterns work too. The lure or fly is cast at an angle upstream and allowed to sweep downstream with the current until the end of the drift. This sweeping motion creates the illusion of a swimming baitfish or aquatic insect, or even a tumbling salmon egg or piece of salmon flesh.

## Rules & Regulations

Roadside waters have strict closures in place on flowing waters in order to protect populations of spawning resident fish. These regulatory restrictions are established by the ADF&G through the Alaska Board of Fisheries. Rainbow and steelhead trout, being two of the top game species in the state, are especially species of concern and have seasonal closures from mid-April into mid-June in some areas, such as the Kenai Peninsula and Matanuska Valley. Some waters are open during the spring spawn but have catch-and-release restrictions instead.

Dolly Varden are protected in a few drainages on the Kenai Peninsula during the fall spawning period. Check state regulations yearly for possible changes.

The following chapter sections describe the most popular resident species in Alaska and details the process of sport fishing for them, including brief information on biology. There are certain methods and techniques that can be used not just for resident fish but other species as well and these are illustrated in the section on Angling Strategies at the end of this chapter in order to eliminate redundancy.

# Steelhead Trout

**Highlights:** Perhaps the alpha fish of the sporting species, targeted for its very powerful and unrelenting runs, sounding deeply with headshaking and rolling before going aerial, often flying several feet into the air in several consecutive leaps. These sea-run trout give their best performance in autumn.

**Common Name:** Rainbow, Trout
**Timing:** May, and September to November
**Size:** 5 to 10 pounds, up to 18 pounds

**State Record:** 42 pounds, 3 ounces
**Gear:** Medium rod/reel; 8- to 14-pound test
**Tackle:** Lures and flies

Steelhead trout have a very limited range of distribution along the road system in Southcentral Alaska compared to other areas of the state, present only in a half-dozen streams. While angling success is only mediocre on average, when finally hooked the steelhead puts on a show that is worthy of pursuit under the most stringent water and weather conditions.

There is a limited spring fishery for steelhead, usually coinciding with the early run of king salmon, yet it is the fall opportunities that really make this species shine. The months of September and October have traditionally been the best time to be on the water as the fish are bright and strong and fresh out of the sea, but steelheading can be productive all the way through fall up to freezeup.

The only fishable drainages on the continuous road system are the lower Kenai Peninsula streams, notably the Kasilof, Ninilchik, and Anchor rivers and Deep Creek. Some fish are also present in Stariski Creek. A smaller run occurs in the Gulkana River in Copper Valley with anglers catching steelhead incidentally to fishing for other species.

Steelhead are not regarded as a food item and regional regulations currently prohibited anglers from killing these fish in most waters.

## Biology

**Scientific Name:** *Oncorhynchus mykiss*
**Description:** Numerous small black spots present on upper sides, back, top of head, and both lobes of tail fin.
**Size:** Common weight 4 to 13 pounds, averaging 6 to 11 pounds in most waters. Maximum weight generally 15 to 18 pounds; known to reach 40 pounds or more.
**Habitat/Abundance:** Clear coastal and inland drainages. Important populations are found in rivers and streams on the Kenai Peninsula and tributaries of Copper River.
**Adult Diet:** Primarily fish and crustaceans.
**Presence:** April to November offshore, peaking in September. Fish enter streams from late March to early June and early August to mid-December, peaking in mid-late September.

**Feeding Phase:** Back is almost black, sides silvery, belly white. A very distinct horizontal pinkish band appears on sides after a few days of freshwater residence. Flesh color is orange.
**Spawning:** Rivers and streams from mid-March to mid-July, most May. Females deposit 100-12,000 eggs, hatching in summer and early fall. May reproduce more than once, up to four times.
**Life Span:** 1 to 4 years in freshwater, 2 to 5 years at sea; up to 7 years of age.

**Spawning Phase:** Black spots are more pronounced. Sides and cheeks are dirty red, back greenish yellow or gray. Post-spawn fish often return to a silvery shine on the sides, belly turning white and back dark. Flesh color is white.

## Identification

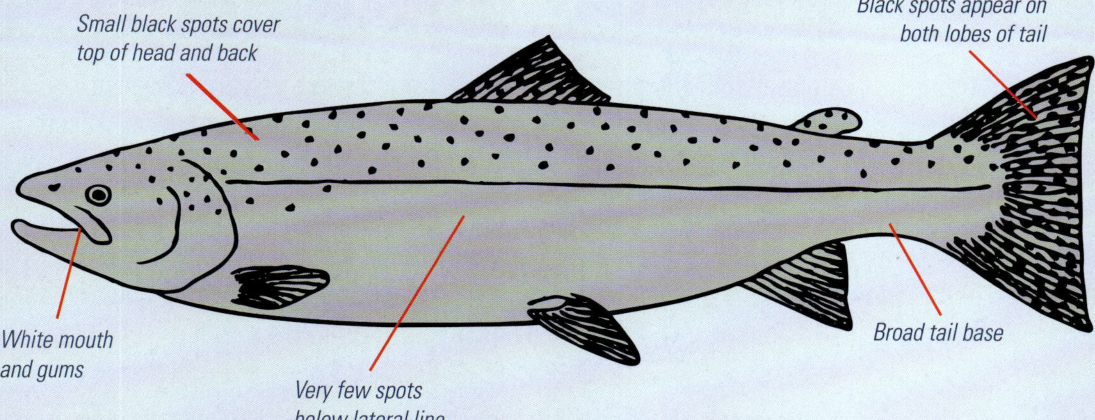

*Small, round spots present on neck and top of head, sometimes on upper gill plate; white mouth and gums.*

*Abundance of black spots cover back and upper sides, few spots below lateral line.*

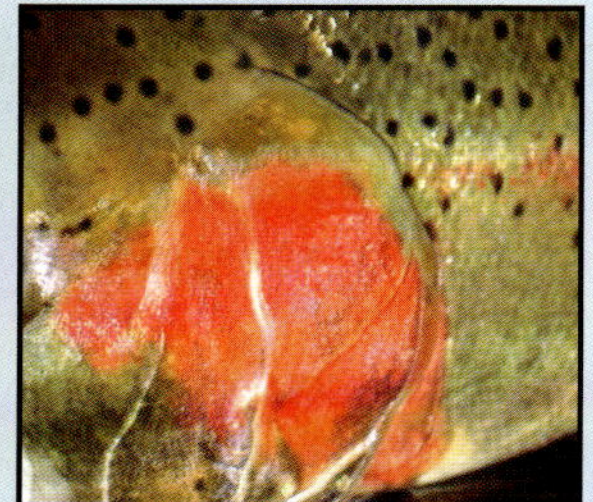

*Spawning fish, spots pronounced on back,upper sides. Red gill plates and horizontal band.*

*Small black spots cover both lobes of tail fin; often iridescent silver color.*

## Fishing for Steelhead Trout

**Top Areas:** There are very few places to seek out these sea-run rainbows, almost all of them situated on the Kenai Peninsula. Several of the tidewater and inland rivers streams here support small but very lively populations of wild fish. Copper Valley has very limited opportunities, especially along the road, yet is possible with proper dedication.
**Regulatory Season:** Spring closures or retention restrictions in effect in many flowing waters to protect spawning fish.

Steelhead trout are regarded as the ultimate sport fish wherever found. Not present in numbers like salmon and resident species (and considerably more finicky), steelhead make up for it by being, pound-for-pound, the hardest-fighting fish an angler is likely ever to encounter.

### Saltwater

Angling for steelhead in saltwater is poor. Relatively small runs, unstable autumn weather conditions, and vast expanses of ocean seem to guarantee an exercise in futility. They are obviously there, on their way to spawning streams, but hooking into one is just a matter of pure luck. A few fish are taken incidentally every year by anglers trolling for other species, such as silver salmon, and the only success reported by shore angler is of fish being caught in estuaries and tidal portions of streams on incoming or outgoing tides.

### Freshwater

Steelhead are present in select rivers and streams starting in fall with fish remaining in freshwater all winter and through the spring spawning period. Soon after the reproductive process is completed, the spent fish retreat to sea. Anglers looking to connect with these tremendous sport fish are advised to do so during the fall in-migration when fish are in their prime. The vast majority of steelhead along the road system in Southcentral are fall-run stocks with very few fish entering freshwater from sea during the spring months.

Trickling into coastal waters as early as August and continuing to arrive until freezeup in November or later, the peak of in-migrating fish occurs during the second half of September. Anglers drifting forage, attractor, and egg imitation flies do well on incoming tides, hitting holes and deep runs. Smaller, high-action tackle works early in the season, the lower sections of rivers and streams being best. Later on as the water cools significantly (mid-October on), steelhead become lethargic and less responsive and will favor larger, low-action offerings. Search out deep holes and runs in the middle portions of drainages for fish.

Autumn often means highly variable water conditions, ranging from very low and clear to rain-swollen and turbid. Bright days and low water spurs a preference towards smaller, darker hues such as black, purple, and green, while rainy days and muddy water requires pink, orange, chartreuse, and red colors.

There is some degree of spring opportunities for sea-run rainbows, mainly in May prior to or during the king salmon season. Some surprisingly bright and feisty specimens can

### Areas & Availability

● = High ● = Moderate ● = Low ● = Closed

| Kenai Peninsula | MAY | JUN | JUL | AUG | SEP | OCT |
|---|---|---|---|---|---|---|
| Kasilof River | High, Moderate, Low, Low | Low, Low, Low | | Low, Low, Low, Low | Moderate, Moderate, Moderate, High | High, High, High, High |
| Ninilchik River | Closed, Closed, Closed, Low | Low, Low, Low | | Low, Low, Low, Moderate | Moderate, High, High, High | High, High, Moderate, Moderate |
| Deep Creek | Closed, Closed, Closed, Low | Low, Low, Low | | Low, Low, Low, Moderate | Moderate, High, High, High | High, High, Moderate, Moderate |
| Stariski Creek | Closed, Closed, Closed, Closed | Closed, Closed, Closed | | Low, Low, Low, Moderate | Moderate, High, High, High | High, High, Moderate, Moderate |
| Anchor River | Closed, Closed, Low, Low | Low, Low, Low | | Low, Low, Low, Moderate | Moderate, High, High, High | High, High, Moderate, Moderate |

| Copper Valley | MAY | JUN | JUL | AUG | SEP | OCT |
|---|---|---|---|---|---|---|
| Gulkana River | Low, Low, Low, Low | Low | | Low, Low | Low, Low, Moderate, Moderate | Moderate, Moderate, Moderate, Moderate |

be caught leading up to mid-month; fish hooked thereafter being increasingly colored. Spring trout tend to be aggressive, often slamming large spinners and attractors, inhaling large, gaudy flies and attractors without hesitation. Green, chartreuse, and pink are effective colors this time of year. Nearly all steelhead landed by anglers during the month of June are kelts, or spawned-out ocean-bound fish, and definitely not in their prime for sport.

## Equipment

### Spin- & Bait-Casting

**Rod:** 8–9 ft., medium action casting rod.
**Reel:** High performance medium-heavy freshwater spin-/bait-casting reel.
**Line:** 175 yards of 8–14 lb. test mono or braided line.
**Advice:** Light gear (8-10 lb. test line )is perfect for low and clear water conditions. Heavy current and deep, turbid water may require upgrading to stronger line (14- to 17-pound test) with matching rod and reel.
**Best Lures:** Spinners, plugs, attractors.
Popular Brands
**Spinners:** Vibrax, G.I. Spinner, Aglia, Black Fury, Bang Tail, Flash Glo (Sizes 2-4).
**Plugs:** Kwikfish, Tadpolly, Flatfish, Wiggle Wart, Hot Shot (Sizes 4-10).

**Attractors:** Spin-N-Glo, Cheater, Okie Drifter, 'Lil Corkie, Corkie (Sizes ¼-2 in.).

*Little Cleo*
Green & Silver 1/2 oz.

*Stee-Lee*
Green & Silver 1/4 oz.

*Sy's Jig*
Pink #2

*Spin-N-Glo*
Orange, Pink, Green #4

*Corkie / Bead*
Orange, Pink, Pearl #2

### Fly-Fishing

**Rod:** 7–8 wt., 9–9 ½ ft., medium-fast action fly rod.
**Reel:** Medium salmon/trout class reel; smooth and reliable drag system.
**Line:** 100-150 yards of 20–30 lb. backing, WF full float/performance taper floating, Type II-V or 200-300 grain T-series lines, sink tip, 8–14 lb. tippet.
**Advice:** Ideal water conditions fish well using lighter gear (7 weight, 8-10 lb. test) with floating line or small grain, sink tip. Fast-flowing glacial waters, such as the Kasilof, and rain-swollen streams command heavier gear such as a 8- or 9-weight rod, sink tip line, and 14- to 17-pound test.

**Best Flies:** Attractor, Egg/Flesh, Forage, Specialty.
Popular Patterns (Hook size 1–6)
**Attractor:** Flash Fly, Alaskabou, Sparkle Shrimp, Fall Favorite, Polar Shrimp, Egg Sucking Leech, Green Butt Skunk, Rajah, Woolly Bugger, Popsicle, Everglow, Skykomish Sunrise, Rajah, Mickey Finn.
**Egg/Flesh:** Bunny Leech, Battle Creek, Wiggletail, Babine Special, Two-Egg Sperm Fly, Glo Bug, Marabou Flesh Fly.
**Forage:** Leech, Muddler.
**Specialty:** Marabou Jig.

**Local Favorites:**

*Fish Taco*
Pink #1/0

*Egg Sucking Leech*
Purple #4

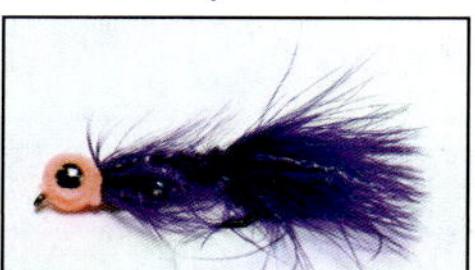

*Garcia Glo Bug*
#2

*Babine Special*
#4

*Pick "Yer" Pocket*
Pink #2

(Courtesy Matt Raye)

# Rainbow Trout

**Highlights:** A very willing and enthusiastic opponent, known for aggressive strikes and lightning quick runs, followed by a series of aerial antics that may include spectacular jumps several feet high. Surface thrashing and incessant rolling is common.

**Common Name:** Trout
**Timing:** May to December
**Size:** 10 to 22 inches, up to 20 pounds

**State Record:** 42 pounds, 3 ounces
**Gear:** Light rod/reel; 4- to 10-pound test
**Tackle:** Lures and flies

Rainbow trout are widely distributed throughout Alaska and may be found in most roadside lakes and streams. It is a superb game fish and one of the most sought-after species among anglers due to their intense temperament when hooked, unmatched by any other fish of similar size.

Although normally associated with the spring and fall fisheries, good action can be had virtually all season long and extending into the early winter months as well. Where allowed, May and June can be hot but many areas are closed to trout fishing during the spring spawning period. The months of August, September, and October are synonymous with exceptional trouting as food sources are abundant and fish engage in a feeding frenzy preparing for the long winter ahead.

Clearwater tributaries of the Susitna River drainage in the Susitna Valley and the mainstem Kenai River and associated streams on the Kenai Peninsula have long been regarded as the top wild trout populations along the road system. Copper Valley has far fewer trout waters but exceptional action still possible in spots with near complete solitude.

Artificial stocks (hatchery fish) are widespread and present especially in lakes and ponds around major towns and cities.

## Biology

**Scientific Name:** *Oncorhynchus mykiss*
**Description:** Numerous black spots present on sides, back, top of head, and both lobes of tail fin.
**Size:** Common length 7 to 23 inches, averaging 10 to 20 inches in most waters. Maximum length generally 25 to 32 inches (6-12 lbs.); known to reach 40 pounds or more.
**Habitat/Abundance:** Clear to glacial coastal and inland drainages. Large or important populations are found in lakes and streams in Matanuska, Copper, and Susitna valleys, the Anchorage area, and on the Kenai Peninsula.

**Feeding Phase:** Coloration and spotting may vary greatly from watershed to watershed. Sides are silvery to copper, light brown, or olive with a light red stripe of varying width and pronunciation. Back is black or dark green. Flesh color is orange.

**Adult Diet:** Primarily fish, fish eggs, and insects.
**Presence:** Year-round in lakes and large rivers; April to December in smaller streams, peaking May to October.
**Spawning:** Rivers and streams from mid-March to early July, most May and June. Females deposit 200-12,700 eggs, hatching in late spring and summer. May reproduce several times.
**Life Span:** Up to 11 years of age.

**Spawning Phase:** Reddish pink on sides and cheeks. Belly is grayish or brown; back black or dirty dark green. Black spots are enlarged or more pronounced. Flesh color is white.

## Identification

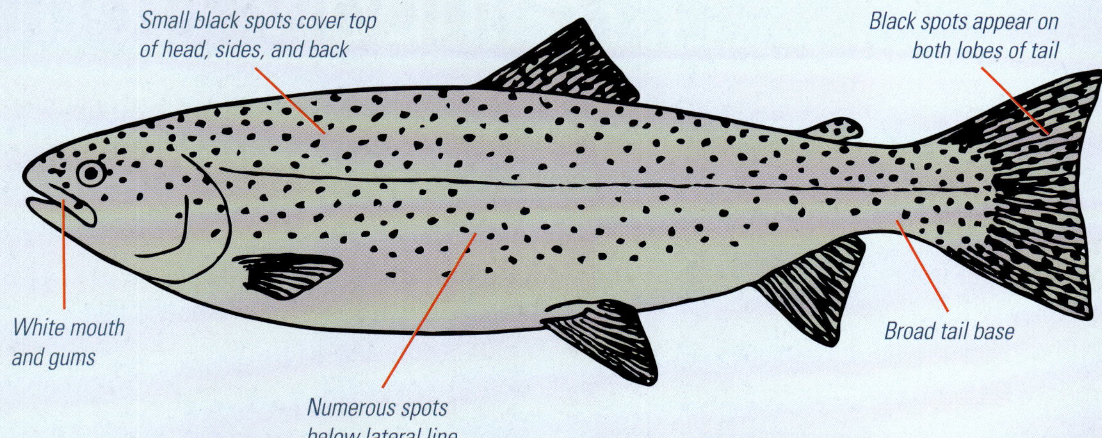

*White mouth and gums; numerous spots cover top of head, neck, and gill plates, sometimes also parts of lower jaw. Pink hue.*

*Many black spots cover back and sides; distinct pink horizontal stripe along lateral line.*

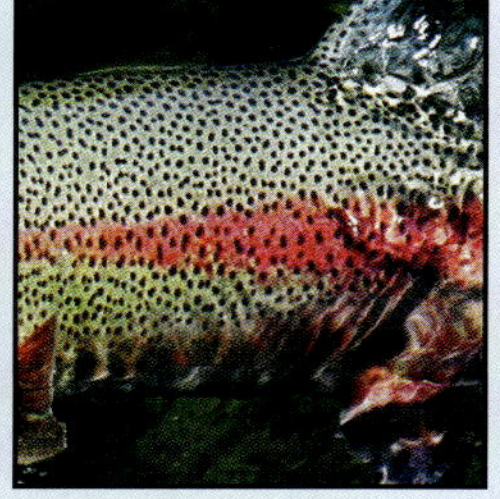

*Breeding fish display red horizontal stripe, dark belly; spots accentuated.*

*Black spots cover entire tail fin area, including both lobes.*

## Fishing for Rainbow Trout

**Top Areas:** Widely distributed with quality angling in most areas, from large glacial rivers to small streams and lakes, rainbows thrive in some of the coastal and nearly all of the inland drainages of the Kenai Peninsula and Matanuska, Susitna, and Copper valleys. They all support very respectable wild trout populations with the addition of stocked fish in area lakes.
**Regulatory Season:** Spring closures or retention restrictions in effect in many flowing waters to protect spawning fish, usually from April 15 to June 15.

(Courtesy Mystic Waters Fly-Fishing)

Rainbow trout are, along with steelhead, viewed as one of the most important game species not only in Alaska but also throughout the Pacific Northwest. Considered abundant in many waters on the road system, rainbows are usually not very finicky in taking artificial lures and flies and will more often than not respond aggressively to these offerings.

### Rivers & Streams

Thriving most in drainages that consists of a combination of clearwater streams and large rivers or lakes, the rainbow is easily targeted by anglers from both shore and boat. A great many waters along the road system are perfect for wade-style fishing with a few rivers also providing drift boat or raft experiences.

Springtime (April into June) means spawning season for trout with many waters being closed to fishing. Some areas, however, remain open to catch-and-release with anglers seeking out migratory streams for a shot at hooking one of these pre- or post-spawning fish. Selection of tackle can be significant, as fish appear both territorially aggressive and hungry. Drifting lures and flies resembling aquatic insects and salmon alevin and smolts are all noteworthy, fished at the mouths of spawning streams and in deeper holes and runs.

Avoid targeting trout that are paired up for spawning or guarding redds, these fish usually spotted in quite shallow reaches with moderate current.

As the spawning season ends and feeding resumes (June/July), rainbows spread out and become very active, mainly in the middle and upper reaches of rivers and streams. Drifting or cast-and-retrieving small spoons, spinners, and forage flies imitating out-migrating juvenile salmon (smolts) typically yield excellent results. The proliferation of insects means that anglers also must consider flies that reflect current hatches or activities in targeted waters. Scan for trout in classical lies, such as deep holes, runs with overhanging banks, and around larger structures consisting of boulders and logjams.

In late summer and fall (August into September), the vast majority of trout streams also support one or more spawning runs of salmon. Flies and attractors/beads in a variety of sizes and shades made to look like free-floating salmon eggs and fished using a dead drift with or without a strike indicator almost guarantees angler success. However, do not neglect using other forage imitations as well, especially in areas with limited or no presence of salmon.

As the weather cools

(Courtesy Beverley & Roy Bailey)

*Spawning salmon are trout magnets. Locate water that has salmon present and trout (as well as char) will be close by. View from Russian River.*

*A float tube or simple watercraft, such as a canoe, is of tremendous value when fishing lakes as it allows anglers to access deeper water and better structure..*

(September into November), trout begin a slow downstream migration, dropping out of the headwaters into the middle and lower sections of rivers and streams. Rainbows will still strike egg imitations and forage flies, primarily larger offerings, yet flesh flies become increasingly important as salmon die off. Anticipating freeze-up, a feeding frenzy ensues and anglers can experience superb catches using a wide range of tackle.

## Lakes

Fishing for rainbow trout in lakes can be highly variable depending on the geographic features of the particular drainage. In lake systems that consist of rivers and large streams, the presence of trout may be minimal during much of the open-water season as fish tend to spawn and feed in flowing waters, only returning to lakes to overwinter. Many roadside lakes, however, are situated within small systems, meaning that the fish may spend the spring in connected streams and return to the lake of origin soon after the spawning period to feed through summer and fall.

After breakup (May/June), rainbows are typically quite aggressive and can be seen patrolling the shallows along the lake shoreline in big schools. Some of the larger, spawn-bound trout, however, may not respond well to angler's offerings at this time, which can be frustrating. Try at or near inlets and outlets.

Come summer (July/August), anglers should try areas around islands and submerged shoals and the edge of steep drop-offs in waters 20 feet or deeper. Trolling or jigging fish imitation lures and flies works well, especially early and late in the day. Bait usually catches fish when nothing else seems to work. A boat, canoe, or float tube may be necessary to reach areas where fish are holding.

Action picks up significantly in fall (September/October) as the trout are found throughout the top layers of water and often close to shore. Focus on locations such as the edge of weed beds, drop-offs, areas with overhanging trees, and stream inlets and outlets. A variety of tackle and techniques may work, with baitfish and aquatic insect imitations cast from shore or boat effective.

Ice fishing in November and December can be excellent using small jigs and bait such as single salmon eggs or clusters of salmon roe.

## Areas & Availability

● = High ● = Moderate ● = Low ● = Closed

| Kenai Peninsula | MAY | JUN | JUL | AUG | SEP | OCT |
|---|---|---|---|---|---|---|
| Rivers/Streams | Closed Closed Closed Closed | Closed Closed Moderate Moderate | Moderate Moderate High High | High High High High | High High High High | High Moderate Moderate Moderate |
| Lakes | Moderate High High High | High High Moderate Moderate | Moderate Moderate Moderate Moderate | Moderate Moderate High High | High High High High | High Moderate Moderate Moderate |

| Matanuska-Susitna Valleys | MAY | JUN | JUL | AUG | SEP | OCT |
|---|---|---|---|---|---|---|
| Rivers/Streams | Moderate Moderate Moderate Moderate | Moderate Moderate High High | High High High High | High High High High | High High High High | High Moderate Moderate Moderate |
| Lakes | Moderate High High High | High High Moderate Moderate | Moderate Moderate Moderate Moderate | Moderate Moderate High High | High High High High | High Moderate Moderate Moderate |

| Copper Valley & Valdez | MAY | JUN | JUL | AUG | SEP | OCT |
|---|---|---|---|---|---|---|
| Rivers/Streams | Low Low Moderate Moderate | Moderate Moderate Moderate High | High High High High | High High High High | High High High High | High Moderate Moderate Moderate |
| Lakes | Moderate Moderate Moderate High | High High High Moderate | Moderate Moderate Moderate Moderate | Moderate Moderate Moderate High | High High High High | High Moderate Moderate Moderate |

## Equipment

(Courtesy Eagle Eye Images)

### Spin- & Bait-Casting

**Rod:** 6–8 ½ ft., medium fast action trout rod.
**Reel:** High performance freshwater spinning/bait-casting reel.
**Line:** 175-200 yards of 4–10 lb. test mono line.
**Advice:** Use at least 10- to 15-pound test on a rod up to 9 ft. when fishing trophy waters and/or large, swift-flowing rivers.
**Best Lures:** Spoons, spinners, plugs, attractors, jigs.
Popular Brands (Lure size 2-3 in., ¼ - ¾ oz., #2-4)
**Spoons:** Pixee, Krocodile, Syclops, Super Duper, Little Cleo, Fiord Spoon, Phoebe (Sizes ¼ - ½ oz.).
**Spinners:** Vibrax, Aglia, Black Fury, Panther Martin, Rooster Tail (Sizes 0 – 4).
**Plugs:** Kwikfish, Tadpolly, Rapala, Flatfish, Wiggle Wart, Hot Shot (Sizes 1 – 10).
**Attractors:** Spin-N-Glo, Cheater, 'Lil Corkie (Sizes ¼ - 1 in.); Bead (6-12mm).
**Jigs:** Kastmaster, Swedish Pimple (Sizes 2 – 3 in.).
Fly-Fishing
**Rod:** 5–6 wt., 8–9 ½ ft., medium-fast action fly rod.

*Rooster Tail*
Silver & Black #1-3

*Black Fury*
Black & Gold #1-3

*Bang Tail*
Pink & Silver #1-3

*Sy's Jig*
*Black #6*

*Corkie / Bead*
Orange, Pearl 6-12mm

### Fly-Fishing

**Reel:** Light-medium trout class reel; smooth and reliable drag system.
**Line:** 100-150 yards of 20–30 lb. backing, WF full floating, intermediate, or short sink tip Type II-IV lines, tapered leader, 4–8 lb. tippet.
**Advice:** Pursuing trophy trout and/or in big rivers with heavy current, use rods up to 9 ½ ft. with steelhead or light salmon class reels, intermediate or sink tip Type III-IV/200-400 grain T-series line, 7- to 9-ft. tapered leader, and 10- to 15-pound test.
**Best Flies:** Attractor, Egg/Flesh, Forage, Dry, Special.
Popular Patterns (Hook size 2–10)
**Attractor:** Polar Shrimp, Egg Sucking Leech, Zonker, Skykomish Sunrise, Woolly Bugger.
**Egg/Flesh:** Battle Creek, Glo Bug, Bead Egg, Babine Special, Two Egg Sperm Fly, Carcass Fly, Bunny Fly.
**Forage:** Alaska Smolt, Alevin, Hare's Ear Nymph, Maggot, Muddler Minnow, Parr Fly, Scud, Woolly Worm, Thunder Creek, Leech.
**Dry:** Adams, Cahill, Elk Wing/Hair Caddis, Midge, Bivisible.
**Special:** Mouse.

**Local Favorites:**

*Glo Bug*
#10

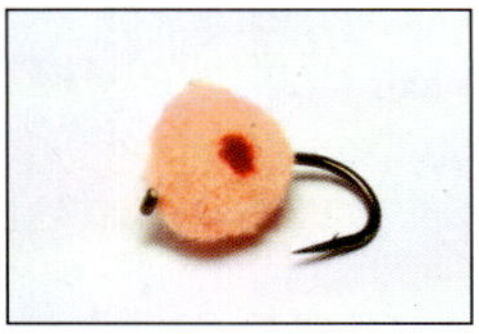

*Dolly Llama*
#6

*Flesh Fly*
#4

*Miles Davis*
#6

*Lord of the Flies*
#6

# Dolly Varden

(Courtesy Alaska Wildland Adventures)

**Highlights:** A brave and reliable fish, always more opportunistic than most other species with enthusiastic strikes and fairly short spurts of energy, often sounding deep during battle before coming to the surface. Rolls often and jumps sporadically. Sea-run fish tend to be more aerial.

**Common Name:** Char and Trout
**Timing:** May to December
**Size:** 10 to 20 inches, up to 10 pounds

**State Record:** 27 pounds, 6 ounces
**Gear:** Light rod/reel; 4- to 8-pound test
**Tackle:** Lures and flies

Dolly Varden are numerous throughout Southcentral as well as the rest of the state, found in nearly every body of water ranging from mere trickles of creeks and beaver ponds to large glacial rivers and deep mountain lakes. Usually not a bit shy about striking artificial lures and flies, these char are a great game fish when other species fail.

Anglers can experience very productive Dolly Varden fishing all season long, from spring through fall in most rivers and streams, with worthwhile action continuing even into mid-winter in lakes. May and June are great for sea-run char while the freshwater fisheries pick up in July and stay strong through September and into October.

The majority of rivers and streams on the Kenai Peninsula support good populations of Dolly Varden with smaller – yet very productive – stocks also found in the Turnagain Arm area and the Matanuska, Susitna, and Copper valleys.

Sea-run populations are present all along the coast of Kenai Peninsula and Prince William Sound.

Dolly Varden do make a good meal, preferably right out of the stream fresh, but are not especially targeted as such given the presence of salmon and the fact that many fishers view these char of more value for catch-and-release sport instead of food.

## Biology

**Scientific Name:** *Salvelinus malma*
**Description:** Spots in varying degrees of color decorate sides only. Scales are small.
**Size:** Common length 8 to 22 inches, averaging 10 to 20 inches in most waters. Maximum length generally 23 to 28 inches (4-8 lbs.); known to reach up to 30 pounds.
**Habitat/Abundance:** Saltwater and clear to semi-glacial coastal and inland drainages. Large or important populations are found on the Kenai Peninsula, in drainages of the Anchorage, and in Prince William. Smaller populations found in Susitna and Copper valleys.

**Feeding Phase:** On sea-run fish are black or dark greenish to blue on back, sides silvery with faint white spots, and white belly. Flesh color is bright orange. In lake and stream populations, fish are dark brown, green, or black on back, and sides yellowish brown with pink spots. Flesh color is light orange.
**Adult Diet:** Primarily fish, fish eggs, crustaceans, plankton, and insects.
**Presence:** Year-round in lakes and large rivers; March to January, peaking May to October in smaller streams. In saltwater, February to October, peaking May and June.
**Spawning:** Rivers, streams, and springs from mid-August to late November, most September and October. May reproduce several times.
**Life Span:** Up to 18 years of age.

**Spawning Phase:** Dirty green or dark on back and upper sides, lower sides and belly bright orange or reddish. Large pink or red spots accent dark sides. Males develop a kype on lower jaw. Pectoral, pelvic, anal, and caudal fins have clear white edges. Flesh color is yellowish white.

## Identification

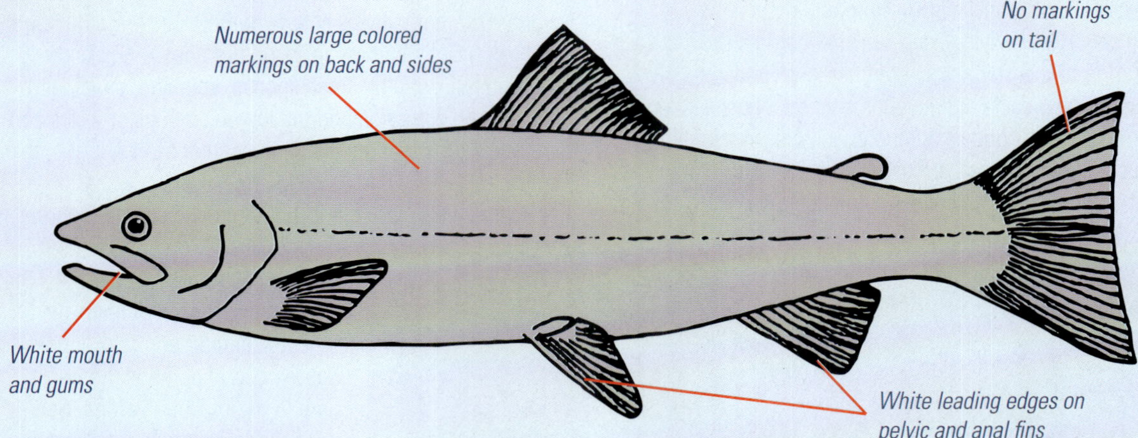

*Blue, green, yellowish-brown, or grey on top of head, no spots or markings present. Mouth and gums are white.*

*Sea-run fish silver sides, dark back. Faint white/light markings visible.*

*Breeding fish distinct orange or red spots on back and sides; belly orange or red. Sides green.*

*No spots present on tail fin; resident fish light pink markings on back/sides.*

## Fishing for Dolly Varden

(Courtesy Shems Jud)

**Top Areas:** The Kenai Peninsula is known as a major producer of char, with most tidewater and inland rivers and streams yielding great angling. Nearshore marine waters here, as well as Prince William Sound, offer very productive action. Some limited opportunities exist in valley drainages of Matanuska, Susitna, and Copper, mainly for resident fish.
**Regulatory Season:** Generally open year-round as a species in most areas. Fall closures (September/October) in a select few streams on the Kenai Peninsula to protect spawning fish.

Dolly Varden are one of the favored game fish on the road system, even targeted exclusively in several popular fisheries. Usually, however, this char is a secondary species after salmon and trout. Abundant in many areas, Dolly Varden are present in all sorts of waters, from rivers and streams to lakes and saltwater, and more often than not very cooperative.

### Rivers & Streams

Anglers may encounter two different populations of Dolly Varden in flowing waters. One is the resident form which are characterized by smaller size (6 to 15 inches), the other are sea-run fish that over-winter in rivers and streams and are typically larger (often several pounds). Dolly Varden are readily caught from both shore and boat.

In spring (April/May), sea-run char begin a downstream migration to the marine environment and feed extensively on emerging insects and juvenile salmon. Thus, casting or drifting small spoons, spinners, and flies can be highly effective. Resident fish are usually not present in any great numbers this early but some locations may provide decent action, such as the confluence of clearwater streams and large glacial rivers. Use same tackle as for sea-run char.

Early summer (June) can be highly variable for anglers seeking Dolly Varden. Sea-run fish are generally absent in freshwater and can be found at sea, and resident fish have yet to make a solid appearance but may still provide worthwhile opportunities in the right areas.

Starting in mid-summer (July), the action begins to improve dramatically as coastal waters see large numbers of sea-run Dolly Varden arrive on the tides. Anglers do exceptionally well on small spoons, spinners, plugs, and flies, hitting estuaries and the lower sections of rivers and streams. Egg imitations become popular after about mid-month.

Resident char are out in full force and can be found at the mouth and lower portion of streams, especially in locations that also receive runs of salmon.

Late summer and fall (August/September) is perhaps the best time to try for Dolly Varden. Sea-run and resident populations are found in concentrations within all areas of their range and respond enthusiastically to a wide range of tackle, including forage, egg, and flesh imitations. Dead drifting is a very effective technique. Additionally, char this time of the

(Courtesy Beverley Bailey)

*Targeting Dolly Varden in salmon spawning streams can be very good in late summer and fall.*

season are in part or full maturity meaning an amazing display of colors.

Starting in late fall and continuing into early winter (October/November), spawning Dolly Varden may be spotted in the shallows and spent or non-reproducing fish hunker down in deep holes and runs. Fishing for them can still be very good but the gradually dropping water temperatures will have an effect on the bite. Resident char begin migrating to over-wintering areas and increasingly more difficult to find. Dead drifting egg and flesh imitations continue to work but casting medium-sized lures and forage and attractor flies work just as well.

## Lakes

As in flowing waters, anglers fishing for Dolly Varden in lakes have to contend with two types of populations: Sea-run and resident. Sea-run fish move into lakes and deep rivers starting in late summer and continuing through fall, over-wintering until spring when a rapid out-migration commences soon after ice-out. Anglers casting small spoons, spinners, plugs, and flies near islands, around points and steep drop-offs, and at lake inlets and outlets usually do very well. In spring soon after breakup, large schools can be found at the main outlet.

Resident char may be found throughout the year and often migrate into inlet and outlet streams during the summer and fall months to feed and reproduce. An assortment of small spinners, plugs, and forage, wet, and dry flies will work.

Ice fishing can be productive using spoons, jigs, and bait such as salmon roe, single salmon eggs, and shrimp.

*Surf-casting from exposed beaches, tidal rips, and stream mouths can be great for sea-run char averaging into the teens. Waters all around the southern section of the Kenai Peninsula as well as much of Prince William Sound are prime areas in late spring and early summer. This is a view from Resurrection Bay in Seward.*

## Saltwater

The appearance of sea-run Dolly Varden along the Southcentral coast is generally quite brief with most anglers doing best during the months of May and June in the majority of locations, although productive action can be found near estuaries through July and into August. Exposed beaches, rocky points, tidal rips, and the mouths of salmon spawning stream are all hot spots. Use anything that resembles a baitfish or small crustacean. Small spoons, spinners, plugs, and jigs are top choices for hardware, fly fishers doing best on forage and saltwater flies imitating salmon smolt and juvenile shrimp.

## Areas & Availability

● = High ● = Moderate ● = Low ● = Closed

| **Kenai Peninsula** | *MAY* | *JUN* | *JUL* | *AUG* | *SEP* | *OCT* |
|---|---|---|---|---|---|---|
| Saltwater | High High High High | High High High High | High High Moderate Moderate | Moderate Moderate Low Low | Low Low Low Low | |
| Freshwater | Low Low Moderate Moderate | Moderate Moderate Moderate Moderate | Moderate Moderate Moderate High | High High High High | High High High High | High High Moderate Moderate |
| **Matanuska-Susitna Valleys** | *MAY* | *JUN* | *JUL* | *AUG* | *SEP* | *OCT* |
| Freshwater | Moderate Moderate Moderate Moderate | Moderate Moderate Moderate Moderate | Moderate Moderate High High | High High High High | High High High High | High Moderate Moderate Moderate |
| **Copper Valley & Valdez** | *MAY* | *JUN* | *JUL* | *AUG* | *SEP* | *OCT* |
| Saltwater | Low Low Moderate Moderate | Moderate Moderate Moderate Moderate | Moderate Moderate Low Low | Low Low Low Low | Low Low Low Low | |
| Freshwater | Low Low Low Low | Low Low Moderate Moderate | Moderate Moderate Moderate Moderate | High High High High | High High High High | High Moderate Moderate Moderate |

## Equipment

### Spin- & Bait-Casting

**Rod:** 5–7 ½ ft., medium fast action trout rod.
**Reel:** High performance freshwater spinning/bait-casting reel.
**Line:** 150 yards of 4–8 lb. test mono line.
**Advice:** Use at least 10- to 14-pound test on a rod up to 9 ft. when fishing trophy waters and/or large, swift-flowing rivers.
**Best Lures:** Spoons, spinners, plugs, attractors, jigs.
Popular Brands
**Spoons:** Pixee, Krocodile, Syclops, Super Duper, Little Cleo, Fiord Spoon, Phoebe (Sizes ¼ -- ½ oz.).
**Spinners:** Vibrax, G. I Spinner, Aglia, Bang Tail, Black Fury, Panther Martin, Rooster Tail (Sizes 0 – 3).
**Plugs:** Kwikfish, Tadpolly, Rapala, Flatfish, Wiggle Wart, Hot Shot (Sizes 1 – 10).

(Courtesy Eagle Eye Photography)

**Attractors:** Spin-N-Glo, Cheater, 'Lil Corkie, Corkie (Sizes ¼ -- 1 in.); Bead (6-12mm).
**Jigs:** Kastmaster, Swedish Pimple (Sizes 1 ½ – 3 in.).

*Swedish Pimple*
Silver #10

*Phoebe*
#6

*Krocodile*
#4

*Bang Tail*
*Pink & Silver* #6

*Corkie / Bead*
Orange, Pearl 6-12mm

### Fly-Fishing

**Rod:** 5–6 wt., 8–9 ft., medium-fast action fly rod.
**Reel:** Light-medium trout class reel; smooth and reliable drag system.
**Line:** 100-150 yards of 20–30 lb. backing, WF full floating, intermediate, or short sink tip Type II-IV lines, tapered leader, 4–8 lb. tippet.
**Advice:** Pursuing trophy char in big rivers with heavy current, use rods up to 9 ½ ft. with steelhead or light salmon class reels, intermediate or sink tip Type III-IV/200-400 grain T-series line, 7- to 9-ft. tapered leader, and 10- to 14-pound test.
**Best Flies:** Attractor, Wet, Egg/Flesh, Forage, Dry, Saltwater, Special.

*Popular Patterns (Hook size 2–10)*
**Attractor:** Polar Shrimp, Egg Sucking Leech, Zonker, Skykomish Sunrise, Woolly Bugger, Fall Favorite.
Egg/Flesh: Battle Creek, Glo Bug, Bead Egg, Babine Special, Two Egg Sperm Fly, Carcass Fly, Bunny Fly.
**Forage:** Alaska Smolt, Alevin, Hare's Ear Nymph, Maggot, Muddler Minnow, Parr Fly, Scud, Woolly Worm, Thunder Creek, Leech, Black Nose Dace, Minnow, Scud, Thunder Creek.
**Wet:** Pheasant Tail Nymph, Caddis, Woolly Worm, Hare's Ear.
**Dry:** Adams, Cahill, Elk Wing/Hair Caddis, Midge, Bivisible.
**Saltwater:** Candlefish, Needlefish, Shrimp.

**Local Favorites:**

*Glo Bug*
#10

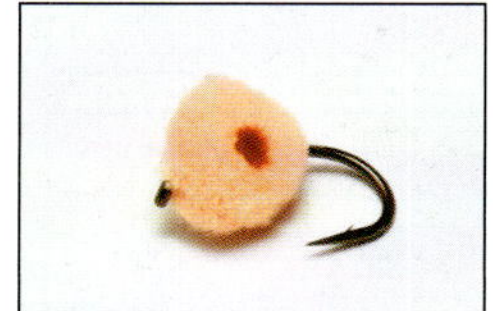

*Dolly Llama*
#6

*Flesh Fly*
#4

*Miles Davis*
#6

*Lord of the Flies*
#6

# Other Char Species

## LAKE TROUT *Salvelinus namaycush*

Contrary to its common name, lake trout are not actually trout at all but a species of char. They thrive in large, deep, and cold inland lakes and when hooked put up a valiant battle. They are targeted by local anglers early and late in the season but may be found in fishable numbers even throughout the summer months.

**Description:** Tail is distinctly forked, and mouth extends well beyond the eye. Sides and back are dark, usually green or brown to black, belly being white. Whitish or yellowish markings are scattered throughout body, including head and some fins. Flesh color is white or light pink. Spawning autumn fish display dark lateral bands on sides and fins take on a slight orange hue. Average weight is 3 to 12 pounds with some specimens reaching 30 pounds or more.

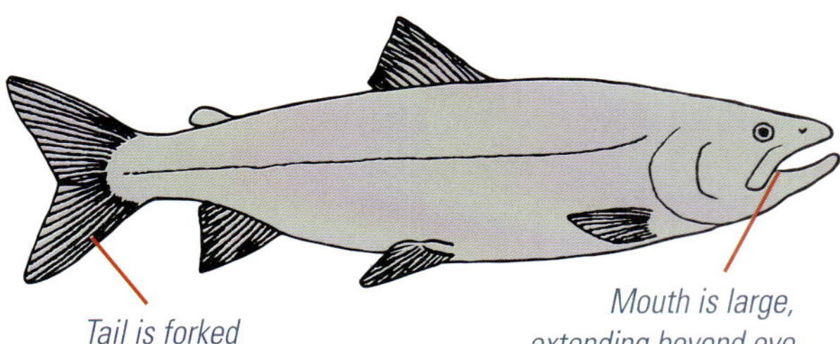


### Fishing for Lake Trout

**Timing:** Year-round inhabitants of deep lakes, occasionally moving into slow-flowing rivers during the summer months. Anglers typically experience the best fishing after breakup in May and early June and again as temperatures cool from late August through November.

**Areas:** Very selective in habitat preference, lake trout are only found in a relatively few lakes throughout its range in Southcentral, being most common in the Copper Valley – most notably Summit, Paxson, and Louise lakes. The Kenai Peninsula has fair populations of char in Kenai, Skilak, and Hidden lakes. Limited opportunities also exist in Susitna Valley.

*(Courtesy Rene Limeres)*

**Equipment:** Light- to medium-sized/weight rod and reel with 6- to 17-pound test line is common gear. Trolling large spoons and plugs is recommended but shore anglers frequently catch these lake char casting chrome and neutral-colored spoons and spinners – even large forage or attractor flies. Ice fishing using jigs, spoons, or single hooks baited with herring or smelt can be good.

**Tips:** Target these lake char in spots with a steep drop-off, near pinnacles or underwater reefs, and around islands. Trolling is best at a depth of 20 to 60 feet although in spring and fall anglers may catch fish considerably shallower. Lake trout often cruise into the mouths of salmon spawning streams. Casting a bait setup – letting it sit on the bottom – at dawn and dusk can be deadly.

## ARCTIC CHAR

*Salvelinus alpinus*

(Courtesy Rene Limeres)

Arctic char are very similar in appearance to Dolly Varden and when in feeding phase may be difficult to tell apart. It is not a common species despite a fairly wide distribution and at first may seem difficult to catch wherever found. However, with the right tackle and methods applied, char are an aggressive species that put up a noteworthy fight.

**Description:** Spots in pink or red decorate sides. Back is dark green to brownish, sides tan or yellowish brown, belly white. Flesh is light orange. Many of the fins have creamy white leading edges. Spawning fish, present in fall and early winter, can display brilliant colors, often being sharp orange with large whitish or creamy markings. Average weight is 2 to 4 pounds, up to 12 pounds or more.

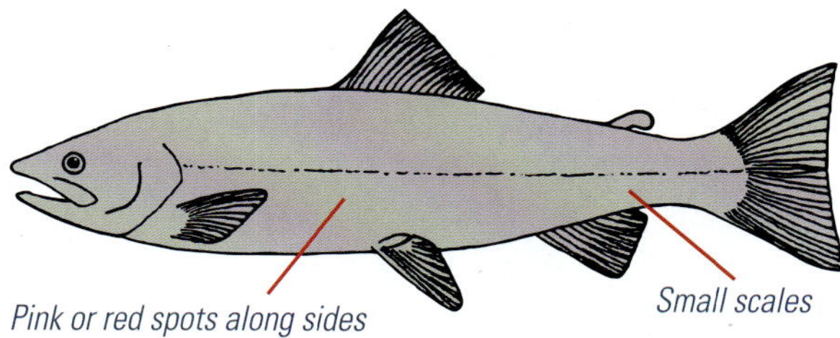


## Fishing for Arctic Char

**Timing:** In Southcentral Alaska, present in lakes year-round with immature specimens also venturing into rivers and streams. Best time is in spring after break-up (May) and in fall (September-October). Ice fishing for char can be extremely productive during the November to January time frame but good catches can still be enjoyed throughout the winter months in some of the deeper lakes.

**Areas:** There are a fair number of lakes in the Matanuska and Susitna valleys and on the Kenai Peninsula that support both wild and stocked populations of char. Planted fish are common in more high-use, urban lakes and ponds. Adult arctic char are generally not encountered in flowing waters in Southcentral. There are no sea-run populations along roadside waters.

**Equipment:** Successful anglers focus efforts on one of the smaller stocked or larger, deeper lakes of the region, trolling spoons and plugs during the open water season, jigging spoons and bait through the ice in winter. Casting medium-sized lures and even large forage flies from boat or shore is most productive in spring and fall when fish concentrate in relatively shallow water. Best bait include pieces of cut herring, small clusters of salmon roe, single salmon eggs, and shrimp on a single hook. Use light to medium-light gear with 4- to 12-pound test line.

**Tips:** Arctic char thrive in deeper portions of lakes, often at 20 to 40 feet, either suspended right above bottom up to the middle layers of water. Larger specimens are rarely found shallow or close to shore. Search steep drop-offs. Serious char anglers use sonar to locate schools of fish. Fly-fishing for these char requires sinking lines with emphasis on spring and fall conditions when fish are located off the bottom in middle stratus water.

*The deep inland and alpine lakes of much of the Southcentral region harbor healthy populations of both arctic char and lake trout. Expect some quality fish to be present as angling pressure is typically light.*

# Other Species

# Freshwater Fish

**Apart from the species typically targeted by anglers along the road system, a few others do not seem to attract very much attention. Arctic grayling, whitefish, northern pike, and burbot are present in varying degrees of abundance but do not play a significant role due to several factors, including general diminutive physical size compared to other species, poor angler access to productive waters, small populations, and/or a general lack of aggressive attitude towards artificial lures and flies. For the most part these species will remain incidental encounters. However, targeting these species with success is possible for anglers willing to put in the time and effort.**

For those not too busy chasing more glamorous species, such as salmon, trout, and char, may look at taking some time to explore other options. If ever around the inland waterways of the Southcentral region, such as the Susitna and Copper valleys, it may be worth gearing down or changing methods, techniques, and tackle to take on these largely ignored species.

Grayling, whitefish, pike, and burbot are synonymous with each other in that they often are located within the same drainages, albeit perhaps in different specific areas. They give anglers a welcome change of pace from the hectic coastal salmon fisheries, showing a more relaxed and peaceful way of enjoying fishing in Alaska.

As the larger inland rivers and lakes are natural migratory channels and spawning areas for salmon and other salmonid species, they also harbor some great opportunities for species that may very much depend on salmon but require drastically different fishing concepts.

Grayling are found throughout the season in clearwater streams and lakes, a true delight for those wanting to experience true dry-fly fishing using ultra-light gear. In some of these same lakes, pike hide in the weeds near shore, waiting to ambush its prey, while burbot occupy the deeper lake sections and, in larger, glacial rivers, often move into the mouths of salmon streams in search of food. Whitefish, not to be outdone, show up in sometimes huge schools during the latter part of the season and invade certain waters en masse, providing a very different and challenging way of enjoying small game on light tackle.

For a growing number of anglers, the solitude (and fast action) these species offer puts a new dimension to enjoying the roadside fisheries.

## Freshwater Species Timing

● = High ● = Moderate ● = Low ● = Closed

| Species | MAY | JUN | JUL | AUG | SEP | OCT |
|---|---|---|---|---|---|---|
| Arctic Grayling | High High High High | High High High High | High High High High | High High High High | High High High High | High High Moderate Moderate |
| Round Whitefish | Low Low Low Low | Low Low Moderate Moderate | Moderate Moderate High High | High High High High | High High High High | High High High Moderate |
| Northern Pike | High High High High | High High Moderate Moderate | Moderate Moderate Moderate Moderate | Moderate Moderate Moderate High | High High High High | High High Moderate Moderate |
| Burbot | Moderate Moderate Moderate Moderate | Moderate Moderate Moderate Moderate | Moderate Moderate High High | High High High High | High High High High | High High High High |

## ARCTIC GRAYLING

*Thymallus arcticus*

The only representative species of the grayling family in Alaska, these fish are typically found in clear and clean inland waters. Arctic grayling has earned a solid reputation among anglers as being a superb game fish due to its aerial antics and aggressiveness towards artificial lures and flies.

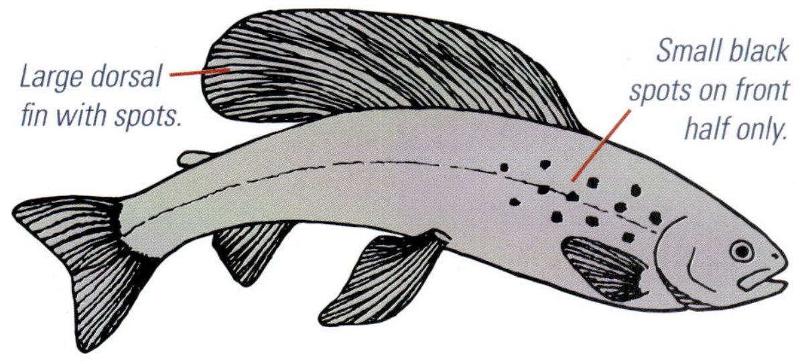


**Description:** Exceptionally large dorsal fin is trademark of the grayling. Numerous black spots are located on sides from gills to almost midway down the fish. Scales are large and tail forked. Color is generally silvery gray, light brown, or copper, belly being white. Flesh color is white. Spawning fish often display a darker overall hue with red or pink spots and stripes on the fins. Average length is approximately 7 to 14 inches, maximum being 18 to 20 inches and a weight of 2 to 3 pounds.

*(Courtesy Chris Cox)*

### Fishing for Arctic Grayling

**Timing:** Available in large, deep rivers and lakes all year long but mainly from spring into fall in smaller streams. Peak action occurs from the spawning runs in May on through the summer season until October when fish are actively feeding. Winter fishing for grayling is typically slow.

**Areas**: Grayling are native to the Susitna and Copper valleys, where the largest populations can be found, but have been introduced in other areas as well, such as around Anchorage, Matanuska Valley, and the Kenai Peninsula. The Gulkana River and Paxson and Summit lakes in upper Copper Valley are some of the best in Alaska. The various clearwater tributaries of Susitna River in Susitna Valley also support good opportunities.

**Equipment:** As grayling are relatively small, ultra-light gear is recommended. In lakes and flowing waters both, use small lures and flies. Size 0 to 3 spinners in neutral colors or metallic finishes is the favorite type of hardware. Dry, wet, and forage flies are superb but when spawning salmon are present grayling will attack egg imitations with abandon. As for bait, try worms or single salmon eggs.

**Tips:** Being heavy insect feeders choose flies to match. In spring and early summer, forage flies and lures resembling salmon smolt can be hot. In lakes, focus effort around vegetated shorelines, underwater reefs, and inlets and outlets. Fish can be found feeding off the surface in the morning and evening, deeper during mid-day. In small streams, look for deep pools and covered water. Rivers and larger creeks usually will find grayling at the head of holes and runs. The mouths of tributary streams and glacial rivers are hot spots early and late in the season. In mid-summer, grayling are most numerous at or near headwaters.

*Grayling fishing is often synonymous with small and fast-flowing, mountainous clearwater streams.*

## NORTHERN PIKE *Esox lucius*

Northern pike is a popular game fish but not found in any abundance in proximity of roads and highways. There are a few productive but isolated populations in various small lakes accessible by car yet none of the famous hot spots in Southcentral support viable numbers of pike. Anglers wishing to target pike in this region of Alaska should consider one of several remote fisheries instead, such as those of Susitna Valley.

**Description:** Dorsal fin is far back on body and long, flat

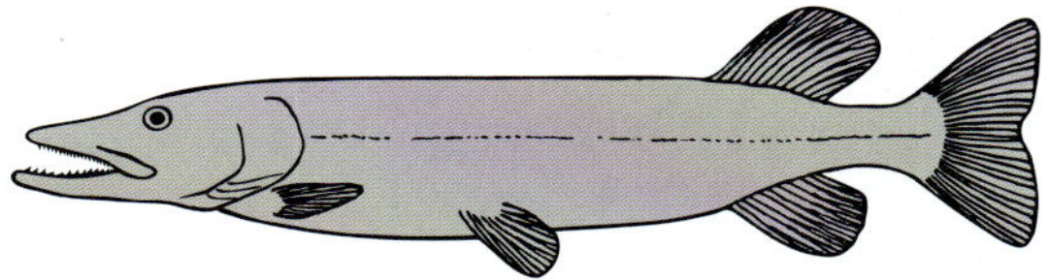

duckbill snout are trademark points of identification. Mouth is large and equipped with long, sharp teeth. Dark grayish green to dark brownish on back and sides; creamy white or yellowish on belly. Numerous yellow spots in irregular longitudinal rows decorate sides. Average weight is three to 10 pounds and may reach 15 to 25 pounds. Maximum size is 50 pounds or more.

### Fishing for Northern Pike

**Timing:** Year-round in lakes and large rivers and typically most active in April, May, and June and again from September into November.

**Areas:** Very few pike waters next to the road provide consistent catches of pike. Roadside lakes and streams

(Courtesy Bryan Allen)

in the Susitna Valley and on the Kenai Peninsula harbor a few fish. Present in a wide range of habitat but seems to proliferate in drainages containing an abundance of slow moving and still water, including lakes and ponds and the lower reaches of rivers and streams. Sloughs are ideal pike hangouts. Dense growths of vegetation, such as weed beds, attract fish.

**Equipment:** Light to medium gear is suitable for most all conditions. Cast-and-retrieve in likely holding areas is effective, as is stationary fishing using a strike indicator and bait. Medium-to large-sized spoons, spinners, plugs, and flies are usually predictable in getting strikes but small whole or plug-cut herring and smelt can be foolproof.

**Tips:** Considering the sharp teeth of pike, a foot-long wire or hard plastic leader is highly recommended.

*Recognizing pike habitat is vital in securing catches. Look in and around weeds beds or any dense shoreline vegetation.*

## ROUND WHITEFISH *Prosopium cylindraceum*

There are several species of whitefish in Alaska, including cisco, but only a few enter the sport fishery to any extent. By far the most common species in Southcentral Alaska is the round whitefish and will be the representative species in this discussion.

**Description:** Body shape is tubular, scales large, and

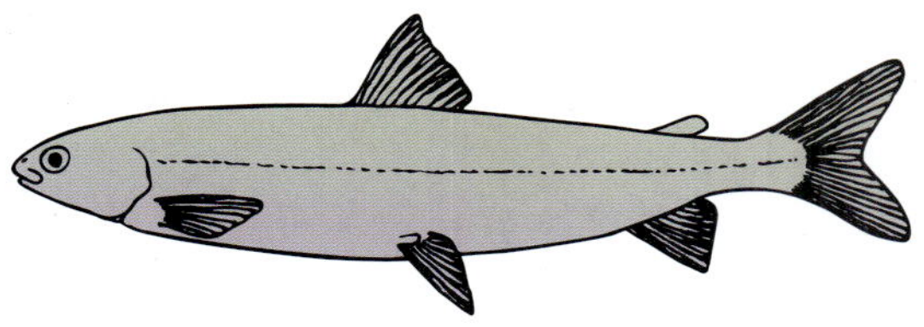

mouth small. Sides are silvery, back dark grey or green, and belly silvery white. Average length is 10 to 15 inches with a weight of two pounds. A few specimens may attain 20 inches and three pounds.

### Fishing for Round Whitefish

**Timing:** Present in freshwater year-round but generally not encountered during the winter months. Peak months of availability are July through October.

**Areas:** Usually found in fishable numbers in tributaries of Susitna River in the Susitna Valley, notably Sheep and Little

(Courtesy Beverley Bailey)

Willow creeks. The Little Susitna River in Matanuska Valley and Upper Kenai River on the Kenai Peninsula also has good populations.

**Equipment:** Due to the diminutive size of whitefish, light or ultra light gear is recommended. These fish also have small mouths so the use of small hooks is necessary. Stationary methods are most productive but some fish are caught while drifting or by casting and retrieving. Tiny spoons and flies (nymphs) are productive, beads, small clusters of salmon roe, and single salmon eggs often proving deadly.

**Tips:** Deep holes and pools in the lower and middle reaches of rivers and streams concentrate fish early in the season (July-August), the more shallow upper stretches being productive later on in fall (September-October). Fish all offerings still or very slowly.

## BURBOT *Lota lota*

Burbot are quite abundant wherever found but the methods used to catch them are generally not compatible with what the majority of anglers look for when fishing with a rod and reel. As a food fish, however, it is superb.

**Description:** Long and slender body, head being wide and

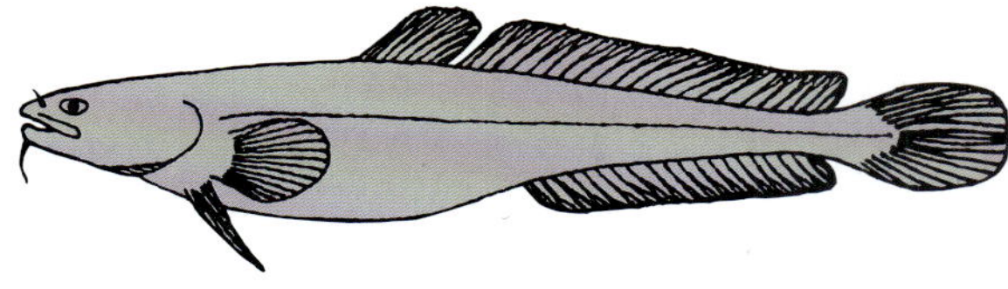

broad. Mouth is large. Characteristic barbell adorns tip of lower jaw. Mottled brown, olive-black, or dark green on back and sides; belly a lighter hue. Numerous dirty yellow patches or markings cover back, sides, and belly in dirty yellow. Flesh color is white. Average weight is two to six pounds, up to 15 pounds. Maximum weight is 75 pounds.

### Fishing for Burbot

**Timing:** Year-round in lakes and large rivers, summer and fall in smaller drainages. Most active during the cooler

(Courtesy Dan Brown)

months. Autumn is a good time to be targeting these cod at the mouths of clearwater streams emptying into larger glacial systems.

**Areas:** Sizable populations are found in the Copper River and Susitna River drainages as well as in a few area lakes. There are only a few locations that may be considered hot spots, such as Paxson, Summit, and Louise lakes in Copper Valley but the mouths of tributaries to the Susitna may be worthwhile as well.

**Equipment:** Light to medium category rod and reel, shorter and stouter rods are used for ice fishing. The vast majority of burbot fishing is associated with stationary methods involving setting bait such as herring or smelt on a single hook right on or immediately above the bottom. Jigging spoons may produce decent catches.

**Tips:** Burbot prefer still/slow-moving water with gravel and mud-covered bottom. Fish at night.

# Saltwater Fish

There are several types of game fish in Alaska's briny, including Pacific halibut, lingcod, rockfish, and salmon shark, and dozens of non-sporting kinds such as cod and flounder. Anglers experience good to excellent action virtually year-round but success tends to be more consistent during the warmer months, primarily from May into September. Although the main game species are not present in any large numbers to roadside anglers, those hiring a charter boat will have access to the best fishing grounds.

Southcentral Alaska has several coastal communities, most of which caters to a prolific fleet of recreational and commercial fishing boats. These communities serve as hubs for essentially all saltwater angling effort, from both shore and more remote locations only accessed by boat.

The primary ports include the towns of Homer and Seward on the Kenai Peninsula and Whittier and Valdez in Prince William Sound. Ninilchik and Anchor Point are two additional communities that offer limited ocean access on the peninsula.

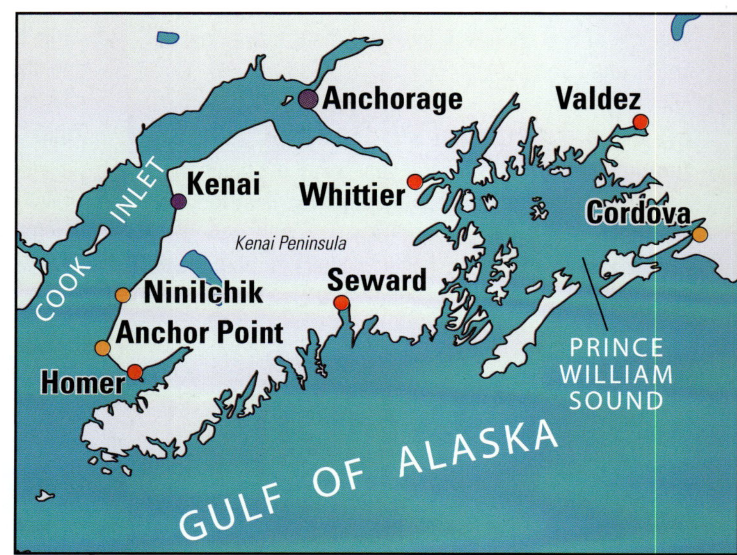


Map Legend

● = *Primary ocean access points. Developed roadside fishing areas and extensive charter fleets.*

● = *Secondary ocean access points. Limited roadside fishing areas; good charter options.*

● = *Ocean access points, limited fishery.*

## Saltwater Species Timing

● = High ● = Moderate ● = Low ● = Closed

| Species | MAY | JUN | JUL | AUG | SEP | OCT |
|---|---|---|---|---|---|---|
| Pacific Halibut | Moderate, Moderate, High, High | High, High, High, High | High, High, High, High | High, High, High, High | High, Moderate, Moderate, Moderate | Moderate, Moderate, Moderate, Moderate |
| Lingcod | Closed, Closed, Closed, Closed | Closed, Closed, Closed, Closed | High, High, High, High | High, High, High, High | High, High, Moderate, Moderate | Moderate, Moderate, Moderate, Moderate |
| Rockfish | Moderate, Moderate, Moderate, High | High, High, High, High | High, High, High, High | High, High, High, High | High, High, Moderate, Moderate | Moderate, Moderate, Moderate, Moderate |
| Salmon Shark | Low, Low, Low, Low | Low, Moderate, Moderate, Moderate | Moderate, High, High, High | High, High, High, High | Moderate, Moderate, Moderate, Low | Low, Low, Low, Low |
| Bottomfish | High, High, High, High | High, High, High, High | High, High, High, High | High, High, High, High | High, High, High, High | Moderate, Moderate, Moderate, Moderate |

## Roadside Fisheries

Pacific halibut, lingcod, and rockfish are present in roadside waters, albeit not in the numbers (or size range) as in more remote offshore waters. Thus, due to limited access of productive fishing areas, the vast majority of saltwater angling in the state occurs from boat. However, non-sporting bottomfish are plentiful in most areas.

For anglers determined to sample what is available will find small populations of rockfish in a few spots in Resurrection Bay (Seward) and Passage Canal (Whittier). The former location also holds a few lingcod, not a viable species since the bay is currently closed by regulation to fishing for the species. Halibut is not a common catch but nonetheless taken time to time by anglers casting bait off exposed beaches and docks in Homer and Seward, usually incidentally to fishing for other species. Most fish are very small, weighing only a few pounds, but can reach considerable proportions on occasion; halibut in the 80- to 100-pound range or more are possible. There have been no reports of any salmon shark being caught from shore.

## Remote Fisheries

To truly experience the best of all the saltwater game fish, hire a charter boat. Prices are reasonable, all necessary gear and bait is provided, and the captain has a vast amount of experience regarding "honey holes," tidal changes, water and weather conditions, and all the other nuances required for success. Another option is to rent a boat, which can be a good solution for those with intimate knowledge of the various species and the target area.

All of the ports mentioned above offer superb fishing and there will be a multitude of guides and lodges advertising their services all along the highway.

Expect the boat ride to take anywhere from 20 minutes to 3 hours or more one way, depending on weather conditions and location of fishing grounds. Come prepared for a long day on the water as charters usually leave port between six and seven in the morning, arriving back at dock in late afternoon.

*For truly exceptional action featuring halibut, lingcod, and rockfish, plan on getting a charter to access deeper, offshore waters.*

(Courtesy Crackerjack Sportfishing)

(Courtesy Roy & Beverley Bailey)

*Soaking bait off beaches is a great way to connect with a variety of bottomfish, including such popular quarries as halibut. This 25-pounder struck a chunk of herring cast from the Homer Spit.*

Half-day charters are available at around half the price as well but generally target inshore areas with an abundance of smaller fish. In contrast, two-day overnight trips are also available, allowing anglers to harvest two limits of fish on one outing. This is a good cost-saving option that may also explore lesser-fished areas too remote for day trips.

Specialized gear being used consists of heavy-duty 5- to 6-foot standup rods, reels outfitted with 50- to 150-pound test line, and hooks baited with herring or salmon heads. Lighter gear and tackle may be available upon request and bringing one's own is another option as well. Saltwater fly-fishing is another opportunity that may be offered.

Always be sure to inquire about specific species being targeted and if combination trips are available. Since halibut, lingcod and rockfish, and salmon shark prefer distinct habitats, anglers must choose what they would like to fish for. Some outfits may not accommodate fishing for certain species.

## PACIFIC HALIBUT

*Hippoglossus stenolepis*

The halibut is the premier target of anglers fishing Alaska's coastal waters. Often very abundant, easy to catch, and a great food fish, the halibut is the perfect species to supplement a harvest trip or any other fishing experience.

**Description:** Largest species of flounder; somewhat elongated body, top side dark gray to dirty brown, bottom side white. The flesh is white and of firm texture. Average weight is 15 to 40 pounds with some of the better locations providing good opportunity for fish ranging from 60 to 100 pounds. Exceptional specimens between 300 and 350 pounds are boated every season and commercial fishers have documented catches up to 550 pounds.

### Fishing for Pacific Halibut

**Main Ports:** Ninilchik, Anchor Point, Homer, Seward, Whittier, and Valdez.

**Timing:** Available year-round (except during the month of January by regulation), the peak abundance in near-shore waters occur from May to September.

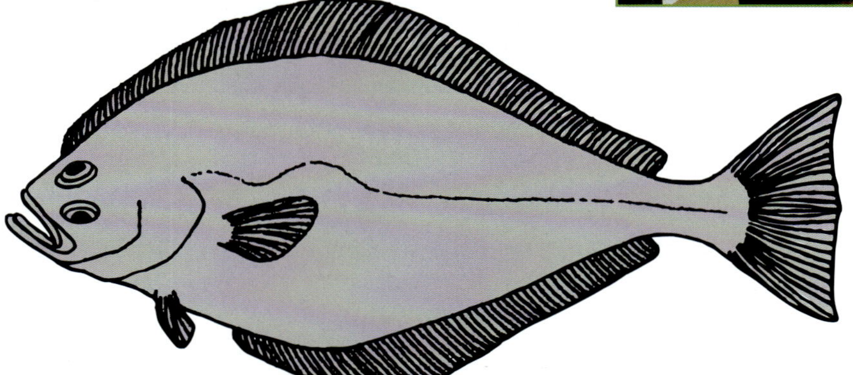

**Areas:** The main halibut hot spots are in 60 to 300 feet of water and include lower Cook Inlet, the coastline of southern Kenai Peninsula, and Prince William Sound, all of which have ideal habitat consisting of pinnacles and sand, gravel, or mud bottoms.

**Gear/Tackle:** The majority of halibut fishing is done with short and stout deep sea rods and reels loaded with 60- to 120-pound test line. An assortment of jigs work well, including metal and lead-heads ("scampi"-style) that are approximately 6 to 10 inches in length. Popular baits include herring, squid, and salmon heads, the latter of which is responsible for many a trophy-sized halibut; however, a chunk of herring is hard to beat for fast action.

Most charter operators will furnish all gear, tackle, and bait as part of the price of trip.

**Methods/Techniques:** Depending on the location and tidal movements, drifting with the current over shoals or banks dragging bait or jigging lures is extremely effective and efficient. If there is little or no current flow, it is possible to anchor in place, using a chum bag to disperse scent and attract fish to the boat. Halibut are frequently caught while trolling for salmon, particularly in more shallow water (20 to 50 ft.) or around structure.

**Note:** Charter captains frequently ask clients if they would like to target smaller halibut, referred to as "chickens" (15-20 pounds), in shallow water for fast and easy action or gamble on deeper locations containing less numerous but bigger fish of 50-60 pounds or more. State intentions or objectives regarding fish size clearly before leaving dock or at time of booking a halibut trip.

**Surf-Casting:** While this species is generally thought of as a mainstay of deeper, offshore waters, a fair number of fish are taken by anglers casting from the surf. A few specimens are taken on regular spinning gear every year; however, for consistent success (and larger fish), proper surf-casting gear and tackle is required.

Choice areas include lower Cook Inlet, along the beaches from the mouth of Kenai River to Anchor Point, as well as Kachemak Bay and the Homer Spit. A few halibut

(Courtesy Beverley Bailey)

*Fishing the surf for halibut using the right gear and tackle can be a thrill, especially if a large fish takes the bait.*

are also taken from shore at the head of Resurrection Bay in Seward, along Lowell Point Road.

Any prospective location ideally should have a fairly steep gradient so to access water that is at least 15 feet or deeper; however, many a fish have been taken in areas that are between 5 and 10 feet, this being especially the case along the beaches of Cook Inlet. Experienced surf-casters have learned to identify structure, such as depressions and deep channels off the mouth of rivers and streams, that may harbor concentrations of halibut.

Although halibut may be caught from shore anytime between April and October, there is definitely a peak season when fish may be found in somewhat greater numbers. In general, the months of June, July, and August are top picks yet seasonal variations do occur as a result of halibut migrations as they target certain types of baitfish or other food sources. For example, the month of May can be relatively productive off the mouth of rivers that support spring runs of hooligan with sizable halibut (to 20-30 lbs.) hunting these little smelt almost into the surf, and again in September as these flatfish seek out food particles from spawned-out salmon that wash out into the briny.

Additionally, land-based fish processing plants act as huge chum sources and will draw a number of halibut close to shore and well within reach of surf-casters. These plants are typically in operation from mid-May to early September.

Anglers casting from shore do best with stationary methods and techniques involving bait. A whole small- to medium-sized herring or a chunk of cod or small salmon head will attract attention. Let it sit on the bottom and check the setup every 20-30 minutes or as needed. Provide some movement to the bait every so often. Remember, these fish are true predators and will move around considerably in their search of food, thus movement and scent are key factors to catching halibut on a consistent basis.

## LINGCOD

*Ophiodon elongatus*

Next to halibut, lingcod is one of the larger bottom dwellers saltwater anglers are likely to encounter. Although not regularly targeted exclusively, they make for a perfect game species along with rockfish since both inhabit the same general structure. Typically very aggressive and of good size, fishing for them is both exciting and rewarding.

**Description:** Lingcod are in reality not a codfish at all but

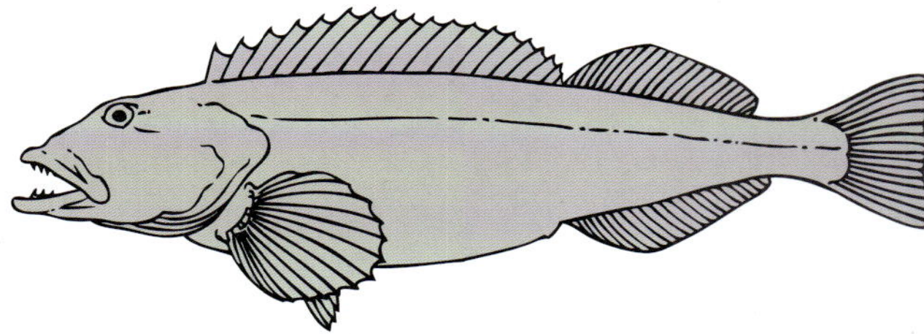

a member of the greenling family. They are characterized by elongated bodies, large heads, and mottled bluish-green to black or brown color. Flesh is white or greenish to even a bluish-white color. Average weight is 10 to 30 pounds with a fair number of fish exceeding 40 pounds. May reach 5 feet in length and 100 pounds.

## Fishing for Lingcod

**Main Ports:** Homer, Seward, Whittier, and Valdez.
**Timing:** Present year-round in offshore waters but available nearshore from July through September. Note, however, that the coastal region of Southcentral Alaska is closed to lingcod fishing from January 1 through June 30.
**Areas:** In the Cook Inlet area, most lingcod are taken at the mouth of the inlet bordering the Gulf of Alaska. The outer coast of Prince William Sound and southern Kenai Peninsula are excellent areas. Hot spots consist of rocky bottom structure with abundant weed beds, pinnacles, and steep drop-offs in 30 to 300 feet of water.
**Gear/Tackle:** Traditional equipment includes short, strong rods with level-wind reels filled with 50- to 80-pound test line. Lingcod respond very favorably to lures and bait both, yet jigs with scampi-style plastic bodies are without a doubt best. Charters furnish these items for their clients.
**Methods/Techniques:** Anglers prefer to drift with the current over and around uneven structure, jigging large lures following the contour of the bottom, thus covering large areas. Very aggressive predators, lingcod are also extremely territorial, often hiding between structure and employing ambush-style hunting tactics on prey. Jigs provide the motion that trigger strikes, which can be savage.
**Note:** Although lingcod and halibut may be found in the same spots, they usually inhabit separate locations. Other bottomfish are commonly found alongside lingcod.
**Surf-Casting:** Anglers casting from shore have very limited opportunities for these fish. Smaller specimens weighing a few pounds are hooked with some regularity in the various costal ports, primarily Seward and Whittier, but closed seasons and areas and size restrictions are keeping harvest levels very low.

While Seward area waters are closed to lingcod fishing, surf-casters may score a few nice fish in Whittier in summer, especially if employing gear facilitating long-distance casting.

Anglers are advised to use very stringent harvest guidelines as populations are easily impacted.

## ROCKFISHES

*Genus Sebastes*

Rockfish are very abundant along coastal waters in Southcentral. Erroneously labeled "snapper" and "sea bass," rockfish is actually a family of fishes that consist of several dozen species in a vast variety of sizes and colors. Anglers generally encounter some 19 species of which only three or four make up the vast majority of sport catches. In Southcentral, the black rockfish is most common, followed by yelloweye, dusky, and quillback.

**Description:** Rockfish generally have a broad body with numerous sharp, spiny rays, large eyes and mouth, and varying shades of color according to species, ranging from carmine red to dark blue to dirty brown. Most rockfish

average 2 to 5 pounds with maximum size between 5 to 10 pounds depending on species. A few species may attain weights of 30 to 40 pounds, this usually being the yelloweye species.

*(Courtesy Miller's Landing)*

## Fishing for Rockfish

**Main Ports:** Homer, Seward, Whittier, and Valdez.
**Timing:** Present year-round in offshore waters, rockfish are generally available in greatest abundance during the warmer summer months as fish are located in more shallow inshore areas. June through September are great months to target most rockfish populations.
**Areas:** The majority of rockfish catches come from the mouth of Cook Inlet and the outer waters of Resurrection Bay bordering the Gulf of Alaska. Rockfish hot spots, however, include virtually the entire coastline of southern Kenai Peninsula and Prince William Sound. Favorite hangouts include rocky areas with plenty of weed beds, underwater reefs, pinnacles, and steep drop-offs in 20 to 400 feet of water.

*Waters off steep, rocky cliffs and pinnacles are prime lingcod and rockfish territory.*

**Gear/Tackle:** Anglers often use equipment that is far too heavy for the general size of rockfish because of high probability of catching much larger game species, such as halibut and lingcod. But if targeted exclusively, the slightly longer and more subtle styles of deep sea rods are sufficient, and reels with 10- to 20-pound test line plenty. Bait is good but jigs are best as they have the perfect motion and flash to draw attention. For pelagic rockfish that frequent the upper layers of water, salmon spoons and standard spinning gear work just fine.
**Methods/Techniques:** For rockfish suspended in and around rock structure, anglers prefer to drift their boats in order to cover large areas and hit schools of fish. Jigging lures is the best way to go, tipped with bait or alone. Bait, such as herring, smelt, or squid are all good.
**Note:** Among the longest-living animals on the planet, rockfish may live up to 100 years of age with some specimens believed to be as old as 150 years. Use discretion with conservation in mind if harvesting fish.
**Surf-Casting:** As with halibut and lingcod, targeting rockfish from shore is generally an exercise for the more patient and determined angler. However, gear is not such a huge issue as these fish tend to keep fairly close to land as that is where structure can be located; the steep cliff walls, boulders, and rock crevasses are ideal hangouts for most species of rockfish and often reached with regular bait-casting rod and reel.

While there are no actual hot spots for roadside rockfish, anglers do well at times catching smaller specimens in such locations as Resurrection Bay in Seward and Passage Canal in Whittier. Successful anglers set up in an area with good structure and move around until fish are found.

## ADDITIONAL SPECIES

There is a vast number of saltwater species in Alaska, of which many are available to boaters as well as the roadside angler. Most readily available during the summer months when found in relatively shallow waters close to shore, the more common catches include one or more members of the cod and flounder families, greenling, and sculpin (Irish Lord). Some are more palatable than others with cod, pollock, greenling, yellowfin and starry flounder, and sablefish (black cod) being quite popular. Wolf eels and skates are caught too. Sharks are represented by several species of which a couple can be very plentiful, especially dogfish, with salmon sharks locally abundant and a huge challenge on sport gear.

All of the above-mentioned species, with the possible exception of nearly all kinds of shark, may be taken by casting from beaches, docks, and breakwater areas bordering waters of at least 5 to 10 feet or more.

While bottomfish are plentiful most anywhere, there are specific locations that draw large concentrations of fish. One such hot spot are the outlets of fish processing plants, providing a natural "chumming" effect that anglers can capitalize on. Several coastal ports have commercial processing plants and fishing near them during the summer months can be no less than superb.

(Courtesy Beverley Bailey)

All species respond best to bait. Cut herring on a single hook is popular, some anglers even rigging two or three hooks on one line, cumulating with a drop sinker. Jigs can be used as well. It is typically the smaller and immature fish of all species that are hooked in nearshore waters; the larger and older specimens found in deeper waters offshore.

A few species thrive in brackish water, such as starry

flounder, often ascending large rivers to a considerable degree and may even be encountered in lakes and ponds closely connected to estuaries.

**Cods:** This is a fairly large family of fish that inhabit a great many regions of the world. Member species in Alaska commonly taken by anglers in Southcentral include the Pacific (true) cod, pollock, and tom cod; all are highly edible, though pollock may have issues with parasites. The flesh is white with a mild taste and even preferred by some.

The Pacific cod may reach very respectable size, up to 20 pounds or more, but generally 3 to 7 pounds near shore. Pollock, constituting the largest fish biomass in the state, can be exceptionally abundant and easy to catch, typically weighing 3 to 5 pounds with some catches to 12 pounds. Tom cod are much smaller, usually 10 to 18 inches and not nearly as prolific as the other cod fishes.

Popular spots include Seward and Homer with some good fishing also in Valdez, Whittier, and Ninilchik.

**Sharks:** These fish are locally abundant along the coast of Southcentral depending on species and time of year, offering excellent possibilities for anglers seeking something out of the ordinary. Several kinds may be encountered or targeted by anglers, with salmon sharks being the most popular due to their aggressiveness, relentless fighting abilities, and tasty flesh.

Dog fish (or mud sharks) are most plentiful and frequently hooked by anglers fishing for other species, such as halibut and salmon, and can be a real nuisance if encountered in large numbers. They are usually around 3 to 5 feet long and 20 to 50 pounds. Although edible, most fish are released.

Salmon sharks are a true game fish. Targeted by the charter industry, fishing for them can be a very exciting as they reach large size, up to 1,000 pounds and 14 feet, and average 150 to 300 pounds. Expect fights to last up to 45 minutes or longer. The meat is very flavorful. Due to the size and potential dangers involved with actually boating one of these jaw-snapping monsters, hiring an experienced guide with appropriate equipment is highly recommended.

The ports of Valdez, Whittier, and Seward provide excellent remote fishing during July, August, and September. There are no great surf-casting spots for salmon shark but good opportunities can be had for spiny dogfish along Cook Inlet beaches, primarily at the mouths of Kenai and Kasilof rivers in mid-summer and fall.

**Skates:** Several species are present in Alaska's waters and frequently tangle with anglers fishing for halibut and other bottomfish. True bottom-dwellers, skate often reach a large size, even in nearshore waters, averaging up to 50 pounds, with specimens up to 100 pounds and more having been caught from the surf.

Edibility varies according to individual taste, and specific species and time of year may affect flavor, and ranges from light and delicate to bland.

All ports yield opportunities for skate, with surf-casters doing best in Homer and along the beaches of Cook Inlet.

**Flounders:** Many types of flounders are present in Southcentral's marine waters, with anglers being very familiar with several of them that inhabit the shallow, inshore areas of the coast that provide sand, mud, and gravel bottom structure, including yellowfin, starry, and turbot. The former two species are highly edible and available in good numbers in many locations. The latter species is also numerous yet not really attracted as a food fish in Alaska; however, it is sold to a great extent on the overseas commercial market.

Starry flounder is the largest species, often weighing several pounds and may attain three feet in length and 20 pounds. The yellowfin flounder averages up to 20 inches.

Best ports are Homer, Ninilchik, and Seward.

**Others:** There is a huge abundance of other species available to surf-casters in areas around the Gulf of Alaska, including many species of sculpin, one of which may reach two feet in length and multiple pounds, greenlings (related to lingcod) that display a mild and almost translucent, light blue or green flesh, and smaller sablefish weighing a couple-three pounds (larger, mature individuals are associated with deep water, to 2,000 feet or more).

*(Courtesy Beverley Bailey)*

*Anglers casting off beaches using bait are often treated to more exotic species, such as this skate caught from Homer Spit. When fishing the briny, big surprises await.*

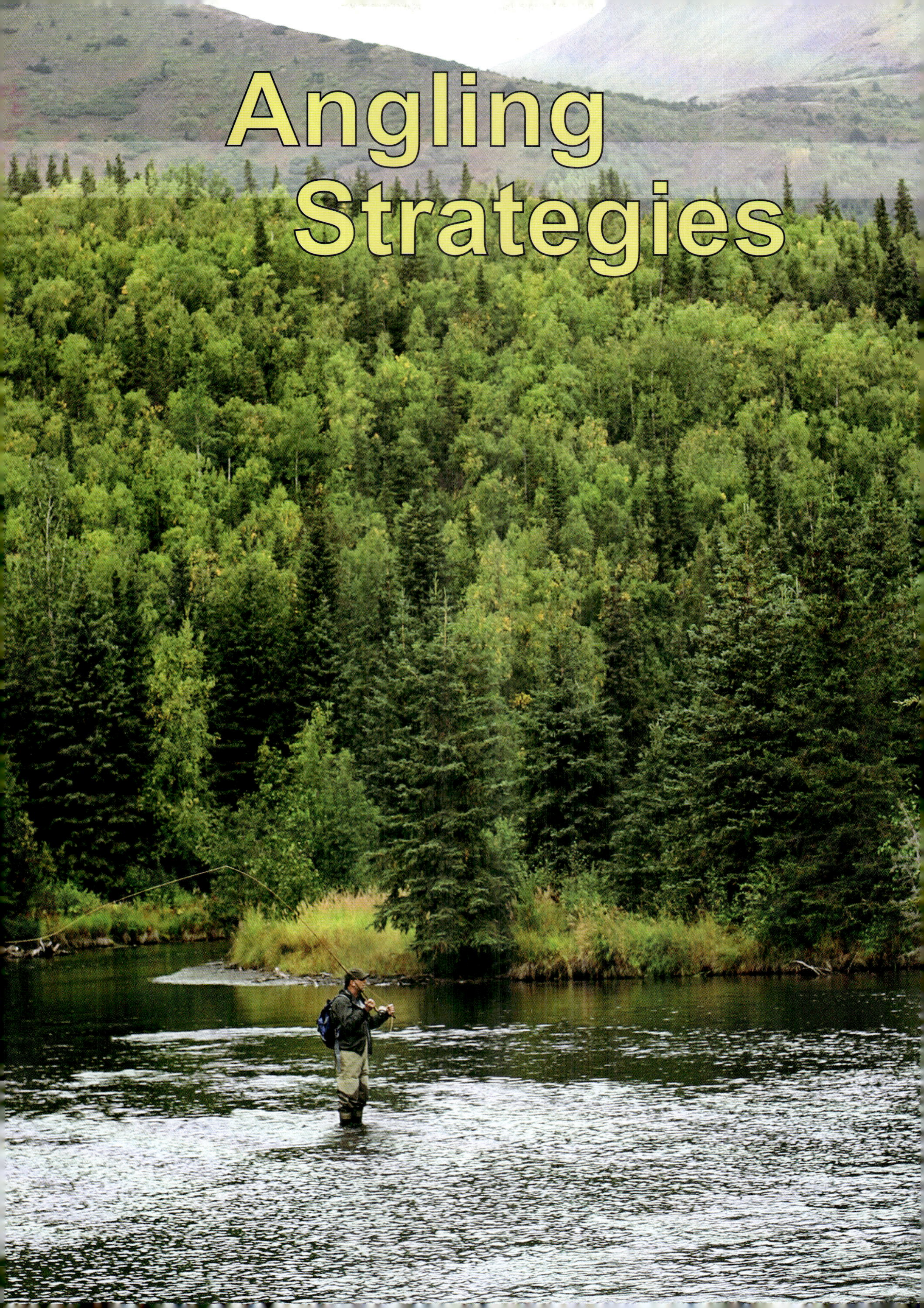
Angling
Strategies

# Introduction

This chapter contains the very basic applications of sport fishing in roadside waters. It is written with the fisher new to Alaska in mind but some aspects within the chapter would probably prove useful for higher skill levels as well. If targeting a specific species of fish in a certain type of water, consult the Roadside Game Fish section (page 22) and the appropriate chapter in this book for details on gear and tackle.

## Terminal Gear

This section will provide anglers with the knowledge how better to select appropriate gear and lists four solid options as a guideline, ranging from medium-length/weight heavy rod and reel setup to light/ultra-light combinations.

It must also be noted that it is very common to use gear, tackle, and techniques interchangeably. For example, anglers sometimes use flies on spinning gear and fly fishers occasionally tie on a lure or piece of bait at the end of the line. The main point of fishing is enjoyment and for many this also means simplicity and functionality.

## Terminal Tackle

Presented here are the three main categories of tackle that are preferred by anglers: Lures, flies, and bait. Although bait is technically not "tackle," it is an important part of most any angler's offering. Each category presents a charts describing various tackle sub-categories and the species that are available. A short list of recommended brand lures and flies are reference as well. Remember that other equally productive lure types or fly patterns that are not listed may certainly be just as effective.

Although bait can easily be used with a variety of lures for extra appeal, bait fished alone on a single hook (avoid trebles) is just as common. Several companies produce hooks with commercially tied bait loops at a very reasonable price and for ease of application.

## Structure & Food Sources

As the correct gear and tackle has been assembled, it is time to look at the various types of structure that fish utilize in their migrations as well as when feeding. This part of the chapter highlights these structures and provides a brief summary why they are important and when and for what species. Analyzed are the environments of rivers and streams, lakes, and saltwater areas.

Finally, there is a brief discussion regarding food sources. This part is especially useful to anglers seeking forage game fish such as trout and char.

The last section of this chapter deals with miscellaneous information that may prove of use and includes tips on tackle, fishing the road system in Alaska, and common catch-and-release techniques.

*Father and son team up to haul a double limit of sockeye to the cleaning table for cleaning and processing.*

## Terminal Gear

To enjoy the whole gamut of opportunities that Alaska has to offer an angler needs to consider four basic fishing rods. Each of the pieces of equipment recommended below shape the essentials of fishing gear in Alaska and one or more may be chosen according to species targeted, water conditions, and angler skill.

If wanting to target only a specific species with optimal equipment, consult the Roadside Species section (page 22)and the appropriate chapter in this book for details.
Anglers wishing to participate in deep-sea fishing for bottomfish, trophy king salmon on the Kenai or Klutina rivers, or any other exclusive trip where specialized gear is often used, should consider hiring a guide. These professionals will have all necessary gear and tackle on hand at no extra charge.

| | *Terminal Gear* | *Line/Tippet* | *Species & Conditions* |
|---|---|---|---|
| **Heavy** | **Rod:** 7 ½–8 ½ ft., medium-fast action, heavy salmon spin-/bait-casting rod; 10–12 wt., 9–10 ft., medium-fast action fly rod with fighting butt section.<br>**Reel:** Heavy freshwater or light saltwater spin-/bait-casting reel; large salmon/tarpon class reel with strong and smooth drag system. | 20 to 25 lb. test or tippet, up to 30 lb. in big waters. | King salmon all waters; other salmon in big rivers with heavy current and/or crowded fishing conditions. This rod should always be on hand if fishing the road system from May through July. Also a good surfcasting option for bottomfish. |
| **Medium** | **Rod:** 7–8 ½ ft., medium weight/action spin-/bait-casting rod; 7-8 wt., 8-10 ft medium/fast-action fly rod.<br>**Reel:** High performance medium action freshwater spin-/bait-casting reel; medium salmon class fly reel with drag system. | 12 to 14 lb. test or tippet, up to 17 lb. in heavy current. | All salmon species (except larger kings), trophy trout, char, and pike. Perfect all-around gear for use on the road system and will work in both fresh and saltwater throughout the fishing season. |
| **Light** | **Rod:** 6 ½–8 ft., medium action salmon spin-/bait-casting rod; 5–6 wt., 8–9 ½ ft., medium-fast action fly rod.<br>**Reel:** High performance freshwater spin-/bait-casting reel; salmon/trout class fly reel. | 6 to 8 lb. test or tippet, up to 10 lb. in heavy current or saltwater. | Small salmon and pike, trout, char, grayling, and other gamefish. This set-up is designed for both lake and stream situations and performs well surfcasting for pink salmon and char in the salt. Good all season. |
| **Ultra Light** | **Rod:** 6-7 ft., medium action spin-/bait casting rod; 2-4 wt., 7-8 ft., medium action fly rod.<br>**Reel:** High performance freshwater spin-/bait casting reel; trout class fly reel. | 2 to 4 lb. test or tippet, all waters. | Perfect gear combination for pink salmon, trout, char, and grayling in smaller rivers, streams, and lakes. Larger game fish may be pursued if angler has matching skill level/experience. |

## Terminal Tackle

(Courtesy Beverley & Roy Bailey)

**Lure Types:** Spoons, Spinners, Plugs, Attractors, Jigs
**Fly Patterns:** Attractor Flies, Wet Flies, Forage Flies, Egg Flies/Beads, Flesh Flies, Dry Flies, Saltwater Flies, Specialty Flies
**Bait Types:** Fish, Fish Eggs, Other Baits

There are three general categories of tackle that are popular in Alaska and in widespread use throughout the roadside fisheries. Lures, flies, and bait all serve the same general purpose although may be preferred or work better in certain areas and conditions. They are great for triggering a range of behavioral reflexes from past and present feeding patterns to generating territorial and/or aggression responses. Understanding the life history or cycle of fish is the key to target the various species successfully.

## Lure Types

| *Spoons* | *Spinners* | *Plugs* | *Attractors* |
|---|---|---|---|
| KS, PS, CS, SS, ST, RT, LT, DV, AC, AG, NP, BB, PH, LC, RF | KS, PS, CS, SS, ST, RT, LT, DV, AC, AG, NP | KS, PS, CS, SS, ST, RT, LT, DV, AC, AG, NP, PH, LC, RF | KS, PS, CS, SS, ST, RT, DV, AG, NP, PH, LC, RF |
| **Pixee**, **Krocodile**, Little Cleo, Syclops, Daredevle, Kastmaster, Super Duper, Coyote, HotRod, Fiord Spoon, NeedleFish, Canadian Wonder, Pot-O-Gold | **Vibrax**, **Aglia**, **G.I. Spinner**, **Kodiak Custom**, Black Fury, Panther Martin, Rooster Tail, Bang Tail, Bolo, **Flash Glo**, Tee Spoon, Blue Streak, Flying C, Trophy | **Kwikfish**, Hot Shot, Tadpolly, Rapala, Magnum FatFish, Zara Spook, Flatfish, J-Plug, **Wiggle Wart**, Crystal Minnow, Foxee Fish, Magnum Wiggler | **Spin-n-Glo**, Aero Drifter, Fenton Fly, Okie Drifter, Lil' Corky, Cheater, Saltwater: Herring, NeedleFish, PowerBait, Squid Bait |

| *Freshwater Jigs* | *Saltwater Jigs* |
|---|---|
| KS, PS, SS, ST, RT, LT, DV, AC, AG, NP, BB | KS, PS, SS, DV, PH, LC, RF |
| **Swedish Pimple**, AeroJig, Rock Dancer, Sy's Jigs, **Krocodile**, Minnow, Dart | **Kodiak Custom**, Super Krocodile, Buzz Bomb, Crippled Herring, Swedish Pimple, Sebastes Jig, **Nordic**, **Dart**, **Minnow**, Stinger, **NeedleFish** |

**Note:** Depending on water conditions, many subsurface patterns tied for salmon are often weighted to aid in getting the fly down in strong or deep currents. Alaska does not allow the use of live bait.
(Species abbreviations are found below)
KS= King Salmon, RS= Red Salmon, PS= Pink Salmon, CS=Chum Salmon, SS= Silver Salmon, ST= Steelhead Trout, RT= Rainbow Trout, LT= Lake Trout, DV= Dolly Varden, AC= Arctic Char, AG= Arctic Grayling, NP= Northern Pike, WF= Whitefish, BB= Burbot, PH= Pacific Halibut, LC= Lingcod, RF= Rockfish, BF= Bottomfish

## Fly Patterns

| Attractor Flies | Wet Flies / Nymphs | Forage Flies | Egg Flies / Beads |
|---|---|---|---|
| KS, RS, PS, CS, SS, ST, RT, LT, DV, AC, AG, NP, LC, RF | RT, LT, DV, AC, AG, WF | KS, RS, PS, SS, RT, LT, DV, AC, AG, NP | KS, RS, PS, CS, SS, ST, RT, DV, AG, WF |
| **Egg Sucking Leech**, Popsicle, **Alaskabou**, Alaska Mary Ann, Polar Shrimp, **Flash Fly**, **Russian River**, **Everglow**, **Sockeye Charlie**, Boss, Woolly Bugger, Bunny Fly, **Comet**, Sparkle Shrimp, Spanker | **Woolly Worm**, **Hare's Ear, Pheasant Tail**, Zug Bug, Lake Leech *(bead headed versions of these flies are also recommended)* | Alaska Smolt, **Black Nose Dace**, Freshwater Clouser Minnow, **Leech**, **Muddler Minnow**, Alevin, Thunder Creek, Woolhead Sculpin | **Fat Freddie**, King Killer, **Glo Bug**, Two Egg Sperm Fly, **Battle Creek**, **Bead Egg**, Iliamna Pinky, Babine Special, Wiggletail |
| **Flesh Flies** | **Dry Flies** | **Saltwater Flies** | **Specialty Flies** |
| SS, RT, LT, DV | RT, DV, AG | KS, PS, CS, SS, DV PH, LC, RF | KS, SS, RT, NP PH, LC, RF |
| Flesh Bunny, **Ginger Bunny**, Battle Bunny, **Carcass Fly**, White Wooly Bugger | **Adams**, Cahill, Gnat, Griffith's Gnat, **Elk Hair Caddis**, **Mosquito**, Humpy, **Wulff** (Royal), | Candlefish, **Deceiver**, Sandlance, Shrimp, Herring, **Clouser Minnow**, Seaducer, Needlefish, Whistler | **Mouse**, Pink Pollywog, Popper, Snake, Dahlberg Diver, Outrageous |

## Bait Types

| Fish | Fish Eggs | Other Baits | Bottomfish Baits |
|---|---|---|---|
| KS, PS, CS, SS, ST, RT, LT, DV, AC, AG, NP, BB | KS, PS, CS, SS, ST, RT, LT, DV, AC, AG, NP | RT, LT, DV, AC, AG, NP | PH, LC, RF, BF |
| **Herring,** Smelt (hooligan), Whitefish, Salmon Parts. | **Salmon Roe,** Single Salmon Eggs | **Shrimp,** Maggots, Worms | **Herring,** Squid, Octopus, Smelt, Cod, Salmon Heads |

## Common Setups Illustrated

**Drift Rigs:** The ideal and most widely used setup for salmon, trout, and char, perfect for rivers and streams with moderate to fast current.

**Indicator Rig:** The setup to use in waters with moderate, slow, or no current. Very productive on practically all game species in both fresh- and saltwater.

**Stationary Rigs:** Setups designed for presenting bait effectively to game fish in both salt- and freshwater.

Shown here are the various types of setups – or rigs – that are in common use. Illustrated for easy duplication, there are four main setups described in detail, several of which also show multiple variations.

Specialized setups as those required for shark hunting, trophy halibut, or other large saltwater fish are not presented as these species do not inhabit roadside waters to any significant degree.

## Drift Rigs

**Example 1:** Standard light to medium-light tackle/sinker rig as used in many roadside streams for salmon, trout, and char. Tackle may consist of a fly, small attractor, or bait.

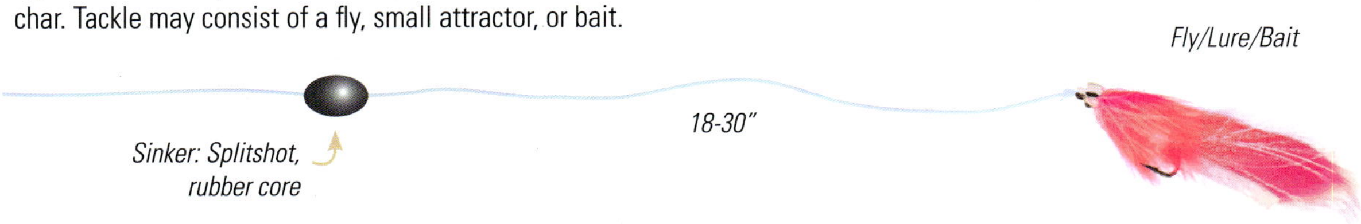

*Fly/Lure/Bait*

*18-30"*

*Sinker: Splitshot, rubber core*

**Example 2:** Medium to heavy tackle/sinker rig, a common setup in larger, swifter waters for king salmon. Tackle is attractor or bait or combination of the two.

*Bait*

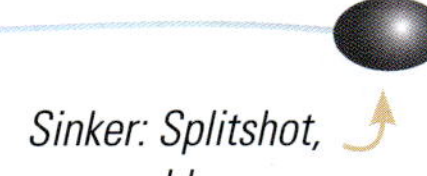

*18-24" leader*

*Sinker: Splitshot, rubber core*

*These two setups are the most common used for stream fishing for salmon, trout, and char. The weight should be just heavy enough to get the lure to the bottom and "tick" along with the current into holding fish or the path of migrating fish.*

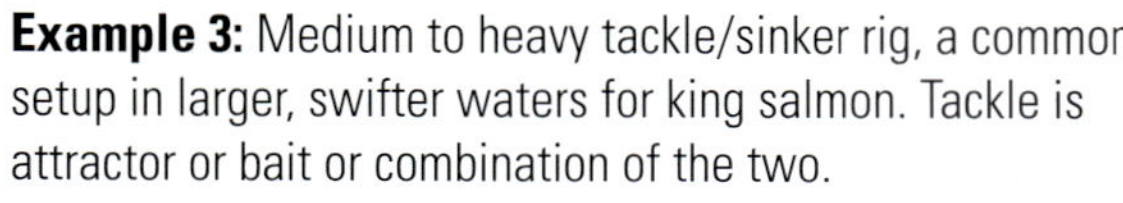

**Example 3:** Medium to heavy tackle/sinker rig, a common setup in larger, swifter waters for king salmon. Tackle is attractor or bait or combination of the two.

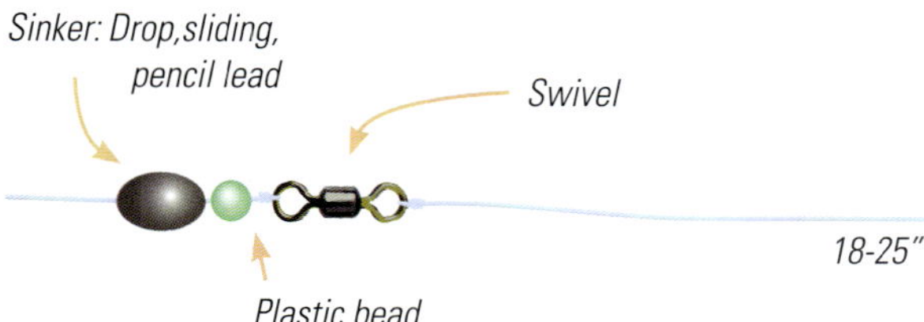


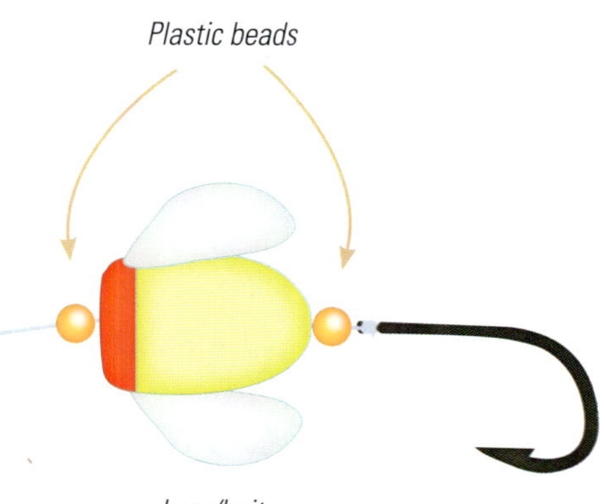


*These three setups are the most common used for stream fishing for salmon, trout, and char. The weight should be just heavy enough to get the lure to the bottom and "tick" along with the current into holding fish or the path of migrating fish.*

## Indicator Rigs

**Example 1:** Light to medium fresh- and saltwater rig, a setup that will work under most conditions. Flies and bait are used for salmon in the salt and in lower reaches of streams, salmon roe in estuaries, flowing waters, and lakes for almost every game fish present.

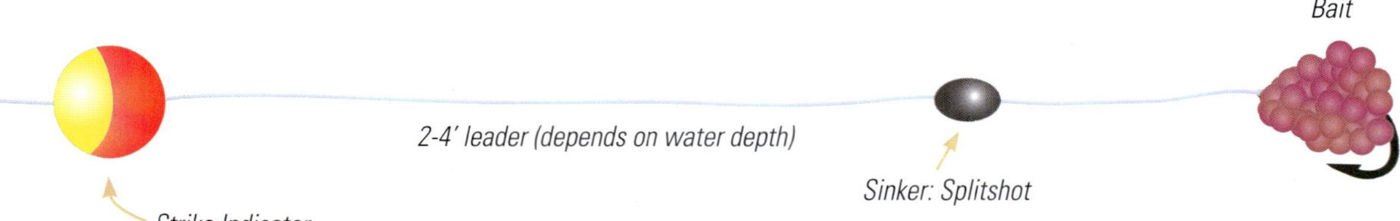


**Example 2:** Light to medium freshwater rig, a setup designed for mainly trout and char in flowing waters but works great for salmon as well. Use for freshwater jigs (no sinker), beads or corkies with single hook, and wet/attractor flies.

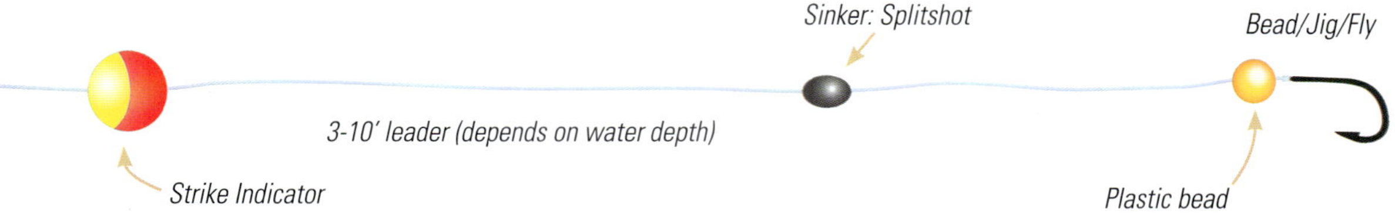


*Bead fishing is a widely used technique by guides. It is a very effective setup when targeting mid-summer and fall trout, char, and grayling. Bead size and color can often be very important; check with a local tackle supplier for what is currently "hot."*

*Note: Make sure to check current regulations for restrictions pertaining to bead use and placement.*

## Stationary Rigs

**Example 1:** Used in both salt- and freshwater; works on salmon, trout, char, and bottomfish. Single hook is baited with salmon roe, whole or pieces of herring or smelt, salmon roe, and shrimp.

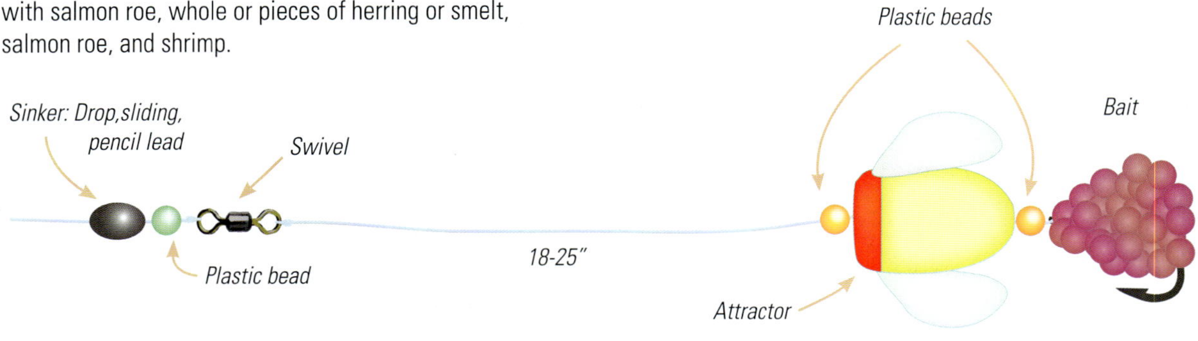


**Example 2:** A hinged light to medium saltwater rig, most effective on various species of bottomfish but shown to do well on trout and char in lakes. Hook is baited with salmon roe and shrimp or pieces of herring and squid.

*Under some circumstances, such as discolored or glaciated water, bait can be about the only way to consistently attract fish. The legal use of bait in freshwater is often seasonal or sometimes suspended depending upon salmon returns and spawning fish in a given area.*

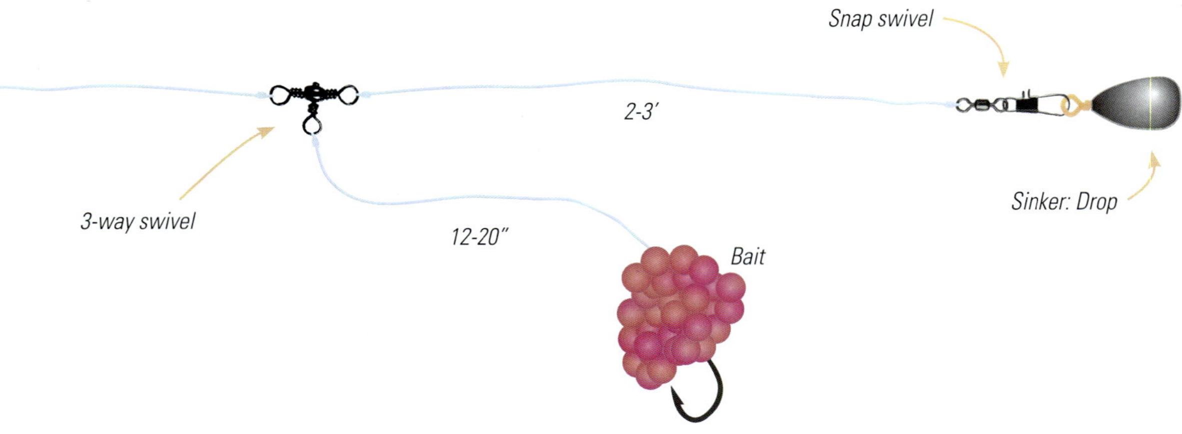


**Example 3:** This particular rig is used primarily for saltwater game fish targeting larger species such as halibut and skate. Hook is baited with pieces of salmon scraps, small salmon heads, or chunks of herring or cod.

*Anglers may consider using several feet of high-impact or shock-absorbent braided line tied between the upper (first) swivel and main line to avoid line breakage that may be experienced with powerful casts using surf-casting gear.*

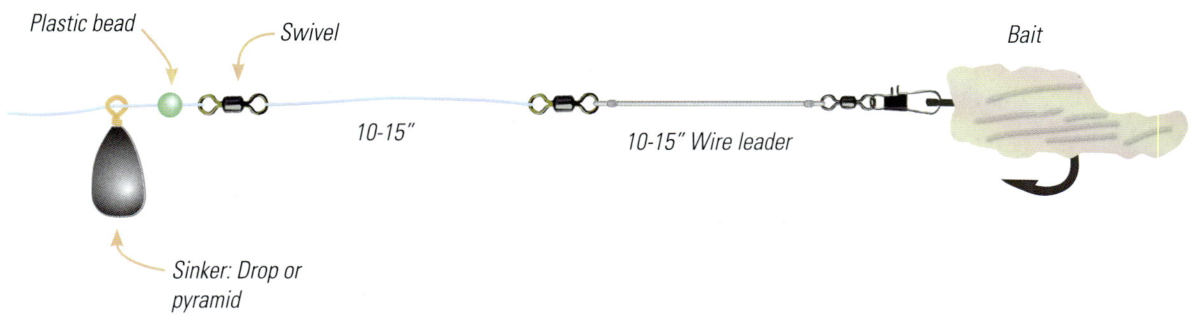

## Structure and Food Sources

**Rivers & Streams:** Emphasis on habits of migrating salmon and feeding resident species in flowing waters.

**Lakes & Ponds:** The habits of fish in still waters are slightly different than elsewhere and a different approach is needed.

**Saltwater:** Ocean fishing presents another perspective for anglers, complete with challenges that are unique.

**Food Sources:** When having recognized the staple diet of resident species, hookup rates improve drastically.

It is well known that fish do have special preferences for the environment they choose to rest, migrate, and feed. Knowing where and at what time in a river, stream, or lake to look for fish is at least as important – if not more so – as having the right gear and skill. Although angling for any species of fish can be productive at any time of the day or year, there are definitely times when the action is better and more predictable. The most common factors to consider are available structure, lighting conditions, current flow, depth, seasonal behavior, and water temperature. Being able to "read" the water is the key to success.

### Rivers & Streams

• **Locate deep holes, pools, and eddies.** Many species have a tendency to congregate in such areas as they find security there while either feeding or migrating to or from spawning grounds. In very long or deep sections, look for fish at the head or tail of pool and around edges.

*(Courtesy Beverley & Roy Bailey)*

• **Fish the tides.** In many coastal waters, fishing can vary greatly according to tidal movements. Work the area starting upstream of stream mouth on an incoming tide as salmon and other sea-run species migrate into fresh water. Also, try deep holes and runs as the tide recedes or upstream areas during or after high tide.

• **Try moderate- to slow-flowing water.** A more passive flow attracts fish since they do not have to fight strong current and unnecessarily burn energy. Avoid very fast flowing, white-water stretches of rivers and streams as fish only pass rapidly through these areas on the way to calmer sections.

• **Concentrate on river and stream confluences.** The mixing zone of larger rivers and smaller streams is a superb location to find all species of fish as it serves as a resting and feeding area. Fish stack up prior to moving up the tributary to spawn or simply use the area to locate food sources.

• **Fish the low light hours.** The best action is generally experienced in early morning and evening and on cloudy/rainy days. Trout, char, grayling, and other species feed most heavily then and salmon are less spooked and respond with more enthusiasm to anglers' offerings.

### Lakes & Ponds

• **Fish according to the seasons.** Late spring, fall, and early winter are probably the best times to fish lakes and ponds because of ideal water temperatures and high oxygen levels. Fish are often lethargic in mid-summer and late winter due to low oxygen levels and too warm or cold water temperatures.

*A father and daughter team try their luck for pinks on an incoming tide in a coastal salmon spawning stream near the town of Whittier.*

• **Fish after break-up.** Trout, char, grayling, and pike are often concentrated fairly close to shore in shallow water as they prepare to spawn, engage in a feeding frenzy, or migrate to summer feeding areas.

• **Try before and after freeze-up.** All resident species are very active at this time, feeding heavily near shore in shallow water. The cool and oxygen-rich water in late fall and early winter sparks the fish to go on the bite.

• **Concentrate on feeding areas.** Fish thrive best in areas of the lake where there is an abundance of feed. Inlets and outlets, vegetated shorelines, and submerged structures such as shoals, pinnacles, and tree trunks are very productive places.

*A pair of coho readies a "nest" to complete their life cycle.*

• **Fish the low light hours.** All species are most active during early morning and evening or on cloudy days, especially in summer. Avoid bright, mid-day sunshine as fish become shy and move into deep water.

• **Focus on water layers.** The upper layer of water is often too warm for fish in summer and they will thus seek out the cooler water at mid-depth or near bottom. In spring and fall, fish are typically quite shallow.

## Saltwater

• **Concentrate on feeding areas.** Salmon, char, and bottomfish all seek out locations that attract baitfish, such as reefs, points, shoals, docks, and similar structures, including the mouths of rivers and streams. Wave activity along the shoreline can have a positive influence on feeding behavior.

• **Fish the tides.** Salmon and bottomfish tend to move close to shore or into shallow water on incoming and high tides. As the tide recedes, the fish move offshore into deeper or more open water.

(Courtesy Jeff Varvil)

*This coho salmon struck a Clouser Minnow, an excellent fly pattern for saltwater or estuary salmon fishing.*

• **Try stream mouths.** The mix of salt and fresh water attracts a number of species, most notably salmon and char. Salmon often congregate here prior to moving upstream and char use the area as a feeding ground. Incoming and high tides are generally the best times to fish these locations.

• **Fish the low light hours.** Salmon and char are most active in the early morning and evening, but all fish respond better to anglers' lures during cloudy or rainy weather. Bright sunshine tends to drive salmon deep and slows the bite.

## Food Sources

• **Spawning salmon.** Resident species largely depend on salmon eggs and flesh to supplement their diet and are often found within a few feet of spawning fish. When the salmon are in the midst of spawning use egg imitations, and when the fish are dying off flesh imitations are better suited.

• **Fish cleaning stations.** These stations are located on many of the more popular fishing spots and action can be hot near or just downstream of them using egg imitation and flesh flies for trout and char seeking a protein-rich meal.

• **Juvenile salmon.** All predatory species in Alaska feed heavily on salmon fry and smolt. In late spring and summer, the smolt migration headed for the ocean peak and anglers should use smolt or forage imitations.

• **Insect hatches.** Clearwater streams and lakes are probably the better option in locating hatches, as non-glaciated habitat is more suitable for insect activity. Hatches occur from April through July with mature insects present through September.

## Miscellaneous Advice

**Fishing Tackle:** Tips on how best to present lures, flies, and bait to maximize hook-ups in a variety of conditions.

**Roadside Fishing:** Learn a few simple rules on how to fish the road system in Alaska in order to find fish and stay safe.

Aside from the usual angler know-how, this section stresses some final points that may be of assistance, including tips regarding tackle and fishing along the road system.

(Courtesy Eagle Eye Images)

### Fishing Tackle

• **Keep offering close to or near the bottom.** Species such as salmon, large trout and char, and whitefish commonly "hug" the bottom and will seldom move much of a distance to intercept a lure or fly floating above their head.

• **Try high-visibility offerings in glacially fed waters.** Lures and flies in fluorescent pink, orange, and chartreuse are best. Sometimes a touch of chrome combination works well. Use bait or bait-scented lures if legal and fish lure slowly or stationary.

• **Use flashy or colorful offerings in murky conditions.** Visibility is important and even more so in glacial waters or during low-light conditions such as rain, heavy clouds, and from dusk to dawn. Main colors are red, orange, chartreuse, pink, yellow, and silver.

• **Use dark or neutral colored offerings in bright conditions.** Too much flash can spook fish, especially in bright sunshine and in clear water or in shallow drainages and when angler pressure is high. Main colors include green, brown, black, copper, purple, blue, and bronze.

• **Match offering size and color with mood of fish.** If fish appear spooked or skittish, try small and/or neutral-colored lures and flies; if aggressive, something larger and more colorful can be used.

• **Presentation of offering must match mood of fish.** When fish are lethargic due to very cold or warm water, use lures and flies with minimal action as well as bait. Present them using slow or stationary methods and techniques. Tackle that display fast action are best when fish are very active.

### Roadside Fishing

• Prior to pursuing a particular type of fish, always take some time to learn the life cycle and other pertinent information concerning the species. Having at least some degree of knowledge of the habits and nuances of the fish can be applied to an advantage using a rod and reel and proper methods and techniques.

• If serious about catching fish, it is a good idea to invest in some hip boots or chest waders. The boots or waders will allow one to move freely around the fishing area, through shallow channels or into deeper waters of a lake or river.

• **Polarized glasses** are ideal when sight fishing for individual fish or schools of fish in clearwater rivers and streams, as well as for salmon migrating close to shore in mainstem Kenai. They also protect eyes from the intense glare off the surface of the water and serve as effective shields from flying lures with sharp hooks.

• Some roadside waters attract considerable crowds, especially during the peak of salmon runs. One way to counter the presence of other anglers is to hike up- or downstream a few hundred yards.

• Many of the lakes along the road system in Alaska offer good fishing but may be somewhat tricky to fish from shore due to very shallow, weedy shorelines. Such areas are best tackled by boat, canoe, inflatable raft, or a float tube.

• **Catch-and-release** is not only a management tool in some waters for certain species; it is also a matter of proper etiquette seeing that a fish not wanted swims away relatively unharmed after having been handled. Always bring a needle-nose plier to safely remove the hook(s), do not play the fish to complete exhaustion, keep it in the water if possible, keep hands and fingers away from gills, and cut the line if hook is embedded too deeply for quick removal. Also, use single hooks, avoid bait, and crimp down barb on hook or use barbless hooks.

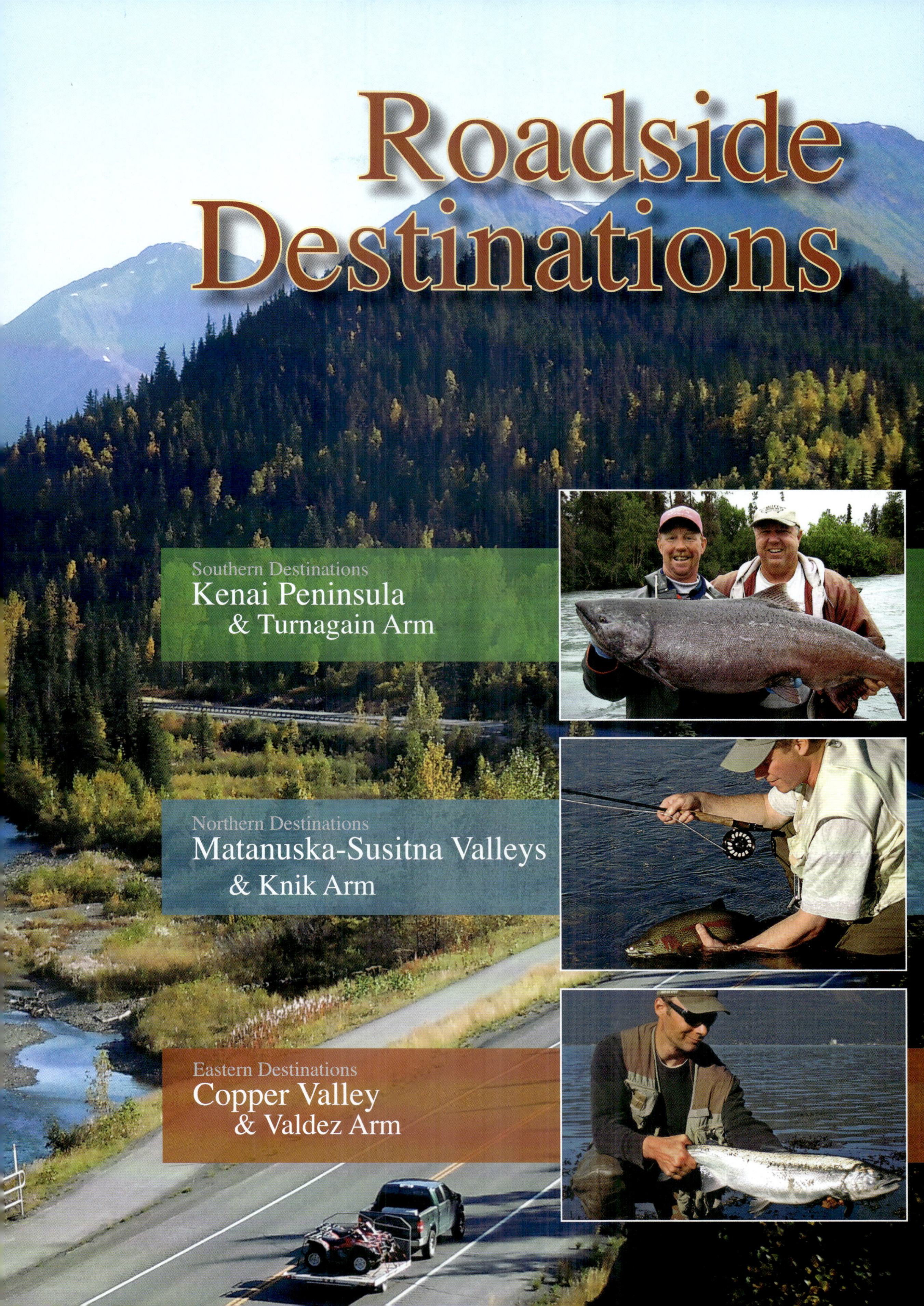
Roadside Destinations
Southern Destinations
Kenai Peninsula
& Turnagain Arm
Northern Destinations
Matanuska-Susitna Valleys
& Knik Arm
Eastern Destinations
Copper Valley
& Valdez Arm

# Introduction

**Alaska is a huge state, bigger than many countries, and the roads and highways here often span hundreds of miles in a specific direction, connecting larger cities with outlying towns and communities. It is along these byways where they cross or parallel lakes, streams, rivers, and saltwater bays that exploring anglers may find a vast richness of fishing opportunities.**

The largest city in Alaska is Anchorage, a hectic commercial center of over 300,000 inhabitants located in what is commonly referred to as the Southcentral region. The vast majority of flights connecting the Lower 48 and other parts of the world to Alaska pass through Anchorage and the major roads of the state originate here as well, making the city a natural hub and spoke for anglers to engage in their pursuit of the regions many fisheries.

Significantly different from most anywhere else in the country, Anchorage has only two major highway arteries heading out of town – one going north, the other south. This is mainly because the city is situated on a small protruding landmass of sorts with water barriers to the north, west, and south, and an impenetrable mountain range to the east. Thus, roads fit where they may. However, these two highways – Glenn and Seward – both directly connect to several more important thoroughfares (Richardson, Parks, Sterling, etc.), and as such open up a virtually limitless panorama of places to fish.

While the fairly busy road system and its population centers may instill a sense of security and peace of mind through the availability or presence of common facilities and amenities, such as large retail stores, chain restaurants, full-service hotels, and RV campgrounds, it is important to remember that this is after all Alaska and true wilderness in the form of bears and moose, ice-cold glacial rivers, and nearly impenetrable boreal rainforests are never too far away. In fact, at some points on the road system, heading out in any direction away from the pavement may mean hundreds of miles of pure undisturbed solitude before any sign of human activity surfaces again, if at all. In this perspective, a great deal of respect need be applied as nature and its elements can be very unforgiving to those who find themselves unprepared.

But for anglers wanting to fish the road system instead of flying out to some extreme remote location, Alaska's highways are just the perfect fit in accessing a very large collection of waters teeming with fish and wildlife. On top of that, rustic campgrounds and cabins, small tackle and fish processing shops, and family-owned guide services are but a slice of what lies await and contributes to why many anglers prefer to fish along the road system. In all, it highlights the human angle, bringing the element of interaction with other people from all over the world, and their common interest in fishing.

As many anglers traveling the road system soon discover, there is a very prominent natural beauty to the Southcentral region that matches perfectly with the awesome fishing opportunities. The landscape can and does vary tremendously, from lowland marshes and dense spruce and birch forests to alpine meadows and tundra, all the while surrounded by jagged mountain ranges, hanging glaciers, and even semi-active volcanoes. Combine all this with abundant wildlife and it is a trip to remember.

For ease of navigation in deciding where to go in search of one or more of Alaska's popular game fish, this book divides the roadside territory into three main geographical sections. These are the "Northern," "Southern," and "Eastern" areas (described in more detail on the next page) that in turn host smaller sub-areas, each with its own unique characteristics in terms of species available, peak timing, geological features of the surrounding landscape, and other distinctions that may appeal to visiting anglers based on various levels of personal interest.

## Southern Destinations: Kenai Peninsula & Turnagain Arm ....................... 109

Features the rich waters of the legendary Kenai Peninsula, including Turnagain Arm, western Prince William Sound, the North Gulf Coast, and lower Cook Inlet.

**Regional Hubs:** Girdwood, Whittier, Hope, Moose Pass, Seward, Cooper Landing, Sterling, Soldotna, Kenai, Nikiski, Kasilof, Ninilchik, Anchor Point, and Homer.

**Main Attractions:** Without a doubt the most visited region and for good reason. A multitude of both freshwater and saltwater species and locations to choose from within close proximity, several of which present great opportunity for trophy catches in magnificent scenic settings. World record-size king salmon and halibut, million-strong runs of red salmon, and fly-fishing for huge rainbow trout are synonymous with the peninsula. Very prolific wildlife in the dense forests and marine waters. Great views of semi-active volcanoes across the inlet.

## Northern Destinations: Matanuska-Susitna Valleys & Knik Arm............. 285

Represented by the vast Matanuska and Susitna valleys, which include drainages of Knik Arm and the mighty Susitna River basin with its near countless tributaries.

**Regional Hubs:** Palmer, Wasilla, Houston, Willow, Talkeetna, and Trapper Creek.

**Main Attractions:** Numerous small clearwater lakes and streams, easy for wading and scouting with excellent float tubing and sight fishing opportunities. King, pink, chum, and silver salmon, rainbow trout, and arctic grayling are the targeted game fish in this region with definite trophy potentials. Do-it-yourself float fishing excursions are popular. Stunning views of the Alaska Range, including Mount Denali (McKinley) at well over 20,000 feet. The large glacial rivers and their tributaries support abundant wildlife to match the semi-wilderness.

## Eastern Destinations: Copper Valley & Valdez Arm.................................. 375

An immense area that encompasses the relatively little-fished Copper Valley and adjoining waterways, such as northern Prince William Sound and the Upper Copper/Upper Susitna River basins.

**Regional Hubs:** Glennallen, Gakona, and Valdez.

**Main Attractions:** This region features a wide range of angling opportunities in terms of both available species as well as scenic surroundings. Whether canoeing the deep lakes for trophy lake trout, hiking in to distant tundra streams jammed with grayling and fish-on-every-cast action, wading or floating expansive forested rivers for king and red salmon and rainbow trout, or surfcasting or boating the briny for pink and silver salmon and halibut, anglers will find plenty to explore. Incredible mountain ranges, including a few of the world's largest volcanoes.

# Kenai Peninsula
## & Turnagain Arm

## Western Kenai....... 193

**Hot Spots:** Middle Kenai River, Lower Kenai River, Kasilof River

**Other Productive Fisheries:** Moose River & Lakes, Swanson River, Swanson Area Lakes

**Additional Opportunities:** Trophy Salmon & Trout Fishing, Remote Fly-In Waters

## Northeastern Kenai & Turnagain Arm.....115

**Hot Spots:** Bird Creek, Passage Canal, Resurrection Creek

**Other Productive Fisheries:** Campbell Creek, Indian Cr., Glacier Cr., Portage Creek, Ingram Creek, Sixmile Creek, Summit Lakes

**Additional Opportunities:** 20-Mile River, Placer River, Turnagain Arm Hooligan

## Central Kenai ........ 145

**Hot Spots:** Upper Kenai River, Russian River

**Other Productive Fisheries:** Quartz Creek, Kenai Lake, Crescent Lake, Trail Lakes & River, Ptarmigan Creek

**Additional Opportunities:** Trophy Trout & Char Fishing, Peninsula Trail System Lakes

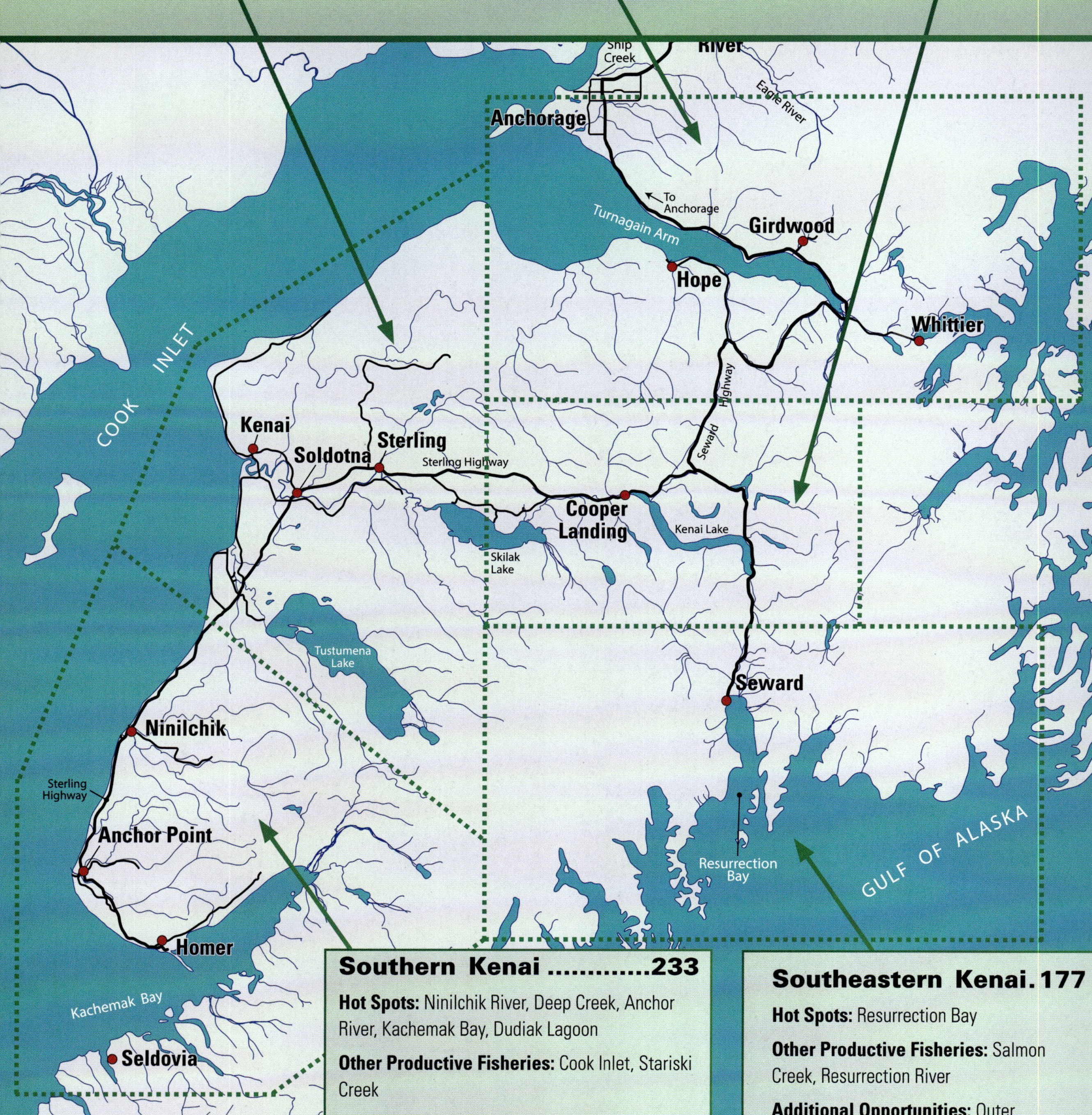


## Southern Kenai .............233

**Hot Spots:** Ninilchik River, Deep Creek, Anchor River, Kachemak Bay, Dudiak Lagoon

**Other Productive Fisheries:** Cook Inlet, Stariski Creek

**Additional Opportunities:** Remote Fly-In Waters, Peninsula Wildlife Viewing, Clam Digging, Lower Cook Inlet Salmon & Halibut

## Southeastern Kenai. 177

**Hot Spots:** Resurrection Bay

**Other Productive Fisheries:** Salmon Creek, Resurrection River

**Additional Opportunities:** Outer Resurrection Bay & North Gulf Coast, Fishing Derbies. Wildlife & Fish Viewing

# Introduction

The Kenai Peninsula is known to possess some of the best roadside fishing in the entire state, coupled with beautiful vistas of snow-covered mountains, ancient glaciers, active volcanoes towering to over 10,000 feet, lowland lakes too numerous to count, and abundant wildlife, including possible close encounters with bear, moose, caribou, beaver, and eagles, among many other kinds of animals, including sea lions, seals, sea otters, and whales. Anglers have liberal access to both salt- and freshwater fisheries that support an impressive variety of game fish, including all five species of salmon, trout and char, grayling, halibut, lingcod, and rockfishes, as well as a multitude of other species such as salmon shark, skate, codfishes, and flounders. The peninsula, along with Turnagain Arm and western Prince William Sound, is indeed a dream recreation area for anglers.

## Area Roads & Highways

The Seward Highway is the main gateway from Anchorage to the interior Kenai Peninsula and the coastal town of Seward. There are a multitude of smaller lakes and streams along this route and the highway also serves the communities of Whittier, by the way of Portage Glacier Road/Whittier Access Road (Milepost 79), and Hope, via Hope Highway (Milepost 56).

It is important to note that the Seward Highway log reflects the distance originating in Seward (Milepost 0) and not Anchorage, unlike most roadways that begin in Alaska's largest city. The total distance is 127 miles.

The majority of productive fisheries, however, can be found along the Sterling Highway that connects to the Seward Highway at Tern Lake Junction. From this junction (Milepost 37), Sterling heads southwest through the communities of Cooper Landing and Sterling to Soldotna, the sport fishing capitol of the peninsula, and continues on to Ninilchik, Anchor Point, and finally Homer (Milepost 173). It is along this highway that one may find the most productive roadside fisheries on the Kenai, if not the entire Southcentral region.

Soldotna is also the junction for Kenai Spur Highway (Milepost 94), leading to the town of Kenai northward 40 miles to the Captain Cook Recreation Area. Decent fishing can be found on this route as well.

## Major Fisheries / Hot Spots

There are over a dozen very popular and productive fishing locales in the greater Kenai Peninsula area, with several more that are not directly road-accessible yet easily within reach by the use of boats or other watercrafts. These peninsula hot spots are among the top fish producers in

*Trophy kings draw many anglers to the Kenai River – the home of the world record and many other very large fish.*

*(Courtesy EZ Limit Guide Service)*

*The rivers and streams of the Kenai Peninsula are a great place of beauty, with an abundance of varied angling opportunities.*

Alaska and receive a good amount of angling pressure, at least part of the year.

The clearwater streams of Turnagain Arm provide great fishing for pink and silver salmon along with good opportunities for chum salmon and Dolly Varden. Bird Creek and Resurrection Creek are among the most popular.

The famed Kenai River is by far the most popular water in Alaska with more than 275,000 angler days spent on this river per season, making it the top drainage in the state based on effort as well as catch statistics. Four species of salmon – king, red, silver, and pink – plus rainbow trout and Dolly Varden are all present in substantial numbers (red salmon can top one million fish and pinks multiple millions), several of which support trophy fisheries (wild rainbows to 30 pounds have been taken here). In fact, the Kenai drainage holds the world record sport-caught king salmon (97 lbs) and the state records for both red salmon (16 lbs) and pink salmon (12 lbs). It also holds the unique distinction of hosting anadromous salmon every day of the year. The river can be waded along the banks in many places and anglers interested in boating the river can do so without any problems, with or without a guide. Floating is a particularly attractive and productive option.

The Russian River (a Kenai River tributary) is the second most popular sport fishery on the peninsula, its gin clear waters boasting two phenomenal runs of red salmon totaling, on average, about 90,000 fish. There is also a smaller but highly productive run of silver salmon and superb fly fishing for rainbow trout and Dolly Varden. Due to its clarity, anglers can easily spot schools of salmon moving upstream and even cast to individual fish if so desired. Russian is exclusively a wade fishery. Bears – both brown and black – are a common sight on the Russian and support great viewing opportunities.

*Angler provides an up-close view of a 13-pound, trophy male sockeye in full spawning regalia. This is a shot from the confluence of the Russian River and Upper Kenai River. The peninsula is known for its trophy potentials.*

Neighboring Kasilof River has long been heralded as a top-notch king and red salmon spot with productive silver salmon, steelhead trout, and Dolly Varden fishing as added bonuses. Wading and floating the river are both possible, lending anglers to experience this river on two levels; the roadside stretches and the more semi-remote section. Additionally, this river harbors some large late-run kings in mid-summer, some of which may top 60 pounds.

The smaller clearwater drainages to the south – Ninilchik, Deep, and Anchor – are known for excellent king and silver salmon, steelhead trout, and Dolly Varden. If there is such as a thing as perfect waters for wading, these are it and anglers are able to move around freely and the streams can generally be crossed with ease. They also hold outstanding opportunities for classic fly-fishing techniques.

The peninsula even offers outstanding saltwater opportunities for sport fishers out of several deep-water ports, including Whitter, Seward, and Homer. These locations offer productive surf-casting for several species, including a mix of wild and hatchery runs of king, red, and silver salmon, and decent action for pink and chum salmon as well. Bottomfish can be abundant. Passage Canal in Whittier, Kachemak Bay and Dudiak Lagoon in Homer, and Resurrection Bay out of Seward are great locations for hatchery runs of king and silver salmon with additional catches of red, pink, and chum salmon and native sea-run char.

## Other Popular Fisheries

There are several other smaller fisheries that do not attract the angling pressure of the hot spots listed above but nonetheless has some good to excellent fishing for one or more species. Indian, Glacier, Portage, Ingram, and Sixmile creeks of Turnagain Arm have some decent pink, chum, and silver salmon and Dolly Varden opportunities.

The Swanson River and Moose River drainages in the western part of Kenai Peninsula near Soldotna and Kenai support substantial populations of silver salmon and rainbow trout, while the Kenai-drainage waters of the central Chugach Mountains – Quartz and Ptarmigan creeks, Trail River, and Crescent Lake – yield a combination of trout, char, and grayling. Around Seward, Resurrection River and Salmon Creek are good spots for sea-run char. South of Soldotna, Crooked Creek is a small stream with quite decent catches of silver salmon and Dolly Varden.

Cook Inlet, located near Homer and along communities to the north, has beach casting for king, silver, and pink salmon as well as sea-run Dolly Varden and halibut. This is also home to the largest charter boat fishery in the state with exemplary salmon and bottomfish action. Nearby Stariski Creek offers a decent chance at pink and silver salmon, steelhead trout, and char.

*The peninsula is synanomous with salt water fishing, with three major ports offering tremendous action for salmon as well as several kinds of marine species. This is a view from Homer.*

## Additional Opportunities

There are tremendous opportunities to find some great fishing other than the more frequented spots mentioned above, especially on the northern half or central portion of the Kenai Peninsula. Some of these waters are quite remote, requiring hours of hiking, yet a few places are next to the road. Additionally, anglers can find excellent action in secluded lakes and streams that are only accessible by plane or boat.

The marine fisheries of western Prince William Sound, Cook Inlet, outer Kachemak Bay, and Resurrection Bay – including the North Gulf Coast – are legendary for a variety of bottomfish, such as halibut, lingcod, and rockfish, as well as all five kinds of salmon. In the coastal ports of Whittier, Seward, Ninilchik, Anchor Point, and Homer, anglers may find a number of charters to hire for a day or overnight trip targeting the above-mentioned species. These type of excursions add significantly to any peninsula fishing trip by providing variety to the overall experience.

Anglers wishing to attempt something a little different may want to do a remote fly-out trip for salmon and trout.

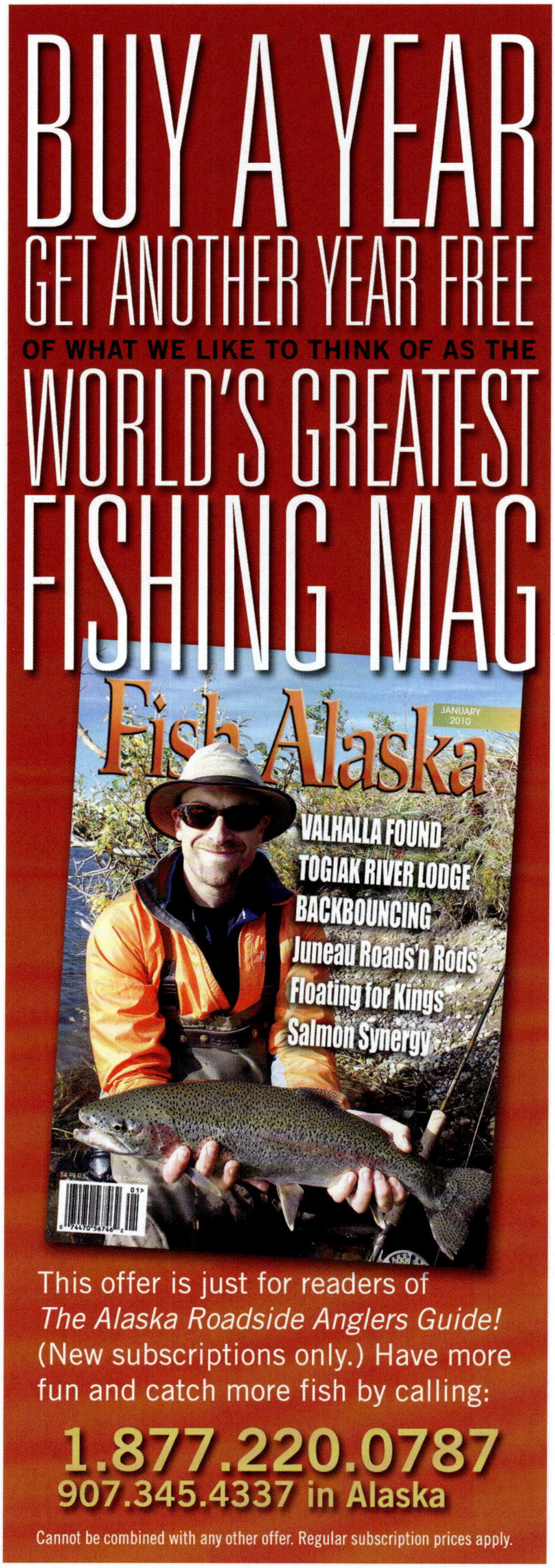

As with the ocean charters, these type of excursions leave from main regional towns and communities. Some operators target waters around the peninsula's gulf coast, including parts of Prince William Sound, while others provide excursions to lesser-fished streams on the west side of Cook Inlet.

## Sport Fishing Regulations

The Kenai Peninsula is part of the Southcentral Alaska management area with restrictions listed under "Anchorage Bowl," "Prince William Sound," and "Kenai Peninsula" sections in the booklet as provided by the Alaska Department of Fish & Game (ADF&G). Open and closed seasons and areas, legal tackle and gear, bag and possession limits, and fish size restrictions may vary from drainage to drainage and between species. Consult a copy of the regulations before fishing or call the ADF&G regional/field offices directly for information.

**Soldotna:** (907) 262-9368
**Homer:** (907) 235-8191
**Anchorage:** (907) 267-2218

**Anchorage • Girdwood • Whittier • Hope**

# Northeastern Kenai & Turnagain Arm

**King Salmon • Pink Salmon • Chum Salmon • Silver Salmon**
**Rainbow Trout • Dolly Varden • Pacific Halibut • Lingcod**
**Rockfish • Shark • Bottomfish**

*Scenic Streams*

*Tidewater Salmon*

*Surf Casting*

*Sight Fishing*

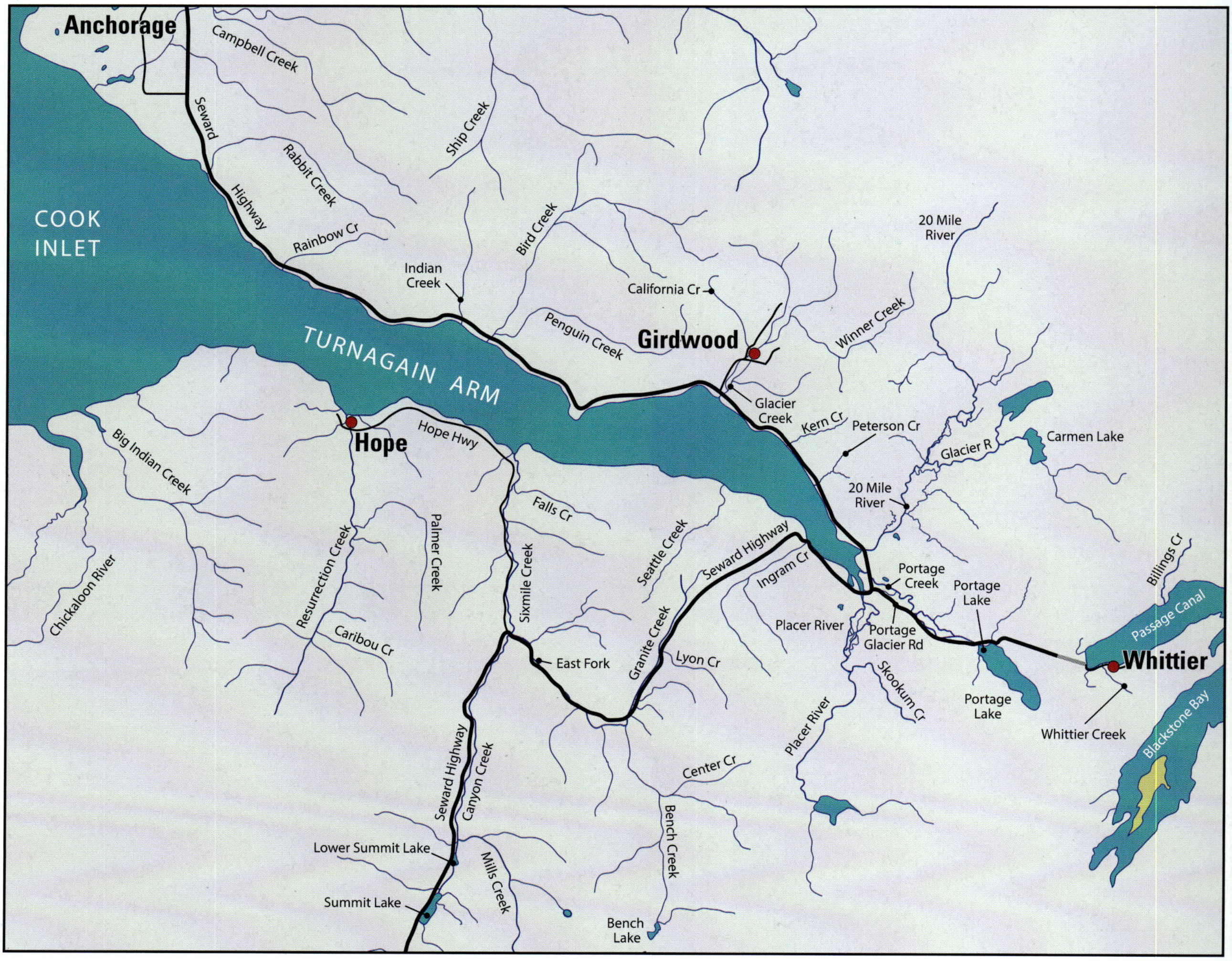

**Area Population Centers:** Anchorage, Indian, Bird, Girdwood, Whittier, and Hope
**Key Species:** King, Red, Pink, Chum, and Silver Salmon, Rainbow Trout, Dolly Varden, and Bottomfish
**Other Species:** Pacific Halibut, Lingcod, Rockfish, and Salmon Shark
**Hot Spots:** Bird Creek, Passage Canal, and Resurrection Creek
**Other Productive Fisheries:** Campbell Creek, Indian Creek, Glacier Creek, Portage Creek, Ingram Creek, Sixmile Creek, and Summit Lakes
**Additional Opportunities:** 20-Mile & Placer Rivers, and Turnagain Arm Hooligan

**Summary of Area Fishing:** Perhaps more known for its extreme tidal fluctuations and awesome scenery, this northernmost part of the boreal Alaska rainforest does offer some great fishing. There are several clearwater streams in the area that support salmon runs along with resident species, albeit few are of any size but most are perfect for wading. In very close proximity to the densest population in the entire state, Turnagain Arm along with Whittier are popular playgrounds for many anglers and a convenient area to spend a few hours to a day for those transitioning between Anchorage and the main sport fisheries of the Kenai Peninsula. However, an increasing number of visitors are discovering the angling charm of this place and dedicate a good portion of their vacation time here.

King and silver salmon and rainbow trout are stocked in area waters, adding to the appeal of anglers seeking fast action and perhaps a way to fill their coolers. Wild fish populations are the norm, however, particularly in streams along Turnagain Arm away from the main city of Anchorage where pinks, chums, silvers, and sea-run char are present. Nearby, the saltwater port of Whittier provides a quick alternative to the busy hubs of Homer and Seward, yielding surf-casting opportunities for all five salmon species and bottomfish. Charters bring anglers in touch with halibut, lingcod, rockfish, and salmon shark, as well as salmon.

The best fishing in this area occurs from June into September.

# Bird Creek

Pink
SALMON

Chum
SALMON

Silver
SALMON

Dolly
VARDEN

**Highlights:** Excellent action for wild and hatchery silver salmon with very productive angling also for pinks, chums, and sea-run char.

**Best Fishing:** Mid-July to early September. **Regulatory Restrictions:** Moderate.

**Location:** Northern Turnagain Arm drainage, community of Bird, Seward Highway, 25 miles south of Anchorage.

**Description:** Bird Creek is arguable the nicest stream in the Anchorage area. It is situated only some 30 minutes from downtown, supports very healthy runs of fish, and cuts through a valley in the scenic Chugach State Park. Spruce and birch surround most of the stream, giving way to rock outcroppings and mudflats at its terminus on Turnagain Arm. The last quarter of a mile is influenced by tidal activity, the water rising up to 20 feet some days.

Bird is a coastal runoff stream with just a tint of green, yet often flows semi-glacial or even fairly silty during prolonged periods of warm weather or heavy rain. As the mid-summer salmon runs begin, expect moderate flows and inviting light turquoise water, perfect conditions for connecting with fish throughout the day. With the onset of fall, stream levels drop significantly and Bird becomes crystal clear barring severe weather conditions.

**Caution:** Anglers fishing the stream mouth need to be aware of extreme tidal activity that may change conditions within seconds. Also, stay off mudflats as some parts may display the consistency of quicksand.

**Facilities:** Parking, camping, and restrooms. Lodging, food, some groceries and gas can be found half a mile southeast of stream in community of Bird.

**Access:** The Seward Highway provides main access within the immediate area. Also access to upper sections of drainage.

**A. Seward Highway Bridge** – Road crosses stream at Milepost 101.2. Developed trails lead from parking and camping areas a few hundred yards to stream. Improvised foot paths present giving anglers good access along both sides. Private property cuts public access near confluence with Penguin Creek about 1/4 mile upstream of highway bridge. Look for posted signs indicating border.

**B. Penguin Creek** – Turn NE on Konikson Road at Milepost 100.6 and proceed 0.6 mile to large parking area with trail continuing 1/4 mile to creek. Faint trail heads upstream from access point. Fast-flowing Penguin is a major tributary of Bird and an important salmon spawning stream. Beware of bears in this area.

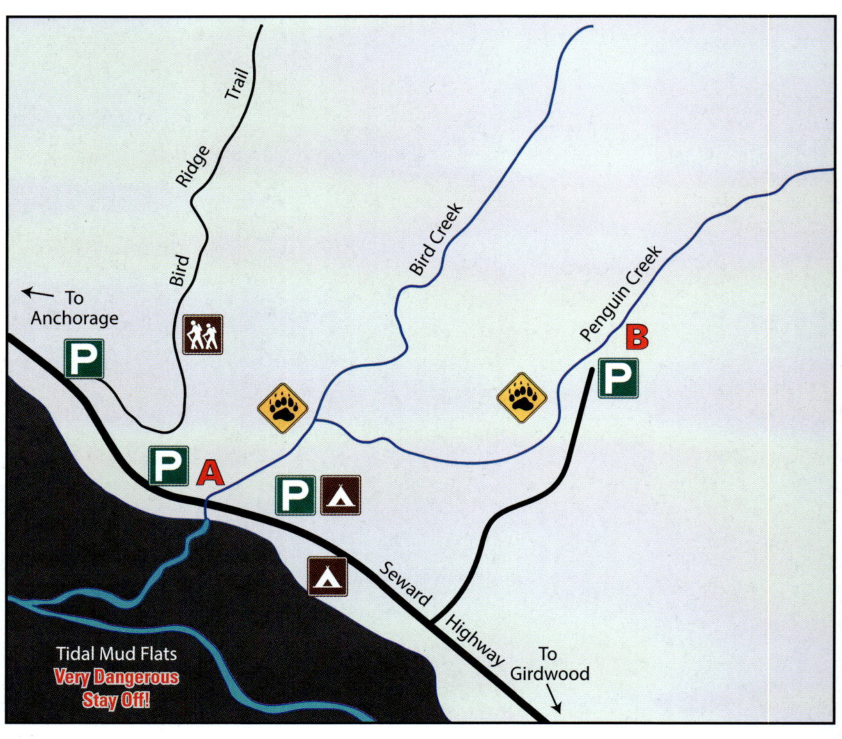

## Rules & Regulations

**Open Season:** July 14 through December 31.
**Open Area:** The entire stream is open to fishing.
**Legal Gear/Tackle:** All gear and tackle, including bait, is allowed.

**All Salmon**

- King salmon fishing is prohibited year-round, including catch-and-release.
- For all other salmon, fishing is open all season (see general "Open Season" above).
- Closed to all salmon fishing year-round upstream of markers 500 yards upstream of the mouth.
- Red, Pink, Chum, and Silver Salmon bag limit is (3) per day and (3) in possession (16 inches or longer). For salmon less than 16 inches (Jacks), the limit is (10).

**Rainbow/Steelhead Trout & Dolly Varden**

- Open all season (see general "Open Season" above).
- For trout, bag limit is (2) per day and (2) in possession, of which only (1) may be longer than 20 inches.
- For char, bag limit is (5) per day and (5) in possession, any size.

*Anglers trying their luck at the mouth of Bird on Turnagain Arm as seen on low tide. Stay along the rocky stream banks if possible.*

## Fishing Bird Creek

**Access:** ★★★
**Scenery:** ★★★★★
**Wildlife:** ★★
**Sight Fishing:** ★★
**Bank/Wading:** ★★★★
**Boat/Floating: N/A**

**Species:** Pink, chum, and silver salmon and Dolly Varden. Rare catches of red salmon and rainbow trout. A run of king salmon enters Bird in June and July.

**Summary:** Next to Ship Creek in downtown Anchorage, Bird is the leading producer of salmon in the area. Strong runs of both pink and silver salmon ascend the stream in mid- to late summer, accompanied by a decent but varied showing of chums. Sea-run char occupy the waters in summer at the same time a small run of king salmon enters the creek.

Due to private property and a lack of fishing opportunity for salmon in the upper reaches of Bird, the majority of anglers fishing here concentrate in the lower quarter mile or so. Salmon fishing, by regulation, is only allowed in the tidal area, hence crowds of anglers are typically present during the peak of the popular silver salmon run. Solitude is very much a possibility on this stream in September and on through the fall, however, even at the road crossing.

Superb silver action is what has made Bird one of the most popular fishing destinations around. Although the stream has always had a modest run of these fish (from mid-August into September), the ADF&G has supplemented the natural run with early-run hatchery salmon that peak slightly earlier (late July to mid-August). The combined effect is a showing of silvers that is available to anglers from mid-summer and well into fall.

Pink salmon used to be the number one attraction at Bird and still draws some level of attention. Expect great action for these smallish salmon as the run enters its peak cycle. Chum salmon is another common species, with anglers often mistaking bright specimens for silvers.

Sea-run Dolly Varden are often ignored in this stream but are present in decent numbers through the summer on the lower stream, and during late summer and fall in the upper reaches and tributaries (such as Penguin Creek).

Due to the small area open to salmon fishing, there are not many holes to choose from. A few of the better spots include the mouth of the creek, the hole right underneath the railroad trestle bridge, the stretch of water adjacent to the rock cliffs, the "boulder" or "big rock" hole, and just downstream of the wire indicating the boundary of private property.

Being in a tidal area, anglers do well here on rising and outgoing tides. When salmon runs are at a peak, outstanding fishing can also be had on low tide. Tides of 29 feet or more flood the entire fishing area, pushing anglers almost completely off the stream. The ideal high tide range is anywhere up to 27 feet.

*A few hopeful anglers cast into the slack current of a rising tide. Fish often congregate in large schools at such times, with sight-fishing to groups of migrating salmon an entertaining challenge.*

## Fish Availability

● = High ● = Moderate ● = Low ● = Closed

| Species | MAY | JUN | JUL | AUG | SEP | OCT | NOV |
|---|---|---|---|---|---|---|---|
| **Pink Salmon** | | Closed | Closed, Closed, High, High | Moderate, Low, Low, Low | | | |
| **Chum Salmon** | | Closed | Closed, Closed, High, High | High, Moderate, Moderate, Low | Low | | |
| **Silver Salmon** | | | Closed, Closed, Moderate, High | High, High, High, Moderate | Moderate, Moderate, Moderate, Low | Low, Low, Low | |
| **Dolly Varden** | Closed, Closed, Closed, Closed | Closed, Closed, Closed, Closed | Closed, Closed, High, High | Moderate, Moderate, Low, Low | Low, Low, Low, Low | Low, Low, Low, Low | Low, Low, Low, Low |
| **Angling Pressure** | | | High, High | High, High, Moderate, Moderate | Low, Low, Low | | |

*A chrome male pink salmon taken at low tide off the stream mouth. Hit the run early on for quality fish.*

## Pink Salmon

**Rating:** ★★★★ Excellent on even-numbered years; good on odd.
**Season:** July 14 through December 31.
**Timing:** July 14 – August 25; peak July 14 – August 1.
**Size:** Average 2 – 4 pounds; up to 6 pounds.
**Tackle:** Spoons, spinners, plugs, and flies.
**Tips:** Lures and flies in green and blue in combination with silver are good when water is clear; try orange or chartreuse if stream is running silty. Incoming and outgoing tides are most productive but when run is at full strength fish can be caught on low tides as well. Large concentrations of fish can typically be located in holes above highway crossing.

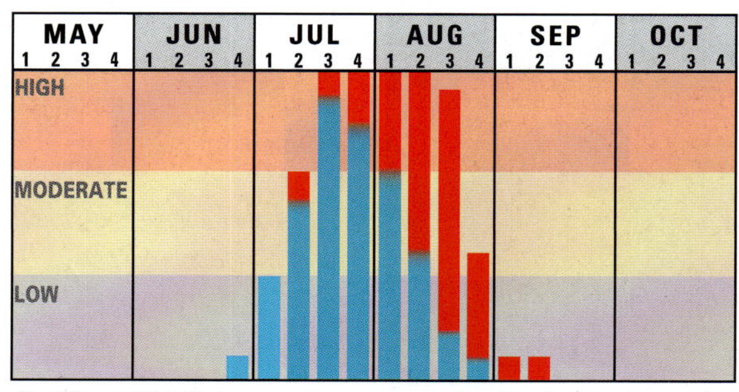


*Bird Creek Pink Salmon.* ● = Fresh ● = Spawning

## Chum Salmon

**Rating:** ★★½ Fair to good.
**Season:** July 14 through December 31.
**Timing:** July 14 – Sept. 5; peak July 14 – August 5.
**Size:** Average 6 – 10 pounds; up to 15 pounds.
**Tackle:** Spoons, spinners, plugs, flies, and bait.
**Tips:** Catches of chums are usually incidental to casting for pinks and silvers. Lures in green, blue, and orange are effective when fished on incoming and outgoing tides. Flies are also good but yield better catches during low tide or when sufficient current is available. Small clusters of salmon roe have a way of taking very fresh specimens.

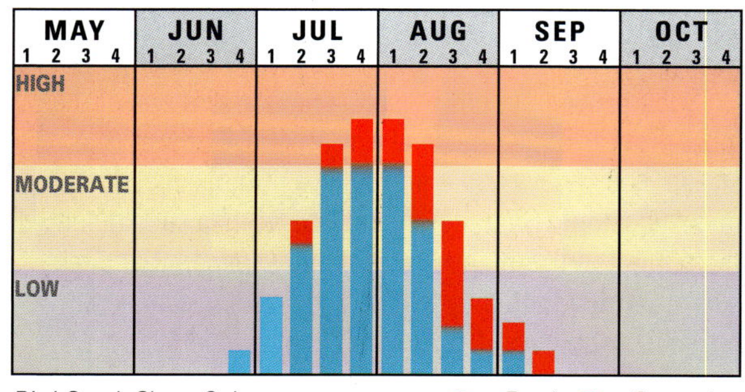


*Bird Creek Chum Salmon.* ● = Fresh ● = Spawning

(Courtesy of Eagle Eye Images)

*A semi-bright Bird chum that struck a large saltwater pattern fly stripped slowly through a school of fish at the edge of high tide.*

*(Courtesy of Eagle Eye Images)*

*A 12-pound male coho, hooked on roe with a strike indicator on a quiet late summer afternoon. Wild, native-run fish continue to enter this stream in small numbers through fall.*

## Silver Salmon

**Rating:** ★★★ Good.
**Season:** July 14 through December 31.
**Timing:** July 14 – October 20; peak July 25 – August 15.
**Size:** Average 5 – 12 pounds; up to 18 pounds.
**Tackle:** Spoons, spinners, plugs, flies, and bait.
**Tips:** Most types of hardware catch fish although spinners are best early in the season while spoons do better in the latter part of the run. Metallic silver, green, blue, orange, and chartreuse are proven colors, with the sharper hues more effective on darker days. Salmon roe fished with a bobber or drifted along the bottom is exceptional for bringing fast action. Flies are best on low tides at the peak of the run when fish are distributed throughout the stream. Try attractor or egg patterns.

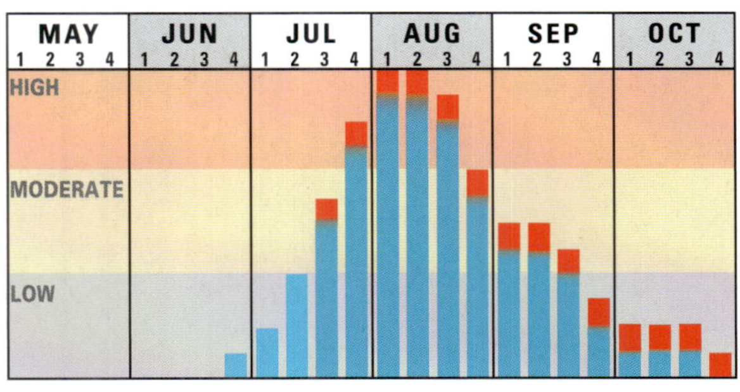


*Bird Creek Silver Salmon.* ● *= Fresh* ● *= Spawning*

## Dolly Varden

**Rating:** ★★½ Fair to good.
**Season:** July 14 through December 31.
**Timing:** July 14 – September 30; peak July 14 – August 1.
**Size:** Average 8 – 16 inches; up to 20 inches.
**Tackle:** Spoons, spinners, flies, and bait.
**Tips:** Smolt and forage imitation lures and flies function best in the tidal area early in the season; incoming and high tides bring char into the stream. Later on, in August and through the fall, use egg and flesh imitations in the upper drainage. The larger fish are caught in July on the tides, the upper stream and tributaries hold smaller specimens.

*Bird is a picturesque stream, situated within the Chugach State Park only 30 minutes from downtown Anchorage. Good, consistent fishing makes this a popular destination among locals and visitors.*

*(Courtesy of Kelsey Gray)*

# Passage Canal

King
SALMON

Red
SALMON

Pink
SALMON

Chum
SALMON

Silver
SALMON

Rockfish

**Highlights:** A large autumn run of silver salmon presents exceptional fishing opportunities for shore-based anglers. Also a good marine fishery for bottomfish.

**Best Fishing:** Mid-June to mid-October.

**Regulatory Restrictions:** Very liberal.

**Location:** Northwestern Prince William Sound, town of Whittier, 58 miles southeast of Anchorage.

**Description:** When the weather is good, Passage Canal can be one of the most scenic places in all of Southcentral Alaska. Tall mountain ridges surround the canal and town of Whittier, ice fields sending small streams cascading down rocky mountainsides to the rainforest below.

The canal has a glacial green tint to it through much of the warm summer months as a result of glacial meltwater from area streams that gives the water its rich turquoise color. Prolonged periods of hot weather or heavy rain often turns the water a greyish hue and slows the fishing considerably. The inner – or west end – of the canal is especially prone to high turbidity. The outer area, from Smitty's Cove and eastward, usually presents better water clarity. In addition, tidal movements play a large role in clarity as high tides bring clear water in from Prince William Sound. Tides range up to 15 feet.

Judging by the steep mountainsides dropping into the canal throughout the area, the water can be very deep just offshore. Passage Canal is at its shallowest at the far west end with depth increasing rapidly towards the town

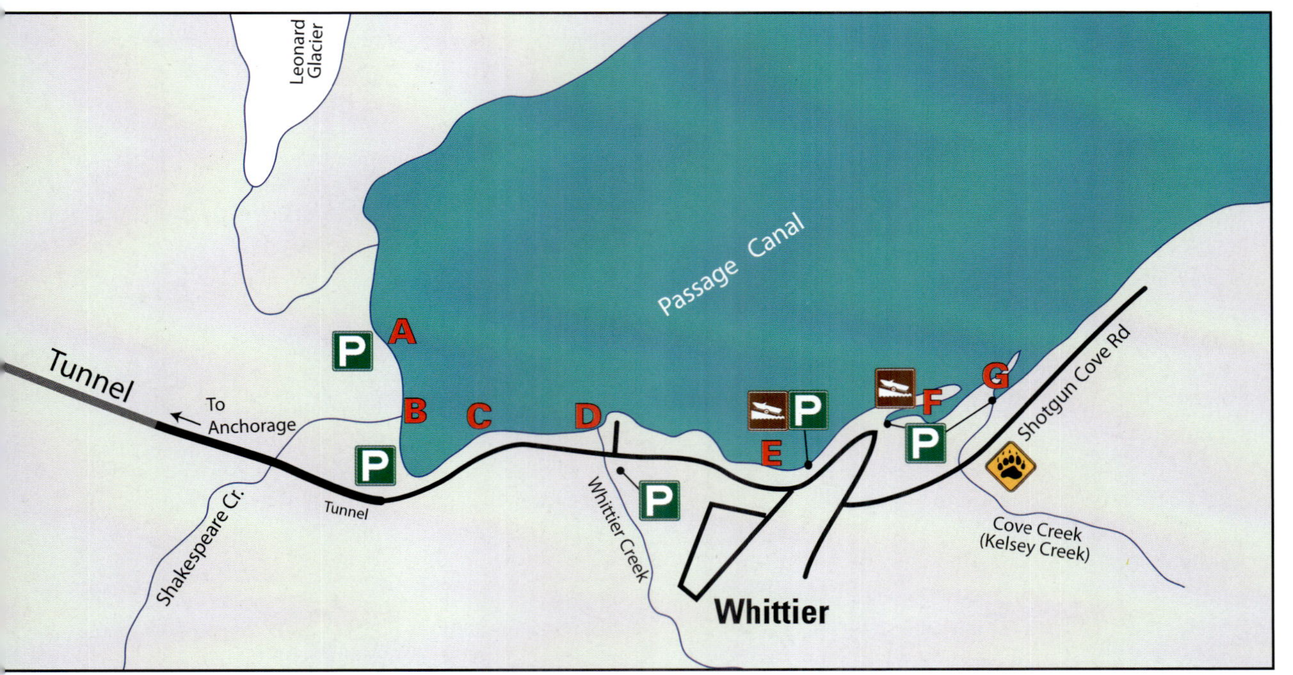


of Whittier. In some spots along the road, such as portions of South Shore to the harbor, the water is quite deep. The depth at mid-canal is 1,000 feet.

**Facilities:** Hotels, motels, groceries, gas, tackle shops, boat rentals, restaurants, guide services, and other amenities available in the town of Whittier.

**Access:** From Milepost 79.2 Seward Highway, turn east on Portage Glacier Road/Whittier Road and proceed straight on main thoroughfare 6.7 miles to toll booth and Bear Valley staging area (Mile 6.8). Openings lasting 15 minutes once an hour lets traffic through Anton Anderson Memorial Tunnel to the Whittier staging area (Mile 9.6). Whittier Road continues from here, paralleling Passage Canal to the town of Whittier (Mile 11.0). The main mileages given are from the Seward Highway junction.

**A. Barge Creek** – Mile 10.0. Northeast on Airstrip Access Road 0.2 miles to end of road and canal. Parking, primitive camping. Mouth of Barge Creek is on the right.

**B. Shakespeare Creek** – Mile 10.2. Road crosses stream. Northeast on access road to large open area and west end of canal. Parking, primitive camping. Mouth of Shakespeare Creek is 150 yards to the left, mouth of unnamed creek on the right.

**C. South Shore** – Mile 10.4—10.8. Road parallels the south shore of Passage Canal. No parking allowed along road and railroad tracks; park at Shakespeare Creek (above) and hike ¼ to ½ mile along paved trail to and along canal.

**D. Whittier Creek** – Mile 11.1. Road crosses stream. South on Whittier Street short distance to paid parking lot. Hike along stream to tidewater area and mouth.

**E. Whittier Harbor** – Mile 11.2. Road parallels harbor area. Parking.

**F. Smitty's Cove** – Mile 11.1. South on Whittier Street 0.5 miles to a "T," left on Depot Road 0.6 miles to end of road and cove. Parking.

**G. Cove Creek** – Mile 11.1. South on Whittier Street 0.5 miles to a "T," left on Depot Road 0.4 miles, right on Blackstone Road 0.1 mile, right on Shotgun Cove Road 0.3 miles to short access road on left immediately before bridge spanning stream. Parking and picnic area.

*(Courtesy Kelsey Gray)*

## Rules & Regulations

**Open Season:** January 1 through December 31.
**Open Area:** The entire canal is open to fishing.
**Legal Gear/Tackle:** All gear and tackle, including bait, is allowed. Snagging is legal (except in Whittier Small Boat Harbor).

**All Salmon**
- Open all season (see general "Open Season" above).
- King salmon bag limit is (2) per day and (4) in possession, any size.
- Red, pink, chum, and silver salmon bag limit is (6) per day and (12) in possession, any size.

**Dolly Varden**
- Open all season (see general "Open Season" above).
- Bag limit is (10) fish per day and (10) in possession, any size.

**Pacific Halibut**
- Open season is February 1 through December 31.
- Bag limit is (2) per day and (4) in possession, any size.

**Lingcod**
- Open season is July 1 through December 31.
- Bag limit is (2) per day and (4) in possession; fish must be minimum 35 inches long to be retained.

**Rockfishes**
- Open all season (see general "Open Season" above).
- From May 1 through September 15, the bag limit is (4) per day and (8) in possession, any size. Note: Only (2) per day and (2) in possession may be non-pelagic.
- From September 16 through April 30, the bag limit is (8) per day and (8) in possession, any size. Note: Only (2) per day and (2) in possession may be non-pelagic.

**Sharks**
- Open all season (see general "Open Season" above).
- Bag limit is (1) per day and (1) in possession.

**Other Saltwater Fishes**
- Open all season (see general "Open Season" above).
- No bag or possession limits.



*Lone angler tries his luck for silver salmon inside the Whittier Harbor. This is a popular and highly productive spot in late summer and early fall. Note that snagging here is prohibited.*

## Fishing Passage Canal

**Access:** ★★★★ **Sight Fishing:** ★★★
**Scenery:** ★★★★★ **Bank/Wading:** ★★★★
**Wildlife:** ★★ **Boat/Floating:** ★★★★★

**Species:** King, red, pink, chum, and silver salmon, Dolly Varden, and rockfish.

**Summary:** The Passage Canal has never been known as an exceptional roadside fishery by any means, the streams in the area being glacial and/or very short and shallow, leaving a fairly hostile environment for many species of migratory fish. The marine waters support some very good fishing for salmon and bottomfish in its outer reaches, with some decent fishing for saltwater species in some parts within the canal. Pink salmon were long the dominant sport fish for roadside anglers in Whittier until certain interest groups implemented a plan to increase opportunity in the area by stocking several species of salmon in various locations, both in Whittier and in other nearby locations.

After a hiatus of a few years, hatchery kings are again returning to the canal with the early summer run expected to build up to full strength by 2014 when larger, full-size fish will arrive in good numbers. Also, there are feeder kings that move into Passage during the spring and summer months, with a few specimens caught from shore, especially in deeper locations such as South Shore and the waterfront right in front of town.

The only true native salmon in this area that can be described as being fairly abundant are pinks. Fishing for them is quite good, this being particularly the case when fish school in front of their spawning streams. Very few bright salmon are available in the streams, however.

Along with the pinks are very modest runs of native red and chum salmon. They can be relatively numerous at times but are usually only encountered incidentally to fishing for pinks or silvers, especially near the mouths of clearwater streams. The best success, however, is enjoyed when schools of hatchery reds and chums provide a small, early-season window of opportunity as they swing by the canal destined for release sites elsewhere in the sound. Fishing success ranges from spotty to great, depending on actual number of fish present and water conditions. Sight-fishing is the way to go with snagging being the preferred harvest method. Waters at the head of the canal are best.

The prized silver salmon draws most attention to Whittier these days. A program was initiated years ago to build an artificial run and it has been a resounding success, with large numbers of dime bright fish being available in coves and stream mouths -- as well as deepwater docks right in front of town -- from late summer into fall.

Bottomfish are not abundant in roadside locations. Some rockfish and lingcod may be taken off the big rocks and cliffs along South Shore and in spots near town, however. Halibut are rare but a few small specimens have been caught at the west end of the canal. Codfish, in contrast, frequent these waters, and are easily caught along with various species of flounder.

(Courtesy Kelsey Gray)

*Angler prospects an incoming tide at Cove Creek for signs of salmon. Hatchery silvers return here, providing great action. Using polarized glasses will enhance success.*

## Fish Availability

● (H) = High ● (M) = Moderate ● (L) = Low ● (C) = Closed

| Species | | MAY | JUN | JUL | AUG | SEP | OCT |
|---|---|---|---|---|---|---|---|
| **King Salmon** | Shore | L L L L | L M H H | H M L L | L L L | | |
| | Boat | L L M M | H H H H | M M M M | M M L L | L L L L | L L L L |
| **Red Salmon** | Shore | L L M | H H M L | L L L M | M L L L | L | |
| | Boat | L L L L | M M L L | L L L L | L L L L | | |
| **Pink Salmon** | Shore | | L L | M H H H | H M L L | L | |
| | Boat | | L L L M | H H H H | H M L L | L | |
| **Chum Salmon** | Shore | L L M | M L L L | L M H H | H M L L | L | |
| | Boat | L L L M | M L L M | H H H H | M L L L | L | |
| **Silver Salmon** | Shore | | | L L | L L M H | H H M M | L L L |
| | Boat | | L | L L L L | M H H H | H M L L | L |
| **Dolly Varden** | Shore | L L L L | M M M M | M M L L | L L | | |
| | Boat | L L L M | M M M M | M M L L | L L L | | |
| **Pacific Halibut** | Shore | L L L L | L L L L | L L L L | L L L L | L L L L | L L |
| | Boat | L L L L | L L M M | H H H H | H H M M | L L L L | L L L L |
| **Lingcod** | Shore | C C C C | C C C C | M M M M | M M M M | M M L L | L L |
| | Boat | C C C C | C C C C | H H H H | H H H H | M M M M | L L L L |
| **Rockfish** | Shore | L L L L | L L M M | M M M M | M M M M | M M L L | L L L L |
| | Boat | M M M M | H H H H | H H H H | H H H H | M M M M | M M L L |
| **Bottomfish** | Shore | L L L L | M M M H | H H H H | H H H H | H M M M | L L L L |
| | Boat | H H H H | H H H H | H H H H | H H H H | H H H H | H H H H |
| Angling Pressure | Shore | | L L M M | M L L L | M M H H | H M L L | |
| | Boat | L L L L | L L L L | L L M M | M M M M | M M L L | L L |

(Courtesy Kelsey Gray)

### King Salmon

**Rating:** ★★ Poor to fair.

**Locations:** Shakespeare Creek, South Shore, and Whittier Harbor.

**Season:** January 1 through December 31.

**Timing:** April 15 – August 15; peak June 15 – July 5.

**Size:** Average 15 – 25 pounds; up to 45 pounds.

**Tackle:** Spoons, spinners, jigs, and bait.

**Tips:** For mature kings, check out the stretch of water around the big boulder at the west end of Passage. Fish often school up here and can be readily caught on herring bait or big spinners in blue or green. Sight fishing is possible. If water clarity is poor, use orange or chartreuse lures.

Feeder kings may be taken from May through July using big spoons or whole herring in deeper water, such as off the rock cliffs at South Shore along the coast to the Whittier Harbor.

*Angler Kelsey Gray tails an 18-pound king. Individual fish can be targeted by sight-fishing at the mouths of streams as well as from points that offer good viewing or prospecting positions, like docks and rock outcroppings. Small schools of five or six kings may be observed and cast to with success. Salmon in Whittier tend to be highly aggressive and respond well to angler's offerings.*

(Courtesy Kelsey Gray)

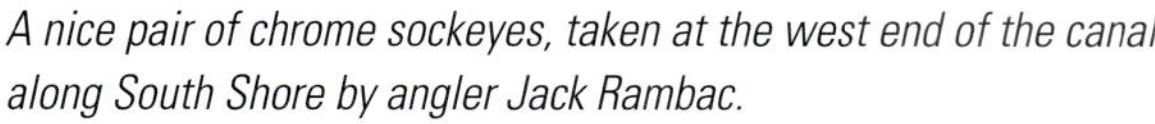

*A nice pair of chrome sockeyes, taken at the west end of the canal along South Shore by angler Jack Rambac.*

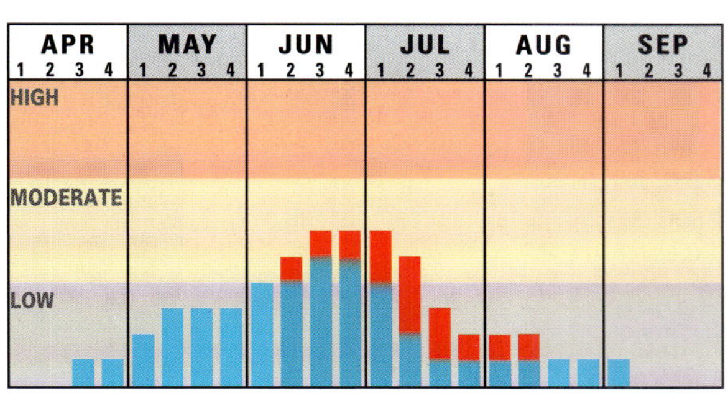


*Passage Canal King Salmon.* ● = Fresh ● = Spawning

## Red Salmon

**Rating:** ★★½ Fair to good.
**Locations:** Barge Creek, Shakespeare Creek, South Shore.
**Season:** January 1 through December 31.
**Timing:** May 15 – September 10; peak June 1 – 15.
**Size:** Average 5 – 7 pounds, up to 12 pounds.
**Tackle:** Flies.
**Tips:** Search out schools of fish at head of canal. These salmon do not readily strike standard tackle but an occasional red may be caught on a properly presented fly; snagging is the preferred harvest method. Sight-fishing can be very rewarding at times.

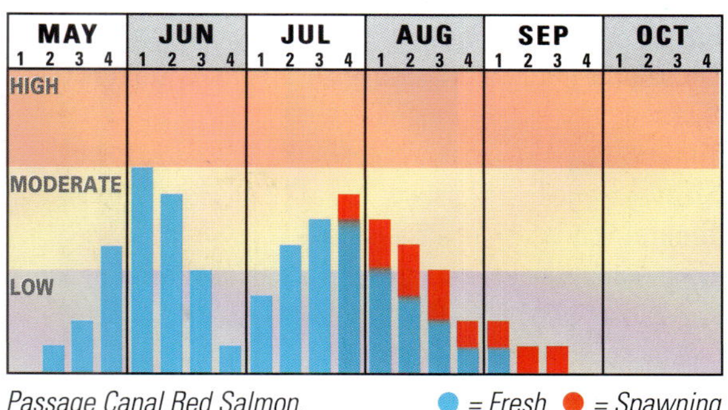


*Passage Canal Red Salmon.* ● = Fresh ● = Spawning

## Pink Salmon

**Rating:** ★★★ Good.
**Locations:** Barge Creek, Shakespeare Creek, South Shore, Smitty's Cove, and Cove Creek.
**Season:** January 1 through December 31.
**Timing:** June 20 – September 5; peak July 15 – August 5.
**Size:** Average 2 – 5 pounds, up to 7 pounds.
**Tackle:** Spoons, spinners, flies, and bait.
**Tips:** Anglers should look for schools of fish near mouths of clearwater streams on an incoming and high tide. Fly-fishers do well in such locations. Chrome and blue spinners and cut herring work well early in the season in deeper areas.

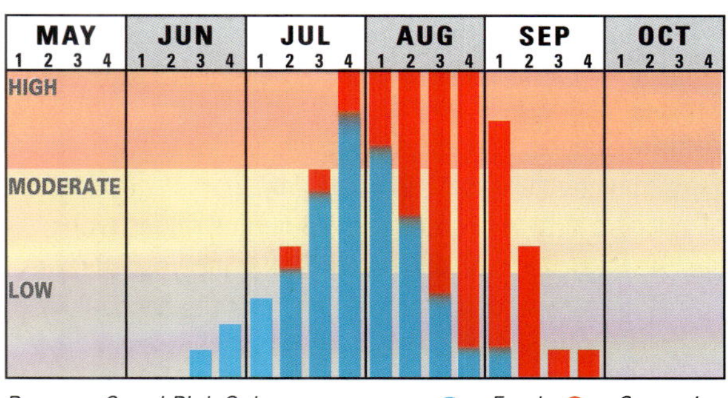


*Passage Canal Pink Salmon.* ● = Fresh ● = Spawning

*A nice and bright saltwater male pink taken off the rocks at South Shore. Larger specimens such as this one are often mistaken for silver salmon. Target these fish early in the season, in July, for prime sporting as well as food quality.*

*(Courtesy Kelsey Gray)*

## Chum Salmon

**Rating:** ★★ Fair.
**Locations:** Barge Creek, Shakespeare Creek, Smitty's Cove.
**Season:** January 1 through December 31.
**Timing:** May 15 – Sept. 10; peak July 20 – August 10.
**Size:** Average 6 – 12 pounds, up to 18 pounds.
**Tackle:** Spoons, spinners, and flies.
**Tips:** Action can be worthwhile if a school of fish can be found. Like with pinks, the best spots would be stream mouths, such as Barge Creek.

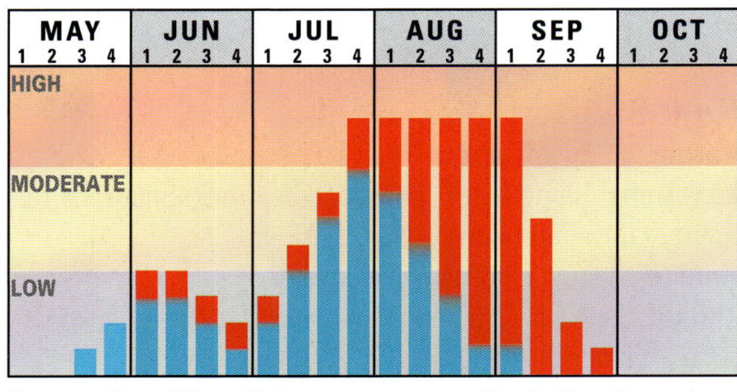


*Passage Canal Chum Salmon.* ● = Fresh ● = Spawning

## Silver Salmon

**Rating:** ★★★ Good.
**Locations:** Barge Creek, Shakespeare Creek, South Shore, Whittier Harbor, Smitty's Cove, and Cove Creek.
**Season:** January 1 through December 31.
**Timing:** July 1 – October 5; peak August 15 – September 5.
**Size:** Average 6 – 11 pounds, up to 16 pounds.
**Tackle:** Spoons, spinners, flies, and bait.
**Tips:** The premier sport fish in the area, particularly fond of spinners in blue or green and cut herring rigged with a bobber. Big schools of silvers often sit at the head of coves and at the far west end of the canal, near the big boulder. Sight fishing is possible in some areas as the salmon often come very close to shore. Look for silvers breaching surface.

Smitty's Cove and South Shore can be good spots early in the season (mid- to late August), while the tail end of the run (early September and later) fishes better at Shakespeare, Whittier, and Cove creeks. During mid-season, all of these locations can yield good fishing. Anglers wanting to catch a silver in freshwater might scout pools in the lower portion of Whittier Creek during the month of September.

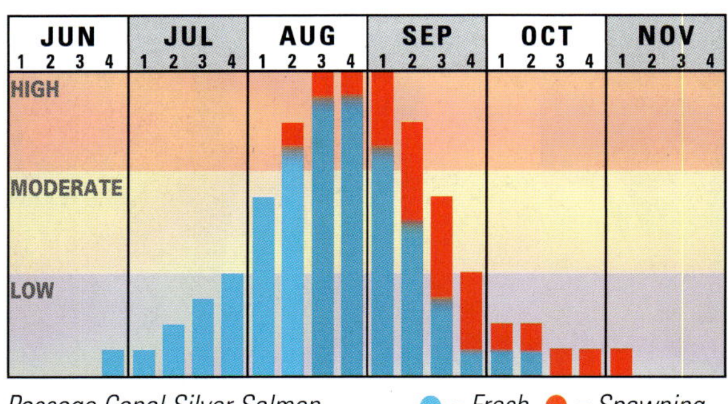


*Passage Canal Silver Salmon.* ● = Fresh ● = Spawning

*(Courtesy Eagle Eye Images)*

## Dolly Varden

**Rating:** ★★ Fair.
**Locations:** Barge Creek, Shakespeare Creek, South Shore, Smitty's Cove, and Cove Creek.
**Season:** January 1 through December 31.
**Timing:** May 15 – August 15; peak June 1 – July 5.
**Size:** Average 8 – 15 inches, up to 22 inches.
**Tackle:** Spoons, spinners, flies, and bait.
**Tips:** Anglers do best targeting these sea-run char at or near the mouths of clearwater streams using small smolt or baitfish imitation lures and flies. Incoming tides are usually most productive. The west end of the canal along the gravel beaches and the rocky shoreline of South Shore traditionally has some decent fishing available.

## Rockfish

**Rating:** ★½ Poor to fair.
**Locations:** South Shore and Smitty's Cove.
**Season:** January 1 through December 31.
**Timing:** April 15 – Oct. 15; peak June 15 – September 1.
**Size:** Average 10 – 20 inches; up to 5 pounds.
**Tackle:** Jigs and bait.
**Tips:** Casting from shore is generally not very rewarding but a few fish can be caught with patience and persistence. Seek out rocky areas with a depth of at least 20 feet or more. Anglers with access to a small boat or inflatable can do quite well scouting hard-bottom structure.

*This bright buck silver struck a blue #4 Vibrax spinner buzzed through a school of fish holding in shallow water near the mouth of Shakespeare Creek. When the water is clear, salmon can easily be spotted and targeted.*

## Other Passage Canal Opportunities

### Western Prince William Sound Excursions

Arguably the most scenic port in all of Southcentral, Whittier and the western portion of Prince William Sound includes the rugged east coast of the Kenai Peninsula with all of its almost countless bays, coves, fjords, and passages, as well as numerous islands of the area; Esther, Culross, Perry, Knight, and northern Montague, among others. Recreational boaters and fishing charters visit these places frequently, targeting salmon and bottomfish with additional opportunities for shark, char, and shrimp.

(Courtesy Alaska Widland Adventures)

Lake Bay at Esther Island is an early-season favorite, with bright hatchery chum salmon returning here from late May to early July, providing intense action. There is also a large run of pinks present, peaking from mid-July to early August, and a smaller appearance of silvers from mid-August through early September.

Coghill River in Port Wells is a favorite red salmon destination with good fishing from late June through mid-July. Pink and silver salmon are also available from mid-July into August and mid-August to mid-September, respectively.

Eshamy Lagoon at the northwest end of Knight Island Passage is a good late-season bet for red salmon. These fish peak from late July through mid-August with decent fishing into September some years. Nearby Main Bay has a slightly earlier run of reds, peaking in late June and early July, in addition to chums in mid-June. Abundant pinks and a fair run of silvers are present in both locations as well.

Other noteworthy locations include Pigot Point (Wells Passage), Bay if Isles (Knight Island), Jackpot Bay (Dangerous Passage), Culross Passage, Port Chalmers (Montague Island), and Perry Island for silver salmon; Cannery Creek (Unakwik Inlet) and Sawmill Bay (Evans Island) for pinks, and Port Chalmers for chums. Expect good to excellent fishing.

Trolling or mooching for feeder king salmon is fair to

good in Prince William Sound. Immature kings ranging from 12 to 25 pounds frequent much of the sound, particularly in late winter and spring, but may be found year-round.

Sea-run Dolly Varden are available in virtually all areas, but are typically most common near the mouths of clearwater streams and associated bays, coves, and points during May and June. For freshwater opportunities, check out streams that are connected to lakes from July into October. Cutthroat trout may be encountered as well, particularly along the western coast of the peninsula in the Eshamy district and nearby islands.

As for bottomfish, halibut, lingcod, and 32 species of rockfish inhabit the sound. For halibut, look in areas consisting of mud, sand, or gravel bottom. Lingcod and rockfish are more common around pinnacles and rocky shoals. Steep drop-offs attract all three types of fish, as well as cod, sablefish, and other species.

Shark fishing can be hot in the sound with the months of July and August prime time to connect with these alpha fish that average 100 to 250 pounds. While a few private vessels target them, the majority of anglers opt to hire an experienced charter boat and crew to assist in locating and landing one of these behemoths.

Shrimping is good in many parts of the sound. Three kinds are available – spot, coonstripe, and northern – with best locations being in hard-surface, debris-covered areas. The mixing zones of glacial and clear water can be great spots to set a shrimp pot.

Charters operating out of Whittier are logical solutions to finding the best fishing in the sound as some of the locations may be difficult to find to the uninitiated (particularly those searching for halibut and other large bottomfish). Specialized trips targeting halibut or salmon shark are widely available and some outfits specialize in salmon/bottomfish combo trips for those wishing to maximize their time and money.

Popular charter destinations include mainland areas of the eastern Kenai Peninsula fjordscape as well as Montague Island. Trolling or mooching for king and silver salmon in one of the numerous bays is a highlight with many anglers, yet some charters may entail anchoring off a river mouth for some fast and furious action for multiple fish species. Adventurous anglers also have the option to rent a boat for a day or more.

Complimenting any fishing trip in this gorgeous area is the scenic aspect. The spectacular fjords along with near countless hidden coves and bays, numerous tidewater glaciers and alpine icefields, and streams cascading down steep mountain sides is a sensory delight and keep anglers coming back time and time again.

Whittier is also a great port to launch kayak expeditions, searching out all of the above in a very personal setting.

The short and narrow tidewater creeks of the sound make for great spots to view salmon in the final stage of maturity and hundreds to even thousands of primarily spawning pinks and chums may be seen churning the shallows during July and August. These places are also focal points for seeing bears feeding on these fish.

Within the community of Whittier, the tiny clearwater streams at the head of Passage Canal often run thick with spawning pink salmon during the month of August and make for good photo opportunities. A few reds and chums may also be spotted, even an occasional silver later on in the fall.

# Resurrection Creek

Pink SALMON

Chum SALMON

Silver SALMON

Dolly VARDEN

**Highlights:** Superb fishing for pink salmon with good opportunities for chums, silvers, and sea-run char in a very scenic area. Great spot to explore and sight-fish.

**Best Fishing:** Mid-June to early September. **Regulatory Restrictions:** Liberal.

**Location:** Northeast Kenai Peninsula drainage, Turnagain Arm, community of Hope, near the end of Hope Highway, 86 miles southeast of Anchorage.

**Description:** Resurrection Creek flows out of a most idyllic valley amidst the Kenai Mountains and through the tiny community of Hope on the shores of Turnagain Arm. It is a rather small clearwater stream, dense vegetation of spruce and birch lining the banks. The stream bottom is rocky and the fish often easy to spot. Ocean tides affect the lower mile of stream, the water often backing up to almost the bridge outside of town.

The lower portion of Resurrection features open space with grasses and mud, eventually giving way deep forest complete with little-worn trails and abundant wildlife. Seals are commonplace at the mouth of the creek on high tides, and brown bears frequent the flats near Turnagain Arm.

This stream is ideal for walking along (and shallow enough in places to cross), scouting deep holes and runs between riffles for schools of salmon. True fly casting may prove difficult in many stretches because of surrounding vegetation but the tidal area is perfectly suitable for it.

Higher up in the drainage, around Resurrection Creek

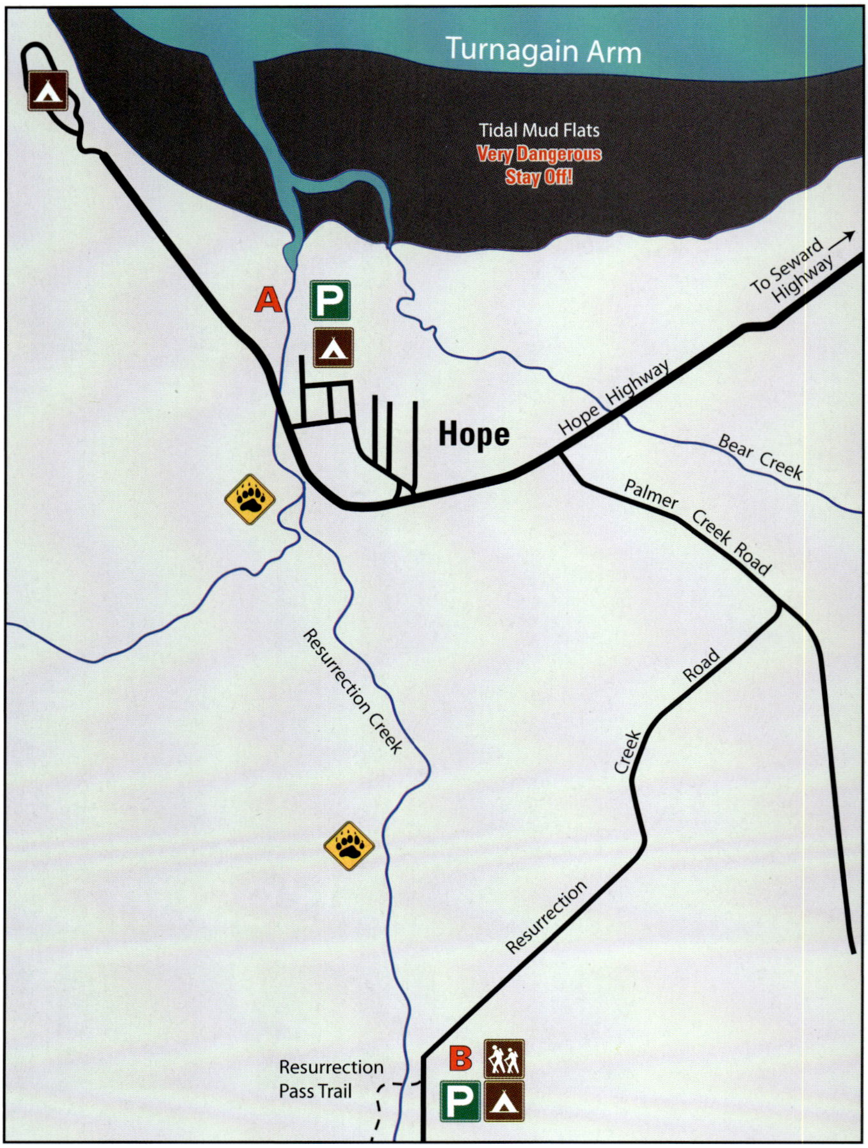

Road and above, the stream is typically fast-flowing and relatively shallow but with enough deeper sections for fish to concentrate. Dense rainforest growth line the narrow and rocky stream banks, sometimes proving almost unpenetrable for those unprepared for the conditions. Expect to do plenty of bushwhacking if venturing much beyond the road access points. Also, be prepared to encounter both brown and black bears in this area since the stream is an important feeding ground during the late summer and fall months.

**Facilities:** Parking, camping, restrooms, lodging, cabins, food, some groceries and gas.

**Access:** From Milepost 56.7 Seward Highway. North on Hope Highway approximately 16 miles to stream access points.

**A. Lower Stream** – Milepost 16.3 Hope Highway. Just prior to stream crossing, turn right and immediate left and follow gravel road to dead end in the community of Hope and tidal area of stream. Undeveloped trails lead along stream from parking and camping areas. Suitable for all size vehicles.

**B. Middle Stream** – The middle section of Resurrection Creek is accessible by the way of Palmer Creek Road at Milepost 16.2 Hope Highway. South on gravel road 0.6 miles to a "Y," then right on Resurrection Creek Road 3.3 miles to stream on right. Road parallels stream next half mile with some parking and primitive camping available. Very large RVs are not recommended beyond Resurrection Pass Trailhead.

## Rules & Regulations

**Open Season:** January 1 through December 31.
**Open Area:** The entire drainage is open to fishing.
**Legal Gear/Tackle:** All gear and tackle, including bait, is allowed year-round.

**All Salmon**

- Closed to fishing for king salmon year-round, including catch-and-release.
- Open to fishing for red, pink, chum, and silver salmon all season (see general "Open Season" above).
- Bag limit is (3) per day and (3) in possession (16 inches or longer), of which only (2) may be silver salmon. For salmon less than 16 inches (Jacks), the limit is (10).

**Rainbow/Steelhead Trout & Dolly Varden**

- Open all season (see general "Open Season" above).
- Bag limit is (2) per day and (2) in possession for each species, of which only (1) trout may be 20 inches or longer.

## Fishing Resurrection Creek

**Access:** ★★★
**Scenery:** ★★★★
**Wildlife:** ★★½
**Sight Fishing:** ★★★★★
**Bank/Wading:** ★★★★
**Boat/Floating: N/A**

**Species:** Pink, chum, and silver salmon and Dolly Varden. Rare catches of red salmon and rainbow trout. A small run of king salmon enters Resurrection in June.

**Summary:** One of the biggest charms about Resurrection is accessibility. The stream can easily be scouted on foot and the lower section at tidewater can even be fished in short boots or even regular shoes. Hiking upstream, above the bridge, an angler can spend hours virtually alone exploring many stretches of stream that rarely see other people. On top of that are the prolific salmon runs, especially pinks which are a top attraction here. There are also smaller runs of chums and silvers to sample in season, and sea-run char are a common catch. Due to water clarity, sight-fishing can be excellent.

This stream has long enjoyed the reputation as one of the best locations on the road system to enjoy catching dime bright freshwater pink salmon. Scores of anglers come to the shores of Resurrection during the month of July to sample the "fish-on-every-cast" action, lining the banks of the lower stream on flooding tides, intercepting huge schools of fish.

But pinks are not the only game as many seasoned anglers here know with fair numbers of large chum and silver salmon mixed in with the masses of fish as well. They are generally caught incidentally to trying for other species but when targeted can provide some decent but challenging sport. Scout for these species around the tides and in deep holes upstream of the highway. Anglers skilled in sight fishing do particularly well catching chrome chums and silvers.

Dolly Varden provide an early-season opportunity before the salmon arrive, with really productive fishing sometimes available at the stream mouth and in the slack water of flooding tides. A few specimens may be hooked higher up in the drainage later in summer and fall along with an occasional rainbow trout.

Resurrection is also home to a small run of kings and a few of these salmon may be spotted during June and July. Targeting these large fish, including for the purpose of catch-and-release, is strictly prohibited.

The lower stream section around the highway crossing and in the community of Hope is the most popular area with anglers and for good reason. The quiet waters of high tide often reveal big schools of salmon with dozens of fish often surfacing at one time. As the water recedes and on low tide, scout the various tidal holes and runs for fish.

Relatively few anglers bother to search out the middle and upper reaches of Resurrection. There are few slow water sections as this is mainly a fast-flowing, run-off stream with only a limited number of spots that concentrate fish. These spots, however, may be black with fish during the height of the salmon runs and the natural beauty of the area is sure to impress. Also, access may be an issue with a lack of roads and trails. Hope is an active mining community and private property are present in some locations. Expect to encounter bears in these reaches.

*The clear waters of Resurrection Creek empties into silty Turnagain Arm, creating a virtual haven for fish and anglers alike as the mixing zone is an important staging area for salmon and char actively feed here. Fish-on-every-cast action is not unusual.*

## Fish Availability

● = High ● = Moderate ● = Low ● = Closed

| Species | MAY | JUN | JUL | AUG | SEP | OCT | NOV |
|---|---|---|---|---|---|---|---|
| **Pink Salmon** | | Low (wk 4) | Low, Moderate, High, High | High, Moderate, Low, Low | | | |
| **Chum Salmon** | | Low (wk 4) | Low, Moderate, High, High | High, Moderate, Moderate, Low | Low, Low | | |
| **Silver Salmon** | | | Low, Low, Low, Low | Moderate, High, High, High | High, Moderate, Moderate, Low | Low, Low | |
| **Dolly Varden** | Low, Low, Moderate, Moderate | High, High, High, High | High, High, High, High | High, High, Moderate, Moderate | Moderate, Moderate, Low, Low | Low, Low, Low, Low | Low, Low, Low, Low |
| Angling Pressure | | Low, Low, Low, Low | Low, Moderate, Moderate, High | High, High, Moderate, Low | Low, Low | | |

## Pink Salmon

**Rating:** ★★★★★ Excellent on even-numbered years.
**Season:** January 1 through December 31.
**Timing:** June 25 – August 25; peak July 15 – August 1.
**Size:** Average 2 – 4 pounds; up to 6 pounds.
**Tackle:** Spoons, spinners, plugs, and flies.
**Tips:** On incoming and high tides, small- to medium-sized spoons and spinners in green, blue, or chartreuse are hot. Orange and pink are good colors at times. On low tide and in upper reaches of stream above tidewater, use an assortment of flies in neutral colors. Pinks usually travel close to the bank.

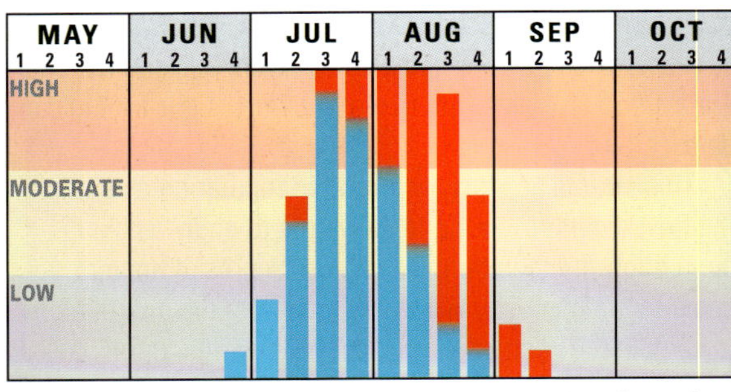


*Resurrection Creek Pink Salmon.* ● = Fresh ● = Spawning

*(Courtesy Eagle Eye Images)*

*Resurrection Creek is an ideal place to go if wishing to find masses of chrome pinks. These little salmon are very abundant on the lower stream and easily targeted.*

## Chum Salmon

**Rating:** ★★½ Fair to good.
**Season:** January 1 through December 31.
**Timing:** June 25 – September 5; peak July 15 – August 5.
**Size:** Average 6 – 10 pounds; up to 15 pounds.
**Tackle:** Spoons, spinners, plugs, flies, and bait.
**Tips:** Most catches of chums are incidental to fishing for pinks. Anglers targeting these salmon can walk away with limits. Green and chartreuse are good colors on bright days while orange and red tend to fish better on dark days or in early morning. Some fish will also hit salmon roe.

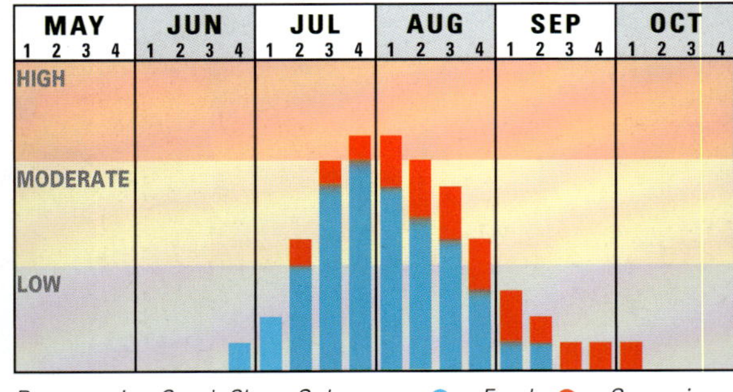


*Resurrection Creek Chum Salmon.* ● = Fresh ● = Spawning

*First-time angler Charles Holness proudly hoists a fresh-off-the-tide silver, spotted holding in a deep pool near the stream mouth.*

## Silver Salmon

**Rating:** ★★ Fair.
**Season:** January 1 through December 31.
**Timing:** July 1 – October 15; peak August 10 – Sept. 5.
**Size:** Average 5 – 11 pounds; up to 16 pounds.
**Tackle:** Spinners, plugs, flies, and bait.
**Tips:** Salmon roe is probably the most effective offering, fished with a bobber on the tides or with a sinker in deep holes upstream. Spinners work well on incoming tides. Fly-fishers score using attractor patterns. Look for silvers to hold in mid-current.

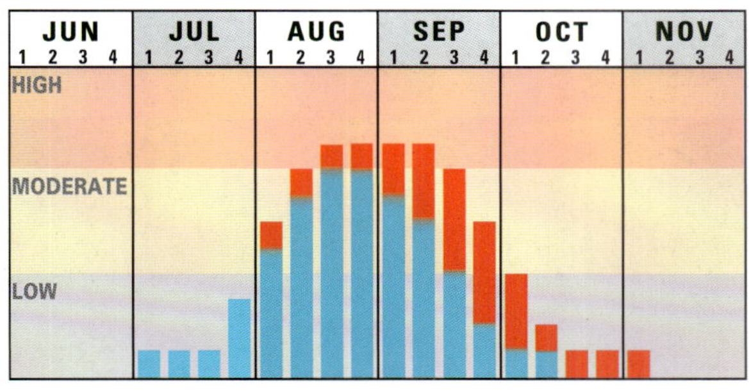


*Resurrection Creek Silver Salmon.* ● *= Fresh* ● *= Spawning*

## Dolly Varden

**Rating:** ★★★ Good in lower stream, fair in upper reaches.
**Season:** January 1 through December 31.
**Timing:** April 25 – September 30; peak June 1 – August 1.
**Size:** Average 8 – 16 inches; up to 20 inches.
**Tackle:** Spoons, spinners, flies, and bait.
**Tips:** From May into July, use smolt and forage imitation spoons and flies in the tidal area. As the salmon begin to spawn from mid-July and on into October, egg and flesh imitations do better in the upper drainage.

*A large school of mainly pinks with some chums and a few silvers hug an inside bend of the stream near the road crossing. Anglers that enjoy sight-fishing will find Resurrection a great destination.*

# Other Productive Fisheries & Additional Opportunities

## CAMPBELL CREEK

**Fishing:** ★★½ **Scenery:** ★
**Accessibility:** ★★★★ **Solitude:** ★★
**Location:** Turnagain Arm drainage, mid-town Anchorage.
**Access:** Many parts of the creek does have private property lining its banks but anglers still have access to many sections of Campbell thanks to parklands and a well-developed trail system. For more detailed information or view of the Anchorage area, consult a city map.

### Lower Campbell Creek

*A. Taku-Campbell Park* – Seward Highway/Dimond Boulevard: Right on Stormy Place 0.1 mile to parking area. Trail leads to and along stream.
*B. Dimond Bridge* – Seward Highway/Dimond Boulevard: Stream crossing. Parking area. Trails lead upstream.

### Middle Campbell Creek

*C. Campbell Creek Park (West)* – Seward Highway/Tudor Road/Lake Otis Parkway: Left on East 48th Avenue short distance to access site on left. Parking, restrooms. Trail leads along stream.
*D. Campbell Creek Parks (East)* – Seward Highway/Tudor Road: Right on Folker Street 0.1 mile to parking area and stream. Developed trail leads upstream and down.

### South Fork Campbell Creek

*E. Campbell Airstrip 1* – Seward Highway or Glenn Highway/Tudor Road: South on Campbell Airstrip Road 1.1 mile, right on access road short distance to parking area. Trail leads 75 yards to stream.
*F. Campbell Airstrip 2* – Seward Highway or Glenn Highway/Tudor Road: South on Campbell Airstrip Road 2 miles, right turn to parking area. Trail leads 50 yards to "Y," right fork leads ¼-mile to stream.
**Facilities:** Parking and primitive camping available.

**Species:** King and silver salmon, rainbow trout, and Dolly Varden.
**Restrictions:** Closed to all salmon fishing, except silver salmon. Consult ADF&G regulations.
**Fishing:** Campbell Creek tumbles out of the Chugach Mountains and flows straight through the middle of Anchorage before dumping into the mouth of Turnagain Arm. It is a relatively small clearwater stream surrounded by a designated greenbelt consisting of trees and brush, deep holes and runs adorn the creek continuously along its winding path.

Populations of salmon, trout, and char still proliferate throughout the drainage, ADF&G boosting the natural stocks of silver salmon and rainbow trout by releasing hatchery fish to increase opportunity and allow for harvest of an otherwise fragile resource. Only the taking of silver salmon is legal at this time, although the state has set up a program in which only youths can participate in a king salmon fishery, held on the last weekend of June every year. Salmon fishing is generally best right after a good rain, helping push fresh fish into the creek from Campbell Lake. When the water is low and clear, sight-fishing can be great.

There are three sections of Campbell: The lower portion from Dimond Boulevard to Seward Highway, the middle portion from Seward Highway to the "Forks" (the confluence of Campbell and the North Fork) near Piper Street, and the upper part above the "Forks" to Campbell Airstrip Road and beyond.

Lower Campbell Creek yields the best silver salmon fishing, in August. The fish are generally brighter here than anywhere else in the drainage and action can be very good at times. There will be some decent fishing available for trout and char during the summer months as well.

Middle Campbell Creek is where anglers start experiencing some good action for rainbows and dollies in summer and fall. Silver salmon are abundant but many fish will be blushing. Scouting for fresh specimens is necessary; late August into September best.

Upper Campbell Creek and the South Fork are closed to salmon fishing but support some very good to excellent trout and char opportunities. Summer through fall is prime. This section of stream is mainly parkland with little or no development, giving a distinct feel of being in a semi-wilderness setting. Anglers should note that brown bears are common in this section of the drainage and encounters are common when spawning salmon are present, mainly from July through October.

**Silver Salmon.** Good; August 10 – September 1; average 6 – 10 pounds. Try the lower access points in mid-August, moving to the middle section starting in late month. Look for a flood of fish to enter stream following a good rain. Spinners, flies, and bait.

**Rainbow Trout.** Good; July 15 – October 10; average 8 – 15 inches. The middle section and south fork yield best catches. Spinners and flies.

**Dolly Varden.** Good; July 15 – October 10; average 8 – 15 inches. Try the middle and south fork access points. Spinners and flies.

## INDIAN CREEK

**Fishing:** ★★ **Scenery:** ★★★
**Accessibility:** ★★ **Solitude:** ★★

**Location:** Turnagain Arm drainage, community of Indian, 24 miles south of Anchorage.

**Access:** The Seward Highway crosses the stream at Milepost 103.0. Short trail from parking area to lower stream and tidal area. **Caution:** Beware of mud at mouth of creek; it acts like quicksand.

**Facilities:** Parking and primitive camping available southeast of highway bridge. Lodging, restaurants, gas, camping, and other amenities situated within a mile in the communities of Indian and Bird.

**Species:** Pink and silver salmon, Dolly Varden. Occasional catches of chum salmon. A few king salmon spawn in Indian during July.

**Restrictions:** King salmon fishing prohibited. Closed to all salmon fishing upstream of highway bridge. Consult ADF&G regulations.

**Fishing:** Indian is a small runoff clearwater stream with very limited angling opportunities. Since the water is so fast and shallow in most places with few holes of any depth, anglers here are usually rendered to fishing on the tides. The lower portion of Indian is situated in the tidal zone with flooding as far upstream as the highway bridge, providing a better angling environment with slower current and deeper water. Stream mouth is located on the other side of the railroad tracks. Sight-fishing can be good on low tide. In waters upstream of the highway, expect scant angling opportunities due to lack of good holding areas.

*(Courtesy Eagle Eye Images)*

Pink salmon is the main species in Indian and considered abundant in mid-summer; an occasional chum may be present at the same time as well. Silvers may show up in numbers on high tide with most fish probably being strays of Bird Creek origin, although a few specimens do spawn in the stream every year. Sea-run char are sometimes abundant early in the season and present throughout the stream.

**Pink Salmon.** Good; July 15 – August 1; average 2 – 4 pounds. Scout mainstream channel right below highway or fish the incoming tide. Spoons, spinners, flies.

**Silver Salmon.** Poor; August 5 – 25; average 5 – 10 pounds. The run is very small and catches usually sporadic at best. Try spinners, flies, and bait.

**Dolly Varden.** Fair to good; June 15 – July 15; average 8 – 15 inches. Hit the mouth on incoming tide or try near the highway bridge on high tide. Spoons, spinners, flies, and bait.

## GLACIER CREEK

**Fishing:** ★★★ **Scenery:** ★★★★★
**Accessibility:** ★★½ **Solitude:** ★★★

**Location:** Turnagain Arm drainage, community of Girdwood, 37 miles south of Anchorage.

**Access:** The Seward Highway crosses the stream at Milepost 89.8. Trail leads upstream and down along creek. Mouth of California Creek is located a quarter mile upstream, just above the railroad tracks.
The upper portion of Glacier Creek can be reached via Alyeska Highway from Milepost 90.0. Head north 2.2 miles to stream crossing. Parking on southwest side of bridge across from fire station. Trails lead short distance from picnic area to creek.

**Facilities:** Small parking area available west of highway bridge. Lodging, hotels, restaurants, sporting goods, groceries, gas, and other amenities can be found in community of Girdwood.

**Species:** Red, pink, chum, and silver salmon, Dolly Varden. Small run of king salmon in June and July.

**Restrictions:** King salmon fishing prohibited. Seasonal and area restrictions on silver salmon. Consult ADF&G regulations.

**Fishing:** Glacier is heavily influenced with meltwater from area glaciers and ice fields, thus its waters are generally flowing high and turbid throughout much of the relatively warm summer season. Angling is often limited to the mouths of clearwater tributaries, such as California Creek, although during cooler periods with little rain the stream itself can clear up enough to allow for good fishing in the stream.

Starting in September and continuing through the autumn, however, Glacier clears up and drops considerably due to lower temperatures and lack of snowmelt (barring heavy rain), exposing many fine holes and runs.

Lures in metallic or fluorescent shades are popular, bait being very productive. As water clears – or at the mouths of clearwater tributaries – the use of neutral colors become more efficient. Mainstem Glacier can be good if water conditions permit; try downstream of highway on incoming or high tide using fluorescent lures.

Glacier Creek has a unique distinction of supporting

(Courtesy Eagle Eye Images)

early and late runs of all primary species of salmon. The early runs are bound for various tributaries while the late runs spawn in select channels and sloughs of mainstem Glacier.

Hiking up California Creek from its mouth can put anglers into some good action for pink salmon and Dolly Varden.

Beware of bears – both black and brown – along Glacier and its tributaries, notably in late summer and fall.

**Red Salmon.** Poor; August 1 – 20; average 4 – 6 pounds. Fairly small population with most fish taken incidentally to fishing for other species. Try mouth of California or mainstem Glacier if water conditions allow. Use spinners and flies.

**Pink Salmon.** Good to excellent; July 15 – August 5; average 2 – 4 pounds. The best spot for pinks is the confluence of California; heavy run of fish most seasons but particularly in even-numbered years. Spoons, spinners, plugs, attractors, and flies.

**Chum Salmon.** Fair; July 15 – August 15; average 6 – 12 pounds. The mouth of California is a relative hot spot. Try spoons, spinners, attractors, and flies. Bait can be very good at times.

**Silver Salmon.** Fair to good; August 10 – September 15; average 5 – 11 pounds. In August, try the mouth of California Creek and high tides (if water conditions are right). Come September, scout mainstem Glacier from tidal area upstream to Alyeska Highway bridge. Use spinners, attractors, or bait.

**Dolly Varden.** Fair to good; June 15 – August 15; average 8 – 12 inches. Incoming and high tides are best in early summer; later on try upstream at mouth of clearwater tributaries. Some nice char are available in autumn. Spinners, attractors, flies, and bait.

## PORTAGE CREEK

**Fishing:** ★★ **Scenery:** ★★★★★
**Accessibility:** ★★ **Solitude:** ★★★★

**Location:** Turnagain Arm drainage, Portage area, 47 miles south of Anchorage.

**Access:** There are several ways to reach Portage Creek, all of them via the Seward Highway. The highway crosses the lower stream at the tidal area while Portage Glacier Road provides road access to the upper reaches, including Portage Lake and a few tributary streams. It is possible to launch a raft or canoe at the upper section and drift down to the main highway, providing access to the more difficult to reach middle section of Portage.

*A. Lower Portage Creek* – Milepost 79.4. Highway crosses stream. Paved parking area south of bridge. Very faint or no trails in the area.

*B. Upper Portage Creek* – Milepost 79.2. Portage Glacier Road begins (mile 0) and parallels Portage creek more or less for several miles to the outlet of Portage Lake. Very few pullouts with limited parking adjacent to stream but developed campgrounds are present nearby.

**Facilities:** Parking only at lower Portage. There are two campgrounds in the upper section: Black Bear USFS Campground is at mile 3.7; Williwaw USFS Campground at mile 4.3. The latter is the larger facility, capable of handling RV vehicles.

**Species:** Red, pink, chum, and silver salmon, and Dolly Varden.

**Restrictions:** King salmon fishing prohibited. Williwaw Creek, a tributary, is closed to salmon fishing. Consult ADF&G regulations.

**Fishing:** Portage is a glacial stream with limited angling opportunities. Turbid water conditions are especially problematic during the warmer summer months; the cooler fall months yielding lower water levels and more pronounced structure. Fish populations are generally not large, with red and silver salmon being the most abundant salmon species.

The majority of fishing on the Portage is confined to the mouths of clearwater streams with little effort along the mainstem. Two of the more productive spots include the mouth of Williwaw Creek and the confluence of a tributary stream (nicknamed Railroad Creek) draining into the more remote middle section of Portage between Williwaw and the main highway bridge.

Anglers using bait and fluorescent lures do well at times for salmon and char on the lower stream, fishing the incoming tide. Silver salmon and Dolly Varden action, in particular, can be very good, but pinks and chums can be hot as well, especially farther upstream in sloughs and quiet water sections. The mouth of tributaries can be fished with an assortment of lures and flies, including bait. These locations attract all available salmon species as well as char. There are relatively few bright salmon available on the upper Portage.

Williwaw Creek is a major spawning stream of red and chum salmon and these fish can be observed from a viewing deck at mile 4.1 Portage Glacier Road. Small char are available in the pretty clearwater creek in fall.

**Red Salmon.** Poor to fair; July 15 – August 1; average 4 – 6 pounds. Can be difficult to get to bite despite seemingly good number of fish present. Spinners and flies may work. Try the mouth of clearwater tributaries or swift current just upstream of holding areas.

**Pink Salmon**. Fair to good; July 20 – August 5; average 2 – 4 pounds. Runs are quite small; even-numbered years yield best fishing. Try spoons, spinners, and flies. The mouth of Railroad Creek is a good bet. Lower Portage may be worthwhile.

**Chum Salmon.** Fair; July 20 – August 15; average 6 – 12 pounds. Best action is at mouth of tributaries where schools of fish concentrate. Use spoons, spinners, attractors, flies, and bait.

**Silver Salmon.** Fair to good; August 25 – September 20; average 6 – 12 pounds. The lower stream and mouth of Railroad Creek supports productive fishing. Bait is tops yet spinners and attractors work too. Upper Portage sees fair action at best with fewer and more blushed fish.

**Dolly Varden.** Fair to good; June 15 – September 15; average 8 – 16 inches. In early summer (June into July) hit lower stream in tidal area, moving upstream to mouth of tributaries starting in mid-July and on into fall. Spinners, attractors, flies, and bait.

## INGRAM CREEK

**Fishing:** ★★★ **Scenery:** ★★★★
**Accessibility:** ★★★ **Solitude:** ★★★
**Location:** Northeast Kenai Peninsula drainage, Turnagain Arm, near Portage, 52 miles from Anchorage.
**Access:** Milepost 75.3 Seward Highway. Southeast on turnout at milepost 75.5 short distance to parking area next to creek. **Caution:** Beware of mud near mouth of creek; it acts like quicksand.
**Facilities:** None; parking only. There is space for primitive camping, RV parking.
**Species:** Pink, chum, and silvers salmon and Dolly Varden.
**Restrictions:** King salmon fishing prohibited. Seasonal and area closure for silver salmon in effect. Consult ADF&G regulations.
**Fishing:** This is a small run-off stream with limited angling opportunity. Much of the stream is quite shallow and can be waded easily with some deep pools and runs throughout its length. The lower stream section is influenced by tides as far upstream as just above the highway bridge. Water clarity is often very good and sight fishing is possible.

Pinks are by far the most abundant species in Ingram and may be encountered in relatively large numbers throughout the lower portion of the stream along with a few scattered chums. Silvers are largely hit-and-miss as the run can be very unpredictable with some years seeing very few fish while other years quite decent numbers. It also depends on the tide as schools of fish from other streams swing by time to time. As a rule for all salmon, try early in the season, preferably on an incoming or high tide, for brightest specimens.

Sea-run char are present throughout the summer and fall months but generally taken in the tidewater section in early summer or upstream on the salmon spawning beds later on in the season.

**Pink Salmon.** Fair to good; July 15 – August 1; average 2 – 4 pounds. A decent run of fish on even-numbered years, small on odd. Most pinks are found near the highway bridge on downstream to mouth. Small spoons, spinners, and flies work.

(Courtesy Eagle Eye Images)

**Chum Salmon.** Poor; July 25 – August 10; average 6 – 10 pounds. Very small run most years. Also, the few chums that may be present are likely turning color. Check deeper stream sections using spoons, spinners, and flies.
**Silver Salmon.** Fair; August 15 – September 5; average 5 – 10 pounds. Most fish are caught on the tides or in deep tidewater holes; a few fish also present in choice spots above highway. Spinners, flies, and roe do best.
**Dolly Varden.** Fair to good; June 10 – August 15; average 8 – 12 inches. Larger specimens can be found in the deeper parts near the stream mouth. Try small spoons, spinners, flies, and bait.

*A male pink of around 5 pounds, still carrying sea lice, caught in the tidal area of Ingram Creek.*

(Courtesy Eagle Eye Images)

## SIXMILE CREEK

**Fishing:** ★★★ **Scenery:** ★★★★★
**Accessibility:** ★★½ **Solitude:** ★★★
**Location:** Northeast Kenai Peninsula drainage, Turnagain Arm/Pass, 65 miles from Anchorage.
**Access:** There are several access points to various sections of the stream, ranging from the headwaters in Turnagain Pass and Johnson Pass to tidewater off the Hope Highway at Sunrise near Hope. The Seward Highway/Hope Highway Junction is at milepost 56.3.

### Seward Highway

*A. East Fork Sixmile Creek* – Milepost 62.5. Bridge crossing, very limited access; no parking.
*B. Granite Creek USFS Campground* – Milepost 62.9. South on gravel road half a mile to campground. Hike along Granite Creek to Sixmile Creek confluence.
*C. Turnout* – Milepost 59.0. Large parking area next to main Sixmile Creek.

### Hope Highway

*D. Canyon / Sixmile Confluence* – Milepost 0.2. East on paved access road short distance to gravel road on left, 0.5 miles to parking area next to Canyon Creek Bridge. Trail follows Canyon Creek 200 yards to confluence area.
*E. Turnouts* – Milepost 0.6 to 6.5. Several small parking areas on east side of road with trail access to stream.
*F. Lower Sixmile Creek* – Milepost 7.1. East on small dirt road 0.3 miles to stream. Note: This road can be very rough and wet. Faint trails lead from parking area upstream and down.

**Facilities:** Parking at most access points, campground at Granite Creek. Rafts can be launched at milepost 59.0 Seward Highway with takeout at Milepost 7.1 Hope Highway.
**Species:** Pink, chum, and silver salmon and Dolly Varden. Rare catches of red salmon, rainbow trout, and arctic grayling.
**Restrictions:** King salmon fishing prohibited. Consult ADF&G regulations.
**Fishing:** Sixmile is not known as a fishing destination; however, it does harbor some very good fishing in certain areas. Much of the reputation is undoubtedly because of the lack of substantial numbers of fish in its upper reaches along the Seward Highway, yet salmon and char are relatively abundant in the lower stream sections – downstream of the Canyon Creek confluence – with the best action occurring from tidewater and upstream a few miles.

Salmon fishing is considered productive in the deep holes and pools in the lower stream along Hope Highway. Pinks can be very abundant and chums show in formidable numbers time to time as well. This is also the best section to target silver salmon. Many salmon spawn in this section with comparatively few fish venturing much beyond Sixmile Canyon, a stretch of Class IV whitewater popular with the rafting crowd.

The headwater tributaries of Granite Creek (including Lyon Creek), East Fork Sixmile Creek, and Bench Creek – as well as Canyon Creek – mainly have small runs of spawning king and silver salmon along with isolated populations of stunted char.

Sixmile is a moody drainage, the water often turning

(Courtesy Eagle Eye Images)

*In some years, very heavy runs of chum salmon ascend the silty Sixmile, seemingly filling up every bit of slack water with their presence. This smallish but colorful specimen struck a cluster of roe meant to entice silver salmon.*

very turbid following heavy rain or prolonged periods of warm weather. Cool temperatures bring the water to a greenish-blue color, running clear in spring and fall. Anglers are advised to use fluorescent offerings, or bait, retrieved slowly through deep holes when stream is murky.

**Pink Salmon.** Fair to good; July 15 – August 5; average 2 – 4 pounds. The run can be highly variable with decent fishing most years. Fluorescent spoons and spinners are best. Try very low in drainage, preferably at or near tidewater. Few salmon found as far upstream as Canyon Creek and beyond.

**Chum Salmon.** Fair to good; July 15 – August 5; average 6 – 12 pounds. This is probably the most abundant salmon species in Sixmile. Runs in some years can be very heavy with excellent action. Tidewater areas and immediately above is most productive. Flashy spinners, attractors, and roe works best.

**Silver Salmon.** Fair to good; August 10 – 30; average 5 – 11 pounds. Spinners and attractors – flies too if water is not too silty – and roe are all effective. Good, but sometimes spotty, fishing in lower stream near tidewater. Action is generally poor at best in upper stream, in early September.

**Dolly Varden.** Fair to good; July 1 – August 15; average 8 – 15 inches. Try small shiny lures, flies, and bait. There are two populations of char in the drainage, one in the upper section above the canyon (resident fish), and another in the lower stream (sea-run fish). Resident char measure only 8 to 10 inches and are caught on flies.

## SUMMIT LAKES

**Fishing:** ★★½ **Scenery:** ★★★½
**Accessibility:** ★★★★ **Solitude:** ★★★★

**Location:** Northeast Kenai Peninsula drainage, Summit Pass, 80 miles from Anchorage.

**Access:** The Seward Highway parallels both Upper and Lower Summit lakes with a few turnouts present on both.

### Lower Summit Lake

*A. Lake Outlet* – Milepost 47.2. Large parking area; fits RVs as well. Some limited camping available along gravel road.

### Upper Summit Lake

*B. Tenderfoot Creek USFS Campground* – Milepost 46.0. East on access road 0.6 miles to campground and lake.

*C. Summit Lake Lodge* – Milepost 45.8. Large parking area with short trail to lake.

*D. Turnout* – Milepost 45.5. Small parking area by lake.

*E. Turnout* – Milepost 44.5. Large parking area; fits RVs.

**Facilities:** Parking only at all access points. Some primitive camping at Lower Summit. The main campground on Upper Summit has good camping facilities.

**Species:** Rainbow trout and Dolly Varden. Rare occurrences of lake trout.

**Restrictions:** Open to all species, year-round. Consult ADF&G regulations.

**Fishing:** Both lakes contain natural resident Dolly Varden, popularly referred to as Goldenfins. Stocking efforts by the state has also introduced rainbow trout, which thrive very well, and once upon a time even lake trout. The latter species are very rarely reported by anglers.

Only Upper Summit is planted with rainbows although the fish have spread to Lower Summit through the small stream (Canyon Creek) connecting the two lakes. Today there are productive populations in both lakes.

Anglers do best focusing on lures and flies that imitate local food sources. Since there are no salmon runs that access these lakes, the fish depend largely on various forms of insect life for sustenance. However, the trout will consume juvenile char and thus small spoons and spinners and attractor flies do work. Concentrate on the mouths of small streams entering the lakes in summer and fall. A canoe or small inflatable is helpful but casting from shore is possible too.

Canyon Creek, which eventually pours into Sixmile Creek, has some worthwhile action for rainbow trout and Dolly Varden, particularly near the lakes.

Breakup is generally late in spring, around the first of June, with freezeup starting in mid-October.

**Rainbow Trout.** Good; June 1 – July 1 and August 15 – September 30; average 10 to 16 inches. Forage imitation flies can be exceptional. Small spoons and spinners and bait are also effective. Big rainbows in excess of 25 inches (6 pounds) are not unheard of from Upper Summit Lake. Try the south end of both lakes.

**Dolly Varden.** Good; June 1 – July 1 and August 15 – September 30; average 8 to 10 inches. The char in these lakes are resident fish and typically small. Flies, both wet and dry, can be deadly at dawn and dusk.

## ADDITIONAL OPPORTUNITIES

### Turnagain Arm Hooligan

Every spring a large run of hooligan enters the cold, silty waters of Turnagain, bound for spawning grounds in rivers at the head of the arm. Armed with dip nets and dressed in layered clothing and warm gloves and hats, anglers descend on the shores in droves to scoop up buckets – or even coolers – full of these silvery little smelt, averaging only six to eight inches long.

Although some fish begin arriving as early as mid-April, the run kicks into high gear by the second week of May and usually continues strong through the season closure at the end of the month (May 31). At this time, dipping shifts to freshwater locations, such as 20-Mile River. Excellent fishing can be had there through early June with worthwhile opportunities until the river closes to hooligan dipping on June 15.

Aside from the main run at 20-Mile, fishing is sporadic elsewhere but can sometimes be decent in Placer River and the far lower reaches of adjoining waterways.

### Salmon Viewing

Observing salmon in the final forays of their life cycle is possible in several of the clearwater streams within the Turnagain Arm area; however, only a few of them have developed walkways and platforms for viewing purposes.

**Rabbit Creek:** The Seward Highway provides access to Boardwalk Wildlife Viewing area from Milepost 117.4, at Potter Point State Game Refuge. King and red salmon are present during June and July, pinks mid-July to mid-August, and silvers latter part of July through September. This is a popular bird watching spot as well.

**Williwaw Creek:** From Milepost 78.9 of the Seward Highway, turn onto Portage Glacier Road to viewing area off mile 4.1. Excellent viewing. Developed trail leads from parking area along stream to Williwaw Lakes. Reds and chums peak in numbers from mid-August to mid-September, while a trickle of silvers appear in October. Use caution; bears feed on salmon in this area and often cross trail.

### 20-Mile River

The 20-Mile (Twentymile) River, at Milepost 80.7 Seward Highway, is home to all five species of salmon as well as sea-run char. Currently closed to king fishing, the remaining four types of salmon provide rich and varied angling opportunities from mid-summer through fall. It is a glacial river, flowing heavy with silt, rendering most sport angling to the mouths of clearwater tributaries and sloughs.

20-Mile supports one of the largest silver salmon fisheries within the greater Anchorage area, the run peaking

from mid-August into early September. Red, pink, and chum salmon are present from early July to mid-August, yielding fair to good action. Dolly Varden are available from July into October.

The Seward Highway crosses the far lower end of the river at tidewater and all angling activity is achieved by boating up the 20-Mile to the mouth of clearwater tributaries and the upper sections of river where salmon and char congregate. While the majority of anglers here use powerboats to reach their destinations, a small number of people utilize canoes as well.

Hiking up the river from the highway bridge is possible yet extremely strenuous as heavy brush, no trails, and mud serve as an effective barrier to reaching prime angling locations miles up the drainage.

### Placer River

Only a few miles away from the larger 20-Mile, Placer River, at Milepost 78.4 and 77.9 Seward Highway, supports runs of four species of salmon species and sea-run Dolly Varden. The main fishing season extends from mid-summer to late autumn. Like other area rivers, the Placer runs turbid with glacial silt, thus the majority of fishing takes place at or near the confluence of clearwaters streams and sloughs.

Salmon runs here are smaller than at 20-Mile but less angler interest means that fishing can still be very good. Reds along with lesser numbers of pinks and chums run the Placer from mid-July to mid-August, while silvers show in force starting in late August and continuing until mid-September. Dolly Varden can be abundant with good action possible between July and October.

The brunt of anglers visiting Placer access the river and its tributaries from the Seward Highway crossing at tidewater. Small watercraft can be launched at one of the two channels in order to reach the best fishing areas a few miles upstream.

There are no trails that head up the Placer from the highway though some anglers do bushwhack their way. A couple of spots can be found within a 2-mile reach.

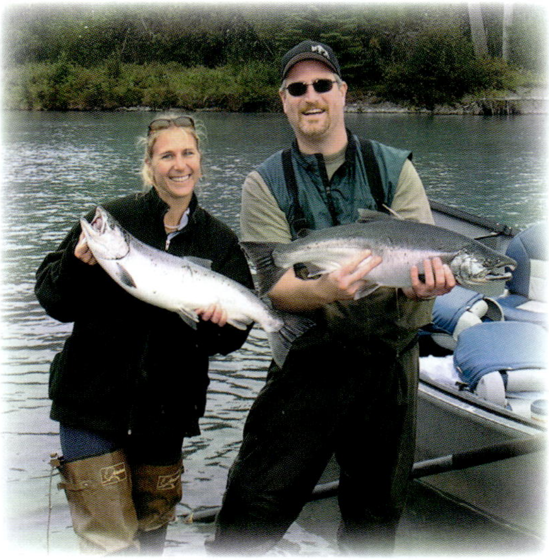

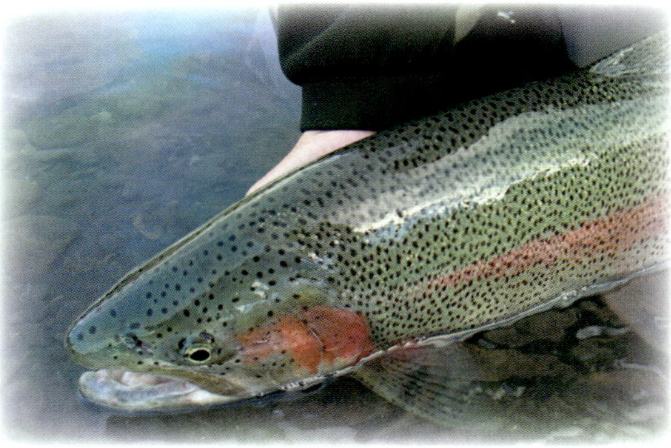



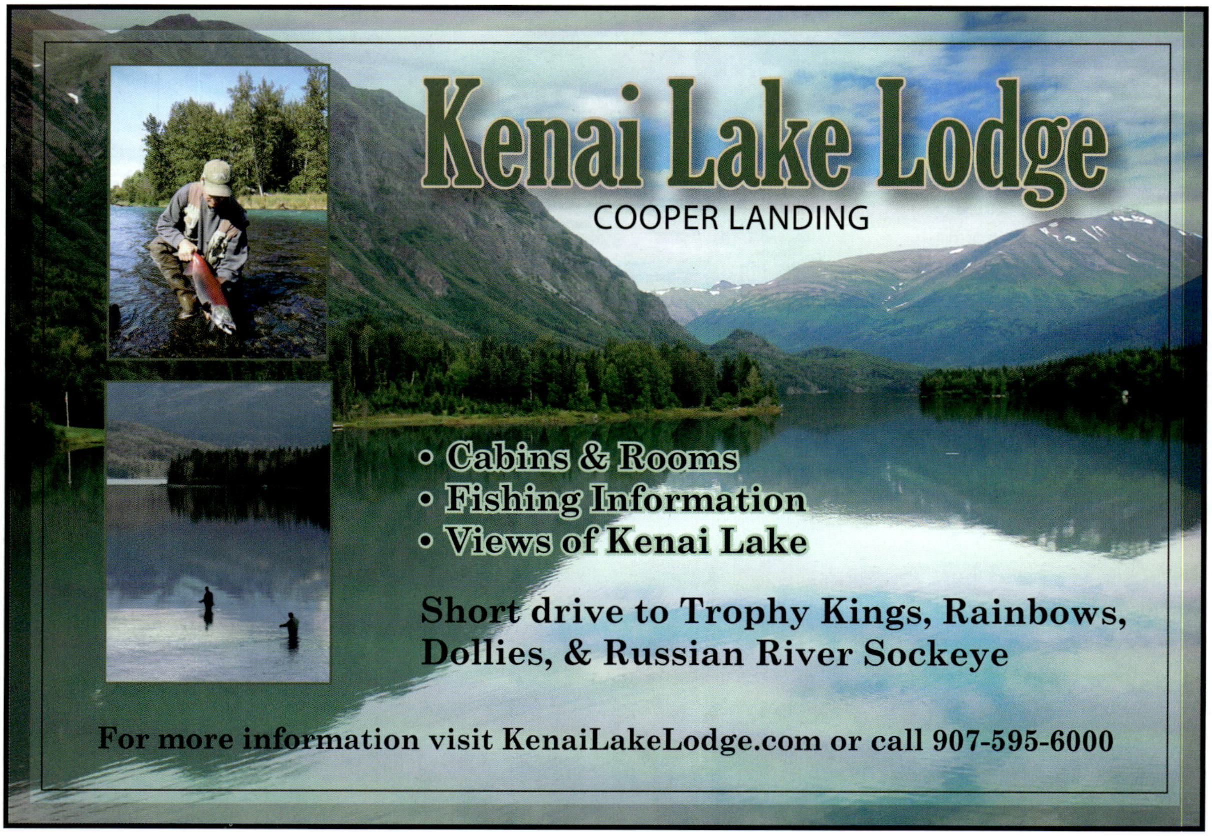
Kenai Lake Lodge
COOPER LANDING
• Cabins & Rooms
• Fishing Information
• Views of Kenai Lake
Short drive to Trophy Kings, Rainbows, Dollies, & Russian River Sockeye
For more information visit KenaiLakeLodge.com or call 907-595-6000

Cooper Landing • Moose Pass

# Central Kenai

**Red Salmon • Silver Salmon • Rainbow Trout • Dolly Varden**

*Trophy Fishing* *Wildlife Viewing* *Fly-Fishing* *River Rafting*

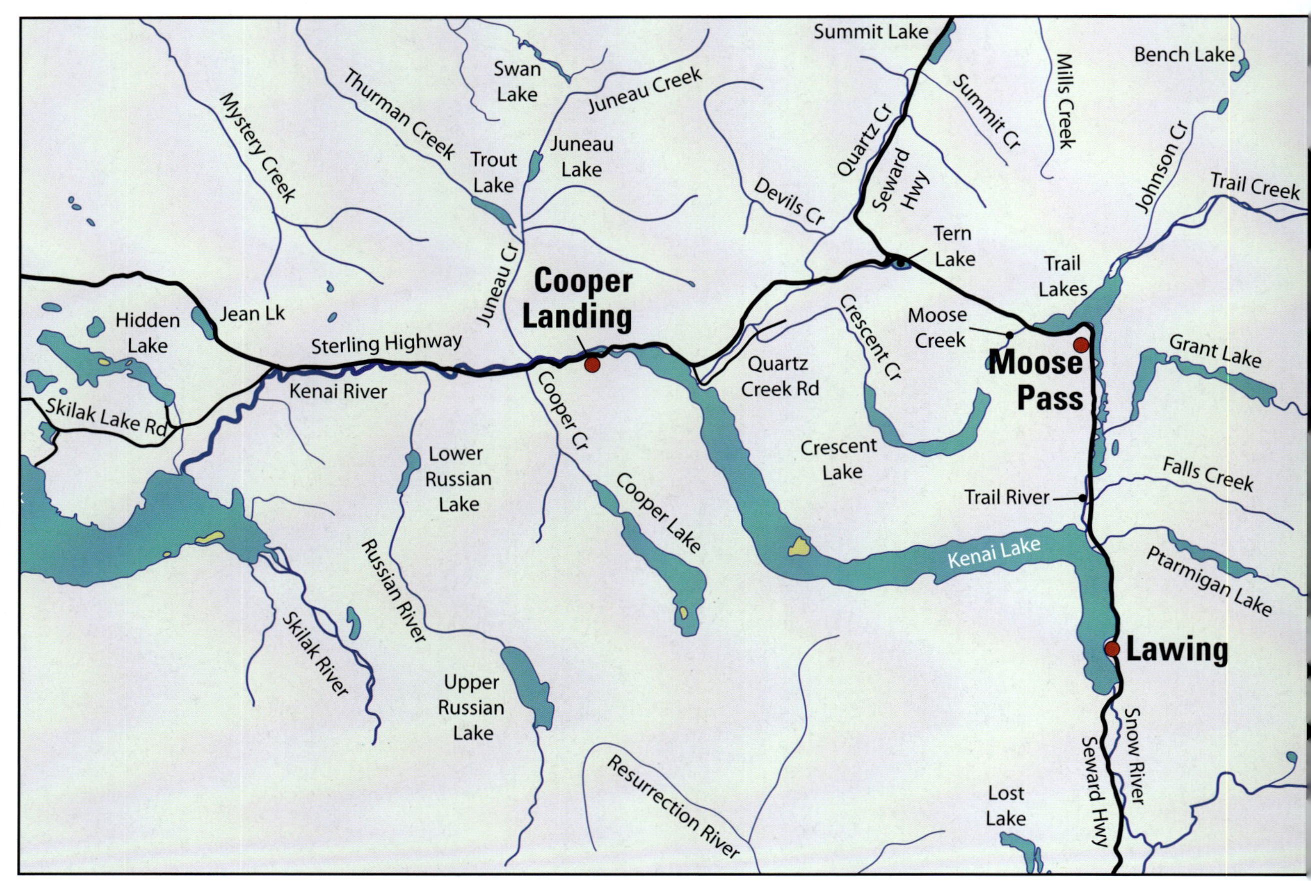


**Area Population Centers:** Cooper Landing, Moose Pass, Lawing
**Key Species:** Red and Silver Salmon, Rainbow Trout, Dolly Varden
**Other Species:** Pink and Chum Salmon, Lake Trout, Arctic Grayling, Round Whitefish, Burbot
**Main Destinations/Hot Spots:** Upper Kenai and Russian rivers
**Other Destinations:** Trail River & Lakes, Quartz and Ptarmigan creeks, Kenai, and Crescent lakes
**Additional Opportunities:** Fly-In Fishing, Trophy Trout & Char Fishing, Peninsula Trail System Lakes

**Summary of Area Fishing:** Central Peninsula has long enjoyed a reputation of being a top angling destination in Alaska as the waters teem with opportunities for those that enjoy wading as well as boating. Like areas to the northeast, the backdrop here consists of rugged mountains and forested valleys that are home to a great plethora of wildlife, which adds immeasurably to the fishing experience. Although Cooper Landing is the main center of angling activity, excellent catching remains at hand throughout the area, be it a glacial river for trophy trout, sight-fishing for salmon on a wading stream, or canoeing across a quiet mountain lake.

Indisputably, the top draw to the area are the multiple pulses of wild red and silver salmon destined for Kenai and Russian rivers in and around Cooper Landing, the former often arriving in waves of tens of thousands, providing fantastic action lasting for several weeks at the height of the runs. Reds and silvers both support two distinct runs.

Not to be outdone, the rainbows and Dollies here are exceptionally abundant even by Alaska standards and offer anglers the perfect opportunity to set personal records and, if luck and skill prevails, even state recognized trophies.

Wade and float fishing around here is among the best anywhere on the road system, the latter becoming an increasingly popular option for the do-it-yourself crowd.

Another aspect not often recognized are the numerous area trail systems taking anglers to clear mountain lakes and streams that support very healthy populations of trout, char, and even grayling – all in spectacular vistas. These trails make for a perfect compliment to any fishing excursion and are in and of themselves also prime main destinations. Bringing a small watercraft is the optimum way of exploring these waters although fishing off the bank is very possible as well.

The fishing in central peninsula drainages peak from June through October.

On the Kenai River since 1977.
Kenai River Trips
ALASKA WILDLAND ADVENTURES
16520 Sterling Hwy, MP 50.1 Cooper Landing, AK 99572
800.478.4100
www.alaskarivertrips.com/road

Kenai Riverside
CAMPGROUND
RV PARK
B&B ROOMS
RAFTING · FISHING
Kenai Riverside
CAMPGROUND & RV PARK

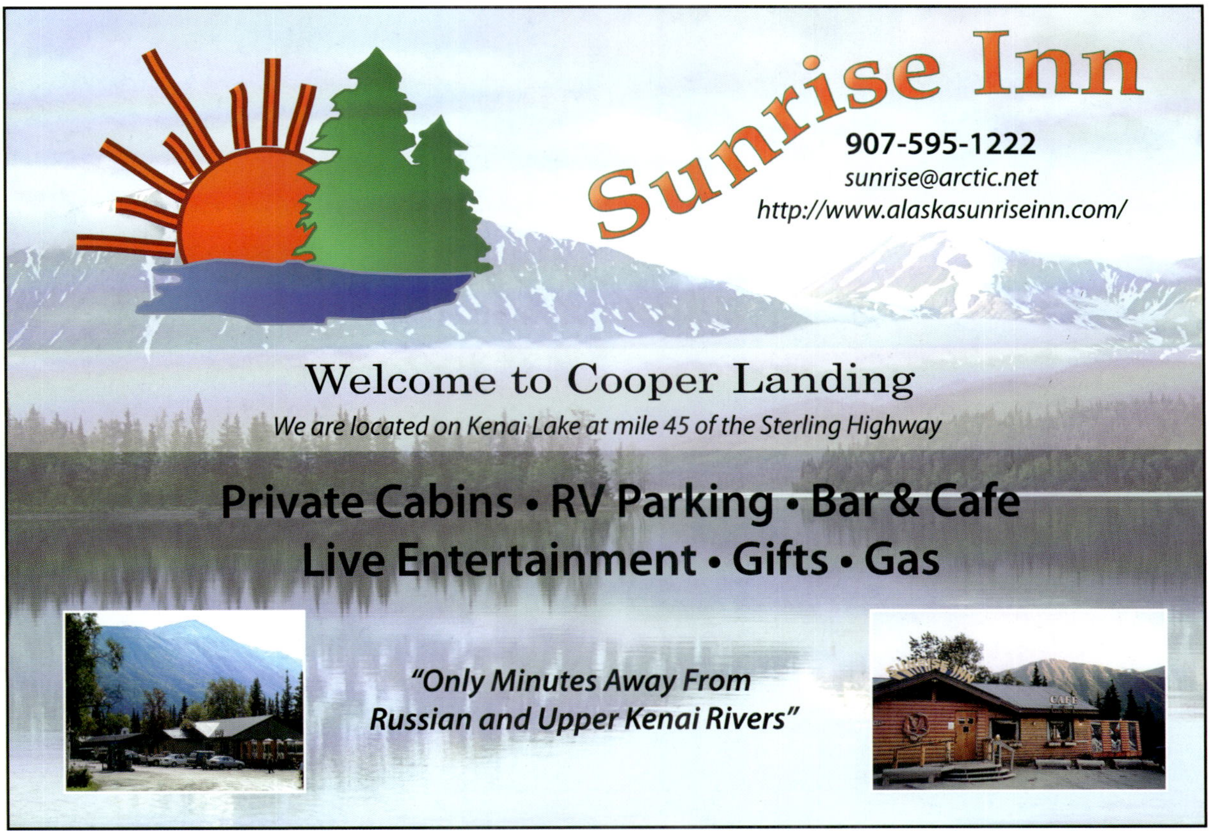

# *UPPER* Kenai River

Red
SALMON

Silver
SALMON

Rainbow
TROUT

Dolly
VARDEN

**Highlights:** Exceptional fly-fishing water for targeting rainbows and char, among the best in the state, with great opportunities for red and silver salmon. Abundant wildlife.

**Best Fishing:** Mid-June to late October. **Regulatory Restrictions:** Conservative.

**Location:** Central Kenai Peninsula drainage, Cooper Landing area, Sterling Highway, 100 miles south of Anchorage, 36 miles east of Soldotna.

**Description:** The stretch of Kenai River that runs between Kenai and Skilak lakes is popularly known as the Upper Kenai River, the glacial water displaying a very characteristic bluish-green or turquoise tint. From the Sterling Highway Bridge at the outlet of Kenai Lake in Cooper Landing downstream to the Skilak Lake inlet the distance is 17.3 river miles. The river flows through a valley carved amidst the Chugach Mountains, parts of which are situated in the Chugach National Forest and Kenai National Wildlife Refuge. Much of the land surrounding the Upper Kenai consists of spruce, cottonwood, and birch forests, making any excursion by trail into the river or a float downstream a sense of at least semi-wilderness.

As the Kenai pours out of Kenai Lake, the current is very slow and steady, the river wide and fairly deep in places. This continues until the "chute" at Fisherman's Bend (river mile 80.5), where the flow picks up speed and the river narrows. Class I water dominates most of the river (which makes it reasonably easy to navigate for a novice rafter/

boater) until the Kenai Canyon below Jim's Landing, where Class II and III water takes hold for two miles before the river slows down again the next three miles prior to dumping into Skilak Lake. Scouting the rapids is not necessary. The average stream gradient between the lakes is 13.9 feet per mile.

Water levels can fluctuate greatly, summer and fall flows often being several feet higher than what they are in winter and early spring. Prolonged periods of heavy rain or high temperatures can elevate river to near flood stage. Additionally, every three to four years the Upper Kenai is subject to flood waters from an ice dam near its headwaters.

Although vegetation can be quite dense along the river, there are a multitude of open spaces with gravel bars that are ideal for shore-bound anglers.

One unique aspect to the Upper Kenai is that it remains ice free throughout the winter, with open-water angling thus possible virtually all year long.

Wildlife such as bears, moose, waterfowl, and other animal species are a common sight along this stretch of river. Eagles can be spotted anytime during the year but perhaps particularly so during the winter and early spring months when the birds congregate to feed on late-spawning silver salmon.

**Facilities:** There are a multitude of facilities and services available along the Upper Kenai River, chiefly in Cooper Landing near the outlet of Kenai Lake. Both government and private campgrounds and boat launches exist along with RV parks, cabins, lodges, restaurants, tackle and gift shops, gas stations, grocery stores, and numerous guide outfits. Large commercial operators are present as well.

**Access:** Sterling Highway parallels almost the entire upper river section, from Milepost 47.7 to 58.0, crossing the river at Milepost 53.0. Foot access poses no immediate problems and most adjoining lands are public with the exception of the Cooper Landing area where private property is encountered. Trails in varying condition lead to and along the river from parking areas and campgrounds and there a few small pull-outs available as well. A cable ferry near the confluence of Kenai and Russian rivers (Milepost 54.9) provides, for a nominal fee, additional access to the southern shore of the river with trails upstream and down.

Boat access is contained to only a few locations with the majority of anglers either putting in at Kenai River Campground or Sportsman's Landing and floating downstream to Jim's Landing. Some boaters elect to continue the float through Kenai Canyon to Skilak Lake and motor across the lake to Upper Skilak Lake Campground for take-out. **Note:** Motorized boats not allowed on upper river.

Additionally, there are private campgrounds, RV villages, guide outfits, and lodges along the highway in Cooper Landing that allow clients bank access to the river.

**A. Kenai River Campground** – Milepost 47.7 Sterling Highway. Road crosses river at outlet of Kenai Lake. North on access road short distance to entrance to campground on right. Parking, camping, restrooms, and boat launch available. Boardwalk leads to river. **Note:** This is a closed riverbank area July 1 – August 15.

**B. Turnout** – Milepost 49.5 Sterling Highway. North to small parking area. River is adjacent to road and anglers can hike upstream or down for quite some distance. Some private property in area. **Note:** High water, such as during the summer months, may prevent access much beyond the immediate road access point.

**C. Cooper Creek Campground** – Milepost 50.7 Sterling Highway. North on road to campground. Developed parking, camping, and restrooms. Trails lead upstream and down along river.

**D. Turnout** – Milepost 53.1 Sterling Highway. North to parking area. Anglers can choose either to fish at road crossing by bridge or hike upstream about a quarter mile to a slough. The east bank of the river provides beach fishing and a good hole can be located a few hundred feet farther upstream.

*Float-fishing the Upper Kenai is extremely popular, particularly for trout and char. This is a perfect river for day trips.*

**E. Turnout** – Milepost 54.7 Sterling Highway. South at sign to small parking area and the river. This access point is located just upstream of the Russian River confluence (see page 125 for information). Main fishing is in channel at turnout.

**F. Sportsman's Landing** – Milepost 54.9 Sterling Highway. South on paved road to developed recreation area and

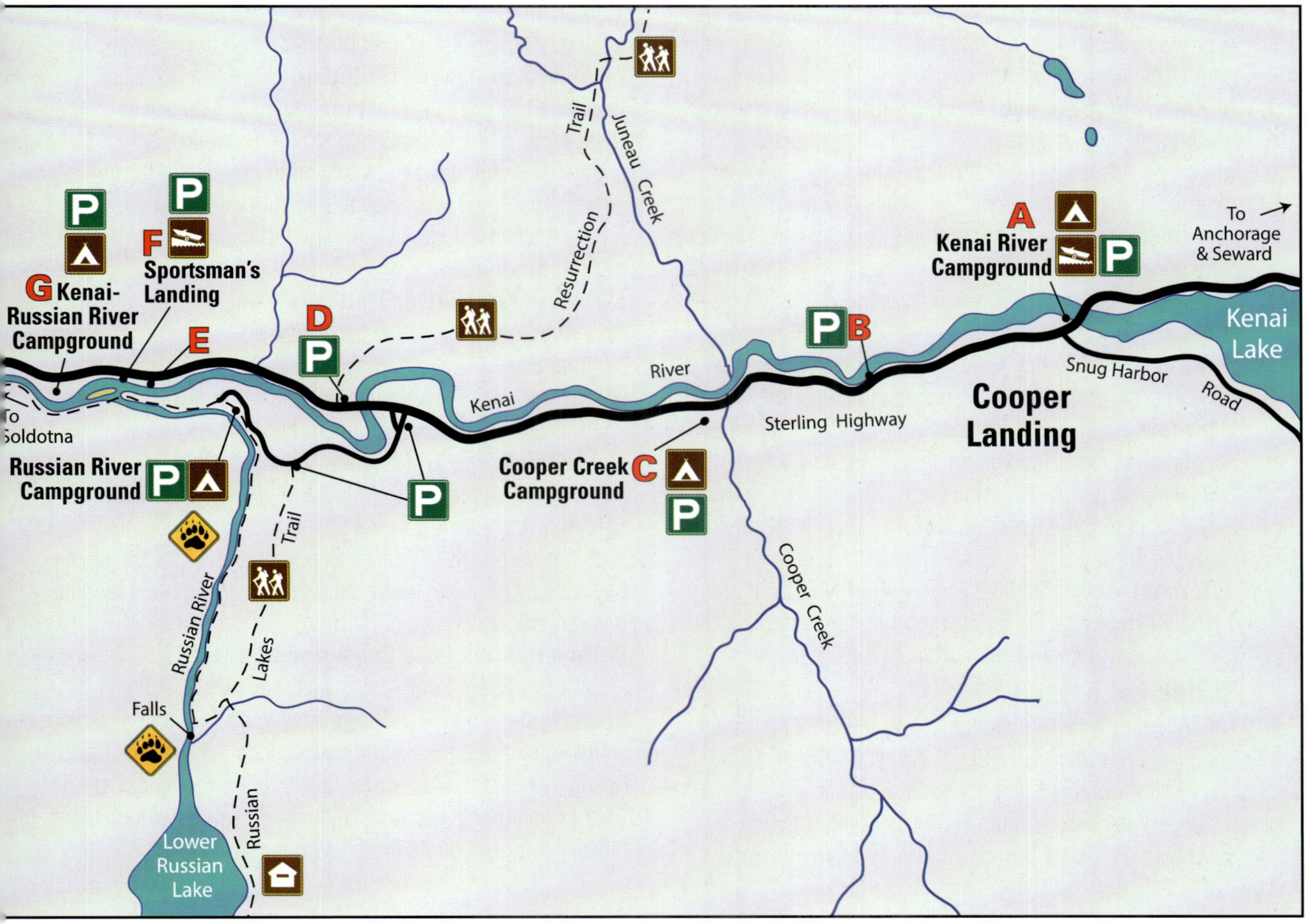

Trail
Juneau Creek
Resurrection
A Kenai River Campground
To Anchorage & Seward
Kenai Lake
F Sportsman's Landing
G Kenai-Russian River Campground
E
D
B
River
Kenai
Snug Harbor Road
Cooper Landing
Sterling Highway
To Soldotna
Russian River Campground
Cooper Creek C Campground
Trail
Russian River
Lakes
Cooper Creek
Falls
Russian
Lower Russian Lake

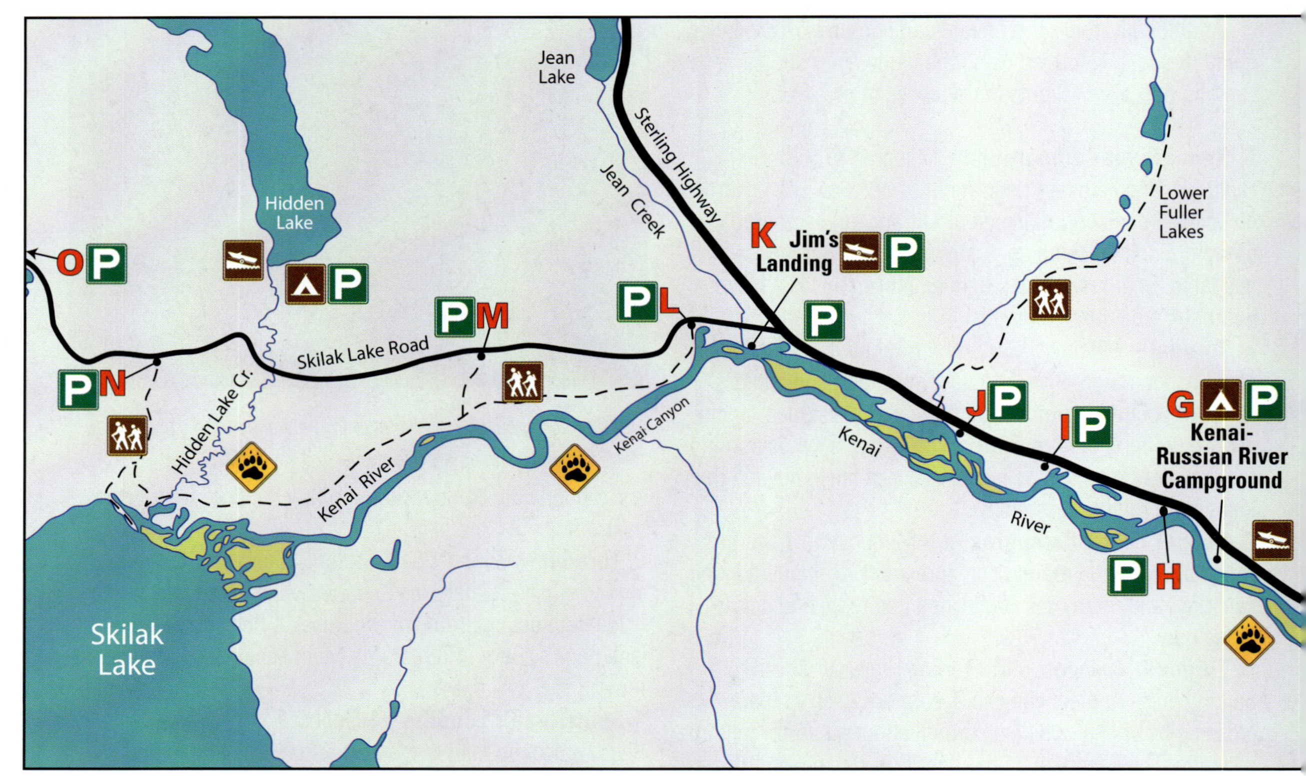


river. Parking, camping, restrooms, and boat launch. This is primarily a put-in/take-out spot for boaters with limited bank fishing available.

**G. Kenai-Russian River Campground** – Milepost 55.0 Sterling Highway. South on paved road short distance to recreation area and river. Developed parking, camping, restrooms, and boat launch. Trail leads downstream along river from campground. Additionally, anglers can take cable ferry across river and hike both upstream and down for two to three miles or more. This is also an access site to the mouth of Russian River.

**H. Turnout** – Milepost 55.5 Sterling Highway. South to parking area. Trails lead upstream and down along the river.

**I. Turnout** – Milepost 56.4 Sterling Highway. South to parking area. Trails lead along slough and through forest 200 yards to river and continue downstream approximately a quarter mile to beach area. **Note:** Trails can be very rough beyond slough.

**J. Turnout** – Milepost 56.9 Sterling Highway. South to paved parking area. Trails lead short distance to river and continue upstream and down along river.

## Skilak Lake Road

The following access points are located off Skilak Lake Road from the Sterling Highway (West Entrance, Mile Post 75.2/East Entrance, Milepost 58.0).

**K. Jim's Landing** – Milepost 58.0 Sterling Highway. Southwest on Skilak Lake Road short distance to access road on left and campground. Parking, camping, restrooms, and boat launch. Trails lead upstream and down along river.

**L. Upper Kenai River Trailhead** – Milepost 0.7 Skilak Lake Road. South at turnout to trailhead. Parking and restrooms. Trail leads 0.25 miles to river. Main trail continues south along river canyon to junction with trail coming from the Lower Kenai River Trailhead and provides further access to Skilak Lake inlet. Little actual river access along most of trail length.

**M. Lower Kenai River Trailhead** – Milepost 2.4 Skilak Lake Road. South at turnout to trailhead. Parking. Trail leads 0.3 mile to a "Y," take right fork 0.5 mile to river area. Trail parallels river next two miles with some undeveloped/improvised trails leading to riverbank.

**N. Hidden Creek Trailhead** – Milepost 4.7 Skilak Lake Road. South at turnout to trailhead. Parking. Trail leads 1.5 mile to a "Y," take left fork 0.5 mile to second juncture, keep left 0.75 mile to river. Trail parallels river for the next two miles with some undeveloped/improvised trails leading to riverbank.

**O. Upper Skilak Lake Campground** – Milepost 8.5 Skilak Lake Road. South on access road by sign 1.9 mile to campground and Skilak Lake. Developed parking and campground, restrooms, and boat launch. Motor from here heading east six miles across lake to inlet and mouth of Upper Kenai River. Locate trail leading upstream along river. **Note:** Motorized boats not allowed on upper river.

## Rules & Regulations

**Note:** *The Kenai River is the most heavily regulated drainage in the state and only a portion of the rules and regulations are listed here.*

**Open Season:** June 11 through May 1, except for the Russian River sanctuary area where the season is July 15 through May 1.
**Open Area:** The entire upper river is open to fishing.
**Legal Gear/Tackle:** Only one unbaited, single-hook, artificial lure is allowed year-round. Gap between point and shank must be less than 3/8 inch.

### Silver Salmon

- Open season is July 1 through October 31.
- Bag limit is (2) per day and (2) in possession (16 inches or longer) from July 1 through August 31; and (3) per day and (3) in possession from September 1 through October 31. For salmon less than 16 inches (Jacks), the limit is (10).

### All Other Salmon

- King salmon fishing is closed year-round.
- Red, pink, and chum salmon open all season (see general "Open Season" above).
- Red and chum salmon bag limit is (3) per day and (3) in possession (16 inches or longer), and pink salmon (6) per day and (6) in possession. For salmon less than 16 inches (Jacks), the limit is (10).

### Rainbow/Steelhead Trout & Dolly Varden

- Open all season (see general "Open Season" above).
- Bag limit is (1) per day and (1) in possession for each species.
- Retained fish must be less than 16 inches long for each species.

### Other Fishes

- Open all season (see general "Open Season" above).
- Arctic grayling bag limit is (5) per day and (5) in possession, any size.
- Whitefish has no bag or possession limit, no size restrictions.

## Fishing Upper Kenai River

**Access:** ★★★★★ **Sight Fishing:** ★★
**Scenery:** ★★★★★ **Bank/Wading:** ★★★★
**Wildlife:** ★★★★ **Boat/Floating:** ★★★★★

**Species:** Red and silver salmon, rainbow trout, and Dolly Varden. Other species present include king, pink, and chum salmon, arctic grayling, and whitefish.

**Summary:** The Upper Kenai River is a top-notch fishery that attracts anglers from around the world. Ease of access, splendid scenery, abundant wildlife, a variety of services, and great fishing all help contribute to the reputation of being one of the most popular angling destinations in the entire state. Although many different types of tackle and techniques are employed, the vast majority of anglers prefer fly-fishing as the river and its species lends perfectly to the utilization of this type of gear.

With the Sterling Highway paralleling much of the river, foot access is easy and abundant. Many anglers, however, prefer to use rafts and drift boats to thoroughly enjoy the ample opportunities available.

The river receives phenomenal runs of salmon accompanied with large populations of trout, char, and other lesser-known resident species. Although all five salmon species are represented to one degree or another, reds are most abundant followed by silvers. Upper Kenai does contain a good number of kings but these fish are currently closed to sport fishing. All three of these species are also represented in two main populations each, defined as early and late runs.

Red salmon are present in two distinct runs, each lasting about two to three weeks. The early run in June consists mainly of fish bound for the Russian River drainage while the late run in July and August is made up of both mainstem Kenai and tributary salmon and is the larger of the two runs. They are usually targeted from gravel bars and in more shallow river channels as they proceed upstream in schools of fish ranging from just a few individuals to bands of salmon consisting of hundreds to even thousands of specimens.

(Courtesy Roy & Beverley Bailey)

Silver salmon, like reds, are available in two distinct runs. The first – or early – run moves through in August and September while the second – or late – run occurs in October and November. The early silvers are bound for tributaries of the Kenai, including Russian River, while the late-running salmon are primarily of mainstem origin. Exceptional silvers weighing into the mid-20s have been reported in late fall. A winter pulse of coho streams through during the winter months (December into March), bound for spawning grounds at the outlet of Kenai Lake. Currently protected by law, these unique salmon are often encountered by anglers fishing for trout and char.

King salmon also appear in two runs, the early component being present in June and July (tributary fish) and the late one from July into September (mainstem Kenai fish). These huge fish (some of which may weigh up to 80-90 pounds or more) are frequently observed migrating through or spawning in the river. Fishing

*Although a relatively large river, the Kenai has an abundance of areas in which to successfully fish from the bank, like this spot near the Russian River confluence. Despite the river flowing a little off-color, sight fishing for salmon can be very exciting and rewarding.*

for them is prohibited.

Smaller runs of pink and chum salmon come through starting in July and continuing into September, the latter a relatively rare species bound for spawning grounds in Kenai Lake tributaries. Neither species has any sporting value on the Upper Kenai due to low abundance and fish being in or near spawning condition.

The crown glory for many anglers on the Upper Kenai, however, is the late summer and fall fly-fishing season targeting rainbows and Dolly Varden. The river hosts a massive population of these game species, particularly trout, and the action can be nothing short of stupendous at times with some highly skilled Kenai veterans claiming triple-digit days at the peak of the feeding binge in August and September. The majority of anglers use beads along with strike indicators.

This is mainly a catch-and-release fishery (although a one-fish under 16 inches limit is allowed by regulation), and anglers spending a few days on the river in late summer and fall stand a reasonable chance to land at least one fish in the 30-inch range. In fact, trout and char between 20 and 25 inches are considered abundant and the opportunity to hook into a native, trophy Kenai-class rainbow of more than 20 pounds always a possibility (see page 158 for more information).

The Upper Kenai also supports a long open-water season as the mainstem very rarely freezes over and regulations allow anglers access continuously from early summer into spring, only closing during the period of May and early June to protect spawning rainbow trout.

## Fish Availability

● = High ● = Moderate ● = Low ● = Closed

| *Species* | *MAY* | *JUN* | *JUL* | *AUG* | *SEP* | *OCT* | *NOV* |
|---|---|---|---|---|---|---|---|
| **Red Salmon** | Closed, Closed | Closed, Moderate, High, High | Moderate, Moderate, High, High | High, Moderate, Low, Low | Low, Low, Low, Low | Low | |
| **Silver Salmon** | | | Low, Low | Low, Moderate, High, High | High, Moderate, Low, Moderate | High, High, High, High | Closed, Closed, Closed, Closed |
| **Rainbow Trout** | Closed, Closed, Closed, Closed | Closed, High, High, High | High, High, High, High | High, High, High, High | High, High, High, High | High, High, Moderate, Moderate | Moderate, Moderate, Moderate, Moderate |
| **Dolly Varden** | Closed, Closed, Closed, Closed | Closed, Low, Low, Low | Moderate, Moderate, Moderate, High | High, High, High, High | High, High, High, High | High, High, Moderate, Moderate | Moderate, Moderate, Moderate, Moderate |
| **Whitefish** | Closed, Closed, Closed, Closed | Closed, Low, Low, Low | Moderate, Moderate, Moderate, Moderate | Moderate, Moderate, Moderate, Moderate | Moderate, Moderate, Moderate, Moderate | Moderate, Moderate, Moderate, Moderate | Low, Low, Low, Low |
| Angling Pressure | | High, High, High | High, Moderate, High, High | High, High, High, High | High, High, High, High | Moderate, Moderate, Moderate, Moderate | Low, Low, Low, Low |

(Courtesy Mystic Water Fly-Fishing)

*An angler displays a large male sockeye in full nuptial coloration. The Upper Kenai has an abundance of water ideal for catching these acrobatic salmon.*

### Red Salmon

**Rating:** ★★★★ Good to excellent (early run) to excellent (late run).

**Season:** June 11 through May 1. Additional seasonal restrictions are in effect for the Russian River area.

**Timing:** June 11 – October 5; peak June 15 – 25 (early run) and July 25 – August 5 (late run).

**Size:** Average 6 – 7 pounds, up to 12 pounds (early run); 4 – 8 pounds, up to 14 pounds (late run).

**Tackle:** Flies.

**Tips:** Salmon usually travel within four to ten feet of shore and can often be observed moving through the shallows in dense schools by anglers wearing Polaroid glasses. Water about two to four feet deep is ideal for finding salmon. Blushed reds typically swim closer to shore than bright ones. The best fishing can be had in the section of water downstream of the mouth of Russian River to Skilak Lake. From the Russian confluence upstream to Kenai Lake, the fishing is typically fair to good at best and the season tends to be more abbreviated, with more blushed salmon than elsewhere on the river.

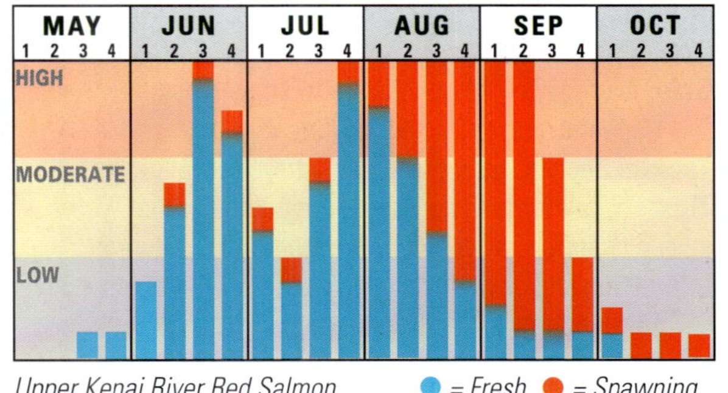


*Upper Kenai River Red Salmon.* ● = Fresh ● = Spawning

There are numerous flies that are effective, one of the most popular being the Coho streamer, but other patterns may work just as well if not even better. Generally the darker or neutral hues (blue, green, black, brown, purple, white) are good on sunny days or if the river runs slightly clear; sharply colored and fluorescent (red, orange, pink, yellow) flies tend to do well on cloudy/rainy days, at dawn and dusk, or if the water is somewhat turbid. Yarn flies work great.

*(Courtesy Eagle Eye Images)*

*A typical late-run October coho, fooled by a #4 spinner buzzed through a slackwater section of river. Dense numbers of fish and a lack of crowds ensure prospecting anglers of fast action in relative solitude. Most any hole or slough will produce fish.*

## Silver Salmon

**Rating:** ★★★½ Good (early run) to excellent (late run).
**Season:** July 1 through October 31. Additional seasonal restrictions are in effect for the Russian River area.
**Timing:** July 20 – October 31; peak August 15 – September 5 (early run) and October 1 – 31 (late run).
**Size:** Average 5 – 10 pounds, up to 15 pounds (early run); 6 – 15 pounds, up to 22 pounds (late run).
**Tackle:** Spoons, spinners, plugs, attractors, and flies.
**Tips:** Focus efforts in areas just upstream of quiet water, in side channels, at or below the mouth of clearwater tributaries, and downstream of islands. Water about three to four feet deep is ideal for locating migrating silvers in late summer. Although early run fish are fixated on holding structure near shore, late run salmon tend to run deeper and can be found most anywhere across the main river current providing water conditions are correct. The mouth of sloughs and quiet water on the inside of river bends are perfect holding areas in late fall.

Action for early-run silvers seems to be most intense from the mouth of Russian River downstream to Skilak Lake. It is less productive between Kenai Lake and the Russian River confluence. Various attractor and forage pattern flies, but also spinners, are in clear favor. The late run offers opportunities throughout the length of the river at the peak of the run, preferring flashy spinners and attractor flies.

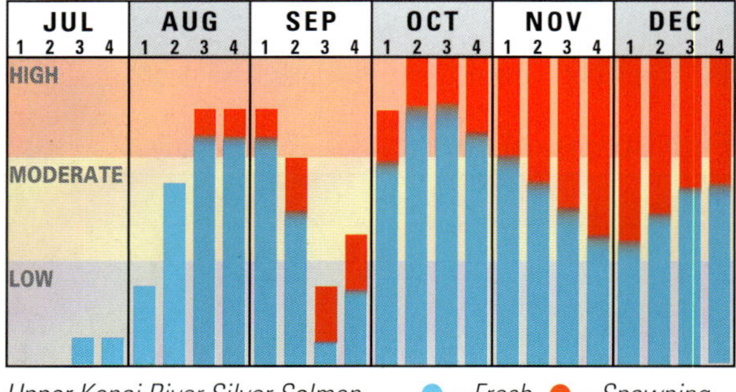


*Upper Kenai River Silver Salmon* ● = *Fresh* ● = *Spawning*

## Rainbow Trout

**Rating:** ★★★★★ Excellent.
**Season:** June 11 through May 1. Additional seasonal restrictions are in effect for the Russian River area.
**Timing:** June 11 – May 1; peak July 25 – October 15.
**Size:** Average 10 – 20 inches, up to 35 inches (20 pounds).
**Tackle:** Spinners, plugs, attractors, and flies.
**Tips:** Almost exclusively a fly-fishing experience. Early in the season (spring/early summer) smolt and forage

*Anglers admire a husky 35-inch autumn rainbow trout before release, estimated to have weighed between 20 and 25 pounds. Fish of this caliber are landed every season.*

*(Courtesy Mystic Waters Fly-Fishing)*

(Courtesy Beverley Bailey)

*An upper river char about to be released after careful admiration. Although rainbow trout may be king on this section of the Kenai, a very healthy population of Dolly Varden is present to add excitement to any trip.*

imitation flies are best, followed by egg imitations in late summer and fall. Most successful anglers on the river use a variety of beads along with strike indicators. Flesh and forage patterns are especially productive starting the latter part of September and on into winter as salmon die off. In areas near Kenai Lake where trout can be found even throughout the winter months feeding on a late run of silver salmon, egg and flesh imitations are good.

The larger catches are usually made in late summer and fall during and after the seasonal feeding binge with 30-inch trophies weighing 12 pounds or more possible. Several rainbows up to 15 pounds are landed every season and ultimate trophy specimens to 25 pounds have been caught.

The mouth of Russian River downstream to Skilak Lake inlet, including Kenai Canyon, is the hot section of water. From the outlet of Kenai Lake to the Russian River confluence, the fishing is typically slightly more subdued.

## Dolly Varden

**Rating:** ★★★★ Excellent.
**Season:** June 11 through May 1. Additional seasonal restrictions are in effect for the Russian River area.
**Timing:** June 11 – May 1; peak July 25 – October 15.
**Size:** Average 10 – 20 inches, up to 30 inches (10-12 pounds).
**Tackle:** Spinners, plugs, attractors, and flies.
**Tips:** The best area is from the mouth of Russian River downstream to Skilak Lake, yet can be productive most anywhere along the river pending food sources are available. Prior to the arrival of salmon, smolt and forage pattern flies and small silvery spoons and spinners take fish. When salmon are present, egg imitation flies and beads are the rule for consistent catches. In fall as salmon begin to die off, try flesh imitations. Forage patterns also work well this time of year and will continue to produce fish through fall and winter. Near the outlet of Kenai Lake, egg and flesh imitations, as well as nymphs, work well during the winter and spring months.

The larger specimens – to 30 inches or more – are most commonly seen later in the season (August to October) with many char exceeding 24 inches and five pounds. Trophy catches of 15 pounds-plus are reported every year with specimens in the 18-pound range possible.

*A very scenic autumn view of where the upper Kenai flows into Skilak Lake, a popular spot with the drift boat and hike-in crowd. This location not only offers spectacular trout fishing in gorgeous vistas, but action for red and silver salmon can be no less than incredible as well.*

(Courtesy Mystic Waters Fly-Fishing)

## Other Upper Kenai Opportunities

### Trophy Trout & Char Fishing

The Upper Kenai River is legendary in providing outstanding opportunities for trophy-sized rainbow trout and Dolly Varden, and it is a fact that these fish are among the biggest not only in Alaska but North America. Additionally, there are large numbers of these species available and the action can be outstanding as red salmon begin to spawn in August and September. Egg and flesh imitation flies (and beads) are the ticket as trout and char gorge themselves on free-floating salmon eggs and pieces of decomposing salmon flesh. The average angler can expect to catch about a dozen or so fish during the course of a day with skilled anglers routinely landing 30 to 50 or more fish at the height of the feeding period.

Rainbow trout commonly reach a length of 25 inches (5-6 pounds) and specimens over 30 inches are taken with regularity. During the peak of activity in September and early October, expect to see a few hogs in the 32- to 36-inch range and up to 20 pounds or more. Late-season trout are loaded with food, often appearing disproportionately round, almost football shaped.

Dolly Varden, equally with rainbows, tend to run on the heavy side on the Kenai. Char to 25 inches are not uncommon with a few fish exceeding 30 inches (10-12 pounds) a possibility. Again, September and early October are the best times to catch trophy Dollies as the fish are bloated from the abundant feed. Occasional catches in the mid-30s range and up to 18 pounds.

### Float Fishing the Upper Kenai

For a growing number of anglers it has become a popular trend to float the river instead of hiking in from one of the numerous roadside access sites. Developed boat launches are present in three different locations on the river to ensure maximum enjoyment for those wishing to sample as much water (and fishing) as possible. Depending on how much time an angler would like to be on the water, these access points are perfectly spaced as to provide for half-day as well as full-day trips with an abundance of fishing time.

For all practical purposes, the upper Kenai can be divided into three separate sections, each offering a variety of water conditions and types of fishing. The first is the stretch of river from the outlet of Kenai Lake (Kenai River Campground) downstream to the Russian River confluence (Sportman's Landing), a relatively mild and easy float that has plenty of slackwater with some areas of Class II conditions. Fishing can be very good but generally not as hectic as lower down on the river. Also, lesser number of anglers float this section compared to the next.

(Courtesy Mystic Waters Fly-Fishing)

The second portion is from the Russian confluence area (Sportman's Landing) downstream to Jim's Landing off Skilak Lake Road, the last take-out point on the river that is readily road accessible. This is by far the most popular stretch of the river and reputed to hold the best salmon and trout action. Expect Class I and II water. Wildlife viewing is excellent with sightings of bear, moose, and eagles commonplace.

The final portion is that stretch of water from Jim's Landing to the inlet of Skilak Lake, taking the angler through Kenai Canyon, a Class III set of rapids that can be negotiated without concern by most skill levels. Scouting the rapids is not necessary. As there is no take-out point at the inlet, floaters must negotiate a section of Skilak Lake to the Upper Skilak Lake Campground via Skilak Lake Road, a trip of several miles. Wise floaters that do this leg always bring a small outboard to complete the journey across the lake part as rowing would take hours. Fishing can be outstanding for all available species.

(Courtesy Alaska Clearwater Sportfishing)

*A drift boat works its way through Kenai Canyon on a blue-bird autumn day. Fishing this stretch of the river can be legendary.*

*Two fishermen enjoy the calm off-season peace swinging flesh flies at the outlet of Kenai Lake where the Kenai River commences. Even if the fishing is on the slow side, the magnificent scenery of the snow-clad Kenai Mountains and the potential for catching a nice trout in mid-winter is all worth it.*

## Fishing the Kenai in Winter

Although most are certainly familiar with the great summer and fall angling for salmon, trout, and char, few know that the Upper Kenai is a great winter fishery as well, at least relatively speaking. While the vast majority of rivers and streams in Southcentral Alaska are frozen over during the long, cold winter months, the Upper Kenai has the distinction of flowing mostly ice free – barring any extended periods of bitter chill (10 to 20 below) – and supporting a viable and welcome opportunity for rainbows and dollies.

In an average year, anglers are able to launch drift boats at the outlet of Kenai Lake and float downstream to either Sportman's Landing or Jim's Landing, the former stretch being most popular in winter as that is where fish concentrations are highest. However, quite a few anglers also park along the highway where turnouts are available and hike in to the river through the snow.

The trout and char are not in the river by accident; they are simply following a major food source – spawning silver salmon. Kenai River is very unique (by Alaska standards) in hosting migratory salmon on any given day of the year, even the coldest winter days. A population of winter-run coho is present on the Upper Kenai throughout the dark months and even into early spring (April), providing plenty of much-needed protein for the river's resident fish.

Successful winter anglers use a variety of offerings to entice a strike, yet beads in various colors, flesh flies, and big, black leech patterns are most popular. In addition, starting in April, chromomid imitations become a hot item.

A good place to fish is the portion of water from the lake outlet and approximately 3-4 miles downstream as this is a major spawning area for salmon during the January to March time frame. Although action can be excellent, the usual catch for a day of fishing is perhaps two or three fish, maybe more depending on skill level and experience. The majority of fish caught are generally in the 15- to 22-inch range with occasional lunkers to 30 inches or more.

While the Kenai is closed to silver fishing in winter and spring (including catch-and-release), the likelihood of tagging one of these unique salmon is high as they share space with the river's trout and char. The number of silvers present can be almost staggering at times in certain spots and hooking up practically unavoidable. Expect to release a fair number of spawners, including a few that may still be dime bright as late as March in some years.

With the advent of spring (April), anglers focusing on the lake outlet using smolt patterns enjoy potential good catch rates for trout as they feed actively on outmigrating juvenile salmon. This is also the time of year when oversized rainbows begin to stage in anticipation of their spawning migration.

Another window of opportunity is the November fishery targeting lake trout, also situated at the Kenai Lake outlet. There are typically not a lot of fish present and the size of the fish only averaging three to five pounds. Successful anglers use baitfish imitation spoons and flies. Some bigger char may be present around the powerplant dam off Snug Harbor Road.

Professional Guided Fishing Trips • Scenic Rafting • Tackle & Fly-Shop
Fish Processing & Freezing • Shuttle Service • Lodging
Kenai Cache Outfitters
TACKLE & GUIDING
Outfitting Fishermen for over 28 years
Kenai River Russian River
HEADQUARTERS
(907) 595-1401
Lamiglas
St. Croix
Abu Garcia

# Russian River

Red SALMON

Silver SALMON

Rainbow TROUT

Dolly VARDEN

**Highlights:** One of the world's best fly-fisheries for red salmon combined with excellent opportunities for rainbow trout in a semi-wilderness setting. Great sight-fishing water.

**Best Fishing:** Mid-June to mid-September. **Regulatory Restrictions:** Very conservative.

**Location:** Central Kenai Peninsula drainage, Cooper Landing area, Sterling Highway, 110 miles south of Anchorage, 39 miles east of Soldotna.

**Description:** The Russian River is one of the most renowned fishing hot spots in all of Alaska, endowed with gorgeous mountain and deep forest scenery, a clearwater drainage teeming with salmon and trout, easy access, and abundant wildlife. Draining out of Upper Russian Lake, the river flows through a wilderness area with no human activity to Lower Russian Lake. At the outlet of this lake is a set of falls and rapids that fish must negotiate, making for excellent photo opportunities of jumping salmon with the added possibility of seeing bears catching their meal out of the river.

Russian continues another few miles north until it joins with the glacial Upper Kenai River, one of the most popular and productive salmon fisheries in the state. It is near this confluence that Russian River Campground is situated.

Despite heavy rains or snow runoff, the Russian is always dependable for anglers as it flows clear and free of debris, largely due to the Russian lakes serving as buffers for any flooding.

*The Russian River Ferry operates from the Kenai-Russian River Campground, taking anglers from the highway side of the river across to the confluence area of the two waters. At peak of runs, expect crowds.*

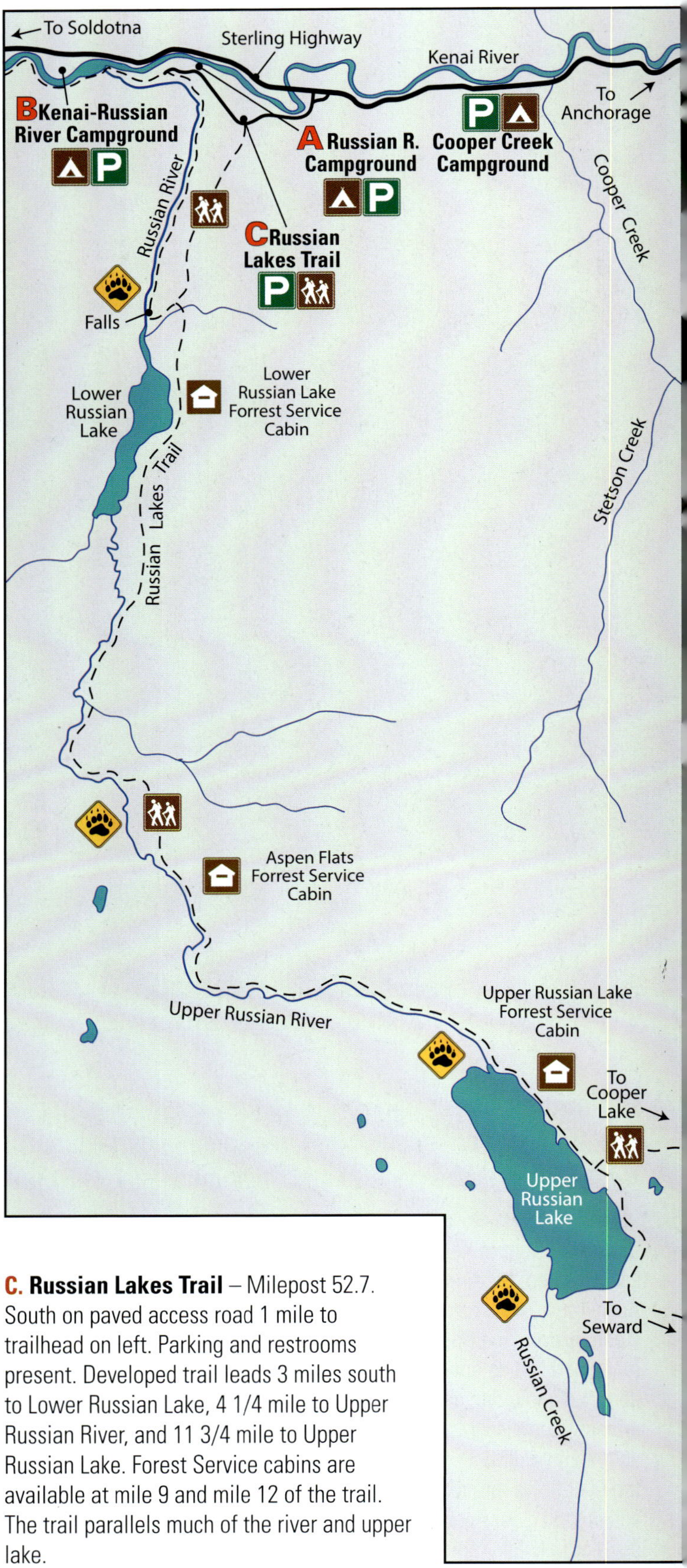

The lower section of river by the campground has become an attraction of sorts not only to anglers but also photographers and wildlife viewers alike as good numbers of both black and brown bears roam the shoreline looking for an easy meal of salmon.

**Facilities:** Developed campgrounds, parking, and restrooms available at or immediately near river. Apart from the campgrounds listed below, within minutes is Cooper Creek Campground at Milepost 50.5. Other facilities and services are available in nearby community of Cooper Landing, including lodging, cabins, motels/hotels, guide services, laundromats, grocery stores, tackle shops, gas stations, and fish processors.

**Access:** There are two points of access from the Sterling Highway; one heading to the USFS campground on the main Russian, the other near the mouth on Upper Kenai.

**A. Russian River Campground** – Milepost 52.7. South on paved access road 1.4 miles to campground. Developed parking, camping, and restrooms with several trails leading to and along river.

**B. Kenai-Russian River Campground** – Milepost 54.9. South on paved road by sign 0.1 miles to campground. Take ferry across Kenai River to confluence area and Russian River.

To Soldotna
Sterling Highway
Kenai River
To Anchorage
B Kenai-Russian River Campground
A Russian R. Campground
Cooper Creek Campground
C Russian Lakes Trail
Russian River
Cooper Creek
Falls
Lower Russian Lake
Lower Russian Lake Forrest Service Cabin
Russian Lakes Trail
Stetson Creek
Aspen Flats Forrest Service Cabin
Upper Russian River
Upper Russian Lake Forrest Service Cabin
To Cooper Lake
Upper Russian Lake
To Seward
Russian Creek

**C. Russian Lakes Trail** – Milepost 52.7. South on paved access road 1 mile to trailhead on left. Parking and restrooms present. Developed trail leads 3 miles south to Lower Russian Lake, 4 1/4 mile to Upper Russian River, and 11 3/4 mile to Upper Russian Lake. Forest Service cabins are available at mile 9 and mile 12 of the trail. The trail parallels much of the river and upper lake.

## Rules & Regulations

**Note:** *The Russian River is one of the most heavily regulated drainages in the state and only a portion of the rules and regulations are listed here.*

**Open Season:** June 11 through May 1, except the "sanctuary" area (Kenai-Russian confluence) where the season is July 15 through May 1. Upper and Lower Russian lakes are open to fishing year-round.
**Open Area:** The entire river is open to fishing.
**Legal Gear/Tackle:** Only one unbaited, single-hook, artificial lure is allowed in entire drainage. The lower river, from a marker below the Russian River Falls to just above the sanctuary, is a fly-fishing-only area from June 11 through August 20. Gap between point and shank must be less than 3/8 inch.

**King Salmon**
- Closed to fishing year-round, including catch-and-release.

**Red Salmon**
- Open season in main river is June 11 through August 20.
- Open season in sanctuary is July 15 through August 20.
- Bag limit is (3) per day and (3) in possession (16 inches or longer). For salmon less than 16 inches (Jacks), the limit is (10).

**Pink & Chum Salmon**
- Open all season (see general "Open Season" above).
- Pink salmon bag limit is (6) per day and (6) in possession (16 inches or longer).
- Chum salmon bag limit is (3) per day and (3) in possession (16 inches or longer).
- For salmon less than 16 inches (Jacks), the limit is (10).

**Silver Salmon**
- Open season in main river is July 1 through Sept. 30.
- Open season in sanctuary is July 15 through October 31.
- Bag limit is (1) per day and (1) in possession (16 inches or longer). For salmon less than 16 inches (Jacks), the limit is (10).

**Rainbow/Steelhead Trout & Dolly Varden**
- Open all season (see general "Open Season" above).
- In main river, bag limit is (1) per day and (1) in possession for each species.
- In main river, retained fish must be less than 16 inches long for each species.
- In Upper and Lower Russian lakes, bag limit is (2) per day and (2) in possession, of which only (1) may be 20 inches or longer.

**Other Fishes**
- Open all season (see general "Open Season" above).
- Arctic grayling bag limit is (5) per day and (5) in possession, any size.
- Whitefish has no bag or possession limit, no size restrictions.

## Fishing Russian River

**Access:** ★★★★ **Sight Fishing:** ★★★★★
**Scenery:** ★★★★ **Bank/Wading:** ★★★★★
**Wildlife:** ★★★★ **Boat/Floating: N/A**

**Species:** Red and silver salmon, rainbow trout, and Dolly Varden. A very small run of king salmon is present in July and August. A few arctic grayling are caught every summer. Chum salmon and round whitefish have been reported but are extremely rare.

**Summary:** The Russian River is arguably one of the best spots anywhere to fish for red salmon. An abundance of fish, often numbering 100,000 or more, swarm the clear and relatively shallow river almost continuously from early summer into fall. Superb action can be experienced with dozens of hookups not only possible but at the height of the two runs actually predictable. A smaller run of silver salmon follows but in no terms offer any less excitement and fly-fishing for rainbow trout can be exceptional throughout the summer into early fall.

The Russian River is a fly-fishing only stream during the entire red salmon season (mid-June to late August) with other types of tackle allowed earlier and later in the year. While salmon fishing is only allowed on the lower river section, resident species may be targeted in all reaches of water, including Upper and Lower Russian Lakes.

Two distinct runs of red salmon move through the Russian. The first run is chiefly present in June and bound for spawning tributaries of Upper Russian Lake, the second in July and August comprises mainstem Russian River and lower Russian Lake fish. On the lower river, September marks the time when the river is flooded with spawning reds and a novelty in viewing.

Silver salmon, although not nearly as abundant as reds, move upstream just as the late red run begins the spawn. Anglers skilled at sight-fishing can experience excellent fishing as individual fish as well as small schools are easily spotted and targeted in the clear Russian.

If water levels are high due to a late spring or heavy snows (as sometimes is the case during the early red run), schools of salmon move into the Russian all day long and can be targeted without difficulty. The run during such conditions can be abbreviated as fish escape upstream to the lakes. Very low water, however, has an opposite effect and prevents or slows down upstream migration from the Kenai confluence. Fish will hold at the mouth for days to even weeks, only moving upstream at night or right after

*An angler scouts for schools of chrome sockeye salmon working their way through the shallows. Low and clear water conditions mean superb sight-fishing opportunities; dark or neutral colored streamer flies in purple or black are perfect.*

*(Courtesy Eagle Eye Images)*

a rainfall. During such conditions, be on the river at dawn in order to intercept schools of reds and silvers heading upstream.

Fishing for trout and char can be exceptional with flyfishers responsible for the majority of catches. Some of the bigger rainbows are traditionally caught early in the season (June) as big fish left from the spring spawn have yet to vacate the river. It has been noted that a few of these specimens may weigh well into the teens. The char, however, are more common later in season as the late run of red salmon enters the Russian.

The upper section of river, between the lakes, provide a great destination for those wanting to get away from the salmon crowds of the lower Russian. Fishing here is generally very good for rainbow trout and Dolly Varden during the late summer and early fall months and anglers willing to hike the few miles by trail are sure not to be disappointed. In addition, anglers will find decent action in area lakes, most notably Upper Russian Lake.

The bear density on the Russian is well known with multiple sightings commonplace during a day of fishing. Animals may approach at close proximity. Be cautious.

## Fish Availability

● = High ● = Moderate ● = Low ● = Closed (H = High, M = Moderate, L = Low, C = Closed)

| *Species* | *MAY* | *JUN* | *JUL* | *AUG* | *SEP* | *OCT* | *NOV* |
|---|---|---|---|---|---|---|---|
| **Red Salmon** | C | C M H H | H M M H | H H M C | C C C C | | |
| **Silver Salmon** | | | L | L M M H | H H M L | L L | |
| **Rainbow Trout** | C C C C | C H H H | H H H H | H H H H | H M M M | L L L L | L L L L |
| **Dolly Varden** | C C C C | C L L L | L L L M | M M H H | H H M M | M L L L | L L L L |
| Angling Pressure | | H H H | H M M H | H H H H | H M M L | L L | |

## Red Salmon

**Rating:** ★★★★★ Excellent.
**Season:** June 11 through August 20.
**Timing:** June 11 – August 20; peak June 15 – 25 (early run) and July 25 – August 15 (late run).
**Size:** Average 5 – 7 pounds, up to 11 pounds (early run); 4 – 10 pounds, up to 12 pounds (late run).
**Tackle:** Flies.
**Tips:** In low-water years, however, the action in the Russian proper may be subdued because of low numbers of fish moving up from the Kenai River confluence and successful anglers either fish the very early morning hours or hike down to the mouth.

Since the water in the Russian is so clear, darker flies seem to work the best. Black, green, purple, and blue are good. Egg imitations can also be very good and fish will sometimes actually strike the offering. Some anglers prefer sharper colors in order to see the fly in the water to more effectively line fish in the mouth.

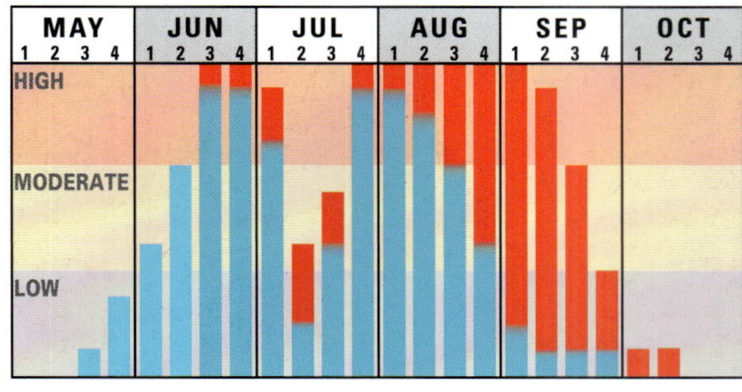


*Russian River Red Salmon.* ● = *Fresh* ● = *Spawning*

*Early-run reds generally appear big and bright and in concentrated form, more so than late-run fish that often tend to be slightly smaller in size and more spread out timing wise.*

*(Courtesy Eagle Eye Images)*

(Courtesy Eagle Eye Images)

*A typical late summer coho, taken on the fly at the confluence of Russian and Kenai rivers. This is an area hot spot for the species where individual as well as groups of fish can be spotted and targeted. Carefully scout the mixing zone of the two rivers.*

## Silver Salmon

**Rating:** ★★★ Good.
**Season:** July 1 through September 30.
**Timing:** July 25 – September 30; peak August 25 – September 10.
**Size:** Average 6 – 11 pounds, up to 16 pounds.
**Tackle:** Flies and spinners.
**Tips:** Scout the river at dawn as schools of silvers can often be found in many of the holes and runs. The upstream migration usually halts as soon as the sun rises. During the day, try at the confluence or hike upstream and search holes just below the falls. The majority of silvers are caught at the river mouth or in holes immediately upstream.

Late-run silvers do not enter the river proper but are frequently encountered in October at the river mouth.

Due to the usually low water levels in the Russian during the silver run, flies in subdued colors are most effective in hooking fish. Black, olive, and purple shades are good. Roe imitations are good bets early in the morning at the river mouth. Spinners in plain silver, green, and blue work in deep holes.

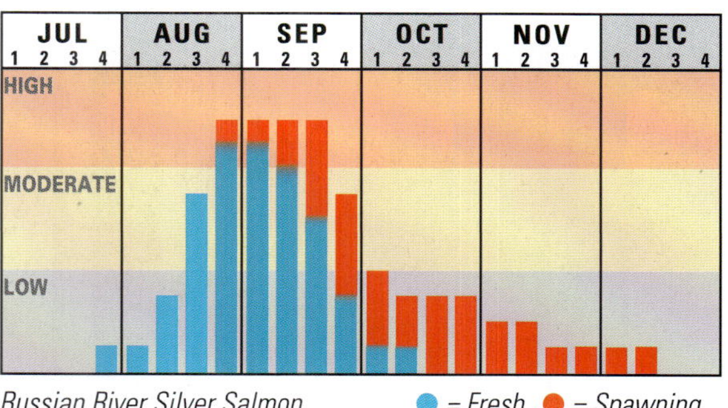


*Russian River Silver Salmon.* ● = Fresh ● = Spawning

## Rainbow Trout

**Rating:** ★★★½ Good to excellent.
**Season:** June 11 through May 1.
**Timing:** April 1 – May 1 and June 11 – November 30; peak July 25 – September 15.
**Size:** Average 8 – 20 inches, up to 30 inches (10-12 pounds).
**Tackle:** Flies and spinners.
**Tips:** For quick action, fly-fishers should focus on areas just downstream of salmon cleaning stations (or wherever fish are being gutted) using egg and flesh imitation flies. Be on the water early, this being especially important during low water conditions common from mid-summer into fall. Trophy rainbows weighing into the teens are not unheard of in June at the season opener but big trout may be present all season long. Some of the bigger mid-season catches have come out of the deeper and swifter river section in the canyon area between the falls and the upper campground, this being especially the case if the Russian is very low and clear as it often is that time of year and later on in the season. Sight-fishing for larger trout is very possible.

(Courtesy Robert Laskodi)

*A heavily-spotted rainbow, caught on a bead. The Russian offers great opportunities for catching trout on the fly, especially in late summer. Do not neglect dry flies, however, as they fish great before the salmon make their grand appearance.*

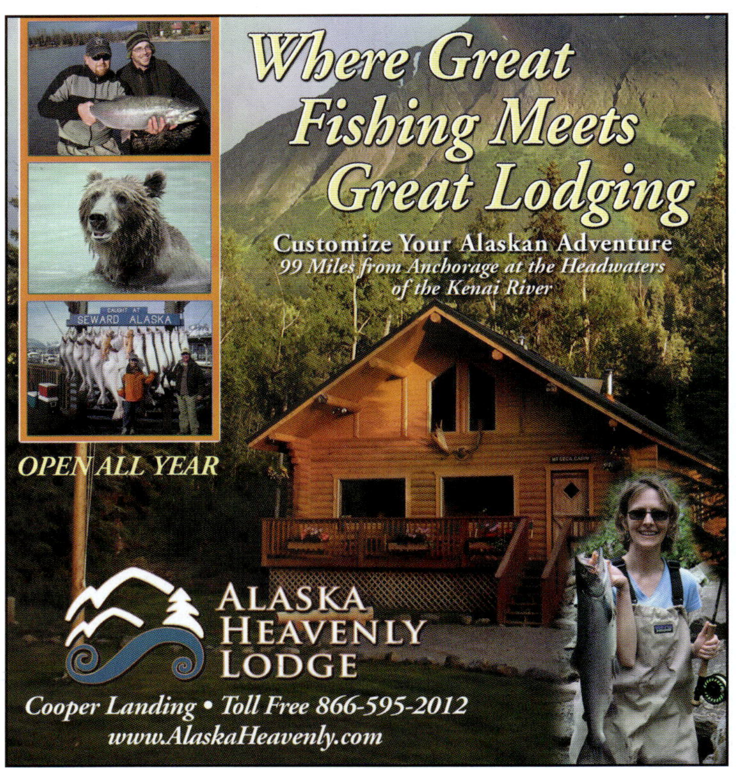

(Courtesy Beverley Bailey)

### Dolly Varden

**Rating:** ★★★ Good.
**Season:** June 11 through May 1.
**Timing:** June 11 – November 30; peak August 10 – September 10.
**Size:** Average 8 – 20 inches, up to 27 inches (7-8 pounds).
**Tackle:** Flies and spinners.
**Tips:** There are very few large char in the river prior to August and the in-migration of spawning late-run sockeye with early-season fish being for the most part confined to the river mouth. As usual, egg and flesh patterns are most popular. In fall, look for big spawners (20+ inches) entering the Russian and remaining into October. Schools of fish are sometimes encountered yet individual char are more common.

*Late season char are often large and colorful, such as this pink-spotted 24-inch specimen, caught on a black wolly bugger.*

## Other Russian Opportunities

### Bears of the Russian River

The Russian has become known for its population of bears, both black and brown. During the salmon runs, bears are frequently spotted wandering the river banks scouting for food, creating excellent sighting and photo opportunities not just for anglers but anyone interested in seeing these large mammals in their natural environment.

While bears may be present anytime between April and November, they are most prevalent when food sources are abundantly available and usually appear just as the salmon runs enter the river. Black bears are common throughout the season yet brown bears tend to show more often starting in mid-summer (July) and on into fall (September), reflecting the peak migration and spawning period of late-run sockeye salmon.

Spottings can be had throughout the day but generally the morning and evening hours are the best times to see these impressive animals. For the most part, it is younger bears or females with cubs that fish the lower Russian around the campground; the larger and older boars tend to avoid people and keep to the upper section of the drainage above Lower Russian Lake.

*(Courtesy Arild Nielsen)*

In viewing bears at the Russian, keep in mind that safety is the number one priority. Never approach bears within very close range in order to get the "best" photo. Respect their space; always yield. Remember, they are neither tame nor friendly; these bears are only tolerant of humans on a very primitive level and can still act in very unpredictable (and dangerous) ways if feeling threatened or surprised.

Because of the close interaction between people and bears on the Russian, special regulations concerning angler conduct, such as proper fish cleaning and storage, are in effect and enforced. Look for posted information.

Anglers should be prepared for the possibility of encounters at all times, especially at dawn and dusk. Avoid walking along river at night. Some brown bears will approach anglers in order to take their fish. Always be aware of surroundings, particularly if fishing alone or on any river section away from the campground.

## Russian Lakes Trail

For anyone planning to spend some time in the Cooper Landing area, this well developed US Forest Service trail will lead anglers and sightseers into the upper portion of the Russian River drainage, including Upper and Lower Russian lakes.

The main trailhead is approximately 1 mile in on the Russian River Campground road off Milepost 52.7 Sterling Highway. The first three miles is easy going with a spur off to the right leading to the Russian River Falls. The main trail continues to a Forest Service cabin on Lower Russian Lake and onward to Upper Russian River, which it parallels more or less for several miles, before reaching two additional Forest Service cabins on Upper Russian Lake (about a 12 mile trip).

Fishing for rainbow trout and Dolly Varden is good to excellent with very few other anglers present. Please note this is a major salmon spawning area and that salmon fishing is prohibited year-round, including catch-and -release.

Bears (specifically brown) are common in these parts and precautions must be taken; make plenty of noise when traveling and avoid venturing out alone along the river unless armed.

## Salmon Viewing

Although migrating and spawning salmon may be seen in a great many waters along the road system, few offer the superb viewing opportunities of the clear and shallow Russian River. There are two primary ways to observe this most extraordinary life cycle of salmon; one is the migration of pre-spawning adults, another the actual breeding act of mature fish.

Four species of salmon spawn in the Russian drainage, the best viewing being of reds (or sockeyes). A set of falls just downstream of Lower Russian Lake provides a great spot to see salmon leaping high in the air while attempting to negotiate their way upstream. The Russian Lakes Trail is the easiest path to the falls but walking along the river is possible too. Best viewing here is in mid-June to early July (first run) and again from early August to early September (second run).

From late August until mid-September, the lower Russian between the Russian River campground and the Kenai River confluence is a prime location to see salmon spawning up close. Thousands upon thousands of reds occupy this shallow river section, making for perfect photo opportunities. Also, this is the perfect time and place to observe bears catching salmon.

*Whether wading and fishing or just hiking along the banks of the river, seeing these bright-bodied salmon in the final stages of the life cycle is an experience not soon forgotten. This angler, in his search for chrome silver salmon, finds himself literally surrounded by crimson-bodied sockeye.*

# Other Productive Fisheries & Additional Opportunities

## QUARTZ CREEK

**Fishing:** ★★★½ **Scenery:** ★★★★
**Accessibility:** ★★★★ **Solitude:** ★★½

**Location:** Central Kenai Peninsula drainage, tributary of Kenai Lake, Cooper Landing area, 94 miles south of Anchorage, 49 miles east of Soldotna.

**Access:** The Sterling Highway provides multiple access points to the middle and lower stream sections while the Seward Highway offers some limited access to the upper stream. Undeveloped or improvised trails are common at most access points, particularly along the middle and lower portions.

(Courtesy Beverley Bailey)

### Seward Highway

*A.* The highway parallels the stream between milepost 42.2 and 41.0. Park on the shoulder of the road. No developed trails present. Stream is on west side of highway and can be difficult to see because of dense foliage.

*B. Devils Pass Trailhead* – Milepost 39.5. West on access road to paved parking area and trailhead. Trail leads half a mile to stream crossing.

### Sterling Highway

*C. Sterling Highway Bridge* – Milepost 44.0. Road crosses stream, paved turnout.

*D.* The highway parallels the stream more or less from milepost 42.0 to 44.0. Pullouts are present. Limited parking.

*E. Quartz Creek Road Bridge* – Milepost 45.0. South on Quartz Creek Road 0.7 miles to stream crossing. Small pullout with limited parking.

*F. Quartz Creek Campground* – Milepost 45.0. South on Quartz Creek Road 0.6 miles to campground on right and lower end of stream. Paved parking, camping, restrooms, and boat launch on Kenai Lake.

*G. Crescent Creek Campground* – Milepost 45.0. South on Quartz Creek Road 2.7 miles to small campground on left. Trail leads short distance to creek.

**Facilities:** Most access points have parking available with developed campgrounds available. Lodging, RV facilities, and other services can be found nearby in Cooper Landing.

**Species:** Rainbow trout and Dolly Varden. Arctic grayling and whitefish are present in small numbers. All five species of salmon spawn in the stream; reds are most abundant followed by silvers.

**Restrictions:** Salmon fishing prohibited. Closed to all fishing from May 2 through June 10. Other restrictions apply. Consult ADF&G regulations.

**Fishing:** This is a premier fly-fishing stream for char but can be productive for trout as well. From mid-summer through fall, large Dolly Varden are targeted in the stretch of water from Kenai Lake upstream to the Sterling Highway bridge where Quartz displays an abundance of deep holes and pools that concentrate fish. The far upper reaches of the stream, along the Seward Highway, however, is quite fast and shallow with multiple braids and not as productive.

Anglers willing to bushwhack a distance away from the road will find superb opportunities. Quartz is a major salmon spawning stream and much of the fishing is done with beads and egg/flesh pattern flies; however, dry flies work exceptionally well at times before the salmon show up. Trophy specimens are not unheard of and the largest Dolly Varden to come out of this stream weighed 15 pounds.

The area around the mouth of Quartz at Kenai Lake is a great spot to connect with lake trout. Although bait is most effective, some fish can also be coaxed to strike lures and flies. Fish average only a few pounds but are plentiful, especially in early morning and evening.

Overall, the upper and middle sections are perfect for sight-fishing. Kings spawn in July-August, reds August-September, and silvers October-November; match the hatch. Anglers should also be aware that this is prime brown bear habitat and several of these animals regularly patrol the stream in late summer and fall.

**Rainbow Trout.** Fair to good; July 15 – September 15; average 10 – 15 inches. Forage patterns recommended in mid-summer, egg and flesh imitations in August and September. Big fish to 25 inches or more present.

**Dolly Varden.** Excellent; July 15 – September 15; average 10 – 20 inches. Forage patterns work throughout season but egg/flesh imitations are best in late summer and fall. Char in excess of 30 inches possible in September when large spawners enter stream.

## KENAI LAKE

**Fishing:** ★★ **Scenery:** ★★★★★
**Accessibility:** ★★★ **Solitude:** ★★★★

**Location:** Central Kenai Peninsula drainage, Cooper Landing area, 98 miles south of Anchorage, 23 miles north of Seward, 46 miles east of Soldotna.

**Access:** Given the size of this lake and two major highways paralleling its shores, there are several places to access the lake with varying degrees of ease or difficulty. However, there are only a few that are noteworthy in terms of angling and those are listed below.

*A. Ptarmigan Creek* – Milepost 23.2 Seward Highway. East on gravel road to Ptarmigan Creek Campground. Parking for all size vehicles, restrooms. Trail parallels stream about ½ mile to outlet at Kenai Lake.

*B. Trail River* – Milepost 24.1 Seward Highway. West on gravel road 1.2 mile to Trail River Campground. Parking for all size vehicles. Trail leads along river ¼ mile to outlet at Kenai Lake.

*C. Quartz Creek* – Milepost 45.0 Sterling Highway. Southwest on Quartz Creek Road 0.6 mile to Quartz Creek Campground on right. Parking for all size vehicles, restrooms, boat launch. Trail leads ¼ mile along creek to outlet at Kenai Lake.

*D. Kenai Lake Outlet* – Milepost 47.7 Sterling Highway. North on paved access road at Milepost 47.8; short distance to Kenai River Campground next to highway bridge at lake outlet. Parking for all size vehicles, restrooms, boat launch.

**Facilities:** Parking, camping, restrooms, and boat launch available on site with guide services, lodging, restaurants, and other services present in town of Cooper Landing.

**Species:** Rainbow and lake trout, Dolly Varden. An occasional arctic grayling and whitefish may be caught. All five species of salmon are present.

**Restrictions:** Salmon fishing prohibited. Consult ADF&G regulations.

**Fishing:** Kenai Lake is a long and relatively narrow body of water, parting the Kenai Mountains to a depth of nearly 700 feet. The second largest lake on the peninsula, Kenai is the headwater to Kenai River. Due to its size and glacial green water, finding proper structure that hold fish can be challenging but definitely worthwhile.

Starting in mid-summer and continuing through fall, prospective anglers can locate reasonably good action for several species of game fish, including rainbow trout, lake trout, and Dolly Varden. The best fishing spots are typically in and around the mouths of clearwater salmon streams where they empty into the lake, as well as the lake outlet where the Kenai River forms. Casting small spoons, spinners, plugs, and forage imitation flies, including bait, all bring results. Early mornings and late evenings are best.

**Rainbow Trout.** Fair to good; July 1 to October 15; average 8 to 20 inches. Small spoons, spinners, plugs, and flies work. Forage patterns work early and late in the season. Occasional lunkers to 30 inches plus.

**Lake Trout.** Fair to good; July 15 to November 30; average 3 to 6 pounds. Bait is superior, especially bits of herring and salmon roe. Spoons work well in autumn.

**Dolly Varden.** Fair to good; July 25 to November 30; average 10 to 20 inches. Small spinners, spoons, and flies best. Try smolt imitations for char to 25 inches or more.

## CRESCENT LAKE

(Courtesy Beverley Bailey)

**Fishing:** ★★★★ **Scenery:** ★★★★★
**Accessibility:** ★★½ **Solitude:** ★★★★
**Location:** Central Kenai Peninsula drainage, Cooper Landing and Moose Pass areas, 95 miles south of Anchorage, 5 miles east of Cooper Landing, 33 miles north of Seward.
**Access:** Two main routes lead to Crescent Lake; one starting at Seward Highway near Moose Pass and the other at Sterling Highway in Cooper Landing.
*A. Carter Lake Trailhead* – Milepost 33.1 Seward Highway. West at turnout to trailhead. Parking. Developed trail leads 3 miles south to lake inlet (hikers will pass Carter Lake en route).
*B. Crescent Lake Trail* – Milepost 45.0 Sterling Highway. South on Quartz Creek Road 3.4 miles to trailhead on right. Developed trail leads 6.5 miles east along Crescent Creek to lake outlet.
**Facilities:** Parking available at trailheads with lodging, restaurants, sporting goods, and other services and amenities in nearby communities.
**Species:** Arctic grayling. A few Dolly Varden also present.
**Restrictions:** Lake is closed to all fishing from May 2 through June 10. Consult ADF&G regulations.
**Fishing:** Crescent Lake is situated in an exceptionally beautiful part of the peninsula, its clear waters surrounded by steep mountain slopes. The main species here is the arctic grayling, which arguably provide the best fishing for the species in the region.

Once stocked by ADF&G, the grayling population is now self-sustaining and yield not only some very noteworthy action by any Alaskan standards but also the potential for trophy specimens.
**Arctic Grayling.** Excellent; June 15 – September 15; average 8 – 17 inches. Small spinners and flies.

## TRAIL RIVER & LAKES

**Fishing:** ★★ **Scenery:** ★★★★
**Accessibility:** ★★ **Solitude:** ★★★★
**Location:** Central Kenai Peninsula drainage, Moose Pass area, 95 miles south of Anchorage, 24 miles north of Seward.
**Access:** There are several places in which to reach the lakes and river as Seward Highway parallels and crosses these waters to a great extent.
*A. Upper Trail Lake* – Milepost 32.3, 31.9, and 30.3 Seward Highway. Lake is reached by short gravel roads and turnouts. Parking, picnic areas, and primitive boat launch present.
*B. Lower Trail Lake* – Milepost 25.3 Seward Highway. East on gravel road at Milepost 2.2 leading 0.1 mile to lake. Parking available at Vagt Lake Trailhead. Trail leads along lake for about ½ mile.
*C. Upper Trail River* – Milepost 25.3 – 24.1 Seward Highway. Road crosses river at Milepost 25.3, paralleling it for almost a mile. Limited parking.
*D. Lower Trail River* – Milepost 24.1 Seward Highway. West on access road 0.4 mile to river crossing and limited parking. Continue another 0.8 mile to Trail River Campground and river. Parking and developed campsites. Numerous trails lead from campground to river and outlet at Kenai Lake.
**Facilities:** Parking, camping, restrooms, and primitive boat launch available in area with guide services, lodging, restaurants, and other amenities present in town of Moose Pass.
**Species:** Rainbow and lake trout, Dolly Varden. An occasional arctic grayling and whitefish may be caught. All five species of salmon are present.
**Restrictions:** Salmon fishing prohibited. Consult ADF&G regulations.
**Fishing:** Situated within the Chugach National Forest and

Kenai Mountains, Trail River and Lakes are perhaps better noted for their scenic beauty than fishing; however, some decent angling can be had still. Even more glacial than nearby Kenai River, the Trail is a moody piece of water, anglers having to match their offerings not only with the "hatch" of the day but also making sure it presents proper visibility in the grayish-green water. The fish are there and with the right perspective in terms of structure and fish habits, action for trout and char will not be disappointing.

The Trail River is best for rainbows and Dolly Varden yet fishing for them at the inlets of clearwater tributaries in the lakes can be productive as well. From mid-summer and into fall, target these gamesters with the knowledge that salmon will be spawning in these waters. A few large char (5-7 pounds) are landed in this river every autumn by anglers using colorful corkies.

Lake trout gather at the mouths of tributaries throughout the season and using smolt imitation lures and flies is the way to go. Herring and salmon roe are good baits and will almost certainly produce strikes when fished on the bottom in early morning and evening.

The Trail lakes are perfect for canoe and kayak excursions to more remote parts away from the main highway thoroughfare. This allows for exploring one or more of the several clearwater streams that empty into the lakes, such as Johnson Creek.

**Rainbow Trout.** Fair to good; July 15 – September 30; average 8 – 16 inches. Small spoons, spinners, plugs, and flies work. Forage patterns work early and late in the season.

**Lake Trout.** Fair to good; July 25 – November 1; average 2 – 4 pounds. Bait is best, especially bits of herring and salmon roe. Spoons may well at times.

**Dolly Varden.** Fair to good; July 25 – October 10; average 8 – 18 inches. Small spinners, spoons, and flies. Try smolt imitations for char to 25 inches or more.

## PTARMIGAN CREEK

**Fishing:** ★★★ **Scenery:** ★★★★

**Accessibility:** ★★★ **Solitude:** ★★★

**Location:** Central Kenai Peninsula drainage, Kenai Lake tributary, Moose Pass area, 104 miles south of Anchorage, 23 miles north of Seward.

**Access:** Ptarmigan Creek Campground, Milepost 23.2 Seward Highway. Turn east to campground and trailhead. Faint angler trails parallel creek up- and downstream. Developed trail leads northeast from campground along stream 3 miles to outlet of Ptarmigan Lake.

**Facilities:** Parking, camping, restrooms.

**Species:** Rainbow trout and Dolly Varden. An occasional arctic grayling and whitefish may be present. All five species of salmon spawn in the stream, reds being most abundant.

**Restrictions:** Salmon fishing prohibited. Closed to all fishing from May 2 through June 10. Consult ADF&G regulations.

**Fishing:** This is primarily a late summer and fall fishery for rainbow trout and Dolly Varden. Since the stream is a major spawning area for red salmon, predatory species are quite abundant and aggressive. Anglers do well scouting deep holes and runs early in the season, focusing on shallower water later on as the salmon begin laying their eggs. The first couple of miles from Kenai Lake on upstream are most rewarding but fair numbers of char can be found throughout the creek up to Ptarmigan Lake.

The outlet of Ptarmigan Lake is a local hot spot for char in late summer and fall. In addition, anglers may also find lake trout at the outlet of the stream at Kenai Lake; decent

action available during the early morning and late evening hours in summer when fish come into the shallows to feed.

Kings spawn here in July-August, reds August-September, and silvers October-November. Match bead size and color for greatest success, switching to flesh accordingly after the spawn.

**Rainbow Trout.** Fair to good; July 25 – September 15; average 10 – 15 inches. Best fishing is when salmon are present using egg and flesh imitations. Forage patterns work early and late in the season. Occasional lunker to 25 inches.

**Dolly Varden**. Good; July 25 – September 15; average 10 – 15 inches. This is the premier sport fish in this stream. Try smolt imitations early before salmon arrive, egg and flesh patterns later on for char to 25 inches or more. Biggest fish are taken in early autumn.

## ADDITIONAL OPPORTUNITIES

### Fly-In Fishing

There are several small air taxis and outfits in Cooper Landing and Moose Pass that offer fly-in trips to remote waters, both in the local area as well as more remote trips.

Trout, char, and grayling fishing in pristine mountain lakes of the peninsula is a popular option, especially the scenic valleys of the Kenai Mountains and the immense flats of the northern peninsula. Although the spring and fall months are generally the most productive, fishing can be excellent throughout the summer season, this being particularly the case in highland and alpine waters. The fish tend to be very abundant and aggressive considering the lack of angling pressure, providing a superb experience. Additionally, if flying in to one of the mountain lakes (such as Paradise Lakes), be prepared to see some astounding scenery that is on par with anything in Alaska.

Longer excursions targeting salmon, trout, and char on the western edge of Prince William Sound and on the west side of Cook Inlet is also possible. The former is a prime area targeting ocean-fresh silvers, pinks, and chums in addition to sea-run char and cutthroat trout. Casting or jigging for bottomfish is even possible off the floats of aircraft resting in one of the many secluded bays and coves of the region. In contrast, the latter area offer the choice of small clearwater streams to big glacial rivers scouting for all five species of salmon as well as rainbow trout and Dolly Varden. The volcanoes of Spurr, Redoubt, and Iliamna provide spectacular backdrops.

Some of these trips may be coupled with bear viewing or other wildlife observations such as whales and seals. Half- or full-day and longer adventures are available.

### Resurrection Pass Trail Lakes

This 38-mile long US Forest Service trail extends from the trailhead at Milepost 53.2 of Sterling Highway at Cooper Landing to Resurrection Creek Road trailhead near the community of Hope. Hikers and prospective anglers will pass several highland lakes that harbor a variety of fish, most notably trout, char, and grayling with excellent opportunities at hand. Also, there are 8 public-use cabins scattered along the trail.

Trout and Juneau lakes connect to each other through Juneau Creek and are in the Upper Kenai River drainage. Both yield good rainbow and lake trout action from late spring through fall and hold the distinction of supporting the only documented burbot population on the Kenai Peninsula. They are situated at Mile 7.5 and 9, respectively.

At Mile 13, Swan Lake comes into view. Anglers will find very productive fishing for rainbows and dollies; reds

(Courtesy EZ Limit Guide Service)

and silvers also move into Swan starting in mid-summer and continuing into fall but may be difficult to catch. This beautiful mountain lake is part of the Chickaloon River drainage and connects with Turnagain Arm. It is also the last body of water along the route providing worthwhile sport fishing opportunities.

### Johnson Pass Trail Fishing

There are limited spots to fish along this 22-mile US Forest Service trail; however, there are a couple of noteworthy locations that are definitely worth trying.

From the southern trailhead access point at Milepost 32.6 Seward Highway, Johnson Pass Trail leads north along Upper Trail Lake and Johnson Creek to Johnson Lake where very good trouting awaits in summer and fall. It is a 12 mile long hike but worth it as very few if any other anglers will be present and rainbows to 20 inches or more being common; however, do not be surprised to catch fish weighing as much as 6 to 8 pounds.

Another place that is a must-fish is Bench Lake, about 1/2 mile north of Johnson Lake. Expect fast action for grayling up to 16 inches. For a shortcut to this lake, begin hike from the northern trailhead access point at Milepost 63.8 of Seward Highway.

### Salmon Viewing

Although spawning salmon may be seen in a great many waterways of central peninsula, the following locations have viewing platforms specifically for the purpose. Proceed with caution if hiking along streams in autumn as brown bears will be feeding on fish.

**Daves Creek:** From Milepost 37.4 Seward Highway, south on gravel access road to stream area at outlet of Tern Lake. Red run peaks from late July to mid-August, silvers all of October. Occasional king salmon present in July.

**Ptarmigan Creek:** Turn west to access site at Milepost 23.3 of the Seward Highway. This is primarily a red salmon spawning stream with peak viewing between late August and mid-September. A few kings may be present in July, and silvers in October.

Seward

# Southeastern Kenai

**King Salmon • Pink Salmon • Chum Salmon • Silver Salmon**
**Dolly Varden • Pacific Halibut • Lingcod • Rockfish**
**Shark • Bottomfish**

*Deep Sea Fishing*

*Saltwater Salmon*

*Wading Streams*

*Surf Casting*

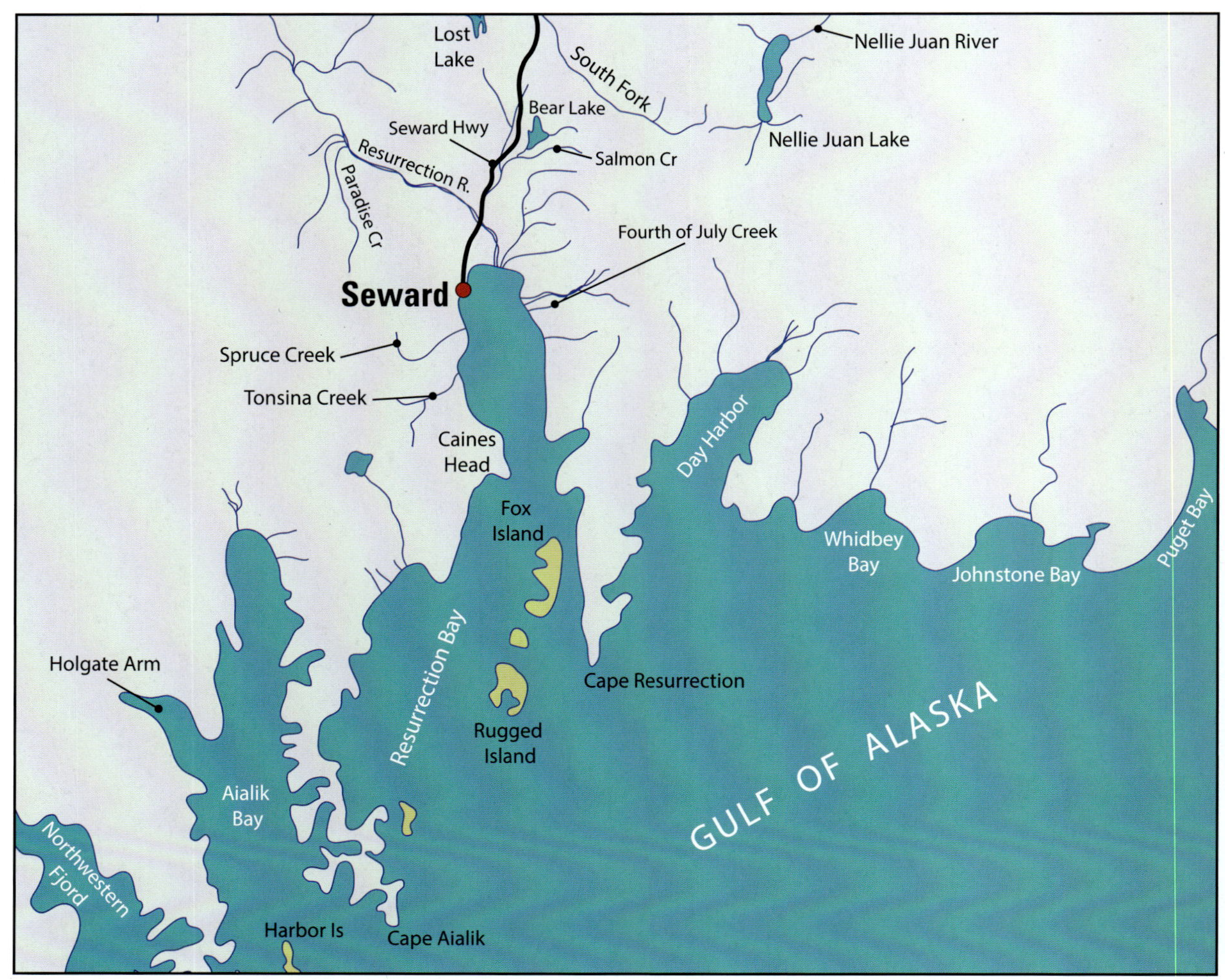


**Area Population Centers:** Seward
**Key Species:** King, Red, Pink, Chum, and Silver Salmon, Dolly Varden, Pacific Halibut, Lingcod, Rockfish, Shark, Bottomfish
**Other Species:** Rainbow Trout and Arctic Grayling
**Main Destinations/Hot Spots:** Resurrection Bay
**Other Destinations:** Salmon Creek and Resurrection River
**Additional Opportunities:** Outer Resurrection Bay & North Gulf Coast Fishing and Fishing Derbies

**Summary of Area Fishing:** For some of the most impressive saltwater action in the state, look no further than Seward at the heart of Southeastern Peninsula. With five species of salmon, sea-run char, and a series of popular ocean species readily present, anglers can expect to have a good time. On top of that, there are several small streams and lakes in the area that support populations of salmon and char for those wanting a break in the saltwater action.

Those equipped with boats call this area a major hub from spring into fall, while anglers casting from shore do reasonably well at the height of the prospective salmon runs. The beaches here offer a variety of bottomfish in addition to salmon and char; in fact, catching halibut (and rockfish) off the bank is not only possible but probable if using surf-casting gear.

Silver salmon is the main species of interest in Seward and a very lucrative derby is held here every August honoring these gamesters; however, runs of chrome kings, reds, pinks, and chums may be found throughout the area too and can be readily targeted from the bank and by boat.

Decent halibut, lingcod, rockfish, and shark opportunities are at hand if traveling offshore and Seward is host to a large fleet of charter outfits specializing in bottomfish and salmon trips. Also, boats and other types of watercraft can be rented on a per day basis for the do-it-yourself angler.

There is a number of waters in the area offering salmon and char fishing for those wishing to wade a small stream instead of or in addition to Seward's marine fisheries.

Prime time is May into September area-wide.

# Resurrection Bay

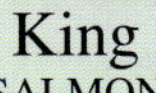
King SALMON

Pink SALMON

Chum SALMON

Silver SALMON

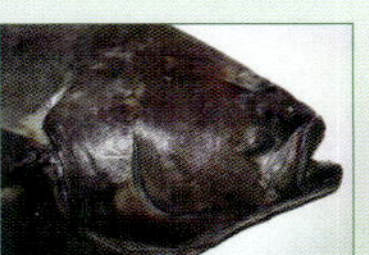
Halibut

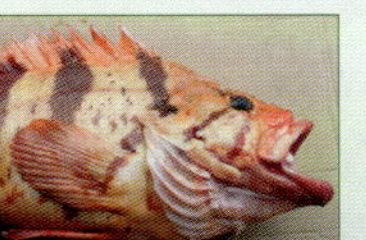
Rockfish

**Highlights:** Very good surf-casting for salmon and sea-run char with spectacular views of the bay area and surrounding mountain ranges. Deep-sea fishing is top notch.

**Best Fishing:** Mid-May to mid-September. **Regulatory Restrictions:** Very liberal.

**Location:** Southeastern Kenai Peninsula, town of Seward, beginning of Seward Highway, 127 miles south of Anchorage.

**Description:** The northern portion of Resurrection Bay is bordered with the town of Seward at the head of the bay. The bluish-green waters are home to a rich ocean fauna consisting of a multitude of fish species and wildlife such as whales and seals. Mountains in this area rise to a height of well over 4,000 feet, a thick carpet of spruce decorating the slopes and valleys down to the edge of tidewater.

There is a heavy utilization in this area of commercial fishing boats and one of the largest sport fishing fleets in Alaska are based here. Seward Harbor in downtown is the center of attention, complete with a myriad of stores or services catered to sport fishing and sightseeing.

Although the bay shoreline is somewhat void of much vegetation in Seward, the area just south and east of town is much more striking in natural appearance. The boulder-strewn water front of Seward eventually give way to a more pleasant marine environment void of commercial activity that features pebble and sand beaches and a dense rainforest that is home to black bears, moose, and eagles.

The water is not deep in most places around the bay, perhaps 10 to 15 feet at most within casting range, yet the shoreline along Lowell Point Road between Lowell Creek Falls and Spruce Creek does border depths of 20 to 30 feet. The bay proper, however, is measured to several hundred feet or more.

**Facilities:** There is an abundance of parking and camping areas next to the bay, complete with RV facilities and other services associated with the town of Seward. Boats and kayaks may be rented from area businesses.

**Access:** The Seward Highway ends in the town of Seward, Milepost 0. Several of the town streets lead east to the shores of Resurrection Bay with ample points of access within the town itself as well as along Lowell Point Road and Nash Road.

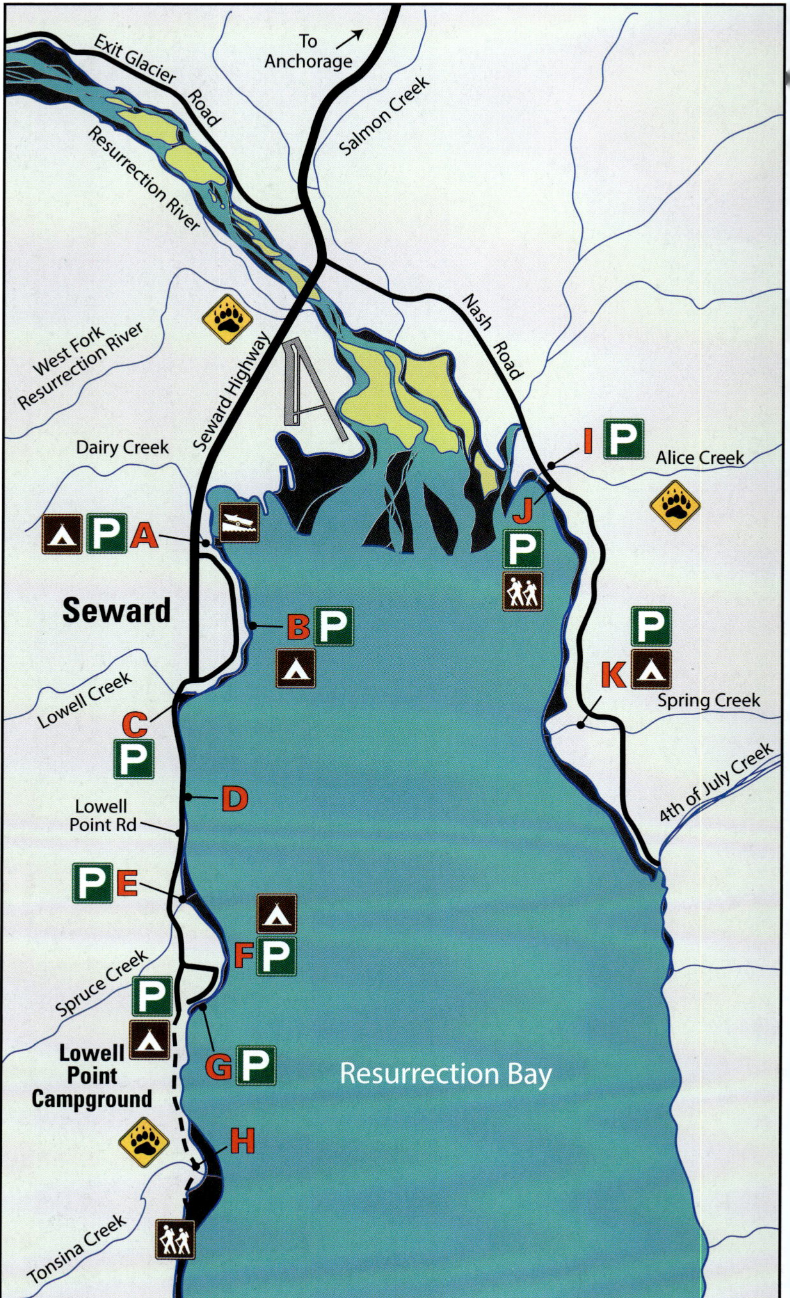


## Downtown Seward

**A. Scheffler Creek** – Downtown Seward. From Third Avenue (Seward Highway), turn left on S. Harbor Street, short distance to Fourth Avenue on right, 0.1 mile to access road on left, 0.2 miles to stream mouth and bay. Parking, camping, restrooms.

**B. Seward Waterfront** – Downtown Seward. From Third Avenue (Seward Highway), turn left on D Street 0.1 mile, cross Fourth Avenue and onto Ballaine Boulevard/Railway Boulevard. The road parallels the bay for the next half mile. Developed parking and camping areas, restrooms.

## Lowell Point Road

The road begins near downtown Seward at the far northwest corner of Resurrection Bay (Mile 0) and ends at Lowell Point south of town (Mile 2.4).

**C. Lowell Creek Falls** – Mile 0.3. Road crosses stream. Parking.

**D. West Resurrection Bay** – Mile 0.5 to 1.5. Road parallels a portion of the west side of Resurrection Bay. Limited parking; pullouts present.

**E. Spruce Creek** – Mile 1.5. From parking area, hike down to bay and follow shoreline 200 yards southeast to stream mouth.

**F. Lowell Point** – Mile 2.4. Left to private campground with beach access. Parking, camping, RV parking, restrooms, and boat rentals.

**G. South Beach** – Mile 2.3. Turn right on Martins Road, continue 0.3 miles to beach access. Developed parking, restrooms.

**H. Tonsina Creek** – Milepost 2.1. Take Martins Road on right leading to access road on right to Lowell Point Recreation area parking lot and trailhead. Developed parking, restrooms. Trail leads 2 miles due south to tidal area of stream and bridge crossing. Follow stream 200 yards to mouth. Anglers should note that bears frequent this area during salmon spawning season from latter July into September. (Trail continues another 3 miles to Caines Head area.)

## Rules & Regulations

**Open Season:** January 1 through December 31.
**Open Area:** The entire bay is open to fishing.
**Legal Gear/Tackle:** All gear, tackle, and methods are allowed, including snagging.

**All Salmon**
- Open all season (see general "Open Season" above).
- King salmon bag limit is (1) per day and (1) in possession; there is no seasonal or annual limit.
- All other salmon bag limit is (6) per day and (6) in possession.

**Dolly Varden**
- Open all season (see general "Open Season" above).
- Bag limit is (5) per day and (5) in possession.

**Pacific Halibut**
- Open season is February 1 through December 31.
- Bag limit is (2) per day and (4) in possession.

**Lingcod**
- Closed to fishing year-round inside of Resurrection Bay.
- Open season is July 1 through December 31 outside of Resurrection Bay.
- Bag limit is (1) per day and (1) in possession outside of Resurrection Bay.

**Rockfishes**
- Open all season (see general "Open Season" above).
- Bag limit is (4) per day and (8) in possession; except only (1) per day and (2) in possession may be non-pelagic.

**Sharks**
- Open all season (see general "Open Season" above).
- Bag limit is (1) per day and (1) in possession.

**Other Saltwater Fishes**
- Open all season (see general "Open Season" above).
- No bag or possession limits.

## Nash Road

The road begins at Milepost 3.3 Seward Highway (Mile 0) and ends at a commercial facility just south of Spring Creek (Mile 5.3).

**I. Resurrection River** – Milepost 2.0. South to private access site. Parking. Trail leads 1.5 mile to river mouth. Be prepared to ford stream channels and make note of tidal conditions before venturing.

**J. Alice Creek** – Milepost 2.3. Small parking area. Hike along stream a hundred yards to its mouth and beach area. There is some private land near this stream; look for posted signs.

**K. Spring Creek** – Milepost 5.1. West on gravel road paralleling stream 0.2 miles to large parking area and creek mouth. Primitive camping.

*Couple of anglers enjoying the lazy morning surf of the bay while casting for silver salmon.*

THE
FISH HOUSE
EST. 1974
FISHING CHARTERS
WWW.THEFISHHOUSE.NET
PERSEVERANCE
SERVANT
REVELATION
PROVIDER
ENDURANCE
• FULL DAY & HALF DAY TRIPS FOR SALMON OR HALIBUT
• COMBINATION TRIPS ALSO AVAILABLE.
CALL TOLL FREE
1-800-257-7760
P.O. BOX 1209 • SEWARD, AK 99664 • (907) 224-3674

## Fishing Resurrection Bay

**Access:** ★★★★
**Scenery:** ★★★★
**Wildlife:** ★★★
**Sight Fishing:** ★
**Bank/Wading:** ★★★★
**Boat/Floating:** ★★★★★

**Species:** King, pink, chum, and silver salmon, Dolly Varden, and rockfish. Occasional catches of red salmon and pacific halibut.

**Summary:** The fishing picks up a little bit slower on this side of the Kenai Peninsula compared to drainages of Cook Inlet. Although feeder king salmon and halibut, among other bottomfish species, are available throughout the year, it is the arrival of hatchery king salmon in June that truly signals the start of the season for road-bound anglers. The season quickly progresses from here on out through the summer and into fall, followed by runs of red, pink, chum, and silver salmon as well as sea-run char.

The kings return to one main site where they were released as smolts – the Seward Lagoon in front of town near the small boat harbor – and anglers successfully target them at the mouth of Scheffler Creek. This site carries little aesthetic value to speak of but is nonetheless a productive harvest location.

As the king migration peaks, other salmon runs are just starting to build. Reds, despite being present in relative abundance, are difficult to catch in the glacial waters of Resurrection Bay with some anglers resorting to snagging (which is legal throughout area marine waters year-round) in order to harvest these seemingly tight-lipped salmon. Although a few are caught incidentally to fishing for other salmon species, more consistent catches are made near the mouths of spawning streams. Both early and late runs occur in the area, the former being the larger by far and bound for Bear Lake in the Resurrection River drainage.

(Courtesy Eagle Eye Images)

The pinks are very reliable and will strike artificial lures and flies with aggression. They are taken throughout the bay all season long and commonly occur in great concentration as many of these smallish salmon spawn in short and shallow tidewater streams.

Chums often suffer the same plight as reds as they too can be difficult to get to bite. Yet when encountered in large schools in or near clearwater streams or at the head of small bays, fishing can be very good. Most runs occur in mid summer with many fish spawning in intertidal waters.

Silver salmon are native to the area but the natural runs have been greatly augmented with hatchery fish, giving Seward a reputation for some of the finest angling in the state for the species. Many of these fish return to Seward Lagoon by the way of Scheffler Creek and Bear Lake through Resurrection River and Salmon Creek. Anglers should keep in mind that both hatchery king and silver salmon, despite only headed to two specific locations, may be found most anywhere along the shoreline. Boaters experience the best action for this species but surf-casting can be worthwhile at the peak of the run.

Sea-run Dolly Varden are in actuality the first game fish available to roadside anglers,

*Anglers try their luck for silver salmon along South Beach at Lowell Point. Look for indications of the presence of fish by "jumpers" – silvers breaching the surface, often vertically several feet into the air.*

leaving area lakes where they overwintered and head out to Resurrection Bay to feed, returning back to the freshwater environment in late summer and fall. They are often taken incidentally to fishing for salmon but when targeted the action can be good.

Marine species are numerous in Resurrection Bay. For the most part it is non-sporting species that are most frequently encountered (flounder, sole, cod, skate, sablefish, greenling, etc.), yet both halibut and a few species of rockfish are present as well and caught time to time from shore by anglers casting bait. Boaters, with better access to deeper water, experience fair to excellent opportunities within the bay. Shore anglers usually do only fair at best.

Anglers putting in the time and effort targeting halibut from shore are often rewarded with fish under 10 pounds, yet catches to 80 pounds or more are possible. The western side of the bay generally fishes better than the eastern side because the water is deeper near shore.

As for rockfish, a few small specimens (less than 5 pounds) can be taken with consistency by anglers focusing on steep, rocky bottom structure. Again, the western bay side is best. Black rockfish is the most common species.

If using bait, anglers will sooner or later hook up with lingcod, which are present in fair numbers. It is reminded that all of the bay area is closed to lingcod fishing.

## Fish Availability

● = High ● = Moderate ● = Low ● = Closed

| Species | | MAY | JUN | JUL | AUG | SEP | OCT |
|---|---|---|---|---|---|---|---|
| **King Salmon** | Shore | L L L L | M M M M | M L L L | L L L – | L L – – | |
| | Boat | L L M H | H H H M | M M M M | M M M M | M L L L | L L L L |
| **Red Salmon** | Shore | L L M H | H H M M | L L L M | M M L L | L L L L | |
| | Boat | L L L L | L L L L | L L L L | L L L L | L L – – | |
| **Pink Salmon** | Shore | | – – L L | L M H H | H H M L | L L L L | |
| | Boat | | L L L M | H H H H | H M M L | L L L – | |
| **Chum Salmon** | Shore | | – L L M | H H H H | H M L L | L – – – | |
| | Boat | – – L L | L M M H | H H H H | M L L L | L – – – | |
| **Silver Salmon** | Shore | | | – L L L | M M H H | H H M M | L L L L |
| | Boat | | L L L M | H H H H | H H H H | M M L L | L L L – |
| **Dolly Varden** | Shore | L M H H | H H H H | H H H H | M M L L | L L – – | |
| | Boat | L L M M | M M M M | M M M L | L L L L | L – – – | |
| **Pacific Halibut** | Shore | L L L L | M M M M | M M M M | M M M M | M M L L | L L L L |
| | Boat | M M H H | H H H H | H H H H | H H H H | H H M M | L L L L |
| **Rockfish** | Shore | L L L L | L L M M | M M M M | M M M M | M L L L | L L L L |
| | Boat | H H H H | H H H H | H H H H | H H H H | H H H H | M M M M |
| **Bottomfish** | Shore | M M M M | H H H H | H H H H | H H H H | H H M M | M M L L |
| | Boat | H H H H | H H H H | H H H H | H H H H | H H H H | H H H H |
| Angling Pressure | Shore | – – – L | L M M L | M M M M | M M M H | H H M M | L – – – |
| | Boat | L L M M | H H H H | H H H H | H H H H | M M L L | L L – – |

## King Salmon

**Rating:** ★★ Fair.
**Locations:** Scheffler Creek and Lowell Creek Falls.
**Season:** January 1 through December 31.
**Timing:** April 15 – September 15; peak June 10 – 25.
**Size:** Average 12 – 25 pounds, up to 50 pounds.
**Tackle:** Spoons, spinners, and bait.
**Tips:** Hardware (especially spinners) and attractor flies worked near stream mouths on an incoming tide takes fish. Bait – salmon roe cluster or whole herring – suspended underneath a bobber can be deadly. Look for schools of kings at the release sites on an outgoing tide.

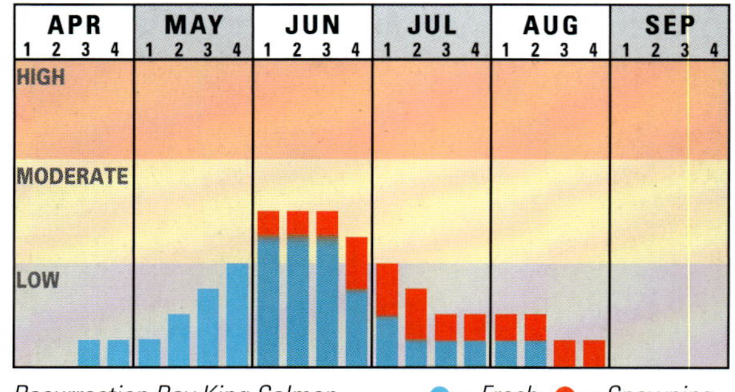


*Resurrection Bay King Salmon.* ● = Fresh ● = Spawning

*Salty sockeyes offer unequalled tablefare and fight; however, in Seward most are caught by snagging near the mouth of streams.*

## Red Salmon

**Rating:** ★★★½ Good to excellent.
**Location:** Resurrection River and Spring Creek.
**Season:** January 1 through December 31.
**Timing:** May 10 – September 20; peak May 25 – June 15 (early run) and July 5 – August 5 (late run).
**Size:** Average 4 – 7 pounds, up to 11 pounds.
**Tackle:** Snag hooks.
**Tips:** The primary fishery for sockeye (early run) in the Seward area is in May and June at the mouth of Resurrection River at the head of the bay. Another location with decent catch rates is at the mouth of Spring Creek in June and July. A few late-run sockeyes are also caught at the mouth of Seward Lagoon Creek in July and August. Although some fish are successfully caught using sporting methods and tackle (flies), the vast majority of salmon are taken by snagging. Anglers interested in sport should consider smaller, neutral-colored flies and fish when water conditions are optimal (clear).

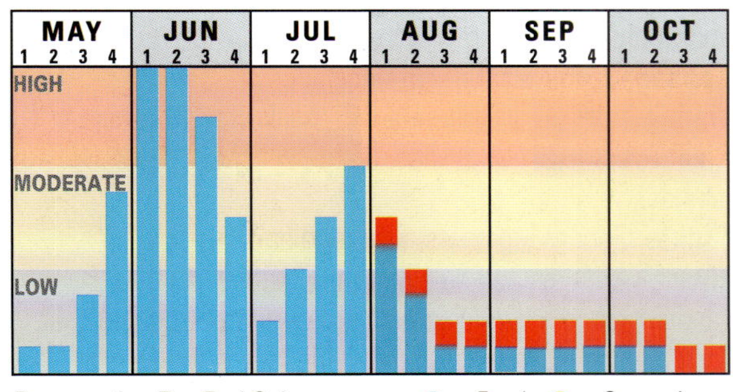


*Resurrection Bay Red Salmon.* ● = Fresh ● = Spawning

## Pink Salmon

**Rating:** ★★★★ Excellent on even-numbered years, good on odd.
**Locations:** Scheffler Creek, Seward Waterfront, Lowell Creek Falls, West Resurrection Bay, Spruce Creek, Lowell Point, South Beach, Tonsina Creek, Alice Creek, and Spring Creek.
**Season:** January 1 through December 31.
**Timing:** June 20 – Sept. 30; peak July 15 – August 15.
**Size:** Average 2 – 5 pounds, up to 9 pounds.
**Tackle:** Spoons, spinners, flies, and bait.
**Tips:** Pinks can be caught anywhere along the shoreline but look for concentrations in small bays or coves and at or near the mouth of spawning streams. Schools of pinks are often spotted and targeted. Casting hardware and attractor flies is good, as is fishing a piece of cut or whole herring with a bobber (especially early in the season).

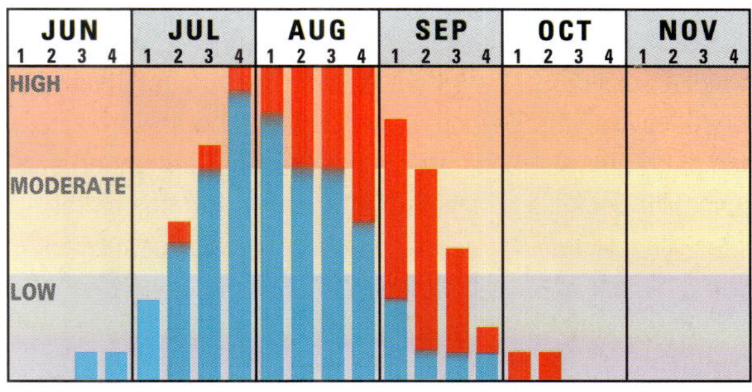


*Resurrection Bay Pink Salmon.* ● = Fresh ● = Spawning

## Chum Salmon

**Rating:** ★★½ Fair to good.
**Locations:** Seward Lagoon Creek, Spruce Creek, South Beach, Tonsina Creek, Alice Creek, and Spring Creek.
**Season:** January 1 through December 31.
**Timing:** June 15 – September 5; peak July 1 – August 5.
**Size:** Average 6 – 12 pounds, up to 18 pounds.
**Tackle:** Spoons, spinners, flies, and bait.
**Tips:** Fish can be numerous at times but hard to catch. Most are caught by snagging but when found in concentration lures and flies in green, chartreuse, or purple can be effective. Look for salmon surfacing as an indicator. Target stream mouths on incoming tide, always watching for jumpers.

Spring Creek peaks the first half of July (early run), other locations in late July to early August (late run). Spring Creek and Tonsina Creek support the heaviest and most accessible runs in the bay area.

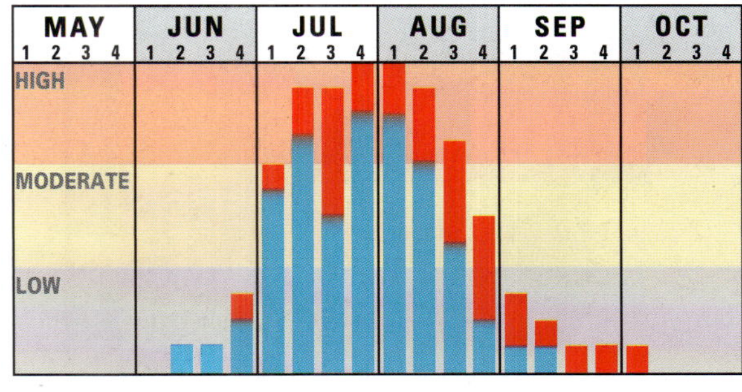


*Resurrection Bay Chum Salmon.* ● = Fresh ● = Spawning

## Silver Salmon

**Rating:** ★★½ Fair to good.
**Locations:** Scheffler Creek, Seward Waterfront, Lowell Creek Falls, West Resurrection Bay, South Beach, and Spring Creek.
**Season:** January 1 through December 31.
**Timing:** July 10 – November 15; peak August 25 – September 15.
**Size:** Average 6 – 12 pounds, up to 22 pounds.
**Tackle:** Spoons, spinners, flies, and bait.
**Tips:** Incoming and outgoing tides produce most fish. Scout surface for signs of salmon jumping or surfacing. Schools of silvers frequent the shoreline and sightfishing is at times a possibility in a few locations. The hatchery-fish locations (Seward Lagoon, Lowell Falls) generally produce fish in greater numbers later in the season (September) and schools of fish can be located entering the mouths on the tides. On low tide, try deeper, offshore waters for success. Size 5 blue or green spinners are effective as is herring fished with a bobber. If water conditions are silty, try casting high-visibility spinners in orange or chartreuse with silver blades; sunny weather tend to drive fish deep and off the bite – use bait or neutral-colored lures. Fly-fishers tend to fare better where concentrations of fish are present, such as hatchery release sites.

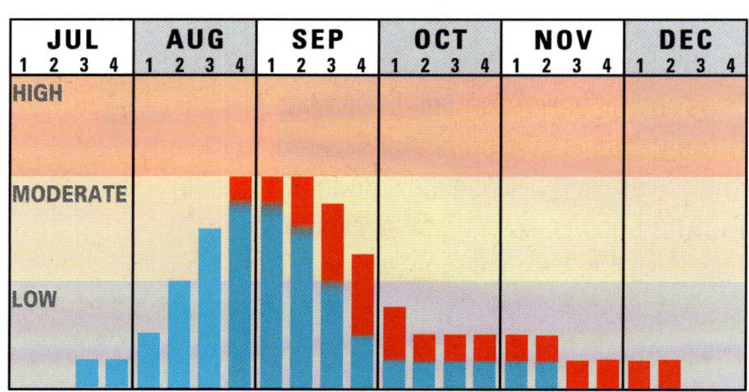


Resurrection Bay Silver Salmon.

(Courtesy Roy Bailey)

*Silvers approach area beaches in late summer, headed for hatchery release sites as well as the numerous clearwater drainages at the head of the bay. This 11-pound specimen hit a size 4 chartreuse spinner at South Beach, a popular mid-season spot for schooling coho.*

(Courtesy Beverley Bailey)

*Halibut are not abundant along Seward's beaches but a few fish are available to those who target them specifically. This 40-pounder was caught off the rocks along Lowell Point Road.*

## Dolly Varden

**Rating:** ★★★ Good.
**Locations:** Scheffler Creek, Lowell Creek Falls, West Resurrection Bay, Spruce Creek, Lowell Point, South Beach, and Spring Creek.
**Season:** January 1 through December 31.
**Timing:** April 20 – September 15; peak May 10 – August 1.
**Size:** Average 8 – 20 inches, up to 30 inches (10-12 pounds).
**Tackle:** Spoons, spinners, flies, and bait.
**Tips:** Small lures and flies imitating baitfish such as sandlance and juvenile salmon are perfect for hungry char. Try locations close to town early and late in the season (May and August) and farther out in mid-summer (June-July). Tidal rips and stream mouths are good spots as fish gather here to feed on salmon fry and smolts, while exposed beaches yield good results where char prey on sandlance.

### Pacific Halibut

**Rating:** Poor to fair.
**Locations:** West Resurrection Bay.
**Season:** February 1 through December 31.
**Timing:** April 15 – October 15; peak June 15 – Sept. 1.
**Size:** Average 5 – 10 pounds, up to 50 pounds.
**Tackle:** Jigs and bait.
**Tips:** Seek out deep water, such as the ferry dock or along Lowell Point Road around the processing plant, for consistent catches. Waters adjacent to Spring Creek can also yield a few fish to surf-casters. Moving around trying different spots and having patience is the key. Use bigger bait to avoid the abundance of non-sporting bottomfish.

### Rockfish

**Rating:** Poor to fair.
**Locations:** West Resurrection Bay.
**Season:** January 1 through December 31.
**Timing:** April 15 – October 15; peak July 1 – September 1.
**Size:** Average 10 – 15 inches, up to 5 pounds.
**Tackle:** Spoons, jigs, and bait.
**Tips:** Small silvery lures (saltwater spoons and jigs) with blue, green, or black insets are good but a piece of herring is usually best. Try the stretch of deep water from near the mouth of Lowell Creek and approximately a quarter mile down the shoreline along Lowell Point Road; this area has structure that rockfishes prefer.

## Other Resurrection Opportunities

### Outer Resurrection Bay & North Gulf Coast

Being only a two-and-a-half hour drive from Anchorage, Seward is one of the most popular gateways in all of Alaska for anglers seeking some of the best saltwater salmon action found anywhere, with multiple species to target from May into September. It is also a prime location to base a trip out of for deep sea fishing, which includes and variety of bottomfish as well as shark. And to top it all off, the scenery is gorgeous and wildlife such as seals and whales commonplace.

Resurrection Bay makes for a fantastic silver salmon experience, which helped build the reputation of this coastal port. Expect to fill limits of these chrome fighters, with excellent action the norm during July and August within 30 minutes of the harbor. The best of it usually occurs at the mouth of the bay and the numerous bays and coves adjacent to the Gulf of Alaska. Many of these fish are bound for waters outside of this area, adding substantially to the overall success rate of the marine fleet.

Most charters focus attention around the outer bay early in the season (June into August), the various coves of the Aialik Peninsula and Eldorado Narrows being hot spots. Later on, mid-August into September, the head of the bay usually produces the bulk of fish as silvers approach area spawning streams.

This coho bounty often coincides with the return of huge numbers of pinks as well, in late summer. Boat captains will often hit up these smallish salmon if action for other fish is slow or if limits have already been reached. Using ultra-light gear for chrome pinks can be an awesome experience and provides hours of non-stop entertainment.

King salmon are available year-round but the fastest action is during May and June as mature spawners return

(Courtesy of Crackerjack Sportfishing Charters)

*Proud angler and deckhand display a trophy halibut, caught on a jig. Fish of this size are not uncommon out of Seward.*

to the bay. This is also the time when larger catches are noted with specimens to 40 or even 50 pounds a possibility. The standard feeder king, however, is much more conservative in size with fish typically ranging from 10 to 20 pounds. The nice part about these fish, however, is that they are aggressively feeding in these waters not only in summer but during the winter months as well.

Schools of chums and reds may be encountered in certain locations but are not targeted specifically by boaters. Chums are more common catches than the reds as the gear and tackle used are specifically meant for the more aggressive silvers.

Bottomfish is big business in Seward. There is a flotilla of charters to choose from, most all of them targeting halibut, lingcod, and rockfish on the very outer edge of Resurrection Bay and along the North Gulf Coast. When the weather cooperates, longer excursions to the mouth of Prince William Sound – primarily the southern section of Montague Island – becomes a good possibility. The bigger halibut (commonly exceeding 100 pounds) are taken at Montague. Expect a long boat ride, however (three hours one way is typical), but it is definitely worth it. Fish in the 300- to 350-pound range are boated every season. Mid-May to early September is the peak.

If the weather is too rough, some boats opt to stay closer to home, such as around Aialik Bay and Day Harbor, jigging for a multitude of bottomfish.

It should be noted here that the rocky coastline of the peninsula supports ideal lingcod and rockfish habitat and anglers report outstanding catches during the summer and early fall months. In fact, this area has held numerous state and trophy records for lingcod with fish between 50 and 70 pounds possible. A great variety of rockfishes are present with light gear, shallow water opportunities possible for some pelagic species.

Another more exotic species is the salmon shark. This tremendous fighter averages 150 pounds, with some specimens weighing half a ton or more. July and August are the months to zero in on them in this area with boaters focusing on the numerous coves and small bays along the southern section of Resurrection Bay. These gargantuan fish are here for the same reason many anglers are – to locate and eat salmon. Generally, wherever there are concentrations of salmon (pinks especially), there will be salmon sharks. In fact, schools of dozens or even hundreds of individual fish may be encountered.

A bonus for anglers plying the remote waters of Resurrection Bay and outlying areas are the abundance of bottomfish, such as Pacific cod. This delicious species is available in great numbers and may be targeted by charters when other fish are not cooperating or if limits have already been reached of salmon and halibut. They may be found in a many types of structure and very often caught incidentally to fishing for halibut and lingcod.

Other bottomfish include several species of flounder, pollock, and sablefish, the latter of which are present in decent numbers in the deeper areas of the bay and the southern coast of the peninsula.



### Seward Silver Salmon Derby

One of the largest, longest-running, and profitable fishing derbies in Alaska is the annual Seward Silver Salmon Derby. Started in 1956, it has become a tradition with a great many local anglers (and even visiting) as the cash stakes are high and fishing excellent.

Commencing the second week of August, the derby lasts for some ten days and offers a wide range of categories in which to participate, including women and kids divisions and daily prizes. Of course, tagged fish valued up to $50,000 are available and anglers always have a shot at catching the heaviest fish of the derby, a catch usually in the 18- to 20-pound range. Bigger fish are out there as silvers up to a monstrous 25 pounds have been caught yet none have been entered in the derby weighing more than about 22 pounds.

Whenever in this are during derby season, always be prepared and pick up a ticket -- whether casting from boat or shore. And remember, these salmon are often caught by anglers targeting other species.

# Other Productive Fisheries & Additional Opportunities

## SALMON CREEK

**Fishing:** ★★½ **Scenery:** ★★★★
**Accessibility:** ★★ **Solitude:** ★★★★
**Location:** Southeastern Kenai Peninsula drainage, Seward area, 121 miles south of Anchorage.
**Access:** The Seward Highway provides two main points of access; one on the upper stream and one on the lower. Respect private property.
Upper Stream
*A. Seward Highway Bridge* – Milepost 5.9. Road crosses stream, very limited parking.
Lower Stream
*B. Nash Road Bridge* – Milepost 3.3 Seward Highway. East on Nash Road 0.5 mile to stream crossing. Limited parking.
**Facilities:** None available at access points but lodging, RV facilities, and other services can be found nearby.
**Species:** Pink, chum, and silver salmon, Dolly Varden. Also red salmon and rare rainbow trout.
**Restrictions:** King salmon fishing is prohibited. Salmon fishing prohibited upstream of Nash Road bridge; open below bridge from June 16 through December 31. Single hook, artificial lures only below bridge. Consult ADF&G regulations.
**Fishing:** This multi-faceted, semi-glacial stream supports runs of most salmon species as well as spring and late summer/fall migrations of sea-run char. Although the upper section flows low and clear throughout the year, the lower portion is much more unpredictable with turbid water conditions the norm during the warmer summer months. The majority of angling effort occurs higher up in the drainage, near and around the Seward Highway crossing.

As salmon fishing is only allowed in the far lower end of the stream near tidewater, the best fishing is in late summer and fall when the water clears, exposing a decent run of silver salmon. Pinks can be targeted successfully earlier in the season using high-visibility lures.

*(Courtesy Eagle Eye Images)*

For those chasing Dolly Varden, head to the upper reaches, around the highway crossing. Starting in mid-summer and continuing into fall, anglers can cast to likely structure with good results. Sight-fishing is possible too; look behind spawning salmon. Pinks and chums spawn here during August and September; use appropriate bead size and color.

**Pink Salmon.** Good; July 25 – August 5; average 3 – 4 pounds. Fluorescent spoons, spinners, attractors, and flies are best if murky water.
**Chum Salmon.** Fair; July 25 – August 10; average 6 – 12 pounds. Fluorescent spoons, spinners, attractors, and flies
**Silver Salmon.** Fair to good; September 1 – 20; average 6 – 11 pounds. Brightly colored spinners and flies when water is glacial, darker hues if clear.
**Dolly Varden.** Good; July 25 – September 15; average 8 – 20 inches. Egg/flesh imitations are best in late summer and fall. Occasional trophy specimens to 28 inches or more.

## RESURRECTION RIVER

**Fishing:** ★★ **Scenery:** ★★★★
**Accessibility:** ★★ **Solitude:** ★★★★

**Location:** Southeastern Kenai Peninsula drainage, Seward area, 123 miles south of Anchorage.

**Access:** The Seward Highway provides limited points of access to lower reaches at bridge crossings with additional access to river mouth off Nash Road and upper river along Exit Glacier Road. Respect private property.

Upper River

*A. Exit Glacier Road* – Milepost 3.7 Seward Highway. West on Exit Glacier Road; road parallels river for several miles. Limited parking and primitive camping.

River Mouth

*B. Nash Road* – Milepost 3.3 Seward Highway. East on Nash Road 0.4 mile to private access site on right with parking. Hike 1 mile to tidal area of river.

Lower River

*C. Seward Highway Bridge #1 & 2* – Milepost 3.0/2.9. Road crosses river, very limited parking.

West Fork

*D. Seward Highway Bridge #3* – Milepost 2.8. Road crosses stream, limited parking next to Railroad bridge off Airport Road.

**Facilities:** None available at access points but lodging, RV facilities, and other services can be found nearby.

**Species:** Red, pink, chum, and silver salmon, Dolly Varden. Also a few rainbow trout.

**Restrictions:** King salmon fishing is prohibited. Salmon fishing prohibited upstream of Seward Highway; open below bridge from June 16 through December 31. Single hook, artificial lures only below bridge. Consult ADF&G regulations.

**Fishing:** Created mainly by meltwater from the Exit Glacier and surrounding ice fields, the Resurrection flows high and silty during the summer months with most sport fishing occurring at the mouths of clearwater tributaries. The West Fork Resurrection, however, typically runs semi-glacial with fishing available throughout the season. Come fall, the main river begins to clear up, presenting angling opportunities to those willing to put in time and effort scouting the various sections of river for late-arriving salmon and char.

Four species of salmon and sea-run Dolly Varden call Resurrection home, with pink and chum salmon finning upstream in late summer, followed soon after by a descent run of silvers in fall. Red salmon are primarily targeted in a snag fishery at the river mouth in early summer, although late-run fish may be taken in the main river later in the season as well. Schools of Dollies may be encountered in autumn, resulting in fast action. Salmon fishing is limited by regulation to the downstream side of Seward Highway but char may be caught in all sections of the river.

In total, Resurrection is hit-and-miss for sport fishing purposes due to water conditions, yet the West Fork probably offer anglers the best and most consistent opportunity.

**Red Salmon.** Good to excellent; May 25 – June 15; average 4 – 7 pounds. The early run fish are taken by snagging in the tidal area of the lower river; use flies in late summer on the West Fork.

**Pink Salmon.** Good; July 25 – August 5; average 3 – 4 pounds. Use spoons, spinners, and flies in the West Fork.

**Chum Salmon.** Fair; July 25 – August 10; average 6 – 12 pounds. Spoons, spinners, flies in West Fork best bet.

**Silver Salmon.** Fair; September 1 – 20; average 6 – 12 pounds. Spinners and flies at the mouth of West Fork. Main river has a few fish when water clears in fall.

**Dolly Varden.** Fair to good; July 25 – September 30; average 8 – 20 inches. Flies generally work best; forage/attractors in mid-summer, egg/flesh patters later on. Occasional trophy specimens to 28 inches or more possible.

*This blushed male silver struck a fly drifted through a deep hole. Expect many autumn fish to show some color, yet a few chromers will be available up until the snow flies.*

## ADDITIONAL OPPORTUNITIES

### Salmon Viewing

The Resurrection Bay area has a plethora of waters perfect for observing migrating and spawning salmon, with viewing possible from late May through November. All five salmon species can be spotted, yet kings are a somewhat rare species; red, pink, chum, and silver salmon are the most prevalent. Be mindful that these streams have frequent bear sightings.

The following is a listing of some of the better places to go and see salmon (and possibly bears too).

**Grouse Creek:** The Seward Highway parallels this small and shallow clearwater stream between Milepost 10.5 and 8.1 with some limited parking available. Grouse is primarily home to late summer runs of red salmon, with peak viewing during the month of August. Some pink and chum salmon may also be present; a few silvers may be spotted in October.

**Bear Creek:** From Milepost 6.6 of Seward Highway, Bear Lake Road leads about a mile to stream crossing next to weir. Parking available. This is a great spot to see both bright fish in the early stages of their migration and spawners. Reds come through starting in late May and peaking in numbers from mid-June to mid-July. Large run of pinks in latter part of August into September on even-numbered years. Decent spot for silvers beginning in mid-September and lasting through October.

**Spring Creek:** Turn onto Nash Road at Milepost 3.2 of Seward Highway and follow 5.2 miles to stream crossing. Best viewing is from the Spring Creek parking/campground on the right. This is the perfect spot for early-run chums with peak spawning from mid-July into August; pinks run heavy in even years, from mid-August to mid-September.

**Seward Lagoon:** At Milepost 1.3 Seward Highway, turn onto Dairy Hill Lane short distance to Benny Benson Memorial and observation platform on left at the head of the lake and mouth of Dairy Creek. Multiple species present, including a few kings (in July/August), with good viewing of reds, pinks, and chums from mid-August to mid-September. Silvers spawn here in fair numbers from mid-October into November.

**Tonsina Creek:** From downtown Seward just west of the Alaska SeaLife Center, turn onto Lowell Point Road at intersection of Railway Avenue heading south along bay to Tonsina Creek Trailhead at mile 2.1. It is a 2-mile hike from here to footbridge crossing stream. Great spot to see fish as water is shallow and crystal clear. Pinks are most plentiful from mid-August to mid-September, chums from late July to late August; a few silvers may be present during September and October.

(Courtesy Roy & Beverley Bailey)

### Wildlife In and Around Seward

Very few marine ports in Southcentral Alaska can match Seward and Resurrection Bay in terms of wildlife viewing. The best time to be out spotting is generally from May to October, although some species (such as seals and sea otters) are year-round residents of the area.

Brown and black bears are present from spring though fall in and around the community of Seward and frequently observed during August and September alongside small salmon spawning streams. For best viewing, be out at dawn and dusk.

Seals, sea lions, and sea otters inhabit all areas of the bay and often seen right up along the waterfront in town, including the small boat harbor. Porpoises and whales do come close to shore on occasion but are much more common in the outer reaches of Resurrection Bay and the Gulf of Alaska; killer whales sometimes come close to town and spotted from area beaches.

(Courtesy Roy & Beverley Bailey)

Sterling • Soldotna • Kenai • Kasilof

# Western Kenai

King Salmon • Red Salmon • Pink Salmon • Silver Salmon
Steelhead Trout • Rainbow Trout • Dolly Varden

Canoe Lakes

Bank Fishing

Tidewater Rivers

Trophy Salmon

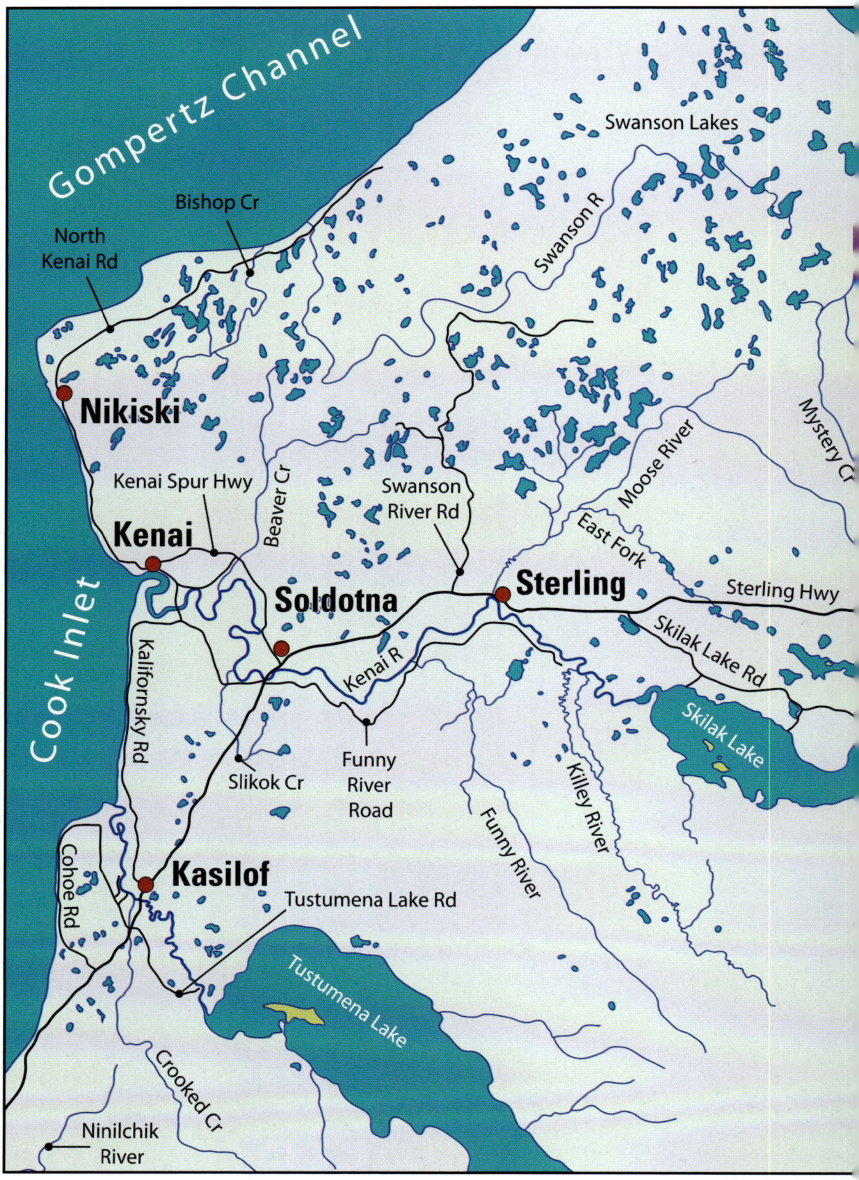

**Area Population Centers:** Kenai, Soldotna, Kasilof, Sterling, Nikiski

**Key Species:** King, Red, Pink, and Silver Salmon, Steelhead and Rainbow Trout, Dolly Varden

**Other Species:** Chum Salmon, Arctic Char, Round Whitefish, Northern Pike, Pacific Halibut, Bottomfish

**Main Destinations/Hot Spots:** Kenai and Kasilof rivers

**Other Destinations:** Moose and Swanson rivers, Crooked Creek, Skilak Lake

**Additional Opportunities:** Trophy Salmon & Trout Fishing, Fly-In Fishing

**Summary of Area Fishing:**
Completely different in surrounding scenery than the mountainous eastern half of the peninsula, the Western section is rather flat in comparison. The fishing, however, is definitely top-notch as literally millions of ocean-bright salmon enter area rivers during a few short months, yielding superior action from both shore as well as boats. Large, glacial rivers dominate the landscape along with a few smaller clearwater streams, yet lakes containing wild and stocked populations of trout and char are plentiful. The twin cities of Kenai and Soldotna, a mere few miles distance from each other, make for perfect hubs in which to thoroughly explore the surrounding area.

At the center of the western portion of the peninsula lies two relatively large glacial systems, the Kenai and Kasilof, both of which sports some incredible angling opportunities on so many levels. Being only 15 minutes driving time apart, they share the distinction of receiving massive sockeye runs that even outpace kings and rainbows in popularity. Despite attracting what undoubtedly are the heaviest crowds on the road system, there is a reason why anglers keep coming back to this area year after year, some even for decades. Huge salmon runs that often support very liberal bag limits has earned the Kenai and Kasilof as the go-to fisheries to fill freezers with salmon fillets, something that keep anglers (and dip netters) swarming the area every July.

What made this area of Alaska world famous is trophy and record-class fishing. The record sport-caught king salmon was taken in the Kenai and more large kings than any other river in the world have been caught here. On top of this, trophy-sized reds, pinks, silvers, rainbows, and Dollies are present for good measure.

For those wanting a more peaceful setting, day-long to a week or more duration trips are possible in the lowland rivers and near countless tributary lakes of the northern section of the peninsula. Canoeing and kayaking is an incredibly efficient way to explore these waters that are teeming with silver salmon, rainbow trout, Dolly Varden, and Arctic char.

May through October are the best months.

# *MIDDLE* Kenai River

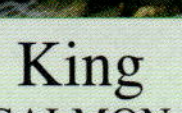
King SALMON

Red SALMON

Pink SALMON

Silver SALMON

Rainbow TROUT

Dolly VARDEN

**Highlights:** Fabulous fall trophy trout and char action along with some of the best silver salmon fishing on the peninsula. Semi-wilderness setting with high scenic values.

**Best Fishing:** Mid-June to late October.

**Regulatory Restrictions:** Very conservative.

**Location:** Central Kenai Peninsula, adjacent to the communities of Sterling and Soldotna, Sterling Highway, 111 miles south of Anchorage.

**Description:** The middle portion of the Kenai River is from the outlet of Skilak Lake downstream to the Sterling Highway Bridge in Soldotna. Parts of the south bank and the first few miles of river below the lake is believed to be the most remote area of the mainstem Kenai with very few access roads, little to no settlement (outside the communities of Sterling and Soldotna), and not nearly the crowds of other anglers so common on the lower river – even during the height of the fishing season.

The stream gradient between the lake and Naptowne Rapids near Sterling (10.5 river miles) is 3.3 feet per mile, which translates to minimal current. There are an abundance of large, well-defined holes and runs that support huge concentrations of salmon, with some fish staging here preparing to run up the clearwater tributary of Killey River. But for late-run kings, reds, and silvers, along with pinks, this is a major spawning area and anglers fishing these respective runs often report phenomenal catch rates. Trout and char are very abundant (and large).

The 19.4-mile portion of the Kenai from Naptowne Rapids to the Sterling Highway Bridge is much different in characteristics. Apart from being more populated, the river does not meander nearly as much and the speed of the current picks up substantially, with stream gradient being 5.4 feet per mile. Holes and runs are no longer as well defined but are still present and have a way of concentrating fish heading upstream. It pays to have experience in this area in order to find the hot spots.

Wildlife such as moose, eagles, bears, waterfowl, and other animal species are a common sight along this stretch of river, primarily along the south bank and areas of Kenai Keys to the Skilak Lake outlet. The largest concentration of bald eagle in Southcentral Alaska can be observed here in late fall and winter as  hundreds of eagles feed on a late run of silver salmon.

*A view of the upper section of Naptowne Rapids in Sterling. Trout and char fishing in this area can be exceptional in fall.*

Early in the season (May into June), the Kenai River usually flows very low with many spots that can make boat travel difficult. By July the volume increases dramatically and peaks in August. Water levels drop again toward the end of September and October.

**Facilities:** The ten main access points generally have the same facilities across the board which includes parking, camping, restrooms, and developed trails. Several also have boat launches available. Since the communities of Sterling and Soldotna are situated right on the river, there are many other amenities present to anglers, such as hotels/motels, RV parks, lodging, cabin and boat rentals, fishing guides, fish processing, and emergency services.

**Access:** The Sterling Highway parallels the river to some extent yet there are relatively few public access points due to private property and undeveloped land. Funny River Road runs along the south side of the river with a couple of places offering public access. It must be noted that there is an abundance of charter/guide operators in the area, most of which allow clients to fish off the bank at their properties.

## Sterling Highway

**A. Torpedo Lake** – Milepost 78.2. South on Feuding Lane 2 miles, left on Kenai Keys Road 1.5 miles, continue left 1.2

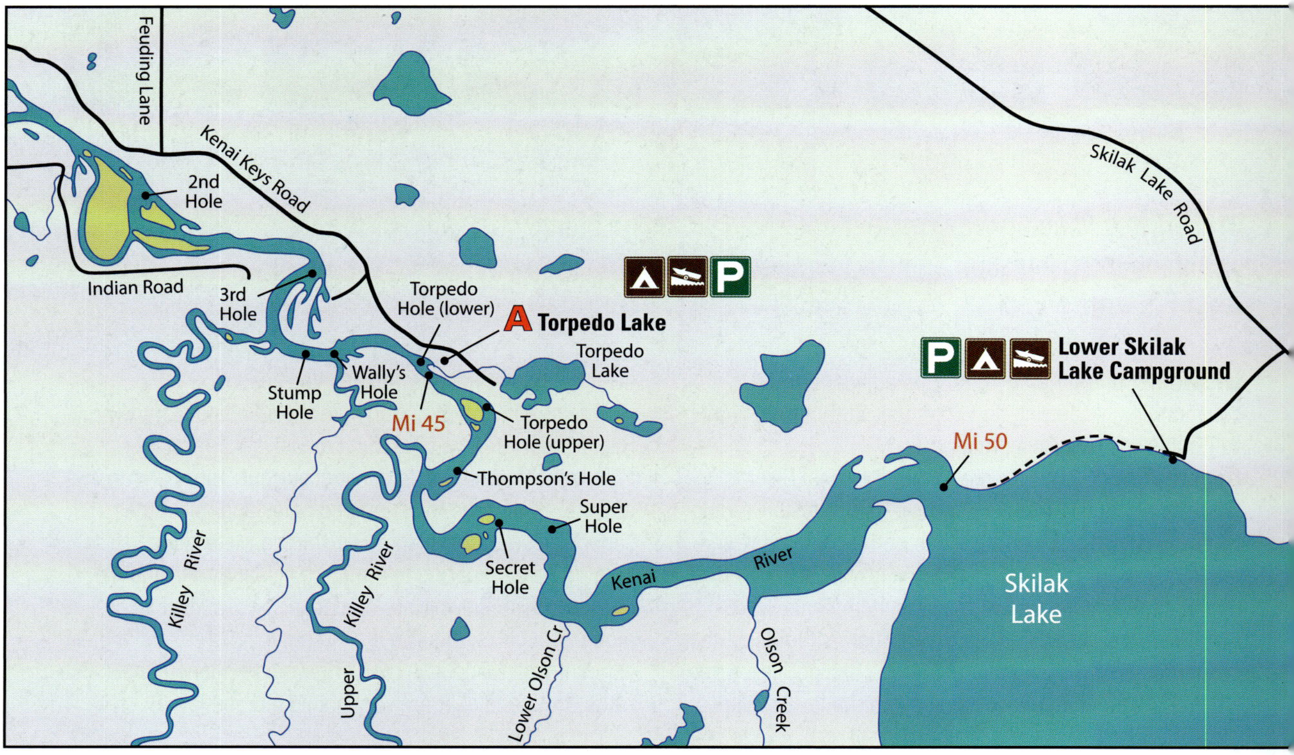

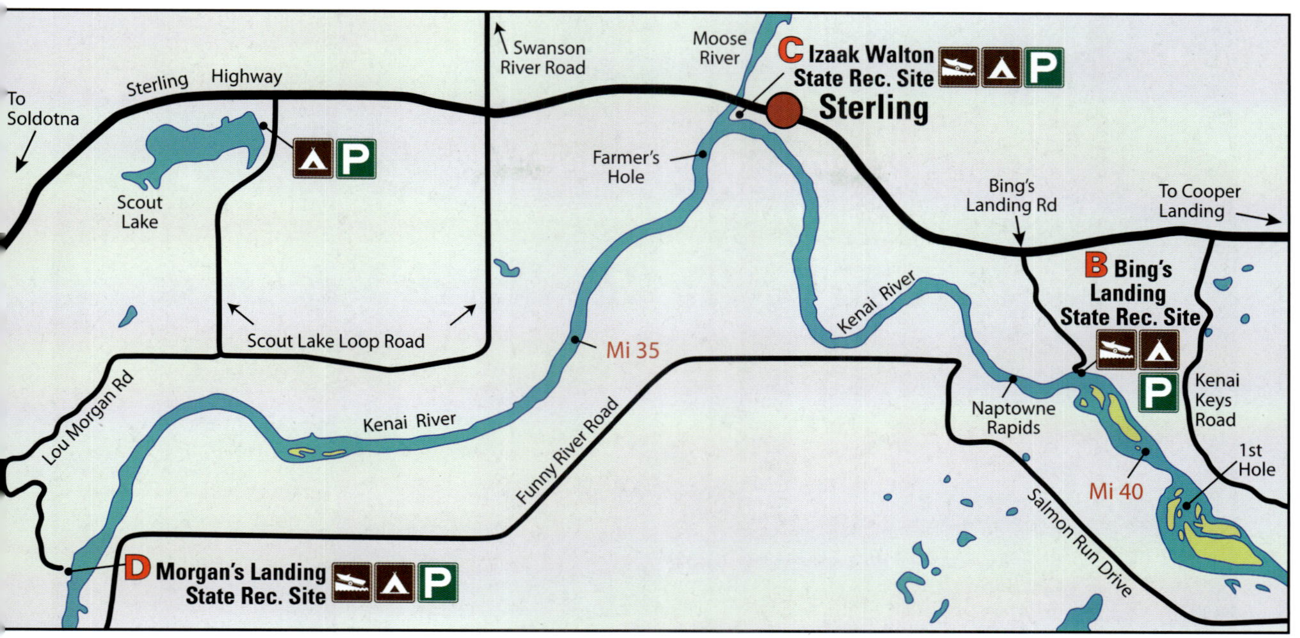


miles to end of road. Parking. Locate trail leading 0.2 mile to river.

**B. Bing's Landing** – Milepost 80.2. Turn south on Bing's Landing Road by sign 0.8 miles to large parking area and river. Camping, restrooms, and boat launch available.

**C. Izaak Walton Campground** – Milepost 82.3. South on access road short distance to campground and the confluence of Kenai and Moose rivers. Parking, camping, boat launch, picnic tables, and restrooms. Trails lead to mouth of Moose and the banks of Kenai River.

**D. Morgan's Landing** – Milepost 84.9. South on Scout Lake Road 1.6 miles to a "T," right on Lou Morgan Road 2.4 miles, right on access road 1.5 miles to campground and parking area. Parking, camping, boat launch, picnic tables, and restrooms. Trails lead from parking and camping areas to and along the river.

**E. Swiftwater Campground** – Milepost 94.1. East on Redoubt Avenue 0.6 miles, right on Griffin Avenue 0.8 miles, right on access road leading to campground and river. Parking, camping, picnic tables, and restrooms. Trails lead to river. Developed boardwalk present.

**F. Moose Meadows #1** – Milepost 94.1. East on Redoubt Avenue 1.5 miles, road becomes Keystone Drive after curve, proceed another 2.1 miles to access site

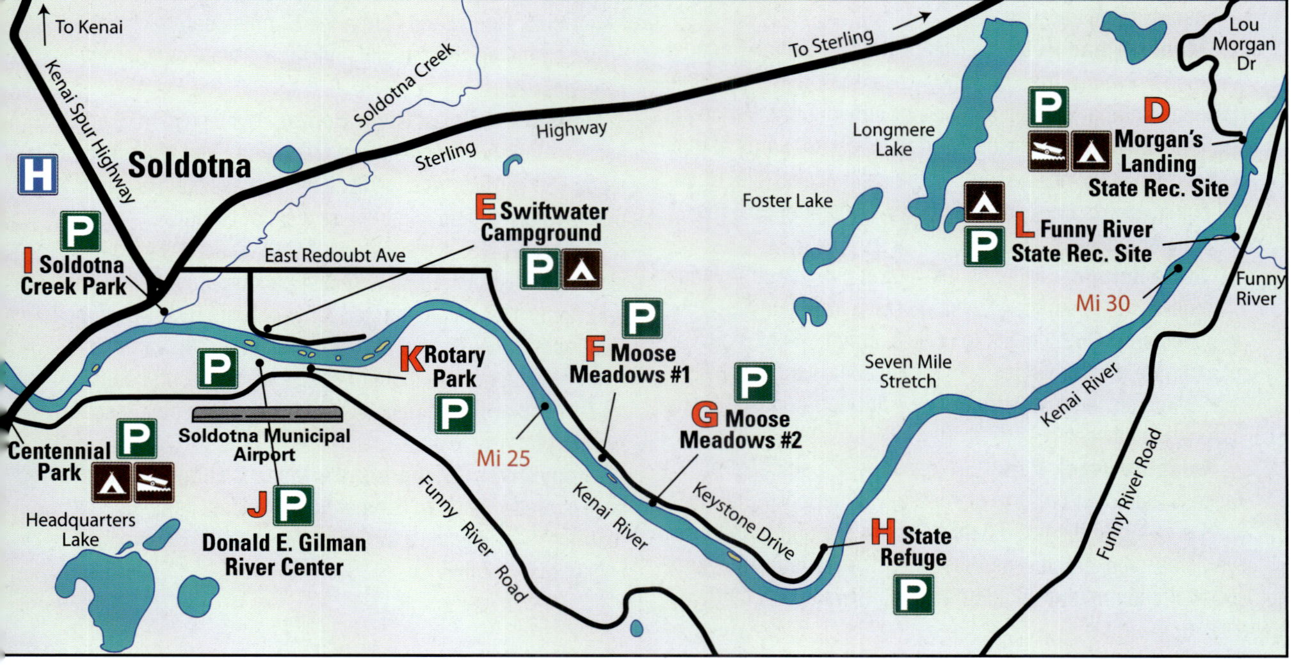

on right. Parking, restrooms. Developed trail leads 100 yards to fishing area with walkways spanning river bank. Wheelchair accessible. Open to public access from July 1 through September 30. Respect private property in area. Free parking and access.

**G. Moose Meadows #2** – Milepost 94.1. East on Redoubt Avenue 1.7 miles, road becomes Keystone Drive after curve, proceed another 3.0 miles to access site on right. Parking is on left side of road; restrooms. Trail leads 200 yards to river. Developed walkway present. Wheelchair accessible. Open to public access from July 1 through September 30. Free parking and access.

**H. State Refuge** – Milepost 94.1. East on Redoubt Avenue 1.7 miles, road becomes Keystone Drive after curve, proceed another 3.5 miles to access site at end of road. Parking for all size vehicles, primitive boat launch. Public easement closed to use from July 1 through August 14. Free parking and access.

**I. Soldotna Creek Park** – Milepost 94.4. Southeast on access road next to State of Alaska Maintenance Station and proceed to the left 0.2 mile to park. Parking for all size vehicles, picnic tables, and restrooms. Trails lead 200 yards to river and mouth of Soldotna Creek. Developed boardwalk present. Free parking and access.

## Funny River Road

The road begins at Milepost 96.1 Sterling Highway (Milepost 0) at the main intersection just south of the Kenai River Bridge and continues 17 miles before changing street name, and eventually ends at a private campground (Milepost 22).

**J. Donald E. Gilman River Center** – Milepost 1.6. Left on access road to science center parking lot. Trail and walkway leads 150 yards to river. Wheelchair accessible. RV parking, primitive camping available just west of center.

**K. Rotary Park** – Milepost 2.4. North on access road by sign short distance to large gravel parking area. Parking and restrooms. Not recommended for very large RVs. Developed trail leads 50 yards to a "T," left fork heads 200 yards to river; must negotiate flight of stairs. Right fork proceeds 1/4 mile to walkway and river. Wheelchair accessible. Respect private property in area.

**L. Funny River Campground** – Milepost 11.4. North on access road by sign to campground. Parking, camping, and restrooms. Trail leads short distance to Kenai River and Funny River confluence.

## Rules & Regulations

**Note:** *The Kenai River is the most heavily regulated drainage in the state and only a portion of the rules and regulations are listed here.*

**Open Season:** January 1 through December 31; except from the outlet of Skilak Lake downstream to the mouth of Lower Killey River, which is closed to all fishing from May 2 through June 10.
**Open Area:** The entire middle river is open to fishing.
**Legal Gear/Tackle:** Only one unbaited, single-hook lure is allowed from January 1 through July 14. Additional bait, tackle, and area restrictions apply.

**King Salmon**
- Open season is January 1 through July 31.
- Bag limit is (1) per day and (1) in possession (20 inches or longer); seasonal limit is (2). For kings less than 20 inches (Jacks), the limit is (10).
- From January 1 through July 14, fish must be less than 42 inches or longer than 55 inches to be retained.

**Silver Salmon**
- Open season is July 1 through November 30.
- Bag limit is (2) per day and (2) in possession (16 inches or longer) from July 1 through August 31; and (3) per day and (3) in possession from September 1 through November 30.

For salmon less than 16 inches (Jacks), the limit is (10).

**All Other Salmon**
- Open all season (see general "Open Season" above).
- Red salmon bag limit is (3) per day and (6) in possession (16 inches or longer), and pink salmon (6) per day and (6) in possession. For salmon less than 16 inches (Jacks), the limit is (10).

**Rainbow/Steelhead Trout & Dolly Varden**
- Open season for trout and char is January 1 through December 31.
- Bag limit is (1) per day and (1) in possession for each species.
- Retained fish must be less than 18 inches long for each species.

**Other Fishes**
- Open all season (see general "Open Season" above).
- Arctic grayling bag limit is (5) per day and (5) in possession, any size.
- Whitefish has no bag or possession limit, no size restrictions.

*Anglers prepare to launch at Bing's Landing to access more remote sections of the river.*

## Fishing Middle Kenai River

**Access:** ★★★
**Scenery:** ★★★
**Wildlife:** ★★★
**Sight Fishing:** ★
**Bank/Wading:** ★★★
**Boat/Floating:** ★★★★★

**Species:** King, red, pink, and silver salmon, rainbow trout, and Dolly Varden. Catches of chum salmon, steelhead trout, and northern pike are rare. A few lake trout and round whitefish are present, the former mostly near Skilak Lake.
**Summary:** The middle Kenai has a combination of factors that make it a very special place for anglers. Of course, salmon runs are highly prolific and trout and char concentrations among the most dense in the entire drainage. Parts of the river give the impression of being quite remote from the road system, while other sections are distinctly urban. While most of the bank fishing is done near populated areas, much of the river is only accessible by boat. One of the best ways to enjoy this river is to float it from the outlet of Skilak Lake, taking out at Bing's Landing or any other point farther downstream.

As with any stretch of the Kenai River, there are two runs each of king, red, and silver salmon, reflecting the various populations within the drainage. There can also be said to be two runs of pink salmon yet they do not seem to be as distinct as that of other species. Chum salmon, however, are rare.

The early runs of salmon are primarily tributary fish and migrate through the middle Kenai on the way to the spawning streams of Funny, Moose, Killey, and clearwater drainages of the upper Kenai River and Kenai Lake. The late returns of kings and silvers are almost strictly mainstem Kenai fish unlike that of reds which are both tributary and mainstem salmon. The outlet of Skilak Lake and the first few miles below hosts a rare winter run of silver salmon that remains present all winter long into spring.

(Courtesy Mystic Waters Fly-Fishing)

(Courtesy Mystic Waters Fly-Fishing)

Fish of the late runs are in general physically larger than those of early runs, of which the vast number of trophy sport catches in the Kenai River derive from. Trophy – even near-record – catches of king, red, pink, and silver salmon are possible. Some of the kings in the area may reach 80 to 90 pounds or more while reds routinely top 12 to 14 pounds. Silvers of 20 pounds are caught every season and are reported to reach weights of 24 pounds. Pinks, although not targeted to any degree, are among the largest in the state. The Alaska record pink was caught at the confluence of Moose River and Kenai rivers and weighed well over 12 pounds.

Trout are present year-round in the middle section of Kenai River, predominantly in the area above Naptowne Rapids and the Kenai Keys. The fishing stays relatively subdued until the salmon runs arrive. By late summer (mid-August), the action really heats up as the salmon begin to spawn and the trout respond in a feeding frenzy. This activity stays strong through the fall months. The September-October fishery near Skilak Lake is legendary for trophy trout. Some of the largest rainbows in Alaska have been caught here, known to weigh into the mid-twenties with historical catches of 30 pounds or more.

There are two populations of char in the Kenai River; resident and sea-run fish. The former stay in the river year-round, migrating into the middle Kenai sometime in late spring and early summer, returning to wintering areas in late fall. The sea-run char, however, move out of Skilak Lake and into the river in spring and do not return again until July and August. Anglers encounter the best fishing starting in mid-July with the onslaught of late-run king and red salmon, with action staying excellent through fall.

*Anglers enjoy a double hookup in a section of water right downstream of Skilak Lake. Action can be legendary here, especially for large trout and char. Late-season coho offer stupendous fishing.*

## Fish Availability

● = High ● = Moderate ● = Low ● = Closed

| Species | MAY | JUN | JUL | AUG | SEP | OCT | NOV |
|---|---|---|---|---|---|---|---|
| **King Salmon** | Low Low Low Low | Moderate Moderate High High | High Moderate Moderate High | Closed Closed Closed Closed | Closed Closed Closed | | |
| **Red Salmon** | Low Low Low | Moderate High High Moderate | Low Moderate High High | High Moderate Low Low | Low Low Low Low | Low | |
| **Pink Salmon** | | Low | Low Moderate Moderate Moderate | High High High Moderate | Low Low Low Low | | |
| **Silver Salmon** | | | Low Low Low | Low Moderate High High | High Moderate Moderate High | High High High Moderate | Moderate Moderate Moderate Moderate |
| **Rainbow Trout** | Closed Closed Closed Closed | Closed High High High | High High High High | High High High High | High High High High | High High High Moderate | Moderate Moderate Moderate Moderate |
| **Dolly Varden** | Low Low Low Low | Low Low Low Low | Moderate Moderate High High | High High High High | High High High High | High High High Moderate | Moderate Moderate Moderate Moderate |
| **Whitefish** | Low Low Low Low | Low Low Low Low | Moderate Moderate High High | High High High High | High High High High | High High High Moderate | Moderate Moderate Low Low |
| Angling Pressure | Low Low Low Moderate | Moderate High High High | High Moderate High High | High High High High | High High High High | High High High Moderate | Moderate Moderate Low Low |

(Courtesy EZ Limit Guide Service)

*Guide and client show off another trophy Kenai king. The middle section of the Kenai offers some less crowded conditions for those targeting these giant fish. Late July is best time to go.*

### King Salmon

**Rating:** ★★½ Fair to good from boat, poor from shore.
**Season:** January 1 through July 31.
**Timing:** May 1 – July 31; peak June 15 – July 5 (early run) and July 20 – 31 (late run).
**Size:** Average 20 – 40 pounds (early run) and 30 – 50 pounds (late run), up to 90 pounds.
**Tackle:** Spoons, spinners, attractors, plugs, flies, and bait.
**Tips:** Angler participation on the middle Kenai is much lower than that seen on the lower river. Drifting, back-trolling, and back-bouncing are all effective techniques here. Using bait such as salmon roe will increase catch rates substantially. Focus efforts on holes and runs in the stretch of water between Soldotna and Naptowne Rapids.

If casting from shore, sporadic success can be had at Swiftwater, Morgan's Hole, and at or near the confluence of clearwater tributaries such as Funny, Moose, and Killey rivers. Drift an attractor with eggs or use large spinners in size 6. Flyfishers need to use large, gaudy attractor patterns.

Beware of seasonally closed areas in the vicinity of Funny and Killey rivers that protect ready to spawn early-run kings.

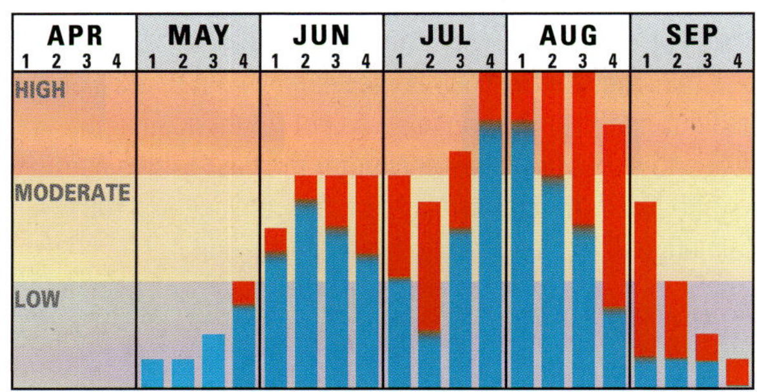


*Middle Kenai River King Salmon.* ● = Fresh ● = Spawning

### Red Salmon

**Rating:** ★★★★★ Excellent (late run) and fair (early run).
**Season:** January 1 through December 31.
**Timing:** May 10 – October 15; peak June 5 – 15 (early run) and July 15 – August 10 (late run).
**Size:** Average 6 – 7 pounds, up to 11 pounds (early run); 6 – 8 pounds, up to 14 pounds (late run).
**Tackle:** Flies.
**Tips:** Anglers are advised to focus their casts (or flips) near the shoreline, about four to 15 feet out. Most often, schools of red salmon migrate close to the bank and making long casts are generally unproductive. Occasionally, though,

salmon do move through mid-river as well, this being particularly the case with large, bright fish. The darkest, or pre-spawn salmon, are found near the bank. The lake outlet, due to its slow current, is not known as a particularly productive area despite heavy concentrations of reds.

Chartreuse or fluorescent green are preferred but flaming red or orange can be remarkably effective in low light conditions. Anglers opting for more traditional patterns do well with streamers and attractors in more neutral shades of color, such as blue, green, black, purple, and white.

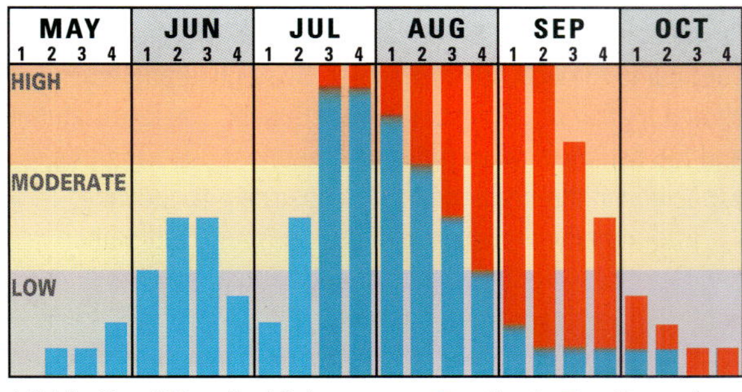


*Middle Kenai River Red Salmon.* ● = *Fresh* ● = *Spawning*

*The Kenai is known for its larger-than-average sockeye and the current state record of 16 pounds was taken here. Expect many of these fish to be the size of a hefty silver salmon and a great challenge on any gear. Here, a proud angler displays her first salmon.*

*Anglers line the banks of the river at a popular access point near Soldotna in hopes of intercepting schools of salmon migrating near shore. Despite potential crowds, action can be superb.*

## Pink Salmon

**Rating:** ★★★★ Excellent on even-numbered years, poor to fair on odd.
**Season:** January 1 through December 31.
**Timing:** June 25 – September 25; peak August 10 – 25.
**Size:** Average 3 – 6 pounds, up to 9 pounds.
**Tackle:** Spoons, spinners, plugs, and flies.
**Tips:** The majority of pinks will avoid strong currents, migrating close to shore and resting in water with slow or still flow. If salmon appear finicky, try darker-colored lures in river with more current. Although the run will be thick as far upstream as Skilak Lake, the better fishing is downstream between Sterling and Soldotna where pinks tend to be brighter and scrappier.

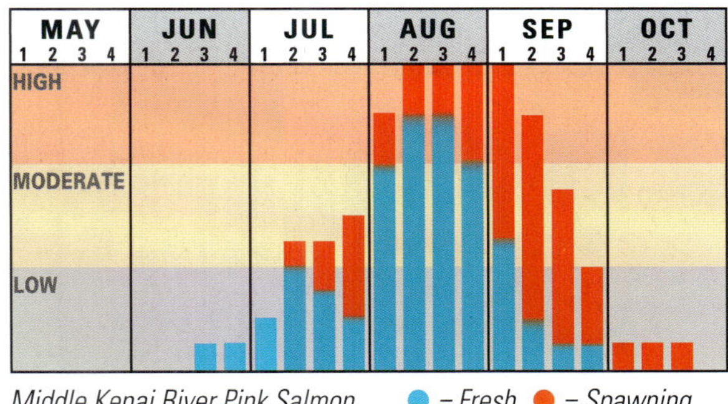


*Middle Kenai River Pink Salmon.* ● = *Fresh* ● = *Spawning*

*(Courtesy of EZ Limit Guide Service)*

*Delighted angler with a trophy coho, caught on a size 5 spinner during an early fall outing. Although trophies are possible all season long, they are especially common during the late run.*

## Silver Salmon

**Rating:** ★★★½ Good to excellent.
**Season:** July 1 through November 30.
**Timing:** July 10 – November 30, peak August 20 – September 5 (early run) and September 25 – October 25 (late run).
**Size:** Average 5 – 10 pounds, up to 15 pounds (early run); 6 – 15 pounds, up to 22 pounds (late run).
**Tackle:** Spoons, spinners, plugs, attractors, flies, and bait.
**Tips:** The silvers in this stretch of the Kenai have a tendency to migrate fairly close to the bank but may be found in mid-current as well. Late-run silvers often tend to hold in deeper water with more current. The mouth of sloughs and quiet water on the inside of river bends are perfect holding areas, as are confluences of clearwater tributaries. The Kenai Keys area has long been heralded as one of the best locations in this stretch of river with heavy concentrations of fish present, especially late-run salmon.

Size 4 and 5 spinners in blue, green, and chartreuse are all good while more visible hues such as orange, red, and pink are good during low light conditions and most anytime for late-run fish. Copper or metallic silver work if fish appear very finicky. Flash flies or any other attractor fly with some level of visibility can be equally productive. Salmon roe drifted through holes or fished stationary on the bottom is deadly.

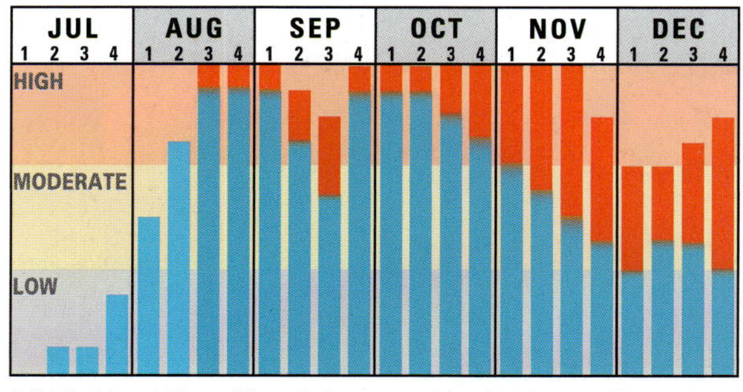


*Middle Kenai River Silver Salmon.* ● = *Fresh* ● = *Spawning*

## Rainbow Trout

**Rating:** ★★★★★ Excellent.
**Season:** June 11 through May 1.
**Timing:** June 11 – May 1; peak July 20 – October 20.
**Size:** Average 10 – 20 inches, up to 35 inches (20+ pounds).
**Tackle:** Spoons, spinners, plugs, attractors, and flies.
**Tips:** The fish are distributed throughout river section in late spring and early summer but become more focused on salmon spawning areas starting in late summer and continuing through fall into winter. By August, anglers should try fishing above Naptowne Rapids. The late summer and fall fishery is rated tops with excellent opportunities, especially in the Kenai Keys area upstream to the lake.

Traditionally, the larger fish are caught in September and October when the seasonal glut of food sources is at a peak. Expect to see some fish in the 30-32-inch range and 10-12 pounds. The largest trophy catches in middle Kenai come from the upper reaches right below Skilak Lake where 20-25-pound fish are beached every season.

*Client and guide are satisfied with the catch of the day. With literally millions of spawning and dying salmon often clogging the river during the late summer and fall months, Kenai's wild rainbows grow to respectful length and weight.*

*(Courtesy Mystic Waters Fly-Fishing)*

## Dolly Varden

**Rating:** ★★★★ Excellent.
**Season:** January 1 through December 31.
**Timing:** All year, peak July 20 – October 20.
**Size:** Average 10 – 20 inches, up to 30 inches (10-12 pounds).
**Tackle:** Spoons, spinners, plugs, attractors, and flies.
**Tips:** Imitate food sources for best success. Small spoons and spinners and flies resembling juvenile salmon will take fish with regularity. Downstream of salmon cleaning stations are good in July, salmon spawning beds in late summer and fall. If char become immune to certain offerings, try something completely different.

Fishing can be terrific most anywhere along the river in July, the better action occurring above Naptowne Rapids from August on into the fall as fish congregate to feed on the salmon and their byproducts. From the Skilak Lake outlet downstream a few miles, superb opportunities exist. Char up to 15 pounds are caught every year and 18-pounders are reported on occasion.

(Courtesy Roy Bailey)

*Angler Beverley Bailey holds up a fine specimen of Dolly Varden. Using beads with a strike indicator is a sure-fire way of connecting with these fish in late summer and fall as the salmon get into the spawn. Match the "hatch" relative to salmon species.*

## Other Kenai Opportunities

(Courtesy Mystic Waters Fly-Fishing)

### Trophy Trout & Char Fishing

A fishing trip to this section of the Kenai River drainage would not be entirely complete without mentioning the stupendous opportunities that exist for catching much larger than normal trout and char, even a shot of what arguably could be the largest rainbows in Alaska. In fact, here it is the potential for mammoth-sized 'bows that attract trophy hunters instead of king salmon.

The entire length of the river between Soldotna and the outlet of Skilak Lake hosts a very healthy population of resident fish where fast-paced, solid double-digit days is the norm at the height of the season. Long synonymous with over-sized rainbows and Dolly Varden, anglers show a strong spirit of advocacy for catch-and-release, measuring their catches not so much in pounds but inches.

With an almost overwhelming food supply driven by salmon and its byproducts, Kenai rainbow trout grow big and sometimes almost absurdly fat, with catches in the mid-20s range common for a days outing. Thirty-plus-inch (10-12 pounds) specimens are hooked and released regularly, especially during the late summer and fall months, with the heaviest trout of the year estimated at 20-22 pounds and at least 34-36 inches. There have been several specimens reported at more than 25 pounds the last several years with historic catches of rainbows measuring around 40 inches and pushing 30 pounds, including one robust 39-incher landed only a few years ago.

Dolly Varden, both sea-run as well as resident, flourish in big numbers on the middle Kenai. Perhaps not as glamorous as its cousin, the rainbow trout, these husky char are nonetheless very worthy sporting opponents and achieve notoriety through their willingness to strike a wide assortment of lures and flies. There have been many a day when trout fishing appears slow that anglers have kept busy hooking and landing Dolly Varden, many of which reach proportions similar to rainbows. Fish between 20 and 25 inches are common with an occasional trophy stretching to 30 inches or more.

Keep in mind that Kenai's trout and char are all wild, native fish, something any angler would be able to respect and cherish when accounting for their abundance and size.

Dead-drifting beads, egg patterns, and flesh flies is undoubtedly best in late summer and fall (August-October), yet swinging big, black leeches can be absolutely deadly at times, particularly early and late in the season (November-April).

Although action can be hot throughout the length of the river, it is the particular portion of water immediately downstream of Skilak Lake to the vicinity of Bing's Landing just upstream of Sterling that is considered top notch. Holding water is abundant with plenty of very deep holes and pools, shoals, and riffles, perfect habitat for big game fish. Also, adding to the importance of trout and char production, is the fact that a significant portion of Kenai's salmon runs spawn in this area.

### Float Fishing

Perhaps the best way to approach the fabulous fishing on the middle Kenai is by boat. Many anglers launch their watercraft in the Sterling or Soldotna area and power to their favorite holes; however, an increasing number of people are choosing to experience the semi-wilderness of the river by drift boat, a very quiet and peaceful tool of access.

Putting in at the Lower Skilak Lake Campground off mile 13.8 Skilak Lake Road, anglers proceed a few miles to the outlet of the lake where the river begins. This first section can be rowed by those so inclined, yet the most practical and fastest (and safest) way is by using a low-powered outboard engine, such as an electric unit, to cover the distance. Be informed, however, that the first several miles of river starting at the lake outlet is a "drift-only" area from March 15 through June 14 (check regulations).

Take-out can be a number of various locations in the Sterling area (including private, guest-only facilities), but the vast majority of anglers use the Bing's Landing State Recreation Site off Milepost 80.2 Sterling Highway, a distance of 10.5 river miles from the lake outlet.

The middle Kenai is an easy float with an abundance of Class I water that lends perfectly to do-it-yourself trips. Many guides also operate in this area, a great solution for those without boats.

## Kenai's Kings: A Unique Breed

(Courtesy Greg Brush)

While it is well known within the world of sportfishing that the Kenai produces what is believed to be the largest strain of king salmon in the world, it was not always so. Up until overfishing, pollution, and habitat degradation overwhelmed and – ultimately – destroyed unique populations of mammoth-size kings in the Pacific Northwest, the Kenai was only one of several river drainages on the continent that supported runs of salmon where specimens up to 100 pounds were recorded with regular frequency. In fact, commercial catches of gargantuan kings between 110 and 120 pounds occurred from time to time.

These days, apart from very rare occurrences, only the Kenai remains as the ultimate destination for record-size fish; however, this is changing. During the hey-day of the 80s and 90s when kings over 70 pounds were relatively common, salmon of such proportions are much more rare today. Decades of targeting and killing these big fish may finally be catching up with the angling populace as the gene pool responsible for yielding 80-plus-pound fish is slowly being eroded.

Many anglers are seeing this as an opportunity to play a leading role in conservation of this unique breed of kings by voluntarily releasing all trophy-sized fish so they will have a chance to procreate and hopefully continue to maintain and even build up the run of giant fish to what it used to be only a brief decade or two ago.

This call to action is a noble cause, especially considering that it really is not necessary to kill these big fish in order to take home a trophy. Very exact replicas or mounts can be made by taking pictures and documenting length and girth of fish to be released, thereby facilitating the taxidermy process and helping to restore the genetic integrity of Kenai's kings.

With many anglers having written off the Kenai as a

destination for kings, the river still remains a viable option for those wanting the opportunity to potentially hook into a world-class fish, despite the current downturn in numbers of salmon available. True, the runs are smaller and the average size has decreased as well, yet there continues to be reports of kings being boated (and set free) every season that would on a scale have weighed between 70 and 90 pounds. Very few other rivers anywhere – if at all – can make such claims. In addition, commercial nets in Cook Inlet near the mouth of the Kenai snare their fair share of over-sized fish every summer, lending more credibility to the point that the genetic component producing these special salmon is alive yet.

Although today's strict regulatory environment prohibits anglers from harvesting the vast majority of huge kings, there is a retention provision for the lucky angler that happens to catch a fish of at least 55 inches in length. A king of such dimensions is likely to weigh at least 85 pounds or more and the provision would easily cover any new world record; however, a growing percentage of guides and anglers advocate for release of any mammoth salmon caught, record or not. In the end, it really is up to the individual angler to make their own decision whether to keep such a magnificent fish or letting it go.

## Kenai's Top 10 Giant Kings

The following is a list of the biggest kings caught by rod and reel in the Kenai River, including dates caught.

| | Lbs - Oz. | Inches | Date |
|---|---|---|---|
| 1. | 97-4* | 58.75 | May 17, 1985 |
| 2. | 95-10 | 59.50 | July 17, 1990 |
| 3. | 92-4 | 57.25 | July 9, 1985 |
| 4. | 91-10 | 58.25 | July 5, 1988 |
| 5. | 91-4 | 53.00 | N/A, 1987 |
| 6. | 91-0 | 57.50 | June 27, 1995 |
| 7. | 90-4 | 59.50 | July 19,1995 |
| 8. | 89-4 | 57.50 | July 31, 2002 |
| 9. | 89-3 | 57.50 | July 5, 1989 |
| 10. | 89-1 | 57.00 | July 15, 1995 |

***Current State of Alaska and IGFA world record**

# LOWER Kenai River

King SALMON

Red SALMON

Pink SALMON

Silver SALMON

Rainbow TROUT

Dolly VARDEN

**Highlights:** Alaska's premier location for record-size king salmon as well as trophy catches of reds, pinks, and silvers. Great spot for catching tidewater reds on the fly.

**Best Fishing:** Late May to late September.

**Regulatory Restrictions:** Very conservative.

**Location:** Western Kenai Peninsula drainage, towns of Soldotna and Kenai, Sterling Highway, 147 miles south of Anchorage, 83 miles north of Homer.

**Description:** The lower Kenai River is defined as the section of water from the Sterling Highway Bridge in Soldotna downstream to its terminus at Cook Inlet outside the city of Kenai. This is by far the most populated portion of the river; private and commercial land are spread throughout the length as the cities of Soldotna and Kenai surround the waterway. Yet there is still an abundance of vegetation to be found, recreational parkland and wooded parcels of land are commonplace, and being on the river does not give the impression of fishing in an area of fairly dense settlement.

The Kenai flows swiftly from the highway bridge downstream to approximately Beaver Creek with numerous mid-river islands and famed angling spots along the way. As the river flows out onto the Kenai River Flats and the intertidal area, the current slows down considerably, and the banks of the river a combination of rock and mud as a sign of large tidal fluctuations of many feet.

Although the Kenai is quite wide and deep in many

places, there are spots where large rocks or boulders and sandbars can be a hazard to boaters, this being particularly the case in spring when water levels are very low. Unless having a fair amount of experience navigating the river, a high level of caution is a must. Additionally, watch out for boat traffic, which can be an issue during the peak of the king salmon runs, specifically on the more popular tidewater holes.

The average stream gradient from Soldotna to the river mouth is 2.6 feet per mile, a distance of 21 miles total.

Wildlife is a possibility even in this section of the Kenai. Moose are a common sight, and a few bears amble along the river's edge in summer and fall. Caribou are not unusual on the Kenai River Flats and eagles frequent the river mouth. Beluga whales and seals swim up the lower river on high tides, often for several miles, in pursuit of salmon.

**Facilities:** There are numerous public and private campgrounds in the area surrounding lower Kenai River, especially in Soldotna. Parking is readily available along with several boat launches. Retail stores of all kinds abound in towns of Kenai and Soldotna, including services such as guides, boat and cabin rentals, B&Bs, hotels/motels, lodging, and emergency care. Commercial airports are present in both Kenai and Soldotna with daily scheduled flights operating to and from Anchorage, Homer, and Kodiak.

**Access:** Several road and highway spurs from the Sterling Highway provide public access to various section of the Kenai River. Many of these points of access also feature developed parking and campgrounds with a few having boat launches as well. The lower Kenai is the most populated stretch within the Kenai drainage with an abundance of private land. Please respect private property.

Seasonal riverbank closures are in effect from July 1 through August 15 in a number of locations in order to protect riparian habitat. Consult sport fishing regulations.

## Sterling Highway

The highway crosses the river in Soldotna.

**A. Soldotna Visitor Center** – Milepost 96.0. Northwest on short access road to Soldotna Visitor Information Center and large parking area. Trail leads 200 yards to river. Developed walkway present. Restrooms.

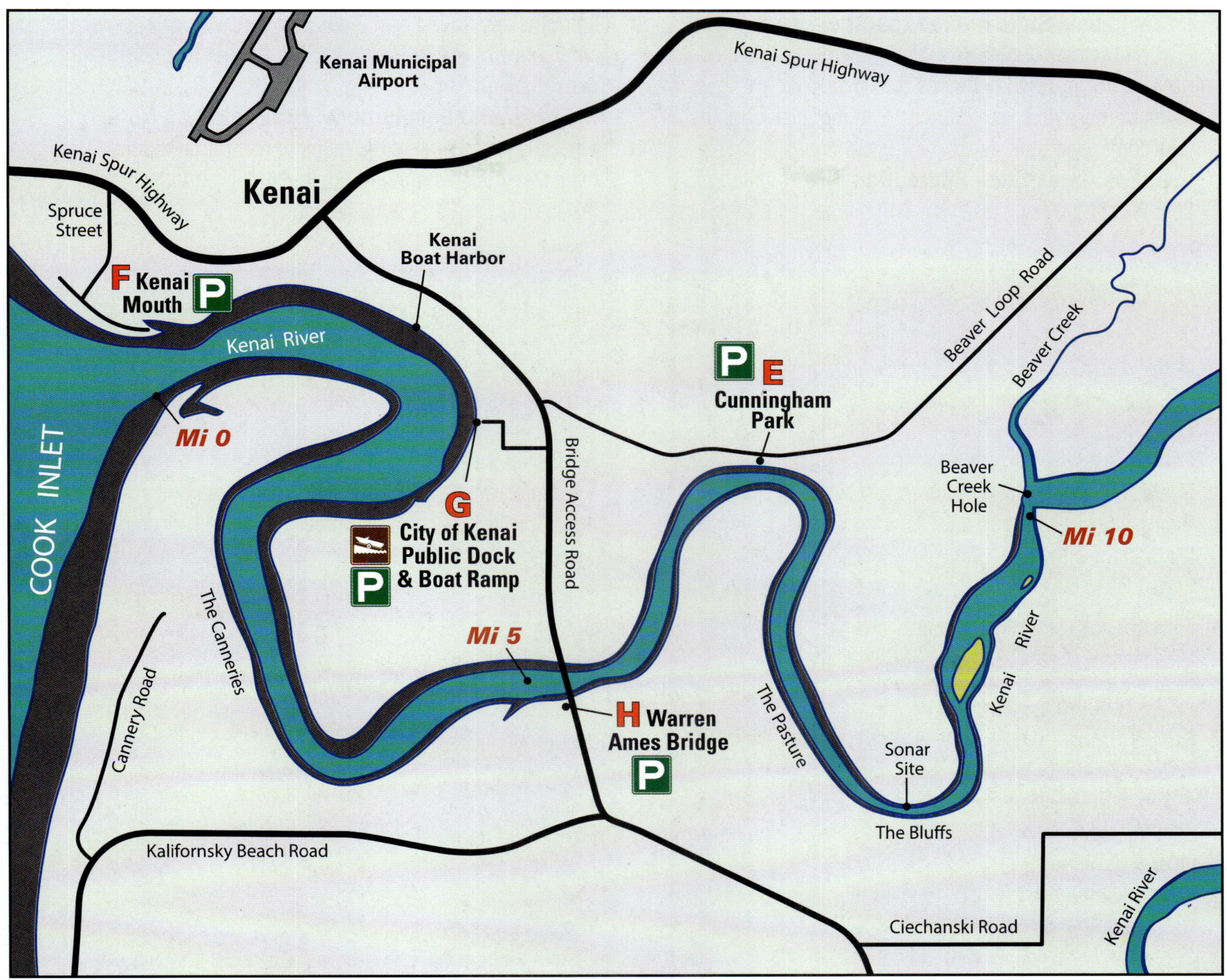


## Kenai Spur Highway

The highway begins at the "Y" intersection of the Sterling Highway, Milepost 94.1 in Soldotna (Mile 0) and ends in the town of Kenai (Mile 10).

B. **Big Eddy State Recreation Site** – Milepost 1.8. West on Big Eddy Road 1.4 miles to recreation site on left. Parking and restrooms. Limited bank fishing.

C. **The Pillars State Park** – Milepost 4.2. West on Silver Salmon Drive 0.5 miles to river. Parking, limited camping, boat launch, and restrooms. No bank fishing; this is primarily a river access point for boaters.

D. **Eagle Rock Campground** – Milepost 5.1. West on Eagle Rock Drive 0.4 miles to river. Parking, limited camping, boat launch, and restrooms. Excellent fishing off the bank.

E. **Cunningham Park** – Milepost 6.4. South on Beaver Loop Road 2.7 miles to access road on left leading to parking area and river. Restrooms and primitive boat launch. Excellent bank fishing.

F. **Kenai Mouth** - Milepost 11.7. South on Spruce Drive 0.5 mile to beach area with access to river mouth. Parking and restrooms. Space for all size vehicles. Not a good option to fish from the bank during dip net season in July. Fair fishing off the shore.

## Bridge Access Road

The road begins at Milepost 10.8 Kenai Spur Highway (Mile 0) and ends at Milepost 16.2 Kalifornsky Beach Road (Mile 3.4).

G. **City of Kenai Public Dock & Boat Ramp** – Mile 1.6. West on access road to launch area. Parking, restrooms, and boat launch. **Note:** The launch is in tidal area of the river and can be unusable during very low tides. Limited bank fishing.

H. **Warren Ames Bridge** – Mile 2.8. West on access road to parking area and river. Restrooms. Fair to good bank fishing.

## Kalifornsky Beach Road

The road intersects the Sterling Highway at Milepost 96.1 (Mile 22.2), just south of the Kenai River Bridge.

**I. Ciechanski State Recreation Site** – Milepost 17.5. East on Ciechanski Road 2.6 miles to split in road, continue right on Porter Road 0.4 miles to access road on right, 0.2 miles to recreation site on right. Parking, picnic tables, restrooms, and boat docks.

**J. Slikok Creek State Recreation Site** – Milepost 20.5. North on Endicott Drive 0.8 mile to recreation area on right. Developed trail leads 250 yards to walkway at the confluence of Slikok Creek and the Kenai River. Excellent bank fishing.

**K. Centennial Campground** – Milepost 22.1. North on access road at sign 0.8 miles to campground and river. Developed campground, parking, boat launch, and restrooms. Excellent bank fishing.

## Rules & Regulations

**Note:** *The Kenai River is the most heavily regulated drainage in the state and only a portion of the rules and regulations are listed here.*

**Open Season:** January 1 through December 31.
**Open Area:** The entire lower river is open to fishing throughout the year.
**Legal Gear/Tackle:** Only one unbaited, single-hook lure is allowed from January 1 through June 30. During the month of July, bait is allowed but only one single-hook lures may be used. Additional bait, tackle, and area restrictions apply.

**King Salmon**
- Open season is January 1 through July 31.
- Bag limit is (1) per day and (1) in possession (20 inches or longer); seasonal limit is (2). For kings less than 20 inches (Jacks), the limit is (10).
- From January 1 through June 30, fish must be less than 42 inches or longer than 55 inches to be retained.

**Silver Salmon**
- Open season is July 1 through November 30.
- Bag limit is (2) per day and (2) in possession (16 inches or longer) from July 1 through August 31; and (3) per day and (3) in possession from September 1 through November 30. For salmon less than 16 inches (Jacks), the limit is (10).

**All Other Salmon**
- Open all season (see general "Open Season" above).
- Red salmon bag limit is (3) per day and (6) in possession (16 inches or longer), and pink salmon (6) per day and (6) in possession. For salmon less than 16 inches (Jacks), the limit is (10).

**Rainbow/Steelhead Trout & Dolly Varden**
- Open season for trout and char is January 1 through December 31.
- Bag limit is (1) per day and (1) in possession for each species.
- Retained fish must be less than 18 inches long for each species.

**Other Fishes**
- Open all season (see general "Open Season" above).
- Arctic grayling bag limit is (5) per day and (5) in possession, any size.
- Whitefish has no bag or possession limit, no size restrictions.

*Mouth of Kenai River as seen from bluffs near town of Kenai*

## Fishing Lower Kenai River

**Access:** ★★★★ **Sight Fishing:** ★
**Scenery:** ★★★ **Bank/Wading:** ★★★
**Wildlife:** ★★ **Boat/Floating:** ★★★★★

**Species:** King, red, pink, and silver salmon, rainbow trout, and Dolly Varden. Minor occurrences of chum salmon, steelhead trout, and whitefish.

**Summary:** It is the Lower Kenai that placed the river on the map with its run of giant king salmon and fly-happy reds that in some years top one million fish. The entire area buzzes with activity starting in late May and continues right through July and even into August as anglers and guides plow the turquoise-colored water in search of trophy kings and filling the cooler with red salmon fillets. But there are other species that are present in formidable numbers as well, such as silver and pink salmon, the latter which is chiefly available in even-numbered years. Apart from salmon, anglers can easily find very productive action for both rainbow trout and sea-run Dolly Varden during the summer months.

The lower Kenai is a large chunk of river, wide and swift in many places. Since salmon are only hours away from the salt of Cook Inlet, it is imperative that anglers are aware of tidal movements and time their presence on the river accordingly, particularly the first 10 to 12 miles which are in the tidal zone.

There are two runs each of the primary salmon species (king, red, pink, and silver) on the lower Kenai. The first – or early – runs are generally headed for tributaries of Kenai River and Kenai Lake, while the late appearances consist mainly of mainstem Kenai fish.

Although some kings are taken from the bank every season, anglers wishing to catch these mammoth salmon on the Kenai are advised to hire a guide. The king fishery here is vastly different both in methods and techniques than any other roadside waters and intimate knowledge of the fish and their habits critical to success.

The majority of Kenai River guides that fish for kings do so on the lower river with many heading straight down to the better holes between river mile 7 (The Pastures) and river mile 19 (Slikok Creek). This stretch of water harbors legendary hot spots, such as Eagle Rock, The Pillars, Big Eddy, Poacher's Cove, and Sunken Island, all of which may by very congested with boat traffic during the height of the king runs and on the weekends during June (early run) and July (late run).

It is the late run of reds in July that draw the majority of bank anglers to the lower Kenai. A sonar unit at river mile 21 tallies the number of salmon entering the river, with results posted in the media on a daily basis to assist anglers in targeting these fish. A daily count of 20-25,000 red salmon is necessary in order to produce good fishing. At the peak of the run, up to 100,000 or more reds may enter the river during a single 24-hour period, creating phenomenal angler success.

In contrast, the early run (June) bound for Russian River and a few other tributaries only offers fair fishing at best, yet a few skilled anglers may do better. The run is significantly smaller than the late run, hence a lower angler success rate.

Pinks show in exceptional numbers and it is believed that up to four or five million or more of these littlest of salmon enter the Kenai in a good season and action is superb with fish-on-every-cast not only possible but commonplace. Like Kenai's other salmon species, pinks here grow large and typically weigh twice that of pinks

*(Courtesy EZ Limit Guide Service)*

*A chrome female sample of Kenai chinook, taken from the far lower end of the river during the season peak. Mid- to late July is perfect timing to encounter large, bright fish such as this specimen.*

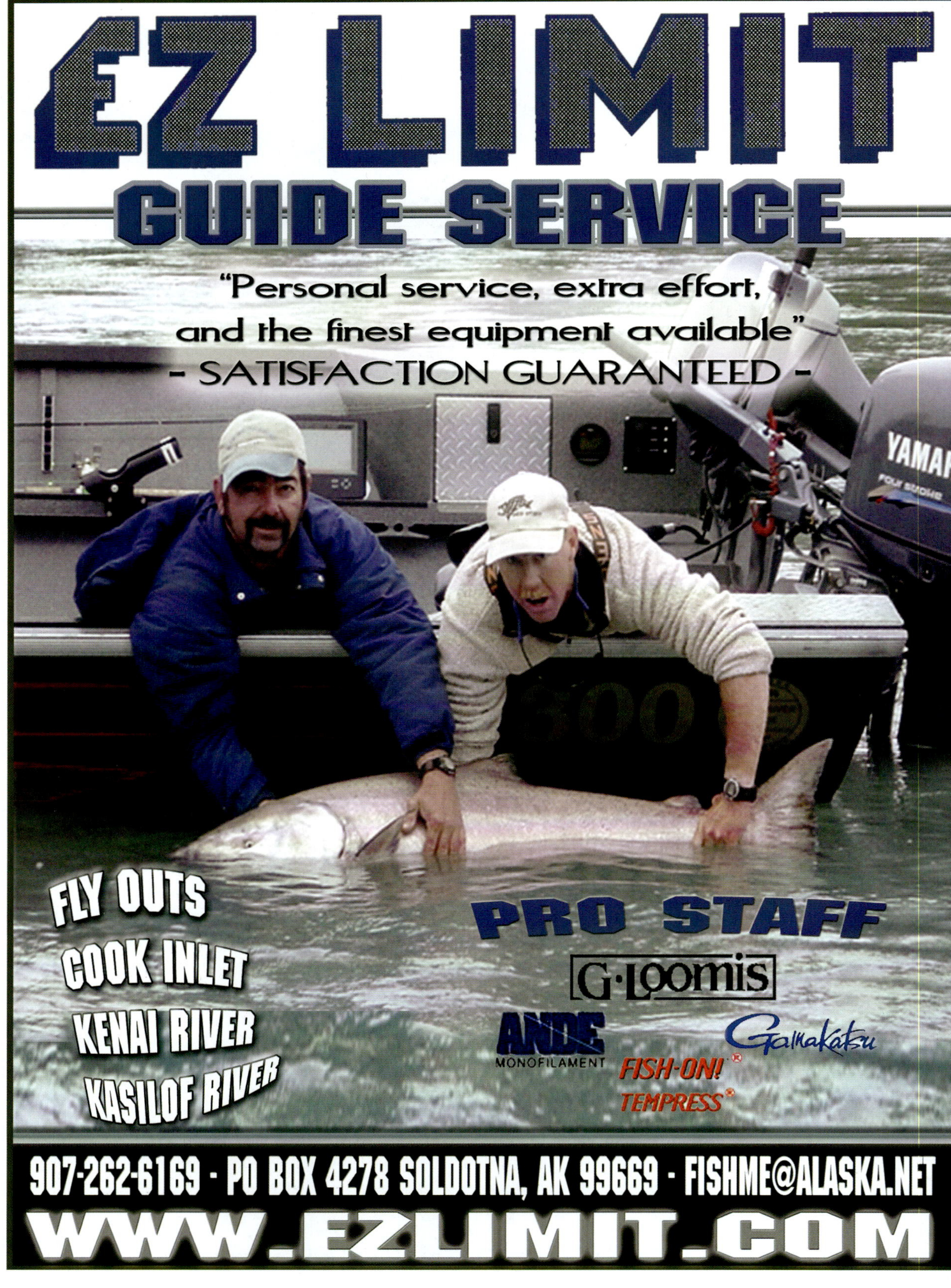
EZ LIMIT
GUIDE SERVICE
"Personal service, extra effort, and the finest equipment available"
- SATISFACTION GUARANTEED -
YAMAHA
FLY OUTS
COOK INLET
KENAI RIVER
KASILOF RIVER
PRO STAFF
G·Loomis
ANDE MONOFILAMENT
Gamakatsu
FISH-ON!
TEMPRESS
907-262-6169 - PO BOX 4278 SOLDOTNA, AK 99669 - FISHME@ALASKA.NET
WWW.EZLIMIT.COM

elsewhere in the region. The early run (in July) usually fishes only fair at best, while the late run (August) provides superb action.

Anglers quickly turn to silver salmon as the king season wraps up and the red run tapers off, with these gamesters providing best sport in August (early run) and September (late run). The tidewater locations are most popular as large schools of fish move into the river and briefly pause in some of the deeper holes and runs. Expect the fishing to be solid throughout both of the runs, with slightly bigger fish the norm later in the autumn season.

Many local and visiting anglers actually prefer to fish for Kenai's silvers as the typical summer salmon crowds are gone and the river a much more solemn place to spend time, this being particularly the case in September.

As for other species, sea-run char appear in big numbers during July near tidewater and as the season progresses disperse throughout the lower river and beyond. They are often overlooked but their sheer numbers are sometimes astounding. Also, rainbow trout stack into some of the better holes when the various salmon runs move through and can yield fast and fun fishing in a starkly different environment compared to the middle and upper portions of the river.

## Fish Availability

● = High ● = Moderate ● = Low ● = Closed

| Species | APR | MAY | JUN | JUL | AUG | SEP | OCT |
|---|---|---|---|---|---|---|---|
| **King Salmon** | Low | Low, Low, Low, Moderate | High, High, High, Moderate | Low, Moderate, High, High | Closed, Closed, Closed, Closed | Closed, Closed, Closed | |
| **Red Salmon** | | Low, Low, Low | Moderate, High, High, Moderate | Low, Moderate, High, High | High, Moderate, Moderate, Low | Low, Low, Low, Low | Low |
| **Pink Salmon** | | | Low, Low | Low, Moderate, Moderate, High | High, High, High, Moderate | Low, Low, Low, Low | |
| **Silver Salmon** | | | | Low, Low, Low | Moderate, High, High, High | Moderate, High, High, High | Moderate, Moderate, Low, Low |
| **Rainbow Trout** | Low, Low, Low, Low | Closed, Closed, Closed, Closed | Closed, Low, Low, Moderate | Moderate, Moderate, High, High | High, High, High, High | High, Moderate, Moderate, Moderate | Moderate, Moderate, Low, Low |
| **Dolly Varden** | Low, Low, Low, Moderate | Moderate, Moderate, Low, Low | Low, Low, Low, Moderate | Moderate, High, High, High | High, High, High, High | High, Moderate, Moderate, Moderate | Moderate, Moderate, Low, Low |
| Angling Pressure | | Low, Low, Moderate, Moderate | High, High, High, High | Moderate, Moderate, High, High | High, High, High, High | High, High, High, Moderate | Moderate, Moderate, Low, Low |

## King Salmon

**Rating:** ★★½ Fair to good from boat, poor from shore.
**Season:** January 1 through July 31.
**Timing:** April 20 – July 31; peak June 1 – 20 (early run) and July 10 – 31 (late run).
**Size:** Average 20 – 40 pounds (early run) and 30 – 50 pounds (late run), up to 90 pounds.
**Tackle:** Spoons, spinners, attractors, plugs, flies, and bait.
**Tips:** The prime king action is from the tidal area below the mouth of Beaver Creek on upstream, the far lower end (Warren Ames Bridge down) considered to be far less productive. Prior to mid-June, avoid lures with too much chrome as kings are largely immune to the flash as the river is filled with millions of silvery smelt. Back-trolling medium-sized plugs in the tidewater holes is best early in the run, hitting holes upstream closer to Soldotna starting in mid-June. Large attractors in combination with salmon roe clusters and plugs in various fluorescent/metallic hues are hot come July.

Drifting and back-trolling are popular methods during the early run, while back-bouncing works better when water volume increases current flow as is the case when the late

(Courtesy EZ Limit Guide Service)

*A blushed trophy king. Fish of such proportions are taken from the Kenai on a regular basis, especially during the late run in July. It is these large catches that put the river on the map and attracts anglers from all over the world to the river during the season.*

run arrives in July.

Anglers fishing from shore have decent opportunities to land kings in a couple of locations; the Centennial Campground and the Kenai River Bridge in Soldotna (see access information above). Best time is the second half of July using attractors and roe or large spinners.

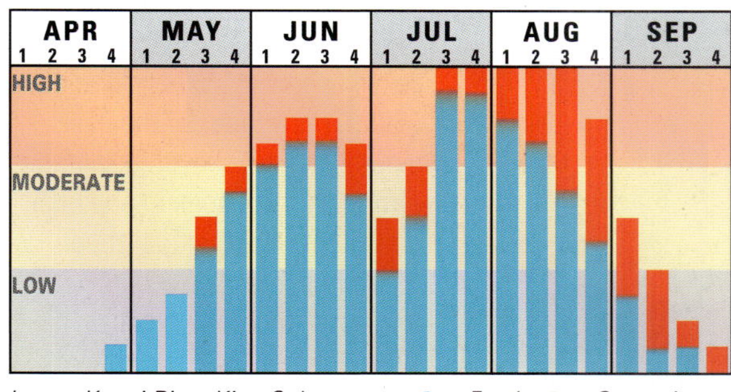


*Lower Kenai River King Salmon.* ● = *Fresh* ● = *Spawning*

## Red Salmon

**Rating:** ★★★★★ Excellent (late run), fair (early run).
**Season:** January 1 through December 31.
**Timing:** May 10 – October 5; peak June 5 – 15 (early run) and July 15 – August 5 (late run).
**Size:** Average 6 – 7 pounds, up to 11 pounds (early run); 6 – 8 pounds, up to 14 pounds (late run).
**Tackle:** Flies.
**Tips:** Red salmon on the lower Kenai, as elsewhere in the drainage, do not swim far from shore, the majority of fish seemingly prefer a corridor about four to 15 feet off the bank in water that is three to four feet deep. Often it is possible to spot fish moving through the shallows near land. Flies must be drifted near the bottom for hookups to be made.

The action is generally poor for early-run salmon but may be fair to good at the peak in mid-June in years when there is a large run. Some anglers that have learned where exactly on the lower Kenai the early run fish have a habit of resting or being channeled through can do quite well. The late run provides the best fishing by far, with excellent angling success being normal during the second half of July. Good fishing often persists into August. Every year there are a few reds caught in the 14 pound range and big males weighing as much as 15 pounds or more have been landed here.

Fluorescent green yarn flies tied on a single hook is preferred but red or orange hues sometimes yield exceptional results, particularly when tied in a ball representing a small cluster of roe.

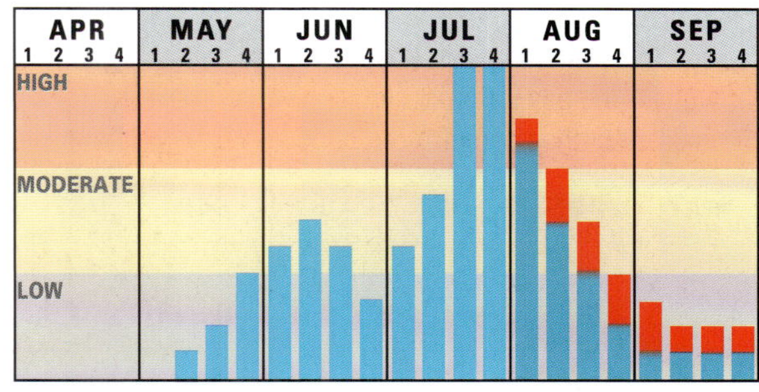


*Lower Kenai River Red Salmon.* ● = *Fresh* ● = *Spawning*

## Pink Salmon

**Rating:** ★★★★★ Excellent on even-numbered years, poor to fair on odd.
**Season:** January 1 through December 31.
**Timing:** June 15 – September 25; peak August 5 – 25.
**Size:** Average 3 – 6 pounds, up to 9 pounds.
**Tackle:** Spoons, spinners, plugs, and flies.
**Tips:** Pinks can be readily caught anywhere along the lower Kenai with the tidal zone (River Mile 12 and downstream)

*(Courtesy Eagle Eye Images)*

*Ready to release a fresh-from-the-sea sockeye, hooked on a simple yarn fly drifted along the bank in three feet of water. These fish are relatively easy to catch with the perfect "lure" often being no more than a small tuft of colored yarn tied on a single hook. However, some purists may opt to use more traditional flies in various color schemes for their angling pleasure. While reds can be coaxed into striking a fly (or even a lure or bait), the vast majority of catches on the Kenai are done by "lining." Yet the most enjoyable method and technique is the simple flip-and-drift, letting the current work the line and fly into the mouth of the fish.*

(Courtesy Eagle Eye Images)

*A semi-bright male pink salmon taken on a size 4 spinner. During even-numbered years, the Kenai becomes practically inundated with literally millions of these fish. Expect fast and exciting action on light gear for pinks that often weigh up to 8 pounds.*

being the prime area for fast action with dime bright fish. Incoming and outgoing tides are best. Upstream of the estuary, focus on locations with slower water than the main current. Early mornings are best but action can be superb throughout the day if rain or cloudy weather prevails. Fluorescent orange and pink are good lure and fly colors.

*Lower Kenai River Pink Salmon.* ● *= Fresh* ● *= Spawning*

## Silver Salmon

**Rating:** ★★★½ Good to excellent.
**Season:** July 1 through November 30.
**Timing:** July 5 – November 30, peak August 10 – 25 (early run) and September 10 – 25 (late run).
**Size:** Average 5 – 10 pounds, up to 15 pounds (early run); 6 – 15 pounds, up to 22 pounds (late run).
**Tackle:** Spoons, spinners, plugs, attractors, flies, and bait.
**Tips:** Early-run silvers often hug the shoreline like reds do, unlike late-run salmon that can just as well be distributed throughout the width of the river. The common link with both strains, however, is that they prefer slow-moving water such as that found around sloughs, side channels, and mouths of tributary streams.

Great action can be experienced in both runs of silvers, yet the first often appears to be more predictable than the second showing. When fishing within a few miles of the river mouth, anglers should focus their efforts on the incoming and high tides in or near the tidal zone.

Salmon roe clusters are without a doubt the biggest silver killer on the lower Kenai. Although they can be drifted through deep, slow holes and runs, most anglers prefer to fish the offering stationary on the bottom. Spinners also function very well and sometimes even outperform bait. Size 4 and 5 are perfect, metallic and neutral colors being best. Blue, green, and plain silver are hot. Flyfishers can do well in certain locations where salmon attractor patterns can be worked efficiently.

(Courtesy Eric and Suzie Mauro)

*Pete Mauro holds up a chrome buck coho taken on a cluster of salmon roe drifted along the bottom with the use of a strike indicator. Many local anglers prefer these late season fish as the summer crowds are gone and the action excellent.*

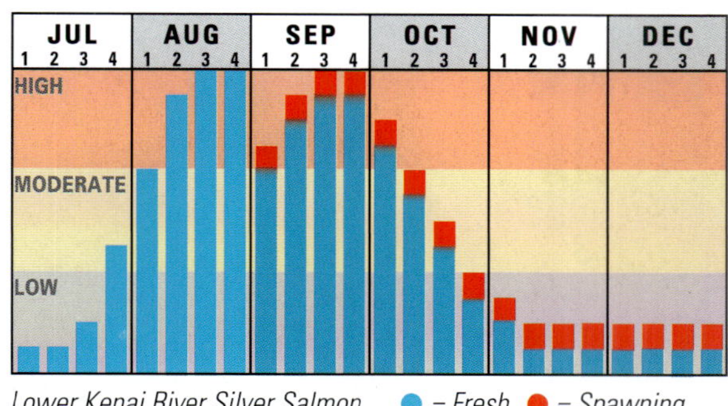


*Lower Kenai River Silver Salmon.* ● *= Fresh* ● *= Spawning*

## Rainbow Trout

**Rating:** ★★★ Good.
**Season:** June 11 through May 1.
**Timing:** March 15 – May 1, June 11 – January 1; peak July 15 – September 15.
**Size:** Average 10 – 20 inches, up to 32 inches (15 pounds).
**Tackle:** Spoons, spinners, plugs, attractors, and flies.
**Tips:** Most trout are found upstream of the tidal reach at river mile 15. Try small chrome spoons and spinners and forage pattern flies early in the season (June), egg patterns later on. During the months of July and August, the Soldotna area can be exceptional for nice-sized rainbows. Casting downstream of fish cleaning stations using flesh flies and beads is a sure way to connect with trout.

(Courtesy Eric and Suzie Mauro)

*Big rainbows also thrive on the Lower Kenai. Suzie Mauro shows off a very colorful specimen.*

## Dolly Varden

**Rating:** ★★★½ Good to excellent.
**Season:** January 1 through December 31.
**Timing:** March 15 – January 1; peak July 10 – Sept. 15.
**Size:** Average 10 – 20 inches, up to 30 inches (10-12 pounds).
**Tackle:** Spoons, spinners, plugs, attractors, and flies.
**Tips:** Fish the slack water on the tides for sea-run char from May into July using baitfish or smolt imitation lures and flies, moving upstream toward Soldotna in latter July, August, and September as king and pink salmon begin to spawn. Starting about mid-July, egg and flesh patterns become more effective.

*Anglers cast from one of several Soldotna area "fishwalks," built by the community to specifically to protect vegetation and facilitate easier access. A few also support wheelchair usage.*

## Other Kenai Opportunities

### Trophy Salmon Fishing

Perhaps nowhere in Alaska are there such outstanding opportunities to catch trophy-sized salmon and trout as what one may find on the Kenai River. It is the reputation of producing huge fish that has earned the river its "world famous" status, lead foremost by a steady and growing list of king salmon that regularly tip the scales at 60 pounds or more. As a matter of fact, the Kenai holds the current state and IGFA world record for the species at 97 pounds, 4 ounces. Additionally, trophy specimens of red, pink, and silver salmon and rainbow trout and many IGFA line-class records all contribute to the river's notoriety.

King salmon is indeed king on the Kenai River. Of the top ten largest sport-caught kings ever documented in Alaska, nine have come from the Kenai. Not only that but the vast majority of trophy kings reported every year also stem from this river. Invariably, the season's biggest salmon usually weighs in excess of 75 pounds. Whereas the minimum trophy weight for king salmon across the state is pegged at 50 pounds, a king must weigh at least 75 pounds to be recognized as a true "Kenai Trophy."

Although anglers may hook into trophy kings anytime during the May through July regulatory season (the world record was caught on May 17), it is the late run in July that really has the spotlight concerning big kings. Yet it should be noted that the Kenai is not a quantity fishery, but quality. That is, the average time it takes to hook into one king is estimated at some 20 hours. With the invaluable assistance of an experienced guide, however, that time can be reduced to 12 hours or less. That is not a good catch rate for kings most anywhere in Alaska but consider that when an angler does finally land one of these behemoths, it could be a potential trophy – even the next world record.

(Courtesy EZ Limit Guide Service)

But it is not only kings that grow big in the Kenai; the drainage also holds the state record for red and pink salmon, at 16 pounds and 12 pounds, 9 ounces, respectively. These are not fluke catches as the average weight of these two species tends to be quite a bit more than that seen in other waters. The late run of red salmon in July and August produces a relatively good number of big males in the 12-pound category, with occasional specimens between 14 and 15 pounds. Pink salmon, not to be outdone, commonly average up to 6 pounds with some larger males exceeding 8 pounds. Ten-pound fish are reported from the Kenai every season (month of August). Red salmon are available throughout the Kenai River, pinks are best on the middle and lower river sections.

One salmon species that really has not been touted much in the trophy standings is the silver salmon. The late run of silvers in the Kenai has long been known among local anglers to produce some very hefty specimens on a regular basis. In September and October, look for fish averaging as much as 12 to 14 pounds with fair chances of seeing an 18-pounder. A few hogs may surpass 20 pounds. Huge catches to 24 pounds are known, only a few pounds shy of the state record.

Anglers should be reminded, however, that trophy-sized salmon may be genetically inclined, thus the killing of large specimens may be detrimental to future production. This is particularly true with king salmon and many anglers, including a growing number of prominent guides, are advocating for a voluntary catch-and-release policy in order to ensure that the river will continue to yield exceptional catches for generations yet to come.

# Kasilof River

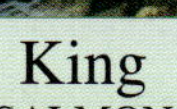
King SALMON

Red SALMON

Pink SALMON

Silver SALMON

Steelhead TROUT

Dolly VARDEN

**Highlights:** Great opportunities for salmon and featuring the only true spring fishery for steelhead on the peninsula. Late summer and fall silvers and trout is exceptional.

**Best Fishing:** Late April to mid-October.

**Regulatory Restrictions:** Conservative.

**Location:** Western Kenai Peninsula drainage, community of Kasilof, Sterling Highway, 13 miles south of Soldotna, 162 miles south of Anchorage.

**Description:** The Kasilof is a short glacial river, stemming from the peninsula's largest lake – Tustumena – at the base of the Kenai Mountains. Although not quite of the same size as neighboring Kenai River to the north, the Kasilof is the second greatest drainage in terms of volume of water and one of the leading producers of red salmon. Rolling hills and marshland line the riverbanks with an abundance of small spruce and birch growth.

From the outlet of Tustumena Lake, the greenish-gray river meanders at a fairly steady clip some 20 miles westward to Cook Inlet. The first few miles of river consists of very slow current, eventually picking up speed until reaching the estuary. There are two small rapids between the lake and the Sterling Highway bridge, named Silver Salmon Rapids and Moosehead Rapids, both of which are easily negotiated by boat and rafts.

There are only two clearwater tributaries of the Kasilof; Crooked Creek and Coal Creek, the latter only supporting small populations of salmon and char. Crooked, however, is

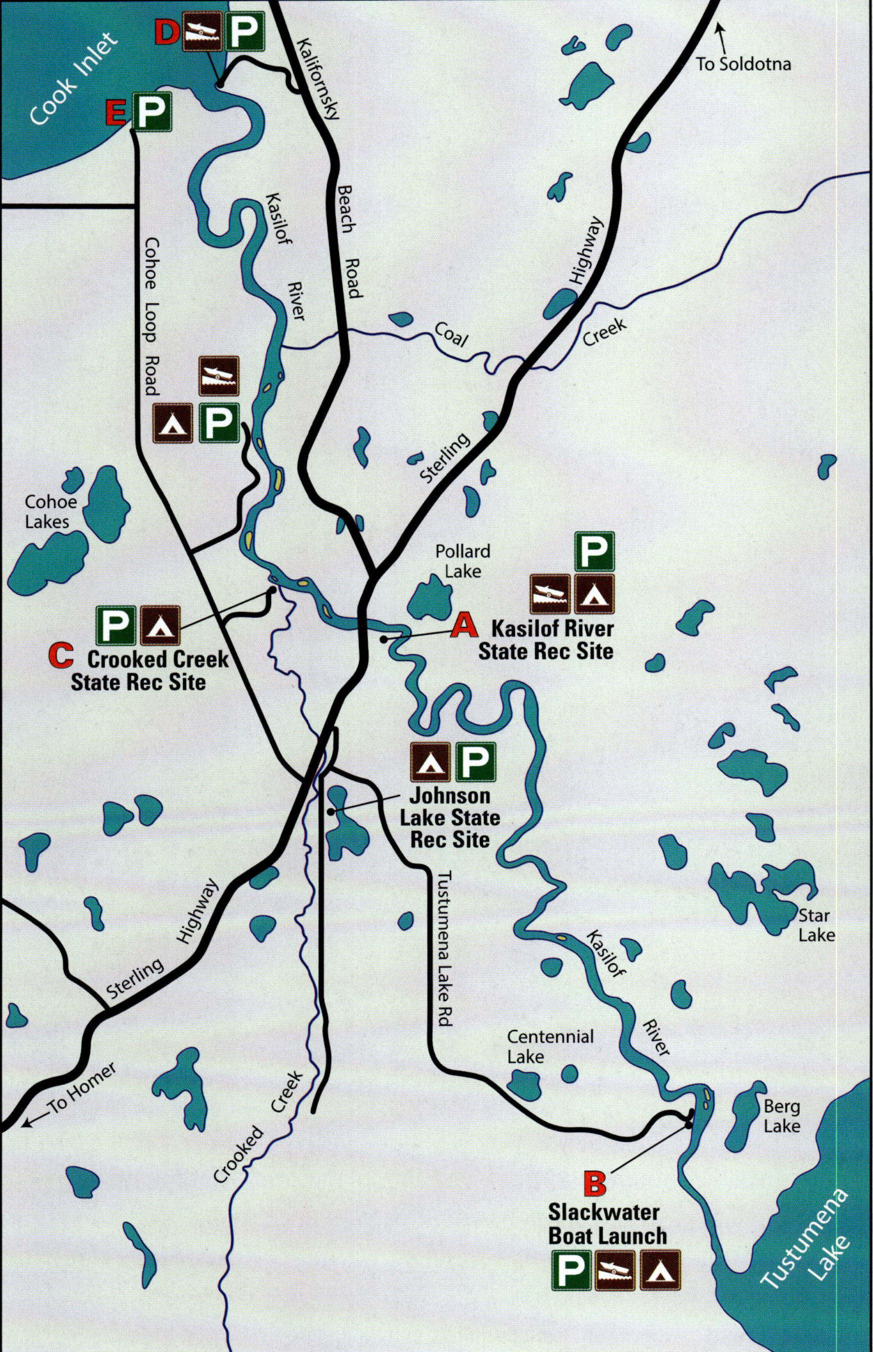


a major producer of king, red, and silver salmon along with a very healthy presence of Dolly Varden.

The river displays a greenish-gray colored appearance throughout the year, even more so than its glacial twin, the Kenai. As much of the volume is based on meltwater from ice fields and glaciers, the Kasilof runs high and turbid during the warmer summer months, water levels dropping by several feet in late fall and remain low through winter into spring. Flows begin to increase in late May and early June and builds steadily up to July.

The lower river is influenced by tides as far upstream as the People Hole below the mouth of Crooked Creek.

**Facilities:** Public and private parking areas, campgrounds, RV parks, and boat launches. Guide services, lodging, restaurants, gas, tackle shops, groceries, and other amenities located nearby.

**Access:** There are three main access points from the Sterling Highway, all presenting significant public access along the shoreline. Private campgrounds with river access are available in the area.

**A. Kasilof River State Recreation Site** – Milepost 109.4. The highway crosses the river. Turn east on Spetz Avenue short distance to access road on left leading to large parking area. Restrooms, picnic tables, and boat launch present. Trail leads upstream along river to productive fishing holes.

**B. Slackwater Boat Launch** – Milepost 110.0. Turn south on Johnson Lake Loop Road 0.8 miles, left on Tustumena Lake Road 5.9 miles to end of road and river. Parking, primitive campsites, and boat launch. Tustumena Lake is approximately 3 miles upstream. Fair to good bank fishing opportunities. Improvised footpaths lead downstream along river.

**C. Crooked Creek State Recreation Site** – Milepost 111.4. Turn west on Cohoe Loop Road 1.7 miles, right on Rilinda Road 1.5 miles to recreation site. Developed trail leads 200 yards to confluence of Crooked Creek and Kasilof River. Developed parking, campground, RV parking, picnic tables, restrooms, and guide services. Excellent bank fishing available in this area.

**D. Kasilof River Mouth (North)** – Milepost 108.8 Sterling Highway. North on Kalifornsky Beach Road 4.9 miles, left on Kasilof Beach Road 1.0 mile to beach area. Primitive launch point for small craft at river mouth. Very limited bank fishing here.

**E. Kasilof River Mouth (South)** – Milepost 111.0 Sterling Highway. West on North Cohoe Road 5.9 miles to end of pavement, continue on dirt road 0.7 mile to parking area at beach. Not recommended for large RVs. Improvised road continues along beach another 1/2 mile to mouth of Kasilof River. No boat launch point present. Some bank fishing opportunities, primarily for bottomfish but also salmon.

*Determined anglers try their luck for early spring steelhead at the mouth of Crooked Creek. Fishing the Kasilof in March and April can be a chilly affair with success ranging from dead slow to fabulous, landing two or three trout usually seen as a good catch.*

## Rules & Regulations

**Open Season:** January 1 through December 31.
**Open Area:** The entire river is open to fishing throughout the year.
**Legal Gear/Tackle:** All gear and tackle, including bait, is allowed, except that only one unbaited, artificial lure may be used from September 16 through December 31.

**King Salmon**
- Open season is January 1 through July 31 from the highway bridge downstream to the mouth.
- Open season is January 1 through June 30 from the highway bridge upstream to the outlet of Tustumena Lake.
- Native (non-hatchery) fish may be retained only on Tuesdays, Thursdays, and Saturdays.
- Bag limit is (2) per day and (2) in possession (20 inches or longer), of which only (1) may be a native, non-hatchery fish. For kings less than 20 inches (Jacks), the limit is (10).

**All Other Salmon**
- Open all season (see general "Open Season" above).
- Bag limit is (3) per day and (3) in possession (16 inches or longer), of which only (2) may be silver salmon. For salmon less than 16 inches (Jacks), the limit is (10).

**Rainbow/Steelhead Trout**
- Open all season (see general "Open Season" above).
- Downstream of the highway bridge, retention of trout is not allowed and fish may not be removed from the water. All fish caught must be released.
- Upstream of the highway bridge, trout may be retained. Bag limit is (2) per day and (2) in possession, of which only (1) may be 20 inches or longer.

**Dolly Varden**
- Open all season (see general "Open Season" above).
- Bag limit is (2) per day and (2) in possession, any size.

**Other Fishes**
- Open all season (see general "Open Season" above).
- Whitefish has no bag or possession limit, no size restrictions.

## Fishing Kasilof River

**Access:** ★★★
**Scenery:** ★★★
**Wildlife:** ★★
**Sight Fishing:** ★
**Bank/Wading:** ★★★
**Boat/Floating:** ★★★★★

**Species:** King, red, pink, and silver salmon, steelhead and rainbow trout, and Dolly Varden. Rare catches of lake trout and round whitefish.

**Summary:** Kasilof River is one of a very few drainages on the Kenai Peninsula that is open to fishing throughout the year. While most streams have seasonal closures in order to protect spawning rainbow trout or other species, the Kasilof remains a solid spring option to many early-season angling enthusiasts. Additionally, it is a very friendly river to boaters/floaters and bank anglers both, making it one of the most popular waters on the whole peninsula and, at times, the most productive as well.

Since the river flows so turbid with glacial silt, the use of bait and fluorescent lures and flies are popular. The People Hole, a large run of slackwater just downstream of Crooked Creek, is favored by bank anglers due to easy access.

King salmon are generally present in fishable numbers by mid-May but are occasionally caught as early as April by anglers casting for trout. These fish are primarily of hatchery origin and bound for Crooked Creek, a clearwater tributary. They tend to congregate at or near the mouth of this stream for weeks, creating a virtual angler's bonanza that lasts through early summer. Fishing is best from boats during May with shore action picking up come June.

Like the Kenai River, the Kasilof also has a late run of kings, in July. The run is small, yet quite productive, with salmon over 50 pounds caught regularly. These mainstem spawners may be difficult to approach from shore as the river runs high and turbid in mid-summer but are readily available by anglers using boats.

Red salmon can be very abundant and are present during a prolonged period of time lasting from May and well into September. These salmon also have a two-run pattern, with early fish present starting in May and peaking in June. The late fish arrive in July and August and typically peaks about a week earlier than the late red run on the Kenai, with several hundred thousand salmon streaming through on their way to spawning beds on the upper Kasilof and in tributaries of Tustumena Lake.

Sockeye anglers are successful anywhere there is sufficient current flow with relative hot spots around the mouth of Crooked Creek and a ways upstream of the Sterling Highway bridge. However, the more remote upper river holds some great water too with plenty of fish and little or no company, such as around Silver Salmon Rapids and Moose Rapids.

In late summer, productive runs of silver and pink salmon show up but attract much less attention than other species in the river. Fishing for pinks is generally best on the lower river, below Crooked Creek, but can be productive in certain holes up to Tustumena Lake.

Anglers casting from shore usually target silvers at the main access points (such as Crooked Creek) during the month of August and into the early part of September. The majority of these fish are tributary spawners,

*Angler battles a large July king in a narrow channel right below Crooked Creek Campground.*

heading to streams emptying into Tustumena Lake. Boaters do well fishing the tides on the lower river all the way up to the lake at this time.

However, there is a late component of mainstem silvers that peaks later, in autumn. Moving rapidly through the lower river, they are almost exclusively fished from boat on the upper Kasilof. Outstanding angling awaits those who launch near Tustumena Lake and drift down to the highway.

As soon as the ice goes out in March, anglers begin plying the glacial waters in search of steelhead. The Kasilof supports the northernmost documented run in Cook Inlet with decent shore opportunities for these over-wintering fish during April and May. The clearwater tributaries of Crooked Creek and Nikolai Creek host spring spawning runs of steelhead but are closed to sport fishing throughout the reproductive period.

These sea-run trout are absent during the summer but become available again in the fall, which is the best time to target them as they ascend the Kasilof fresh from the salt. The stretch of water between Tustumena Lake and Sterling Highway is prime with very productive angling, mainly from boats. Fish are available until freeze-up, usually in the latter part of November or December.

Coinciding with the late-run salmon and steelhead are anadromous Dolly Varden. Expect good fishing in spring and fall as fish move from and to the lake, respectively.

## Fish Availability

● = High ● = Moderate ● = Low ● = Closed

| Species | APR | MAY | JUN | JUL | AUG | SEP | OCT |
|---|---|---|---|---|---|---|---|
| **King Salmon** | Low | Low Low Moderate Moderate | High High High Moderate | Moderate Moderate High High | Closed Closed Closed Closed | Closed Closed Closed | |
| **Red Salmon** | | Low Low Low | Moderate High High Moderate | Low Moderate High High | High Moderate Low Low | Low Low Low Low | |
| **Pink Salmon** | | | Low Low | Low Moderate Moderate High | High High Moderate Moderate | Low Low Low | |
| **Silver Salmon** | | | | Low Low Low | Moderate Moderate High High | High Moderate High High | High Moderate Moderate Low |
| **Steelhead** | Low Moderate Moderate High | High Moderate Moderate Low | Low Low Low | | Low Low Low | Low Moderate Moderate High | High High High High |
| **Rainbow Trout** | Low Low Low Moderate | Moderate Moderate Low Low | Low Low Moderate Moderate | Moderate Moderate Moderate Moderate | Moderate Moderate Moderate Moderate | Moderate Moderate Moderate Moderate | Moderate Moderate Low Low |
| **Dolly Varden** | Low Low Low Low | Moderate Moderate High High | High Moderate Low Low | Moderate High High High | High High High High | High Moderate Moderate Moderate | Moderate Moderate Low Low |
| Angling Pressure | Low Low Moderate Moderate | High High High High | High High High Moderate | Moderate Moderate Moderate High | High High High High | High Moderate Moderate Moderate | Moderate Moderate Low Low |

## King Salmon

**Rating:** ★★★ Good (early run); fair to good from boat, poor from shore (late run).
**Season:** January 1 through July 31.
**Timing:** April 20 – July 31; peak June 1 – 20 (early run) and July 15 – 31 (late run).
**Size:** Average 12 – 28 pounds, up to 50 pounds (early run); 25 – 40 pounds, up to 70 pounds (late run).

*Two anglers carry out a 50-pound late-run king, caught off the bank at the Crooked Creek Campground in July while red fishing..*

**Tackle:** Spoons, spinners, plugs, attractors, flies, and bait.
**Tips:** Plugs with sardine wraps are favored in May, attractors with salmon roe in June and July. Shore anglers do best in June when kings are found in abundance close to the bank. Use small attractors and flies in areas with current, fish attractors and roe stationary on the bottom and cast hardware in slack water. Fishing for kings from shore is difficult in July as salmon are large and water levels high and current swift.

Early-run kings can be found in largest concentrations within a quarter of a mile of the Crooked Creek confluence while late-run fish are more scattered from the tidal zone upstream to the Sterling Highway Bridge.

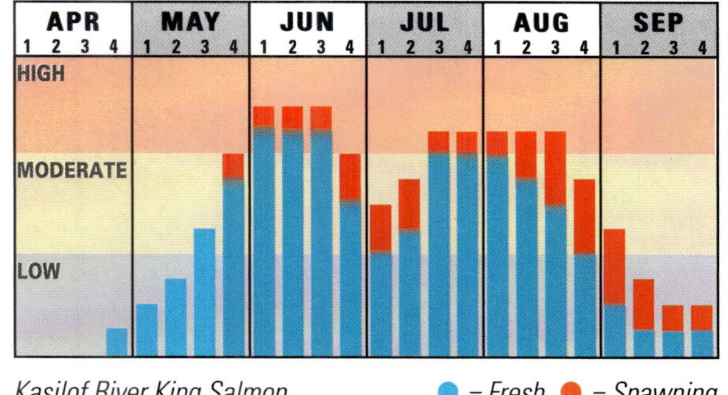


*Kasilof River King Salmon* ● = Fresh ● = Spawning

*Kasilof lends itself perfectly to fishing both off the bank as well as boats. Here, a flyfisher swings for kings holed up in a channel.*

## Red Salmon

**Rating:** ★★★½ Good to excellent.
**Season:** January 1 through December 31.
**Timing:** May 15 – September 25; peak July 5 – 25.
**Size:** Average 4 – 7 pounds, up to 12 pounds.
**Tackle:** Flies.
**Tips:** Anywhere along the river where there is some good current flow is suitable for catching reds using fluorescent flies in orange or chartreuse. Avoid slackwater areas. Salmon travel close to the bank (6 to 15 feet) in relatively shallow water. Popular spots with shore anglers include the fast water just below Crooked Creek and an area a quarter mile upstream of the highway bridge.

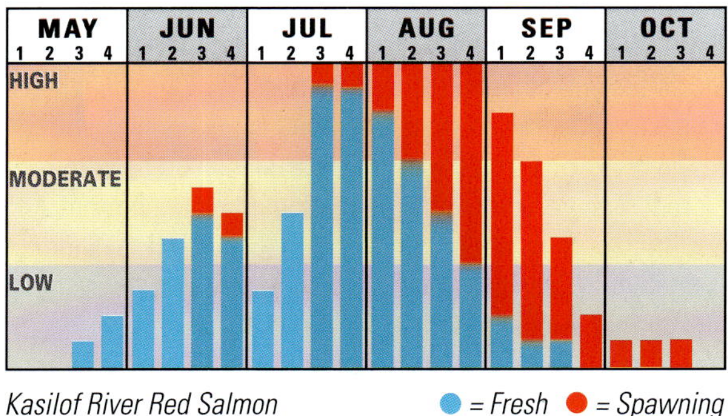


*Kasilof River Red Salmon* ● = Fresh ● = Spawning

*A fresh-off-the-tide sockeye, caught off the bank on a yarn fly.*

*(Courtesy Eagle Eye Images)*

## Pink Salmon

**Rating:** ★★★ Good on even-numbered years, fair on odd.
**Season:** January 1 through December 31.
**Timing:** June 15 – Sept. 15; peak July 20 – August 10.
**Size:** Average 2 – 5 pounds, up to 7 pounds.
**Tackle:** Spoons, spinners, plugs, attractors, and flies.
**Tips:** Cast fluorescent lures and flies into sloughs or backwater channels where the current is slow and fish have a tendency to concentrate.

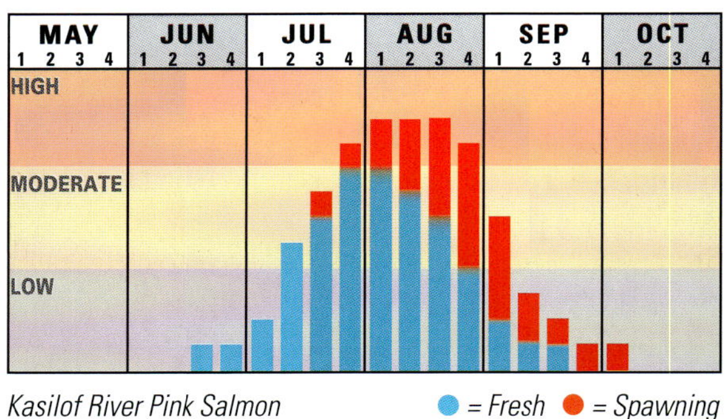


*Kasilof River Pink Salmon* ● = Fresh ● = Spawning

## Silver Salmon

**Rating:** ★★★ Good.
**Season:** January 1 through December 31.
**Timing:** July 15 – November 1; peak August 15 – September 5.
**Size:** Average 5 – 10 pounds, up to 15 pounds.
**Tackle:** Spinners, plugs, attractors, and bait.
**Tips:** Hit the tides using fluorescent hardware or set a cluster of salmon roe on the bottom. Shore anglers experience best results at the mouth of Crooked Creek, although some fish can also be taken on the upper river near Tustumena Lake.

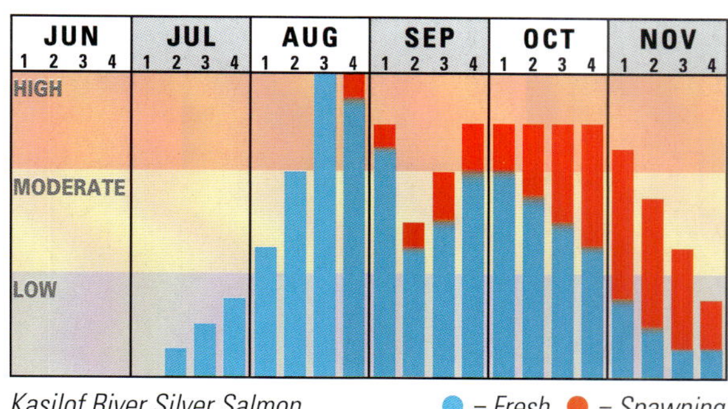


*Kasilof River Silver Salmon* ● *= Fresh* ● *= Spawning*

## Steelhead Trout

**Rating:** ★★½ Fair to good.
**Season:** January 1 through December 31.
**Timing:** August 10 – June 20; peak September 25 – November 30 and April 20 – May 10.
**Size:** Average 4 – 8 pounds, up to 32 inches (15 pounds).
**Tackle:** Spinners, attractors, and flies.
**Tips:** Trout can be located throughout the river from fall into spring, the greatest concentration of fish being near Crooked Creek in April and May. Fluorescent orange or metallic pink and chartreuse attractors and flies are good.

*Angler shows off a bright hen steelie, landed on a purple Egg Sucking Leech at the mouth of Crooked Creek. Early in the spring, look for a combination of chrome fish such as this and blushed pre-spawners. Spring steelheading on the Kasilof is a welcome open-water opportunity after a long Alaska winter.*

*(Courtesy Eagle Eye Images)*

*Fishing off the bank can be great in many parts of the river but access is especially good on the lower river around Crooked Creek.*

## Rainbow Trout

**Rating:** ★½ Poor to fair.
**Season:** January 1 through December 31.
**Timing:** March 15 – Dec. 15; peak June 15 – August 1.
**Size:** Average 8 – 16 inches, up to 25 inches (5-6 pounds).
**Tackle:** Spinners, attractors, and flies.
**Tips:** Look for signs of spawning salmon in summer and fall and try egg imitations. Shore anglers usually connect with these fish in spring at the mouth of Crooked Creek.

## Dolly Varden

**Rating:** ★★★ Good.
**Season:** January 1 through December 31.
**Timing:** April 1 – January 1; peak May 15 – June 10 and July 10 – September 5.
**Size:** Average 8 – 20 inches, up to 25 inches (5-6 pounds).
**Tackle:** Spoons, plugs, attractors, flies, and bait.
**Tips:** Egg imitations and bait tend to work best in late summer and fall. Smolt patterns do quite well in spring and summer before salmon spawn. A good number of char are caught in May, usually incidentally to fishing for king salmon and steelhead trout, as fish out-migrate from headwaters to sea. Targeting these char in the tidal area can be hot in the latter part of July.

## Other Kasilof Opportunities

### Drift Fishing

An increasingly popular mode of access is by employing a drift boat or raft in reaching some of the better stretches of water. Long a mainstay of neighboring Kenai, drifting the Kasilof has become the preferred way of connecting with the river's salmon and trout populations with viable water available from Tustumena Lake down to tidewater.

The months of April, May, and June are superb for floating the lower Kasilof as the river flows slow and low compared to mid-summer levels. Several guides operate on the river this time of year and the water conditions lend to a great experience, even for novice drifters. Come July, the river runs several feet higher with strong current.

The majority of anglers choosing this peaceful way of fishing the Kasilof launch at the Sterling Highway bridge and take out on the far lower end of the river, in tidewater. It is a great trip easily accomplished in a day and half-day floats are possible too with many hours of fishing accounted.

However, drifting the upper river is also a great experience, particularly from mid-summer through fall when red and silver salmon and steelhead trout dominate the scene, providing excellent, semi-remote fishing perfect for day-long trips.

Launch point is near the Tustumena Lake outlet, taking out at the Sterling Highway bridge.

Anglers must read up on special regulations on this river before going as there are restrictions in place governing drift boats as well as boating in general.

For put-in and take-out locations, refer to the area map and access description at the beginning of this section.

# Other Productive Fisheries & Additional Opportunities

## MOOSE RIVER & LAKES

**Fishing:** ★★★ **Scenery:** ★★★
**Accessibility:** ★★ **Solitude:** ★★★★

**Location:** Western Kenai Peninsula drainage, 121 to 135 miles south of Anchorage, 13 to 28 miles east of Soldotna.

**Access:** There is a limited number of roadside spots in which to approach this drainage, most of which are in the East Fork Moose River drainage and includes several lakes. With the exception of the Sterling Highway crossing on the far lower end of the mainstem Moose River, this vast lake system remains relatively remote with main modes of access being a watercraft such as a canoe or kayak.

*A. Moose River* – Milepost 82.3. Turn south on paved side road leading short distance to Izaak Walton Wayside and recreation area at the confluence of Moose and Kenai rivers. Developed parking, campground, firepits, picnic tables, restrooms, and boat launch. Suitable for all size vehicles. Fish from the bank or launch watercraft to explore the upper river and associated lakes.

*B. East Fork Moose River* – Milepost 71.4. Sterling Highway crosses stream; for primary access, use Watson Lake turnout east of crossing. Hike to and along small stream.

*C. Watson Lake* – Milepost 71.3. North on access road 0.7 mile to recreation area and lake. Parking, camping, boat launch, and restrooms. Some shore fishing possible but mainly by canoe.

*D. Egumen Lake* – Milepost 70.8. South to gravel parking area and trailhead. Marked trail leads 1/4 mile to lake. Some shore fishing possible but mainly by canoe.

*E. Peterson & Kelly Lakes* – Milepost 68.4. South on gravel road by sign 0.3 mile to a "Y"; left fork leads 0.3 mile to Kelly Lake, right fork 0.2 mile to Peterson Lake. Parking, camping, and boat launch available. Some shore fishing possible but mainly by canoe.

**Facilites:** The main area for recreational purposes featuring developed facilities is the Izaak Walton Wayside right in the community of Sterling. Some primitive parking and camping, including boat launches, may be available in drainage lakes. Motels, guide services, gas stations, convenience stores, and other amenities are present in Sterling as well as Soldotna a few miles to the west.

**Restrictions:** Closed to all fishing from May 2 through June 10 upstream of Sterling Highway bridge; open year-round downstream. King salmon fishing is prohibited. Consult ADF&G regulations.

**Species:** Red, pink, and silver salmon, rainbow trout, and Dolly Varden. A few arctic char, whitefish, and northern pike reported in drainage.

**Fishing:** This typical lowland drainage harbors some fantastic lake fishing opportunities for those having access to a canoe or kayak, but casting from shore is possible in some roadside locations with varying results. While fishing for rainbow trout and other resident game species is definitely better in the lakes of West, North, and East forks, salmon are more cooperative for the road-bound angler.

Several waters of the West and North fork drainages are in the Swan Lake Canoe Route and are known for decent access with very productive early and late season action for trout and char averaging the the high teens. In fact, some of the larger and more remote lakes in the Moose system contain rainbows up to 28 inches and 7-8 pounds. Exploring the upper reaches of Moose using watercraft is an incredible and sensible way to experience some awesome fishing at very low cost.

Anglers restrained to the main road access points can still engage in good fishing, however. The confluence area of Moose and Kenai is a hot spot for salmon while the East Fork drainage lakes can be very good for nice-sized trout.

Red salmon run thick at the mouth of Moose from June into August, and pinks stage here during August in huge numbers on even-numbered years, followed by a very decent showing of silvers that lasts throughout fall.

For roadside trout, hit Peterson, Kelly, Watson, and Egumen lakes, the latter accessed by trail. Expect fishing to be decent with some exceptional days in mid-autumn.

**Red Salmon.** Fair; June 5 – 15 and July 15 – August 1; average 4 – 8 pounds. Two runs present. Use flies.

**Pink Salmon.** Excellent; August 10 – 25; average 3 – 5 pounds. River mouth is best. Spoons, spinners, and flies.

**Silver Salmon.** Good; August 20 – September 5 and September 20 – October 10; average 6 – 15 pounds. Two runs present at river mouth. Spinners, flies, and bait.

**Rainbow Trout.** Good to excellent; June 15 – October 15; average 8 – 20 inches. Flies (attractors and egg patterns), spoons, and spinners.

**Dolly Varden.** Fair to good; July 15 – October 15; average 8 – 16 inches. Use attractor flies early, egg imitations later in the season; spinners.

## SWANSON RIVER

**Fishing:** ★★★½ **Scenery:** ★★★½
**Accessibility:** ★★★ **Solitude:** ★★★

**Location:** Western Kenai Peninsula drainage, 151 to 187 miles south of Anchorage, 16 to 39 miles north of Soldotna.

**Access:** There are two main access points to Swanson. The mouth and lower river can be reached through Kenai Spur Highway while the middle section is best accessed from Swanson River Road near the community of Sterling. Anglers wishing to experience the river at its best can launch a canoe from the Swanson River Road access point and paddle/drift downstream to Swanson Canoe Landing off Kenai Spur Highway.

### Kenai Spur Highway

This road begins in Soldotna (Milepost 0) and ends just after the Clint Starnes Memorial Bridge crossing the Swanson River (Milepost 39.0). The lower river and surrounding land is within the Captain Cook State Recreation Area, starting at Milepost 35.5.

*A. Swanson Canoe Landing* – Milepost 38.6. Turn east on access road 0.6 miles to parking area with toilets. Limited turnaround for large RVs. This is the end of the Swanson River Canoe Trail system.

*B. Swanson River Crossing* – Milepost 38.7. The road crosses Swanson River. Some limited parking by bridge.

*C. Discovery Campground* – Milepost 39.0. Road ends here. Turn left 0.4 miles to campsites and picnic area. Trails lead to river.

### Swanson River Road

The road begins at Milepost 83.4 of the Sterling Highway (Milepost 0) and ends at Swan Swanson River.

*D. Swanson River* – Milepost 17.7. End of road. Parking, camping, small boat launch, and wheelchair access available.

**Facilities:** The only on-site facilities are situated on the lower end of Swanson as indicated above. The community of Sterling at the beginning of Swanson River Road has public and private campgrounds, RV parks, gas stations, canoe rentals, grocery stores, tackle shops, and other amenities.

**Species:** Red and silver salmon, rainbow trout, and Dolly Varden. Small run of pink salmon in lower river.

**Restrictions:** King salmon fishing is prohibited. Closed to all fishing from April 15 through June 14. Consult ADF&G regulations.

**Fishing:** Swanson River is a relatively small, slow-flowing drainage that supports a very healthy run of silver salmon during late summer and early fall along with outstanding fly-fishing for rainbow trout, particularly in its middle and upper reaches. Lesser numbers of red salmon and Dolly Varden are also present in season.

The salmon fishing is for the most part a lower Swanson affair as there are relatively few bright specimens and mostly turning fish available higher up in the drainage. Anglers casting in the tidal area or the first few miles of river are treated to some exceptional action, particularly for silver salmon. Hiking upstream on trails from the tidal area, beaver dams and a multitude of holes and pools hold significant numbers of silvers. Reds, although sometimes present in fishable numbers, are generally not targeted to any extent since this slow-flowing river is not conducive to methods or techniques required for successful fishing. As for pinks, the run is small with most fish caught incidentally to casting for silvers.

Rainbow trout are most prolific in the upper and middle reaches of the Swanson where a number of feeder streams and lakes connect to the river. Fall fly-fishing on the middle and upper reaches of the river can be legendary for trout averaging in the teens. Dolly Varden are not as numerous as trout but can still yield some decent opportunities throughout the length of the Swanson.

One quite popular way to enjoy the fishing on this peaceful river is to launch a canoe at the upper access point and paddle downstream scouting for schools of salmon and hungry trout.

**Red Salmon.** Fair; July 10 – 25; average 3 – 6 pounds. Look for water with at least some current. Try upstream edge of incoming tide on the lower river. Use flies.

**Pink Salmon.** Poor to fair; July 20 – August 5; average 2 – 4 pounds. Even-numbered years are best. Cast spoons, spinners, and flies on incoming/outgoing tide.

**Silver Salmon.** Good to excellent; August 15 – September 10; average 5 – 12 pounds. Incoming tides can produce great catches using spinners, flies, and bait. Look for schools of fish in holes in middle and upper river. Brightest salmon are found in the lower river.

**Rainbow Trout.** Good to excellent; August 15 – October 10; average 8 – 18 inches. Best action is on the upper and middle river, action being poor to fair on the lower end. Flies and spinners. A few large specimens to 25 inches present in fall.

**Dolly Varden.** Fair; August 15 – October 10; average 8 – 16 inches. Decent fishing for sea-run char on the lower river in July. In fall, try the upper river. Use attractor patterns early, switching to egg imitations later.

## SWANSON AREA LAKES

**Fishing:** ★★★★ **Scenery:** ★★★½
**Accessibility:** ★★★ **Solitude:** ★★★★

**Location:** Western Kenai Peninsula drainage, 140 miles south of Anchorage, 11 miles east of Soldotna.

**Access:** The Sterling Highway is the main artery of access to the northern sections of the peninsula through the Swanson River Road and Swan Lake Road, both of which are gravel surface. Swanson River Road begins at Milepost 83.4 Sterling Highway in the community of Sterling and head northward to Swan Lake Road Junction at Mile 17.2. From here, Swan Lake Road continues to end of road at Mile 12.2.

Some lakes are situated close to the road, others require a hike up to a mile or more. Parking spaces at locations or trailheads are limited with large RVs not recommended.

### Swanson River Road

*A. Mosquito Lake* – Milepost 7.9. Parking. Trail leads 200 yards to lake. Rainbow trout.

*B. Silver Lake* – Milepost 9.1. Parking. Trail leads 1 mile due west to lake. Rainbow trout and arctic char.

*C. Finger Lake* – Milepost 9.8. Parking. Trail leads 2.3 miles due west to lake. Arctic char.

*D. Forest Lake* – Milepost 10.7. Parking. Trail leads 200 yards due northwest to lake. Rainbow trout.

*E. Dabbler, Skookum, & Drake Lakes* – Milepost 13.3.

(Courtesy Max Root)

Parking. Trail leads due east 1/4 mile to Dabbler, continues 1 mile to a fork; left fork heads 1/2 mile to Drake, right fork 1/4 mile to Skookum. Rainbow trout and arctic char.

*F. Dolly Varden Lake* – Milepost 14.1. Parking and camping. Access site on right to lake. Rainbow trout and arctic char.

*G. Rainbow Lake* – Milepost 14.8. Parking. Take right fork at "Y" 0.8 mile, road on right leads to lake. Parking and camping. Rainbow trout and Dolly Varden.

### Swan Lake Road

*H. Ice Lake* – Mile 4.0. Parking south of road. Cross road and locate trail heading due north 1/2 mile to lake. Rainbow trout and arctic char.

*I. Campfire Lake* – Mile 7.0. Parking. Trail leads 1/2 mile due north to lake. Rainbow trout.

*J. Nest Lake* – Mile 8.3. Park on shoulder of road. Trail leads 1/2 mile due north to lake. Rainbow trout.

*K. Paddle Lake* – Mile 12.2. Parking. Trail leads 1/4 mile due north to lake. Rainbow trout and arctic char.

**Facilities:** Parking and primitive camping present at most sites. The community of Sterling has public and private campgrounds, RV parks, gas stations, canoe rentals, grocery stores, tackle shops, and other amenities.
**Species:** Rainbow trout, Dolly Varden, and arctic char. Red and silver salmon may be present in a few lakes.
**Restrictions:** General restrictions apply. Consult ADF&G regulations.
**Fishing:** The string of forested lakes along area road are known to produce some exceptional catches, particularly in late summer and fall. Although the lakes closest to the road do receive a fair amount of angling pressure, the spots a ways off the road can be legendary fishing at the height of the season with some robust trout and char pushing 28 inches and 7 to 8 pounds.

Casting from shore is possible at a few of the lakes, yet the best fishing can definitely be had using a float tube or light watercraft to access deeper water where fish concentrate. Canoes can be rented in Sterling.
**Rainbow Trout.** Good to excellent; August 25 – January 1; average 8 – 22 inches. Spoons, spinners, flies, and bait.
**Dolly Varden.** Fair; August 25 – January 1; average 10 – 20 inches. Spinners, flies, and bait.
**Arctic Char.** Good to excellent; August 25 – February 1; average 10 – 22 inches. Spoons, plugs, jigs, and bait.

## ADDITIONAL OPPORTUNITIES

### Remote Fly-In Fishing

There are a multitude of air services in the towns of Kenai and Soldotna, and to some degree also Sterling, that operate both wheel as well as float planes to angling destinations across Cook Inlet. Guided as well as drop-off trips are available, with excursions lasting from half a day to a week or more depending on clients' wishes. A few have rustic tent camps set up for shelter on the banks of area waters and there are a couple of lodges in operation too. These outfits mainly target the five species of salmon in addition to trout and char.

Popular hot spots include Chuit River and clearwater tributaries of Beluga River for kings and silvers, Kustatan River, Shelter Creek, and Crescent River/Lake for silvers, Big River Lakes for reds (a great location for bear viewing), and Silver Salmon Creek for – what else – silver salmon. All of these drainages produce some phenomenal catches based on numbers of fish present and general lack of angling effort; however, it should be noted that one must always expect company on any one of these waters, particularly at the peak of the respective runs, considering the relatively close proximity to the Kenai Peninsula and Anchorage.

The run timing for these drainages is June into July for king and red salmon and early August to mid-September for silvers. Several of the locations described above also produce some noteworthy fishing for rainbow trout and Dolly Varden throughout the summer and fall months, as well as some fast action for pink and chum salmon (mid-July to mid-August).

Some companies offer sightseeing and bear viewing separately or in combination with their fishing trips, as many of these far-flung drainages of western Cook Inlet support very healthy bear populations and awesome views of the region's active volcanoes.

*(Courtesy Beverley Bailey)*

*Remote fly-in drainages typically offer excellent fishing and spectacular vistas. This view is from Shelter Creek.*

### Fly-In Bear Viewing

The remote western shore of Cook Inlet is not just all about fishing; viewing wildlife -- in particular bears -- is as good as it gets. Daily bear watching trips are arranged through various charter flight companies in the area and quite a few of them offer guided fishing trips all in the same package.

Flying out of the peninsula communities of Soldotna, Kenai, and Homer, bear watchers are treated to a short 30 minute flight across the inlet to a few select destinations known for their reliable sightings. Spotters can expect to see several of these large animals on their trip which may include both the black and brown varieties. At the height of the viewing season, it is even possible to see a dozen or more bears at relatively close range.

A couple of the more popular spots are Big River Lakes and Hallo Bay where bears gather starting in mid-June and lasting through the summer and into fall. Observations are done from planes, area beaches, and boats depending on location. Both of these locations experience a fair amount of viewing activity. There are also several other places to go viewing that are not as busy but still offer great opportunities to see bears.

Ninilchik • Anchor Point • Homer

# Southern Kenai

**King Salmon • Pink Salmon • Silver Salmon • Dolly Varden**
**Pacific Halibut • Lingcod • Rockfish • Shark • Bottomfish**

*Clam Digging* *Surf Casting* *Deep Sea Fishing* *Tidewater Streams*

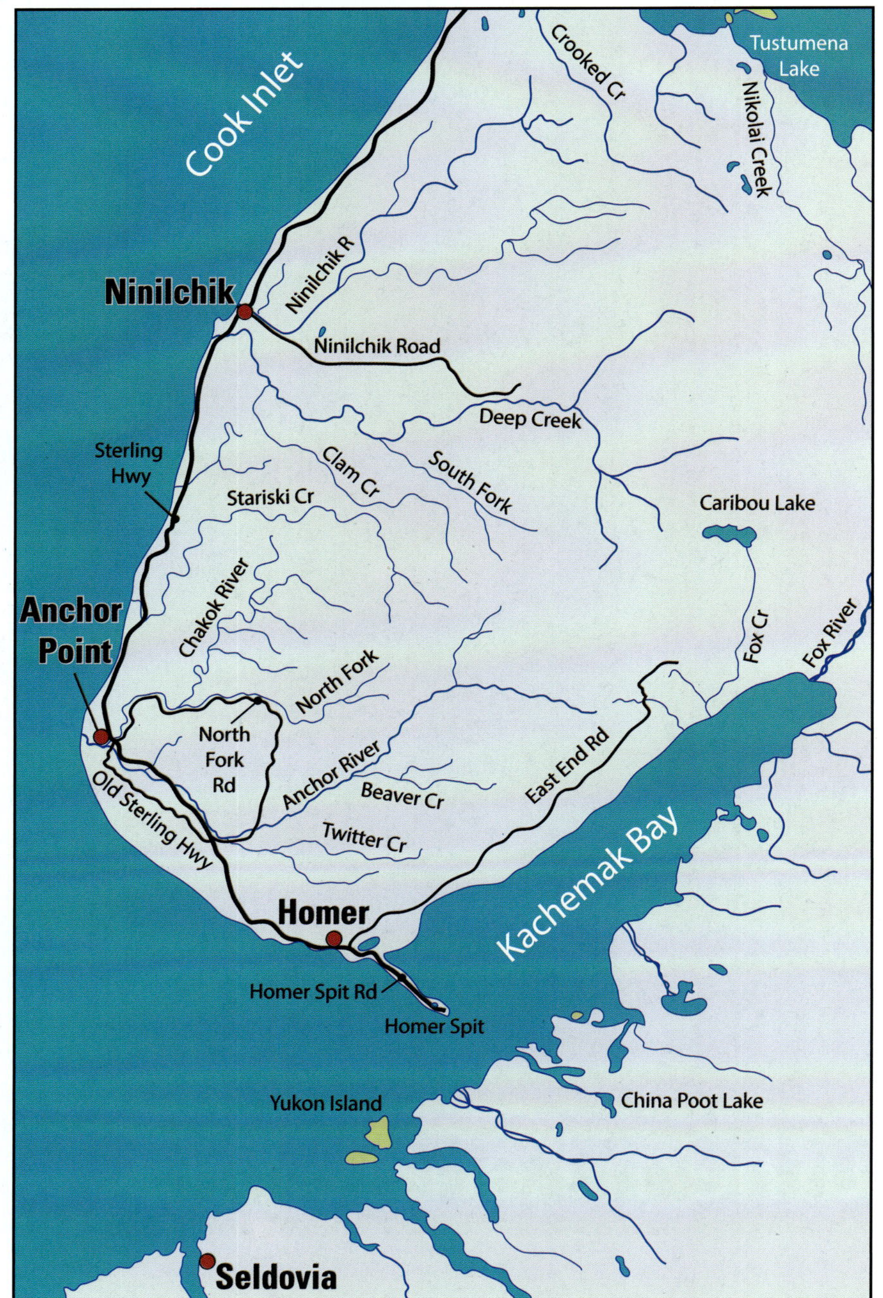


**Area Population Centers:** Homer, Anchor Point, Ninilchik

**Key Species:** King, Red, Pink, and Silver Salmon, Steelhead Trout, Dolly Varden, Pacific Halibut, Lingcod, Rockfish, Bottomfish

**Other Species:** Chum Salmon, Rainbow Trout, Shark

**Main Destinations/Hot Spots:** Ninilchik and Anchor rivers, Deep Creek, Kachemak Bay, Dudiak Lagoon

**Other Destinations:** Stariski Creek and Cook Inlet

**Additional Opportunities:** Clam Digging, Remote Fly-In Waters, Peninsula Wildlife Viewing

**Summary of Area Fishing:** Where the southern peninsula lacks some of the grandeur of mountain ranges and rainforests at close range, the setting is on a different scale entirely. Here, lush green rolling hills, thin black spruce, marshland, and charcoal soaked bluffs dominate along with small iron-stained rivers and streams that run full of salmon, sea-run trout, and char from spring through fall, while the ocean provides a plethora of activity concerning not only salmon but bottomfish as well.

However, the view is no less stunning as a row of semi-active volcanoes -- some of which reach heights of 10,000 feet or more -- splendidly decorate the western shores of Cook Inlet not many miles away. In addition, across from Kachemak Bay and bordering the Gulf of Alaska, jagged mountains complete with ice fields and cutting fjords, bring even more intrigue to an area steeped with a long history of human settlement.

There can be said to be two aspects to fishing the southern peninsula, the first being the small-stream atmosphere that caters to an enthusiastic and loyal group of anglers targeting ocean-bright salmon only minutes from the salt and classic fly-fishing opportunities for steelhead trout and Dolly Varden. Part of the charm is not only the superb fighting (and eating) conditions of the available species, but the physical attraction of these waters. They are all easily waded with literally dozens of fishable stream miles per water to really hike to and along and explore, with just enough roadside influence to enjoy relative solitude together with easy access.

Fishing the saltwater areas here is no less than fantastic. Homer and the smaller communities immediately to the north have a solid reputation of producing world-class action for halibut, lingcod, rockfish, and two species of salmon (kings, silvers) with trophy and record size fish present. Wildlife, too, is abundant.

Peak season is May into October.

# Ninilchik River

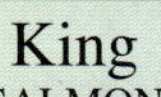
King
SALMON

Red
SALMON

Pink
SALMON

Silver
SALMON

Steelhead
TROUT

Dolly
VARDEN

**Highlights:** Excellent action for kings, silvers, and steelhead. Also, great salmon and halibut fishing off the river mouth and clam digging on area beaches.

**Best Fishing:** Late May to mid-October.

**Regulatory Restrictions:** Moderate.

**Location:** Southern Kenai Peninsula drainage, community of Ninilchik, Sterling Highway, 188 miles south of Anchorage, 45 miles north of Homer.

**Description:** The Ninilchik is a small river in comparison to Deep and Anchor to the south and could probably be classified as a creek or stream more than anything else. The river meanders considerably through the shallow valley hence it flows, while every bend or twist in the river reveal deep holes and runs perfect for hiding and concentrating fish, a fact that anglers familiar with Ninilchik know intimately well.

Because of the somewhat diminutive size of the river, casting or classic fly-fishing is not practical (except for in the tidal zone) with anglers resorting to the basic "flipping" technique so common elsewhere.

The far lower end of the river is influenced by Cook Inlet tides, the water rising 10-15 feet at the mouth. A wide and deep artificial lagoon has been created here and used as a harbor for small commercial fishing boats, the fleet moving in and out on high tide during the brief July season. Heading upstream from the tidal area, the Ninilchik quickly narrows with dense vegetation surrounding the slightly

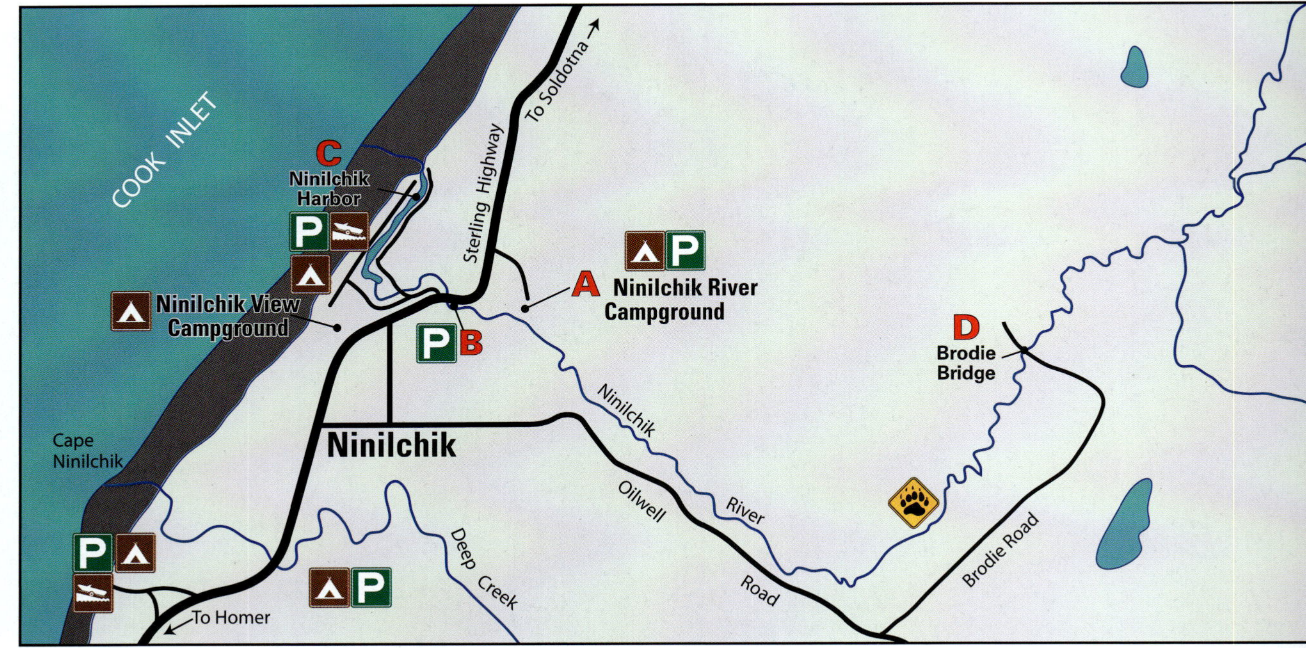


tannic waters.

Upstream of the highway bridge, the Ninilchik continues for miles into the valley with faint trails paralleling both sides of the river. Some sparse settlement is obvious along the ridges overlooking the valley but none as apparent as what can be seen in Ninilchik Village near the mouth.

The greatest volume of water is during the spring months as snowmelt fills the river and help push king salmon in from Cook Inlet. Water levels retreat sometime in early June and typically stay very low and clear until the late summer and fall rains swell the river yet again, this time sending pulses of silver salmon and steelhead trout upstream.

**Facilities:** There is a developed campground present just north of the river, complete with picnic tables and restrooms, with trail access to the lower and middle Ninilchik. A very large gravel parking lot is present at the Sterling Highway bridge. There is also a state-run campground on the beach near the mouth of the river at Ninilchik Village. Many other facilities and services are available in the community of Ninilchik less than a mile away.

**Access:** The Sterling Highway offers easy and convenient access to the lower Ninilchik and the river mouth. There are three main areas of public access as listed below. The upper river is far more difficult to access, impeded by private land and difficult terrain.

**A. Ninilchik River Campground** – Milepost 134.5. Turn east at sign to campground. Trails lead 200 yards to river.

**B. Sterling Highway Bridge** – Milepost 135.0. Highway crosses river. Parking areas located north and south of bridge with camping also available.

**C. Ninilchik Harbor** – Milepost 135.1. Turn west on Mission Avenue (Beach Access Road) south of the highway bridge and follow 1.2 miles to end of road and river mouth. Road parallels the entire lower river with several parking areas and a campground present.

**D. Brodie Bridge** – Milepost 135.9. East on Oilwell Road 3.4 miles, turn left on Brodie Street and proceed 0.5 mile to bridge at stream crossing. Small pullout next to bridge. Faint, improvised trail leads downstream along river.

*Anglers try their luck for king salmon on a couple of tidewater holes just upstream of the boat harbor along Mission Avenue. Easy access and good fishing on a small clearwater river is trademark of the Ninilchik. Several salmon species, steelhead, and char await.*

## Rules & Regulations

**Open Season:** Memorial Day weekend and the following two weekends, including Mondays, and July 1 through October 31. Closed to all fishing from November 1 until Memorial Day weekend and all weekdays through May and June (except Mondays).

**Open Area:** From the mouth of the river to a marker two miles upstream, salmon fishing is allowed. Upstream of this marker, salmon fishing is prohibited and only open for other species from August 1 through October 31.

**Legal Gear/Tackle:** All gear and tackle, including bait, is allowed, except that only unbaited, single-hook, artificial lures may be used from September 1 through October 31.

**King Salmon**

- Open season is Memorial Day weekend and the following two weekends, including Mondays, and July 1 through July 31.
- Bag limit is (1) per day and (1) in possession (20 inches or longer). For kings less than 20 inches (Jacks), the limit is (10).

**All Other Salmon**

- Open all season (see general "Open Season" above).
- Bag limit is (3) per day and (3) in possession (16 inches or longer), of which only (2) may be silver salmon. For salmon less than 16 inches (Jacks), the limit is (10).

**Rainbow/Steelhead Trout**

- Open all season (see general "Open Season" above).
- Retention of trout is not allowed. All fish caught must be released.
- Trout may not be removed from the water at any time.

**Dolly Varden**

- Open all season (see general "Open Season" above).
- Bag limit is (2) per day and (2) in possession, any size.

## Fishing Ninilchik River

**Access:** ★★★★ **Sight Fishing:** ★★★
**Scenery:** ★★★★ **Bank/Wading:** ★★★★★
**Wildlife:** ★★ **Boat/Floating: N/A**

**Species:** King, red, pink, and silver salmon, steelhead and rainbow trout, and Dolly Varden. Occasional catches of chum salmon.

**Summary:** The Ninilchik is a productive stream, attracting large numbers of anglers to its banks starting in late May with the opening of king salmon season and lasting through much of June. It has been said that the otherwise quiet community and its surroundings become Alaska's fourth largest city on Memorial Day weekend, speaking volumes of its popularity and great fishing. Although the crowds can be overwhelming at times with shoulder-to-shoulder activity, there are miles of water open to fishing and for the patient angler willing to do some walking, some relatively undisturbed stretch of water can be found.

After the king season has ended, however, the Ninilchik turns into something entirely different. The few fishers that decide to visit the river from July on through the rest of the summer and into fall are treated to a peaceful, small-stream atmosphere complete with sea-run char, a variety of salmon species, and even the opportunity to hook into a steelhead trout.

*Working the tidal movements of the Ninilchik is often key to success as schools of salmon and trout gather in preparation for their run into the narrow and shallow river.*

(Courtesy Gary Sinnhuber)

This is one of those rivers that remain almost forgotten or ignored much of the year in people favoring the larger drainages to the north or south for their angling needs. While it is true that the fish populations may be smaller here than elsewhere, fishing is still good and the solitude may be more than worth it.

Ninilchik is an easy river to fish due to liberal access and a multitude of holes, pools, and runs. The harbor area is a popular spot for kings in May and June and also attracts some degree of attention in August during the silver salmon run. Many anglers target the incoming waves of fish on the rising tide, keeping up with the schools of migrating salmon and trout as they move upstream from hole to hole.

Fishing on the Ninilchik can be good to excellent but anglers have to watch water and weather conditions a little bit more closely here than other places, focusing efforts on the early morning bite, the tides, and during and right after a good rainfall.

The king salmon run are comprised of wild-stock fish supplemented by a run of hatchery salmon. The timing trend of the hatchery fish is somewhat later than the native kings so the allotted regulatory season is often prolonged through June or even into July if the numbers of fish returning warrants additional harvest.

The red run into Ninilchik is much abbreviated compared to other streams. Some of these fish do swim up the river itself to spawn yet many are of Kenai and Kasilof origin and only sweep by the river on high tides before continuing their journey.

Steelhead are largely fall-running fish in this river. The number of fish present is not as great as in neighboring waters but action can be good nonetheless. Trophy trout to 25 pounds are known to be present but are exceedingly rare. The largest fish to have come out of here recently (landed during the spring king season) measured 40 inches, a monster in regards to Kenai Peninsula standards.

## Fish Availability

● = High ● = Moderate ● = Low ● = Closed

| Species | MAY | JUN | JUL | AUG | SEP | OCT | NOV |
|---|---|---|---|---|---|---|---|
| King Salmon | Closed, Closed, Closed, High | High, High, Closed, Closed | Moderate, Low, Low, Low | Closed, Closed | | | |
| Red Salmon | | Closed | Low, Moderate, Moderate, Low | Low, Low, Low, Low | | | |
| Pink Salmon | | Closed | Low, Low, Moderate, High | High, High, Moderate, Low | Low, Low, Low | | |
| Silver Salmon | | | Low, Low, Low | Moderate, High, High, High | High, Moderate, Moderate, Low | Low, Low, Low, Low | Closed |
| Steelhead Trout | Closed, Closed, Closed, Moderate | Low, Low | | Low, Low, Low, Moderate | Moderate, High, High, High | High, High, High, High | Closed, Closed, Closed, Closed |
| Rainbow Trout | Closed, Closed, Closed, Low | Low, Low, Closed, Closed | Moderate, Moderate, Moderate, Moderate | High, High, High, High | High, High, High, High | High, High, Moderate, Moderate | Closed, Closed, Closed, Closed |
| Dolly Varden | Closed, Closed, Closed, Low | Low, Closed | Low, Moderate, Moderate, High | High, High, High, High | High, High, High, High | High, High, Moderate, Moderate | Closed, Closed, Closed, Closed |
| Angling Pressure | High | High, High | Low, Low, Low, Low | Moderate, High, High, High | High, Moderate, Moderate, Moderate | Moderate, Low, Low, Low | |

### King Salmon

**Rating:** ★★½ Fair to good.
**Season:** Late May (Memorial Day weekend) into mid-June, weekends only, including Mondays (wild/hatchery fish), and July 1 through October 31 (hatchery fish only).
**Timing:** Late May – mid-June; peak May 25 – June 15.
**Size:** Average 12 – 25 pounds, up to 55 pounds.
**Tackle:** Spinners, attractors, flies, and bait.
**Tips:** The first two weekend openers are often said to be the best as water conditions are perfect and kings plentiful. The fishing can be equally productive throughout the river. Early mornings are hot for kings, the bite usually being active from about four o'clock to nine or so. Later in the season, with increased daylight (mid-June) and low water conditions, anglers can do very well from midnight and the next few hours. On any one given weekend, the fishing slows later on opening day (Saturday) and is usually poor on Sunday and Monday in the river upstream of the highway bridge. However, anglers pursuing these salmon on incoming tide and the far lower stream reaches can experience productive fishing any day.

Use bait or fluorescent orange lures and flies if river flows high and muddy, as it sometimes does after a heavy rain or if snow runoff is still ongoing. Very low and clear water conditions command darker hues such as black or metallic blue and green. In the harbor, action is often very good about two hours after high tide.

*Angler lifts two fine specimens, one wild and a smaller hatchery fish. Hatchery fish are recognized by a missing adipose fin.*

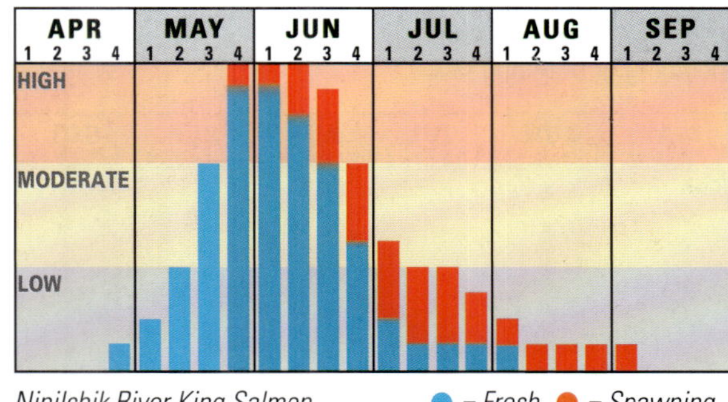


*Ninilchik River King Salmon.* ● = Fresh ● = Spawning

### Red Salmon

**Rating:** ★★ Fair.
**Season:** Late May (Memorial Day weekend) into mid-June, weekends only, and July 1 through October 31.
**Timing:** July 1 – September 1; peak July 10 – 20.
**Size:** Average 5 – 8 pounds, up to 12 pounds.
**Tackle:** Flies.

**Tips:** A decent current is necessary in order to experience productive red action, with anglers recommended to find holes or runs with at least a moderate flow. Avoid calm pools. Casting into areas just above tidewater is good for fish heading upstream, while targeting the outgoing tide at the river mouth on the ocean side of the harbor can be surprisingly good. Appearances of fish can be sporadic and the fishing can vary greatly from tide to tide. The far lower end of the river (below highway bridge) is generally best.

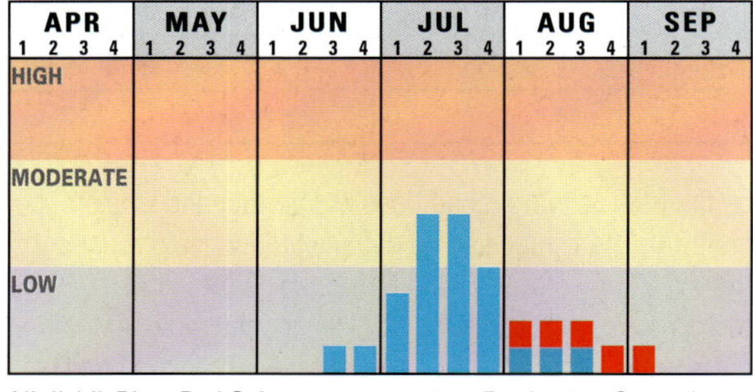


*Ninilchik River Red Salmon.* ● = Fresh ● = Spawning

## Pink Salmon

**Rating:** ★★★½ Good to excellent on even-numbered years, fair to good on odd.
**Season:** Late May (Memorial Day weekend) into mid-June, weekends only, and July 1 through October 31.
**Timing:** July 1 – September 25; peak July 20 – August 10.
**Size:** Average 2 – 4 pounds, up to 7 pounds.
**Tackle:** Spoons, spinners, attractors, and flies.
**Tips:** Most of the run is confined to the lower few miles of river, with pinks spawning anywhere between the headwaters and the river mouth. The brightest specimens are generally caught below the highway bridge – particularly the tidal area – and best intercepted on an incoming or outgoing tide.

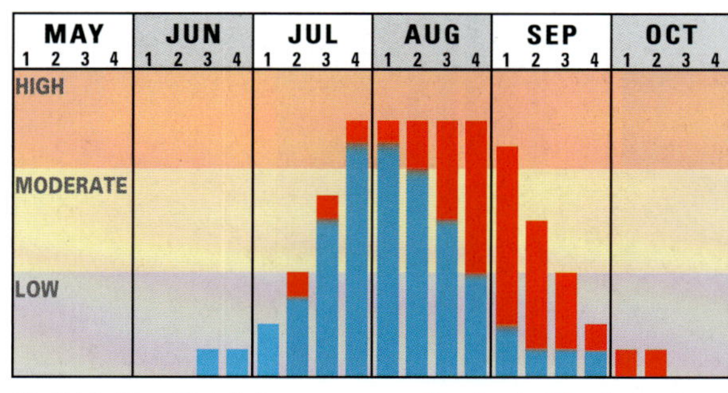


*Ninilchik River Pink Salmon.* ● = Fresh ● = Spawning

*The rocky bend just downstream of the boat harbor is a hot spot to tie into kings and other salmon about two hours after high tide. Floating salmon roe under a strike indicator and casting spinners are proven methods in catching these fish coming in fresh from Cook Inlet. Skilled flyfishers may also do well using flies.*

## Silver Salmon

**Rating:** ★★★ Good.
**Season:** Late May (Memorial Day weekend) into mid-June, weekends only, and July 1 through October 31.
**Timing:** July 15 – November 15; peak August 15 – September 5.
**Size:** Average 6 – 12 pounds, up to 18 pounds.
**Tackle:** Spinners, attractors, flies, and bait.
**Tips:** Silvers can appear very finicky, thus it is very important to be on the river at dawn or to fish the tides. Darker pattern flies are sometimes the only thing that will work consistently (except bait). Strong numbers of salmon often flood the tidal area and the lower river following a good rain.

If water is high and muddy (as is often the case in fall), vibrant colors in pink, orange, and red are good. Bait fished stationary in slow current is deadly. Drifting a cluster of salmon roe is arguably the best way to connect with these fish, yet a great many silvers are also taken using attractor flies. In the harbor, tossing spinners on the tides (as well as bait such as roe or cut herring) can be very effective. Fly-

*Partial view of Ninilchik Village, a leisurely community situated on the banks of the lower river. This spot is a favorite haunt among salmon anglers. Cook Inlet can be seen in the background.*

fishing at the mouth on an outgoing tide is a proven way to hook up with salmon.

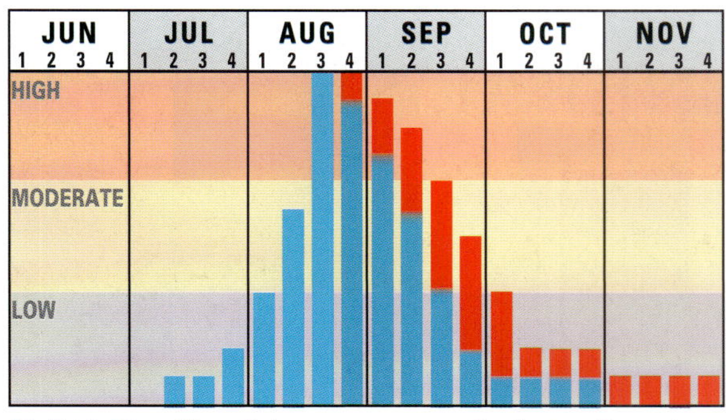


*Ninilchik River Silver Salmon.* ● *= Fresh* ● *= Spawning*

## Steelhead Trout

**Rating:** ★★½ Fair.
**Season:** Late May (Memorial Day weekend) into mid-June, weekends only, and July 1 through October 31 (lower river); August 1 through October 31 (upper river).
**Timing:** Late May – mid-June, August 1 – October 31; peak September 15 – October 31.
**Size:** Average 5 – 10 pounds, up to 20 pounds.
**Tackle:** Spinners, attractors, and flies.
**Tips:** Flies are most popular. A variety of forage patterns are commonly used, with some anglers resorting to more colorful attractor patterns and egg imitations if water is slightly high and off-colored. If no rain is in the forecast, use dark flies and hit the river at dawn. Spinners have a way of enticing stubborn fish. During the king season, many steelhead are caught on green flies and attractors.

*Steelheading on the Ninilchik can be a solitary experience as the autumn crowds focus mainly on larger waters to the south.*

*(Courtesy Eagle Eye Images)*

## Rainbow Trout

**Rating:** ★★ Fair to good in upper parts of drainage.
**Season:** Late May (Memorial Day weekend) into mid-June, weekends only, and July 1 through October 31 (lower river); August 1 through October 31 (upper river).
**Timing:** Late May – mid-June, August 1 – October 31; peak August 1 – September 30.
**Size:** Average 8 – 15 inches, up to 25 inches (5-6 pounds).
**Tackle:** Spinners, attractors, and flies.
**Tips:** A few trout are sometimes caught in the lower river near the highway bridge during the king season and later on in summer. The best fishing, however, occurs higher up in the drainage during August and September. Successful anglers usually hike a mile or two or more up from the Brodie Bridge. Caution is advised hiking along upper Ninilchik as brown bears are a very common sight.

## Dolly Varden

**Rating:** ★★★½ Good to excellent.
**Season:** Late May (Memorial Day weekend) into mid-June, weekends only, and July 1 through October 31 (lower river); August 1 through October 31 (upper river).
**Timing:** Late May and early June, August 1 – October 31; peak July 15 – October 15.
**Size:** Average 8 – 20, up to 25 inches (5-6 pounds).
**Tackle:** Spoons, spinners, attractors, and flies.
**Tips:** Very good fishing can typically be experienced at the mouth of the river in summer (July) using forage or smolt imitations as fish in-migrate from sea, and from August into October in the middle and upper sections. Try egg and flesh patterns. Small spoons and spinners imitating juvenile fish and larger aquatic insects are also known to work well.

# Deep Creek

King
SALMON

Pink
SALMON

Silver
SALMON

Steelhead
TROUT

Rainbow
TROUT

Dolly
VARDEN

**Highlights:** Fast-paced action for early season king salmon and late summer and fall silvers, steelhead, and char. Kings, halibut excellent off mouth; great clam digging spot.

**Best Fishing:** Late May to mid-October.

**Regulatory Restrictions:** Moderate

**Location:** Southern Kenai Peninsula drainage, community of Ninilchik, Sterling Highway, 190 miles south of Anchorage, 43 miles north of Homer.

**Description:** There is some classic small stream water available, complete with deep holes and long runs between stretches of minor rapids and riffles. There are trails that lead both upstream and down with lots of room to really explore Deep in detail. Hiking up from the road crossing, anglers are treated to a fairly narrow perspective of Deep Creek with a few pools that earned the stream its name. Some private property is present.

Heading downstream of the bridge, the stream runs fast and quite shallow with few holding spots for fish (due in part to a tremendous flood years ago) until nearing the tidal zone. The creek slows down considerably with quite a few sharp bends revealing prime habitat for salmon and trout. The far lower section and the mouth are in a wide open area with beach and grassland.

Ocean tides push as far as at least a quarter of a mile inland and bring an increase of water level up to 10-15 feet or more at the mouth.

Deep is often plagued by very high and muddy water

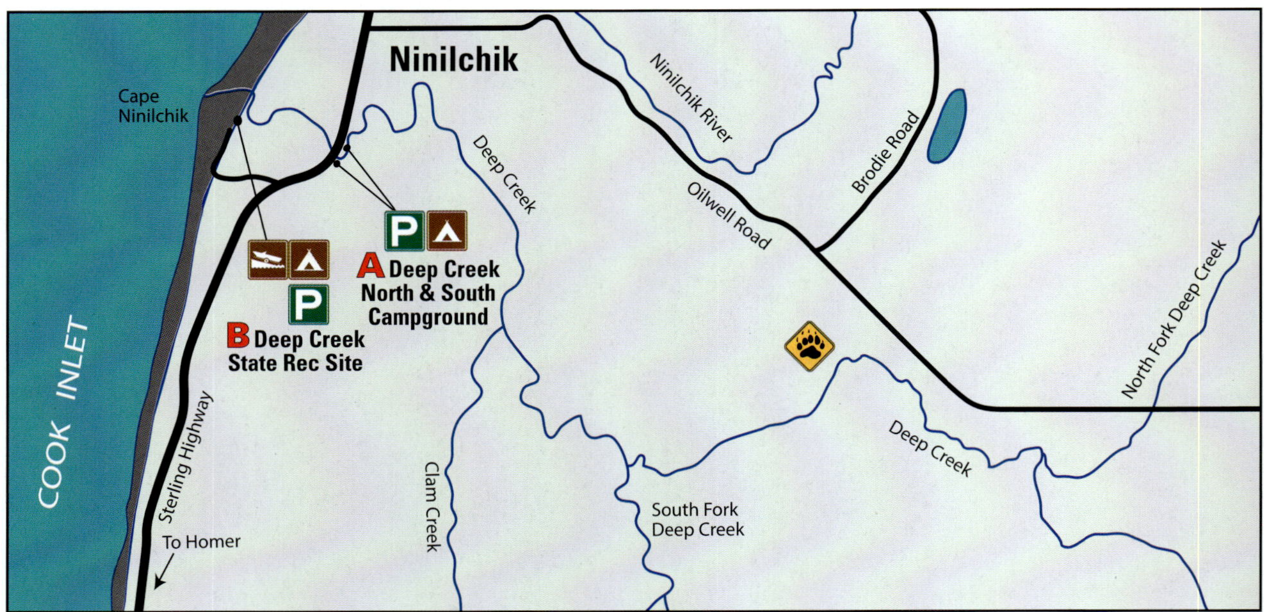


from snow runoff early in the season which may disrupt the first weekend of the king salmon season. Water levels drop as June progresses, becoming low and crystal clear by mid-month. The stream is still a very moody one, churning up a good amount of silt during prolonged periods of rain that are so common during August and September. Yet there is a blessing behind this as well, because salmon and trout will enter Deep Creek in large numbers during and following a good downpour, with anglers experiencing some phenomenal catches as water drops and clears.

**Facilities:** There are two campgrounds located at Deep, one at the highway crossing and another at the mouth of the stream. Parking and restrooms available at both.

**Access:** The Sterling Highway provides two main points of access to the lower section of Deep Creek.

**A. Sterling Highway Bridge** – Milepost 136.8. Highway crosses stream. There are two camping areas here; Deep Creek North Scenic Overlook and Deep Creek South Scenic Overlook. Both border on the stream next to bridge. Parking and restrooms available.

**B. Deep Creek State Recreation Area** – Milepost 137.3. Turn west on Beach Access Road 1 mile to lower stream area, beach, and the mouth of Deep Creek. Parking, primitive camping, and restrooms available. Launching of boats from the beach.

## Rules & Regulations

**Open Season:** Memorial Day weekend and the following two weekends, including Mondays, and July 1 through October 31. Closed to all fishing from November 1 until Memorial Day weekend and all weekdays through May and June (except Mondays).

**Open Area:** From the mouth of the river to a marker two miles upstream, salmon fishing is allowed. Upstream of this marker, salmon fishing is prohibited and only open for other species from August 1 through October 31.

**Legal Gear/Tackle:** All gear and tackle, including bait, is allowed, except that only unbaited, single-hook, artificial lures may be used from July 1 through July 15 and September 1 through October 31.

**King Salmon**
- Open season is Memorial Day weekend and the following two weekends, including Mondays.
- Bag limit is (1) per day and (1) in possession (20 inches or longer). For kings less than 20 inches (Jacks), the limit is (10).

**All Other Salmon**
- Open all season (see general "Open Season" above).
- Bag limit is (3) per day and (3) in possession (16 inches or longer), of which only (2) may be silver salmon. For salmon less than 16 inches (Jacks), the limit is (10).

**Rainbow/Steelhead Trout**
- Open all season (see general "Open Season" above).
- Retention of trout is not allowed. All fish caught must be released.
- Trout may not be removed from the water at any time.

**Dolly Varden**
- Open all season (see general "Open Season" above).
- Bag limit is (2) per day and (2) in possession, any size.

## Fishing Deep Creek

**Access:** ★★★
**Scenery:** ★★★★
**Wildlife:** ★★
**Sight Fishing:** ★★★
**Bank/Wading:** ★★★★
**Boat/Floating:** N/A

**Species:** King, pink, and silver salmon, steelhead and rainbow trout, and Dolly Varden. Occasional catches of red and chum salmon.

**Summary:** The almost legendary fishing reputation Deep Creek has earned goes back many decades (to the days when Sterling Highway was first built), being a favorite haunt among anglers targeting king and silver salmon and steelhead trout. It is the first true clearwater stream of any size one encounters in this area and contains healthy populations of several very sought-after game species.

Kings are the first salmon to return to spawn and the number one game fish at Deep Creek, a very apparent fact if visiting the area in late May and June as campgrounds run at capacity and anglers stand shoulder-to-shoulder in some of the better holes. Even so, anglers willing to put in some time hiking will usually find their own piece of water, especially in the latter part of the season.

A lull in activity follows in mid-summer but is soon offset by a good push of pink salmon. Although not targeted to any extent, pinks may fill the tidewater holes on even-numbered years (in July) along with Dolly Varden. These sea-run char are considered abundant in Deep, with good opportunities beginning in July and lasting through the summer and fall. Incoming tides are great early in the season with better opportunities higher up in the drainage later on in autumn.

*View of the lighthouse on the bluffs overlooking the lower portion of Deep near its mouth. This is a great area to intercept schools of salmon, steelhead, and sea-run char moving in from Cook Inlet.*

The late season entails fast-paced action for silver salmon and steelhead trout, a time preferred by many local anglers as there is plenty of elbow room and an atmosphere of tranquility dominating the fishing scene. The silvers arrive just as the pink run winds down and keeps the area busy until about Labor Day and the first genuine appearance of steelhead. The tidewater holes are good for both species with silvers best in August and steelhead in September. Starting in October, look for steelhead to be present throughout the drainage and provides a welcome extension to the fishery that lasts until the snow flies.

Deep Creek offers a variety of angling disciplines, spin fishing as well as fly-fishing. Although the upper stream sections can be heavily vegetated and largely inaccessible, the lower stream has ample room to move around between holes and casting is not a problem. A few anglers opt to hike in to the upper reaches by the way of Oilwell Road and will literally have miles of water to themselves.

But it is not just the stream that has put Deep Creek on the map for Alaska; the marine fishery off the mouth of the creek in spring and summer for salmon and halibut is exceptional and some of the best found anywhere. It is fully possible to try for salmon and trout on the stream at dawn, then launch a boat from the beach in the afternoon to access the fabulous bottomfish action. Additionally, clam digging is a popular activity on the beach north of the stream mouth from April to October.

## Fish Availability

● = High ● = Moderate ● = Low ● = Closed

| Species | MAY | JUN | JUL | AUG | SEP | OCT | NOV |
|---|---|---|---|---|---|---|---|
| **King Salmon** | Closed Closed Closed High | High High Closed Closed | Closed Closed Closed Closed | Closed Closed | | | |
| **Pink Salmon** | | – – – Closed | Low Low Moderate High | High High Moderate Low | Low Low Low | | |
| **Silver Salmon** | | | – Low Low Low | Moderate High High High | High Moderate Moderate Low | Low Low Low Low | Closed |
| **Steelhead Trout** | Closed Closed Closed Low | Low Low | | Low Low Low Moderate | Moderate High High High | High High High High | Closed Closed Closed Closed |
| **Rainbow Trout** | Closed Closed Closed Low | Low Low Closed Closed | Moderate Moderate Moderate Moderate | High High High High | High High High High | High High Moderate Moderate | Closed Closed Closed Closed |
| **Dolly Varden** | Closed Closed Closed Low | Low – – Closed | Low Moderate Moderate High | High High High High | High High High High | High High Moderate Moderate | Closed Closed Closed Closed |
| Angling Pressure | – – – High | High High | Low Low Low Low | Moderate High High High | High Moderate Moderate Moderate | Moderate Moderate Moderate Moderate | |

## King Salmon

**Rating:** ★★½ Fair to good.

**Season:** Late May (Memorial Day weekend) to mid-June, weekends only, including Mondays.

**Timing:** Late May – mid-June; peak May 25 – June 15.

**Size:** Average 12 – 28 pounds, up to 55 pounds.

**Tackle:** Spinners, attractors, flies, and bait.

**Tips:** Fishing is traditionally best early on Saturday morning but later in the season, toward mid-June, it can be good at the midnight opener and throughout the night until the sun rises. If the water conditions are high and muddy, use salmon roe with fluorescent cure, possibly along with orange and red attractors for a high-visibility effect. Focus on slow-moving water, such as on a high tide. If water is very low and clear, try flies and small attractors in black or dark metallic green. Herring can be excellent for bait.

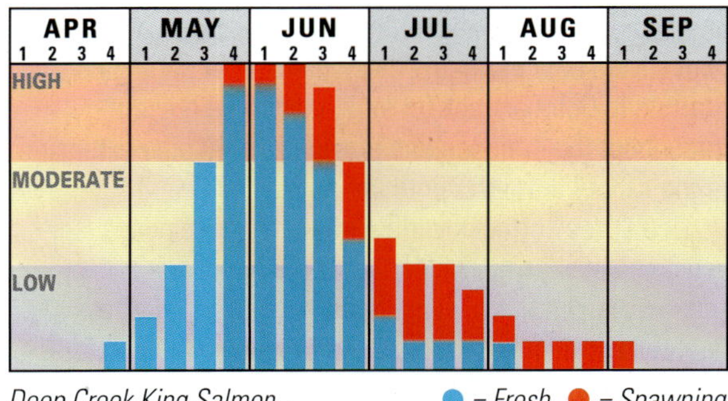


*Deep Creek King Salmon* ● = Fresh ● = Spawning

## Pink Salmon

**Rating:** ★★★★ Excellent on even-numbered years, good on odd.

**Season:** Late May to late June, weekends only, and July 1 through October 31.

**Timing:** July 1 – September 25; peak July 20 – August 10.

**Size:** Average 2 – 4 pounds, up to 6 pounds.

**Tackle:** Spoons, spinners, attractors, and flies.

**Tips:** Since the majority of the pink run is confined to the lower and middle stream, focus attention on areas below the highway bridge. The lower river will usually see the most (and brightest) pinks early on, the middle and upper reaches turning on somewhat later and the fish will more than likely be heading into the spawning phase.

*When the stream runs murky with spring runoff, brightly colored flies (as well as lures and bait) draw consistent strikes.*

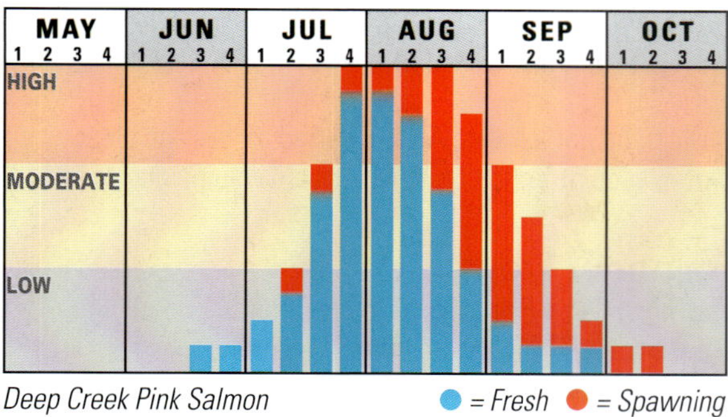


*Deep Creek Pink Salmon* ● = *Fresh* ● = *Spawning*

## Silver Salmon

**Rating:** ★★★ Good.
**Season:** Late May to late June, weekends only, and July 1 through October 31.
**Timing:** July 15 – November 15; peak August 15 – Sept. 5.
**Size:** Average 6 – 12 pounds, up to 18 pounds.
**Tackle:** Spinners, attractors, flies, and bait.
**Tips:** When water levels are very low, tone down size and color of lure or fly. Bait usually outperforms anything else. Hit the stream early before the sun rises. Darker pattern flies are very consistent in getting hookups between dawn and dusk. During murky water conditions, bait and sharply-colored offerings are good. Watch stream for increased signs of activity soon after a good rain. The most consistent daytime action is during incoming tides.

(Courtesy Monte Waite)

*Happy angler showing off a chrome buck coho, taken on a cluster of salmon roe in a tidal hole. Month of August is perfect timing.*

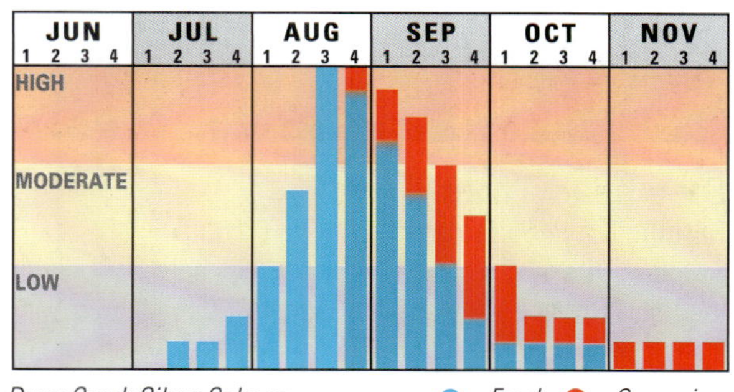


*Deep Creek Silver Salmon* ● = *Fresh* ● = *Spawning*

*Drifting beads and swinging flies is the way to go on Deep during the autumn months. The holes and pools of the upper reaches of tidal influence and above are sure to hold sea-run trout and char.*

(Courtesy Eagle Eye Images)

(Courtesy Robert Laskodi)

An ocean-fresh hen steelie taken near the road crossing. Anglers willing to hike a bit will find an abundance of holding water.

## Steelhead Trout

**Rating:** ★★½ Fair to good.
**Season:** Late May to late June, weekends only, and July 1 through October 31 (lower river); August 1 through October 31 (upper river).
**Timing:** Late May – mid-June, August 1 – October 31; peak September 15 – October 31.
**Size:** Average 5 – 10 pounds, up to 20 pounds.
**Tackle:** Spinners, attractors, and flies.
**Tips:** Be prepared to hit the stream at dawn in order to experience the best action, yet fishing on the tides at mid-day can be hot as well. After a period of low and clear water, keep attention on rising stream volume due to rain.

## Rainbow Trout

**Rating:** ★★½ Fair to good in upper parts of drainage.
**Season:** Late May to late June, weekends only, and July 1 through October 31 (lower river); August 1 through October 31 (upper river).
**Timing:** Late May – mid-June, August 1 – October 31; peak August 1 – September 30.
**Size:** Average 8 – 15 inches, up to 25 inches (5-6 pounds).
**Tackle:** Spinners, attractors, and flies.
**Tips:** It can be tough going to reach areas that have good rainbow fishing considering the lack of developed trails and access roads. Bushwhacking in from the highway is one way; another is to find small dirt roads that lead to portions of the upper drainage.

## Dolly Varden

**Rating:** ★★★★ Excellent.
**Season:** Late May to late June, weekends only, and July 1 through October 31 (lower river); August 1 through October 31 (upper river).
**Timing:** Late May – mid-June, August 1 – October 31; peak September 15 – October 31.
**Size:** Average 8 – 20 inches, up to 25 inches (5-6 pounds).
**Tackle:** Spinners, attractors, and flies.
**Tips:** In July and August, try in the vicinity of the highway bridge and below to the tidal zone. Later on through the fall until freezeup, the upstream reaches above the highway are most productive.

*Lone angler enjoys battling a mid-season king salmon.*

## Other Ninilchik Area Opportunities

### Cook Inlet Salmon & Halibut

The marine fishery north of Anchor Point is about as productive as it gets. Quite different in nature from any other coastal port, the gentle gradient of the inlet's beaches along with huge tidal fluctuations create an environment that is very distinct both in access as well as timing and techniques. Here, anglers can expect to launch right off surf-swept beaches and not from protected harbors and docks. This in itself is an experience not to be missed and one that many anglers tend to favor after having spent a few days on one of several area streams.

Fishing is generally divided by species according to tidal movements. When the tides rush in and out of the inlet, salmon fishing is best, but as the water comes to a slack, anglers jig for halibut. It is common to limit out on both kings or silvers and halibut, taking full advantage of the cost of a trip. However, the most sought-after species here include king salmon and halibut.

The coarse sand and gravel bottom of Cook Inlet is virtually halibut heaven, with perfect depth and habitat to attract massive numbers of flatfish. Despite its angling popularity for decades, Cook Inlet remains the top destination in Alaska for the species with success rates being consistently described as "excellent."

The majority of halibut caught in this area are in the 10- to 40-pound range with reasonable opportunity to hook much bigger specimens. Catches in the triple digits are not unusual at the height of the season with trophies between 200 and 300 pounds possible. As a note, flatties weighing as much as 450 pounds have been boated out of Ninilchik/ Deep Creek.

The halibut season may be slightly abbreviated in this part of Cook Inlet in contrast to other ocean ports in Southcentral, yet anglers can expect quick action at any time between early May and early September. The shoulder seasons of latter April and September can be productive as well, albeit average size of fish caught tends to decrease.

Trolling for salmon can be very worthwhile along the peninsula coastline. King salmon come through in two runs, the first comprised of fish from all area streams and peaks from mid-May to early June with good catch rates. In late June and early July, look for late-run kings headed to the Kenai and Kasilof rivers. There are not as many fish in this run with fair action the norm, but the size of kings is impressive – up to 60 pounds or more. Past years have seen trophy specimens weighing in the mid-80s range.

Silvers are usually not targeted to the degree of their larger brethren but nonetheless can offer some quite impressive action. From the first part of August on through the month until about Labor Day, anglers score trolling along area beaches for migrating fish destined for local rivers and streams. Look for fish surfacing or pick up schools of migrating salmon on the sonar. It is not uncommon to find them within a stone's throw of the surf, so trolling close and shallow works.

As for other species, the inlet is home to good numbers of true cod, spiny dogfish, and skate, in addition to sea-run Dolly Varden. A few charters in the area offer extended trips to more remote locations, offering a mix of both lingcod and rockfish as well as halibut. Charters generally go anywhere from 10 minutes to an hour or more offshore.

# Anchor River

King
SALMON

Pink
SALMON

Silver
SALMON

Steelhead
TROUT

Rainbow
TROUT

Dolly Varden
CHAR

**Highlights:** Top-notch bank fishing for kings, silvers, steelhead, and Dolly Varden. Premier fly-fishing stream. Marine waters off mouth very productive for kings, halibut.

**Best Fishing:** Late May to mid-October. **Regulatory Restrictions:** Moderate

**Location:** Southern Kenai Peninsula drainage, community of Anchor Point, Sterling Highway, 210 miles south of Anchorage, 23 miles north of Homer.

**Description:** Draining out of a broad valley north of Bald Mountain, the Anchor flows approximately 34 miles through spruce and cottonwood forests before emptying into Cook Inlet. It is a moody river, sensitive to hard rain which makes the water turn a chocolate brown and can bring the water level up by a couple of feet or more in a relatively short period of time. Usually, however, the Anchor runs clear with a tint of iron reflecting the muskeg surroundings in parts of the drainage.

There are two main branches of the Anchor, which includes the main fork (sometimes referred to as South Fork) and the North Fork. The main fork is the larger of the two and also supports the most fish. Sterling Highway parallels the river for several miles, with pull-outs and small parking areas scattered along the way. Comparatively, North Fork is much smaller in appearance and does not contain the numbers of fish compared to the main Anchor.

The brunt of angling activity takes place on the lower two miles of river, or from the confluence of the main river

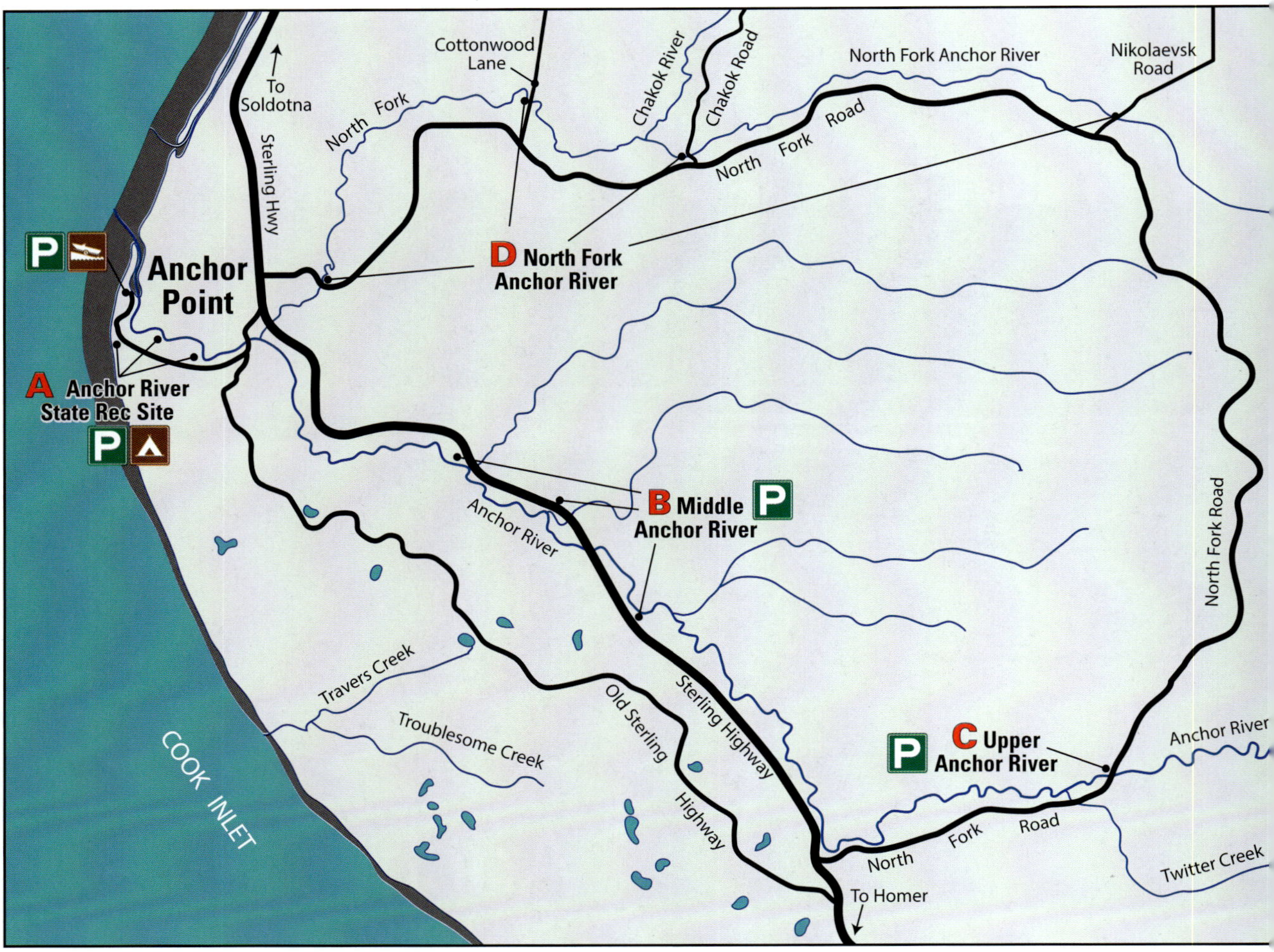

To Soldotna
Cottonwood Lane
Chakok River
Chakok Road
North Fork Anchor River
Nikolaevsk Road
North Fork
Sterling Hwy
North Fork Road
Anchor Point
D North Fork Anchor River
A Anchor River State Rec Site
B Middle Anchor River
Anchor River
North Fork Road
Travers Creek
Troublesome Creek
Old Sterling Highway
Sterling Highway
COOK INLET
C Upper Anchor River
Anchor River
North Fork Road
Twitter Creek
To Homer

and North Fork downstream to Cook Inlet, since this is the only area that is open to salmon fishing.

As is common with coastal run-off streams, the Anchor is ever-changing with old holes disappearing or being altered by spring floods while new pools or runs are continuously being created. The river is especially popular with the fly-fishing crowd as there is some classic water to be found, with an abundance of deep portions ideal for holding schools of fish along relatively open areas for casting.

Breakup occurs sometime in March or the beginning of April, the river running very turbid from snowmelt through much of May, even into June in some years. By mid-June the Anchor has settled to summer levels and won't see much fluctuation until the late season rains in the latter part of August and September. Freezeup commences in the second half of October, the river totally iced over by late November. During seasons experiencing above-average temperatures, however, the river may not freeze until December or later.

The mouth of the river also serves as a launching point on high tide for anglers with boats seeking to troll for king and silver salmon and jig for halibut in the marine waters of Cook Inlet.

*The weir immediately upstream of the Old Sterling Highway bridge provides sonar and visual fish counts from spring into fall, mainly following the health of king and silver salmon runs.*

**Facilities:** The lower portion of Anchor River at Anchor Point has several campgrounds available, while the upper sections only provide limited parking. Motels, lodging, cabin rentals, groceries, guides, and other amenities can be found in the community of Anchor Point.

**Access:** The Sterling Highway provides several points of access in and around Anchor Point as well as to the south towards Homer. Lower Anchor River, from the Old Sterling Highway, is the busiest area.

**A. Lower Anchor River** – Milepost 156.9. Turn southwest on Old Sterling Highway 0.7 mile to river crossing. Anchor River (Beach) Road on right just after bridge parallels river 1.5 miles, ending near river mouth and Cook Inlet. Developed campgrounds at the Anchor River State Recreation Area with picnic tables and restrooms, and parking areas available. Parking for all size vehicles. Primitive boat launch present in tidal area near river mouth.

**B. Middle Anchor River** – Milepost 159.9—164.3. Highway parallels river, crossing it at Milepost 161.0. Turnouts and limited parking, primitive camping present. Not recommended for large RVs.

**C. Upper Anchor River** – Milepost 164.3. Turn east on North Fork Road (South Junction) 2.8 miles to river crossing. Limited parking. Not recommended for large RVs.

**D. North Fork Anchor River** – Milepost 156.7. Turn east on North Fork Road (North Junction) 0.7 miles to stream crossing. Several additional points of access available: Mile 4.1, Cottonwood Lane; Mile 5.0, Chakok Road; and Mile 9.0, Nikolaevsk Road. River is within half a mile on all roads. Limited parking. Not recommended for large RVs.

(Courtesy Eagle Eye Images)

*The Anchor has an ample supply of long, deep runs and pools that tend to congregate migratory fish, particularly on the lower river in and near tidewater. Here, an angler casts into such a holding area containing dozens of hefty chrome-bodied chinooks, fresh in from the salt of Cook Inlet. The quality of salmon (as well as steelhead and sea-run char) on the Anchor is superb.*

## Rules & Regulations

**Open Season:** The last weekend before Memorial Day weekend and the following three weekends, including Mondays, and July 1 through October 31. Closed to all fishing from November 1 until mid-May and all weekdays through May and June (except Mondays and Wednesday).

**Open Area:** From the mouth of the river to the confluence of the North and South forks, salmon fishing is allowed. Upstream of the forks, salmon fishing is prohibited and only open for other species from August 1 through October 31.

**Legal Gear/Tackle:** All gear and tackle, including bait, is allowed, except that only one unbaited, single-hook, artificial lure may be used from July 1 through July 15 and September 1 through October 31.

**King Salmon**

- Open season is the last weekend before Memorial Day weekend and the following four weekends, including Mondays and Wednesdays.
- Bag limit is (1) per day and (1) in possession (20 inches or longer), seasonal limit is (2). For kings less than 20 inches (Jacks), the limit is (10).

**All Other Salmon**

- Open all season (see general "Open Season" above).
- Bag limit is (3) per day and (3) in possession (16 inches or longer), of which only (2) may be silver salmon. For salmon less than 16 inches (Jacks), the limit is (10).

**Rainbow/Steelhead Trout**

- Open all season (see general "Open Season" above).
- Retention of trout is not allowed. All fish caught must be released.
- Trout may not be removed from the water at any time.

**Dolly Varden**

- Open all season (see general "Open Season" above).
- Bag limit is (2) per day and (2) in possession, any size.

## Fishing Anchor River

**Access:** ★★★★
**Scenery:** ★★★★
**Wildlife:** ★★
**Sight Fishing:** ★★★
**Bank/Wading:** ★★★★
**Boat/Floating:** N/A

(Courtesy Roy & Beverley Bailey)

**Species:** King, pink, and silver salmon, steelhead trout, and Dolly Varden. Some rainbow trout in upper stream. Occasional catches of red and chum salmon.

**Summary:** The Anchor represents one of the largest clearwater streams on the peninsula. It offers some solid action for several salmon species and boasts the most intense steelhead fishery available on the road system in Southcentral Alaska. It is particularly the early season king salmon fishery and the late season silver salmon, trout, and char opportunities that draw anglers to the Anchor.

The lower two miles of river sees the heaviest utilization, anglers staging their efforts around tidal movements and plying the holes just upstream. Above the "forks," or where the main Anchor meets the North Fork Anchor, salmon fishing is prohibited but can be dynamite for steelhead and Dolly Varden starting in mid-September and lasting until freeze-up. Anglers scouting the far upper reaches of Anchor (along North Fork Road) will more than likely have the river to themselves.

The season begins in May with big numbers of kings usually rolling into the lower river by Memorial Day weekend. The in-migration continues to be heavy into mid-June, a good year seeing around 10-12,000 kings come through. When water levels are high early in the season, a lot of fish will quickly shoot through the lower section of Anchor. But as the river drops down to summer levels, the upstream migration slows considerably with many fish holding in deep water waiting for an increase in stream volume, such as after a good rain. Fishers begin to see a drop in success after mid-June, but good opportunities still abound as there is considerably less angling pressure to contend with. The officially largest king to have come out of the Anchor weighed 62 pounds.

Pink salmon and sea-run char follow in mid-summer, providing some intense action using ultra-light gear. It is not unusual to experience fish-on-every-cast success at the peak of the in-migrations. The char will continue to provide sport into autumn, just as silvers and steelhead begin to enter on the tides.

The silver salmon run on the Anchor can be exceptional in some years, in excess of 10,000 fish, with some awesome action all the way from tidewater up to the mouth of North Fork. Usually, however, the appearance of these autumn salmon is a little less extravagant but will still yield very good fishing.

Anchor River is synonymous with steelhead trout fishing. The largest run of this species on the road system in Southcentral Alaska can be found here, with sea-run rainbows occasionally numbering into the thousands. Although every year varies to some extent, anglers can expect some days with half a dozen hookups or better. Hit the peak in-migration in late September, focusing on the upper tidal holes and pools.

During times of high and muddy water conditions, anglers may want to consider trying at the confluence of the main river and North Fork. The headwaters of North Fork is not as susceptible to heavy snowmelt and rainfall, thus running clearer than the main fork, creating a relative hot spot.

*A salmon takes to the air much to the delight of a lucky angler. This scene is near the beach at the mouth of the river, a popular spot for anglers drifting bait, casting spinners, and swinging flies.*

## Fish Availability

● = High ● = Moderate ● = Low ● = Closed

(H = High, M = Moderate, L = Low, C = Closed)

| Species | MAY | JUN | JUL | AUG | SEP | OCT | NOV |
|---|---|---|---|---|---|---|---|
| **King Salmon** | C C C H | H H H C | C C C C | C C | | | |
| **Pink Salmon** | | C | L M M H | H H M L | L L L | | |
| **Silver Salmon** | | | L L L | M H H H | H M M L | L L L L | C |
| **Steelhead Trout** | C C C L | L L | | L L L M | M H H H | H H H H | C C C C |
| **Rainbow Trout** | C C C L | L L C C | M M M M | H H H H | H H H H | H H M M | C C C C |
| **Dolly Varden** | C C C L | L C | L M M H | H H H H | H H H H | H H M M | C C C C |
| Angling Pressure | H | H H H | L L L L | M H H H | H H H H | H H H H | |

## King Salmon

**Rating:** ★★½ Fair to good.
**Season:** Mid-May (the weekend before Memorial Day weekend) to late June, weekends only, including Mondays.
**Timing:** Mid-May – late June; peak May 25 – June 20.
**Size:** Average 12 – 30 pounds, up to 60 pounds.
**Tackle:** Spinners, attractors, flies, and bait.
**Tips:** Dark metallic green or blue, also black, are good hues on any lure or fly when river is low. Try fluorescent orange, red, or chartreuse in early morning or anytime when Anchor flows high and muddy. Fish any deep hole or run from midnight on until the sun rises, then focus on the tidal area for incoming kings. Herring is excellent bait, especially early on in the season when kings are just returning from sea. Spinners can be formidable starting the second week of June and through the rest of the king season. Attractors are very popular and can be fished alone or with roe. Flies in various king patterns are highly effective, particularly so if water is clear.

The first and second weekend opener (including Memorial Day Weekend) can be good if the river does not run too dirty with snowmelt but in general expect fair success considering water conditions and that the run is just starting to build. The following weekend openers promise good to excellent action. Traditionally, the first opening day on any weekend (Saturday) is best, the action cooling significantly through the remainder of the opener that week.

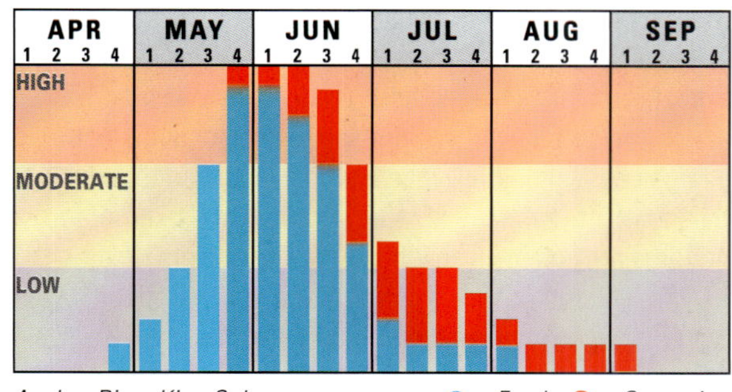


*Anchor River King Salmon* ● = Fresh ● = Spawning

*The streams of lower Kenai Peninsula are known for quality salmon, such as this chrome Anchor chinook taken from the Upper Grass Hole, a favorite tidewater location. Both spin- and fly-fishing can be very productive.*

## Pink Salmon

**Rating:** ★★★★ Excellent on even-numbered years; good on odd.
**Season:** Mid-May to late June, weekends only, and July 1 through October 31.
**Timing**: Late June – Sept. 25, peak July 20 – August 10.
**Size:** Average 2 – 4 pounds; up to 6 pounds.
**Tackle:** Spoons, spinners, attractors, and flies.

(Courtesy Roy & Beverley Bailey)

*A deep-bodied male coho that inhaled a size 4 chartreuse spinner buzzed through a deep hole on an incoming tide.*

**Tips:** Most of the run is confined to the lower few miles of river, with pinks spawning anywhere between the headwaters and the river mouth. The brightest specimens are generally caught in the tidal area and best intercepted on an incoming or outgoing tide.

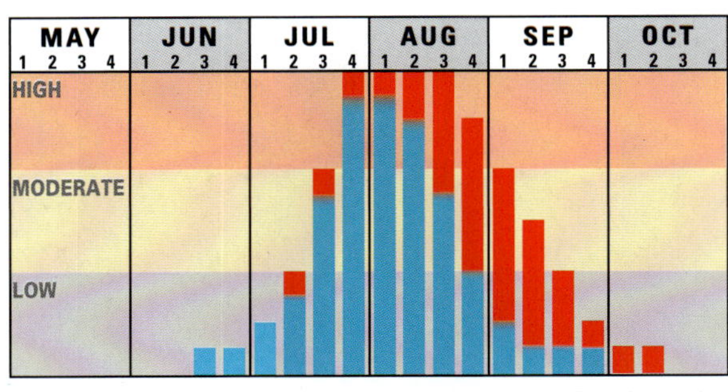


*Anchor River Pink Salmon* ● = *Fresh* ● = *Spawning*

## Silver Salmon

**Rating:** ★★★ Good.
**Season:** Mid-May to late June, weekends only, and July 1 through October 31.
**Timing:** July 15 – November 15; peak August 15 – September 5.
**Size:** Average 6 – 12 pounds; up to 18 pounds.
**Tackle:** Spinners, attractors, flies, and bait.
**Tips:** Silvers usually enter the Anchor in large numbers following a good downpour, especially in years with low water. Action is best at dawn but incoming tides fish well too. Chrome or copper spinners and various colored attractor flies take salmon. A cluster of salmon roe is indisputably the top silver killer on the river. After Labor Day, focus efforts on holes upstream of tidewater.

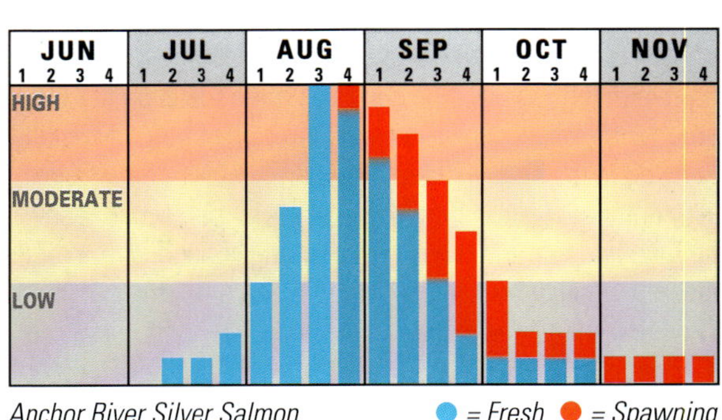


*Anchor River Silver Salmon* ● = *Fresh* ● = *Spawning*

## Steelhead Trout

**Rating:** ★★½ Fair to good.
**Season:** Mid-May to late June, weekends only, and July 1 through October 31 (lower river); August 1 through October 31 (upper river).
**Timing:** Mid-May – late June, August 1 – October 31; peak September 15 – October 31.
**Size:** Average 5 – 10 pounds; up to 20 pounds.
**Tackle:** Spinners, attractors, and flies.
**Tips:** Morning or evening tides produce good action during the second half of September, anglers doing better in areas above the tidal zone and the middle river during the month of October and later. A variety of darker forage patterns are commonly used, with some anglers resorting to more colorful attractor patterns and egg imitations if water is slightly high and off-colored. Spinners have a way of enticing stubborn fish. During the king season, many steelhead are caught on green flies and attractors.

(Courtesy Christian Ormt)

*Second only to kings in popularity, steelhead trout draw anglers from all over Southcentral to the Anchor every fall. This image shows a blush-cheeked October buck.*

## Rainbow Trout

**Rating:** Fair to good in upper parts of drainage.
**Season:** Mid-May to late June, weekends only, and July 1 through October 31 (lower river); August 1 through October 31 (upper river).
**Timing:** Mid-May – late June, August 1 – October 31; peak August 1 – September 30.
**Size:** Average 8 – 15 inches; up to 25 inches (5-6 pounds).
**Tackle:** Spinners, attractors, and flies.
**Tips:** There is a fair population of resident trout that inhabit the upper Anchor. Anglers encounter these fish during late summer and fall using egg and forage imitations, preferably in areas upstream of the Sterling Highway bridge. Very few rainbows are available on the lower river.

## Dolly Varden

**Rating:** Excellent.
**Season:** Mid-May to late June, weekends only, and July 1 through October 31 (lower river); August 1 through October 31 (upper river).
**Timing:** Mid-May – early June, August 1 – October 31; peak July 15 – October 15.
**Size:** Average 8 – 20 inches, up to 26 inches (7 lbs.).
**Tackle:** Spoons, spinners, attractors, and flies.
**Tips:** The Anchor has outstanding action for sea-run char during incoming tides in July using smolt and forage imitations. Later in the season, look for colorful Dolly Varden in the middle and upper river sections as fish follow salmon to the spawning grounds. Egg and flesh patterns are good enticements starting in August on through the fall.

*An angler takes time to relax on the banks of the river to survey the water and the success of others. In the background, snow-clad Mount Iliamna volcano provides a majestic relief to the tidewater grasslands of lower Anchor.*

# Kachemak Bay

King SALMON

Pink SALMON

Silver SALMON

Dolly VARDEN

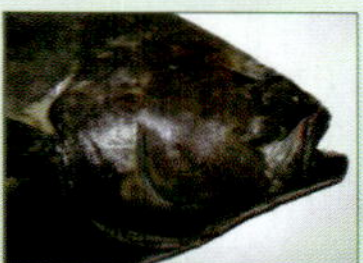
Halibut

**Highlights:** A renowned destination featuring excellent surf-casting for primarily bottomfish, with reasonable opportunity for salmon, halibut, and sea-run char.

**Best Fishing:** Mid-May to early September. **Regulatory Restrictions:** Liberal.

**Location:** Southern Kenai Peninsula, community of Homer, end of Sterling Highway, 231 miles south of Anchorage, on the Homer Spit.

**Description:** A very scenic body of water situated at the southern end of the Kenai Peninsula, Kachemak Bay is an angler's hot spot, or hub, in several different ways. The town of Homer serves as a gateway to the bay and all recreational opportunities in the area, which includes not just the multifaceted types of fishing available but also such activities as clam digging, boating, kayaking, bird watching, and bear viewing.

Usually appearing clear with a slight bluish-green tint, the bay is home to a considerable fauna of game fish as well as non-sporting species. Significant numbers of marine mammals, such as whales, seals, sea otters, and porpoises, are present. While the Homer or roadside portion of Kachemak is predominantly bluffs with rolling hills, the southern half offers splendid natural beauty as snowclad mountain peaks complete with icefields, remnants of glaciers, and numerous short fjords and protected bays come clearly to view. Additionally,the mountainous landscape is draped in a lush boreal rainforest.

However, as there are areas of fine grain sand and mud, deriving from the influence of glacial rivers at the head of the bay, the water may become somewhat silty during times of heavy rain or prolonged warm periods.

The main method of gaining access to Kachemak is by the way of Homer Spit, a narrow and naturally occurring landmass extending from the mainland for several miles into the heart of the bay. This gives roadside anglers significant opportunities to explore the gravel and sand beaches and surf.

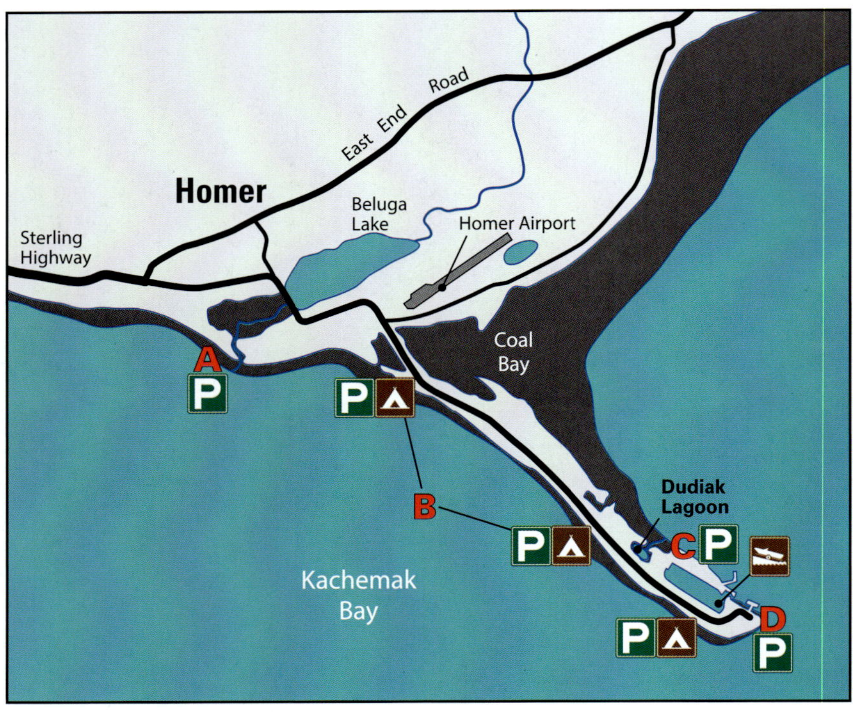


**Facilities:** Visitors to the Kachemak Bay area have a significant variety of facilities and services at disposition. Homer is a sizable town and offers hotels and motels, lodges, restaurants, cafes, bed & breakfasts, RV parks, a commercial airport, grocery and sporting good stores, emergency clinics, processors, and a myriad of other amenities usually associated with important commercial hubs. The population center at the tip of Homer Spit also features tent campgrounds, parking, boat launches, restrooms, guide/charter services, restaurants, cafes, gift shops, fish processors, and lodging.

**Access:** From the town of Homer and the end of Sterling Highway at Milepost 179.5. That portion of the road extending out onto Homer Spit is referred to as Spit Road and has its own mile markers, indicated here as Mile (0) following the Sterling Highway markers.

**A. Bishop's Beach** – Milepost 173.1. Turn south on Main Street, left on E. Bunnell Avenue, then right on Beluga Avenue to end of road and Bishop's Beach Park and the bay. Parking, picnic tables, and restrooms. Beluga Slough trailhead. Limited surf-casting opportunities; this is not a highly regarded fishing area. Some pinks, char, and general bottomfish present.

**B. Ocean Beach** – Milepost 175.4 (4.1). Continue 3.1 miles along southwestern shore of spit facing the ocean with extensive beach area open to public. Parking and primitive camping; space for all size vehicles. Surf-casting for pink and silver salmon, char, and some bottomfish.

**C. Harbor Breakwater** – Milepost 178.2 (1.3). Turn northeast on gravel road leading to large parking area with access to the bay side of the spit. Parking for all size vehicles, primitive camping, restrooms. Boat launch nearby at Homer Harbor. Casting off boulders or hike to beach area in front of Dudiak Lagoon. King, pink, and silver salmon, Dolly Varden, and bottomfish available.

**D. Ferry Dock** – Milepost 179.5 (0). End of road at resort with gravel parking area on left. Public access to beach; no fishing access to dock. King, pink, and silver salmon, Dolly Varden, halibut, and bottomfish.

*View of the Homer Spit and Kachemak Bay as seen from the bluffs.*

## Rules & Regulations

**Open Season:** January 1 through December 31.
**Open Area:** The entire bay is open to fishing.
**Legal Gear/Tackle:** All gear, tackle, and methods are allowed, including snagging.

**All Salmon**
- Open all season (see general "Open Season" above).
- King salmon bag limit is (2) per day and (2) in possession; consult regulations for size and area seasonal restrictions.
- Silver salmon bag limit is (3) per day and (3) in possession.
- All other salmon bag limit is (6) per day and (6) in possession.

**Dolly Varden**
- Open all season (see general "Open Season" above).
- Bag limit is (5) per day and (5) in possession.

**Pacific Halibut**
- Open season is February 1 through December 31.
- Bag limit is (2) per day and (4) in possession, no size limit.

**Lingcod**
- Open season is July 1 through December 31.
- Bag limit is (2) per day and (4) in possession, must be 35 inches or longer.

**Rockfishes**
- Open all season (see general "Open Season" above).
- Bag limit is (5) per day and (10) in possession; except only (1) per day and (2) in possession may be non-pelagic.

**Sharks**
- Open all season (see general "Open Season" above).
- Bag limit is (1) per day and (1) in possession, with an annual limit of (2) fish, except for spiny dogfish which is (5) per day and (5) in possession, no seasonal limit.

**Other Saltwater Fishes**
- Open all season (see general "Open Season" above).
- No bag or possession limits.

## Fishing Kachemak Bay

**Access:** ★★★★
**Scenery:** ★★★★
**Wildlife:** ★★
**Sight Fishing:** ★
**Bank/Wading:** ★★★★
**Boat/Floating:** ★★★★★

**Species:** King, pink, and silver salmon, Dolly Varden, halibut, and various species of bottomfish on the spit side of the bay. Occasional catches of red and chum salmon.

**Summary:** The emerald green waters of Kachemak Bay have an almost endless variety of fishing opportunities for anglers. Salmon and several species of bottomfish are available year-round, with sea-run char and clams rounding out the bounty. It should be noted that the fishing opportunities described in this section are mainly for anglers casting from shore and small watercraft right off the road system, primarily along Homer Spit.

While it is definitely true that the fishing is better from boat in the more remote parts of the bay, hatchery runs of salmon bound for Dudiak Lagoon on the spit ensures surf-casting opportunity for at least two of Alaska's most popular game species, and a fish processing plant churning out fish parts attracts significant numbers of bottomfish, including some halibut. Anglers will find plenty of action when putting to use various methods and techniques proven effective on the various fish species present. In fact, very few places on the road system are able to show the consistent beach catches of halibut that Homer Spit supports. However, timing , gear, and location are of utmost importance in determining success, this being especially the case for king and silver salmon and halibut.

For those able to launch skiffs, boats, and even kayaks will find a plethora of opportunities along the south side of the bay that includes both deep sea as well as tidewater stream fisheries. For more on this, see page 266.

(Courtesy Beverley Bailey)

Mature hatchery king salmon start their migration along the northern shore of Kachemak in spring, destined for Dudiak Lagoon. Successful anglers target these fish near the outwash channel of the lagoon but fish staging in the salt are frequently taken at the breakwater in front of the boat harbor and may even be encountered in small schools around the ferry dock in May. Generally, the closer to the lagoon one makes an attempt, the higher ratio of hook-ups.

On occasion, anglers may tie into an immature feeder king, especially if casting into deeper waters along the spit. Plug-cut herring fished near bottom may tempt a fish.

Schools of pink salmon hit the beach area from around the end of the spit up along the surf towards town in mid-summer (mid-late July), providing decent light tackle action. These are fish bound for bay area streams as well as drainages higher up in Cook Inlet.

There are two showings of silver salmon at Homer Spit. The first occurs in July and the first part of August and comprises hatchery salmon headed to Dudiak Lagoon. As with kings, the best success can be had along the beach area near the lagoon, yet schools of fish may be encountered most anywhere along the spit, usually the eastern shore.

The second showing follows right on the heels of the first and contains less numerous but slightly heavier silvers preparing to enter spawning streams within the bay and adjoining waters. Best fishing for these occurs in the latter half of August near the end of Homer Spit along the western shoreline.

One of the earliest opportunities in Kachemak Bay occurs when sea-run char hit the beaches, arriving to feed for the short summer from their wintering areas in area rivers and streams. Targeting Dolly Varden using baitfish patterns can be a great experience.

*Angler walks a 20-pound king towards shore, taken on a herring and double-hook set-up.*

The highlight for the majority of shore-bound anglers visiting this area is the astounding fishery for the various kinds of bottomfish. Although they may be caught anywhere along the spit, the densest concentration of fish can be located at the end of the spit, right around the ferry dock.

For the most part, just tossing out a piece of bait on one or more single hooks is assured instantaneous action. Cut herring, shrimp, or squid make perfect baits. Common catches include several species of flounders, codfishes, and giant sculpins. Action is usually fast and furious, with fish on every cast to be expected all summer long. This is a great spot to introduce youngsters to fishing.

Halibut frequent these waters at the end of the spit and are caught on a regular basis by anglers with the proper equipment. Skilled surf-casters often walk away from here with at least one fish, if not a limit. The average shore-caught halibut is usually relatively small, in the 10- to 25-pound range, with occasional bigger fish mixed in.

Other fish that are common along the spit include skate, which may reach 100 pounds or more, and Pacific cod up to 15 pounds.

*A handful of anglers gather at the end of the spit, casting into the surf targeting a variety of bottomfish, including halibut.*

## Fish Availability (Homer Spit Area)

● = High ● = Moderate ● = Low ● = Closed

| Species | | MAY | JUN | JUL | AUG | SEP | OCT |
|---|---|---|---|---|---|---|---|
| **King Salmon** | Shore | Low Low Moderate High | High Moderate Low Low | Low Low Low Low | Low Low Low Low | Low Low Low Low | Low Low Low Low |
| | Boat | Moderate Moderate Moderate High | High High High Moderate | Moderate Moderate Moderate Moderate | Moderate Moderate Moderate Moderate | Moderate Moderate Moderate Moderate | Moderate Moderate Moderate Moderate |
| **Pink Salmon** | Shore | | Low Low | Low Moderate High High | High High Moderate Low | Low Low Low | |
| | Boat | | Low Low Low Moderate | High High High High | High Moderate Moderate Low | Low Low | |
| **Silver Salmon** | Shore | | Low Low | Low Moderate High High | High High Moderate Moderate | Moderate Low Low Low | |
| | Boat | | Low Low Low | Moderate High High High | Moderate Moderate High High | Moderate Moderate Low Low | Low Low Low |
| **Dolly Varden** | Shore | High High High High | High High High High | High High Moderate Moderate | Moderate Moderate Low Low | Low Low Low Low | Low Low |
| | Boat | Moderate Moderate Moderate Moderate | Moderate Moderate Moderate Moderate | Moderate Moderate Moderate Low | Low Low Low Low | Low Low Low Low | |
| **Pacific Halibut** | Shore | Low Low Moderate Moderate | Moderate Moderate Moderate Moderate | Moderate Moderate Moderate Moderate | Moderate Moderate Moderate Moderate | Moderate Low Low Low | Low Low |
| | Boat | Moderate Moderate High High | High High High High | High High High High | High High High High | High High Moderate Moderate | Low Low Low Low |
| **Bottomfish** | Shore | Moderate Moderate High High | High High High High | High High High High | High High High High | High Moderate Moderate Moderate | Low Low Low Low |
| | Boat | High High High High | High High High High | High High High High | High High High High | High High High High | High High High High |
| Angling Pressure | Shore | Moderate Moderate Moderate Moderate | Moderate Moderate Moderate Moderate | Moderate Moderate Moderate Moderate | Moderate Moderate Moderate Moderate | Moderate Low Low Low | |
| | Boat | Low Low Moderate Moderate | High High High High | High High High High | High High High High | Moderate Moderate Low Low | Low Low Low Low |

## King Salmon

**Rating:** ★★ Fair.
**Locations:** Harbor Breakwater and Ferry Dock.
**Season:** January 1 through December 31.
**Timing:** Year-round; peak May 25 – June 5.
**Size:** Average 12 – 25 pounds, up to 50 pounds.
**Tackle:** Spoons, spinners, and bait.
**Tips:** Hardware, like spinners, do take some fish, especially if a school can be located. However, the majority of salmon are taken on cut herring suspended beneath a strike indicator. The breakwater area can be productive with most kings coming to shore on an incoming or outgoing tide.

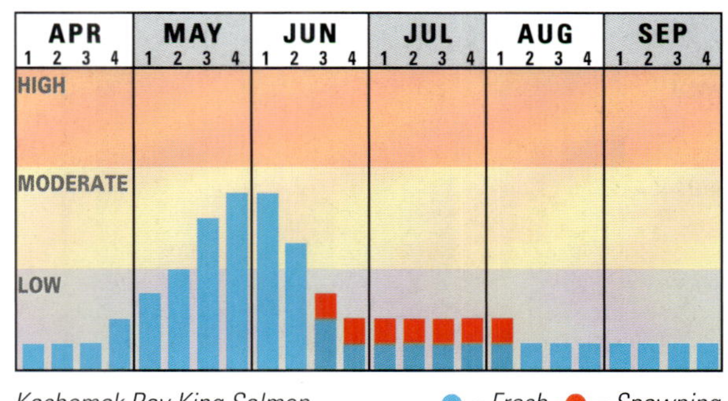


*Kachemak Bay King Salmon.* ● = Fresh ● = Spawning

(Courtesy Beverley Bailey)

*Summer-run silvers are typically smaller than their late-season brethren (5-6 pounds) but show in greater numbers . This specimen struck a spinner fished within 20 yards of the surf.*

## Pink Salmon

**Rating:** ★★★ Fair to good.
**Locations:** Harbor Breakwater, Ferry Dock, Ocean Beach, and Bishop's Beach.
**Season:** January 1 through December 31.
**Timing:** June 15 – Sept. 20; peak July 10 – August 10.
**Size:** Average 2 – 4 pounds, up to 7 pounds.
**Tackle:** Spoons, spinners, flies, and bait.
**Tips:** Look for surfacing pinks around high tide as schools come closer to the shore. Anglers able to cast out a ways beyond the surf stand a greater chance of hooking fish. Bait such as small herring can do well yet size 3 spinners or 1/2 ounce spoons are best.

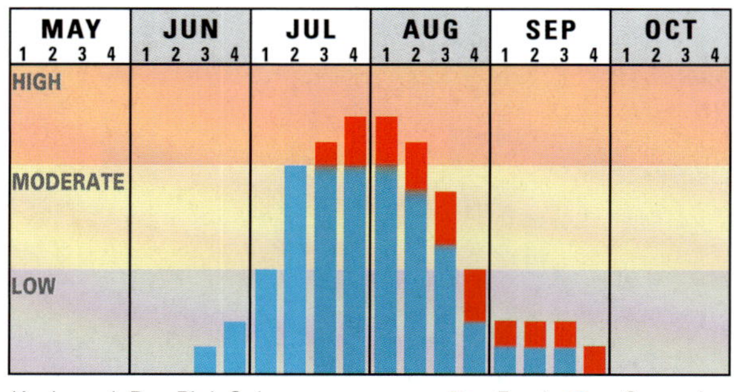


*Kachemak Bay Pink Salmon* ● = Fresh ● = Spawning

## Silver Salmon

**Rating:** ★★½ Fair to good.
**Locations:** Harbor Breakwater, Ferry Dock, Ocean Beach.
**Season:** January 1 through December 31.
**Timing:** June 15 – October 25; peak July 15 – August 25.
**Size:** Average 5 – 11 pounds, up to 18 pounds.
**Tackle:** Spoons, spinners, flies, and bait.
**Tips:** Incoming and high tide is generally best. Scout water for signs of salmon breaching the surface. Long casts are usually necessary to connect with fish although hookups can be made closer to shore on overcast or rainy days. Sizable schools of silvers can sometimes be spotted around the breakwater area.

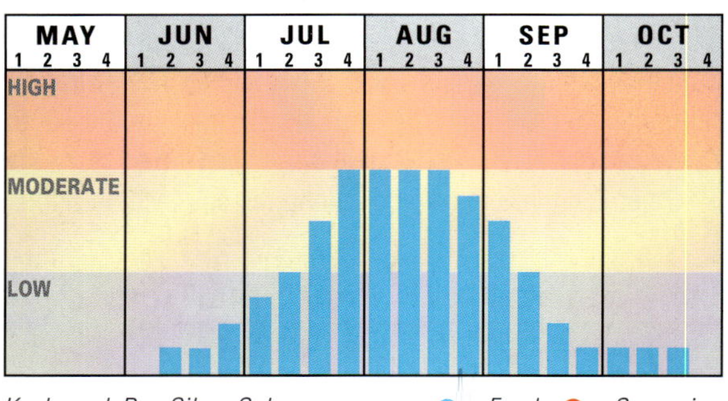


*Kachemak Bay Silver Salmon* ● = Fresh ● = Spawning

(Courtesy Beverley Bailey)

*Probably the most exciting part about fishing the salt is the unknown: This surprise skate was beached while halibut fishing.*

*Smaller halibut are fairly common along the sandy beaches of Homer Spit. Anglers using the right gear stand a decent chance of hooking one of these delicious flatfish.*

(Courtesy Beverley Bailey)

## Dolly Varden

**Rating:** ★★★ Good.
**Locations:** Bishop's Beach, Ocean Beach, Ferry Dock, and Harbor Breakwater.
**Season:** January 1 through December 31.
**Timing:** February 15 – October 15; peak May 1 – July 10.
**Size:** Average 8 – 20 inches, up to 28 inches (6-7 pounds).
**Tackle:** Spoons, spinners, flies, and bait.
**Tips:** Use lures and flies imitating baitfish for hungry char, such as 1/4 ounce or smaller spoons or jigs. The surfline of area beaches and around the pilings of the ferry dock hold fish. Long casts are not necessary as fish travel close to the beach in search of food; successful anglers often wade out a bit and cast almost parallel to the shoreline.

## Pacific Halibut

**Rating:**  Fair.
**Location:** Ferry Dock.
**Season:** February 1 through December 31.
**Timing:** April 15 – October 15; peak June 15 – Sept. 1.
**Size:** Average 10 – 25 pounds, up to 40 pounds.
**Tackle:** Jigs and bait.
**Tips:** A few halibut are taken on regular gear by anglers targeting other bottomfish, yet for consistent catches proper surf-casting gear is required. Distance casting is a must in order to reach depth that hold fish. Use large baits in order to persuade flatfish to strike and smaller species to stay off.

The discharge area from the fish processing plant next to the ferry dock is a relative hot spot as halibut are drawn here by scent and food particles, including feeding baitfish. Focus on low tides as this puts anglers within close range to the discharge plume.

*The Irish Lord is a bottom scavenger that all surf-casters soon come to know; they are very opportunistic feeders and will engulf most any bait or lure tossed their way, being quite a nuisance.*

(Courtesy Beverley Bailey)

## Other Kachemak Opportunities

### Remote Kachemak Bay Fishing

The south side of Kachemak Bay is unique compared to the north, with an abundance of bays and islands and small clearwater streams perfect for creating a vast brew of species. This rich ocean fauna is responsible for immature king salmon ranging between 12 and 25 pounds providing respectable action every month of the year. Anglers trolling along various points and channels here as well as the bluffs just northwest of Homer towards Anchor Point experience some fine fishing for off-season salmon. There is even a winter king salmon derby held out of Homer every March.

There are other south-side fisheries worth exploring as well. Seldovia Bay and Halibut Cove Lagoon both have good runs of mature hatchery king salmon from late May through mid-June, while China Poot Bay supports a showing of red salmon from mid-July into early August. Although difficult to get to strike in the bay, most successful anglers target these reds in the stream at the head of the bay. Tutka Bay and Lagoon is the place to be during the first half of July for some fish-on-every-cast action for dime-bright pink salmon. The deeper parts of these bays also harbor halibut and rockfish among other types of bottomfish. Expect fair to good fishing.

Anglers willing to search the estuaries and lower reaches of area creeks may find Dolly Varden during the months of May and June and many pinks (in July) and small runs of chum and silver salmon in late summer and fall.

Clam digging is productive in some spots, such as China Poot Cove, Sadie Cove, Tutka Bay, Kasitsna Bay, and Seldovia Bay.

### Seldovia Fishing

An angling opportunity not often sought by visitors to the Homer area is that which can be found in the community of Seldovia just across the bay. Locals here target a prolific run of hatchery king salmon early in the season, right in town. Late May to mid-June is prime time. Later in the season, fishing is also good for other species right off the shore, such as pink salmon, Dolly Varden, and various kinds of bottomfish, primarily flounders and codfishes but also the more popular lingcod and rockfish. In addition, charter boats are available.

Access is nearly effortless once in town but requires prospective roadside anglers to hire a water taxi to get there from Homer. The ride is about 30 minutes in duration and available at reasonable cost. Taxi operators can be found at the end of Homer Spit.

*A boat heads out at the break of dawn from Homer Harbor, destined for the popular salmon and bottomfish grounds on the south side of the bay.*

# Dudiak Lagoon

King
SALMON

Silver
SALMON

Dolly
VARDEN

**Highlights:** A great spot to target hatchery runs of early season king and silver salmon. Easy access for the mobility challenged and young anglers.

**Best Fishing:** Late May to late August. **Regulatory Restrictions:** Liberal.

**Location:** Southern Kenai Peninsula, community of Homer, end of Sterling Highway, 231 miles south of Anchorage, on the Homer Spit, 1.5 miles south of Homer.

**Description:** Dudiak Lagoon, also known as the Homer Spit Lagoon and "The Fishing Hole," is a man-made body of water near the tip of Homer Spit. Appearing as a saltwater lake, the lagoon is connected to Kachemak Bay via a narrow channel where the flooding water of high tide enters and exits the lagoon.

Depending on the actual height of the tide, the water level in the lagoon itself can fluctuate from several feet up to 10 feet or more. There is little to no tidal movement through the channel into the lagoon if the high tide is less than 14 feet. With tide levels of 17 feet or more, the channel becomes more of a river as water flushes in and out of the lagoon.

Since the water in the lagoon is essentially identical in color and clarity as the bay, anglers can expect a slight bluish-green tint with minimal silt. After periods of heavy winds and strong tidal surges, however, the water can easily turn quite murky.

There is no vegetation to speak of, aside from patches

of grass, with the surrounding area being the typical beach landscape of sand, gravel, and rock. The lagoon is of very sparse physical beauty in itself although the scenic value of Kachemak Bay and the mountain chain across the bay adds immeasurably to the overall experience.

Wildlife is surprisingly common as some marine mammals frequent the lagoon. Both harbor seals and sea lions use the channel connecting the lagoon with the bay on high tides to access the abundance of salmon present within the lagoon. Additionally, eagles are sighted around the edges of the lagoon, particularly at dawn, feeding on scraps of fish, and up to a dozen birds may be seen at once.

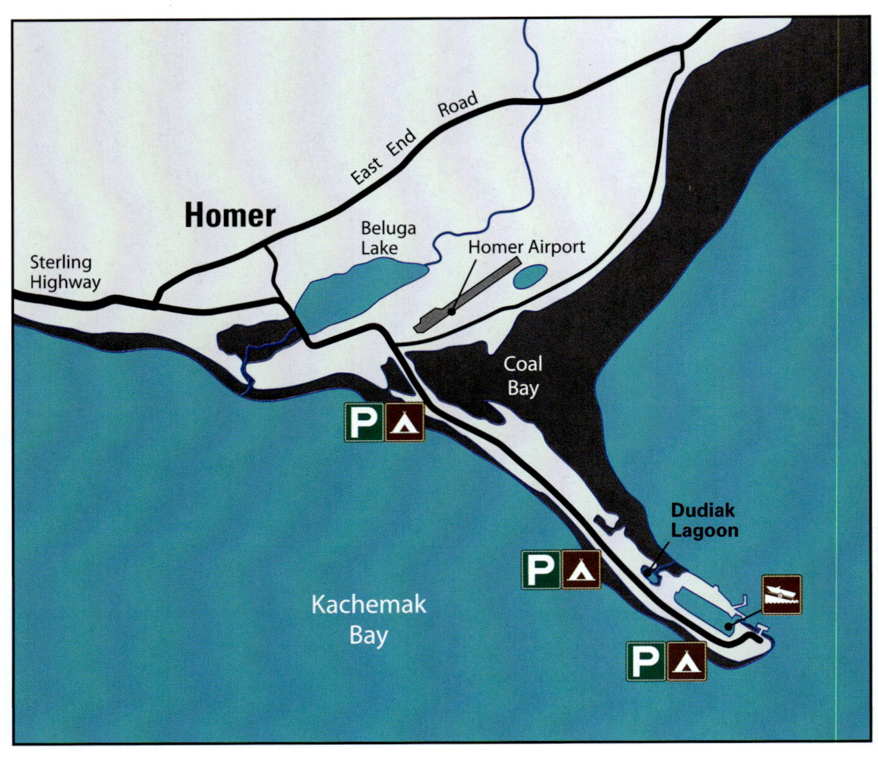


**Facilities:** RV camping, primitive campgrounds, parking, restrooms. Many other amenities available on the Homer Spit and in Homer.
**Access:** From the town of Homer and the end of Sterling Highway. Continue main right of way, becoming Spit Road, 4.3 miles out onto Homer Spit. The lagoon is located on the left beyond parking area.

*Dudiak Lagoon is stocked with both king and silver salmon that return every summer between May and September.*

## Rules & Regulations

**Open Season:** January 1 through December 31; no closed periods.
**Open Area:** The whole lagoon is open to fishing throughout the year.
**Legal Gear/Tackle:** All gear and tackle, including bait, is allowed year-round. Snagging is permitted by emergency order only.

**King Salmon**
- Open all season (see general "Open Season" above).
- Bag limit is (2) per day and (2) in possession (20 inches or longer). For kings less than 20 inches (Jacks), the limit is (10).

**All Other Salmon**
- Open all season (see general "Open Season" above).
- Bag limit for red, pink, chum, and silver salmon is (6) per day and (6) in possession (16 inches or longer). For salmon less than 16 inches (Jacks), the limit is (10).

**Dolly Varden**
- Open all season (see general "Open Season" above).
- Bag limit is (5) per day and (5) in possession, any size.

## Fishing Dudiak Lagoon

**Access:** ★★★★★
**Scenery:** ★★★★
**Wildlife:** ★★
**Sight Fishing:** ★★★
**Bank/Wading:** ★★★★★
**Boat/Floating: N/A**

**Species:** King and silver salmon, Dolly Varden. Occasional catches of red and pink salmon and various species of bottomfish.

**Summary:** The Dudiak Lagoon has become one of the most popular sport fisheries on the Kenai Peninsula with excellent runs of both king and silver salmon returning almost continuously from May to October. The lagoon was originally stocked with salmon in the 80s as a means of taking angling pressure off local streams and native fish populations as well as providing more diversity.

Although the lagoon at one point had early and late runs of both king and silver salmon, only the early segments are present today as the late runs were discontinued due to lower than expected returns and/or cost considerations. The late run of silvers may be re-established again in the future pending availability of funding.

Most anglers visiting Dudiak Lagoon utilize hardware and bait with spinning rods and do very well, with the majority of the action concentrated according to tidal movements. Fishing can be hot for the first hour or two on the inside of the lagoon as water begins to pour through the channel. Right at high or low tide the fishing is generally quite slow, unless at break of dawn.

There is also significant effort on the bay-side of the spit where the washout from the lagoon through the channel creates an optimal staging area for salmon as well as sea-run char. Fly-fishers can also participate in this fishery with most effort occurring in the channel during changes to or from high tide, on incoming tide right at the mouth of the channel where it enters the lagoon, and outgoing tide on the ocean side.

Schools of salmon tend to hold on the ocean side near the channel, sometimes coming very close to the beach as the tide rises. When water in the channel has reached critical depth (around three to four feet), the fish begin to pulse through.

Sight-fishing is possible in the channel when the current is strong and the water not too deep, this being especially the case on the outgoing tide.

King salmon begin trickling into the lagoon in spring, the run lasting primarily during the months of May and June, reflecting the general timing of most Kenai Peninsula stocks. The push of silvers begins just as the king run dwindles, generally by the first half of July, and peaks around the first of August. These fish have a run timing that is typical of stocks found in northern Cook Inlet.

Anglers may also catch a number of sea-run char here and appearances of other salmon species (mainly reds and pinks) do occur as well.

An emergency order allowing snagging may be instituted toward the tail end of the respective salmon runs if it is determined that a surplus of fish remains available within the lagoon. After the snagging period has ended, which usually lasts only a few days, the number of fish still left in the lagoon is usually negligible with only a few salmon present through the rest of the season.

*Two young anglers negotiate how best to net a rampaging 20-pound king salmon, newly arrived from the briny of Kachemak Bay. The lagoon is an exceptional location for youngsters to fish.*

## Fish Availability

● = High ● = Moderate ● = Low ● = Closed

| Species | APR | MAY | JUN | JUL | AUG | SEP | OCT |
|---|---|---|---|---|---|---|---|
| **King Salmon** | Low | Low, Low, Moderate, High | High, High, High, Moderate | Low, Low, Low, Low | Low, Low | | |
| **Silver Salmon** | | | Low | Low, Moderate, High, High | High, High, Moderate, Moderate | Low, Low, Low, Low | |
| **Dolly Varden** | Low, Low, Low, Low | Moderate, Moderate, Moderate, Moderate | Moderate, Moderate, Moderate, Moderate | Moderate, Moderate, Low, Low | Low, Low, Low, Low | Low | |
| Angling Pressure | | Low, Low, Moderate, High | High, High, High, Moderate | Moderate, Low, Low, Moderate | High, High, High, Moderate | Low, Low | |

## King Salmon

**Rating:** ★★½ Fair to good.
**Season:** January 1 through December 31.
**Timing:** April 25 – August 5; peak May 25 – June 20.
**Size:** Average 12 – 25 pounds, up to 50 pounds.
**Tackle:** Spoons, spinners, flies, and bait.
**Tips:** Fish tend to travel in deeper water and respond with less enthusiasm during bright sunny days. Periods of rain and heavy cloud cover usually bring big schools of kings into the channel during the tide changes. Inside the lagoon, fishing is best as the tide comes in. There is also a smaller "bite" that occurs in the early morning before the sun comes up. The fish have a tendency to mill around the lagoon, often traveling in large schools around the edges several feet from shore. Most kings develop lockjaw at such times and slackwater techniques are employed for consistent success.

Small whole or plug-cut herring can be extremely effective early in the season (May/early June) while clusters of salmon roe tend to work better starting around the first of June and continuing through the season. Most bait is used with a strike indicator but can be cast or drifted alone whenever there is current present. Size 5 spinners in blue, green, silver, and copper can be deadly on newly-arrived fish. Flies and small attractors are used in the channel on the tide changes.

Kings in the 15- to 20-inch range (Jacks) may be very abundant in some years.

*Satisfied angler holding a catch of king salmon. Liberal bag limits makes the lagoon a great place to harvest salmon for the freezer.*

*(Courtesy Eagle Eye Images)*

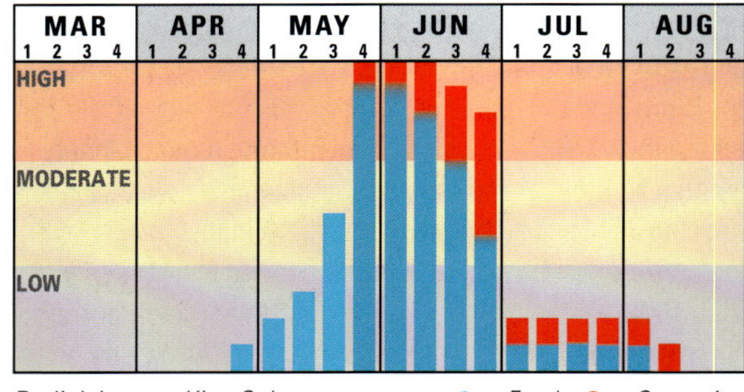


*Dudiak Lagoon King Salmon* ● = Fresh ● = Spawning

## Silver Salmon

**Rating:** ★★★ Good.
**Season:** January 1 through December 31.
**Timing:** June 20 – Sept. 30; peak July 15 – August 10.
**Size:** Average 5 – 10 pounds, up to 18 pounds.
**Tackle:** Spinners, flies, and bait.
**Tips:** The most productive catches are made on rainy and cloudy days, especially combined with a rising or outgoing tide. Silvers inside the lagoon respond best in the very early morning and when the tide begins to flood. Sometimes anglers can experience good fishing along the beach on the bay side of the lagoon. Look for salmon jumping.

Cut herring fished alone in current or with a strike

indicator works well early in the season when the salmon are first arriving, with more success later on using small clusters of salmon roe. Size 3 and 4 spinners in blue, green, and chartreuse are most efficient on incoming tides. The use of flies and attractors is possible in the channel on an outgoing tide.

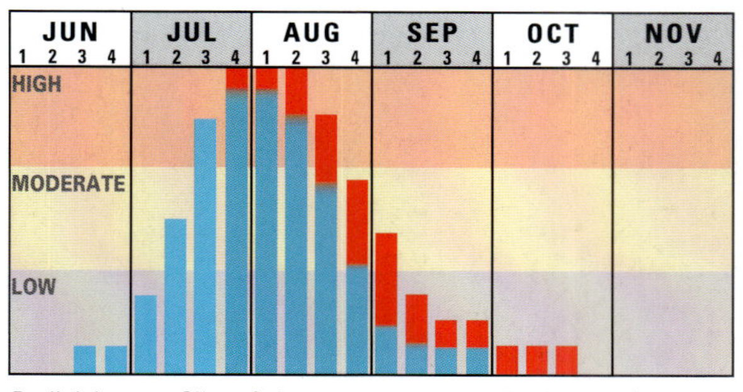


*Dudiak Lagoon Silver Salmon* ● *= Fresh* ● *= Spawning*

## Dolly Varden

**Rating:** ★★ Fair.
**Season:** January 1 through December 31.
**Timing:** April 1 – September 1; peak May 1 – June 30.
**Size:** Average 8 – 20 inches, up to 28 inches (7-8 pounds).
**Tackle:** Spoons, spinners, flies, and bait.
**Tips:** Work offerings at the mouth of the channel on an outgoing tide and along the beach on incoming and outgoing tide for results. Fishing for Dolly Varden inside the lagoon is poor. The fish are often keyed in on salmon byproducts flushed into the bay and the scent of salmon roe. The natural prey, however, are salmon smolts migrating out to sea from area streams. Whenever juvenile salmon are stocked in the lagoon, usually in late spring/early summer, the char fishing can be good.

*Angler beaches a king salmon. The gravel shoreline, free of obstructions, makes landing big fish an easy task.*

Both herring and salmon roe are effective. Targeting these fish is better using small silvery-blue spoons and smolt imitation flies.

## STARISKI CREEK

(Courtesy Gary Simhuber)

**Fishing:** ★★½ **Scenery:** ★★½
**Accessibility:** ★★ **Solitude:** ★★★★★

**Location:** Southern Kenai Peninsula drainage, Anchor Point area, 204 miles south of Anchorage, 29 miles north of Homer.

**Access:** The Sterling Highway crosses the stream at milepost 150.8. Some parking available for smaller vehicles. Trails lead up- and downstream. Note: Respect private property in area.

**Facilities:** There is some undeveloped parking by highway crossing. Stariski State Recreation Site located at Milepost 151.9 has camping and restrooms.

**Species:** Pink and silver salmon, steelhead and rainbow trout, and Dolly Varden.

**Restrictions:** King salmon fishing prohibited. Salmon fishing prohibited upstream of highway. Closed to all fishing January 1 through July 31. Consult ADF&G regulations.

**Fishing:** This is one of the lesser-fished streams on the entire southern Kenai Peninsula. Smaller than surrounding waters and with fish populations not quite as dense, Stariski does offer, however, a more secluded angling experience. It is primarily a late summer and fall fishery for silver salmon, trout, and char. Anglers hiking in from the highway crossing will find suitable fish holding structure, albeit the stream is small and easily waded throughout most parts near the road.

Anglers should focus on the lower or tidal section of the stream when attempting for salmon and steelhead, but access is by boat only via Cook Inlet. The lower end has a reasonable abundance of holes and runs prime for concentrating fish. Much of the angling activity here coincides with the tides.

The upper reaches, however, have fewer deep slots with more fast water and private property may pose a problem. Also, the salmon may not always be as bright here as farther downstream but nonetheless offers very decent fishing at times. Trout and char can be numerous with some large resident rainbows available at the headwaters.

**Pink Salmon.** Fair to good; August 1 – 15; average 3 – 4 pounds. Small spoons, spinners, and flies take fish. Even-numbered years are best, odd years are generally only mediocre.

**Silver Salmon.** Fair to good; August 25 – September 15; average 6 – 10 pounds. Spinners, flies, and bait are the general rule. Try for silvers following a good rain, scouting holes and pools for fresh salmon.

**Steelhead Trout.** Fair to good; September 15 – October 31; average 5 – 10 pounds. Flies and attractors draw attention. Best fishing down low in the stream, near tidewater.

**Rainbow Trout.** Fair; August 1 – October 15; average 7 – 15 inches. Small spinners and flies outperform all else. Fish are concentrated high up in the drainage.

**Dolly Varden.** Good; August 1 – October 10; average 8 – 15 inches. Spinners, attractors, and flies are good. Egg imitations are effective in fall.

## COOK INLET

**Fishing:** ★★★★ **Scenery:** ★★★★
**Accessibility:** ★★★ **Solitude:** ★★★

**Location:** Southern Kenai Peninsula, Kasilof to Anchor Point, 166-211 miles south of Anchorage, 8-63 miles south of Soldotna.

**Facilities:** The communities of Kasilof, Ninilchik, and Anchor Point have developed state and private campgrounds as well as parking areas for all size vehicles. Sporting good and other retail stores are available, as well as charter services.

**Access:** The Sterling Highway provides numerous points of access to the east side of Cook Inlet along Kenai Peninsula, from the city of Kenai south to Homer. Primarily, however, the major access areas to fishing grounds are situated around various towns and communities, such as Ninilchik, Anchor Point, and of course, Homer. The foremost method of access is by boat (charter as well as private) yet some anglers also cast from shore or even use kayaks.

*A. Kasilof River Beach (North)* – Milepost 108.8 Sterling Highway. Northwest on Kalifornsky Beach Road 4.9 miles, left on Kasilof Beach Road 1.0 mile to beach area. Primitive launch point for small craft at river mouth.

*B. Kasilof River Beach (South)* – Milepost 111.0 Sterling Highway. West on North Cohoe Road 5.9 miles to end of pavement, continue on dirt road 0.7 mile to parking area at beach. Improvised road continues along beach another 1/2 mile to mouth of Kasilof River. No boat launch point present.

(Courtesy Eagle Eye Images)

*C. Ninilchik Beach* – Milepost 135.1 Sterling Highway. West on Mission Avenue 1.2 mile to the village of Ninilchik and the harbor at the mouth of the river. Primitive launch point mostly used by small private craft (also commercial fishing boats).

*D. Deep Creek Beach* – Milepost 137.3 Sterling Highway. West on Beach Access Road 0.5 mile to state recreation site and boat launch area near stream mouth. Commercial and state launches used by charter and private watercraft.

*E. Whiskey Gulch Beach* – Milepost 152.7 Sterling Highway. West on steep access road 0.4 mile to beach area. Primitive launch point used by small private craft.

*F. Anchor Point Beach* – Milepost 156.7 Sterling Highway. West on Old Sterling Highway 0.4 mile, turn right on Anchor River (Beach) Road immediately after bridge crossing river, proceed 1 mile to beach area. Commercial launch used by charter and private watercraft. Continue another 0.5 mile to small boat launch on the lower Anchor River.

**Fishing:** A highly productive fishery for salmon and bottomfish, Cook Inlet has earned tremendous respect among anglers the last several decades. The cold, greenish-grey waters often rip along the peninsula's western coast more like a river than anything else, creating challenging yet dynamic opportunities for those prepared to take on the elements involved. While it is true that anglers using boats have a significant advantage in successfully locating the area's major game fish species, it is entirely possible to do well surf-casting off the beaches between Kasilof and Anchor Point using the right equipment and some basic

*A 26-pound halibut, caught in mid-May on a regular spinning rod and a piece of salmon scrap in only seven feet of water at the mouth of Kasilof River. Flatfish of this size are not uncommon during the spring and early summer months; as the season progresses the larger fish tend to move to slightly deeper water.*

knowledge of structure and fish habits.

The following information applies directly to anglers casting from shore; for boat fishing, see the "Additional Opportunities" section on next page.

As the majority of the coastline features a gentle graded slope that reveals extensive tidal flats of sand, gravel, and mud, anglers casting from shore generally do best about two hours before to two hours after high tide as the water tends to be deeper, bringing migrating salmon and feeding bottomfish closer to the surf. Schools of salmon often travel within 20-30 yards of the beach in their search for spawning streams, while halibut and other bottomfish use flooding tides in order to locate various food sources, frequently moving into surprisingly shallow water.

Anglers dressed in chest waders and equipped with long rods and level-wind reels designed for distance casting stand a much greater chance of hooking up as this setup allows them to best reach the zone where fish travel.

The best way to target salmon is usually near the mouths of rivers and creeks flowing into the inlet, particularly on incoming and high tides, although some fish are consistently caught off beaches with a slightly steeper gradient, such as Whiskey Gulch. Lucky anglers have managed to catch king salmon up to 50 pounds here. As always, scout the surface of the water for signs of fish and cast accordingly. However, a lack of indications does not necessarily mean that no fish are present; hit-and-miss is the general rule with Cook Inlet salmon.

Sea-run char follow the shoreline and easily within casting range as they search for prey during the short summer feeding season. Many of these fish derive from local drainages and migrate south towards Kachemak Bay in spring and back north again in mid-summer to spawn and over-winter in their home waters. It is during these migrations that anglers may score using small lures and flies imitating baitfish.

In spring (latter April-May), halibut begin moving into the shallows chasing schools of herring and hooligan and are at times caught in water less than six feet deep (although deeper is generally better). In fact, it is common for halibut to enter the mouths and outwash of rivers and streams on high tides, this being especially the case on the Kasilof River (and to some extent Kenai River as well), something anglers can and do capitalize on. Herring and chunks of salmon parts routinely catch fish at such times with limits even possible. A big fish would be anything over 25 pounds. In some areas, small halibut (5-15 pounds) continue to be available to surf-casters throughout summer and into fall.

Other species that frequent the inlet's waters include several kinds of bottomfish, including Pacific cod, pollock, flounders, and Irish Lord, with fair to good opportunities in certain locations. Generally, it is the smaller specimens of these species that are taken from shore. Spiny dog fish ("mud shark") are sometimes landed, along with skate. The latter species is a worthy adversary, commonly reaching weights up to 100 pounds.

*(Courtesy Roy & Beverley Bailey)*

*Hopeful angler casts for silver salmon off the beach near the mouth of Anchor River at Anchor Point.*

Anglers wanting to maintain a light and easy way of fishing Cook Inlet resort to launching skiffs or other small watercrafts right off the beach. An increasingly popular method is the use of kayaks, which will put anglers into the thick of most salmon and bottomfish action.

**King Salmon.** Poor to fair; May 15 – June 5; average 12 – 40 pounds. Use large, silver/red or silver/green spoons and spinners, working them with the tidal currents. Apply fluorescent colors if water is murky from silt. Cut herring may be effective.

**Pink Salmon.** Fair; July 15 – August 15; average 3 – 6 pounds. Cast fluorescent, medium-sized spoons and spinners to concentrations of fish near shore.

**Silver Salmon.** Poor to fair; August 10 – September 5; average 6 – 15 pounds. Brightly colored spinners traditionally work best. Cut herring may do well.

**Dolly Varden.** Fair; May 1 – July 15; average 12 – 20 inches. Small, silvery spoons, spinners, and flies are best. Wade out a distance and cast parallel to beach.

**Pacific Halibut.** Poor to good; April 25 – October 10; average 10 – 25 pounds. Large whole or chunks of herring are proven; lures are generally less effective. Pieces or strips of salmon scraps make for outstanding baits.

**Caution:** As tides fluctuate up to 25 feet or more twice a day, the strong and sometimes unexpected currents of the inlet can be dangerous. Be aware of tidal movements at all times, as well as wave activity, particularly if in a small watercraft.

## ADDITIONAL OPPORTUNITIES

### Lower Cook Inlet Salmon & Halibut

The area of Cook Inlet south of Ninilchik is commonly referred to as the "Lower" portion and without a doubt yields some terrific angling for a multitude of game fish as well as non-sporting species. Here, the silty waters dominating the upper section of the inlet gives way to the mostly clearwater influence of the Gulf of Alaska that is home to many species of bottomfish and a major migration corridor and feeding ground for all five kinds of salmon as well as steelhead trout and sea-run Dolly Varden. However, the most sought-after species include king and silver salmon, halibut, lingcod, and rockfish.

There are two types of charters utilizing this fishery. The first operates out of Homer and targets fishing grounds about an hour to three hours out of port, usually shoals near the middle of the inlet or feeding areas around Chugach and Barren islands at the mouth of Cook Inlet and the Gulf of Alaska.

The second type of charter mainly hits fishing locales closer to shore along the bluffs of the peninsula from Anchor Point northward and are described separately in more detail on page 273.

Generally, the average weight of halibut caught by anglers increases the farther away from the harbor the boat travels (30-40 pounds) and "barn door"-size trophies occur with greater frequency. Halibut holes closer to dock are known for smaller (15-20 pounds) and more numerous catches, a fact that the charter boat captain will often point out, leaving clients to decide if they want to enjoy quantity or quality.

Although a few halibut will be sounding in the inlet

throughout the year, by far the best time to be out on the water in search of these colossal flounders is from mid-May to early September. Also recognized is the fact that the bigger fish usually come to boat during the peak season, smaller specimens rounding out the shoulder months.

A large halibut is considered anything over 100 pounds with a small number of 200-pounders available. Every season reports of "barndoor"-size flatfish caught between 250 and 350 pounds peaks angler's interest.

Cook Inlet also harbors some great salmon action. Many of these fish are headed to spawning streams along coastal Kenai Peninsula, giving anglers a good shot to intercept migrating schools of kings, silvers, and pinks. Giant masses of red salmon are sometimes encountered in July but these tight-lipped fish generally do not offer the same level of sport as the other species.

Feeder – or immature – king salmon are present in lower Cook Inlet (including Kachemak Bay) year-round. Fishing for them is typically fair to good on any given day but can be excellent at times with multiple hook-ups per angler. Generally smaller than spawn-bound fish, they tend to average around 12 to 25 pounds with some 35-plus-pound specimens mixed in. A few charters specifically target these kings and, in March, there is even a derby dedicated to them. A good percentage of these fish are "white" kings as indicated by the light or pearl colored flesh tone.

Angling for silvers can be very good as well. The whole month of August and into early September is hot as a series of different runs keep anglers busy. Although generally targeted along inshore waters, large schools of fish can often be found offshore as well and always a welcome bonus on any halibut trip. Best results may be had mooching for them when spotted relatively near the surface on the open seas.

Fishing for lingcod and rockfish is among the best in the region, with boaters heading out to the steep and rocky coastline around the southern tip of the peninsula (including Chugach and Barren islands) in order to find suitable structure. Expect fast and furious action with trophy lings a definite possibility. Specimens in the 40- to 50-pound category are relatively common and record-size fish to 70 pounds or more are present.

Several species of rockfish are available with fish-on-every-cast action a very real possibility. Since they tend to inhabit the same hard-surface structure as lingcod, anglers can easily switch gear as needed and go for one or the other.

Many charters offer combination trips for salmon and bottomfish or halibut and lingcod/rockfish. Overnight excursions to the southern shore of the peninsula is also possible, where anglers will have the opportunity to take home two limits of fish on one trip.

Unlike the fisheries north of Anchor Point, tides are less important out of Homer and Seldovia with fishing being productive all day long. In fact, some spots may yield better action when the tide rips as the moving water stirs up feed, resulting in a feeding frenzy.



There are several salmon and halibut derbies in the area from May through September. See separate entries for derbies in this section (pages 280-281).

## Peninsula Clam Digging

One of the most favorite outdoor activities among Alaska residents to initiate the fishing season is to go clam digging and the beaches along the western side of the Kenai Peninsula are the perfect spots to do so.

From just south of the mouth of the Kasilof River all the way down the coast to Anchor Point and on the east side of the Homer Spit in Kachemak Bay, clam diggers gather during minus tides, buckets and clam

*Clam diggers descend on Ninilchik Beach near the mouth of Ninilchik River. This area is known for big clams, May to August being best. Mount Redoubt volcano looms in the background.*

guns or shovels in hand. Digging is best on tides of -2.0 feet or lower. The exact time and tidal range of clam tides can be determined by using a tide book, available in most sporting good, tackle shop, gas station, and grocery stores around the peninsula.

There are several species of clams that are targeted, the most popular being the razor clam. The razor thrives in the sandy beaches north of Anchor Point, accessed from the Sterling Highway. Hot spots to dig include Clam Gulch (Milepost 117.4), Ninilchik (Milepost 135.1), Deep Creek (Milepost 137.3), and Anchor Point (Milepost 156.9).

Mud Bay on the east side of Homer Spit near the end of Sterling Highway has a population of cockles. These shellfish are not nearly as popular as razors but just as good eating. Using a rake is most effective way of harvesting cockles.

Note, however, that the tides of Cook Inlet can vary upwards of 25 to 35 feet so all diggers need to be aware of their location in respect to islands and channels as not to be caught off guard. Being stranded on a sand island surrounded by strong tidal currents can have deadly consequences.

Bag limit for razor clams is the first 45 clams dug. Check ADF&G regulations for details.

## Remote Fly-In Waters

There are several good rivers and streams at disposal for anglers wanting to fly out and experience some wilderness fishing away from the road system. Most of these waters are located on the west side of Cook Inlet while at least one is on the southern part of the tip of Kenai Peninsula.

First off is Crescent River, a beautiful bluish-green drainage that supports very good sport for red and silver salmon in July and August-September, respectively, and Dolly Varden throughout the summer season. The scenery around this semi-glacial system is nothing short of gorgeous.

To the south, Silver Salmon Creek is a popular late summer and fall destination, providing intense action for big silver salmon fresh off the August and September tides.

Shelter Creek has several species of salmon available, most importantly silvers during the August-September time frame, but also good runs of both pinks and chums in July and August. Situated at the base of Mount Iliamna, a 10,000-foot semi-active volcano, the views at Shelter are as tremendous as the fishing.

In Kamishak Bay, with Mount Augustine volcano rising abruptly from the center, there are several streams and one river worth considering for a day or two or longer excursions. Amakdedori Creek has a good showing of silvers in late summer as well as a small and rarely fished fall run of steelhead trout that adventurous anglers really should consider.

Farther down the coast are Little Kamishak River and Kamishak River, two clearwater drainages both known for their tremendous runs of silver salmon and great Dolly Varden action. They also have sizable showings of pinks and chums in late summer as well as small appearances of steelhead in autumn that are virtually untapped.

(Courtesy Roy & Beverley Bailey)

*A Cessna Caravan prepares to touch down on a Cook Inlet beach. The flying can be as exciting as the fishing and a great adventure in and of itself, flying over some of the most remote areas of the state, complete with deep, lush forests and active, snow-capped volcanoes towering to 10,000 feet or more.*

## Fly-In Bear Viewing

The remote western shore of Cook Inlet is not just all about fishing; viewing wildlife -- in particular bears -- is as good as it gets. Daily bear watching trips are arranged through various charter flight companies in the area and quite a few of them offer guided fishing trips all in the same package.

Flying out of the peninsula communities of Soldotna, Kenai, and Homer, bear watchers are treated to a short 30 minute flight across the inlet to a few select destinations known for their reliable sightings. Spotters can expect to see several of these large animals on their trip which may include both the black and brown varieties. At the height of the viewing season, it is even possible to see a dozen or more bears at relatively close range.

A couple of the more popular spots are Big River Lakes and Hallo Bay where bears gather starting in mid-June and lasting through the summer and into fall. Observations are done from planes, area beaches, and boats depending on location. Both of these locations experience a fair amount of viewing activity. There are also several other places to go viewing that are not as busy but still offer great opportunities to see bears.

(Courtesy Roy & Beverley Bailey)

*A family of coastal brown bears graze a field in Hallo Bay on the west side of Cook Inlet. These open spaces provide excellent viewing potential of the large animals in a relatively safe environment. There are several outfitters that specialize in taking visitors to the remote sections of the inlet as well as the Katmai wilderness of Southwest Alaska.*

## Peninsula Wildlife Viewing

Several of the roadside waters of southern Kenai Peninsula offer ample viewing of several different kinds of wildlife, primarily birds and marine mammals. Anglers are privileged to be able to observe these creatures -- very often up close -- at such locations as the tidal rivers and streams in and around Ninilchik and Anchor Point and the beaches of Kachemak Bay in Homer.

Perhaps the most prominent icon of anglers and photographers alike is the bald eagle. The charcoal-studded bluffs all along the western coast of the peninsula are ideal eagle habitat and these majestic birds can be seen in great numbers during the spring and summer months as they raise their young and feed off the scraps of salmon and halibut left on the beaches by the sport fishing fleets.

In fact, the area of Ninilchik and Deep Creek is sometimes referred to as "Eagle City" by the locals as hundreds of birds gather on the beach, perched in trees and on the bluffs, and along the banks of salmon streams every April, May, and June. Observing several dozen birds a day is common.

Eagles also frequent Anchor Point and the Homer Spit, the latter often harboring birds all year long yet tend to be more abundant from May through August.

Seals and sea otters swim the waters of Cook Inlet and Kachemak Bay and seem especially prevalent around the Homer Spit. Harbor seals, as well as sea lions, plow the briny just off the surf, chasing schools of salmon and bottomfish in full view of anglers and other outdoor enthusiasts. They even enter the Dudiak Lagoon and the small boat harbor on high tides, making a nuisance of themselves by scaring up the fish and even snatching salmon off the line from unfortunate anglers.

Frequently, humpback and killer whales and porpoises can be seen from the beach at Homer Spit. To watch these animals in greater numbers up close, taking a charter boat trip out of Homer is the way to go.

(Courtesy Eagle Eye Images)

*Adult bald eagle methodically devouring the remains of a spawned-out silver salmon. Keep an eye on fish left unattended on the beach or along stream banks: eagles have a way of snatching them from unsuspecting anglers.*

*Tent camping on Kenai Beach.*

# Kenai Peninsula Fishing Derbies

*The coastal ports of Seward, Ninilchik, and Homer all have salmon and halibut derbies during the season. Make certain to purchase a derby ticket before heading out.*

## FISHING DERBIES

### Northeastern Kenai Peninsula

July
**Hope Pink Salmon Derby**
**Approximate Dates:** July 15 through August 15.
**Area/Location:** Hope; Resurrection Creek.
**Prizes/Categories:** 1 troy ounce of gold. Additional categories include other species and a youth division.
**Ticket Fees:** None – free.
**Note:** Winning fish range 4 to 5 pounds.
**Contact Information:** BJW Mining & Gifts, (907) 782-3268.

### Southeastern Kenai Peninsula

May – July
**Seward Jackpot Halibut Derby**
**Approximate Dates:** May 1 through July 31.
**Area/Location:** Seward; Resurrection Bay, North Gulf Coast.
**Prizes/Categories:** Prizes awarded based on selected weights between 60 and 120 pounds. Also prizes for tagged fish and weekly winners.
**Ticket Fees:** $5 day, $35 entire derby.
**Note:** Computer randomly generates new weights every week.
**Contact Information:** Seward Chamber of Commerce, (907) 224-8051.

August
**Seward Silver Salmon Derby**
**Approximate Dates:** Held during the second and third week of August.
**Area/Location:** Seward; Resurrection Bay.
**Prizes/Categories:** $150,000 in cash and prizes. Categories include $50,000 tagged fish, 50 heaviest silvers, and mystery drawings.
**Ticket Fees:** $10 day, $35 entire derby.
**Note:** This is the largest derby in Alaska and on the US West Coast. Winning fish range 16 to 19 pounds.
**Contact Information:** Seward Chamber of Commerce, (907) 224-8051.

### Southern Kenai Peninsula

March
**Winter King Salmon Tournament**
**Approximate Dates:** On a Saturday, the third week of March.
**Area/Location:** Homer; Kachemak Bay.
**Prizes/Categories:** Jackpot winnings, largest fish $10-15,000; $60,000 in cash and prizes.
**Ticket Fees:** $100 entire derby.
**Note:** This is a one day event. Winning fish range 25 to 35 pounds.
**Contact Information:** Homer Chamber of Commerce, (907) 235-7740

April – June
**Ninilchik King Salmon Derby**
**Approximate Dates:** May 1 through June 15.
**Area/Location:** Ninilchik; Lower Cook Inlet saltwater between Deep Creek and Stariski Creek.
**Prizes/Categories:** $1,000 and free mount for the largest king weighed in; second and third place finishers cash winnings. Other categories include weekly prizes for largest and smallest fish.
**Ticket Fees:** $3 per day.
**Note:** Winning fish range 50 to 60 pounds.
**Contact Information:** Ninilchik Chamber of Commerce, (907) 567-3571.

May – September
**Homer Jackpot Halibut Derby**
**Approximate Dates:** May 1 through September 30.
**Area/Location:** Homer; Kachemak Bay and lower Cook Inlet.
**Prizes/Categories:** $150,000 or more in cash and prizes. Categories include five largest halibut every month, largest

# Derbies & Directory

derby fish, largest released halibut, and 100 tagged fish.
**Ticket Fees:** $7 per day.
**Note:** The derby record is 379 pounds.
**Contact Information:** Homer Chamber of Commerce, (907) 235-7740 or www.homerhalibutderby.com.

## June

**Kid's All-American Fishing Derby**
**Approximate Dates:** The Saturday of the National Fishing Week (the first full week of June).
**Area/Location:** Anchor Point; Anchor River.
**Prizes/Categories:** Prize for largest king salmon weighed in; also categories in casting expertise.
**Ticket Fees:** Free.
**Note:** Derby is open only to kids younger than 16 years of age.
**Contact Information:** Anchor Point Chamber of Commerce, (907) 235-2600.

## June – September

**Ninilchik Halibut Derby**
**Approximate Dates:** Father's Day (mid-June) through Labor Day (early September).
**Area/Location:** Ninilchik; Lower Cook Inlet.
**Prizes/Categories:** $2,500 and tail mount for largest halibut.
**Ticket Fees:** $5 per day, $20 per week.
**Note:** Winning fish exceed 250 pounds.
**Contact Information:** Ninilchik Chamber of Commerce, (907) 567-3571.

## July

**Homer July 4th Halibut Tournament**
**Approximate Dates:** July 4 (one-day event).
**Area/Location:** Homer; Kachemak Bay, lower Cook Inlet.
**Prizes/Categories:** Prizes based on percentage of ticket sales; 1st 40%, 2nd 20%, and 3rd 10%.
**Ticket Fees:** $100 entire derby.
**Note:** Proceeds benefit The Fishing Hole Silver Salmon Enhancement Program.
**Contact Information:** Homer Chamber of Commerce, (907) 235-7740.

## FISHING GUIDES & CHARTERS

### Whittier: Western Prince William Sound

**Whittier Marine Charters**
www.fishwhittier.com (907) 440-9510

### Cooper Landing/Kenai/Soldotna/Sterling: Kenai & Kasilof Rivers

**Alaska Clearwater Sportfishing**
www.alaskaclearwater.com (888) 662-3336

**Alaska River Adventures**
www.alaskariveradventures.com (888) 836-9027

**Alaska Trout Fitters**
www.aktroutfitters.com (907) 595-1212

**Alaska Wildland Adventures**
www.alaskarivertrips.com (800) 478-4100

**Capt. Bligh's Beaver Cr. Guide Service**
www.captainblighs.com (888) 480-7919

**D-Ray Personal Guide Service**
www.d-ray.com (907) 235-4374

**EZ Limit Guide Service**
www.ezlimit.com (907) 262-6169

**Kenai Cache Outfitters**
www.fishkenairiver.com (907) 595-1401

**Kenai River Drifter's Lodge**
www.drifterslodge.com (866) 595-5959

**King of the River**
www.kingoftheriver.com (800) 478-9901

**Mystic Waters Fly Fishing**
www.mysticfishing.com (907) 227-0549

### Homer/Anchor Point: Cook Inlet & Kachemak Bay

**A-Ward Charters**
www.awardcharters.com (888) 235-7014

# Kenai Peninsula Directory

## FISHING GUIDES & CHARTERS CONT.

**Big Bear Halibut Charters**
www.bighalibut.com (907) 235-7222

**Bob's Trophy Charters**
www.bobstrophycharters.com (800) 770-6400

**Silverfin Guide Service**
www.silverfinguides.com (907) 235-7352

### Ninilchik/Deep Creek: Cook Inlet

**Ninilchik Saltwater Charters**
www.alaskabigfish.com (800) 382-3611

**Silverfin Guide Service**
www.silverfinguides.com (907) 235-7352

### Seward: Resurrection Bay & Gulf Coast

**Crackerjack Fishing Charters**
www.crackerjackcharters.com (800) 566-3912

**The Fish House Charters**
www.thefishhouse.net (800) 257-7760

**J-Dock Seafood Processing**
www.jdockseafood.com (888) 22J-DOCK

**Miller's Landing**
www.millerslandingak.com (877) 541-5739

## CAMPGROUNDS & RV PARKS

**Alaska Wildland Adventures** *(Cooper Landing)*
www.alaskarivertrips.com (800) 478-4100

**Beluga Lookout Lodge & RV Park** *(Kenai)*
www.belugalookout.com (907) 283-5999

**Kenai Riverside Campgr. & RV Park** *(Soldotna)*
www.kenairv.com (888) 536-2478

**Sportsman's Supply & RV Park** *(Homer)*
(907) 235-2617

## ACCOMMODATIONS

**Alaska Heavenly Lodge** *(Cooper Landing)*
www.alaskaheavenly.com (866) 595-2012

**Beluga Lake Lodge** *(Homer)*
www.belugalakelodging.com (888)795-6343

**Captain Bligh's Beaver Creek Lodge** *(Soldotna)*
www.captainblighs.com (888) 480-7919

**Kenai Lake Lodge** *(Cooper Landing)*
www.kenailakelodge.com (907) 595-6000

**Kenai Rivers Drifter's Lodge** *(Cooper Landing)*
www.drifterslodge.com (866) 595-5959

**Land's End Resort** *(Homer)*
www.lands-end-resort.com (800) 478-0400

**Marina Motel** *(Seward)*
www.sewardmotel.com (907) 224-5518

**Sunrise Inn** *(Cooper Landing)*
www.alaskasunriseinn.com (907) 595-1222

## TACKLE & SPORTING GOODS

**Alaska Trout Fitters** *(Cooper Landing)*
www.aktroutfitters.com (907) 595-1212

**The Fish House** *(Seward)*
www.thefishhouse.net (800) 257-7760

**Kachemak Gear Shed** *(Homer)*
www.reddenmarine.com/homer/ (800) 478-8612

**Kenai Cache Outfitters** *(Cooper Landing)*
www.kenaicache.com (907) 595-1401

**Ninilchik General Store** *(Ninilchik)* (907) 567-3378
www.facebook.com/pages/Ninilchik-General-Store

**Soldotna Hardware & Fishing** *(Soldotna)*
www.soldotnahardware.com (907) 262-4655

**Sportsman's Supply & RV Park** *(Homer)*
(907) 235-2617

**Sweeney's Clothing** *(Soldotna)* (907) 262-5916

## FISH PROCESSORS

**J-Dock Seafood Processing** *(Seward)*
www.jdockseafood.com (888) 22J-DOCK

**Kenai Cache Outfitters** *(Cooper Landing)*
www.kenaicache.com (907) 595-1401

**Ed's Kasilof Seafoods** *(Kasilof/Soldotna)*
www.kasilofseafoods.com (800) 982-2377

**Fee's Custom Seafoods** *(Whittier)*
www.feescustomseafoods.com (907) 472-5055

**Tanner's Fresh Fish Processing** *(Ninilchik)*
www.tannersfish.com (907) 567-3222

## WATERCRAFT RENTALS

**Alaska Raft & Kayak** *(Anchorage)*
www.alaskaraftandkayak.com (800) 606-5950

**Miller's Landing** *(Seward)*
www.millerslandingak.com (877) 541-5739

**Whittier Boat Rental**
www.alaska-boat-rentals.com (907) 232-2783

## RESTAURANTS

**St. Elias Brewing Company** *(Soldotna)*
www.steliasbrewingco.com (907) 260-7837

## GENERAL INFORMATION

**Alaska Department of Fish & Game** *(Homer)*
www.sf.adfg.state.ak.us (907) 235-8191

**Alaska Department of Fish & Game** *(Soldotna)*
www.sf.adfg.state.ak.us (907) 262-9368

**Alaska State Parks**
www.dnr.state.ak.us/parks/ (907) 269-8400

**Anchor Point Chamber of Commerce**
www.anchorpointalaska.info (907) 235-2600

**Chugach National Forest**
www.fs.fed.us/r10/chugach/ (907) 743-9500

**Cooper Landing Chamber of Commerce**
www.cooperlandingchamber.com (907) 595-8888

**Greater Soldotna Chamber of Commerce**
www.soldotnachamber.com (907) 262-9814

**Homer Chamber of Commerce**
www.homeralaska.org (907) 235-7740

**Hope Chamber of Commerce**
www.advenalaska.com/hope (907) 566-5656

**Ninilchik Chamber of Commerce**
www.ninilchikchamber.com (907) 567-3571

**Seward Chamber of Commerce**
www.sewardak.org (907) 224-8051

*View of Deep Creek Campground on the shores of Cook Inlet, a popular spot to camp and fish. Boat operators launch their craft into the surf here and salmon and halibut derbies are held in this area every summer.*

# Matanuska Susitna Valleys & Knik Arm

**Northern Susitna & Chulitna ................. 351**

**Hot Spots:** Byers Creek, East Fork Chulitna River

**Other Productive Fisheries:** Peters Creek, Moose Creek, Talkeetna River, Troublesome Creek, Honolulu Creek, Middle Fork Chulitna River

**Additional Opportunities:** Upper Sustina Drainages

**Central Susitna ..... 321**

**Hot Spots:** Willow Creek, Sheep Creek, Montana Creek

**Other Productive Fisheries:** Willow Area Lakes, Little Willow Creek, Kashwitna River, Caswell Creek, Goose Creek, Sunshine Creek, Rabideux Creek

**Additional Opportunities:** West Side Sustina River Drainage

**Matanuska Valley & Knik Arm........... 291**

**Hot Spots:** Ship Creek, Little Susitna River, Eklutna Tailrace

**Other Productive Fisheries:** Point Mackenzie Area Lakes, Fish Creek, Cottonwood Creek, Wasilla Creek, Jim Creek, Kepler-Bradley Lakes, Matanuska Area Lakes

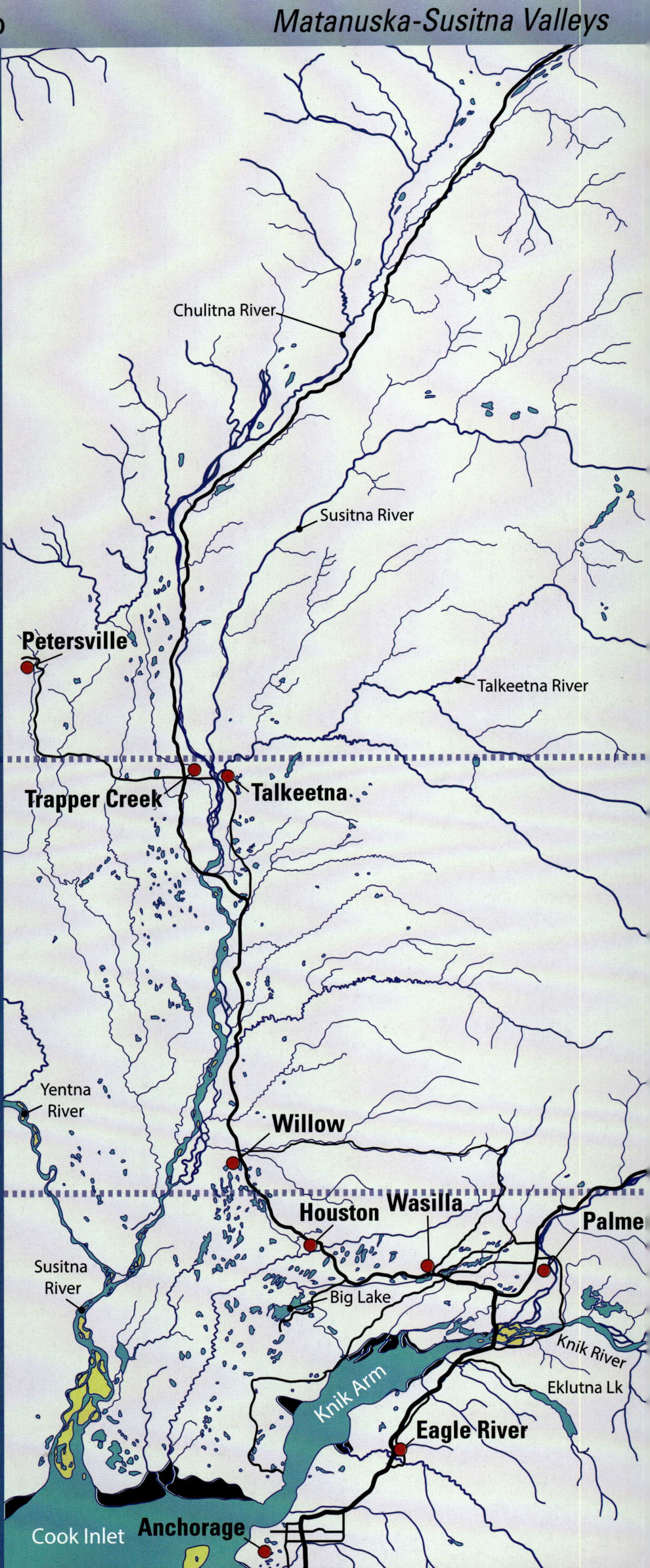

# Introduction

**This expansive region offers dynamic fisheries for many primary game species. The valleys of Matanuska and Susitna, including drainages of Knik Arm and the Chulitna basin, promote easy road access to many prime fishing spots and are known for their great small stream and lake fisheries for salmon, trout, char, and grayling. The scenic value is splendid as jagged mountain peaks of several thousand feet tower above the valley below where the glacially influenced waters of Matanuska, Knik, Susitna, and Chulitna rivers continuously carve new channels through the timeless landscape.**

While there are a handful of waters that support tidewater opportunities for salmon, the majority of waters in this area are situated inland and generally connected to one of several glacial river systems. The trademark of much of this area are the smaller clearwater tributaries of these systems, each teeming with fish and wildlife, including the vast lowlands that are literally covered with lakes and ponds amidst thick spruce, birch, and alder forests. To the north, snow-covered Mount Denali (McKinley) at well over 20,300 feet looms in the distance along with other majestic peaks outlining the horizon.

## Area Roads & Highways

Parks and Glenn highways are both important arteries in accessing any lake or stream in this region with a myriad of side roads. Glenn Highway is the primary gateway out of Anchorage (Milepost 0) to the greater Matanuska Valley area, including the towns of Palmer and Wasilla, and continues heading northeast to the settlement of Glennallen in Copper Valley and the junction with Richardson Highway (Milepost 189).

Serving as the main artery of the Susitna Valley, the Parks Highway cuts through the area vertically, running from Wasilla and Anchorage (Milepost 0) in the south in a northerly direction, intersecting various roadside communities before terminating in the city of Fairbanks (Milepost 362) in the Interior. Important junctions include Willow and Hatcher Pass Road (Milepost 71.2), Talkeetna Spur Highway (Milepost 98.7), Trapper Creek and Petersville Road (Milepost 114.8), and Cantwell and the Denali Highway (Milepost 209.9).

The vast majority of primary stream fisheries for salmon and trout occur along the Parks, the Glenn more renowned for its lake fishing opportunities targeting landlocked salmon, trout, char, and grayling.

*A gorgeous specimen of valley rainbow trout, taken on a bead from a Susitna River tributary. Leopard-spotted trout are abundant.*

*(Courtesy Mike Kersbergen)*

*Matching the great fishing, the scenic qualities of the region are identified by majestic mountain ranges, expansive rivers, and deep, lush forests. Solitude abounds.*

## Major Fisheries / Hot Spots

The "Twin Valleys" region is studded with lakes, streams, and a couple of good-sized rivers, of which some eight of them are considered to be of significant value as true angling destinations. As for the Matanuska Valley and the drainages of Knik Arm, Ship Creek, Eklutna Tailrace, and the Little Susitna River represent the vast majority of angling effort and for good reason as very productive salmon runs keep anglers returning year after year. However, they are also very distinct from each other in appearance, size, species available, and style of fishing.

Ship Creek, located within walking distance of downtown Anchorage, and Eklutna Tailrace, on the outskirts of Palmer, both support wild and hatchery runs of salmon, as well as smaller populations of trout and char. Due to easy access within major population centers, including for those with physical disabilities, these streams enjoy a loyal following of local anglers. In fact, Ship has a reputation of being one of the most visited fishing spots in all of Alaska. King and silver salmon are the top draws but fishable numbers of pinks and chums and char are available too.

Far different are the roadside drainages just to the north; all are semi-remote as they flow through largely undeveloped areas. Susitna Valley offers a plethora of good places to fish, mainly clearwater tributaries draining into the turbid Susitna and Chulitna rivers. There are five of them that really stand out as being exceptionally gifted in terms of numbers of fish and species available, ease of access from the road, and quality of drainage for sport fishing purposes.

Starting with the Little Susitna River and continuing on to the tributaries flowing into the Susitna and Chulitna systems, including Willow, Sheep, and Montana creeks and East Fork Chulitna River. They are known for sizable runs of king and silver salmon, the former which may number in the multiple thousands to even tens of thousands of fish. Even

*(Courtesy Beverley Bailey)*

*Anglers that enjoy small, solitary clearwater streams teeming with fat and aggressive rainbow trout and arctic grayling will find what they are looking for in this region. Here, a native Chulitna drainage 'bow caught and released by Roy Bailey.*

greater densities of pink and chum salmon are present. Byers Creek also sports a sizable red salmon run. The latter species is not widely distributed in these waters but are usually abundant where found. Fly-fishers and others can certainly appreciate the rainbow trout and arctic grayling opportunities that are abundant in the middle and upper reaches of area streams.

All of these northern drainages are perfectly suited for bank fishing with plenty of opportunity for boating, particularly rafting. The Little Susitna is a good place for motor boating and a great place to arrange a multi-day float trip between access points. Willow Creek and East Fork Chulitna are other popular float destinations, but Sheep, Montana, and Byers are generally too small for anything but wading. Additionally, these waters offer some exceptional sight-fishing opportunities.

## Other Productive Fisheries

There are several smaller streams in the valley that do not receive the effort of the hot spots described above yet has some very good opportunities for salmon. Jim Creek, tributary of Knik River, is a popular destination with local anglers, providing decent action for reds, silvers, and Dolly Varden. The weekend-only fisheries of Wasilla, Cottonwood, and Fish creeks, draining into Knik Arm, produce runs of primarily red and silver salmon. Some added trout and char action can be had as well. Equally entertaining are the handful of area lakes where both stocked and wild populations of landlocked salmon, trout, char, grayling, and burbot reside.

Apart from the major roadside hot spots of the Susitna basin, anglers have a good selection of additional waters worth exploring. In the southern section, the drainages of Little Willow, Kashwitna, Caswell, and Goose all support runs of king, pink, chum, and silvers salmon plus good action for trout and grayling. These are mainly wade fishing streams because of their size but the semi-glacial Kashwitna is also a prime spot for floating and motor boating. Anglers wanting to try something different may opt to spend some time on one or more of the small lakes in this area that support primarily rainbow trout but also a chance to tangle with northern pike.

Farther north, there is some productive fishing for salmon to be found, primarily king and silver salmon but also reds, pinks, and chums. Rabideux and Sunshine creeks are two local favorites. Lesser-fished yet equally productive waters include Peters, Moose, Troublesome, Honolulu, and the Middle Fork Chulitna where anglers may find worthwhile opportunities for rainbows and grayling. The small drainages of the upper Susitna and Chulitna drainages are known for their good fishing and lack of crowds.

## Additional Opportunities

From Wasilla, Palmer, Houston, and Willow, anglers have many great fishing destinations to choose from, the majority of them only a short flight away. The Susitna, Yentna, and Talkeetna river drainages have almost countless clearwater tributaries that support runs or populations of all five salmon species, trout, char, grayling, and pike. All of them are remote, yet do receive a fair amount of fishing pressure during the summer months, especially at the height of the king and silver salmon runs.

Some of the remote waters are only accessible by floatplane, landing on lakes or adjoining sloughs, while boats are utilized to reach other spots. Wheel planes usually land on gravel bars along rivers.

## Sport Fishing Regulations

The Matanuska and Susitna valleys, including Knik Arm, are part of the Southcentral Alaska management area with restrictions listed under "Anchorage Bowl," "Knik Arm," and "Susitna River Drainage" sections in the booklet as provided by the Alaska Department of Fish & Game (ADF&G). Open and closed seasons and areas, legal tackle and gear, bag and possession limits, and fish size restrictions may vary from drainage to drainage and between species. Consult a copy of the regulations before fishing or call the ADF&G regional/field offices directly for information:

**Palmer:** (907) 746-6300
**Anchorage:** (907) 267-2218

*Without a doubt, king salmon is the most popular game species in the Mat-Su region and can be targeted successfully in several rivers and streams draining into the Susitna River and Knik Arm.*

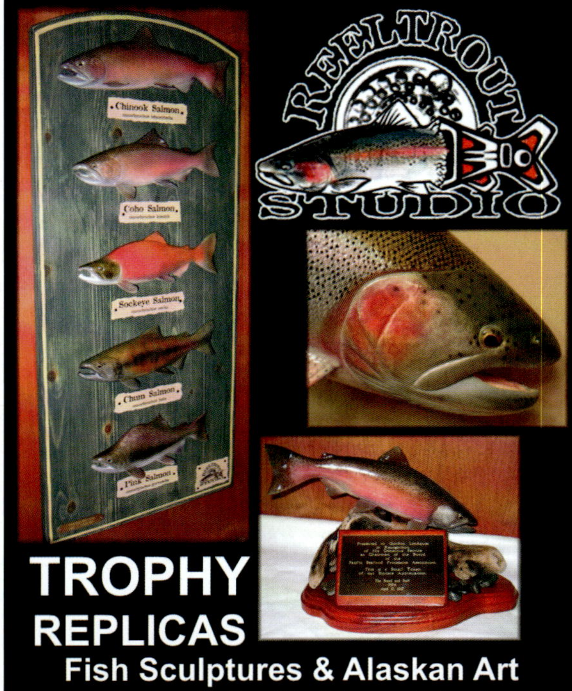

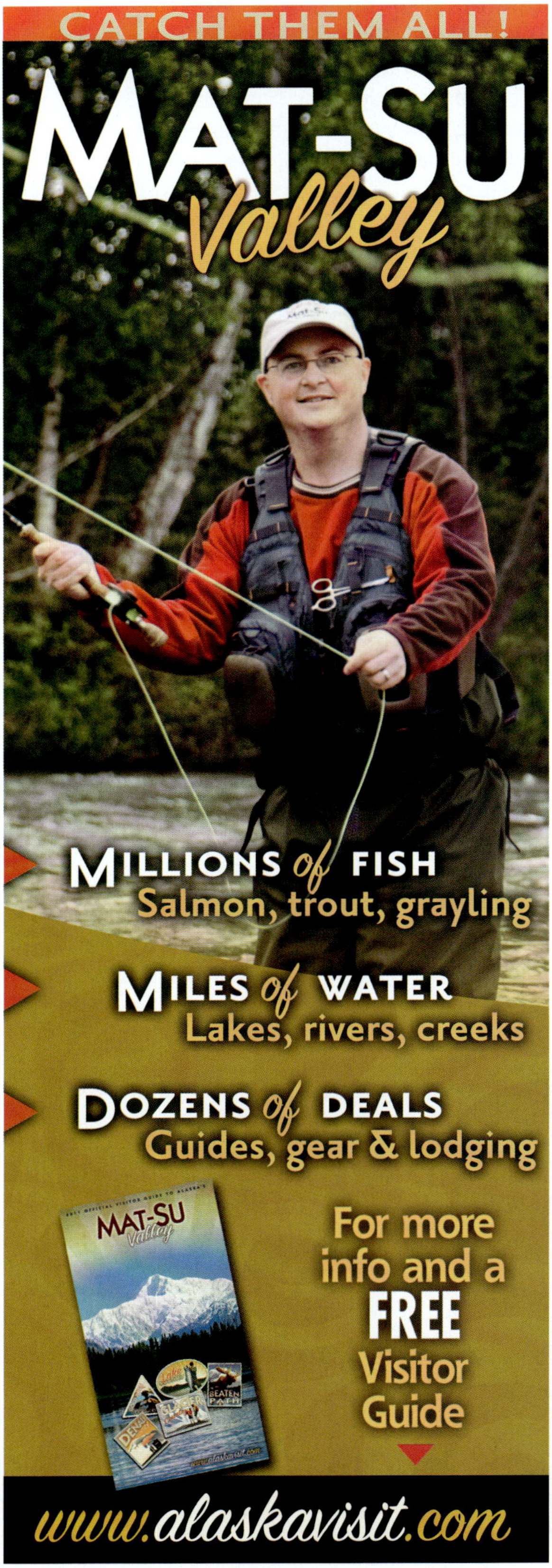
CATCH THEM ALL!
MAT-SU Valley
MILLIONS of FISH
Salmon, trout, grayling
MILES of WATER
Lakes, rivers, creeks
DOZENS of DEALS
Guides, gear & lodging
For more info and a FREE Visitor Guide
www.alaskavisit.com



Chinook Salmon
Coho Salmon
Sockeye Salmon
Chum Salmon
Pink Salmon
REELTROUT STUDIO
TROPHY
REPLICAS
Fish Sculptures & Alaskan Art
On Display & Quality Shops & Lodges
visit us online at: www.ReelTrout.com
(907) 357-1900 or Toll Free: (877) 211-3474

**Anchorage • Palmer • Wasilla • Houston**

# Matanuska Valley
## & Knik Arm

**King Salmon • Red Salmon • Pink Salmon • Chum Salmon**
**Silver Salmon • Rainbow Trout • Dolly Varden • Arctic Grayling**

*Lake Fishing*

*Tidewater Salmon*

*Urban Fishing*

*Fish Viewing*

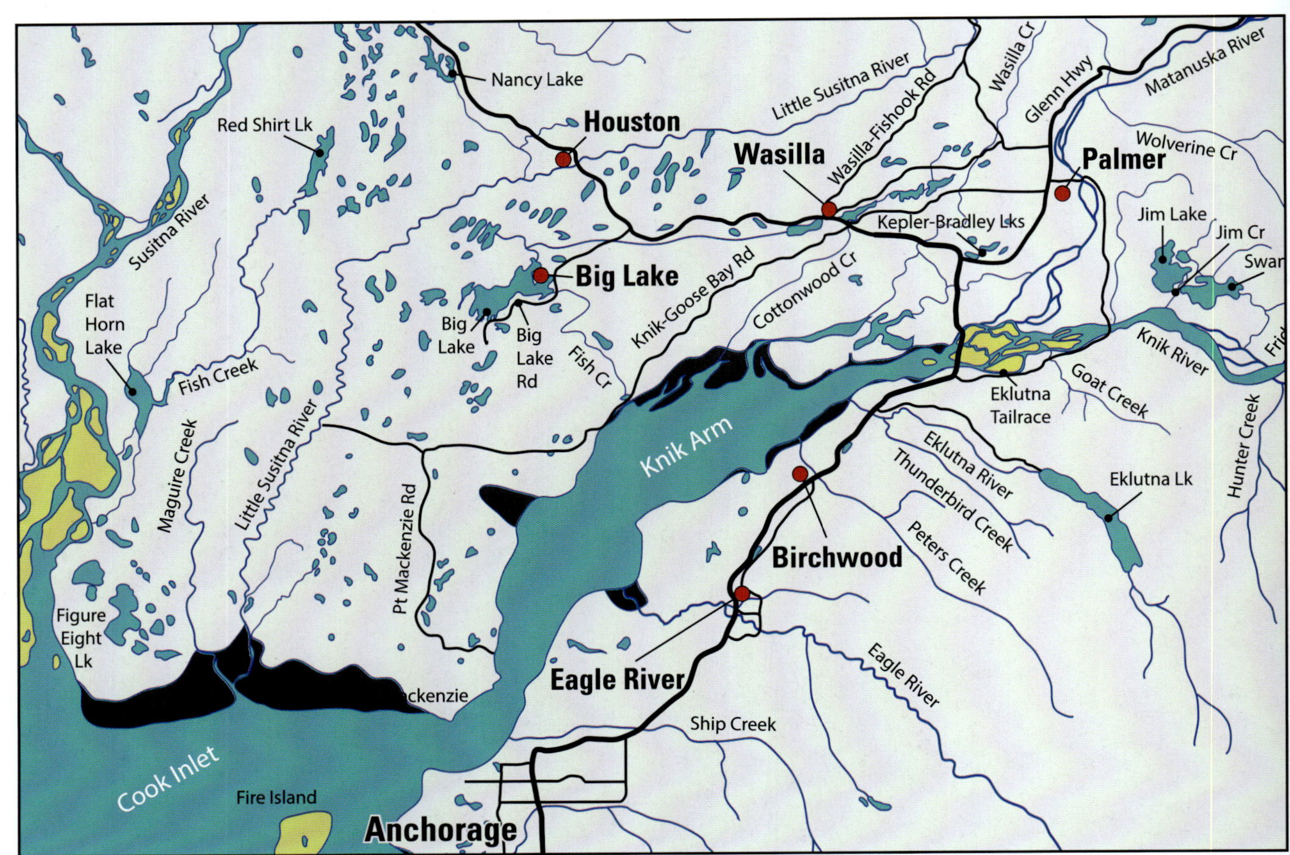


**Area Population Centers:** Anchorage, Wasilla, Palmer, Eagle River, Birchwood, Big Lake, and Houston
**Key Species:** King, Red, Pink, Chum, and Silver Salmon, Rainbow Trout, and Dolly Varden
**Other Species:** Landlocked King and Silver Salmon, Kokanee, Lake Trout, Arctic Char, Arctic Grayling, Round Whitefish, Northern Pike, and Burbot
**Main Destinations/Hot Spots:** Ship Creek, Eklutna Tailrace, and Little Susitna River
**Other Destinations:** Wasilla Creek, Jim Creek, Cottonwood Creek, Fish Creek, Kepler-Bradley Lakes, and Matanuska Area Lakes
**Additional Opportunities:** Fly-In Fishing, Salmon Viewing

**Summary of Fishing:** A place of striking beauty, the Matanuska Valley and the adjoining Knik Arm spur of Cook Inlet is a fairly developed area but still carries a reputation as the lake fishing capital of Southcentral. With the main hubs of Wasilla and Palmer, anglers here will find literally hundreds of trout and char lakes in which to practice their vice as well as several noteworthy streams that support good runs of several species of salmon in season. And, apart from the impressive jagged mountain peaks lining the green valley below, the forest in this area is typical of lowland regions as spruce and birch predominate the scenery, changing to a mix of alder and black spruce at higher and cooler elevations.

With such a relatively populated area, a great many of the smaller lakes especially have been stocked with several popular game fish, such as landlocked king and silver salmon, rainbow trout, arctic char, and arctic grayling, to meet growing demands for angling opportunities. However, there are also many lakes that harbor resident native fish (including lake trout, northern pike, and burbot) so there is always an abundance of spots to go and species to pursue.

As for river and creek fishing, the clearwater tributaries of Knik and Matanuska rivers offer some decent action for red, chum, and silver salmon. One stream is also stocked with hatchery king and silver salmon. Looking at the Knik Arm, there are some very good angling options there as well with all five species of salmon available on top of trout, char, and grayling.

If planning to hit the lakes, preferably come prepared with a float tube or canoe in order to fish them properly, yet this is not required as good action can still be had from shore. The rivers and streams, however, can easily be waded and fished off the bank. A couple of the larger waters also offer the opportunity to launch boats.

Prime time is from May to October.

# Ship Creek

King
SALMON

Pink
SALMON

Chum
SALMON

Silver
SALMON

Rainbow
TROUT

Dolly
VARDEN

**Highlights:** Very good catch rates for king and silver salmon with worthwhile opportunities for pinks and chums as well. Decent trout action above tidewater.

**Best Fishing:** Late May to mid-September.

**Regulatory Restrictions:** Liberal.

**Location:** Knik Arm drainage, downtown Anchorage.

**Description:** Ship Creek is not a typical representation of fishing in Alaska. The stream, which begins in the heart of the Chugach Mountains, flows trough one of the most populated and commercially developed areas of Anchorage before emptying into Knik Arm. Roads and highways crisscross Ship, trees and grassland being very limited anywhere along the creek. The surrounding scenery, especially on the lower end of the stream, is of tall glass buildings and concrete bridges, starkly contrasted by the forest-clad Chugach mountain range in the background.

The tidal area consists of muddy banks with a rock and gravel stream bottom. Running clear most of the year, Ship is prone to shedding some levels of silt during summer warm spells and is also sensitive to prolonged periods of rain. From late fall into spring, the stream is typically very low and clear, water levels not rising until about the middle of May (prompting the salmon migrations) and continuing through June as snowmelt from the mountains fill Ship Creek. Summer levels begin in July and persist into September. Autumn rains often bring the stream to near flood stage, yet the water quickly settles after a day or two.

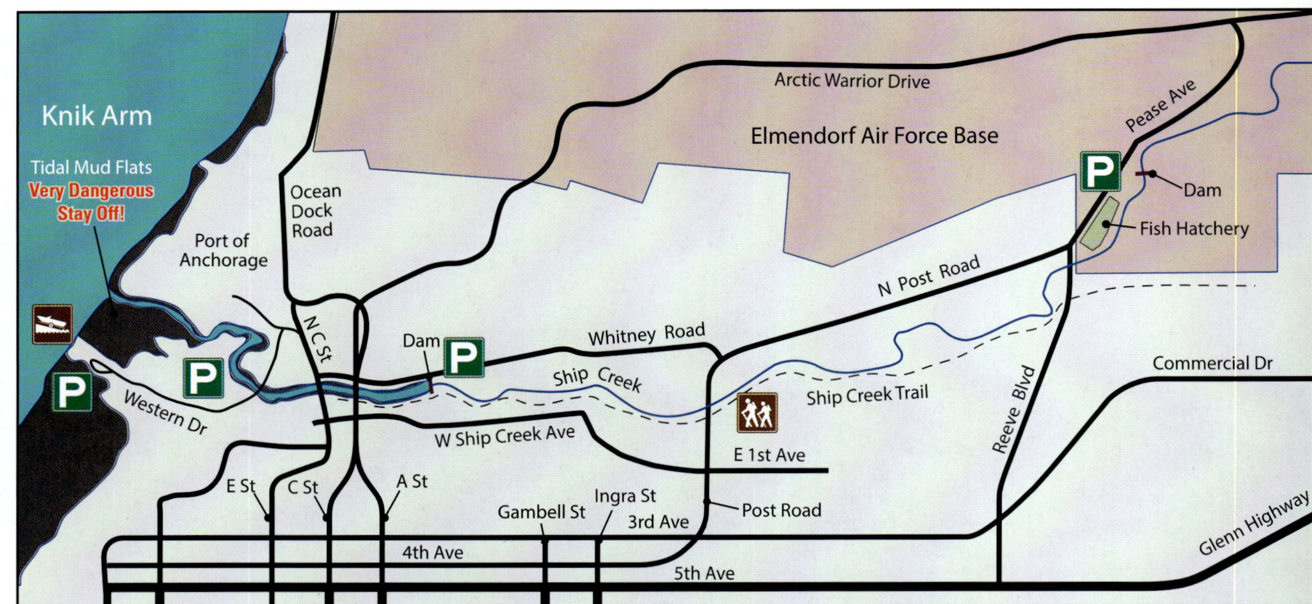


**Facilities:** Pay parking, restrooms, tackle shop, and hotels along stream. Camping, RV services, hotels, sporting goods, and city shopping available within a mile.

**Access:** The lower portion of Ship Creek is located near the Port of Anchorage and the Alaska Railroad Depot just north of downtown. Whitney Road and Ship Creek Avenue by the way of E Street and C Street are the main roadways crossing or paralleling the stream. Ship Creek Avenue provides access to south bank of stream, Whitney Road the north bank. Numerous access points are available along both roads with developed trails present. Western Drive off N C Street has access to far lower end and mouth of stream. For more detailed information or view of the Anchorage area, consult a city map.

## Rules & Regulations

**Open Season:** Downstream of Chugach power plant Dam, season is January 1 through December 31. Between power plant dam and Reeve Boulevard bridge, season is June 15 through April 14. Upstream of Reeve Boulevard bridge to Elmendorf power plant dam, fishing is prohibited year-round. Closed to all fishing between 11:00 p.m. and 6:00 a.m. from May 15 through July 13.

**Open Area:** The entire stream is open to fishing (except as noted above).

**Legal Gear/Tackle:** Lures with multiple hooks and bait are allowed downstream of Chugach power plant dam year-round; only one unbaited, single-hook, artificial lure allowed between Chugach power plant and Reeve Boulevard bridge.

**King Salmon**

- Open season is January 1 through July 13.
- Open area is from mouth to ADF&G marker below Chugach power plant dam; closed to kings above marker.
- Bag limit is (1) per day and (1) in possession (20 inches or longer). For kings less than 20 inches (Jacks), the limit is (10).

**All Other Salmon**

- Open all season (see general "Open Season" above).
- Open area is from mouth to ADF&G marker below Chugach power plant dam; closed to salmon above dam.
- Red, pink, chum, and silver salmon bag limit is (3) per day and (3) in possession (16 inches or longer). For salmon less than 16 inches (Jacks), the limit is (10).

**Rainbow/Steelhead Trout & Dolly Varden**

- Open all season (see general "Open Season" above) downstream of Chugach Power Plant Dam. Upstream of power plant, the season is June 15 through April 14.
- Open area is entire stream.
- Catch-and-release only year-round for trout upstream of Chugach Power Plant Dam.
- Bag limit for trout is (2) per day and (2) in possession, only (1) over 20 inches, and Dolly Varden (5) per day and (5) in possession, only (1) over 12 inches.

## Fishing Ship Creek

**Access:** ★★★★★
**Scenery:** ★★
**Wildlife:** ★
**Sight Fishing:** ★★★
**Bank/Wading:** ★★★★
**Boat/Floating:** ★

**Species:** King, pink, chum, and silver salmon, rainbow trout, and Dolly Varden. Rare catches of red salmon.
**Summary:** Ship Creek, despite being situated in the center of Alaska's largest city, holds the distinction of being one of the most popular fisheries in the state in terms of both angler participation as well as harvest. As a matter of fact, the salmon fishing here rivals even many of the better remote fly-out fisheries in terms of action. Although natural salmon runs are only a fraction of what they once used to be, the ADF&G has initiated an aggressive stocking program of king and silver salmon which is responsible for drawing heavy crowds to the little stream during the brief summer months.

Nearly 100% of the angling effort at Ship Creek takes place in the tidal zone since this is the only area open to salmon fishing, with very little activity occurring anywhere upstream due to access problems and lack of consistent fish populations. Where salmon and other species once proliferated throughout the entire stream into the Chugach Mountains, a dam built only a few miles from the stream mouth near Elmendorf Air Force Base decades ago effectively halted any subsequent upstream migration. Fish runs to this day end at this dam, where the state also maintains a hatchery and salmon viewing area.

The stretch of water from the Chugach dam downstream to the mouth can be a challenge for some anglers since there are only a very few resting areas for fish to hold in and the deep mud along the banks poses a certain level of hazard. Many anglers negotiate the mud by walking in the stream itself.

The majority of king and silver salmon returning to Ship every year are of hatchery origin. Some of these fish spawn on their own in the stream while others are caught and "artificially" spawned to procreate future hatchery runs. There are two showings of silvers at the creek, the first being the hatchery fish but the second are native salmon. The second – and much smaller – run has a timing cycle some three weeks later than the artificial run, yet the two often blend, giving the impression of one run lasting several months.

Whether casting for king or silver salmon, the best fishing is often found on the changing of the tides. Approximately two to three hours before and after high tide is the optimum time. When the respective runs are at a peak, however, fishing can be worthwhile all day long. Casting lures is productive during slack water periods while drifting attractors, flies, and bait is better in current.

Rainbow trout and Dolly Varden may be encountered throughout the lower stream but are more abundant in the stretch of Ship above the Chugach dam up to the state hatchery site.

*View of Ship Creek just below the Chugach Power Plant Dam, the upper limit of tidal activity. When water runs clear, this can be a good spot to sight-fish for schools of salmon.*

## Fish Availability

● = High ● = Moderate ● = Low ● = Closed

| Species | APR | MAY | JUN | JUL | AUG | SEP | OCT |
|---|---|---|---|---|---|---|---|
| **King Salmon** | Low | Low Low Moderate Moderate | High High High Moderate | Moderate Low Closed Closed | Closed Closed | | |
| **Pink Salmon** | | | Low | Low Moderate High High | Moderate Low Low Low | | |
| **Chum Salmon** | | | Low | Low Low Moderate Moderate | Moderate Low Low Low | Low | |
| **Silver Salmon** | | | Low | Low Low Moderate High | High High High Moderate | Moderate Moderate Moderate Low | Low Low Low Low |
| **Rainbow Trout** | Low Low Closed Closed | Closed Closed Closed Closed | Closed Closed Moderate Moderate | Moderate Moderate Moderate Moderate | Moderate Moderate Moderate Moderate | Moderate Moderate Moderate Moderate | Moderate Moderate Low Low |
| **Dolly Varden** | Low Low Low Low | Low Low Low Moderate | Moderate Moderate Moderate Moderate | Moderate Moderate Moderate Moderate | Moderate Moderate Moderate Moderate | Moderate Moderate Moderate Moderate | Moderate Moderate Low Low |
| Angling Pressure | | Low Low Moderate Moderate | High High High High | Moderate Moderate Moderate High | High High High Moderate | Moderate Moderate Low Low | |

## King Salmon

**Rating:** ★★½ Fair to good.
**Season:** January 1 through July 13.
**Timing:** April 25 – July 13; peak June 1 – 25.
**Size:** Average 12 – 30 pounds; up to 60 pounds.
**Tackle:** Spoons, spinners, plugs, flies, and bait.
**Tips:** Drifting flies and attractors, preferably in chartreuse or fluorescent green, is good at any time during the run. Hardware such as spoons and spinners become more effective as the run begins to peak and water temperatures rise, usually sometime in early June. Blue or chrome spinners can be deadly. Bait should be fished stationary early in the season (May) and can be drifted through holes and runs later on (June and July). When the run is going strong, try bait or spinners as the tide comes in and flies or bait when the tide goes out. The stretch of water between the Restaurant Bridge and the stream mouth is best but can be productive all the way up to the dam.

(Courtesy Chris Cox)

*Angler Paul Ferreira holds up a mint-bright female chinook, caught on a flooding tide near the mouth of the creek in late May.*

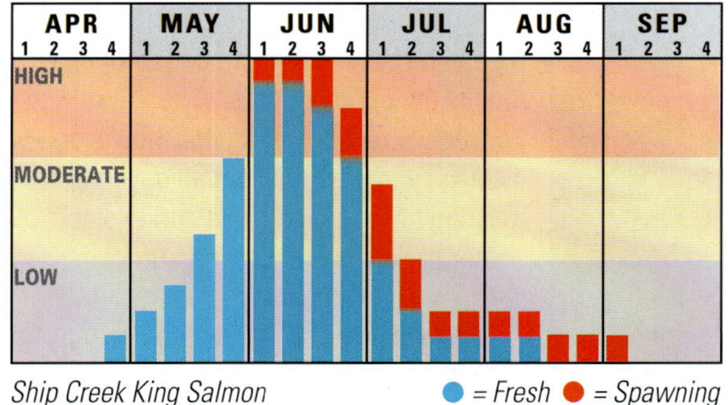


*Ship Creek King Salmon* ● = Fresh ● = Spawning

## Pink Salmon

**Rating:** ★★★ Good on even-numbered years.
**Season:** January 1 through December 31.
**Timing:** June 25 – August 25; peak July 15 – August 1.
**Size:** Average 2 – 4 pounds; up to 6 pounds.
**Tackle:** Spoons, spinners, plugs, and flies.
**Tips:** Scout for small schools of fish in various holes and runs on low tide. Use lures and flies, preferably in green or chartreuse. When tide influences stream, use spoons and spinners in above colors as well as blue and orange depending on water and weather conditions. On high tide, look for fish near the dam.

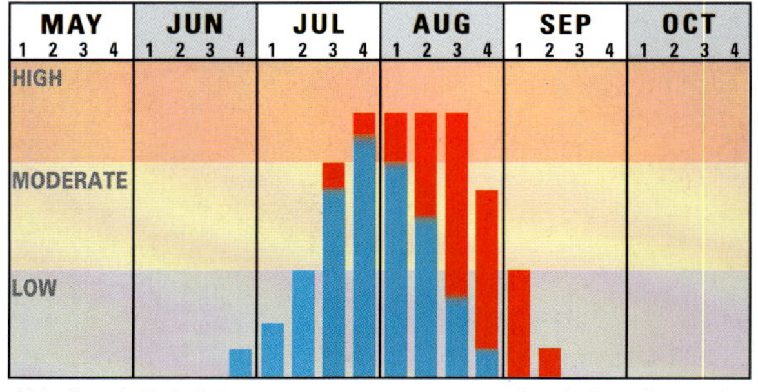


*Ship Creek Pink Salmon* ● = Fresh ● = Spawning

## Chum Salmon

**Rating:** ★★ Fair.
**Season:** January 1 through December 31.
**Timing:** June 25 – September 5; peak July 15 – August 5.
**Size:** Average 6 – 10 pounds; up to 15 pounds.
**Tackle:** Spoons, spinners, plugs, flies, and bait.
**Tips:** Chums are best targeted on low tides. Scout likely structure using lures and flies in blue, green, or orange; sight-fishing is a possibility when water is clear. If the tide is in, catches are sporadic and usually incidental to fishing for other species.

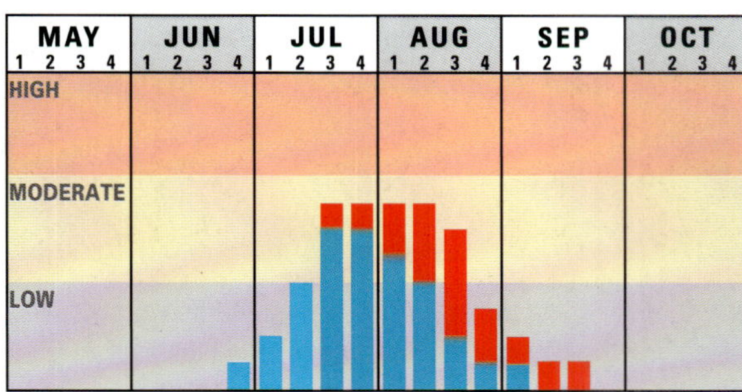


*Ship Creek Chum Salmon* ● = Fresh ● = Spawning

## Silver Salmon

**Rating:** ★★★ Good.
**Season:** January 1 through December 31.
**Timing:** July 1 – November 1; peak August 1 – 25.
**Size:** Average 5 – 10 pounds; up to 18 pounds.
**Tackle:** Spoons, spinners, plugs, flies, and bait.
**Tips:** Orange or red lures and bait are favored with silvers most any time. Try the incoming our outgoing tide. Metallic silver, blue, and green can be good shades for sunny days if the bite is slow. Drift salmon roe with a bobber on high slack tide. On low tide, scout structure for concentrations of fish using flies or bait.

Fishing the late run in September, only incoming and outgoing tides are productive since the silvers typically do not stay in the lower stream on low tides, either moving up into the creek or out again into Knik Arm.

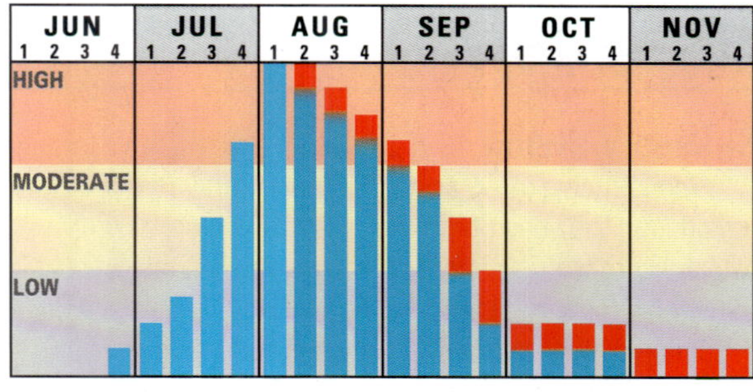


*Ship Creek Silver Salmon*

*A happy, young angler with a limit of early-season silvers, taken on roe fished along with a bobber below the railroad trestle bridge on an incoming tide. Ship is a decent place to take youngsters.*

### Rainbow Trout

**Rating:** ★★ Fair.
**Season:** January 1 through December 31.
**Timing:** Year-round; peak June 15 – October 15.
**Size:** Average 8 – 16 inches; up to 25 inches.
**Tackle:** Spinners and flies.
**Tips:** The best area to try for rainbows include the stretch of Ship Creek between the upper dam at the hatchery (at Elmendorf) and the Chugach dam. Any hole from near tidewater upstream will contain trout with a few larger specimens caught in spring. Use small spinners and smolt imitation flies early in the season (June, first part of July), switching to egg and flesh patterns starting in July and through the fall. Forage imitations are good all season.

Trout can be caught year-round in Ship but fishing for them in winter is typically very slow.

### Dolly Varden

**Rating:** ★½ Poor to fair.
**Season:** January 1 through December 31.
**Timing:** Year-round; peak June 15 – October 15.
**Size:** Average 8 – 16 inches; up to 20 inches.
**Tackle:** Spoons, spinners, and flies.
**Tips:** Some char may be coaxed to strike smolt and forage imitations in late spring and early summer from the upper dam downstream to the mouth of Ship Creek. The late summer and fall opportunities between the upper and lower dams are perhaps the most consistent. Try egg and flesh patterns, focusing on areas where spawning salmon are present.

A few char do overwinter in the stream and, if open water prevails, may be caught.

## Other Ship Opportunities

### Salmon Viewing

When running clear, as it does the majority of the time during the year, Ship Creek provide anglers as well as onlookers with excellent viewing of salmon migrating through the stream to their spawning beds. All five species of salmon may be spotted, yet the most common species include king, pink, and silver salmon.

Several points of access are present, the most popular being at the Chugach Power Plant Dam at tidewater and by the Alaska Department of Fish & Game state fish hatchery at Elmendorf AFB. The former location has great viewing from above as people are able to use the walkway on top of the dam in order to see salmon gathering in the deep pool below. These fish range from chrome and newly fresh in from the sea to dark-colored breeding condition. It is mainly good numbers of kings (mid-June to mid-July), pinks (late July to late August), and silvers (mid-August to mid-September) present with some chums (July-August) mixed in along with an occasional red.

The viewing area at the fish hatchery presents a couple of opportunities, including one not available in most all other roadside places. Foremost, this is a spawning area for many of Ship's salmon. Main species here are kings and silvers, which peak in abundance during mid-July to early August and early September to mid-October, respectively.

The fish hatchery is open to the public with posted visitor hours. Guided tours introduce the functions of the plant and the importance it carries in terms of fish stocking around the region.

For additional viewing, a paved trail parallels the banks of Ship from the Chugach dam to the Reeve Boulevard bridge just downstream of the hatchery. This is a fabulous

way to walk along the stream watching the fish migrations as well as the potential to see wildlife, such as eagles. The full length of the trail (one way) takes about two hours. Many locals use this trail for biking.

### Past, Present, & Future

Prior to having two dams constructed on it, Ship Creek in downtown Anchorage was an incredibly rich salmon stream with thousands of native kings and silvers and an estimated ten thousand or more pinks returning on an annual basis. Fish could move upstream completely unhindered and were known to spawn into the foothills of the Chugach Mountains behind the city.

Today, fish are only able to migrate up to the old dam at Elmendorf. This dam effectively blocks any further migration beyond this point, leaving dozens of miles of prime spawning habitat barren of salmon. Future plans for Ship includes removing the dam in hopes of seeing the stream return to what it once used to be many decades ago.

# Little Susitna River

King
SALMON

Red
SALMON

Pink
SALMON

Chum
SALMON

Silver
SALMON

Rainbow
TROUT

**Highlights:** Outstanding action for four species of salmon, including one of the largest silver runs in all of Southcentral. Good water for a longer float-fishing excursion.

**Best Fishing:** Late May to mid-September. **Regulatory Restrictions:** Liberal.

**Location:** Matanuska Valley/Knik Arm drainage, greater Palmer-Wasilla area, Parks Highway-Knik Goose Bay Road, 73 miles northwest of Anchorage.

**Description:** Draining the south side of the Talkeetna Mountains north of Palmer, the clear Little Susitna flows 110 miles in a southwesterly direction to Cook Inlet and the Susitna Flats near the mouth of Susitna River. The far upper reaches of the river is very fast and rock-bottomed with complete whitewater conditions before spilling out onto the valley floor, where the Little Susitna becomes wider and deeper, meandering considerably on its way to sea. Spruce and birch forests surround the river the entire length.

Sensitive to rain, the river can quickly rise by a foot or two in a relatively short period of time, the water turning turbid, almost chocolate brown.

The Parks Highway intersects the river in Houston, approximately at its halfway point, the stretch of water from above the bridge to the Hatcher Pass area generally referred to as the upper Little Susitna. Downstream of the bridge to within a few miles of the lower access points is the middle section, and from there on to the mouth of the river is the lower part.

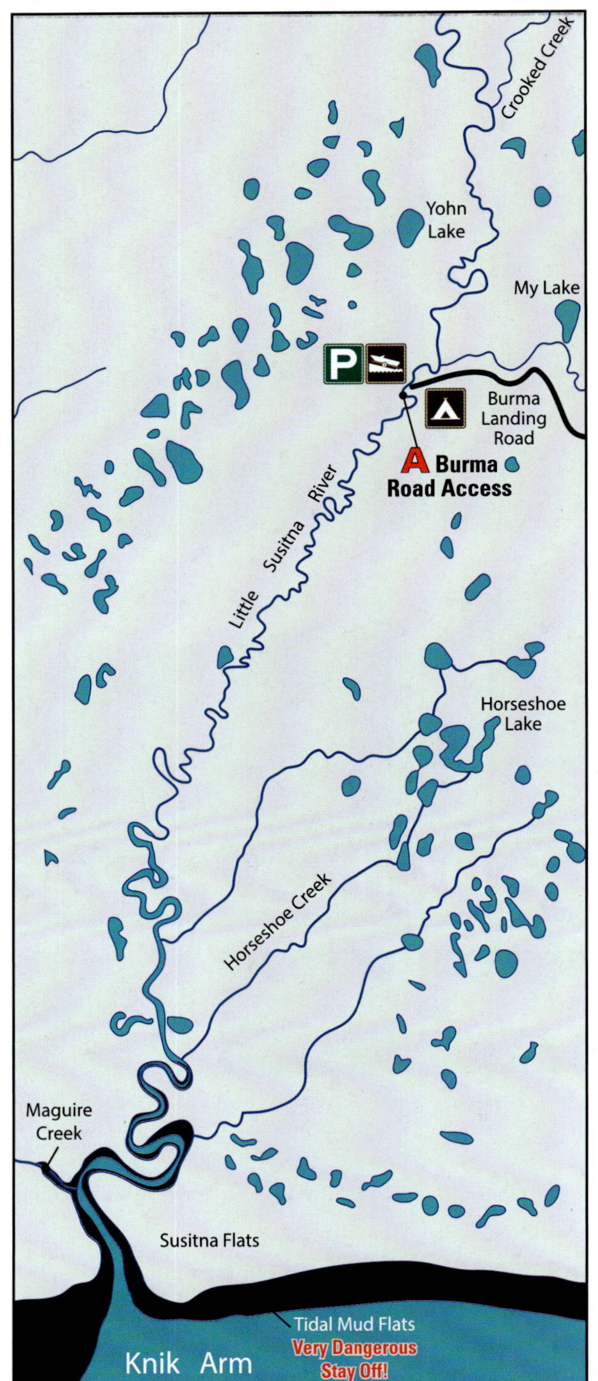

*The Little "Su" as seen from the Fishhook-Willow Road near Palmer. This is the most beautiful section of the river, albeit not the best for fishing. Shallow, fast-flowing and boulder-strewn, some smaller trout and char may be caught on flies and spinners.*

**Facilities:** Parking, camping, and boat launches are available at both access points but the community of Houston also has RV parking, tackle, gas, restaurant, guide services, and convenience stores available.

**Access:** The Parks Highway provides direct and indirect access to the upper, middle, and lower river sections.

**A. Burma Road Access** – Milepost 42.2. South on Main Street/Knik-Goose Bay Road to Milepost 17.2, right on Point Mackenzie Road 7.6 miles to a "T," right short distance to another "T," turn on Ayrshire Road 2.7 miles to a "Y," right on Little Su Access Road 3.3 miles to river. Parking for all size vehicles, camping, boat launch, and restrooms. Trails lead along river bank.

**B. Parks Highway Bridge** – Milepost 57.1. Highway crosses river. Turnout. Main access is off Milepost 57.4; parking for all size vehicles, camping, primitive boat launch. RV parking in area as well as a large developed community campground. Guide service, lodging, restaurant, gas station, and other amenities available in Houston. Trail heads downstream along north bank of river.

**C. Sushana Road Bridge** – Milepost 42.2. Turn north on Main Street (Wasilla Fishhook Road) 3.0 miles, left on E Seldon Road 0.1 mile, right on Schrock Road 4.2 miles, right on Sushana Street 0.6 mile to river crossing. Parking (not recommended for large RVs) and primitive camping. No developed trails in area.

**D. Schrock Road Bridge** – Milepost 42.2. North on Main Street (Wasilla Fishhook Road) 3.0 miles, left on E Seldon Road 0.1 mile, right on Schrock Road 6.7 miles to river crossing. Parking (not recommended for large RVs) and limited camping. No trails in area.

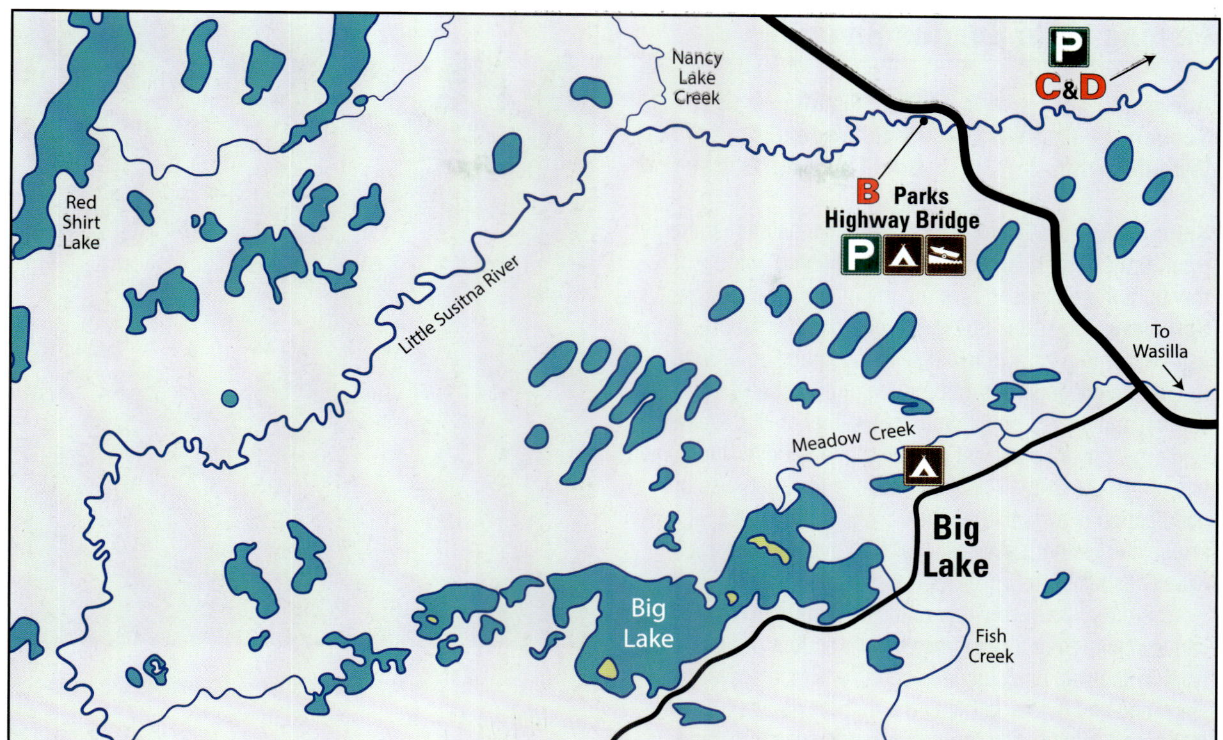

## Rules & Regulations

**Open Season:** January 1 through December 31 on lower river downstream of Parks Highway bridge; June 15 through April 14 on upper river above bridge.
**Open Area:** The entire river is open to fishing.
**Legal Gear/Tackle:** On lower river, only unbaited, artificial lures may be used from October 1 through August 5; bait is allowed from August 6 through September 30. On upper river, only one unbaited, single-hook, artificial lure is allowed.

### King Salmon

- Open season is January 1 through July 13.
- Open area is from river mouth to Parks Highway bridge.
- No fishing allowed between 11:00 pm and 6:00 am from May 15 through July 13.
- Bag limit is (1) per day and (1) in possession (20 inches or longer). For kings less than 20 inches (Jacks), the limit is (10).

### All Other Salmon

- Open all season (see general "Open Season" above).
- Open area is from river mouth to Parks Highway bridge.
- Red, pink, and chum salmon bag limit is (3) per day and (3) in possession (16 inches or longer), and silver salmon (2) per day and (2) in possession. For salmon less than 16 inches (Jacks), the limit is (10).

### Rainbow/Steelhead Trout & Dolly Varden

- Open all season (see general "Open Season" above).
- Open area is entire river.
- Catch-and-release only for trout from April 15 through June 14.
- Bag limit for trout is (2) per day and (2) in possession, only (1) over 20 inches, and Dolly Varden (5) per day and (5) in possession, only (1) over 12 inches.

### Other Fishes

- Open all season (see general "Open Season" above).
- Open area is entire river.
- Arctic grayling bag limit is (2) per day and (2) in possession, any size.
- Whitefish has no bag or possession limit, no size limit.
- Burbot bag limit is (5) per day and (5) in possession, any size.

## Fishing Little Susitna River

**Access:** ★★★ **Sight Fishing:** ★★★
**Scenery:** ★★★½ **Bank/Wading:** ★★★★
**Wildlife:** ★★ **Boat/Floating:** ★★★★★

**Species:** King, red, pink, chum, and silver salmon, rainbow trout, Dolly Varden, arctic grayling, and round whitefish. A few burbot are present; rare reports of northern pike.

**Summary:** The Little "Su" is one of the richest sport fisheries within easy reach of Anchorage and other area towns and communities, supporting all five species of salmon and decent populations of trout, char, and whitefish. Anglers focus for the most part on the lower river for salmon where fish are at their peak in quality and abundance but good action is available all the way up to the Parks Highway bridge. For resident species, the middle and upper river usually fishes better.

There really are very few roadside waters in Alaska that can lay claim to producing worthwhile action for all five salmon species. Runs begin in spring with the arrival of kings and end in late fall with the last trickle of silvers, the rest of the salmon clan arriving during the summer months.

Targeting salmon is best, as stated above, down low in the drainage as fish are dime bright and in prime sporting condition. Little Susitna is actually a very long river with an abundance of bends, thus any salmon arriving at the upper access point at the Parks Highway have already been in freshwater for up to two weeks or longer and often display some sign of maturity.

King salmon move slowly and steadily up the river, the bulk of the run taking approximately two to three weeks to migrate from the tidal area to the highway bridge. Action starts off being good on the lower river and progressively deteriorates as the fish advance upstream, being only fair at best at the upper limit of waters open to king fishing. The run typically peaks in mid-June down low and not until the last week of June or early July higher up. Additionally, very few fresh kings are available as far upstream as the road crossing, most having turned red in color.

(Courtesy Eagle Eye Images)

There are two runs of reds in the Little Susitna. The early run is quite small, peaks in mid-June, with anglers catching these salmon incidentally to fishing for kings. Some early-run fish will be available at the Parks Highway in late June and early July, the fish headed to the upper reaches of the river. The late run is also small, with some fish caught on the more remote middle section of water. Hit the Lake Creek confluence as the vast majority of these fish head up that stream.

Pink salmon run strong on even-numbered years but generally there are enough fish in any given season to produce good to excellent action. Target these small salmon at the lower access point since they mature quickly and only a relatively few semi-bright salmon are available any higher up in the drainage.

Chrome chum salmon fill the river every July. The Little Susitna experiences a heavy run of these underrated salmon, with the most productive fishing occurring on the lower and middle sections of river. Like pinks, chums mature rapidly with the majority of fish around the road crossing already displaying full spawning colors.

The Little Susitna River has one of the largest silver salmon runs on the road system, numbering between 30,000 and 45,000 fish in a good year. Again, the lower river is the prime spot to catch these fish with the run peaking the first half of August. After mid-month, anglers do better

*The middle and upper reaches of Little Susitna are much more conducive to casting off the bank as the river is narrower and holes defined, perfect conditions to locate concentrations of fish.*

in the vicinity of the Parks Highway. A few bright, late-season fish are often found at and right below the mouth of Lake Creek through the month of September, offering anglers one of the last opportunities for the species in the area.

Resident species are not particularly abundant in the Little Susitna. Understanding that these fish are in the river year-round, there is not much potential for population growth as one would see in a lake system. Nevertheless, trout, char, grayling, and whitefish all thrive here in modest numbers, keyed in more or less on the movement of salmon within the drainage. They are typically encountered during the summer and fall months, and big schools of spawning round whitefish can be sighted on the upper river (above Parks Highway) during September and October.

Another species occasionally caught by anglers fishing for salmon and trout is burbot. They are never particularly abundant but can be targeted in slower sections of the river with limited success.

## Fish Availability

● (H) = High ● (M) = Moderate ● (L) = Low ● (C) = Closed

| Species | APR | MAY | JUN | JUL | AUG | SEP | OCT |
|---|---|---|---|---|---|---|---|
| **King Salmon** | L | L L M M | H H H M | M L C C | C C | | |
| **Red Salmon** | | L | L M M M | L L M M | M M L L | L | |
| **Pink Salmon** | | | L | L M H H | M L L L | | |
| **Chum Salmon** | | | L | L M H H | H M L L | L | |
| **Silver Salmon** | | | L | L L M H | H H H H | M M L L | L |
| **Rainbow Trout** | L L L L | L L M M | M M M M | M M M M | M M M M | M M M M | M M L L |
| **Dolly Varden** | L L L L | L L M M | M M M M | M M M M | M M M M | M M M M | M M L L |
| **Whitefish** | L L L L | L L L L | L L L L | M M M M | M M M M | M M M M | M M L L |
| Angling Pressure | | L L M M | H H H H | M M M H | H H H M | M M L L | |

### King Salmon

**Rating:** ★★½ Fair to good.
**Season:** January 1 through July 13.
**Timing:** May 1 – July 13; peak June 1 – 25.
**Size:** Average 15 – 40 pounds, up to 75 pounds.
**Tackle:** Spinners, plugs, attractors, and flies.
**Tips:** On the lower river early in the season, anglers do best fishing plugs and attractors deep and slow. Spinners become more effective as water warms up in June and July. Fly-fishing for kings is better on the middle and upper reaches where the river is narrow, holes more pronounced, and fish concentrated.

When river is high and murky, try fluorescent orange and chartreuse lures. As water conditions improve, blue, green, and black colors are better.

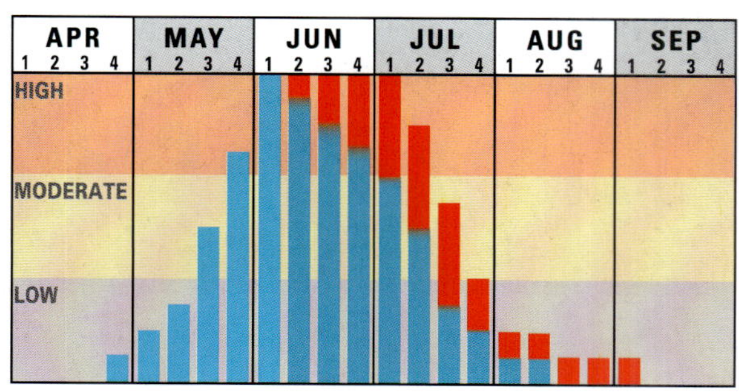


Little Susitna River King Salmon ● = Fresh ● = Spawning

(Courtesy Chris Cox)

*Chris Cox lifts a beautiful specimen of spring chinook, caught from shore at the lower end of the Little Susitna on a size 6 silver/blue spinner. Anglers targeting these big fish do well lower in the drainage during May and June as the fish are brighter and scrappier; kings found higher up, such as around the highway crossing in Houston, generally tend to be increasingly blushed. Casting lures, flies, and bait off the bank can be productive.*

### Red Salmon

**Rating:** ★ Poor.
**Season:** January 1 through December 31.
**Timing:** May 25 – September 1; peak July 15 – August 1.
**Size:** Average 5 – 7 pounds, up to 11 pounds.
**Tackle:** Flies and bait.
**Tips:** Targeting reds can be difficult on the lower river since slow current flow and lack of good structure prevents consistent hookups. Head upstream to the middle river, preferably near the mouth of Lake Creek, where schools of fish gather. It helps to sight-fish, spotting small schools of salmon, increasing the catch rate.

Small flies work wherever there is sufficient current and sometimes a cluster of salmon roe fished stationary on the bottom can be effective in slack water.

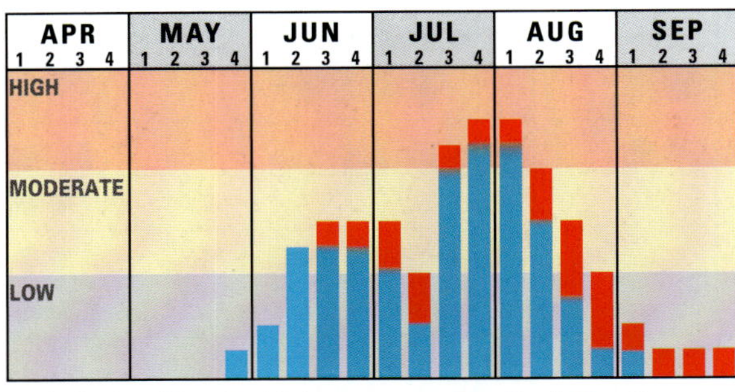


*Little Susitna River Red Salmon* ● = Fresh ● = Spawning

### Pink Salmon

**Rating:** ★★★★ Excellent on even-numbered years, good on odd.
**Season:** January 1 through December 31.
**Timing:** June 20 – September 1; peak July 15 – August 5.
**Size:** Average 2 – 5 pounds, up to 7 pounds.
**Tackle:** Spoons, spinners, plugs, and flies.
**Tips:** Chrome lures and attractor flies with orange or green function well throughout the river. Fish deep and slow.

For brightest fish, try lower access point the second half of July when fish are transitioning into the river on the tides. The run peaks on the middle and upper river after the first of August; expect significant number of semi-bright to blushed fish and prepare to do a lot of catch-and-release.

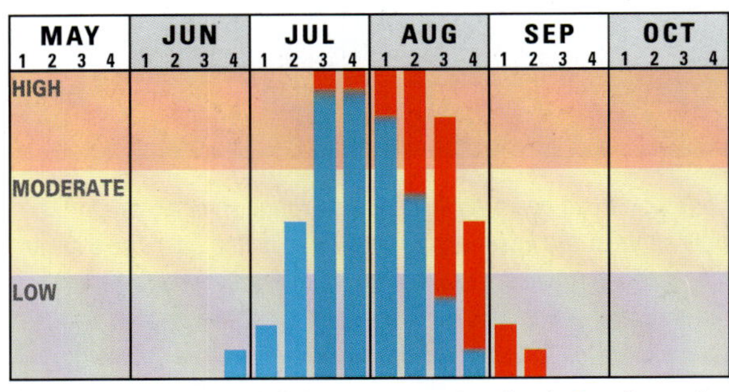


*Little Susitna River Pink Salmon* ● = Fresh ● = Spawning

### Chum Salmon

**Rating:** ★★★★ Excellent.
**Season:** January 1 through December 31.
**Timing:** June 15 – September 15; peak July 15 – August 5.
**Size:** Average 6 – 12 pounds, up to 18 pounds.
**Tackle:** Spoons, spinners, plugs, and flies.
**Tips:** Medium-sized lures in silver with green or chartreuse color inset are popular on fresh chums. Orange may be better on darker days or if river is flowing off color. If fish are skittish, try smaller lures and/or darker hues such as black or purple.

Second half of July is peak for dime bright chums and the lower river is where to target them as they stream through on the way to spawning grounds higher up in the drainage. Some holes may see significant numbers of fish jammed together. The middle and upper river around Houston tend to do better come August, although many chums will be showing signs of sexual maturity at this stage; pick and choose is the rule for quality fish.

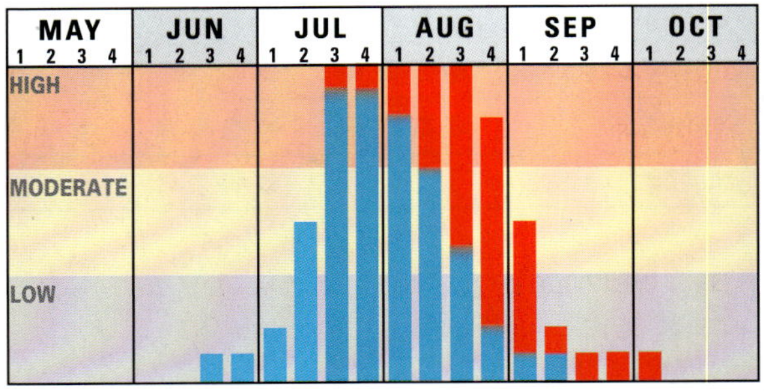


*Little Susitna River Chum Salmon* ● = Fresh ● = Spawning

*A female calico – or chum – salmon. The Little Susitna receives a very large mid-summer run of this species. Target these fish, along with pinks, in the lower river for better sport and eating.*

(Courtesy Eagle Eye Images)

*A lightly blushed late-season coho, taken on the middle river near Houston. It struck an egg sucking leech fished through a school of fish holding in a deep pool. This area frequently offers fabulous sight-fishing for silvers and other salmon species.*

## Silver Salmon

**Rating:** ★★★ Good.
**Season:** January 1 through December 31.
**Timing:** June 25 – October 15; peak July 25 – August 25.
**Size:** Average 5 – 12 pounds, up to 18 pounds.
**Tackle:** Spinners, plugs, flies, and bait.
**Tips:** Before the August 6 bait opener, try plain chrome or chrome and red spinners and plugs. Attractor flies are good throughout river. When bait is legal, soak clusters of salmon roe on the bottom or drift with a strike indicator for fast results. Bait is superior for silvers near the highway access point.

The vast majority of anglers targeting silvers do so on the lower river early in the season as salmon are chrome and in great shape. Fish densities are sometimes even greater on the middle and upper river later on in the season as they crowd into deep holes; do not expect all fish to be in prime condition and many will be showing color.

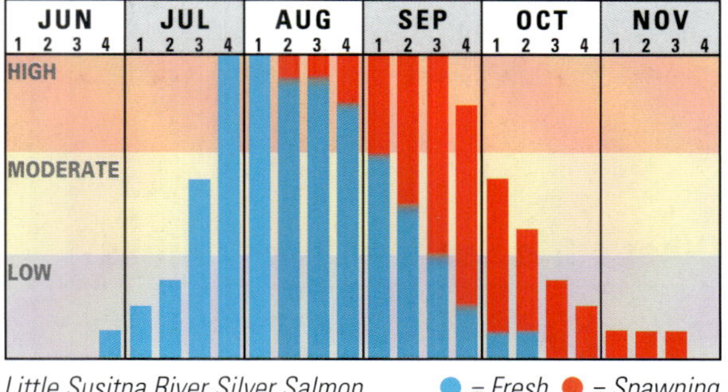


*Little Susitna River Silver Salmon* ● *= Fresh* ● *= Spawning*

## Rainbow Trout

**Rating:** ★★ Fair.
**Season:** January 1 through December 31.
**Timing:** Year-round; peak June 1 – September 30.
**Size:** Average 8 – 20 inches, up to 26 inches.
**Tackle:** Spoons, spinners, and flies.
**Tips:** Search for trout on the middle and upper river using forage and smolt imitation lures and flies prior to mid-July, switching to egg and flesh patters after that into autumn. Although usually caught incidentally to salmon fishing, when targeted the action can be fairly decent. Big specimens to multiple pounds reside in holes upstream of Houston.

*A couple of hike-in anglers enjoy mid-season solitude on a stretch of river just downstream of the Parks Highway crossing. Improvised trails lead along the river to a variety of water away from the road. This is a perfect area for those willing to explore.*

### Dolly Varden

**Rating:** ★★ Fair.
**Season:** January 1 through December 31.
**Timing:** Year-round; peak July 1 – September 15.
**Size:** Average 8 – 15 inches, up to 22 inches.
**Tackle:** Spoons, spinners, and flies.
**Tips:** Try deep holes in lower and middle river early in the season (July) using forage imitations, then higher up in the drainage come late summer and fall with egg patterns.

### Arctic Grayling

**Rating:** ★★ Fair.
**Season:** January 1 through December 31.
**Timing:** Year-round; peak June 15 – September 15.
**Size:** Average 8 – 12 inches, up to 17 inches.
**Tackle:** Spinners and flies.
**Tips:** These fish respond best to small chrome spinners or an assortment of insect and forage imitation flies on the middle and upper river during the summer and fall months.

## Other Little Susitna Opportunities

### Float Fishing

The "Lil' Su" is not known as a particularly popular spot to float fish, primarily because of lack of access points and fairly significant distances between the few that are present, usually requiring one or two nights on the river. Also, the river does lack good and consistent fishing for resident game fish -- such as trout and grayling -- leaving anglers to almost exclusively pursue one or more of the five species of salmon found in the river.

For those wishing to explore some new territory as far as floating a roadside river goes, the Little Susitna does offer a variety of water to challenge. While the far upper end (around Hatcher Pass) is too narrow, fast, and rocky to enjoy if targeting the fishing aspects of the river, that section of water from the Schrock Road-Houston area downstream is certainly worth it.

If salmon is not of any consideration, put-in at any of the two main road-accessible spots along Schrock Road and float downstream to take-out at the Parks Highway Bridge in the community of Houston. This is a relatively short journey, manageable for half- or full-day trips with plenty of fishing time accounted, aimed at the Little Su's native fish populations of rainbow trout, Dolly Varden, arctic grayling, and round whitefish.

There are some nice fish in this section but do not expect fast and furious action; 'bows to 5-6 pounds or more are known to hide in the deeper pools. Also, there are several sweepers and the potential for a few log jams so caution is advised. Different from the lower river section, this area presents generally shallower and faster water.

If wanting a shot at both salmon and trout on a multi-day trip, launch at Houston and float down to the Burma Road access point on the lower river near tidewater. This trip is ideal if aiming to catch a load of salmon with all five species available throughout the summer months. Trout, char, and grayling, while not plentiful, do show up on the end of the line with some frequency.

(Courtesy Jeff Varvil)

Anglers need to be prepared for spending three to five days out in a semi-remote area in relative solitude. The river in this section is heavily wooded and both deeper and slower than the upper portion, exposing an abundance of structure that are almost guaranteed to hold large concentrations of, foremost, salmon. Sweepers and minor log jams may be an obstacle in places, yet the main issue is that the river winds considerably, slowing down the float. There are also many gravel bars where to pull over and fish from and camp.

The confluence with Lake Creek (draining out of Nancy Lake) is a relative hot spot that is especially known for its great red and silver salmon fishery. It is located approximately halfway between Houston and Burma Road.

The last stretch of Little Susitna prior to take-out is where anglers will come across schools of chrome salmon only hours away from the salt. The river flows very slowly here, straightens out somewhat, and becomes wider as well. Expect power boats to be present along with a fair amount of angling pressure, especially on the better holes.

# Eklutna Tailrace

King SALMON

Red SALMON

Chum SALMON

Silver SALMON

Dolly VARDEN

**Highlights:** Productive fishing for king and silver salmon in a very accessible location, ideal for anglers of all ages and those with physical disabilities.

**Best Fishing:** Early June to early September. **Regulatory Restrictions:** Liberal.

**Location:** Matanuska Valley/Knik Arm drainage, Palmer area, Old Glenn Highway, 33 miles northeast of Anchorage, 15 miles south of Palmer.

**Description:** The Eklutna Tailrace is a manufactured structure, the glacial waters originating at Eklutna Lake high in the Chugach Mountains. Channeled through a pipe down to a power plant at the base of the mountain, the water is then released into a long channel that connects with the Knik River. Flowing low, relatively clear, and greenish blue and nearly current free in spring, the Eklutna begins to rise with the advent of warm weather promoting greater snowmelt. The months of June through August see optimal stream conditions as the channel fills with silty glacial green water, encouraging a fair current, prompting salmon migrations to enter the tailrace without any hesitation unlike early in the season when low water largely prevents fish from exiting the Knik. During periods of extended hot or rainy weather, the Eklutna turns almost gray, slowing down the fishing.

Some brush and birch trees line the banks but the tailrace flows mostly through a quite open and accessible area.

*The trailrace is primarily a bait plunking location.*

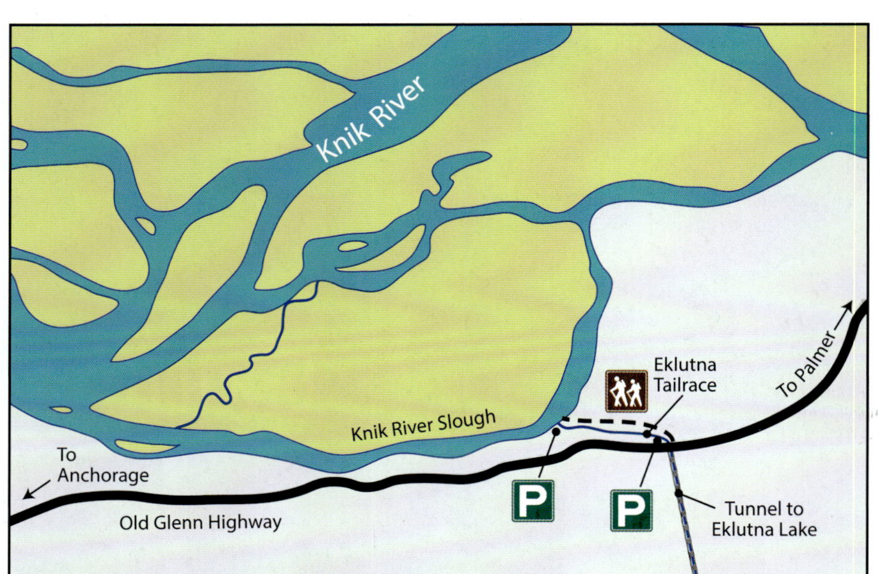


**Facilities:** Developed parking and restrooms.
**Access:** From Milepost 29.6 of the Glenn Highway, turn east onto Old Glenn Highway to Milepost 3.9, left on access road short distance to large parking area and mouth of stream. Additional access by continuing to Milepost 4.1 Old Glenn Highway and stream crossing. Parking available. Trail leads along north side of stream to Knik River confluence.

## Rules & Regulations

**Open Season:** January 1 through December 31.
**Open Area:** The entire tailrace is open to fishing.
**Legal Gear/Tackle:** All types of gear and tackle allowed, including bait.

**King Salmon**
- Open season is January 1 through December 31.
- Bag limit is (1) per day and (1) in possession (20 inches or longer). For kings less than 20 inches (Jacks), the limit is (10).

**All Other Salmon**
- Open all season (see general "Open Season" above).
- Red, pink, chum, and silver salmon bag limit is (3) per day and (3) in possession (16 inches or longer). For salmon less than 16 inches (Jacks), the limit is (10).

**Dolly Varden**
- Open all season (see general "Open Season" above).
- Bag limit is (5) per day and (5) in possession, only (1) over 12 inches.

**Other Fishes**
- Open all season (see general "Open Season" above).
- Whitefish has no bag or possession limit, no size restrictions.
- Burbot bag limit is (5) per day and (5) in possession, any size.

## Fishing Eklutna Tailrace

**Access:** ★★★★
**Scenery:** ★★★★
**Wildlife:** ★
**Sight Fishing:** ★
**Bank/Wading:** ★★★★★
**Boat/Floating: N/A**

**Species:** King, chum, and silver salmon, and Dolly Varden. Small runs of red and pink salmon.

**Summary:** Eklutna Tailrace has become one of the top salmon streams in the Matanuska Valley and one of the better and more liberal roadside freshwater fisheries in Southcentral. Once stocked with red and chum salmon to enhance commercial interests, the tailrace is now home to early-run king and silver salmon to take angling pressure off the area's natural salmon populations. Not all fish in the Eklutna are of hatchery origin, however, as a fair number of salmon bound for upstream tributaries of the Knik River swing by the tailrace to rest and thus become available to anglers.

One of the big bonuses regarding the tailrace is that it is accessible to just about anyone. With a well-developed fishing area intended to free up access to the water by wheelchair users and others with mobility challenges, the Eklutna is a blessing.

The best place to connect with fish in the tailrace is right at the mouth and the first 20 yards or so above and below. Salmon school up here and the action can be outstanding.

King salmon is the main species here in terms of angler participation and elbow-to-elbow crowds are the norm at the height of the run. Whereas many freshwater king fisheries across the region are expanding the number of regulations in an effort to stem harvest levels, the Eklutna is open daily – year-round – and all tackle and methods (except snagging) is allowed.

On the heels of the kings come silver salmon. Considerably more prolific, the silvers show in big numbers by late summer and continue to be present well into autumn thanks in part to the influx of late-run fish headed for other drainages mixing in with the hatchery fish.

Reds, chums, and pinks are for the most part incidental catches to fishing for silver salmon. The runs are small compared to other species, although chums do provide some decent action and a small number of these fish do spawn in the tailrace. Far from ideal for productive red salmon fishing, Eklutna does boast a number of these fish every season, with most fish succumbing to bait.

Opportunistic sea-run Dolly Varden move into the tailrace in summer and remain into fall, feeding on salmon eggs. There are usually not very many of them but enough to provide some decent action should an angler decide to target these char using ultra-light gear.

### Fish Availability

🔴 = *High* 🟠 = *Moderate* 🟣 = *Low* ⚫ = *Closed*

| *Species* | *APR* | *MAY* | *JUN* | *JUL* | *AUG* | *SEP* | *OCT* |
|---|---|---|---|---|---|---|---|
| **King Salmon** | 🟣 | 🟣🟣🟣🟠 | 🟠🔴🔴🔴 | 🟠🟣🟣🟣 | 🟣🟣 | | |
| **Red Salmon** | | | 🟣 | 🟣🟣🟠🟠 | 🟣🟣🟣🟣 | 🟣 | |
| **Chum Salmon** | | | 🟣 | 🟣🟣🟠🟠 | 🟠🟠🟣🟣 | 🟣🟣🟣🟣 | 🟣 |
| **Silver Salmon** | | | | 🟣🟣🟠🟠 | 🔴🔴🔴🟠 | 🟠🟠🟣🟣 | 🟣🟣🟣🟣 |
| **Dolly Varden** | | 🟣🟣🟣🟣 | 🟣🟣🟠🟠 | 🟠🟠🟠🟠 | 🟠🟠🟠🟠 | 🟣🟣🟣🟣 | 🟣🟣🟣🟣 |
| Angling Pressure | | 🟣🟣 | 🟠🔴🔴🔴 | 🔴🟠🟠🟠 | 🔴🔴🔴🟠 | 🟠🟣🟣🟣 | |

## King Salmon

**Rating:** ★★ Fair.
**Season:** January 1 through December 31.
**Timing:** April 25 – August 10; peak June 15 – July 5.
**Size:** Average 12 – 25 pounds, up to 50 pounds.
**Tackle:** Spinners, attractors, and bait.
**Tips:** Casting chrome spinners with a blue or green combination is effective on kings. If the water is very glacial, try something chartreuse or orange. Drifting salmon roe with a bobber or letting the bait sit on the bottom with an attractor can be deadly and is the method of choice by the vast majority of anglers.

If access to a boat, the mouth of Eklutna is a relative hot spot in May and first half of June as water levels and flow in the tailrace are very low, prompting most salmon to hold in the Knik River confluence area. As the water increases in depth and flow, the fish begin migrating upstream to the roadside access points.

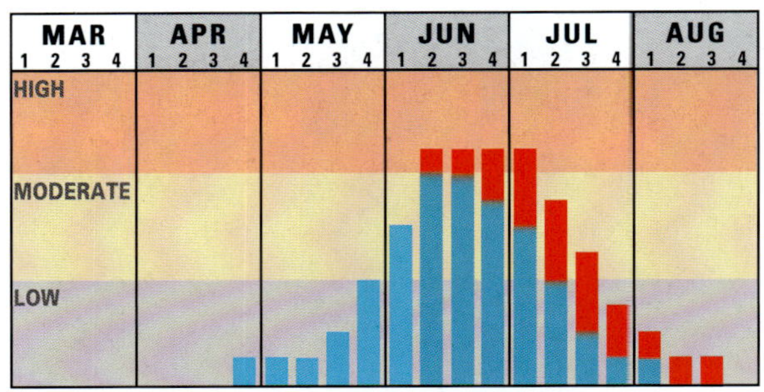


*Eklutna Tailrace King Salmon* ● = Fresh ● = Spawning

(Courtesy Stephen Stidham)

*Many of the kings taken at Eklutna display some degree of color or maturation, such as this large specimen caught by Armendariz Stidham. Brighter, but fewer, fish are available earlier in the summer yet the majority of chinooks arrive here in mid-season (late June/early July).*

## Red Salmon

**Rating:** ★½ Poor to fair.
**Season:** January 1 through December 31.
**Timing:** June 25 – September 15; peak July 15 – August 5.
**Size:** Average 3 – 6 pounds, up to 11 pounds.
**Tackle:** Bait.
**Tips:** These salmon are tough to catch in this location despite being fairly abundant at times. Success can be had by fishing small clusters of salmon roe stationary on the bottom or suspended under a strike indicator. Krill-flavored roe seems to work best.

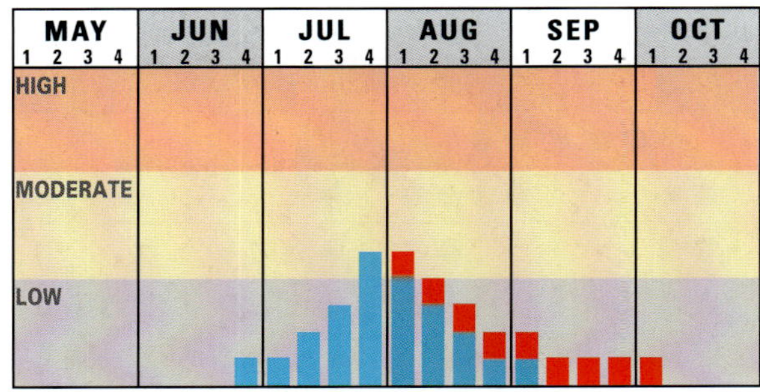

*Eklutna Tailrace Red Salmon* ● = Fresh ● = Spawning

## Chum Salmon

**Rating:** ★★ Fair.
**Season:** January 1 through December 31.
**Timing:** June 25 – October 5; peak July 25 – August 5.
**Size:** Average 6 – 12 pounds, up to 16 pounds.
**Tackle:** Spoons, spinners, attractors, and bait.
**Tips:** As the water is very silty, fish any lure very slowly. Attractor/bait combination can be good at times, either fished stationary on the bottom or allowed to drift along with the current. Fluorescent colors are generally best. Schools of chums generally hold right at the mouth of the creek with smaller numbers available upstream along the tailrace.

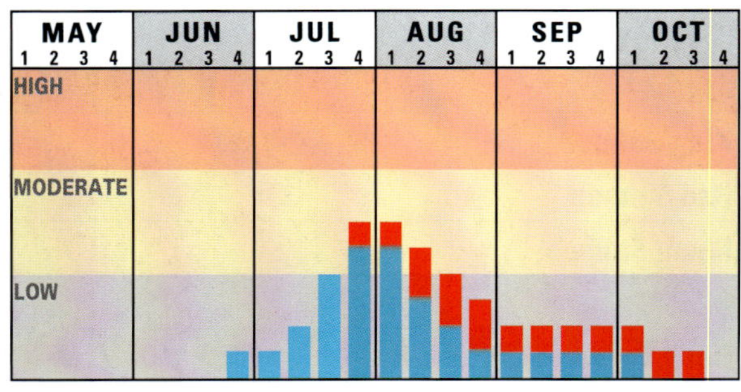

*Eklutna Tailrace Chum Salmon* ● = Fresh ● = Spawning

## Silver Salmon

**Rating:** ★★★ Good.
**Season:** January 1 through December 31.
**Timing:** June 25 – October 25; peak August 1 – 20.
**Size:** Average 5 – 10 pounds, up to 18 pounds.
**Tackle:** Spinners, attractors, and bait.
**Tips:** Letting a small attractor with a chunk of salmon roe sit on the bottom is the most effective way of hooking up with a silver but chrome spinners in sizes 3 and 4 can be hot as well. Some anglers do well using bait with a strike indicator, letting the setup float along the length of the tailrace from the weir down to the mouth.

The sweet spot for silvers tend to be right at the mouth of the tailrace and immediately below. This is a popular area for those soaking bait but some fish are caught on lures too. Up along the banks of the tailrace, anglers sometimes do very well tossing spinners. Do not forget to scout the section of water below the weir.

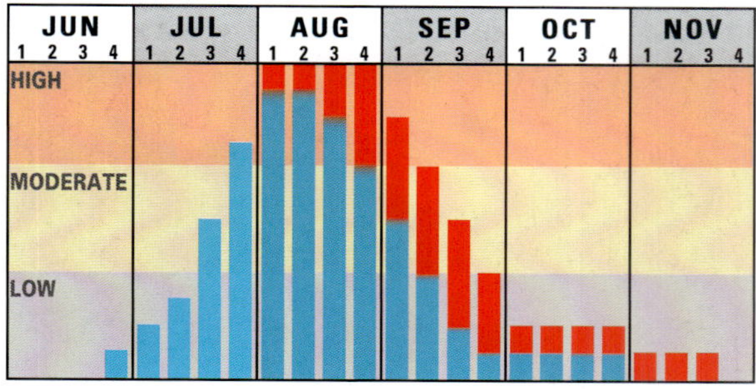

Eklutna Tailrace Silver Salmon ● = Fresh ● = Spawning

## Dolly Varden

**Rating:** ★★ Fair.
**Season:** January 1 through December 31.
**Timing:** May 1 – September 30; peak July 15 – Sept. 1.
**Size:** Average 8 – 14 inches, up to 5 pounds.
**Tackle:** Spinners, attractors, flies, and bait.
**Tips:** Small smolt or forage imitation lures and flies catch fish. During the salmon runs, use beads or corkies. If targeting char to keep, try salmon roe fished stationary on the bottom. The mouth of the tailrace has traditionally been the best spot.

*A couple of local anglers enjoy some early autumn quiet time at the Knik River confluence, hoping to net one or more late-season coho. This is the prime spot for all species of fish moving into the tailrace and a good place to intercept runs destined for areas farther up the Knik drainage.*

# Other Productive Fisheries & Additional Opportunities

## FISH CREEK

**Fishing:** ★★★ **Scenery:** ★★★
**Accessibility:** ★★ **Solitude:** ★★½
**Location:** Matanuska Valley drainage, Wasilla area, 57 miles north of Anchorage, 16 miles south of Wasilla.
**Access:** Milepost 42.2 Parks Highway. South on Knik-Goose Bay Road 16.1 miles to stream crossing. There is considerable private property on the middle and upper stream sections.
**Facilities:** Parking and primitive camping.
**Species:** Red and silver salmon, rainbow trout, Dolly Varden, and whitefish. Also smaller numbers of pink and chum salmon.
**Restrictions:** King salmon fishing prohibited. Closed to all fishing from April 15 through June 14. Weekend-only salmon fishery starting in early August. Consult ADF&G regulations.
**Fishing:** This rather small clearwater stream drains a fairly large area that include several lakes, most notably Big Lake. Anglers here primarily target the late summer run of silvers on the far lower end of the stream near tidewater at the mouth but other salmon species, as well as trout, char, and whitefish, may be found in varying numbers. This is a popular spot among locals.

The salmon season kicks off late on Fish Creek, usually around the second week of August and just in time to intercept the peak migration of silver salmon into the drainage. As the area open to salmon fishing is in or just above the tidal effects of Knik Arm, anglers need to consult the movement of tides carefully in order to hit the waves of chrome salmon arriving fresh from the salt. Although the stream does support a very substantial run of red salmon, due to the late season opener most of these fish have already moved through to spawn in headwater lakes and their tributaries. A few nice reds are available, however. It is the same with pinks and chums.

Much less interest is paid to the resident species of this stream. Decent populations of rainbow trout and Dolly Varden are present and can be found throughout Fish Creek as well as tributary lakes and streams. The upper and middle portions yield fair to good action. In late fall (October and November), a good run of round whitefish moves into the upper section of the creek.

In Big Lake, anglers successfully engage arctic char in addition to trout and burbot. Some northern pike up to 20 pounds or more may be present.

**Red Salmon.** Poor to fair; August 10 – 20; average 3 – 6 pounds. Flies and bait; fish salmon roe on the bottom, drift flies through migration channels.
**Silver Salmon.** Good; August 10 – 25; average 5 – 10 pounds. Spinners, flies, and bait; salmon roe is best in holes and on high tide, cast spinners at mouth, drift flies in faster water upstream.
**Rainbow Trout.** Fair to good; June 15 – October 10; average 8 – 16 inches. Spinners and flies work well. Try using dry flies/insect imitations or egg imitations when salmon spawn.
**Dolly Varden.** Fair; July 15 – October 10; average 8 – 15 inches. Spinners and flies; early in season fish the lower stream, go higher up in late summer and fall.

## COTTONWOOD CREEK

**Fishing:** ★★★ **Scenery:** ★★½
**Accessibility:** ★★½ **Solitude:** ★★½
**Location:** Matanuska Valley drainage, Wasilla area, 45 to 50 miles north of Anchorage, 4 to 7 miles south of Wasilla.
**Access:** Although there are a multitude of smaller roads crossing the stream throughout the Wasilla area, most of these locations have very limited access due to private land. The majority of fishing is done on the lower end of the stream along Knik-Goose Bay Road (from Milepost 42.2 Parks Highway/Main Street) as access is more readily available.
*A. Fern Bridge* – Milepost 1.3; southeast on Fern Street 0.1 mile to stream crossing. Parking for smaller vehicles. Respect private property.
*B. Edlund Bridge* – Milepost 2.6; south on Edlund Road 0.2 mile to stream crossing. Parking for smaller vehicles. Respect private property.
*C. Fairview Bridge* – Milepost 4.0; south on Fairview Loop Road 2.4 miles to stream crossing. Parking for smaller vehicles. Respect private property.
*D. Creek Mouth* – Milepost 4.0; south on Fairview Loop Road 1.9 miles to sharp turn in road, straight on Hayfield Road 1.3 miles, left on access road 0.5 mile to stream. Large parking area. May be very muddy after a rain. This is the tidewater portion of Cottonwood; be cautious.
**Facilities:** Parking and primitive camping available. Hotels/motels, restaurants, sporting goods, retail shopping, and many other services available in town of Wasilla.
**Species:** Red and silver salmon, rainbow trout, and Dolly Varden. Occasional pink salmon.
**Restrictions:** King salmon fishing prohibited. Closed to all fishing April 15 through June 14. Only the lower portion of the stream is open to salmon fishing. Consult ADF&G regulations.
**Fishing:** As with a few of the other smaller streams in the valley, Cottonwood is another weekend-only salmon fishery targeting reds and silvers. Although a decent-sized run of reds makes it up the creek destined for headwater lakes, fishing for them in the slack water near the mouth can be difficult at times. However, if water conditions are correct (clear and moving) and a big school is present, it can be worthwhile. The silvers, on the other hand, are aggressive and prone to strike a variety of lures and bait. Numbers of these fish come in on the tides in late summer.

The lower section of Cottonwood (in and near the tidal zone) is not really known for rainbow trout and Dolly Varden; these species are better targeted in the upper parts. They are widely distributed throughout the stream, from a few miles above the mouth to the lakes and their tributaries. Fishing for trout, especially, can be very productive during the summer and fall months, with some specimens pushing several pounds. Most of the fish are only about a foot long but generally abundant. Char, on the other hand, are not present in any numbers but a few fish are taken, including some really nice ones.

For anglers wanting to expand their Cottonwood trip, include a few of the connecting lakes to the itinerary, such as Wasilla and Cottonwood, both of which harbor native populations of trout and char. A few of these rainbows may weigh 4 to 6 pounds or more.
**Red Salmon.** Fair; July 15 – August 1; average 4 – 6 pounds. Flies and bait; fish salmon roe stationary on the bottom, drift flies through schools of migrating reds on outgoing tide.
**Silver Salmon.** Good; August 5 – 25; average 5 – 10 pounds. Spinners, flies, and bait; salmon roe is best, slow drift or on the bottom. Toss spinners on incoming and high tide, flies on outgoing tide.
**Rainbow Trout.** Fair to good; June 15 – September 30; average 8 – 16 inches. Spinners and flies are popular. Search out upper reaches of the stream using dry flies/insect imitations, egg imitations when salmon spawn.
**Dolly Varden.** Poor to fair; June 20 – September 30; average 8 – 15 inches. Spinners and flies best options. Some fish caught in tidal zone early in season, go higher up in late summer and fall.

## POINT MACKENZIE LAKES

**Fishing:** ★★★½ **Scenery:** ★★★
**Accessibility:** ★★★ **Solitude:** ★★★★
**Location:** Matanuska Valley drainages, Wasilla area, 69-81 miles northeast of Anchorage, 27-39 miles southwest of Wasilla.
**Access:** The paved Knik-Goose Bay Road begins at the Parks Highway junction in downtown Wasilla (Milepost 42.2) and provides easy and convenient access to the entire Point Mackenzie area (including Little Susitna River), with gravel side roads leading to several lakes. The indicated mileposts are for the Knik-Goose Bay Road. None of these locations are recommended for large RVs. Note private land in area and respect posted boundaries.
*A. Carpenter Lake* – Milepost 17.2; west on Point Mackenzie Road 7.6 miles to a "T," turn right, then left on Ayrshire Road 1.2 miles, right on dirt road 0.5 mile to lake. Parking. Landlocked salmon, rainbow trout, arctic char.
*B. Farmer Lake* – Milepost 17.2; west on Point Mackenzie Road 7.6 miles to a "T," turn left, 3.4 miles to Holstein Avenue, turn right, 2.7 miles to access on left. Parking. Locate trail leading short distance to lake. Rainbow trout.
*C. Barley Lake* – Milepost 17.2; west on Point Mackenzie Road 7.6 miles to a "T," turn left, 3.4 miles to Holstein Avenue, turn right, 1.6 miles to Guernsey Road, left at 4-way intersection on Guernsey Road for 1.1 miles, right at second farm lane 0.1 mile. Parking. Locate trail leading short distance to lake. Landlocked salmon, rainbow trout.
*D. Twin Island Lake* – Milepost 17.2; west on Point Mackenzie Road 7.6 miles to a "T," turn left, 8.0 miles to unimproved seismic trail on left, 0.3 mile to southwest corner of Mat-Su Borough lot, east 0.1 mile to lake. Parking. Rainbow trout.
*E. Lorraine Lake* – Milepost 17.2; west on Point Mackenzie Road 7.6 miles to a "T," turn left, 12.3 miles to pullout on left, 0.2 mile by 4-wheel drive vehicle or hike to lake. Parking. Rainbow trout, arctic grayling.
**Facilities:** Parking only at these lakes.
**Species:** Landlocked salmon, rainbow trout, arctic char, and arctic grayling.
**Restrictions:** There are no area or location specific restrictions in place. Consult ADF&G regulations
**Fishing:** Located right across the narrow strait separating Anchorage from the Susitna forelands is a vast area containing dozens upon dozens of little lakes. Not all of them support populations of fish but many do. Also, most are very remote and require special means to access, such as float planes or boats. However, a handful of these are next to or near the limited road system and stocked with several popular game fish species. Yet even so, these waters receive very little angling pressure and are known to produce good to excellent fishing for those taking the drive off the Parks Highway.

With landlocked salmon, trout, char, and grayling being the targets, anglers can expect a nice variety of catches if spending a day or two in this area. The lakes are in close proximity to each other and consistently yield above average-sized fish.

While the lakes can be attempted from shore, those wise to these lowland lakes use float tubes, canoes, or kayaks in order to reach the deeper parts where fish concentrations are greatest. Some of these waters are very shallow along the shoreline.

The month of September is a great time to be out as all species focus on shallower, more accessible waters; even anglers casting off the bank do reasonably well. Expect a few specimens of trout and char to top 5 or 6 pounds, maybe more.

As these lakes are stocked with hatchery fish, there is also an upswing in activity right after plantings are made, usually sometime in early summer. For larger fish stretching into the teens or better, it is advised to search out structure in water between 20 and 30 feet.
**Landlocked Salmon.** Excellent; June 15 – January 1; average 7 – 15 inches. Fish often travel in large schools. Small spoons, spinners, jigs, flies, and bait. Carpenter and Barley lakes are the places to go
**Rainbow Trout.** Good to excellent; May 15 – January 1; average 8 – 22 inches. In spring, look for big trout along shoreline. All lakes have trout. Spoons, spinners, plugs, flies, and bait.
**Arctic Char.** Fair to good; May 15 – January 1; average 8 – 24 inches. Go deep near bottom in summer. Try Carpenter Lake. Spoons, plugs, jigs, bait.
**Arctic Grayling.** Good to excellent; May 15 – September 30; average 8 – 15 inches. Lorraine Lake has fish. Small spinners and flies best options.

## WASILLA CREEK

**Fishing:** ★★½ **Scenery:** ★★½
**Accessibility:** ★★ **Solitude:** ★★½

**Location:** Matanuska Valley drainage, Wasilla area, 36 miles north of Anchorage, 4 miles southeast of Wasilla.
**Access:** Turn off at Trunk Road exit ramp, Milepost 35.8 (northbound) or 36.2 (southbound) Parks Highway, left on E Fireweed Road 1.4 miles to sharp turn and Nelson Road, left on gravel road 0.7 mile to parking area with trail access to lower portion of Wasilla Creek (Rabbit Slough).
**Facilities:** Parking and primitive camping available.
**Species:** Pink and silver salmon, Dolly Varden. A few red and chum salmon, rainbow trout present.
**Restrictions:** King salmon fishing prohibited. Closed to all fishing April 15 through June 14. Fishing for salmon is open downstream of the railroad trestle bridge near the highway bridge, and only on the weekends. Consult ADF&G regulations.
**Fishing:** A local haunt, Wasilla Creek is primarily a weekend fishery as anglers are drawn here in search of silver salmon, the staple species of this small, clear-flowing stream. There is an abundance of private property in the area surrounding the creek, thus focusing nearly all angler traffic to the lower access point at Rabbit Slough on the Matanuska flats.

Draining into the upper end of Knik Arm and the mouth of Matanuska River, Wasilla is a tidewater stream in its lower reaches. Anglers usually concentrate their efforts around the tides but hiking upstream to holes and pools is certainly a valid option at any time of the day. Generally, since Wasilla is a rather diminutive body of water, action is best at dawn – preferably on a Saturday, since this is a weekend-only fishery.

(Courtesy Beverley Bailey)

(Courtesy Kelsey Gray)

Some adventurous anglers choose to launch a small watercraft into the slightly deeper and calmer section of stream below Rabbit Slough in order to access little-fished tidal holes teeming with salmon.

At the upper limit of allowable salmon fishing, anglers do wisely in searching out deeper slots as the stream flows quite rapidly here with numerous shallows limiting salmon holding areas and thus concentrating fish into a few places. Some nice silvers show up towards the end of August.

The far upper reaches of Wasilla, from the Parks crossing and above, is closed to salmon fishing but offers a quite decent shot at small trout and char starting in mid-summer and continuing into fall. Look for spawning salmon and there will likely be fish to be had. This is also an area to watch for private property.

**Pink Salmon.** Fair; July 15 – August 1; average 2 – 4 pounds. Small spoons, spinners, and flies will take fish. Find numbers of pinks in best condition off the Rabbit Slough access; mostly ripe fish higher up.
**Silver Salmon.** Fair; August 5 – 25; average 4 – 7 pounds. Spinners, flies, and bait effective, with salmon roe best. Scout lower stream for schools of incoming fish. Later in season, look in holes downstream of highway crossing.
**Rainbow Trout.** Poor to fair; July 15 – September 1; average 8 – 12 inches. Small spinners and flies draw strikes, primarily in upper reaches.
**Dolly Varden.** Fair to good; July 15 – September 15; average 8 – 12 inches. Small spinners and flies are used from tidewater to upper parts.

*Although being a very small stream, Wasilla supports decent numbers of primarily silver salmon. Check out various deep holes early on a Saturday morning and the fishing might be surprisingly good. Fish range from chrome to lightly blushed.*

## JIM CREEK

**Fishing:** ★★★★ **Scenery:** ★★★★★
**Accessibility:** ★½ **Solitude:** ★★

**Location:** Matanuska Valley drainage, Palmer area, 44 miles north of Anchorage, 11 miles south of Palmer.

**Access:** Turn onto Old Glenn Highway at Milepost 29.6 (northbound) or 42.1 (southbound) of the Glenn Highway and proceed to Milepost 11.5. East on Plumley Road 1.3 mile to a "T," right on Caudill Road 1.0 mile to sharp curve, continue 0.3 mile to gravel access road on left leading to large gravel parking area. There are several roads/ATV trails that lead to the stream at Knik River Flats (0.8 miles), most of which are in very rough shape, especially following a stretch of wet weather. For best driving conditions, select the road at the far west end of the lot, by the large signs.

**Facilities:** A large gravel parking lot is situated next to the road where the dirt road leading to the mouth of Jim Creek starts. Convenience store located nearby.

**Species:** Red, chum, and silver salmon, and Dolly Varden. A few pink salmon and an occasional king salmon, round whitefish, or burbot may be present.

**Restrictions:** King salmon fishing prohibited. Closed to all fishing from the second Saturday in August through December 31. Consult ADF&G regulations.

**Fishing:** Clearly one of the best fisheries in the valley, offering a small variety of salmon as well as char. Primarily a mid- to late summer hot spot, the big drawback to the stream's reputed excellent angling opportunities is the obvious lack of proper access. Thus, it is mainly local anglers fishing here who are prepared to take on the infamous rutted road and deep pot holes. Yet if willing to brave the maze of weathered dirt and mud roads, the scenery on a clear day at the creek mouth is absolutely stunning, with views of jagged mountain peaks and the Knik Glacier.

(Courtesy Chris Cox)

The vast majority of angling effort occurs right at the mouth of the stream where it flows into the glacial Knik River and the area of water immediately below, and for good reason. Salmon mass here prior to moving up the narrow and shallow Jim Creek itself (or other spawning waters farther up the Knik), proving a bonanza of sorts for anglers that line the confluence area in numbers. Also keep in mind that these fish may only be hours from tidewater so the quality for sport and consumption is superb.

It must be pointed out that the confluence area is also subject to frequent flooding from the Knik River, such as following a period of prolonged rain or hot weather that creates an abundance of glacial meltwater. Under such conditions, the usual sand and gravel flats at the creek mouth are completely under a foot or two of water, pushing anglers up against the wooded banks. The fish, however, are still there, sometimes in most surprising places.

The main draw to Jim are the very productive runs of red and silver salmon. Although the reds are not very good biters in the slack water of the stream, they can be caught on conventional tackle and flies with a bit of patience, with small clusters of krill-scented roe being best by far.

Silvers are great sportsters and respond enthusiastically to anglers' offerings. Two runs of these salmon pass through the area, the first in August destined for upper reaches of Jim Creek; the smaller and more unpredictable late run in

*Autumn view of the mouth of Jim Creek where it enters the glacial Knik River. This is a hot spot for salmon enthusiasts and may draw significant crowds at the height of the runs, in August. Gorgeous scenery and good fishing awaits.*

September is bound for side channels and sloughs of mainstem Knik River.

Scouting the creek proper towards the headwater lakes, usually by canoe, anglers will find schools of salmon migrating through the calm, smooth-flowing stream. Unlike the mouth, anyone fishing this part of Jim will likely find near complete solitude. Additionally, action for Dolly Varden is more consistent and can be very good at times in late summer and fall. Jim Lake and the other lakes connected to the creek support populations of these char as well.

**Red Salmon.** Fair to good; July 20 – August 10; average 4 – 7 pounds. Small spinners and flies take a few fish but most are caught soaking salmon roe on the bottom. Use bait at the mouth, artificial upstream.

**Chum Salmon.** Fair to good; July 25 – August 15; average 6 – 12 pounds. Spoons, spinners, flies, and bait all work. Creek mouth is best.

**Silver Salmon.** Good; August 10 – September 1; average 5 – 10 pounds. Spoons, spinners, and flies are effective. Salmon roe is deadly either fished stationary or with a strike indicator.

**Dolly Varden.** Fair to good; July 15 – September 1; average 8 – 15 inches. Bait is best at creek mouth; head upstream for better fishing using small spinners and flies.



## KEPLER-BRADLEY LAKES

**Fishing:** ★★★★ **Scenery:** ★★★½
**Accessibility:** ★★★★ **Solitude:** ★★★★

**Location:** Matanuska Valley drainages, Palmer area, 36 to 39 miles north of Anchorage, 6 miles south of Palmer.

**Access:** All lakes are situated within the Kepler-Bradley Lakes State Recreation Area and reached by side roads and/or trails from the Glenn Highway.

*A. Matanuska Lake* – Milepost 36.4; north on access road 0.2 mile to parking are and lake. Landlocked salmon, rainbow trout, and arctic char.

*B. Victor Lake* – Milepost 36.4; north on access road 0.2 mile to parking lot next to Matanuska Lake. Locate trail leading ½ mile to lake on right. Landlocked salmon.

*C. Klaire Lake* – Milepost 36.4; north on access road 0.2 mile to parking lot next to Matanuska Lake. Locate trail leading ½ mile to lake on left. Landlocked salmon.

*D. Echo Lake* – Milepost 37.1; turnout and parking. Follow trail down hill short distance to lake. Landlocked salmon, rainbow trout, and arctic char.

*E. Kepler & Bradley Lakes* – Milepost 37.3; north on Kepler Road short distance to parking area and private campground. Kepler is on left, Bradley on right. Rainbow

trout and arctic grayling.

*F. Canoe Lake* – Milepost 38.0; north on Colleen Street short distance, left on Bradley Lake Avenue 0.2 mile, right on Green Jade Place short distance, left on Killarney Drive 0.2 mile to access site on right. Short hike to lake. Rainbow trout and arctic grayling.

*G. Irene Lake* – Milepost 38.0; north on Colleen Street short distance, left on Bradley Lake Avenue 0.2 mile, right on

Green Jade Place short distance, left on Killarney Drive 0.4 mile to parking area. Trail leads 50 yards to lake. Rainbow trout and arctic char.

*H. Long Lake* – Milepost 38.0; north on Colleen Street short distance, left on Bradley Lake Avenue 0.2 mile, right on Green Jade Place short distance, left on Killarney Drive 0.6 mile, left on access road 0.1 mile to parking area. Trail leads ¼ mile to lake. Rainbow trout.

**Facilities:** Parking and primitive camping available. Boat rentals.

**Species:** Landlocked salmon, rainbow trout, arctic char, and arctic grayling.

**Restrictions:** No area-specific restrictions. Consult ADF&G regulations.

**Fishing:** This cluster of small lakes has a solid reputation for producing excellent catches of a wide variety of species. Although the general appearance of these waters is similar (surrounded by pristine birch forest), each supports one or two types of game fish, thus providing for a mixed bag depending on specific lake.

Stocked yearly by ADF&G, the Kepler-Bradley lake system has an abundance of smaller, "pan-sized" trout, char, and grayling that provide ample opportunities throughout the year. Thus, this is mainly a put-and-take fishery; however, a fair number of planters do survive to live multiple years and grow to respectable proportions, even by Alaska standards. As these lakes are very fertile, a few rainbows and char may attain 26 to 30 inches in length and weights of 6 to 10 pounds or more. Long Lake, for example, is strictly a catch-and-release water where the trout may average several pounds.

Though locally popular in winter, there is significantly less angling pressure during the summer months given the huge onslaught of salmon available in other nearby waters. In fact, some of these lakes offer a great solitary experience, especially the ones situated away from the main road. Casting from shore can be good but undoubtedly the best way to connect with these fish is by any sort of small watercraft, such as a float-tube or canoe.

Most years, ice-out occurs in late April to early May with freeze-up again in mid- to late October.

**Landlocked Salmon.** Excellent; June 1 – November 30; average 7 – 12 inches. Small spinners, flies, jigs, and bait.

**Rainbow Trout.** Good to excellent; May 15 – January 1; average 8 – 20 inches. Spinners, flies, and bait.

**Arctic Char.** Fair to good; May 15 – February 1; average 8 – 20 inches. Spoons, flies, jigs, and bait.

**Arctic Grayling.** Good to excellent; May 15 – September 30; average 7 – 12 inches. Spinners and flies.

## MATANUSKA AREA LAKES

**Fishing:** ★★★★ **Scenery:** ★★★★★
**Accessibility:** ★★★★ **Solitude:** ★★★★

**Location:** Matanuska Valley drainages, Sutton area, 60 to 88 miles northeast of Anchorage, 12 to 46 miles northeast of Palmer.

**Access:** The lakes in this area are all located along the Glenn Highway, often right next to the road but usually accessed by gravel side roads appropriate for most vehicles, including RVs. A few of them, however can only be reached by trail.

*A. Seventeenmile Lake* – Milepost 57.9; north on 58 Mile Road 0.5 mile, right 1.7 mile, left on Twin Hills Lane 0.3 mile, right on Seventeen Mile Boulevard 0.2 mile, right on Wishbone Place 0.2 mile to lake. Parking for all size vehicles, boat launch. Rainbow trout and arctic char.

*B. Ida Lake* – Milepost 73.0; west on Fish Lake Road 0.2 mile, left on Granvold Drive 0.4 mile, left on Ida Drive 0.2 mile, left on Oline Circle 0.1 mile to parking area. Trail leads down steep hill to lake. Kokanee, rainbow trout, and arctic grayling.

*C. Ravine Lake* – Milepost 83.3; north on Bonnie Lake Road 0.9 mile to lake on right. Parking. Rainbow trout.

*D. Lower Bonnie Lake* – Milepost 83.3; north Bonnie Lake

Road 1.1 mile to a "Y," right fork leads 0.9 mile to lake. Parking for all size vehicles, camping, and boat launch. Rainbow trout.

*E. Upper Bonnie Lake* – Milepost 83.3; north Bonnie Lake Road 1.1 mile to a "Y," right fork leads 0.9 mile to Lower Bonnie Lake and trailhead. Parking for all size vehicles and camping. Trail leads 2 miles east to lake. Rainbow trout.

*F. Long Lake* – Milepost 85.4; south to lake access. Parking for all size vehicles, camping, restrooms, and boat launch. Rainbow trout, lake trout, arctic char, and burbot.

**Facilities:** Depending on location. Parking, camping, restrooms, and boat launch available. Lodging, restaurants, gas, and RV facilities also present within area.
**Species:** Landlocked red salmon (Kokanee), rainbow trout, lake trout, arctic char, arctic grayling, and burbot.
**Restrictions:** No area-specific restrictions. Consult ADF&G regulations.
**Fishing:** The upper section of the valley along the turbid Matanuska River is as scenic as Alaska gets with absolute stunning panoramic views of the river and the surrounding jagged mountain landscape, complete with glaciers and a dense birch and alder forest that perfectly highlights the change of seasons, especially the brilliant colors of autumn.

*The lakes along the Matanuska River are situated in some of the most breathtaking scenery in the state and certainly worthy of being angling destinations for trout and char in and of themselves. This is a September view of Long Lake.*

There are a handful of lakes lining the Matanuska and the highway, offering a variety of game species. Some of the lakes are stocked by ADF&G on a regular basis, while a few support native populations of fish. In all, these scenic waters make for a terrific angling experience.

Most of the lakes are fairly small and easily scouted from the bank or using a float tube or canoe, with only a couple being relatively large and better suited for canoes and boats. Due to the elevation of these waters, break-up arrives late in spring (mid-May to early June) and freeze-up early in fall (October). Apart from being good open-water locations, they are also great spots to ice fish from November through April.

Expect some company on these lakes in summer, especially those next to the road, but anglers will generally find few other people present so a solitary experience is entirely possible, this being particularly the case on hike-in lakes or a couple of the larger ones where pressure tend to spread out.

Fish are typically most active in the early morning and late evening hours in summer with larger catches being made in the deeper and cooler sections of the lakes. While casting from shore can be good for smaller specimens, the bigger ones are taken by anglers using float tubes or other forms of watercraft in order to access proper depth (20-30 feet) and structure. Peak fishing, however, occurs in June and September when the various species are found closer to shore in shallower water and thus readily accessible to anglers using standard methods and techniques.

While stocked lakes have a tendency to produce an abundance of smaller fish (7 to 15 inches), the lack of significant angling pressure along with the fertile conditions of these waters make for very real possibilities of hooking up with larger than average fish, this being especially the case concerning trout and char. Seeing schools of rainbows, some individual fish which may top 25 inches, is common along the shoreline in early summer. Likewise, the larger and deeper lakes (such as Long Lake), contain trophy class specimens of arctic char that may weigh 10 to 15 pounds; lake trout up to 20 pounds or more have been reported.

The Matanuska area lakes are perfect locations to spend a few hours between main fishing destinations. However, for anglers that enjoy lake fishing and want to invest some time exploring these waters fully, rewards can be bountiful.
**Kokanee.** Fair; May 20 – September 30; average 7 – 12 inches. Try proper structure at Ida Lake. Small spinners, flies, and bait.
**Rainbow Trout.** Good to excellent; May 20 – January 1; average 7 – 20 inches. Seventeenmile, Ida, Ravine, and Upper Bonnie lakes are best. Spoons, spinners, plugs, flies, and bait.
**Lake Trout.** Fair; May 25 – January 1; average 3 – 10 pounds. Long Lake is the only spot with this species. Spoons, plugs, jigs, and bait.
**Arctic Char.** Fair to good; May 20 – February 1; average 8 – 23 inches. Seventeenmile and Long Lake only; big fish at Long. Spoons, jigs, and bait.
**Arctic Grayling.** Good to excellent; May 20 – September 30; average 7 – 12 inches. Only Ida Lake has fish. Spinners and flies.
**Burbot.** Fair; September 15 – April 30; average 10 – 20 inches. Long Lake only. Spoons, jigs, and bait.

# ADDITIONAL OPPORTUNITIES

## West Side Susitna River Drainage

There is a multitude of options to consider regarding fishing opportunities on the west side of the vast Susitna River drainage. As the Susitna is a glacial system anglers focus their time on clearwater tributaries where healthy populations of salmon, trout, char, grayling, and pike thrive. During the height of the season, expect to share these waters with other anglers – especially when the kings are running in June and the first part of July.

The means of access to these remote locations include aircraft and boat, primarily from Anchorage but also various towns and communities along the road such as Wasilla. Flying time can range from as little as 15 minutes to over an hour depending on final destination and weather and water conditions.

Alexander Creek near the terminus of the Susitna is a good spot for salmon, primarily silvers (first half of August). It also receives a big run of pinks at the mouth and supports a prolific stock of rainbow trout and arctic grayling in its upper reaches. This is also a great stream to float with little experience needed.

A little ways upstream of Alexander is the renowned Deshka River. The tannic-stained Deshka has a phenomenal late May-June run of kings that may top 40,000 fish in some years, along with a showing of pinks in latter July that can exceed one million. Silvers are also abundant (in August) and all of these species yield excellent angling opportunities. Rainbow trout and arctic grayling are also present in the upper parts of Deshka. A tributary lake of the Deshka – Trapper Lake – is a hot spot for northern pike.

Lake Creek is a swift clearwater stream that holds strong runs of salmon, particularly kings (late June-early July, pinks (late July), and silvers (late August-early September), but can also be good for reds and chums (late July-early August). Important resident species include rainbow trout and arctic grayling, with a large population of northern pike found in Chelatna Lake (headwater to Lake Creek). The creek is tributary of Yentna, which in turn flows into the Susitna.

Also on the Yentna is the Talachulitna River. This clear flowing river is top notch for raft trips and supports big runs of kings in late June-early July, reds and pinks in late July-early August, and silver salmon late August-early September. What put this location on the map was its great summer and fall fly-fishing for rainbow trout and grayling.

Apart from the above-mentioned waters, there are also dozens of other smaller drainages that enjoy good to excellent sport fishing opportunities and less people. Quite a few of the waters mentioned above also have lodges and guide services present.

## Salmon Viewing

Throughout the Matanuska Valley there is an abundance of little clearwater streams and ponds where observing migrating and spawning salmon is a possibility. All five species may be seen in their respective seasons, with the best viewing historically being from July into October.

The following is a listing of some of the better places to go visit with the added chance of seeing bears.

**Eagle River Nature Center:** From Milepost 15.3 Glenn Highway, take the Eagle River exit and head east to Eagle River Road, take right and continue 12.6 miles to end of road at center. Parking for all size vehicles. Developed trail leads to viewing platforms overlooking clearwater stream and the surrounding valley and mountain range. Red and chum salmon are chiefly present from mid-August to mid-September, with silver salmon peaking in numbers during the month of October. Decent opportunity to spot feeding brown bears in autumn. Awesome scenery.

**Bodenburg Creek:** At Milepost 29.6 Glenn Highway, take Old Glenn Highway exit and proceed to large parking area on left at Mile 12.9. Gin-clear stream and a series of small ponds on other side of road receive spawning red and chum salmon from mid-August to mid-September.

**Yellow Creek:** Milepost 69.1 Glenn Highway. Small, elongated pulloff along the Matanuska River flood plain. This shallow clearwater stream is found right next to road. Spawning red and chum salmon are present from mid-August to mid-September and silvers from late September to mid-October. Great spot for picture taking.

**Big Lake & Fish Creek:** Turn west onto Big Lake Road at Milepost 52.3 Parks Highway and continue to pullout on right at Mile 3.5 next to Big Lake outlet. Viewing platform present. Red salmon migrate through creek into the lake from late July through August, with a late run spawning along the lake shoreline from mid-September through early October. Fair number of silvers can be observed in the stream by the bridge during September and October.

Willow • Montana • Talkeetna • Trapper Creek

# Central Susitna

**King Salmon • Pink Salmon • Chum Salmon • Silver Salmon**
**Rainbow Trout • Dolly Varden • Arctic Grayling**

*Canoe Lakes*

*Trophy Kings*

*Hike-In Solitude*

*Trout Streams*

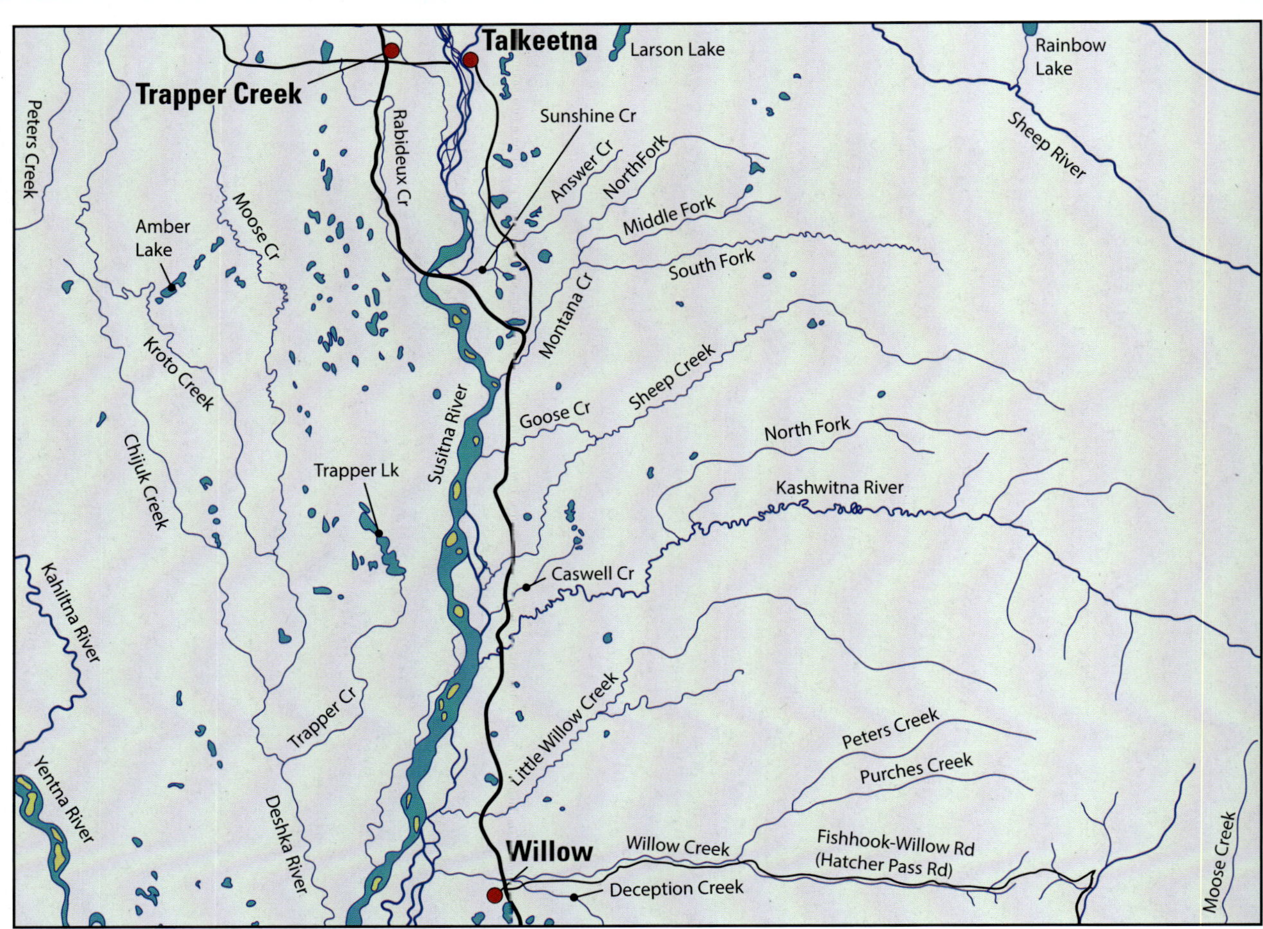


**Area Population Centers:** Willow, Montana, and Talkeetna
**Key Species:** King, Pink, Chum, and Silver Salmon, Rainbow Trout, Arctic Grayling
**Other Species:** Red Salmon, Lake Trout, Dolly Varden, Arctic Char, Round Whitefish, Northern Pike, and Burbot
**Main Destinations/Hot Spots:** Willow, Sheep, and Montana Creeks
**Other Destinations:** Little Willow, Caswell, and Goose Creeks, Kashwitna River
**Additional Opportunities:** Fly-In Fishing

**Summary of Fishing:** With a sparse population, the southern half of the Susitna Valley experiences a wide range of available species and types of water within a relatively small area, making it an awesome destination for visitors and local anglers alike. The broad alluvial flood plain of the glacial Susitna River drainage provides a myriad of smaller clearwater rivers and creeks that receive large and healthy salmon runs along with resident species such as trout, char, grayling, and whitefish. Vegetation in the area is mainly birch, alder, spruce, and cottonwood as distant mountain ranges are obvious on the horizon. Wildlife, such as moose, bear, and beaver, is commonly observed at some of the fisheries.

This is the part of the "Mat-Su" region that stream fishing opportunities begin to flourish. Several main clearwater tributaries of the Susitna are crossed by the Parks Highway and make for great spots to fish for a few hours to a week or more. Despite being right on one of the busiest roads in the state, the streams here are expansive and largely undeveloped, giving anglers generous space in which to hike and explore.

A great many anglers keep coming back here as runs of king, pink, chum, and silver salmon fill area waters during the brief summer season and wild populations of rainbow trout and arctic grayling are present continuously from spring through fall.

For sight-fishing, this is really the area to explore, and for those interested in hiking a distance away from the stream crossings, there are ample opportunities. Yet the fishing is also very productive in the lakes in this area, with both hatchery and native stocks of trout, char, and pike available.

May to October is best time to fish this area.

# Willow Creek

King SALMON

Pink SALMON

Chum SALMON

Silver SALMON

Rainbow TROUT

Arctic GRAYLING

**Highlights:** Renowned salmon and trout stream, yielding runs of multiple salmon species in addition to great fly-fishing for rainbows and grayling. Perfect water for rafting.

**Best Fishing:** Mid-June to late September. **Regulatory Restrictions:** Moderate.

**Location:** Southern Susitna Valley drainage, community of Willow, Parks Highway, 71 miles north of Anchorage, 41 miles south of Talkeetna.

**Description:** Flowing swiftly out of the Talkeetna Mountains, the Willow is a good-sized clearwater run-off stream surrounded by hardwood forest with an abundance of deep pools and runs along its course, home to a myriad of popular game fish species. There are three main parts to the Willow; the upper stream from the headwaters to the confluence with Deception Creek above the Parks Highway bridge, the middle section from Deception Creek to halfway down to the mouth, and the lower section which includes the lower couple of miles and the Susitna River confluence.

The upper creek section along the Hatcher Pass Road is narrow and rocky, a set of rapids near the headwaters effectively blocking fish migrations farther up the drainage. A few ardent king salmon, however, will manage to negotiate the rapids pending ideal water conditions. Fly-fishers in search of trout, char, and grayling frequent this area.

The middle section is accessed from the Parks Highway and is a favorite angling destinations for those seeking

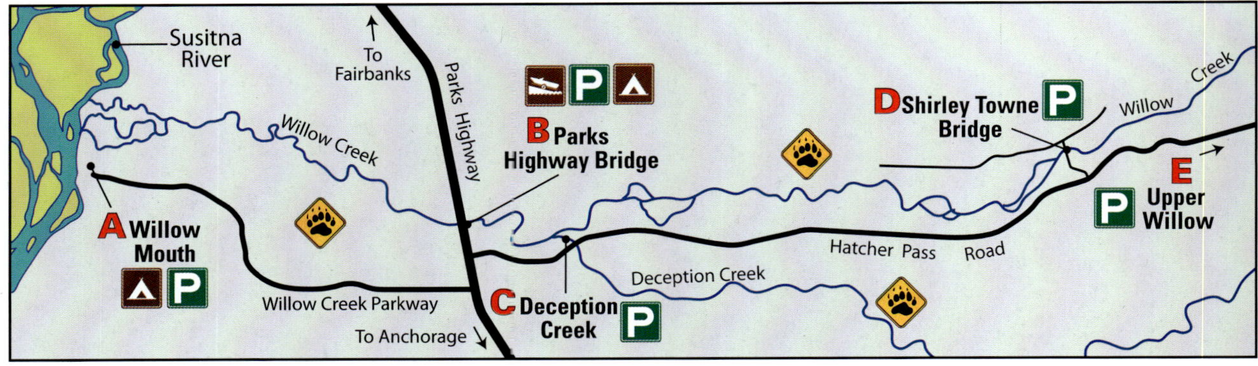


a combination of excellent salmon and trout action. The stream begins to widen below the highway, becoming deep and not quite as swift as the upper areas. Holes and runs are pronounced, holding big schools of fish. Anglers can hike in from the road with miles of water to cover that sees relatively little competition.

Approaching the Susitna River confluence, the Willow splits into three different channels, all of them quite shallow with deeper parts scattered throughout. It is the mouth of this channel, however, that holds the largest concentrations of fish (and anglers). The Willow Creek Parkway provides ample access to the mouth, an area that has slow-flowing water and easy fishing from the bank.

**Facilities:** There are a multitude of facilities and services at the stream and in the community of Willow nearby. Campgrounds, RV parking, guide services, tackle shops, grocery stores, gas stations, boat launches, and lodging among other amenities are available.

*The Willow Creek boat launch as seen from the Parks Highway bridge. Quite a few airboats operate from this location, heading downstream to more remote sections of stream. This is also a good spot to put in or take out rafts.*

**Access:** The Parks Highway provides three areas of access, including the upper and middle reaches and the Susitna confluence. Undeveloped trails at all access points provide anglers with the opportunity to explore many miles of off-the-road water.

Rafters usually put in at the Parks Highway bridge and float down to the mouth, a full-day trip that offers outstanding fishing in a semi-remote setting. Powerboats also negotiate the Willow, jetting downstream to productive holes and the mouth of the Willow and beyond.

**Note:** The Hatcher Pass Road begins in Palmer (Milepost 0) and ends in Willow (Milepost 49.1). Mileage shown in parenthesis is distance from Parks Highway junction in the community of Willow.

**A. Mouth of Willow** – Milepost 70.7. West on Willow Creek Parkway 3.9 miles to recreation area. Developed trails lead ¼ mile to lower channel of stream mouth. Parking for all size vehicles, campground, RV parking, restrooms, firepits, and picnic tables.

**B. Parks Highway Bridge** – Milepost 71.4. Highway crosses river. Parking for all size vehicles, campground, RV parking, restrooms, guide services, convenience store, tackle shop, and boat launch. Improvised trails lead downstream along creek.

**C. Deception Creek** – Milepost 71.2. East on Hatcher Pass (Fishhook-Willow) Road to Milepost 48.2 (Mile 1.7), left on Deception Creek Wayside short distance to parking area. Not suitable for large RVs. Trail leads 50 yards to confluence area of Deception Creek and Willow Creek.

**D. Shirley Towne Bridge** – Milepost 71.2. East on Hatcher Pass (Fishhook-Willow) Road to Milepost 5.8, left on Shirley Town Drive 0.3 mile to stream crossing. Dirt access road on right leads short distance to gravel area with limited parking. Not suitable for large RVs. This is a popular spot to launch rafts to float the upper reaches of the creek.

**E. Upper Willow** – Milepost 71.2. East on Hatcher Pass (Fishhook-Willow) Road to Milepost 34.5—30.0 (Mile 14.6—19.1); road parallels stream. Limited parking at pullouts and along shoulder of road. Some RV space.

## Rules & Regulations

**Open Season:** Downstream of Parks Highway bridge, fishing is allowed from January 1 through mid-June, then weekends only, including Mondays, until July 1 (check regulations for exact dates) and July 14 through Dec. 31.
**Open Area:** The entire stream is open to fishing.
**Legal Gear/Tackle:** Only one unbaited, single-hook, artificial lure may be used year-round, except for stream mouth (check regulations for defined area) where lures with multiple hooks and bait are allowed from July 14 through August 31.

**King Salmon**
- Open season is January 1 through last weekend in June (check regulations for exact dates).
- Open area is from mouth to Parks Highway bridge; closed to kings above bridge.
- No fishing allowed between 11:00 pm and 6:00 am from May 15 through July 13.
- Bag limit is (1) per day and (1) in possession (20 inches or longer). For kings less than 20 inches (Jacks), the limit is (10).

**All Other Salmon**
- Open all season (see general "Open Season" above).
- Open area is from mouth upstream to Deception Creek confluence.
- Red, pink, and chum salmon bag limit is (3) per day and (3) in possession (16 inches or longer), and silver salmon (2) per day and (2) in possession. For salmon less than 16 inches (Jacks), the limit is (10).

**Rainbow/Steelhead Trout & Dolly Varden**
- Open all season (see general "Open Season" above).
- Entire stream is open to fishing.
- Catch-and-release only for trout year-round; retention not allowed.
- Bag limit for Dolly Varden is (5) per day and (5) in possession, only (1) over 12 inches.

**Other Fishes**
- Open all season (see general "Open Season" above).
- Arctic grayling bag limit is (2) per day and (2) in possession, any size.
- Whitefish has no bag or possession limit, no size restrictions.
- Burbot bag limit is (5) per day and (5) in possession, any size.

## Fishing Willow Creek

**Access:** ★★★ **Sight Fishing:** ★★★½
**Scenery:** ★★★ **Bank/Wading:** ★★★★
**Wildlife:** ★★★ **Boat/Floating:** ★★★★★

**Species:** King, pink, chum, and silver salmon, rainbow trout, Dolly Varden, arctic grayling, and round whitefish. Occurrences of red salmon and burbot.

**Summary:** Within close proximity to towns such as Wasilla and Palmer, Willow Creek is the most popular roadside fishing spot in all of the Susitna River drainage. During the king and silver salmon runs, expect anglers to be out in force, especially at the mouth of the creek. Salmon gather here from a few days to several weeks before proceeding up the Willow and fish from other drainages farther up the Susitna will also pull in here to rest, making this a prime angling destination. Additionally, other species such as trout, char, and grayling will concentrate at the confluence in spring prior to entering Willow and again in fall as they drop back down to the Susitna to overwinter.

The middle stretch of water between the mouth and the Deception Creek confluence near the highway crossing does harbor some good fishing, although the quality of salmon may not be as consistent as what can be expected lower down in the drainage. Silver salmon are generally the brightest of all the salmon species. Typically, the peak of the respective salmon runs is brief, only about a week to ten days or so, compared to two weeks at the mouth. Fishing for trout and grayling, on the other hand, is much better in this area.

*The slack water confluence at the mouth of Willow always draws attention. Although crowds can be very heavy at times, the fishing is still surprisingly good as salmon tend to stack up here.*

(Courtesy Roy Bailey)

Upper Willow, between Deception Creek and the canyon, is closed to all salmon fishing but supports some productive action for rainbow trout and arctic grayling during the summer months.

While the fishing at the mouth can be fast and furious at times for salmon, crowds are likely to be out and anglers looking for less company and still a decent shot at landing a few fish may want to hike in or float the stretch of stream between the highway bridge and the confluence. Since the Willow flows clear throughout summer and fall, anglers are successfully able to sight fish for salmon in this stretch.

The king salmon run is typically quite large, comprised of both wild and hatchery fish, with anglers having a fair chance of hooking into a trophy if spending a weekend here at the height of the run. Some of the heavier kings in Susitna Valley come from Willow, with specimens up to 50 pounds not unusual. In fact, fish up to 60 pounds are present every season and several specimens over 70 pounds have been landed over the years. The official heaviest king to have come out of the Willow weighed a whopping 84 pounds, caught at the Susitna confluence.

Pinks and chums often stage in huge numbers at the mouth before ascending Willow and fish-on-every-cast action is the norm some mornings at the peak of the runs. They are abundant throughout the middle and lower stream as well, this being the perfect area for taking them on the fly. Schools of fish are typically present in all of the deeper holes and pools and easily targeted.

After kings, it is the silver that commands the most attention on the Willow. The stream receives a good run of this species and, like other salmon members, congregate at the mouth early in the season before heading upstream. Anglers prefer to fish for them there but the catching can be very good in areas closer to the highway as well, although silvers towards the latter part of the season tend to be showing signs of maturity farther upstream.

Anglers targeting other species do best using an assortment of flies reflecting the particular food conditions in the stream, which is salmon smolt and fry in spring, insects in early summer, and salmon eggs and flesh in late summer and fall.

The Willow has some of the best rainbow action in Southcentral, with a fair number of trout up to 26 inches. Hooking one or even two dozen fish a day is not unrealistic in late summer and early fall with skilled anglers even claiming near triple-digit days. The stretch of water upstream of the highway bridge along Hatcher Pass Road can be phenomenal at times.

A few large Dolly Varden are present when salmon run in July and August, but the upper stream above the rapids has decent fishing for 8- to 10-inch char throughout the entire season. Grayling are numerous in summer, especially high up in the drainage. Big schools of whitefish can be found in the Willow but they are typically very finicky and rarely caught with any consistency unless specifically targeted.

## Fish Availability

H = High M = Moderate L = Low C = Closed

| Species | APR | MAY | JUN | JUL | AUG | SEP | OCT |
|---|---|---|---|---|---|---|---|
| **King Salmon** | | L L L | M M H H | C C C C | C C | | |
| **Pink Salmon** | | | L | L C M H | H M L L | | |
| **Chum Salmon** | | | L | L C M H | H H M L | L L | |
| **Silver Salmon** | | | | L C L M | H H H M | M M L L | L |
| **Rainbow Trout** | L L L M | M M M M | M M H H | H H H H | H H H H | H H H H | M M L L |
| **Dolly Varden** | L L L L | L L L L | L L L M | M M M M | M M M M | M M M M | L L L L |
| **Arctic Grayling** | L L L M | M M M M | M M H H | H H H H | H H H H | H H H H | M M L L |
| Angling Pressure | | L L L L | M M H H | H M M M | H H H M | M M L L | L L L L |

## King Salmon

**Rating:** ★★½ Fair to good.
**Season:** January 1 until mid-June, then every weekend until July 1.
**Timing:** May 10 – late June; peak June 15 – June 30.
**Size:** Average 15 – 45 pounds, up to 80 pounds.
**Tackle:** Spinners, attractors, and flies.
**Tips:** When water is clear, use blue or green spinners and attractors. In murky conditions, chartreuse, orange, and red are favored. Black may also be effective, especially on sunny days and in the mainstem Willow. Flies are best fished in the current above the mouth.

Only a few kings venture upstream beyond the confluence prior to the third week of June, the vanguard of the run holding at the mouth. Expect a big push of kings into the stream proper by the last week of June; this is the ideal time to look for bright fish. Throughout the remainder of the king season, the majority of the run is located just downstream of the highway crossing, but only a very few bright specimens will be available.

*Father and son team up to display a blushed Willow king before releasing it. Kings here frequently top 40 pounds and sight fishing for them can be exceptional.*

(Courtesy Jeff Varvil)

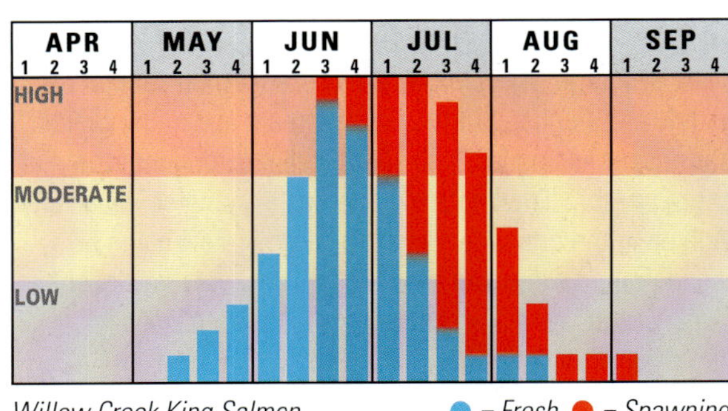


*Willow Creek King Salmon* ● = *Fresh* ● = *Spawning*

## Pink Salmon

**Rating:** ★★★★ Excellent on even-numbered years, good on odd.
**Season:** July 14 until mid-June, then every weekend through July 13.
**Timing:** June 25 – August 20; peak July 15 – August 5.
**Size:** Average 2 – 4 pounds, up to 7 pounds.
**Tackle:** Spoons, spinners, and flies.
**Tips:** Green, blue, and chartreuse lures and flies do well on fresh pinks at the mouth. If water is murky, orange or pink seem to do better. These fish school at the mouth until about the last week of July before rapidly heading upstream. Flies and small spoons are best once the fish have entered the mainstem Willow.

For brightest fish, try at the mouth. Only fair numbers of decent pinks are available as far upstream as the highway bridge.

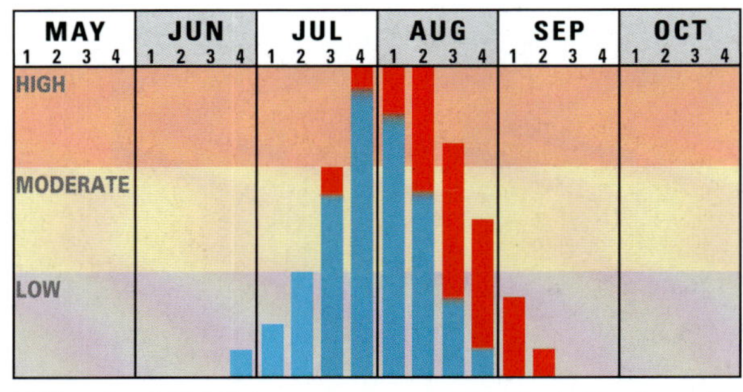


*Willow Creek Pink Salmon* ● = *Fresh* ● = *Spawning*

## Chum Salmon

**Rating:** ★★★★ Excellent.
**Season:** July 14 until mid-June, then every weekend through July 13.
**Timing:** June 25 – Sept. 15; peak July 15 – August 10.
**Size:** Average 6 – 12 pounds, up to 18 pounds.
**Tackle:** Spoons, spinners, attractors, flies, and bait.
**Tips:** Lures such as green and chartreuse spoons and spinners are well received at the mouth but do not work as well upstream. The prime offering for dime bright chums

*(Courtesy Beverely Bailey)*

*The Willow has a great summer run of silvers and chrome fish can be taken throughout the stream area open to salmon fishing.*

is a small cluster of salmon drifted along the bottom. Attractors with or without bait can be good when fished in the murk just downstream of the confluence. In the mainstem Willow, use attractor flies or spoons.

There are only a small number of chrome chums available anywhere in the creek above the mouth; most are semi-bright to slightly blushed.

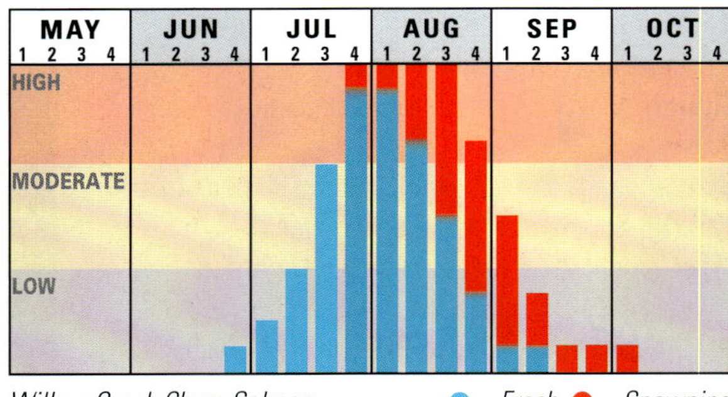


*Willow Creek Chum Salmon* ● = *Fresh* ● = *Spawning*

## Silver Salmon

**Rating:** ★★★ Good.
**Season:** July 14 until mid-June, then every weekend through July 13.
**Timing:** July 1 – October 5; peak August 1 – 20.
**Size:** Average 5 – 10 pounds, up to 15 pounds.
**Tackle:** Spoons, spinners, flies, and bait.
**Tips:** Most silvers hang at the mouth of Willow until about mid-August when a significant upstream migration begins. Most salmon are starting to turn by the first of September, the only bright specimens found at the Susitna confluence.

Clusters of salmon roe are deadly throughout the area

open to salmon fishing, but lures will work perfectly fine during the first half of the season (prior to mid-August). Spinners in red or orange can be hot when run is at a peak, use blue or green ones early in the season. Fly-fishing is best above the mouth in the mainstem Willow.

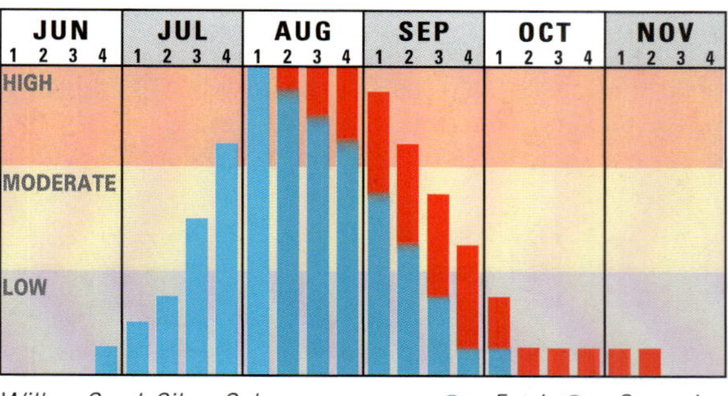


*Willow Creek Silver Salmon* ● = *Fresh* ● = *Spawning*

## Rainbow Trout

**Rating:** ★★★★ Excellent.
**Season:** January 1 through December 31.
**Timing:** April 1 – November 1; peak June 15 – Sept. 30.
**Size:** Average 8 – 20 inches, up to 28 inches (8 pounds).
**Tackle:** Spoons, spinners, and flies.
**Tips:** Forage imitation lures and flies work best in spring and first part of summer before salmon arrive and again in late fall (October on), try egg imitations starting in mid-July through September.

Few trout are in the far lower end in mid-summer; try higher up from highway bridge to the canyon. Starting in August and continuing through September, fish drop down into the middle and lower stream sections. Not many rainbows are in mainstem Willow beyond the first of October but may be abundant at the mouth at this time.

*The Willow supports a healthy population of rainbow trout. Fish of this size and color, as taken by Josh Varvil, are common.*

*(Courtesy Jeff Varvil)*

## Dolly Varden

**Rating:** ★ Poor.
**Season:** January 1 through December 31.
**Timing:** May 1 – November 1; peak June 25 – Sept. 30.
**Size:** Average 8 – 18 inches, up to 24 inches (5 pounds).
**Tackle:** Spinners, attractors, and flies.
**Tips:** Early and late in the season, try forage imitations. Later on as salmon begin to spawn, use egg imitations and then flesh. A number of often stage in huge numbers fish

*A view of the middle section of Willow Creek as seen from the Parks Highway bridge. This is a great spot for families and perfect for introducing youngsters to the sport of fishing.*

are available at the mouth of Willow in spring and early summer, following the salmon upstream to the middle section from July into September. A few large specimens weighing several pounds may be spotted among spawning salmon in August in the highway bridge area.

### Arctic Grayling

**Rating:** ★★★ Good.
**Season:** January 1 through December 31.
**Timing:** April 1 – November 1; peak June 15 – Sept. 15.
**Size:** Average 8 – 14 inches, up to 18 inches.
**Tackle:** Spinners and flies.
**Tips:** Some fish head upstream in spring but most arrive in mid-June. Anglers do best on grayling above the highway bridge, preferably the upper stream along Hatcher Pass Road all the way to the canyon rapids. Use dry flies and forage imitations anytime during the season, egg patterns being productive in late summer and fall when the salmon are on the reds.

## Other Willow Opportunities

### Float Fishing

Probably the most popular float fishing stream on the road system north of Anchorage, the Willow is easily negotiated by most skill levels. There are two main put-in points; one on the upper stream off Hatcher Pass Road, the other on the mid-section at the Parks Highway crossing. Both offer really productive action for a wide range of species depending on the time of season and where the float begins and ends.

The upper stream along the Hatcher Pass Road (Willow-Fishhook Road) is shallow and rocky with numerous sweepers, riffles, and braided channels, interspersed with deep trenches and holes that make perfect habitat for Willow's resident species, such as trout and grayling. A favorite day trip for many anglers is to launch at Shirley Towne bridge and float down to the take-out point at Parks Highway bridge in the community of Willow.

Fishing in this stretch is usually very good with some truly exceptional days presenting almost triple digit catches possible during the mid- to late summer peak. Plan on starting the float at dawn, reaching the highway by evening.

Much different in appearance is lower Willow, or that portion between the Parks Highway and the Susitna River confluence. The stream becomes wider and deeper, with a slower current and combination of sand and rock bottom structure. There are quite a few sweepers going down with logjams present in a couple of spots. Although a relatively easy journey, exercise caution.

The fishing here can be hot for trout, especially in late summer and early fall, and four species of salmon fill many of the holes from July into September. Like upper Willow, this section is a full-day float, taking out near the campground at the mouth of the stream. Anglers should note, however, that there are three branches to the far end of Willow, all of which can be negotiated to varying degrees of success depending on waterflow. Those selecting to exit right above the campground should plan on using the south branch.

(Courtesy Jeff Varvil)

Remember that airboats also share the lower Willow and floaters, particularly those traveling by canoe or kayak, should plan accordingly in order to avoid potentially dangerous situations.

### Deception Creek

A tributary of Willow Creek, Deception flows in from the northeast about a mile and a half above the highway bridge. The main access is off the Hatcher Pass Road, however, with some parking available. It is a small, slightly tannic stream with sand and rock bottom supporting decent populations of trout and grayling.

With a multitude of riffles and relatively deep pools, anglers have little problem negotiating Deception by crossing the stream as warranted, bushwhacking the shoreline. Those that put in the effort to hike a couple of miles or more upstream, fishing semi-remote water completely devoid of other people, report fair to excellent success rates for rainbow trout averaging in the teens. A few of the deeper spots are known to harbor trout to 28 inches. Some arctic grayling are available too. Fishing is best from mid-June to early September.

Since this is a salmon spawning stream from July into October (closed to all salmon fishing), expect bears to be present.

# Sheep Creek

King
SALMON

Pink
SALMON

Chum
SALMON

Silver
SALMON

Rainbow
TROUT

Arctic
GRAYLING

**Highlights:** One of Susitna Valley's most exceptional angling streams, known for its abundant salmon runs and aggressive trout and grayling. Trophy fish potential.

**Best Fishing:** Mid-June to late September. **Regulatory Restrictions:** Liberal.

**Location:** Southern Susitna Valley drainage, Caswell area, Parks Highway, 86 miles north of Anchorage, 26 miles south of Talkeetna.

**Description:** Draining out of the Talkeetna Mountains, Sheep is a moody stream that changes character abruptly according to weather conditions. Surrounded by spruce and birch forests, the sand and gravel-bottomed creek rises sharply in water level during hot and sunny days, often flowing high and turbid with snowmelt until cooler weather prevails. Likewise, heavy rain quickly turns the clear stream high and murky.

The stream meanders considerably along its length, complete with swift water, sweepers, submerged trees, and deep pools, only straightening out and calming down the last half-mile or so before emptying into the glacial Susitna River.

Sheep has much less developed trails and foot-traffic compared to its neighbor Montana to the north and Willow to the south. The section of stream from the highway bridge down to the mouth is quite wild, complete with frequent wildlife such as moose, beaver, and both black and brown bear, the brush infested with biting insects.

**Facilities:** Parking, primitive camping, restrooms, cabins, and restaurant available in the area.

**Access:** There are two major access points for Sheep Creek along the Parks Highway; the mouth (Sheep Creek Slough) and the middle reach at the Parks Highway crossing.

**A. Sheep Creek Slough** – Milepost 85.8. West on Resolute Drive 1.4 miles to large parking area. Primitive camping, restrooms, RV parking, and wheelchair accessible. Trail leads 150 yards to slough and the Susitna River confluence. In addition, a faint trail heads upstream along the bluff above the slough to the middle stream section.

**B. Parks Highway Bridge** – Milepost 88.6. Highway crosses stream. Parking and primitive camping. Faint trails lead downstream along both sides of creek. Some private property on the north side of Sheep.

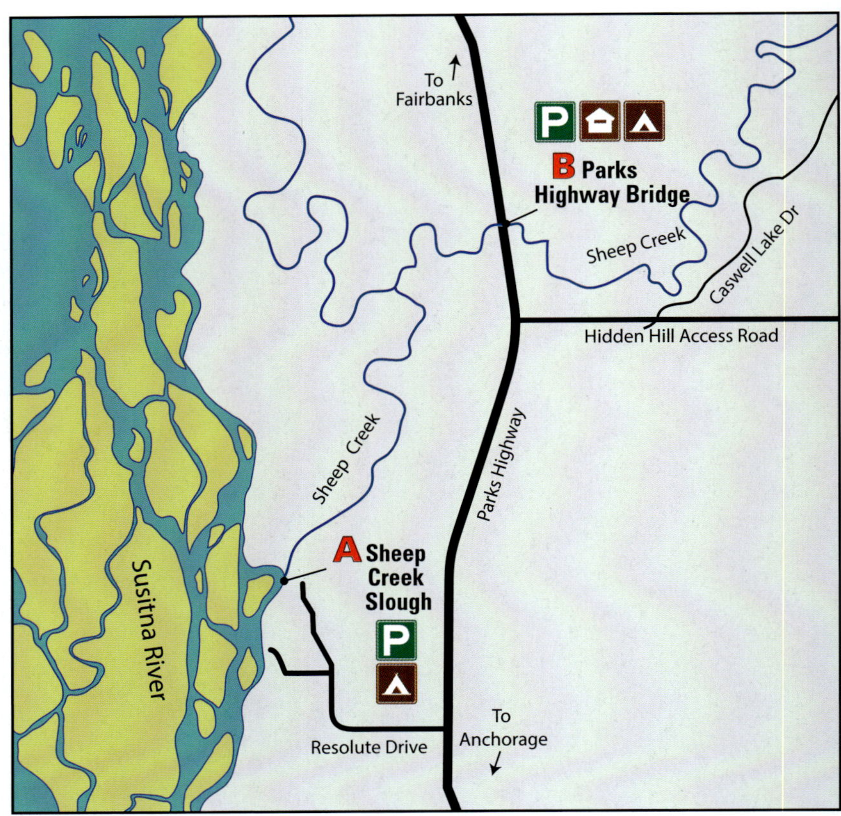

## Rules & Regulations

**Open Season:** Downstream of Parks Highway bridge, fishing is allowed from January 1 through mid-June, then weekends only, including Mondays, until July 1 (check regulations for exact dates) and July 14 through December 31.

**Open Area:** The entire stream is open to fishing.

**Legal Gear/Tackle:** Only one unbaited, single-hook, artificial lure allowed from September 1 through May 31; only unbaited, artificial lures allowed from June 1 through July 13. Lures with multiple hooks and bait are allowed from July 14 through August 31.

### King Salmon

- Open season is January 1 through last weekend in June (check regulations for exact dates).
- Open area is from mouth upstream to Parks Highway bridge; closed to king fishing above bridge.
- No fishing allowed between 11:00 pm and 6:00 am from May 15 through July 13.
- Bag limit is (1) per day and (1) in possession (20 inches or longer). For kings less than 20 inches (Jacks), limit is (10).

### All Other Salmon

- Open all season (see general "Open Season" above).
- Entire stream is open to fishing.
- Red, pink, and chum salmon bag limit is (3) per day and (3) in possession (16 inches or longer), and silver salmon (2) per day and (2) in possession. For salmon less than 16 inches (Jacks), the limit is (10).

### Rainbow/Steelhead Trout & Dolly Varden

- Open all season (see general "Open Season" above).
- Entire stream is open to fishing.
- Catch-and-release only for trout from April 15 through June 14.
- Bag limit for trout is (2) per day and (2) in possession, only(1) over 20 inches; Dolly Varden is (5) per day and (5) in possession, only (1) over 12 inches.

### Other Fishes

- Open all season (see general "Open Season" above).
- Arctic grayling bag limit is (2) per day and (2) in possession, no size restrictions.
- Whitefish has no bag or possession limit, no size restrictions.
- Burbot bag limit is (5) per day and (5) in possession, no size restrictions.

## Fishing Sheep Creek

**Access:** ★★★
**Scenery:** ★★★
**Wildlife:** ★★★
**Sight Fishing:** ★★★
**Bank/Wading:** ★★★★
**Boat/Floating:** ★★

**Species:** King, pink, chum, and silver salmon, rainbow trout, Dolly Varden, arctic grayling, round whitefish, and burbot. Occasional red salmon.

**Summary**: In terms of angling effort, Sheep falls just behind Willow and Montana. However, it frequently outperforms either one as salmon runs and fish populations are just as healthy here as in neighboring waters and the crowds are smaller as well. By far the greatest concentration of anglers is at the slough where the stream hits a channel of the glacial Susitna River. Comparatively, only a small number of anglers fish from the road crossing since a lack of good trails and rough terrain makes the area less than hospitable. The fishing, however, can be very good and anglers willing to explore some new territory would find Sheep very appealing.

Salmon gather in huge numbers at the mouth during the summer months as they wait for the right water conditions to head upstream to the spawning grounds. During this time, anglers can find some exceptional action for four species of salmon, including kings, pinks, chums, and silvers. At the road crossing, the fishing can still be excellent but varies much more than down below at the Susitna. If Sheep is running high, swift, and murky, fishing can be tough in the middle and upper sections, yet the mouth will still yield good action because it is relatively current free.

Some of the largest kings in Susitna Valley stem from the Sheep. As the expansive confluence area consists mostly of slack water and few trees and snags, landing a trophy king is very much possible. Fish in the 60-pound range are landed here every season and specimens up to 70 and even 80 pounds are known to exist. In fact, many of the biggest kings entered in the Susitna Valley King Salmon Derby have come from Sheep.

Pinks and chums arrive on the heel of the kings and more often than not makes the water in the slough boil with activity. Fish densities are greatest on even-numbered years. As with kings, the mouth produces the fastest action and freshest fish. The section of stream around the road crossing is a major spawning area for salmon and thus it can be difficult at times to hook into nice specimens.

Silvers draw a good amount of attention at the mouth but few anglers ever take the time to pursue this salmon in one of the many holes and pools downstream of the highway. The confluence can be very good for bright silvers, with fewer nice fish available up above. Yet with a lack of pressure and releasing darker fish, anglers can find plenty of fresh salmon.

Rainbow trout and arctic grayling are distributed in good numbers throughout Sheep with anglers hooking the most fish in the middle and upper stream sections during the summer and early fall months. The mouth can be productive early in the year (May) and again in fall as these resident fish head back to the Susitna to spend the winter.

*A lucky angler struggles to control a bright, 40-pound chinook, hooked on a corkie and yarn set-up drifted along the bottom at the confluence of Sheep Creek and the muddy Susitna River. In mid- to late June, this is the place to be for kings.*

## Fish Availability

● = High ● = Moderate ● = Low ● = Closed (H = High, M = Moderate, L = Low, C = Closed)

| Species | APR | MAY | JUN | JUL | AUG | SEP | OCT |
|---|---|---|---|---|---|---|---|
| **King Salmon** | | L L | M M H H | C C C C | C C | | |
| **Pink Salmon** | | | | L C M H | H M L L | | |
| **Chum Salmon** | | | | L C M H | H H M L | L L | |
| **Silver Salmon** | | | | C L M | H H H M | M M L L | |
| **Rainbow Trout** | L L L M | M M M M | M M H H | H H H H | H H H H | H H H H | M M L L |
| **Dolly Varden** | L L L L | L L L L | L L L M | M M M M | M M M M | M M M M | L L L L |
| **Arctic Grayling** | L L L M | M M M M | M M H H | H H H H | H H H H | H H H H | M M L L |
| Angling Pressure | | L L L L | M M H H | H M M M | H H H M | M M L L | L L L L |

## King Salmon

**Rating:** ★★½ Fair to good.
**Season:** January 1 until mid-June, then every weekend until July 1.
**Timing:** May 15 – late June; peak June 15 – June 30.
**Size:** Average 15 – 45 pounds, up to 80 pounds.
**Tackle:** Spinners, attractors, and flies.
**Tips:** Some kings will ascend Sheep up to the highway crossing and beyond already by mid-June but the bulk of the run will not commit to the stream proper before the final week of the month or later.

The mouth of Sheep is an obvious hot spot, with anglers tossing hardware to connect with some great king action. As the stream usually runs high and just slightly murky during king season, sharply colored spinners and attractors are best. If the water is low and clear, blue and green work better. Upstream, hit deep holes and pools early in the morning using big spinners, attractors, and bulky flies in orange or red. During the day, green and black works better.

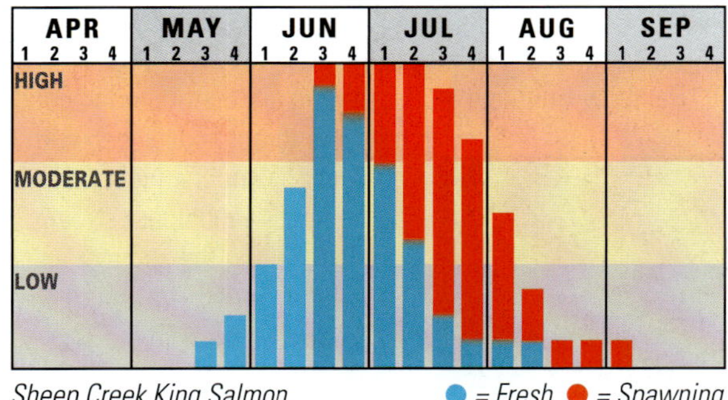


*Sheep Creek King Salmon* ● = Fresh ● = Spawning

## Pink Salmon

**Rating:** ★★★★ Excellent on even-numbered years, fair to good on odd.
**Season:** July 14 until mid-June, then every weekend through July 13.
**Timing:** July 1 – August 20; peak July 20 – August 5.
**Size:** Average 2 – 4 pounds, up to 7 pounds.

(Courtesy Dennis Musgraves)

*Sheep has a reputation of producing some very large kings. Spend a few days here and hooking a fish of 40-50 pounds is very possible. Be willing to experiment and move around the stream.*

**Tackle:** Spoons, spinners, and flies.
**Tips:** Big schools of reasonably fresh pinks are available at the mouth of Sheep during the latter part of July. Come August, relatively few nice specimens are left, but there are still a fair number of semi-bright fish available. In the section of stream around the highway crossing, expect mostly ripe pinks.

Spoons and spinners in orange, red, and chartreuse are effective, some anglers experiencing success with darker colors such as green and blue if the water is very low and clear. Upstream of the Susitna confluence, smaller tackle is better.

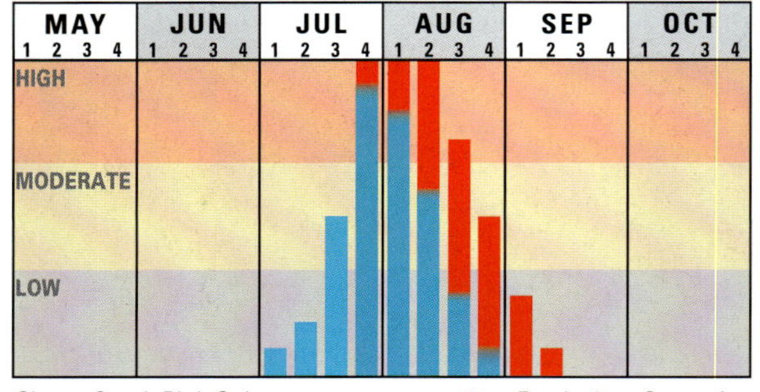


*Sheep Creek Pink Salmon*

### Chum Salmon

**Rating:** ★★★★ Excellent.
**Season:** July 14 until mid-June, then every weekend through July 13.
**Timing:** July 1 – September 15; peak July 20 – August 10.
**Size:** Average 6 – 12 pounds, up to 18 pounds.
**Tackle:** Spoons, spinners, flies, and bait.
**Tips:** Sheep Creek is known as one of the top chum producers of all the roadside Susitna drainages. These fish school in large numbers at the mouth during late July and early August and are very susceptible to medium-sized chrome and orange or green spoons and spinners. In the stream proper above the mouth, use spoons or an attractor and roe combination. Darker pattern flies can be particularly hot. For fresh chums, try the mouth and deep holes on the lower river. Few bright fish are available after the first week of August.

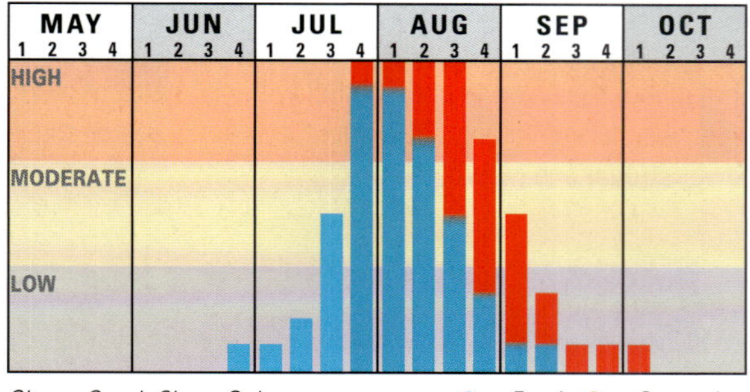


*Sheep Creek Chum Salmon* ● = Fresh ● = Spawning

### Silver Salmon

**Rating:** ★★★ Good.
**Season:** July 14 until mid-June, then every weekend through July 13.
**Timing:** July 5 – September 30; peak August 5 – 20.
**Size:** Average 5 – 10 pounds, up to 15 pounds.

*(Courtesy Beverley Bailey)*

*(Courtesy Dennis Musgraves)*

*Buzzing a spinner through that stretch of water just below the Parks Highway crossing proved the hot item for several chums, including this male displaying characteristic calico markings. Sight fishing to schools of chums is good in this area.*

**Tackle:** Spoons, spinners, flies, and bait.
**Tips:** Silvers often school at the mouth in large numbers early on, shooting upstream to deeper holes and runs below the highway crossing as the season progresses. Most fish head up Sheep in late August and early September, albeit they will not be as bright as earlier in the run.

Use a cluster of salmon roe with or without a bobber at the mouth in early morning or cast a spoon or spinner during the day. Attractor flies do work as well. Orange and red are good colors on Sheep most any time. Upstream, more subdued hues are commonly employed, such as blue and green. Salmon roe fished along the bottom in deep holes can be deadly.

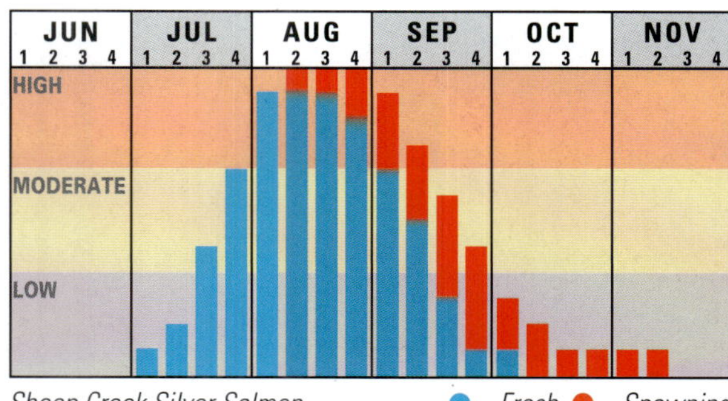


*Sheep Creek Silver Salmon* ● = Fresh ● = Spawning

*The lower end of Sheep has very slow current and drifting flies and other lures is very good for staging silvers. Many of the fish show a tinge of pink, yet some may be pure chrome, especially early on in the run (late July-early August).*

### Rainbow Trout

**Rating:** ★★★★ Excellent.
**Season:** January 1 through December 31.
**Timing:** April 1 – November 1; peak June 15 – Sept. 30.
**Size:** Average 8 – 20 inches, up to 28 inches (8 pounds).
**Tackle:** Spoons, spinners, and flies.
**Tips:** In spring and early summer, use forage and insect imitations and by mid-July, egg and flesh patterns should be increasingly effective. During the months of July and August, look for big rainbows wherever spawning salmon are found, especially on the middle and upper stream section. In fall, lower Sheep and its mouth produce the best action.

*The roadside streams of Susitna Valley harbor some exceptional angling for rainbow trout, such as this heavily spotted specimen.*

### Dolly Varden

**Rating:** ★ Poor.
**Season:** January 1 through December 31.
**Timing:** May 1 – November 1; peak June 25 – Sept. 30.
**Size:** Average 8 – 18 inches, up to 24 inches (5 pounds).
**Tackle:** Spinners, attractors, and flies.
**Tips:** The creek's mouth has some decent spring char action, but anglers usually fare poorly on this species throughout the season. The population is small.

### Arctic Grayling

**Rating:** ★★★ Good.
**Season:** January 1 through December 31.
**Timing:** April 1 – November 1; peak June 15 – Sept. 15.
**Size:** Average 8 – 14 inches, up to 18 inches.
**Tackle:** Spinners and flies.
**Tips:** Grayling pass through the mouth in spring headed to the middle and upper portions of the creek for the summer. Anglers do well using insect and forage imitations throughout the summer and into fall with egg patterns also effective starting in July. After mid-September, search the lower stream and mouth.

*Sheep has an abundance of water that see little angling effort. While the mouth may be congested at times at the height of the salmon runs, the middle and upper reaches harbor some great holding water for salmon, trout, and grayling matched with relative solitude. Hiking in on one of the area foot paths will put anglers onto some potentially great semi-wilderness fishing.*

*(Courtesy Eagle Eye Images)*

# Montana Creek

King
SALMON

Pink
SALMON

Chum
SALMON

Silver
SALMON

Rainbow
TROUT

Arctic
GRAYLING

**Highlights:** Clearwater stream affording sight-fishing with easy access and excellent action for four species of salmon. Very productive for trout in upper reaches.

**Best Fishing:** Mid-June to late September.

**Regulatory Restrictions:** Moderate.

**Location:** Southern Susitna Valley drainage, Montana area, Parks Highway, 96 miles north of Anchorage, 16 miles south of Talkeetna.

**Description:** This clear, gravel-bottomed, mid-sized stream is, next to Willow Creek to the south, one of the most popular fishing spots in all of the Susitna Valley. Draining from the northwest side of the Talkeetna Mountains, many anglers actually prefer Montana over other area waters since it can be easily waded and crossed in several places, and the choice holes are within easy walking distance of the road. Those proficient in sight fishing will find Montana the perfect place to be; the water is crystal clear and schools of salmon are easily spotted.

Although being a run-off stream, Montana is not susceptible to flooding from mountain snowmelt during periods of hot weather. Rain has little influence as well unless the area is exposed to heavy downpour lasting days.

The upper portion of Montana, off Talkeetna Spur Highway, is relatively narrow and somewhat swift in places but there is an abundance of nice holes and runs to scout for resident fish. At the highway crossing, the Montana has widened somewhat with about half a dozen productive holes that are frequented by anglers. The mouth of Montana is a place of change as the vast Susitna River continues to carve new channels and runs during the spring floods. Generally, the current at the confluence is slow throughout the summer season.

Moose frequent the area in spring and fall, black and brown bears being common along the stream above the highway.

**Facilities:** At the main road crossing, parking, camping, RV parking, restrooms, tackle shop, and convenience goods are available. Several miles to the north, hotels, grocery stores, cafes, gas stations, restaurants and many other services are present.

**Access:** The Parks Highway provides access to the lower section of Montana and the Susitna River confluence as well as the upper part via Talkeetna Spur Highway.

**A. Parks Highway Bridge** – Milepost 96.5. Highway crosses stream. Parking, camping, RV parking, and restrooms. Trails lead ¼ mile along stream from bridge parking areas to Susitna River confluence.

**B. Yoder Road Bridge** – Milepost 98.7. North on Talkeetna Spur Highway to Milepost 3.1, right on Yoder Road 2.7 miles to stream crossing. Parking and primitive camping.

**C. Luthman Trail** – Milepost 98.7. North on Talkeetna Spur Highway to Milepost 3.1, right Yoder Road 2.8 miles to Luthman Trailhead on left. Parking and primitive camping. Trail leads 2 to 4 miles to and along Middle Fork Montana Creek, crossing South Fork, ending at falls (mile 4).

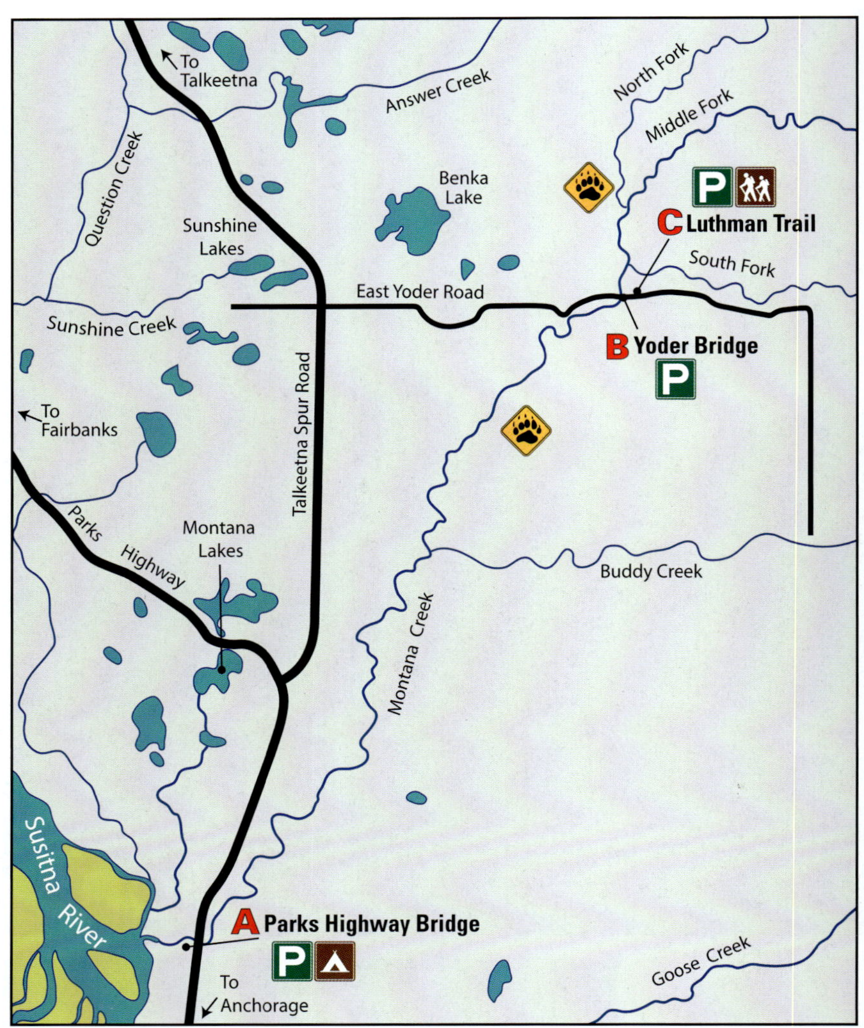

*Overview of the Montana Creek Campground entrance next to the Parks Highway and the stream crossing. Many anglers park here and hike a short distance to the creek.*

## Rules & Regulations

**Open Season:** Downstream of ADF&G markers ½ mile above Parks Highway bridge, fishing is allowed from January 1 through mid-June, then weekends only, including Mondays, until July 1 (check regulations for exact dates) and July 14 through December 31.
**Open Area:** The entire stream is open to fishing.
**Legal Gear/Tackle:** Only one unbaited, single-hook, artificial lure allowed from September 1 through May 31; only unbaited, artificial lures allowed from June 1 through July 13. Lures with multiple hooks and bait are allowed from July 14 through August 31.

**King Salmon**
- Open season is January 1 through last weekend in June (check regulations for exact dates).
- Open area is from mouth upstream to ADF&G marker ½ mile above Parks Highway bridge; closed to king fishing above marker.
- No fishing allowed between 11:00 pm and 6:00 am from May 15 through July 13.
- Bag limit is (1) per day and (1) in possession (20 inches or longer). For kings less than 20 inches (Jacks), the limit is (10).

**All Other Salmon**
- Open all season (see general "Open Season" above).
- Open are is from mouth upstream to ADF&G markers ½ mile above of Parks Highway bridge; closed to salmon fishing above marker.
- Red, pink, and chum salmon bag limit is (3) per day and (3) in possession (16 inches or longer), and silver salmon (2) per day and (2) in possession. For salmon less than 16 inches (Jacks), the limit is (10).

**Rainbow/Steelhead Trout & Dolly Varden**
- Open all season (see general "Open Season" above).
- Entire stream is open to fishing.
- Catch-and-release only for trout year-round; retention not allowed.
- Bag limit for Dolly Varden is (5) per day and (5) in possession, only (1) over 12 inches.

**Other Fishes**
- Open all season (see general "Open Season" above).
- Catch-and-release only for Arctic grayling; retention not allowed.
- Whitefish has no bag or possession limit, no size restrictions.
- Burbot bag limit is (5) per day and (5) in possession, no size restrictions.

## Fishing Montana Creek

**Access:** ★★★★ **Sight Fishing:** ★★★★
**Scenery:** ★★★ **Bank/Wading:** ★★★★★
**Wildlife:** ★★ **Boat/Floating: N/A**

**Species:** King, pink, chum, and silver salmon, rainbow trout, Dolly Varden, arctic grayling, and burbot. Occasional catches of red salmon and whitefish.

**Summary:** Montana Creek has to offer great fishing for four species of salmon as well as rainbow trout and arctic grayling almost continuously from spring through fall. King salmon draw the most attention, crowds of anglers descending on the lower portion of Montana every weekend between mid-June and mid-July. The silver salmon season in August also sees a lot of effort.

There are two sections of the Montana that is covered here, the first being the upper stream off the Talkeetna Highway. Closed to salmon fishing, flyfishers will find productive and largely undisturbed water that feature nice-sized rainbow trout and arctic grayling. This area is also a spawning ground for many of Montana's salmon, hence very good action can be expected if pursuing predatory species.

From about a ¼-mile upstream of the highway bridge to the mouth is referred to as the lower section of Montana. This area is busy with other anglers from about mid-June to mid-August when salmon are present in good numbers. Earlier and later in the season (May and September/October), the stream is largely desolate save a few flyfishers targeting migrating trout, char, grayling, and a few late-arriving silver salmon.

King salmon fishing on the Montana can be extremely productive, especially at the mouth of the creek as fish concentrate in huge numbers waiting to begin their run upstream. Few kings head up the Montana prior to the last week of June, the brunt of the run entering the last few days of June and early July. Like the Willow and Sheep to the south, the kings in Montana also reach very large size. Trophy kings around 50 pounds are reasonably common with specimens between 60 and 70 pounds caught from the bank every season. The biggest king weighed at Montana tipped the scale at 81 pounds.

Pink and chum salmon often gather at the mouth by the thousands and, like the kings, wait for maturity to set in before venturing into the low, clear waters of Montana. Anglers that hit the first half of the run are treated to some phenomenal action for bright and semi-bright fish, particularly at dawn or on a drizzly day. Some fresh specimens may be caught in deep holes in the stream proper following a good rain.

After the king salmon, silvers are the top species on the Montana. These fish habitually school at the mouth and become easy targets for anglers casting from the bank. Action can be very good all day long but generally only in the mornings in holes and pools above the confluence. Silvers retain their sea-bright coloration also in the stream.

Rainbow trout and arctic grayling pass through this area in May and June and again in September and October as they move to and from the headwaters of Montana. There are a few Dolly Varden to be caught during the salmon runs. Burbot do not frequent the clear and shallow Montana itself but can be found at the Susitna confluence in decent numbers.

*Anglers line up just downstream of the mouth of Montana, casting to the "siltline" of the glacial Susitna River. Salmon, trout, and grayling school here.*

## Fish Availability

H = *High* M = *Moderate* L = *Low* C = *Closed*

| *Species* | APR | MAY | JUN | JUL | AUG | SEP | OCT |
|---|---|---|---|---|---|---|---|
| **King Salmon** | | L | L M H H | C C C C | C C | | |
| **Pink Salmon** | | | | L C M H | H M L L | | |
| **Chum Salmon** | | | | L C M H | H H M L | L L | |
| **Silver Salmon** | | | | C L M | H H H M | M M L L | |
| **Rainbow Trout** | L L L M | M M M M | M M H H | H H H H | H H H H | H H H H | M M L L |
| **Dolly Varden** | L L L L | L L L L | L L L M | M M M M | M M M M | M M M M | L L L L |
| **Arctic Grayling** | L L L M | M M M M | M M H H | H H H H | H H H H | H H H H | M M L L |
| Angling Pressure | | L L L L | M M H H | H M M M | H H H M | M M L L | L L L L |

*A duo of chinooks, blushed male and bright female, weighing 40 and 38 pounds, respectively. At Montana Creek – as elsewhere in the Susitna drainage – catching salmon in various stages of maturity is commonplace, particularly in mid- to late season. These fish were taken on a simple green yarn/single hook setup drifted through a hole containing over a hundred fish not far from the road crossing.*

## King Salmon

**Rating:** ★★½ Fair to good.
**Season:** January 1 until mid-June, then every weekend until July 1.
**Timing:** May 20 – late June; peak June 20 – June 30.
**Size:** Average 15 – 45 pounds, up to 80 pounds.
**Tackle:** Spinners, attractors, and flies.
**Tips:** At the Susitna confluence, use large spinners and attractors. Green and blue are good colors early in the season or on sunny days while chartreuse, orange, and red function better later on in the run. In the clear waters of the Montana, smaller attractors and flies in green or black work well.

Kings will hold at the mouth of the creek pending a rise in water level following a day of rain or until maturity has set in. This migration usually commences in earnest by the last week of June but may be later in some years. Expect the majority of the run to start showing some degree of spawning colors by July. For bright kings, go early in the season and try the mouth. Later on, scout holes upstream looking for silvery shapes among the turned kings.

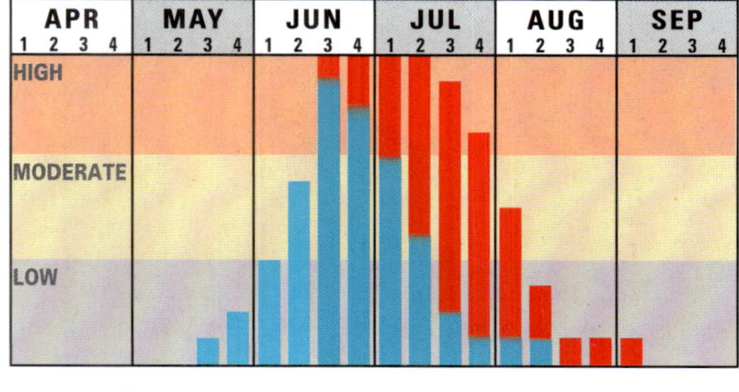


*Montana Creek King Salmon* = *Fresh* = *Spawning*

*Montana chums are vulnerable to most anything green, purple, or black. This nearly chrome specimen inhaled a weighted green/silver Hairball Leech swung through a deep run near the creek mouth. The confluence area and the holes immediately above are hot spots for fresh chums.*

## Pink Salmon

**Rating:** ★★★★ Excellent on even-numbered years, fair to good on odd.
**Season:** July 14 until mid-June, then every weekend through July 13.
**Timing:** July 1 – August 20; peak July 25 – August 5.
**Size:** Average 2 – 4 pounds, up to 7 pounds.
**Tackle:** Spoons, spinners, and flies.
**Tips:** Standard hardware and flies in green, blue, and chartreuse are favored in the clear waters of Montana. Orange and red can do well if cloudy or rain or if water levels are high.

The mouth is the best spot to hook into fresh pinks. Try early in the season just as the majority of fish are starting to arrive – about the second half of July. Fish numbers peak the first half of August but most of the run will be well into the spawning phase by then, but there are still good opportunities semi-bright pinks. Do not expect to find many salmon in upstream holes until after the first of August, the majority of them blushing.

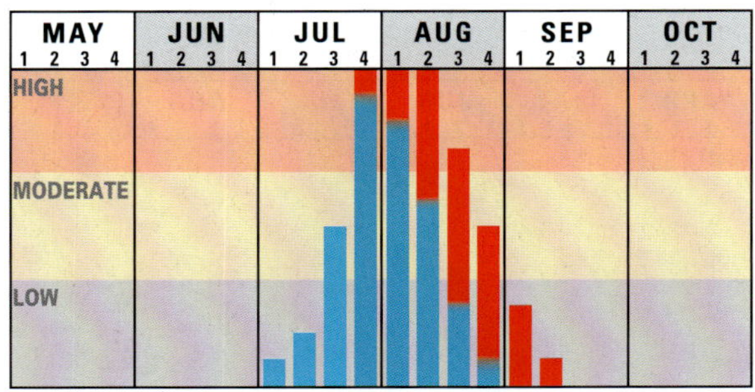


*Montana Creek Pink Salmon*

## Chum Salmon

**Rating:** ★★★★ Excellent.
**Season:** July 14 until mid-June, then every weekend through July 13.
**Timing:** July 1 – September 15; peak July 25 – August 10.
**Size:** Average 6 – 12 pounds, up to 18 pounds.
**Tackle:** Spoons, spinners, flies, and bait.
**Tips:** Green or chartreuse spoons and spinners have always worked well on chums in Montana. Some anglers prefer to drift a small cluster of salmon roe with or without an attractor since it has a way to connect with fresher specimens. If salmon appear finicky, try something smaller in black or purple. A dark pulsating fly can be deadly, especially upstream of the mouth.

The Susitna confluence is always the best spot to hook bright chums but scouting deep holes below the highway at dawn during the peak of the run can be rewarding as well. Fresh chums will move up from the mouth at night.

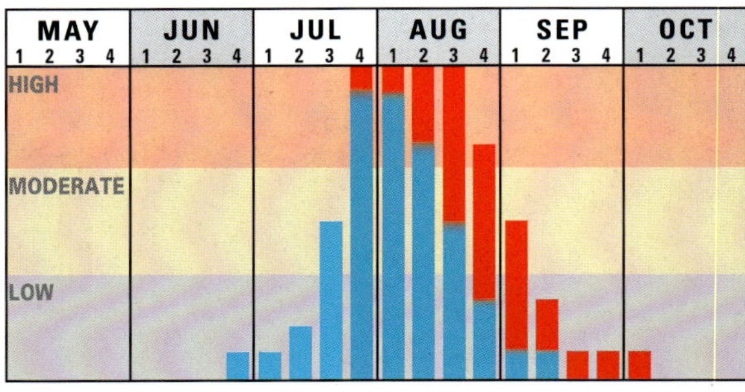


*Montana Creek Chum Salmon* ● = Fresh ● = Spawning

## Silver Salmon

**Rating:** ★★★ Good.
**Season:** July 14 until mid-June, then every weekend through July 13.
**Timing:** July 5 – September 30; peak August 5 – 20.
**Size:** Average 5 – 10 pounds, up to 15 pounds.
**Tackle:** Spoons, spinners, flies, and bait.
**Tips:** Salmon roe fished stationary or drifted along the bottom is tops for producing limits of silvers and may be the only consistent way of taking these salmon once they have entered Montana proper. Spoons, spinners, and flies in chrome and orange or red combinations are best, although blue, green, or black spinners and flies can be hot.

Like other salmon species, silvers have a tendency to wait at the mouth of Montana for days or even weeks before continuing upstream. After a good downpour, check the holes around the highway crossing. Rain or no rain, the migration will commence by mid-August as fish begin to show signs of maturity by then. Anglers always find the brightest silvers at the mouth and the first big hole above (Railroad Hole), with few nice specimens remaining after the first of September.

(Courtesy Eagle Eye Images)

*The warm light of the evening sun highlights the brilliant breeding colors of a male coho. Late season fishing often entails releasing fish such as this in favor of newly-arrived, chrome specimens.*

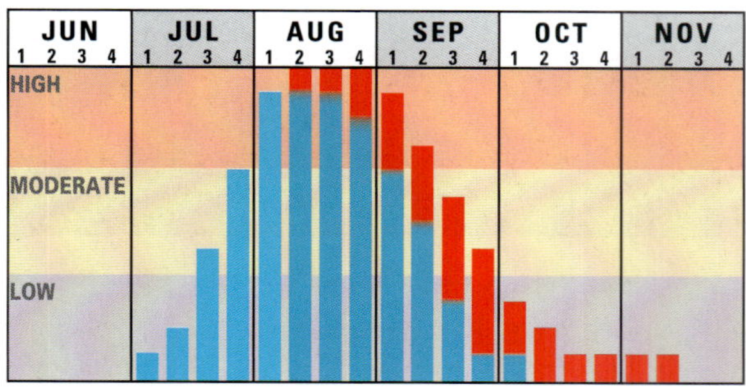


*Montana Creek Silver Salmon* ● = *Fresh* ● = *Spawning*

## Rainbow Trout

**Rating:** ★★★½ Good to excellent.
**Season:** January 1 through December 31.
**Timing:** April 1 – November 1; peak June 15 – Sept. 30.
**Size:** Average 8 – 20 inches, up to 28 inches (8 pounds).
**Tackle:** Spoons, spinners, and flies.
**Tips:** Forage imitation lures and flies are good bets anytime during the season but perhaps especially so in May and June, the fish switching to a primarily egg and flesh diet in summer and fall as salmon spawn and die off.

There is some productive action at the mouth in spring as fish arrive, yet anglers generally target these trout during the summer months (mid-June to mid-August) on the upper section of Montana, and in fall the lower stream and the mouth can be great fishing.

## Dolly Varden

**Rating:** ★ Poor.
**Season:** January 1 through December 31.
**Timing:** May 1 – November 1; peak June 25 – Sept. 30.
**Size:** Average 8 – 18 inches, up to 24 inches (5 pounds).
**Tackle:** Spinners, attractors, and flies.
**Tips:** Look for fish to be available at the creek mouth in spring using smolt imitation spoons and flies, with some quite hefty specimens possible casting egg imitations as the salmon begin to arrive in July and August. The char population in Montana is small with very few fish entering the stream proper much beyond the confluence area.

## Arctic Grayling

**Rating:** ★★★ Good.
**Season:** January 1 through December 31.
**Timing:** April 1 – November 1; peak June 15 – Sept. 30.
**Size:** Average 8 – 14 inches, up to 18 inches.
**Tackle:** Spinners and flies.
**Tips:** May and June can be good months for grayling on the lower stream as the fish move into Montana from mainstem Susitna, with the upper drainage being best from mid-summer to early fall as fish feed actively on insect life and salmon by-products.

By mid-September and later, try lower Montana and the mouth using forage imitation flies.

*The Susitna drainage rainbows have distinct colors and spotting, a truly striking appearance not often seen on other trout in the Southcentral region. This fish hit a bead drifted through a school of spawning king salmon.*

(Courtesy Jeff Varvil)

# Other Productive Fisheries & Additional Opportunities

## WILLOW AREA LAKES

**Fishing:** ★★★ **Scenery:** ★★★★
**Accessibility:** ★★★ **Solitude:** ★★★

**Location:** Lower Susitna Valley drainage, Willow area, 70 miles north of Anchorage, 30 miles north of Wasilla.

**Access:** The Parks Highway is the main thoroughfare to this area where Long Lake Road and Willow Creek Parkway heads west to numerous small lakes. Large RVs not recommended for these locations.

*A. Long Lake* – Milepost 69.2 Parks Highway; west on Long Lake Road 3.2 miles to where it becomes Crystal Lake Road, 0.2 miles to stream crossing. Parking. Follow stream 50 yards to lake. Rainbow trout and northern pike.

*B. Rainbow Lake* – Milepost 69.2 Parks Highway; west on Long Lake Road 3.2 miles to where it becomes Crystal Lake Road, 0.1 mile to unnamed road on left, 0.1 mile to large boulder blocking vehicle access. Parking. Trail leads 0.2 miles from here to lake. Rainbow trout and northern pike.

*C. Crystal Lake* – Milepost 69.2 Parks Highway; west on Long Lake Road 3.2 miles to where it becomes Crystal Lake Road, 0.3 mile to Crystal Lake Alternate on right, 1.1 mile to Crystal View Drive, 0.9 mile to lake access. Parking. Rainbow trout and northern pike.

*D. Florence Lake* – Milepost 69.2 Parks Highway; west on Long Lake Road 3.2 miles to where it becomes Crystal Lake Road, 0.3 mile to Crystal Lake Alternate on right, 1.4 mile to lake access on right. Parking. Trail leads short distance to lake. Rainbow trout and arctic grayling.

*E. Little Lonely Lake* – Milepost 69.2 Parks Highway; west on Long Lake Road 3.2 miles to where it becomes Crystal Lake Road, 1.7 miles to gravel road on left, 0.2 mile to dirt road on left, proceed 0.1 mile to lake access. Trail leads short distance to lake. Rainbow trout.

*F. Vera Lake* – Milepost 70.7 Parks Highway; west on Willow Creek Parkway 2.0 miles to Crystal Lake Road, left 2.4 miles to Deshka Landing Road, right 1.0 mile to 4-wheel-drive section line trail on left leading 0.1 mile to lake. Rainbow trout.

**Facilities:** Parking and primitive camping available.

**Species:** Rainbow trout and northern pike. A few silver salmon present in some of the lakes in fall.

**Restrictions:** Salmon fishing prohibited in area lakes from January 1 through December 31. Consult ADF&G regulations.

**Fishing:** This gathering of small lakes just south of Willow Creek in the vicinity of Willow community all support good fish populations that see relatively little angling pressure and are nice getaways from the salmon buzz of other area waters. A few of these are planted by the ADF&G while others contain naturally reproducing stocks. Also note that some lakes are part of the Willow Creek drainage and as thus have special restrictions regarding salmon.

Casting from shore is possible on any one of these lakes and can be quite productive early and late in the season when the various species are situated closer to shore in shallower water. In summer, however, anglers would be advised to use a float tube or canoe for success.

Several lakes do have decent populations of small pike that can be targeted with moderate success. In waters containing these fish, the trout fishing is generally poor to fair at best as predation is very high. If wanting to chase rainbows, hit the lakes that are stocked with fish. There are a few good-sized trout taken in fall.

**Rainbow Trout.** Good to excellent; May 15 – January 1; average 7 – 20 inches. All of the lakes described have trout; Florence, Little Lonely, and Vera best. Spoons, spinners, flies, and bait.

**Arctic Grayling.** Good to excellent; May 15 – September 30; average 7 – 12 inches. Only Florence Lake has fish. Spinners and flies.

**Northern Pike.** Fair to good; May 15 – October 15; average 2 – 4 pounds. Occasional catches to 15 pounds. Spoons, plugs, jigs, flies, and bait.

## LITTLE WILLOW CREEK

**Fishing:** ★★★★ **Scenery:** ★★½
**Accessibility:** ★★ **Solitude:** ★★★

**Location:** Lower Susitna Valley drainage, Willow area, 75 miles north of Anchorage.

**Access:** The Parks Highway crosses the stream at Milepost 74.7. Respect private property in area.

**Facilities:** Parking and primitive camping available.

**Species:** King, pink, chum, and silver salmon, rainbow trout, arctic grayling, and round whitefish. Smaller numbers or occurrences of red salmon, Dolly Varden, and burbot.

**Restrictions:** King salmon fishing prohibited from July 1 through December 31. Downstream of highway crossing is a weekend-only fishery the last two weeks of June (check exact dates). Upstream of the highway crossing, salmon fishing is prohibited. Consult ADF&G regulations.

**Fishing:** The Little Willow is quite distinct from neighboring Willow Creek, although they both drain out of the Talkeetna Mountains. Muskeg and swamplands around the stream helps shape the character of it, the clear waters stained with iron. Dense brush and a hardwood forest surround Little Willow, making any lengthy excursions away from the road crossing a strenuous activity. Trails lead downstream to some of the better holes but the upper reaches are less accessible with only a very faint trail network available.

The salmon runs on the Little Willow are fairly brief in timing, with fish often holding at the mouth of the creek (about eight miles away) for a week or two before heading upstream. Therefore, it is imperative that anglers hit the early portion of the runs, the farther down from the road crossing the better. Silver salmon retain their color the longest, followed by kings, which usually appear semi-bright to slightly blushed. Pinks and chums, although numerous, are normally well advanced in their spawning phase at this point in their journey, yet some nice specimens will be present early on in the respective runs.

Trout and grayling provide good opportunities throughout the season but perhaps especially so in late summer and fall when spawning salmon are present. Hike upstream for the best fishing; trophy rainbows to 28 inches (6-8 pounds) or more possible. Whitefish can be plentiful in some spots and hit quite well on small beads or nymphs fished deep and very slow along the bottom.

**King Salmon.** Fair to good; June 20 – June 30; average 15 – 45 pounds. Hike downstream about ¼ mile to best holes. Spinners, attractors, and flies.

**Pink Salmon.** Fair to good; July 25 – August 5; average 2 – 4 pounds. Scout holes for schools of fish; few fresh pinks available. Spoons, spinners, flies.

**Chum Salmon.** Fair to good; July 25 – August 5; average 6 – 12 pounds. Scout holes for schools of fish; few fresh chums available. Spoons, spinners, flies.

**Silver Salmon.** Good; August 10 – September 1; average 5 – 10 pounds. Hike downstream about ¼ mile to best holes. Spinners, flies, and bait.

**Rainbow Trout.** Good; June 15 – September 15; average 8 – 20 inches. Early and late in season, try downstream of highway, upstream in mid-season. Spinners and flies.

**Arctic Grayling.** Good; May 15 – September 15; average 8 – 14 inches. In spring and summer, try upstream of road, go downstream in fall. Spinners and flies.

**Round Whitefish.** Fair; July 15 – September 30; average 10 – 15 inches. Schools of fish are present in deep holes during late summer and fall. Flies and bait.

## KASHWITNA RIVER

**Fishing:** ★★½ **Scenery:** ★★
**Accessibility:** ★★ **Solitude:** ★★★★★
**Location:** Lower Susitna Valley drainage, Willow area, 83 miles north of Anchorage.
**Access:** From the Parks Highway, there are two main access points at Kashwitna: the middle section and the mouth. Respect private property.
*A. Mouth of Kashwitna* – Milepost 82.5. West on Susitna Landing Road 0.6 miles to Susitna River confluence. Parking.
*B. Highway Bridge* – Milepost 83.2. Highway crosses river. Parking and primitive camping.
**Facilities:** Camping, guide services, RV parking, restrooms, and a boat launch is available at mouth of river.
**Species:** King, pink, chum, and silver salmon, rainbow trout, arctic grayling, and burbot. Smaller numbers or occurrences of red salmon, Dolly Varden, and round whitefish.
**Restrictions:** King salmon fishing prohibited from July 1 through December 31. Downstream of highway crossing is a weekend-only fishery the last two weeks of June (check exact dates). Upstream of the highway crossing, king salmon fishing is prohibited. Consult ADF&G regulations.

*Fish tend to grow big in the Kashwitna, often topping 40 pounds with 50-pounders being quite common. Shore anglers favor the river mouth for the best shot at landing a big king such as this fresh 25-pounder. June is the month for hooking bright fish.*

*(Courtesy Chris Cox)*

**Fishing:** The Kashwitna River is a glacial stream, typically running greenish-gray with silt during the summer months, but starts to clear up in fall as temperatures drop and the silt load halts. Prolonged periods of hot weather can cause the river to flood.

Fishing can sometimes be difficult in the Kashwitna because of the turbid water conditions with most anglers trying their luck either early in the season or during the autumn months when silt discharge is light. Cooler weather periods in summer usually bring favorable fishing conditions.

Salmon action on the Kashwitna is entirely dependent on water conditions. Many anglers use attractor lures in combination with salmon roe to increase their chances in the murky water, while fluorescent spinners and brightly colored flies may prove effective at times. The river mouth is a good spot to target salmon from the bank but productive fishing can be found throughout the drainage.

As for trout and grayling, anglers target these species primarily in spring during the spawning migrations or in fall as the fish out-migrate to the Susitna River. The river has a history of delivering some very nice-sized rainbows to late-season anglers here, in September and October.

Boaters frequently travel upstream a few miles to holes and eddies that consistently offer good fishing away from the main road access points. This is particularly a popular option with guides pursuing king and silver salmon.

**King Salmon.** Fair to good; June 15 – June 30; average 15 – 45 pounds. Try Susitna confluence

in the latter part of June. Trophy fish possible. Spoons, spinners, plugs, and attractors.
**Pink Salmon.** Fair; July 20 – August 5; average 2 – 4 pounds. Mouth of river is best. Use spoons, spinners, attractors, and flies.
**Chum Salmon.** Fair; July 20 – August 5; average 6 – 12 pounds. Mouth of river is best. Use spoons, spinners, attractors, flies, and bait.
**Silver Salmon.** Fair to good; August 5 – 25; average 5 – 10 pounds. Susitna confluence best first half of August, try upstream during second half. Spinners, attractors, and bait.
**Rainbow Trout.** Fair to good; May 1 – June 1 and September 1 – October 15; average 8 – 20 inches. Mouth can be productive in first part of May and late fall; all of September into October upstream. Spinners and flies.
**Arctic Grayling.** Fair to good; May 1 – June 1 and September 1 – October 15; average 8 – 14 inches. Try river mouth in first part of May and late fall; all of September into October upstream. Spinners and flies.
**Burbot.** Fair; May 1 – November 1; average 2 – 4 pounds. Soak bait at confluence with Susitna and area immediately below for results.

## CASWELL CREEK

**Fishing:** ★★★ **Scenery:** ★★
**Accessibility:** ★★ **Solitude:** ★½
**Location:** Lower Susitna Valley drainage, Caswell area, 84 miles north of Anchorage.
**Access:** From the Parks Highway, there are two main access points at Caswell: the middle section and the mouth.
*A. Mouth of Caswell* – Milepost 84.1. West on dirt road 0.4 miles to parking area. Short hike down bluff to Susitna River confluence.
*B. Highway Culverts* – Milepost 84.9. The highway crosses stream. Limited parking.
**Facilities:** Parking and primitive camping available at mouth of creek.
**Species:** King, pink, chum, and silver salmon, rainbow trout, arctic grayling, and burbot. Smaller numbers or occurrences of red salmon, Dolly Varden, and round whitefish.
**Restrictions:** King salmon fishing prohibited from July 1 through December 31. Downstream of highway crossing is a weekend-only fishery the last two weeks of June (check exact dates). Upstream of the highway crossing, salmon fishing is prohibited. Consult ADF&G regulations.
**Fishing:** Caswell Creek is a small tannic stream that offers productive fishing in a limited area only, at the mouth where it joins the glacial Susitna River. The stream itself much beyond the mouth does not support large numbers of fish of any species, with only a few salmon and trout available.

Anglers focus on the mouth where fish concentrate on their way up the Susitna to their destined spawning streams. There is very little current in Caswell, the confluence area being more of a slough than anything else. Fish often school here for several hours before moving on upstream. Cast-and-retrieve is the favored technique with lures and flies, soaking salmon roe on the bottom also being popular. There is no opportunity for drifting.

During the king salmon season (weekend-only during peak of run), this is a true shoulder-to-shoulder fishery with some effort also during the silver run in August.

**King Salmon.** Fair; June 15 – June 30; average 15 – 40 pounds. The only viable fishing is on the first day (Saturday) of each opener, especially the first few hours after midnight. Action is usually fair at best on Sundays and Mondays. Spinners, attractors, and flies.
**Pink Salmon.** Good; July 20 – August 5; average 2 – 4 pounds. Hit mouth in early morning. Spoons, spinners, and flies.
**Chum Salmon.** Fair to good; July 20 – August 5; average 6 – 12 pounds. Look for schools of fish at mouth. Spoons, spinners, flies, and bait.
**Silver Salmon.** Fair to good; August 5 – 20; average 5 – 10 pounds. Most fish are at confluence but schools can be tracked quite a ways upstream. Spinners, flies, and bait.
**Rainbow Trout.** Fair; September 1 – October 5; average 8 – 18 inches. Try at mouth in fall, only a few fish available upstream. Spinners and flies.
**Arctic Grayling.** Fair; September 1 – October 5; average 8 – 14 inches. Confluence area best bet in fall, a few fish upstream. Spinners and flies.
**Burbot.** Fair; May 15 – October 15; average 2 – 4 pounds. Fish the mouth and the lower hundred yards of stream. Use bait, preferably at night.

## GOOSE CREEK

**Fishing:** ★★★ **Scenery:** ★★
**Accessibility:** ★★★ **Solitude:** ★★★
**Location:** Lower Susitna Valley drainage, Montana area, 93 miles north of Anchorage.
**Access:** The Parks Highway crosses the stream at Milepost 92.7. To reach the Susitna River confluence, find trail on north side of stream leading 1 mile due west to mouth.
**Facilities:** Parking and primitive camping available.
**Species:** Pink, chum, and silver salmon, rainbow trout, arctic grayling, and whitefish. An occasional red salmon, Dolly Varden, northern pike, and burbot may be present.
**Restrictions:** King salmon fishing prohibited. Upstream of the highway crossing, salmon fishing is prohibited. Consult ADF&G regulations.
**Fishing:** The Goose is a small, tannic stained stream that supports runs of four species of salmon plus trout, grayling, and whitefish. It is a popular spot to fish during the silver run in August.

The stream mouth is where fish concentrate (especially salmon) and this is where most anglers go to catch them. There are some holes between the highway and the Susitna confluence containing small schools of salmon and other species but the brightest specimens are usually caught down low in the drainage. Upstream of the highway crossing is an area that is largely ignored by most, the only interest being from an occasional angler looking for trout and grayling. Some nice rainbows reside in the upper reaches, including some surprisingly big fish for this size water.

(Courtesy Roy Bailey)

**Pink Salmon.** Good to excellent; July 20 – August 5; average 2 – 4 pounds. Fish are at their best in July at the mouth, more but darker specimens upstream in August. Use spoons, spinners, and flies.
**Chum Salmon.** Fair to good; July 20 – August 5; average 6 – 12 pounds. Best at mouth, mediocre upstream. Spoons, spinners, and flies work.
**Silver Salmon.** Fair to good; August 5 – 20; average 5 – 10 pounds. During the first half of the run, try mouth; the last part of August is better in upstream holes. Spoons, spinners, flies, and bait at mouth; upstream use flies and bait.
**Rainbow Trout.** Good; May 15 – June 15 and July 15 – September 30; average 10 – 20 inches. In May and September, try lower stream and mouth; from June into September, search above highway. Spinners and flies.
**Arctic Grayling.** Fair to good; June 1 – September 30; average 8 – 14 inches. Hit the mouth early and late in the season, upstream of highway during July and August. Spinners and flies.
**Round Whitefish.** Poor to fair; July 15 – October 5; average 10 – 15 inches. In summer and early fall, fish down low; head upstream in September. Flies and bait.

## SUNSHINE CREEK

**Fishing:** ★★★ **Scenery:** ★★
**Accessibility:** ★★★ **Solitude:** ★½
**Location:** Upper Susitna Valley drainage, Trapper Creek area, 102 miles north of Anchorage.
**Access:** Turn northeast on access road at Milepost 102.5 Sterling Highway, 0.6 mile to parking area. Trail leads 100 yards to Sunshine Creek and Susitna River confluence.
**Facilities:** Some parking and primitive camping. Limited RV parking. Nearby community of Trapper Creek support numerous developed facilities.
**Species:** All salmon species, rainbow trout, arctic grayling, and burbot. An occasional Dolly Varden, round whitefish, and northern pike may be present.
**Restrictions:** King salmon fishing prohibited from July 1 through December 31. The lower quarter mile of stream is a weekend-only fishery the last two weeks of June (check

(Courtesy Beverley Bailey)

exact dates). Upstream of the confluence area, king salmon fishing is prohibited. Consult ADF&G regulations.
**Fishing:** Sunshine is a very small stream that in itself supports only a small population of salmon and other resident species. The mouth of the creek, however, serves as a resting area for many salmon headed to spawning tributaries farther up the Susitna and Talkeetna rivers. The

slow water of the confluence is ideal for holding salmon, a fact that many local anglers take advantage.

Anglers hiking upstream may find fair numbers of small trout, grayling, and silver salmon with some very good fishing at times.

Because Sunshine is limited in size and productive fishing area, it pays to be on the water at dawn before other anglers begin to arrive in numbers. Action at mid-day can be very slow. During king salmon season, however, the best of it occurs at midnight at the main opener. Expect shoulder-to-shoulder crowds. Catching will be hot for an hour or two and then dies down until the next opener the week after.

**King Salmon.** Fair; June 15 – June 30; average 15 – 40 pounds. Spoons, spinners, and attractors are popular. Look for brightest fish early in season.

**Red Salmon.** Poor to fair; June 10 – 20 and July 20 – August 5; average 3 – 7 pounds. Small spinners and flies. Fish can be abundant but hard to catch.

**Pink Salmon.** Good to excellent; July 25 – August 5; average 2 – 4 pounds. Small spoons and spinners, flies. Big run on even-numbered years.

**Chum Salmon.** Fair to good; July 25 – August 5; average 6 – 12 pounds. Try spoons, spinners, flies, and roe. Early morning is best.

**Silver Salmon.** Good; August 5 – 25; average 5 – 10 pounds. Spinners and flies are good but salmon roe is best. Many of these silvers are Sunshine fish and can be found throughout the stream.

**Rainbow Trout.** Fair; August 25 – September 30; average 8 – 12 inches. Flies and small spinners. Search upstream for trout.

**Arctic Grayling.** Fair; June 1 – September 15; average 8 – 10 inches. Usually found in upper stream away from mouth. Spinners, flies.

**Burbot.** Fair; May 15 – September 1; average 2 – 4 pounds. Soak bait such as pieces of herring or smelt right at confluence.

## RABIDEUX CREEK

**Fishing:** ★★★ **Scenery:** ★★★
**Accessibility:** ★★★ **Solitude:** ★★½

**Location:** Upper Susitna Valley drainage, Trapper Creek area, 105 miles from Anchorage.

**Access:** The Parks Highway provides four points of access.
*A. Rabideux / Susitna Confluence* – Milepost 104.4. Turn west on gravel road 0.7 mile to confluence area. Note: Access road is often in poor condition and may at times be impassable due to flooding from the Susitna River. Primitive camping, undeveloped parking.
*B. Rabideux (Lower)* – Milepost 104.5. Turn west on dirt road 0.3 mile to stream. Small parking area.
*C. Rabideux Creek Culvert* – Milepost 105.8. Highway crosses stream. Limited parking.
*D. Rabideux (Upper)* – Milepost 112.6. Highway crosses stream. Park on shoulder of road.

**Facilities:** There is some limited parking and camping opportunities, none of them with RV capabilities. Nearby community of Trapper Creek support numerous developed facilities.

**Species:** All salmon species, rainbow trout, arctic grayling, and burbot. A few Dolly Varden and round whitefish and an occasional northern pike may be present.

**Restrictions:** King salmon fishing prohibited from July 1 through December 31. The lower quarter mile of stream is a weekend-only fishery the last two weeks of June (check exact dates). Upstream of the confluence area, king salmon fishing is prohibited. Consult ADF&G regulations.

**Fishing:** The majority of angling activity occurs on the far

lower portion of the stream, the mouth being a popular spot since salmon school up here waiting to head upstream and fish from other tributaries higher up in the Susitna drainage often pull in and rest in the relatively clear waters of Rabideux. The lower portion of Rabideux is quite wide with a very slow current so spotting fish surfacing indicating a possible school is easy.

This stream is known for its healthy runs of kings and silvers but only the confluence area is open to king fishing.

Fishing is far less productive in respect to salmon in the middle and upper stream reaches, with silver salmon providing the only viable action (in late August). The run actually peaks in September; however, expect most salmon to be turning at least a shade of color at that time.

As for trout and grayling, these species are available throughout the creek and present some level of opportunity upstream of the mouth where there is more current and defined holes and pools. Spawning kings and silvers is the reason these fish are here.

The upper stream (access point D) has a few resident

species and small numbers of spawning salmon and is generally not a good angling option.

**King Salmon.** Fair; June 15 – June 30; average 15 – 40 pounds. The run has a tendency to hold in lower stream until near ripe before moving upstream. Large spinners are great when water is clear, otherwise use fluorescent attractors. Large attractor flies work too.

**Red Salmon.** Poor; July 20 – August 5; average 4 – 7 pounds. Slack water of mouth is not conducive to productive fishing but when fish are abundant at peak of run, some are caught on spoons, spinners, and flies. Most fish are headed to other streams.

**Pink Salmon.** Good; July 25 – August 5; average 2 – 4 pounds. Small spoons and spinners in orange or chartreuse tempt strikes, as do attractor flies.

**Chum Salmon.** Fair; July 25 – August 5; average 6 – 12 pounds. The majority of these salmon are bound for other Susitna tributaries. Spoons, spinners, and flies take fish.

**Silver Salmon.** Good; August 10 – 25; average 5 – 10 pounds. Spinners in orange or chartreuse and small clusters of salmon roe are top producers here. Colorful flies get hits. Decent action can also be had in the middle stream reaches.

**Rainbow Trout.** Fair; July 15 – September 30; average 8 – 12 inches. The mouth is not very productive and successful anglers are targeting the fish in middle stream reaches where there is more structure. Use small spinners and flies.

**Arctic Grayling.** Fair; June 1 – September 15; average 8 – 12 inches. The middle stream portions yield most fish, only a few are caught at mouth. Flies and small spinners take fish.

**Burbot.** Fair; May 15 – November 1; average 2 – 4 pounds. A few fish may be found throughout most of stream but higher concentrations are at mouth. Small pieces of cut fish (herring or smelt) works.

## ADDITIONAL OPPORTUNITIES

### Susitna River Remote Fishing

The communities of Willow north to Talkeetna and beyond offer guided and drop-off fishing trips to remote sections of the vast Susitna River drainage using boats and planes, targeting all five species of salmon, trout, char, grayling, and pike. It is also the ideal area to engage fall hunts from and combination fishing/hunting trips can be arranged as well. On top of this, flightseeing trips to Mount Denali (McKinley) and surrounding glaciers are available.

With such an immense system like the Susitna that encompasses dozens of large glacial drainages and almost too many clearwater tributaries and lakes to count, anglers can expect to find themselves in a very remote wilderness heading out. Boaters primarily access fishing locales within two hour or less from the launch, concentrating on the myriad of small rivers and streams that flow into the Susitna. Those that fly in, however, generally aim for even more distant places, landing on gravel bars, broad rivers, and lakes, sometimes in conjunction with area lodges.

Day trips are most popular and a perfect solution for those traveling the road system, but half-day excursions are available in addition. For anglers seeking a more rustic do-it-yourself experience may choose to be dropped of somewhere for a few days or longer. Many established lodges operate on the Susitna and surrounding waters.

The vast majority of anglers opt to fish for salmon with the months of June to September being prime. Kings come in heavy from late May through mid-July, with locations such as Deshka and Talachulitna rivers and Lake Creek being popular destinations. There are also a lot of smaller, lesser-known streams that harbor good fishing for kings.

The period from mid-July to early August means fishing for red, pink, and chum salmon. These species are very prolific in the Susitna watershed and can be caught in most any clearwater stream in the area. With the possible exception of reds, very few people target them.

Silvers are more sought, running strong from late July to early September. Hot spots, again, include the Deshka and Talachulitna rivers and Lake Creek but most any location with clear water will support excellent fishing.

Resident species, such as rainbow trout and arctic grayling, provide notable stream opportunities during the period from June to October. The Talachulitna is a great fly-in location. Northern pike thrive in this area and are taken in lakes and sloughs of the Susitna from May to October.

Talkeetna • Petersville

# Northern Susitna & Chulitna

**King Salmon • Red Salmon • Pink Salmon • Chum Salmon**
**Silver Salmon • Rainbow Trout • Dolly Varden • Arctic Grayling**

*Wildlife* *Small Stream Trout* *World-Class Scenery* *Solitude*

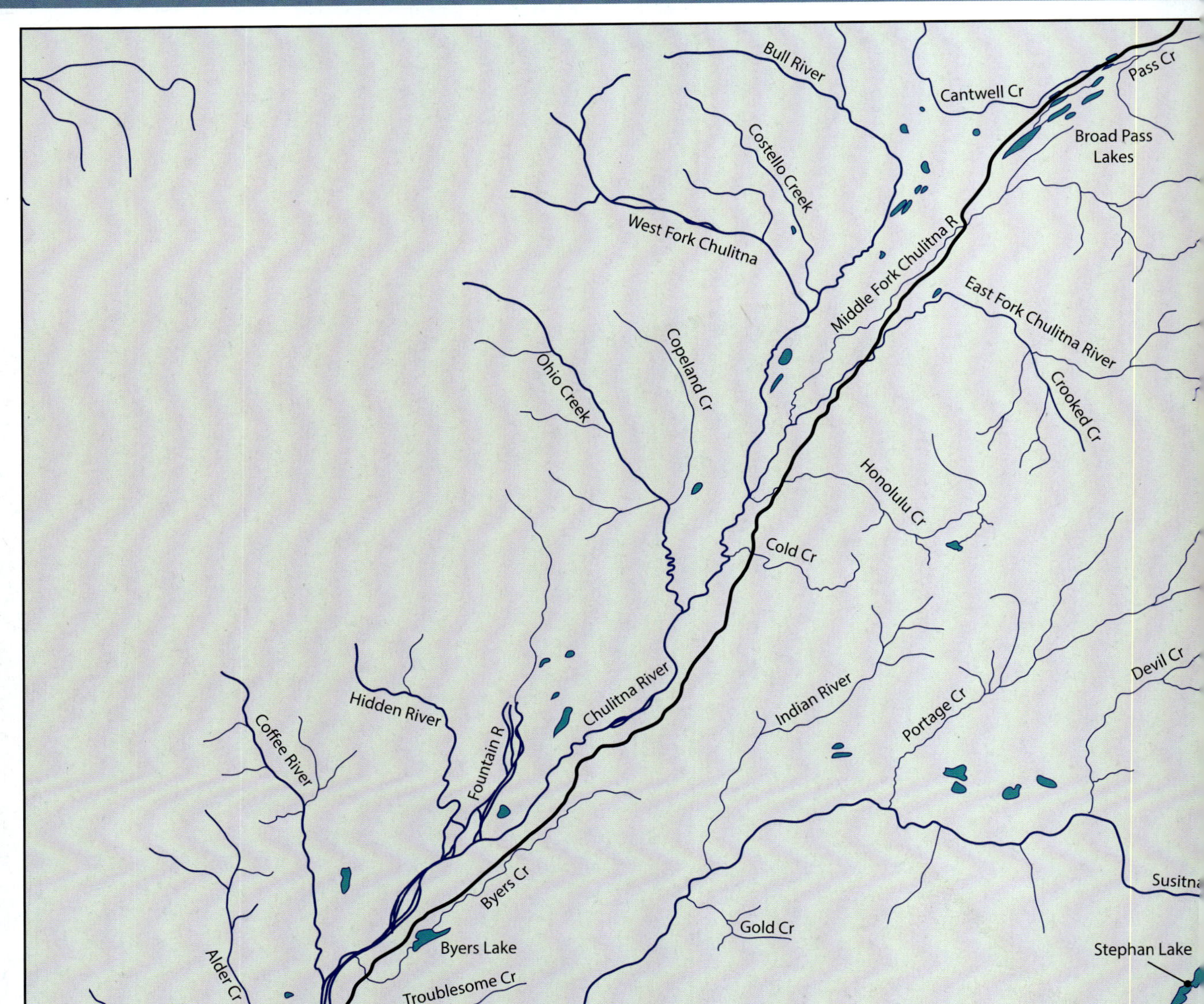


**Area Population Centers:** Talkeetna, Trapper Creek, and Petersville
**Key Species:** King, Red, Pink, Chum, and Silver Salmon, Rainbow Trout, and Arctic Grayling
**Other Species:** Lake Trout, Dolly Varden, Round Whitefish, Northern Pike, and Burbot
**Main Destinations/Hot Spots:** Byers Creek and East Fork Chulitna River
**Other Destinations:** Talkeetna and Middle Fork Chulitna Rivers, Moose, Peters, Troublesome, and Honolulu Creeks
**Additional Opportunities:** Float Fishing Safaris and Upper Susitna River Excursions

**Summary of Fishing:** Very sparse settlements that are hours apart is the trademark of this area that is dominated by spruce-forested valleys where huge rivers flow and magnificent snow-clad mountain ranges, including the 20,300-plus-foot Mount Denali (McKinley) which commands a formidable view from most any location. In this roadside wilderness, anglers will find gin-clear streams that are home to salmon, trout, char, grayling, and whitefish along with abundant wildlife, such as bear, moose, beaver, and wolf. In fact, on some waters it is far more common to fish alongside grizzlies than other anglers.

While the major rivers around here are turbid and full of glacial silt, their tributaries are laden with several key species of game fish. For those that enjoy hiking and wading small clearwater rivers and creeks while casting to wild rainbows and arctic grayling in a stunning setting, this is must-visit area. It is an especially great destination for sight-fishing salmon, with runs of king, red, and silver salmon being the top draw.

Fishing is best from June through September.

# Byers Creek

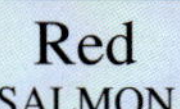

Red SALMON

Pink SALMON

Chum SALMON

Silver SALMON

Rainbow TROUT

**Highlights:** A premier rainbow trout stream offering very productive fly-fishing in a true wilderness setting. Solid action also for red and silver salmon. Abundant wildlife.

**Best Fishing:** Mid-June to early October.

**Regulatory Restrictions:** Liberal.

**Location:** Northern Susitna Valley drainage, Parks Highway, 144 miles north of Anchorage, 52 miles north of Talkeetna, 218 miles south of Fairbanks.

**Description:** Draining from the hilly terrain around the Alaska Range within the Denali State Park, forming Byers Lake along the way, and meandering through a combination of spruce, aspen, and cottonwood forest before emptying into the glacial Chulitna River, Byers Creek is a relatively small and inviting clearwater stream that is perfect for wading and easily forded in most places, even with hip boots. It is home to five species of salmon and several resident species, such as rainbow trout and arctic grayling. In fact, this is the northernmost roadside stream in the Susitna drainage that supports strong runs of reds, pinks, and chums.

The far upper portion of the stream, above Byers Lake, flows slow and steady with an abundance of deep pools and runs, eddies, and cut banks. In addition, coarse sand constitutes much of the bottom structure with rocks in some parts. This section is an important spawning area for mainly reds and silvers.

Lower Byers, from the lake outlet down to the Chulitna

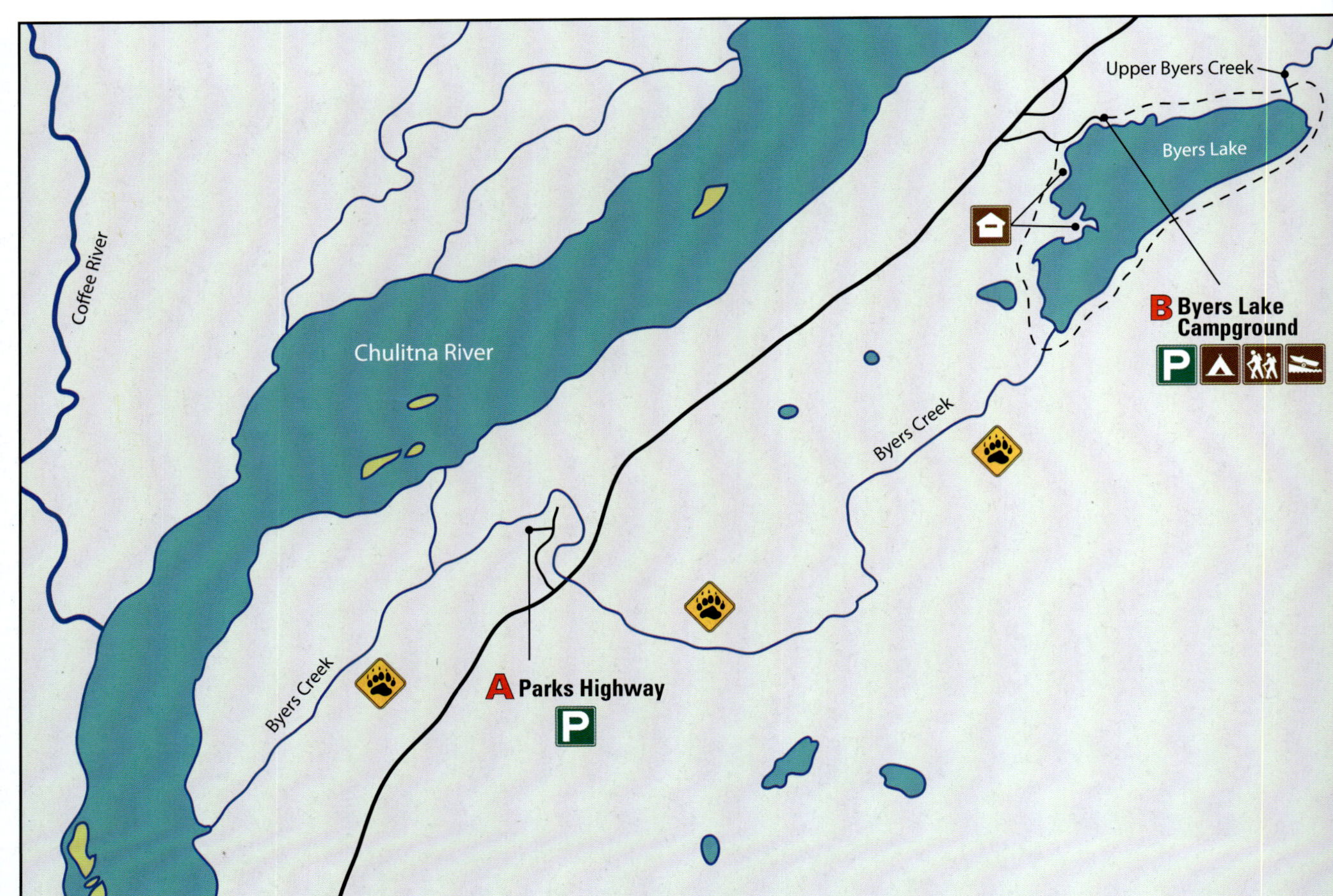


confluence has a much different character altogether, the clear creek meanders less and widens, becoming fairly swift and shallow in places with plenty of riffles and holes. Rock and gravel constitutes bottom structure. This stretch is a major breeding ground for kings, pinks, and chums.

There is little angling activity on Byers, most of it because until very recently private land ownership blocked any public access to the more productive reaches of the lower stream and its mouth. Also, this waterway is in ways somewhat "remote" by roadside standards – situated between the cities of Anchorage and Fairbanks with just as productive waters much closer to either population center and just two access points.

Some angling effort occurs in August when the salmon runs peak and again later on in autumn when a few die-hard flyfishers hit Byers in search of trout. Expect to meet few people on Byers, even in mid-summer.

Visitors to this stream should be aware that this area has an exceptionally high population of bears – both brown and black – and encounters during the height of the salmon runs are not only possible but highly likely. Take necessary precautions before fishing here, especially if deciding to hike away from the road access points to any extent, such as the 2-mile trip to the Byers Creek/Chulitna River confluence or along the upper stream above the lake.

**Facilities:** There is a complete lack of common facilities and amenities at and around the immediate vicinity, except for a lodge several miles to the south and the state-run campground at Byers Lake just up the road.

**Access:** The Parks Highway provides general stream access near the crossing; however, the better bet is to use the Byers Creek Landing Road south of the bridge (Access Point A).

**A. Parks Highway/Lower Byers Creek** – Milepost 143.9. Turn west on Byers Creek Landing Road and follow to a split where one fork is chained off. Take left fork short distance to cul-de-sac. Parking. Not recommended for large RVs. Locate trailhead with dirt path leading 100 yards down steep slope to stream. Wade in the stream and/or use faint footpath on the south shore of Byers to navigate along the stream. The 2-mile hike to the mouth may require bushwhacking and fording the creek.

**B. Byers Lake Campground/Upper Byers Creek** – Milepost 147.2. Northeast on gravel road 0.3 mile to lake. A developed trail begins at the campground and circles the lake, providing access to the upper part of Byers Creek as well as the lake outlet. Parking, camping, restrooms, primitive boat launch at the lake.

## Rules & Regulations

**Open Season:** Fishing is allowed from January 1 through December 31.
**Open Area:** The entire stream is open to fishing.
**Legal Gear/Tackle:** Only unbaited, artificial lures allowed from September 1 through July 13; lures with multiple hooks and bait are allowed from July 14 through August 31.

**All Salmon**

- Open all season (see general "Open Season" above), except for kings.
- King salmon fishing is prohibited, including catch-and-release.
- Open area is from mouth upstream to Parks Highway bridge; closed to salmon fishing above bridge (including Byers Lake).
- Red, pink, chum, and silver salmon bag limit is (3) per day and (3) in possession (16 inches or longer); for salmon less than 16 inches (Jacks), the limit is (10).

**Rainbow/Steelhead Trout & Dolly Varden**

- Open all season (see general "Open Season" above).
- Entire stream is open to fishing.
- Bag limit for trout is (2) per day and (2) in possession, only (1) over 20 inches, and Dolly Varden (5) per day and (5) in possession, only (1) over 12 inches.

**Other Fishes**

- Open all season (see general "Open Season" above).
- Arctic grayling bag limit is (2) per day and (2) in possession, any size.
- Whitefish has no bag or possession limit, no size restrictions.
- Burbot bag limit is (5) per day and (5) in possession, any size.

## Fishing Byers Creek

**Access:** ★★
**Scenery:** ★★★½
**Wildlife:** ★★★★
**Sight Fishing:** ★★★★★
**Bank/Wading:** ★★★★
**Boat/Floating: N/A**

**Species:** Red, pink, chum, and silver salmon, and rainbow trout. A few grayling present. Small run of king salmon during July.
**Summary:** Byers Creek is perhaps the uppermost drainage of the Susitna-Chulitna basin to receive significant numbers of multiple salmon species and is a relative hot spot for trout as well. Primarily a late summer opportunity for salmon, relatively few anglers visit this idyllic stream. Although rainbow fishing is good throughout most of the open water season, salmon runs here are short in duration, with productive action usually lasting no more than ten days to two weeks at the most for any one species.

With salmon fishing only allowed downstream of the highway crossing, anglers are limited to a few short miles of water in which to focus their efforts. Four species of salmon are available, three of them (red, pink, and chum) run relatively at the same time while silvers are the last to arrive. On Byers, as is the case with many inland and interior waters, it is wise to tempt the various species early in their respective seasons if seeking prime sport and food quality fish, preferably as low down in the drainage as possible, such as at or near the stream mouth.

The red run is usually very good and many of the fish still sporting a silvery shine upon entering Byers Creek.

*A small school consisting of four species of salmon in varying phases of maturity hug the siltline of Chulitna River and clear Byers Creek.*

Anglers often intercept these fish as they migrate in schools between deeper and calmer stream portions. Bound for spawning beds on upper reaches of Byers, including the lake, these salmon usually move through the lower stream rapidly compared to other species.

Right as the red run peaks, large numbers of pinks and chums ascend Byers, the former being especially prevalent on even-numbered years. These fish are typically well into their nuptial coloration at this point in their life cycle and generally not the best fish for table fare; however, if caught early enough in the run, chrome bright salmon are possible. The main spawning area for pinks and chums are low in the drainage (below Parks Highway bridge) and salmon often clog sections of the stream with spawning activity.

The majority of silvers pulling into Byers are in decent shape – silvery to semi-bright – early in the season but tend to blush quickly as the run progresses. A few nice specimens will continue to arrive into fall, however. For anglers hitting this run at its peak, expect days of exceptional action. Like reds, most silvers are bound for the lake outlet and the upper stream.

Very few anglers continue to ply these waters into the cooler fall months, yet this is when rainbow trout are at a peak. Although available from spring on through summer, late season opportunities present aggressive fish and even sight-fishing opportunities in some stretches of the stream. In fact, Byers ranks very high among all of the Susitna system streams in terms of numbers of fish present and the size of some of the specimens.

Byers Lake supports a fair population of lake trout along with smaller numbers of rainbows, grayling, and burbot. The upper portion of the stream above the lake can be good at times for rainbows and a few arctic grayling when salmon are spawning in late summer and fall.

## Fish Availability

● = High ● = Moderate ● = Low ● = Closed

| Species | APR | MAY | JUN | JUL | AUG | SEP | OCT |
|---|---|---|---|---|---|---|---|
| **Red Salmon** | | | | Low, Low, Moderate | High, High, Moderate, Low | Low | |
| **Pink Salmon** | | | | Low, Low, Moderate | High, Moderate, Low, Low | | |
| **Chum Salmon** | | | | Low, Low, Moderate | High, High, Moderate, Low | Low | |
| **Silver Salmon** | | | | Low | Low, Moderate, High, High | Moderate, Low, Low, Low | |
| **Rainbow Trout** | Low, Low, Low, Moderate | Moderate, Moderate, Moderate, Moderate | Moderate, Moderate, High, High | High, High, High, High | High, High, High, High | High, High, High, High | Moderate, Moderate, Low, Low |
| **Arctic Grayling** | Low, Low, Low, Low | Low, Low, Low, Low | Moderate, Moderate, Moderate, Moderate | Moderate, Moderate, Moderate, Moderate | Moderate, Moderate, Moderate, Moderate | Moderate, Moderate, Moderate, Moderate | Moderate, Moderate, Low, Low |
| Angling Pressure | | | Low, Low, Low, Low | Low, Low, Low, Low | Moderate, Moderate, Moderate, Moderate | Low, Low, Low, Low | |

(Courtesy Eagle Eye Images)

*Byers Creek is the leading road-accessible sockeye water in the Susitna-Chulitna Valley. Anglers skilled at sight-fishing will find this stream a delight, scouting for schools of fish or even individual specimens possible.*

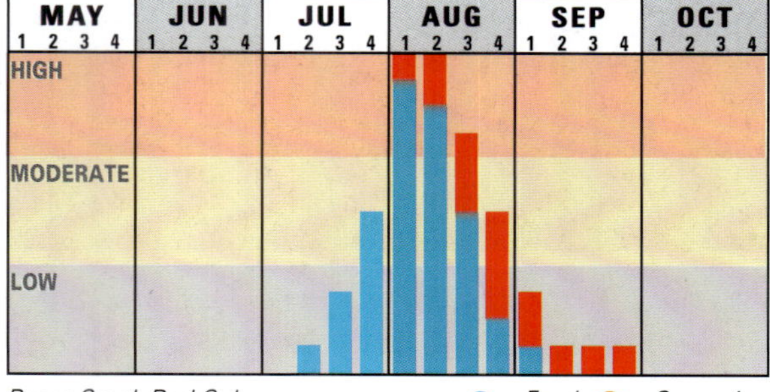


*Byers Creek Red Salmon* ● = Fresh ● = Spawning

### Red Salmon

**Rating:** ★★½ Fair to good.
**Season:** January 1 through December 31.
**Timing:** July 15 – September 15; peak August 1 – 10.
**Size:** Average 4 – 7 pounds; up to 11 pounds.
**Tackle:** Flies.
**Tips:** Intercept fish when they are moving through shallower stream sections and migratory channels. Look for concentrations of resting fish in deeper areas where there is some current flow as well. Flies in darker colors are usually best, as stream is small and very clear.

### Pink Salmon

**Rating:** ★★ Fair; expect few bright specimens, many spawners. Even-numbered years are best.
**Season:** January 1 through December 31.
**Timing:** July 15 – August 25; peak August 1 – 10.
**Size:** Average 2 – 4 pounds; up to 5 pounds.
**Tackle:** Spoons, spinners, and flies.
**Tips:** Fish at or near mouth early in run if interested in quality fish. Search out deeper holes and runs; the spawners are mainly in the shallows. Lures in green, pink, and black work.

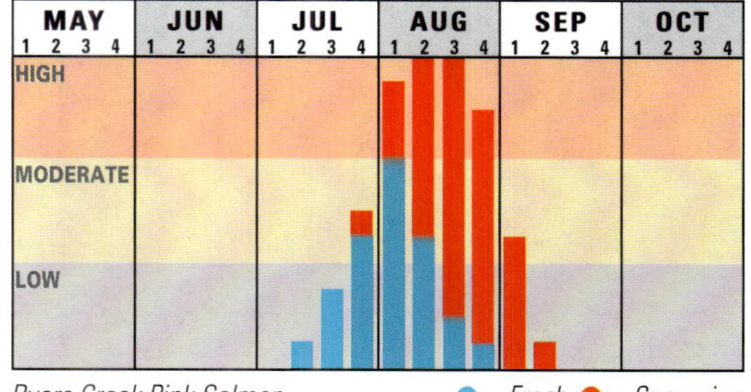


*Byers Creek Pink Salmon* ● = Fresh ● = Spawning

(Courtesy Beverley Bailey)

*A blushed male coho is returned to the water. Be prepared to sort through darker fish if targeting brighter specimens. The month of August is great for a variety of salmon species, as well as trout.*

## Chum Salmon

**Rating:** ★★ Fair; expect few bright specimens, many spawners.
**Season:** January 1 through December 31.
**Timing:** July 15 – September 5; peak August 5 – 15.
**Size:** Average 6 – 12 pounds; up to 15 pounds.
**Tackle:** Spoons, spinners, and flies.
**Tips:** Fish at or near mouth early in run if interested in quality fish. Scout deeper parts of the stream using lures and flies in neutral colors, such as green, purple, and black.

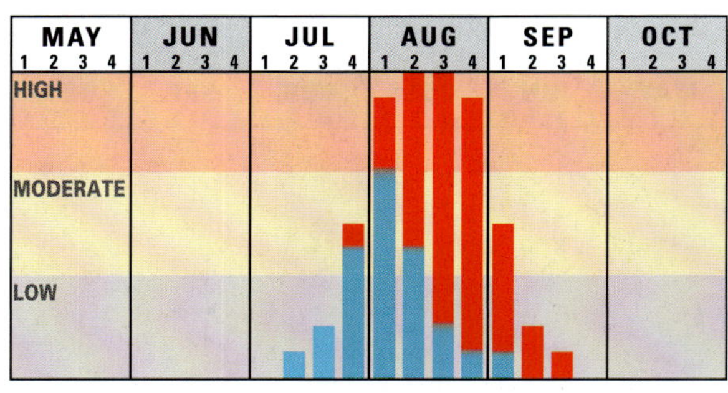


*Byers Creek Chum Salmon*

## Silver Salmon

**Rating:** ★★½ Fair to good.
**Season:** January 1 through December 31.
**Timing:** July 25 – September 30; peak August 25 – Sept. 5.
**Size:** Average 5 – 10 pounds; up to 15 pounds.
**Tackle:** Spinners, flies, and bait.
**Tips:** Bright specimens are scattered throughout area open to salmon fishing but most nice fish are found lower down in drainage closer to the mouth. Look for aggressive salmon in early morning using lures and flies in orange and green; purple and black hues do well during the day. Sight-fishing to individual silvers amongst masses of other salmon species can be exciting and challenging.

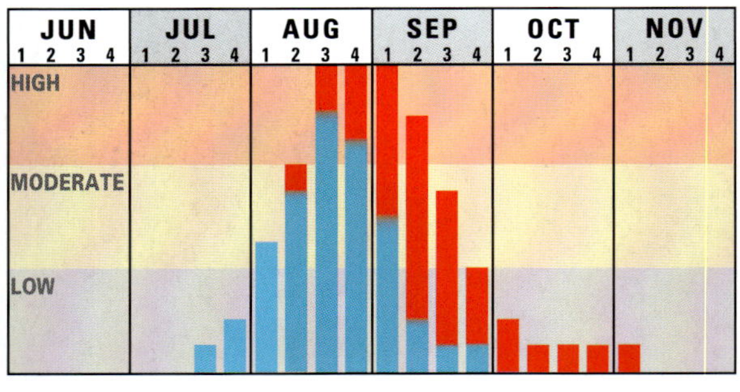


*Byers Creek Silver Salmon* ● = *Fresh* ● = *Spawning*

## Rainbow Trout

**Rating:** ★★★½ Good to excellent.
**Season:** January 1 through December 31.
**Timing:** May 1 – November 15; peak August 1 – Sept. 30.
**Size:** Average 10 – 16 inches; up to 28 inches and 10 pounds.
**Tackle:** Spinners and flies.
**Tips:** Scout deeper stream sections early and late in the season using attractor/forage imitations, switching to egg/flesh patterns from the latter part of July into September when salmon spawn. Schools of trout are sometimes encountered in holes downstream of highway bridge.

*A typical heavily spotted Byers rainbow, caught on an Egg Sucking Leech. Byers is a late season favorite with many trout enthusiasts.*

# East Fork Chulitna River

King
SALMON

Silver
SALMON

Rainbow
TROUT

Arctic
GRAYLING

**Highlights:** A yet to be fully discovered roadside drainage, featuring exciting sight-fishing opportunities for big kings and silvers. Great late-season fishery for trout and grayling.

**Best Fishing:** Late June to late September. **Regulatory Restrictions:** Liberal.

**Location:** Northern Susitna Valley drainage, Parks Highway, 177 miles north of Anchorage, 85 miles north of Talkeetna, 138 miles south of Fairbanks.

**Description:** Quite variable in appearance, the upper section of Chulitna River constitutes three main branches, namely the glacial West Fork draining out of the foothills of the Alaska Range, the small and shallow Middle Fork, and the slightly larger and swifter East Fork, the latter two pouring out of the narrow valleys of the Alaska Range just southeast of Broad Pass. Of these three, it is the East Fork that carries the best potential for exemplary fishing as it flows relatively deep and clear with plenty of gravel bars, long runs, cutbanks, some sweepers, and overhanging brush all adding to the charm of this rocky-bottomed stream.

With a highland spruce and alder forest lacking any sign of human settlement lining the river, the East Fork Chulitna is clearly as remote as can be for a roadside waterway. The surrounding scenery is absolutely gorgeous and arguably one of the most picturesque in all of Alaska, complete with jagged mountain ranges displaying ice fields and glaciers, and the 20,300-foot Mount Denali (McKinley) looming

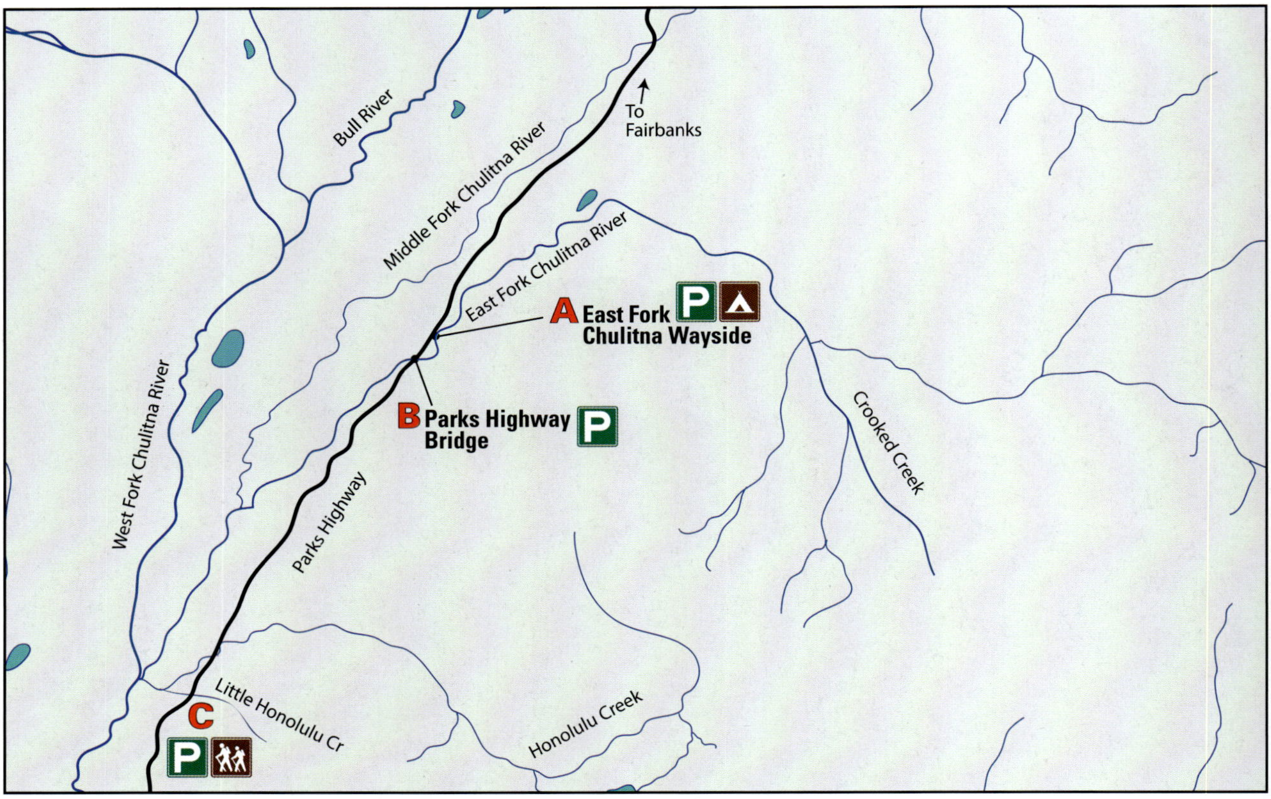

Bull River
Middle Fork Chulitna River
To Fairbanks
East Fork Chulitna River
A East Fork Chulitna Wayside
B Parks Highway Bridge
West Fork Chulitna River
Parks Highway
Crooked Creek
Little Honolulu Cr
Honolulu Creek
C

immediately to the northwest.

A terrific location to hike in and wade, those spending time on this river can wander its banks for literally days to a week or more completely unhindered, scouting for new and productive stretches of water without concerns for closed or restricted fishing areas. Angling effort on this branch of the Chulitna is still very low as developed access is minimal to near non-existent. Because of this, East Fork is an increasingly popular destination for those wanting a more rustic fishing excursion without the commercialization prevalent on so many other roadside waters.

Wildlife is abundant as moose, beaver, and both black and brown (grizzly) bear are common sights along the river. It is not unusual to hear wolves howling in the distance.

**Facilities:** There is nearly a complete lack of infrastructure of any kind in this area, yet a developed rest area is located near the Parks Highway crossing. Guide services operating on the river may be found in the Trapper Creek and Talkeetna area.

**Access:** As with facilities, developed access, too, is very limited on the East Fork Chulitna. The Parks Highway does parallel the middle and upper river for a few miles, even

(Courtesy Eagle Eye Images)

*Left: The trail leading to the lower reaches of Honolulu Creek and the East Fork confluence. Come prepared for wet trail conditions and fording a couple of shallow creeks may be necessary. Also pay attention to private property in the area.*

*Right: Anglers work the deep run at the Honolulu confluence, a favorite spot for kings and silvers. Always expect company at the peak of the runs. For solitude, fish the river where it parallels the highway, scouting for quiet water between fast flows.*

## Rules & Regulations

**Open Season:** January 1 through December 31.
**Open Area:** The entire river is open to fishing.
**Legal Gear/Tackle:** Only one unbaited, single-hook, artificial lure allowed from January 1 through July 13; lures with multiple hooks and bait are allowed from July 14 through December 31.

**King Salmon**

- Open season is January 1 through July 13; retention of kings is allowed until July 1, weekends only (check regulations for exact dates).
- The entire river is open to king fishing, including Middle Fork Chulitna River and the first 1/4 mile of Honolulu Creek.
- Bag limit is (1) per day and (1) in possession (20 inches or longer). For kings less than 20 inches (Jacks), the limit is (10).

**All Other Salmon**

- Open all season (see general "Open Season" above).
- The entire river and its tributaries are open to salmon fishing, including Middle Fork Chulitna River and Honolulu Creek.
- Red, pink, chum, and silver salmon bag limit is (3) per day and (3) in possession (16 inches or longer). For salmon less than 16 inches (Jacks), the limit is (10).

**Rainbow/Steelhead Trout & Dolly Varden**

- Open all season (see general "Open Season" above).
- Entire river is open to fishing.
- Retention of rainbow trout is allowed from June 15 through April 14; catch-and-release only from April 15 through June 14.
- Bag limit for rainbow trout is (2) per day and (2) in possession, only (1) over 20 inches.
- Bag limit for Dolly Varden is (5) per day and (5) in possession, only (1) over 12 inches.

**Other Fishes**

- Open all season (see general "Open Season" above).
- Entire river is open to fishing.
- Bag limit for arctic grayling is (2) per day and (2) in possession, no size restrictions.
- Whitefish has no bag or possession limit, no size restrictions.
- Burbot bag limit is (5) per day and (5) in possession, no size restrictions.

crossing it at one point, and a primitive trail provides access to the lower river.

**A. East Fork Chulitna Wayside** – Milepost 185.6 Parks Highway. East on paved access road that loops 0.5 mile through rest area. Parking for all size vehicles, primitive camping, restrooms, fire pits, and picnic tables and shelters present. Trails lead short distance to river.

**B. Parks Highway Bridge** – Milepost 185.0 Parks Highway. Road crosses river. Limited parking near bridge.

**C. East Fork Chulitna/Honolulu Confluence** – Milepost 177.0. West to gravel/dirt parking area with space for smaller RVs. Locate ATV trail to south of parking leading 1 mile to confluence of East Fork Chulitna River and Honolulu Creek, just upstream of West Fork Chulitna River.

*(Courtesy Eagle Eye Images)*

## Fishing East Fork Chulitna River

**Access:** ★★★
**Scenery:** ★★★★★
**Wildlife:** ★★★
**Sight Fishing:** ★★★
**Bank/Wading:** ★★★★
**Boat/Floating:** ★★★★★

**Species:** King and silver salmon, rainbow trout, and arctic grayling. Some chum salmon, whitefish, and burbot present.
**Summary:** The East Fork Chulitna is a superb sportfishing stream that has yet to hit stride in popularity as far as roadside waters are concerned. Despite only supporting two salmon species in any numbers (with kings the dominant and most targeted catch), the river holds its own as the trout and grayling populations are very healthy and virtually untapped.

East Fork (along with Middle Fork Chulitna) represents the uppermost extent of salmon migrations in the Susitna River drainage and anglers should expect many fish to be at least slightly blushed upon arriving. Typically, specimens caught early in the respective runs tend to be in reasonably good shape with some fish even being nearly dime bright. But as the runs progress, the salmon increasingly display nuptial coloration; however, they are still nowhere close to spawning and put up a great fight when hooked.

Anglers also need to keep in mind that East Fork Chulitna is a fairly long river, meaning that if targeting salmon for both sport and consumption, a focus on the lower reaches of the river is preferable as the fish tend to be in better shape than higher up in the drainage.

King salmon is the primary game fish on East Fork, with excellent opportunities possible from the Parks Highway bridge all the way downstream to where the river hits the turbid West Fork. Sight-fishing can be exceptional when the river flows low and clear as it often does in mid-summer.

(Courtesy Eagle Eye Images)

In fact, few places on the road system can compare in excitement; casting streamers to big, aggressive kings weighing up to 40-50 pounds using a fly rod.

Silvers, on the other hand, can be abundant but are generally not much of a sought-after species on the East Fork. Good action await those that traverse this river in late season when this species finally shows up, the best of it taking place low down in the drainage at or near the confluences of main tributaries.

Other game species include rainbow trout and arctic grayling, the former of which is reasonably plentiful and may attain a respectable average size. As the East Fork is a salmon spawning ground, expect these opportunistic fish to be present in good numbers and highly aggressive. The trout are relatively abundant, being most prominent in the upper river in summer, lower down come fall. Kings peak breeding the latter part of July and into August, silvers starting in mid-September, and the trout will be there.

Grayling are seasonally abundant, with prime fishing occurring in late summer and fall when significant numbers of fish begin to withdraw from feeding grounds at the headwaters of East Fork and the larger tributaries, such as Middle Fork Chulitna and Honolulu, and migrate downstream to the lower reaches of river. Expect a number of whitefish to show as well.

As any seasoned angler that has spent some time in autumn on East Fork can attest to, the schools of trout and grayling occupying the deeper holes and pools often create fantastic action.

*A small group of anglers focus on a large school of salmon spotted holding at the head of a run.*

## Fish Availability

● = High ● = Moderate ● = Low ● = Closed

| Species | APR | MAY | JUN | JUL | AUG | SEP | OCT |
|---|---|---|---|---|---|---|---|
| **King Salmon** | | | Low Low Moderate | High High Closed Closed | Closed | | |
| **Silver Salmon** | | | | Low | Low Moderate High High | Moderate Low Low Low | |
| **Rainbow Trout** | Low Low Low Moderate | Moderate Moderate Moderate Moderate | Moderate Moderate High High | High High High High | High High High High | High High High High | Moderate Moderate Low Low |
| **Arctic Grayling** | Low Low Low Low | Low Low Low Low | Moderate Moderate Moderate Moderate | Moderate Moderate Moderate Moderate | Moderate Moderate Moderate Moderate | Moderate Moderate Moderate Moderate | Moderate Moderate Low Low |
| Angling Pressure | | | Low Low Low Low | Low Low Low Low | Moderate Moderate Moderate Moderate | Low Low Low Low | |

## King Salmon

**Rating:** ★★★ Good.
**Season:** January 1 through July 13.
**Timing:** June 5 – July 13; peak June 25 – July 10.
**Size:** Average 15 – 40 pounds, up to 75 pounds.
**Tackle:** Spinners, attractors, and flies.
**Tips:** Scout all deeper areas of the river as kings usually stack up here with individual fish or small schools scattered throughout. The largest concentrations are typically found lower in the drainage, around the Honolulu confluence as well as where the East Fork meets the Middle Fork Chulitna, this being a good stretch of water for fresher kings as the water is deeper and slower. Sight-fishing is better in the middle and upper reaches of the drainage, however, as river is narrower, of moderate depth, and fish easy to spot.

Big, flashy spinners in plain metallic finishes and/or neutral colors (blue/green) are generally best, especially when buzzed through some of the deeper holding areas, such as what can be found on the lower river. On the upper river, use flies with base colors of green, purple, or black. When water flows slightly silty, use chartreuse or orange colors for lures and flies.

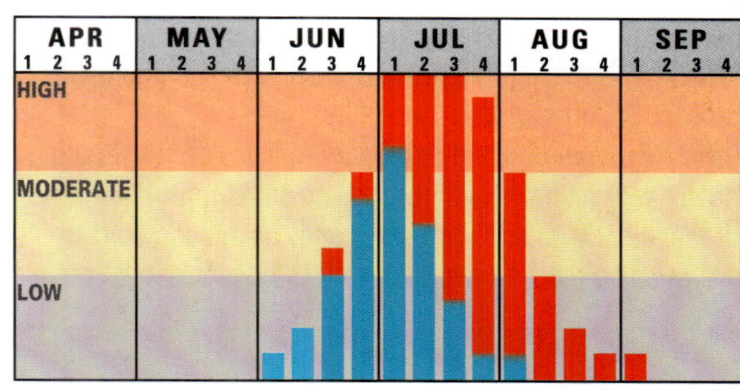


*East Fork Chulitna King Salmon* ● = Fresh ● = Spawning

## Silver Salmon

**Rating:** ★★½ Fair to good.
**Season:** January 1 through December 31.
**Timing:** August 1 – Sept. 30; peak August 25 – Sept. 10.
**Size:** Average 5 – 10 pounds; up to 15 pounds.
**Tackle:** Spinners, flies, and bait.
**Tips:** As with kings, the lower river is the prime stretch to focus on for quality fish, both in brightness as well as fighting capacity. The mouth of Honolulu is the hot spot yet good fishing can be had quite a ways upstream in years when there is a large run. When working the upper reaches, search out deeper water where fish concentrate; these fish tend to be fairly blushed at this point but sight-fishing very effective and efficient.

The standard color fare is, again, much the same as for

(Courtesy Eagle Eye Images)

*This visiting angler hefts a blushed 35-pound male chinook, landed on the East Fork just downstream of the Honolulu confluence. Spend a day at the height of the run and tangling with up to a half dozen fish or more is very much a possibility. Move around and scout for the dark bulks of salmon holding in the deep pools of the greenish-clear river. Sight-fishing can be outstanding.*

kings; try darker or neutral hues when water is clear and/or on a sunny day, brighter if water flows more turbid. Soaking or drifting eggs may be an option in all holding areas but perhaps especially so in the deep pools near the mouth.

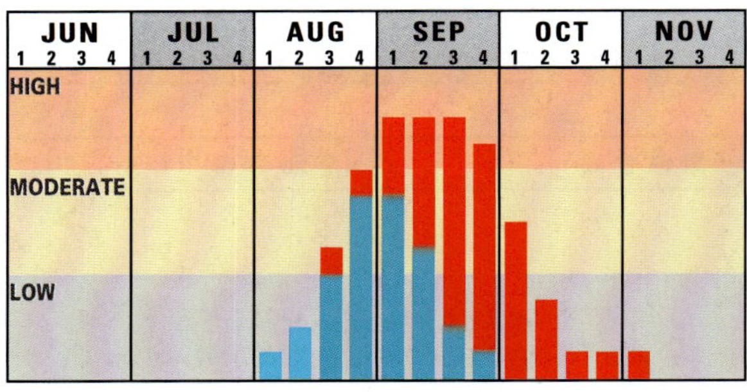


*East Fork Chulitna Silver Salmon* ● = *Fresh* ● = *Spawning*

*A healthy rainbow trout about to be released. These fish are relatively abundant in East Fork. Deep pools and the presence of salmon equals bead-hungry, leopard-spotted trout.*

*(Courtesy Jeff Vanvil)*

## Rainbow Trout

**Rating:** ★★★½ Good to excellent.
**Season:** January 1 through December 31.
**Timing:** April 15 – November 1; peak June 25 – Sept. 30.
**Size:** Average 8 – 22 inches, up to 28 inches (8 pounds).
**Tackle:** Spoons, spinners, and flies.
**Tips:** The upper and middle stream reaches are best during the summer months, with forage and smolt imitations effective early on and flesh and beads as salmon start to spawn and die off. Come fall, scout the water downstream of the highway using flesh and forage patterns. Late in the season, for a brief period, the Honolulu confluence down to West Fork Chulitna can be terrific as fish stack up in the deep pools waiting to exit the drainage.

There are a few trophy-sized fish in East Fork; locate them in the deeper river sections that has an abundance of cover, such as logjams and fallen trees.

*The most idyllic section of water is that of the upper river around the highway crossing. Sight-fishing is the rule for salmon.*

*(Courtesy Eagle Eye Images)*

### Arctic Grayling

**Rating:** ★★★ Good.
**Season:** January 1 through December 31.
**Timing:** April 5 – November 1; peak June 25 – Sept. 30.
**Size:** Average 8 – 15 inches, up to 20 inches.
**Tackle:** Spinners and flies.
**Tips:** Fish tend to focus around the mouths of Middle Fork Chulitna and Honolulu creeks in May and early June as these tributaries are important summer feeding grounds for grayling. Try smolt, insect, and forage imitations. There is also plenty of action in fall as fish exit the streams and move downstream to the East Fork. In mid-summer, grayling tend to concentrate high up in the system, well beyond the road crossing, striking beads when salmon are running and insect/forage imitations throughout the season. Come fall, fish school up again in the lower river.

## Other East Fork Chulitna Opportunities

### Float Fishing

The East Fork Chulitna is perhaps best known as a float-fishing destination as road access points are very scarce in relation to the size of the drainage. It is a relatively mild piece of water technically speaking, making for a perfect beginner or family style excursion. Fishing is typically good for salmon and trout but can range from fair to incredible depending on water flows and fish timing. For those wanting to experience a semi-remote fishing trip with road access, the East Fork delivers.

Water and fishing conditions are typically at a peak during the summer and fall months (June through September), with May and October seeing open water but usually a lot of snow along the banks and river sometimes running high with silt. Being significantly smaller than most other true rafting rivers, those venturing downstream can expect plenty of brush and sweepers along with some boulders and log jams to negotiate around. It is considered a safe float but as with any journey such as this close attention is a must.

Launching at the Parks Highway crossing (Milepost 184.8), anglers have a few options which to consider concerning take-out locations; it all depends on what an angler wants out of the trip in regards to type of fishing, species sought, and trip duration.

The shortest trip block is that from the highway bridge to the mouth of Honolulu Creek, the take-out point. This encompasses the best of East Fork fishing and can be accomplished in as little as one day. There are a few outfitters in the area, including Talkeetna, that run fishing and rafting trips on this stretch. Some floaters decide to spend a couple of days out on the river and cover the better fishing spots in detail. For die-hard anglers, an overnighter on the East Fork is definitely the way to go. There are plenty of good holding water to fish with two hot spots being the confluence with Middle Fork and, at the end of the trip, the mouth of Honolulu Creek.

Option two is definitely an over-night trip if serious about fishing. This block follows the same put-in at Parks Highway but with take-out at the mouth of Troublesome Creek and a 1/2 mile hike to parking lot at Milepost 137.4. This can be a challenging trip and requires good rafting skills and knowledge of navigating large, swift, glacial rivers safely. There is some great fishing to be found for salmon, trout, and grayling at the mouth of virtually every sizable clearwater stream entering the Chulitna.

The third option is to allow for a multi-day trip, putting in at the Parks Highway bridge, floating down to the West Fork Chulitna confluence, and continuing on to the Chulitna River Bridge at Milepost 132.8 for take-out. Although this block can be done in a long day of just floating, those wanting to put in some good fishing time need to plan for at least two to three days or more.

The only uncertainty with the last take-out point is access status as much of the land around the bridge is private property. Local outfitters have permission by land owners to take-out at parking lot; others haul their gear out from river bank next to bridge up the hill to the highway. Do not enter or park within the gated area without permission.

Instead of taking out at the Chulitna Bridge, anglers may want to consider a fourth option by extending their journey to the Parks Highway bridge across the Susitna River just downstream of the mouth of Rabideux Creek, Milepost 104.2. Free parking here on the beach and easy to pull gear out. Expect to add another day of travel time for this block.

The East Fork Chulitna, along with the mainstem Chulitna, is a true and affordable float fishing safari.

## MOOSE CREEK

**Fishing:** ★★½ **Scenery:** ★★★
**Accessibility:** ★★★ **Solitude:** ★★★

**Location:** Upper Susitna Valley drainage, Petersville area, 122 miles north of Anchorage, 80 miles north of Wasilla.
**Access:** At Milepost 114.9 Parks Highway, turn west on Petersville Road 7.1 miles to stream crossing. Footpaths lead upstream and down to various holes. The mid-section of Moose can be accessed by the way of Oilwell Road from Mile 6.3 of Petersville Road, heading south 0.5 mile to stream crossing.
**Facilities:** Parking and primitive camping and boat launch available in immediate area.
**Species:** Pink and silver salmon, rainbow trout, and arctic grayling. A few red and chum salmon, Dolly Varden, northern pike, and round whitefish present. Good run of king salmon (protected).
**Restrictions:** King salmon fishing prohibited. Trout may not be retained upstream of Moose/Kroto confluence. Gear restrictions in effect. Consult ADF&G regulations.
**Fishing:** Flowing out of the foothills and a few muskeg lakes between the communities of Trapper Creek and Petersville, the Moose is one of two forks of the upper Deshka River drainage, the other being Kroto Creek. It has long been heralded as a major producer of king and silver salmon with large numbers of these species utilizing the stream as a spawning ground, a fact that also inspires a small contingent of anglers to scout for opportunistic trout and grayling during the summer and fall months.

Although technically a clearwater stream, the Moose carries a distinct iron tint to its flow, reflecting the muskeg influence of area lakes. The Moose is also a fairly popular spot to launch rafts in order to access the more remote sections of the upper and middle Deshka River.

Being a salmon breeding area, the Moose does yield some decent fishing for salmon, primarily silvers. A few reds and chums come through here along with a mass of pinks but they are not particularly in any good shape for angling purposes. Having spent two weeks or more migrating up the Deshka, they generally appear in their nuptial coloration and sub-par for consumption; however, the silvers tend to be brighter and can be targeted.

Rainbows spawn here in the spring and continue to be present through summer and well into fall. There is an abundance of lies in which are perfect hiding spots for trout and anglers hiking upstream or down will find them without too much effort. The grayling is not a particularly abundant species but found in decent numbers throughout the open water season and frequently hooked while trouting.

Anglers wanting a true float fishing experience can launch small rafts or kayaks at the road crossing or the end of Oil Well Road and drift to a designated take-out point on the middle or lower Deshka River. Expect a multi-day journey covering mostly shallow and slow-flowing water that features a range of species, including king salmon on the far lower end of the river along with excellent action for chrome pinks and silvers. Trout and grayling fishing can also be good, especially at the confluence of Moose and Kroto creeks where they form the mainstem Deshka River.

**Silver Salmon.** Fair; August 15 – September 1; average 5 – 10 pounds. Focus on structure that concentrate fish. Use spinners and flies.

**Rainbow Trout.** Good; June 15 – September 25; average 8 – 18 inches. Hit riffles and the in- and outflows of holes. Spinners, attractors, and flies.

**Arctic Grayling.** Fair to good; June 15 – September 15; average 8 – 14 inches. Search out riffles and the head and tail of deep holes. Small spinners and flies.

## PETERS CREEK

**Fishing:** ★★★ **Scenery:** ★★★½
**Accessibility:** ★★★ **Solitude:** ★★★★

**Location:** Upper Susitna Valley drainage, Petersville area, 130 miles north of Anchorage, 88 miles north of Wasilla.

**Access:** At Milepost 114.9 Parks Highway, turn west on Petersville Road 18.7 miles to a fork in the road. Left fork leads 0.2 mile to parking area next to bridge crossing river. The right fork leads 0.8 mile to pullout on left. Hike down hill to river.

**Facilities:** Parking, primitive camping, restaurant, and lodging available in immediate area.

**Species:** King, pink, chum, and silver salmon, rainbow trout, and arctic grayling. Some red salmon and round whitefish present.

**Restrictions:** King salmon fishing prohibited at roadside access point; open at lower end of stream. Bait restrictions are in effect. Consult ADF&G regulations.

**Fishing:** Located off the beaten path and away from the high-traffic Parks Highway, Peters Creek is a jewel of a stream. The water runs gin clear with a rocky bottom structure and supports very healthy populations of salmon and resident species. King and silver salmon are both abundant in Peters, yet fishing for the former is legal only in the very lower end of the stream which is only accessible by plane or boat. Silvers, however, are fair game throughout the stream. For most anglers, however, Peters is a trout and grayling destination and few northern waters can match the thrill of fishing this largely ignored roadside stream.

While various species of salmon appear in Peters from early summer on into fall, the vast majority of fish do show signs of sexual maturity due to the distance traveled. Pinks and chums, although abundant, are likely to be in too far gone to be targeted, leaving anglers the option to tangle with a heavy run of silvers and even an occasional red as these species tend to be semi-bright still upon arriving. If wanting salmon for consumption, expect to do a bit of catch-and-release for quality fish.

Trout and grayling are numerous and move into the area in force just as the salmon begin to enter the stream. Fishing can be worthwhile before then but it really picks up as the salmon spawn and die off. There are some very large rainbows present in late summer and fall and anglers scouting proper structure a little ways away from the road access points may find several trout measuring 25 inches or more along with a slew of smaller fish and arctic grayling.

*(Courtesy Jeff Varvil)*

For the adventuresome, launch a small raft and do the two- to three-day float down to the Kahiltna River confluence where anglers will find excellent opportunities for both kings and silvers as well as rainbow trout.

As this is a relatively shallow salmon spawning stream, anglers should be prepared to encounter grizzly bears.

**Silver Salmon.** Fair to good; August 15 – September 1; average 5 – 10 pounds. Hike along stream and find holes containing big schools of fish. Spinners, flies, and bait.

**Rainbow Trout.** Good; June 25 – September 15; average 8 – 20 inches. Small spinners and flies. Beads or egg imitation flies are deadly when salmon spawn from late July to late September. Biggest fish are in deepest holes.

**Arctic Grayling.** Good; June 15 – September 15; average 8 – 14 inches. Spinners and flies. Try forage flies early in season, egg imitations when salmon appear.

## TALKEETNA RIVER

**Fishing:** ★★★ **Scenery:** ★★★★
**Accessibility:** ★★★ **Solitude:** ★★★
**Location:** Upper Susitna Valley drainage, Talkeetna area, 113 miles north of Anchorage, 70 miles north of Wasilla.
**Access:** At Milepost 98.7 of Parks Highway, turn north on Talkeetna Spur Highway 14.5 miles to end of road in town of Talkeetna. The community borders the river with main point of access from end of Main Street. Wide trail leads to far end of river and the Susitna confluence area. Hike upstream or down on open beach.
**Facilities:** Parking and primitive camping, restrooms, lodging, cabins, hotels, restaurants, guide services, and sporting good stores available. Many other amenities in town of Talkeetna.
**Species:** King, red, pink, chum, and silver salmon, rainbow trout, Dolly Varden, arctic grayling, and round whitefish. A few burbot in lower drainage.
**Restrictions:** King salmon fishing is open from January 1 through July 13. Consult ADF&G regulations.
**Fishing:** The Talkeetna, a fairly large glacial river flowing out of the Talkeetna Mountains, is a gifted drainage in terms of beauty as well as fish numbers. The mainstem river and its several forks and multitude of tributaries are surrounded by some of the most majestic scenery in the state, with marvelous views of Mount Denali (McKinley) immediately to the northwest and lush boreal forests covering the numerous valleys cut by the waters of this system.

Being a glacier-born river influenced by meltwater from area ice fields, Talkeetna flows greenish-grey during the warmer summer months and crystal clear the remainder of the year as temperatures cool and bring the silt discharge to a halt. This cycle is typical of many Alaska waters, rendering the majority of angling effort to the vast array of clearwater tributaries and where they enter the turbid Talkeetna, at least from mid-June to mid-September.

There is little actual roadside fishing on the Talkeetna despite being accessed through the buzzing tourist town of the same name situated directly on the river banks near the confluence with the larger Susitna River. Here, the predominant mode of access is by jet boat that can be launched in town to explore the more remote parts of the drainage. Some roadside opportunities still exist, yet they are limited in scope in terms of access points and favorable water conditions.

A remarkably productive system, Talkeetna hosts good runs of all five kinds of salmon in addition to healthy populations of resident species such as rainbow trout, Dolly Varden, arctic grayling, and round whitefish. Fishing generally takes place on the lower and middle portions of mainstem Talkeetna as access by riverboat is easiest; the upper river, however, is another story as Class IV and V whitewater makes travel difficult and even dangerous, in some instances next to impossible. Only experienced river runners should tempt the Talkeetna on their own as boulders, sweepers, and standing waves are the norm and the river channels change to

(Courtesy Beverley Bailey)

*Angler Roy Bailey tests a promising spot on a clearwater tributary and gets lucky. The Talkeetna has an abundance of smaller rivers and streams that are ideal for scouting on foot, several of which support very healthy fish populations and little, if any, angling pressure. If hiking up these waters, however, always carry bear protection.*

some degree every season. But for those that do venture up this wilderness system on their own or by one of the several guide outfits in town, the fishing is nothing short of spectacular and certainly worthy a day or two of exploration.

Early runs of king and red salmon infiltrate the Talkeetna starting around the first of June and usually peak by the end of the month, although the former may stay productive well into July in some areas of the river. It is particularly kings that draw angler's attention as fish often top 40 pounds and provide plenty of fast action throughout much of the drainage that is accessible by boat. The reds are primarily targeted towards the end of July with the arrival of more numerous late-run fish; this is also a time when large numbers of pink and chum salmon move in along with the first few silvers. Reds, pinks, and chums continue to be prevalent until mid-August, at which time the silvers begin to arrive in force and stay very active into September.

As for other types of fish, the Talkeetna is renowned for its superlative trout opportunities. Rainbows are typically encountered at the mouth of clearwater streams throughout the summer months. Many of these smaller tributaries offer great trouting for those able to negotiate their way upstream either by boat or on foot; yet a growing number of fly fishers prefer the autumn months of September and October when trout are found throughout the mainstem in big numbers. Expect fast and furious action for rainbows that may top eight to 10 pounds.

As with trout, char and grayling are present in the same areas and times of the season and fishing for them can be stellar as well. Look for the char within close proximity of the main river, while grayling are more often found higher up in tributaries, at least in mid-summer. Whitefish, although very abundant at times (especially in fall), can

*Dennis Musgraves shows off a blushed male calico. These tough fighters are among the most abundant of Talkeetna salmon.*

*(Courtesy Dennis Musgraves)*

*(Courtesy Eagle Eye Images)*

*A near-chrome female chinook taken from the lower reaches of a clearwater stream near the Talkeetna confluence. Do not only focus on creek mouths; scout deep pools just upstream as well.*

be a challenge to get to strike on standard trout and char presentations but when proper enticements are used, the fishing can be quite good. A few burbot may also be available.

One great way to experience some of the best fishing on the Talkeetna River is to do a drop-off trip at Clear Creek, and there are operators that specialize in exactly this. The stream is a short boat ride up from the town of Talkeetna and offers excellent fishing for all available species in season. It is the perfect solution for low-cost, do-it-yourself type of anglers with half- and full-day and overnight excursions popular. Expect company of other anglers, especially at the peak of the king and silver salmon runs, but those willing to hike upstream along Clear Creek may find a piece of solitude.

Anglers casting off the bank right in front of town can do quite well on resident species in spring (April to early June) as these fish migrate out of the Susitna into the mainstem Talkeetna destined for their summer feeding grounds. At this time, the river still flows clear enough to fish throughout much of its length. By mid-June, the water rises and becomes increasingly silty, yet anglers using large, colorful attractors may tie up with an early king or two with some patience and luck.

The next opportunity for roadside salmon is in late August and September as waters begin to drop and clear up. At this time there will still be a few silvers streaming by town, but do not expect anything too spectacular as most fish have already passed this area. A little later, end of September and into October, trout, char, and grayling again become available as these fish begin their downstream migration to overwintering areas in the Susitna River.

**King Salmon.** Good; June 25 – July 10; average 15 – 40 pounds. Best fishing at mouths of sloughs and clearwater tributaries. Spinners, attractors, plugs, and flies. Use fluorescent colors in silty water.
**Red Salmon.** Fair to good; June 15 – 25 (early run) and July 20 – August 10 (late run); average 4 – 7 pounds. Search out clearwater stream mouths with some current. Use flies; sometimes spinners and salmon roe work.
**Pink Salmon.** Excellent; July 25 – August 5; average 2 – 4 pounds. For brightest fish, hit lower river early in the season. Spoons, spinners, and flies.
**Chum Salmon.** Excellent; July 20 – August 10; average 6 – 12 pounds. Best color fish are caught in July leading up to run peak. Spoons, spinners, attractors, and flies. Salmon roe is good in turbid water.
**Silver Salmon.** Good; August 15 – September 5; average 5 – 11 pounds. Tributary mouths best but also good fishing higher up some streams. Spinners, attractors, flies, and roe.
**Rainbow Trout.** Excellent; June 15 – October 10; average 10 – 23 inches. Tributaries best June, July, and August; mainstem September and October. Spinners, attractors and flies.
**Dolly Varden.** Good; August 1 – 10; average 4 – 7 pounds. Stream mouths best bet. Spoons, spinners, flies, and bait.
**Arctic Grayling.** Excellent; May 25 – September 15; average 8 – 15 inches. Mainstem in early and late season; tributaries in mid-season. Spinners and flies.
**Whitefish.** Fair; July 1 – October 15; average 10 – 15 inches. Search out stream mouths in summer, tributaries and mainstem in fall. Attractors and flies.

## TROUBLESOME CREEK

**Fishing:** ★★½ **Scenery:** ★★★★
**Accessibility:** ★★★ **Solitude:** ★★★
**Location:** Upper Susitna Valley drainage, Chulitna River tributary, 137 miles north of Anchorage.
**Access:** The Parks Highway crosses stream at Milepost 137.4. To reach mouth of Troublesome, take marked trail from parking area 0.6 mile to Chulitna River confluence.
**Facilities:** Developed parking, some camping, and restrooms available. Lodging in area.
**Species:** Red, pink, chum, and silver salmon, rainbow trout, and arctic grayling. A small run of king salmon is present in June and July. Whitefish and burbot may be encountered.
**Restrictions:** King salmon fishing prohibited. Consult ADF&G regulations.
**Fishing:** This small clearwater stream receives small runs of salmon and supports decent populations of resident fish

(Courtesy Beverley Bailey)

such as trout and grayling. It is not a very popular fishing hole as most salmon are confined to the mouth and action can at times be inconsistent. Also, Troublesome is far from any settlement, there are better fishing spots to the south, and it has a high concentration of bears.

The majority of salmon this far up the Susitna drainage will be showing signs of spawning color but a few dime bright specimens will always be present early in the respective runs. For fresh salmon, try the mouth; upstream reaches have mostly spawners. Anglers hitting the confluence and the holes immediately upstream at dawn can be rewarded with some very good action. Note, however, that many of the fish seen crowded into the mouth are actually bound for other tributaries of the Chulitna.

Rainbow trout and arctic grayling inhabit the stream all season and fishing for them can be worthwhile, especially if hiking away from the road crossing a mile or two.

**Red Salmon.** Fair; August 1 – 10; average 4 – 7 pounds. Available at mouth of stream only. Small spinners and flies are effective.

**Pink Salmon.** Fair to good; July 25 – August 5; average 2 – 4 pounds. Most pinks are near or in spawning condition. Spoons and flies.

**Chum Salmon.** Fair; July 25 – August 10; average 6 – 12 pounds. Run can be very heavy at mouth but few bright fish available. Spoons and flies.

**Silver Salmon.** Fair; August 15 – September 1; average 5 – 10 pounds. Spinners, flies, and roe are all good. This is the premier salmon species at Troublesome.

**Rainbow Trout.** Fair; August 15 – September 30; average 8 – 16 inches. Search structure throughout stream. Spinners and flies.

**Arctic Grayling.** Fair to good; May 25 – September 15; average 8 – 15 inches. Try upper stream in summer, lower in fall. Spinners and flies.

## HONOLULU CREEK

**Fishing:** ★★ **Scenery:** ★★★
**Accessibility:** ★★½ **Solitude:** ★★★★

**Location:** Upper Susitna Valley drainage, Chulitna River tributary, 178 miles north of Anchorage.

**Access:** The Parks Highway crosses stream at Milepost 178.1. Lower creek and mouth accessed by trail from Milepost 177.0. Parking for all size vehicles. Hike 1 mile to stream; respect private property in this area.

**Facilities:** Limited parking with primitive camping possible. Lodging and restaurant available in area.

**Species:** King salmon, rainbow trout, and arctic grayling. A few chum and silver salmon and whitefish present.

**Restrictions:** King salmon fishing is prohibited, except in lower quarter mile of the stream. Consult ADF&G regulations.

**Fishing:** This beautiful clearwater stream, due to its distance from sea, does not support any great numbers of salmon; however, fishing for resident species such as trout and grayling can be worthwhile, especially if scenery and lack of crowds is what is important. Both king and silver salmon spawn in Honolulu but the runs are small and the fish usually in less than stellar condition upon reaching this point in their migration. Chums occasionally nose into the creek, too, but do not swim much beyond the mouth.

There is some very decent opportunity to be had for rainbows and grayling for those up to hiking and exploring the stream. The most consistent action can be had when salmon infiltrate the drainage starting in July and continuing well into September. There are a handful of spots within a mile radius of the highway bridge that are always good for a few fish.

(Courtesy Beverley Bailey)

For anglers willing to hike the distance to the lower portion of Honolulu and the mouth are welcomed to some quite decent king salmon action. Semi-bright and light blush specimens may be present early in the season (late June-early July) in a few of the deeper holes.

**Rainbow Trout.** Fair to good; June 20 – September 15; average 8 – 18 inches. Hit deep holes or search for spawning salmon. Spinners and flies.

**Arctic Grayling.** Fair to good; May 25 – September 15; average 8 – 12 inches. Go upstream in mid-summer, downstream in fall. Spinners and flies.

## MIDDLE FORK CHULITNA RIVER

**Fishing:** ★★★ **Scenery:** ★★★★★
**Accessibility:** ★★ **Solitude:** ★★★★★
**Location:** Upper Susitna Valley drainage, Chulitna River tributary, 195 miles north of Anchorage.
**Access:** The Parks Highway crosses the river at Milepost 194.5. Faint foot trails lead along banks of the river.
**Facilities**: Parking and primitive camping.
**Species:** Rainbow trout and arctic grayling. A few silver salmon and an occasional whitefish may be caught. Small run of kings (protected).
**Restrictions:** King salmon fishing prohibited. Consult ADF&G regulations.
**Fishing:** Flowing through a truly magnificent piece of Alaska wilderness, the Middle Fork is one of the least fished productive waters directly accessible by a major highway. Smaller than nearby East Fork, this stream is much more conducive to bank anglers and wading is possible in many places without any problems. Water clarity is also greater, meaning opportunities for sight-fishing and targeting resident species is generally more consistent.

Distance hiking either upstream or down will put anglers onto promising holes for trout and grayling. A few anglers may embark on floating the river down to the Chulitna and beyond; however, low water conditions in mid-summer create persistent issues of having to drag a raft through many parts.

This small clearwater river entertains anglers with some very productive grayling action, generally more so than rainbow trout. Get away from the road a little ways and the fishing is often excellent, and the size of fish is bigger too. For fly-fishing enthusiasts, this is prime water.

Although salmon runs infiltrate the drainage from mid-summer into fall, Middle Fork Chulitna is not really the place to target them. The numbers of fish present is relatively small and, due to the distance traveled from the ocean, are also quite advanced into the reproductive phase. The silvers present are likely to be quite blushed with very few or no bright or semi-bright specimens available. Instead, focus efforts on trout and grayling.

**Rainbow Trout.** Fair to good; June 20 – September 15; average 8 – 18 inches. Search out salmon and try egg imitation flies, beads; also spinners.

**Arctic Grayling.** Good to excellent; June 15 – September 10; average 8 – 14 inches. Scout holes and areas with slower water. Spinners and flies.

## ADDITIONAL OPPORTUNITIES

*(Courtesy Jeff Varvil)*

### Upper Susitna River Safari

The mainstem Susitna River splits into three branches right outside the town of Talkeetna, the west being Chulitna, the north Upper Susitna, and the west Talkeetna. All three are glacial systems and support strong populations of game fish. While there is limited road access to the Chulitna and Talkeetna rivers, the Upper Susitna River is a true wilderness drainage with the only means of access being by boat from the community of Talkeetna.

Several clearwater tributaries enter the river that host a variety of game fish, including five species of salmon, trout, char, grayling, and whitefish. What brings anglers to these remote parts, however, are the big runs of king and silver salmon and prolific rainbow trout. Because access to the area is so limited, very few anglers share these waters and experiencing excellent fishing in complete solitude is very much the norm.

Anglers have the option to do one-day trips as well as week-long, drop-off excursions. Guides specializing in the Upper Susitna offer a variety of package trips that cater to various species, types of water, and preferred gear.

There are several clearwater tributaries that may be worth checking out, a few of the better ones are Indian River and Portage, Whiskers, and Fourth of July creeks, although great fishing can be expected at the mouth of any clearwater stream entering the river.

# Matanuska-Susitna Valleys Fishing Derbies and Directory

## FISHING DERBIES

**MatSu Valley King Salmon Derby**
**Approximate Dates:** May 20 through July 13.
**Area/Location:** Wasilla/Houston/Willow/Talkeetna; Susitna River and tributaries, Little Susitna River.
**Prizes/Categories:** Cash and merchandise.
**Ticket Fees:** $10 three-day, $20 entire derby; $15 youth fee.
**Note:** Multiple categories; winning fish based on selected random weight.
**Contact Information:** Sheep Creek Lodge, (907) 337-1979 or www.pseakingderby.com

**Mat-Su Pike Derby**
**Approximate Dates:** February 1 through March 31.
**Area/Location:** Wasilla/Houston/Willow/Talkeetna; Susitna River area lakes and tributaries.
**Prizes/Categories:** Split-the-pot cash, locally made products, and sponsor donated sporting good merchandise.
**Ticket Fees:** $20 entire derby.
**Note:** Multiple categories; largest fish generally measure 35 to 40 inches.
**Contact Information:** Houston Chamber of Commerce, (907) 373-0826 or www.houstonakchamber.com

## FISHING GUIDES & CHARTERS

**D-Ray Personal Guide Service**
www.d-ray.com (907) 230-6348

**Mahay's Riverboat Service** *(Talkeetna)*
www.mahaysriverboat.com (800) 736-2210

**Susitna Valley River Guides**
www.susitnavalley.com (907) 495-2699

## CAMPGROUNDS & RV PARKS

**Alaskan Trails RV & Camper Park** *(Wasilla)*
www.aktrailsrvpark.com (907) 376-5504

**Big Bear Campground & RV Park** *(Wasilla)*
www.bigbearrv.net (907) 745-7445

**Mary's McKinley View Lodge** *(Trapper Creek)*
www.McKinleyViewLodge.com (907) 733-1555

*(Courtesy Mike Larsen)*

*Mike Larsen lifts a 54.4-pound king salmon, taken off the bank at Willow Creek. The fish placed third in the 2005 Susitna Valley King Salmon Derby.*

## TACKLE & SPORTING GOODS

**3 Rivers Fly & Tackle** *(Wasilla)*
www.3riversflytackle.net (907) 373-5434

**Boondock Sporting Goods & Outfitters**
*(Eagle River)* (907) 694-2229

**Mountain View Sports** *(Anchorage)*
www.mtviewsports.com (907) 563-8600

**World Wide Angler** *(Anchorage)*
www.akflyshop.com (907) 561-0662

## WATERCRAFT RENTALS

**Alaska Raft & Kayak** *(Anchorage)*
www.alaskaraftandkayak.com (800) 606-5950

# Matanuska-Susitna Valleys Directory

## AIR TAXI OPERATIONS

**Rust's Flying Service** *(Anchorage)*
www.flyrusts.com (800) 544-2299

## CAMPGROUNDS & RV PARKS

**Midnight Sun Car & Van Rental** *(Anchorage)*
www.ineedacarrental.com (888) 877-3585

## GENERAL INFORMATION

**Alaska Department of Fish & Game** *(Palmer)*
www.sf.adfg.state.ak.us (907) 746-6300

**Alaska State Parks**
www.dnr.state.ak.us/parks/ (907) 745-3975

**Greater Palmer Chamber of Commerce**
www.palmerchamber.org (907) 745-2820

**Greater Wasilla Chamber of Commerce**
www.wasillachamber.org (907) 376-1299

**Houston Chamber of Commerce**
www.houstonakchamber.tripod.com (907) 373-0826

**Matanuska-Susitna Convention & Visitor's Bureau**
www.alaskavisit.com (907) 746-5000

**Sunshine Chamber of Commerce**
www.sunshinecitylimits.com (907) 733-1416

**Talkeetna Chamber of Commerce**
www.talkeetnachamber.org (907) 733-2330

**Willow Chamber of Commerce**
www.willowchamber.org (907) 495-6800

*Early winter view of a salmon spawning stream near the Eagle River Nature Center in Chugach State Park.*

Copper Valley
& Valdez Arm

**Northern Copper ............ 381**

**Hot Spots:** Gulkana River

**Other Productive Fisheries:** Lake Louise, Upper Copper River Streams, Gulkana Area Streams, Paxson Lake, Summit Lake, Tangle Lakes & River

**Additional Opportunities:** Midde Fork & West Fork Gulkana River, West Fork Gulkana Lakes, Copper & Tanada Lakes, Susitna & Tyone Lakes

**Southern Copper ............ 397**

**Hot Spots:** Klutina River and Tonsina River

**Other Productive Fisheries:** McCarthy and Tazlina Area Lakes, Little Tonsina River, Tolsona Creek, Mendeltna Creek

**Additional Opportunities:** Tebay & Hanagita Rivers

**Valdez Arm ..... 419**

**Hot Spots:** Port Valdez

**Other Productive Fisheries:** Robe River

**Additional Opportunities:** North Prince William Sound, Valdez Wildlife, Salmon Viewing

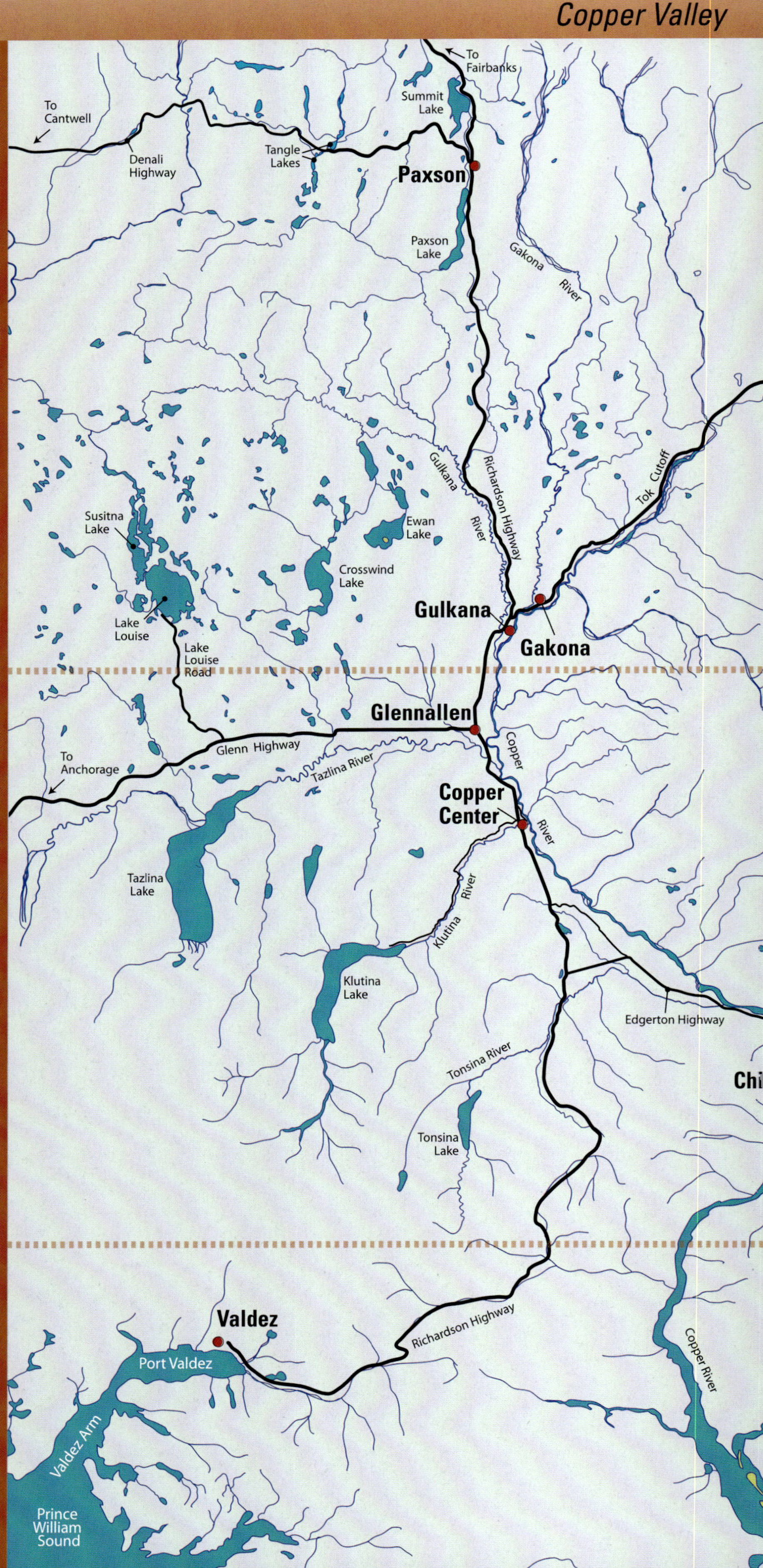

# Introduction

The greater Copper Valley area along with Valdez Arm is the least-fished on the road system in the Southcentral region. It is certainly not because of a lack of fish or scenery; the valley and its surrounding waterways have angling quality and scenic beauty to match any roadside fishery in the state, offering both top-notch freshwater as well as saltwater opportunities. In addition, several of the largest volcanoes in Alaska can be found here and, along with the snow-covered Wrangell Mountains, provide a majestic backdrop to most any angling excursion. The fjord-like landscape of Valdez at the northern edge of Prince William Sound has aptly earned the nickname of "Little Switzerland."

Lakes and clearwater streams are generously spread throughout the area, most of which flow into the vast Copper River, a major glacier-fed body of water cutting its way from the Interior of the state all the way to the North Gulf Coast. These waters are rich in salmon runs, particularly kings and reds, and help drive an entire ecosystem supporting healthy populations of rainbow trout, lake trout, Dolly Varden, and arctic grayling. Situated to the south is Valdez Arm, a destination entirely of its own sporting tremendous runs of primarily pink and silver salmon and world-class bottomfish opportunities for halibut, lingcod, and rockfish.

Those visiting this area of the state will appreciate the rustic feel of the fisheries as population centers are far and few compared to other roadside angling destinations. Services and amenities offered are relatively minimal, with the possible exception of Valdez that supports good infrastructure for even the most discriminate traveler.

## Area Roads & Highways

Several highways connect the small towns and settlements in the area with other parts of the state as well as Canada and the Lower 48. Richardson Highway is the main artery, originating in the coastal port of Valdez (Milepost 0) at the head of Valdez Arm and cuts vertically through the entire Copper Valley, joining the Glenn Highway in Glennallen (Milepost 115), Tok Cutoff in Gakona (Milepost 128), Denali Highway in Paxson (Milepost 185), and Alaska Highway in Delta Junction (Milepost 266) before terminating in the Interior city of Fairbanks (Milepost 362). Nearly all of the most important sport fisheries in the area can be found along this highway. Glenn Highway,

*Two satisfied anglers displays a catch of lightly blushed August sockeye, caught from the Gulkana River. This river and a couple of other drainages in the region are known for their great salmon fishing. With some work, it is very possible to experience solitude on these waters.*

*(Courtesy Kingfisher's Perch)*

originating in Anchorage (Milepost 0), heads eastward and joins the Richardson Highway in the town of Glennallen (Milepost 189). Small lakes and clearwater creeks are plentiful along the Glenn.

There area many side roads of the Richardson and Glenn highways that anglers can capitalize on, leading to more remote sections of various featured drainages, as well as providing additional access to smaller and perhaps lesser-fished waters.

## Major Fisheries / Hot Spots

Almost a couple of dozen productive fishing spots line the road system in the Copper Valley/Valdez area; however, only three of them experience large runs of salmon and productive populations of resident game species that attract significant angling effort.

Clear-flowing Gulkana River north of Glennallen supports two runs of red salmon lasting from early summer into fall, an early run of kings, and has some noteworthy rainbow trout action and arguably some of the best arctic grayling fishing in the entire state. Moreover, just to the south, the larger and swifter glacial-green Klutina is home to huge late-run king salmon, many specimens of which exceed the 50-pound trophy mark, and two red runs that span the entire summer. Both of these systems are easily fished from the bank at the various access points but the use of rafts and powerboats are common as well. The Tonsina River is a highly productive yet rarely fished system, supporting runs of late-run kings, reds, and silvers as well as Dolly Varden and arctic grayling. Good populations of bear, moose, and other wildlife are present.

*An early autumn view of the lower Klutina River as seen from the Richardson Highway near Copper Center. Fall fishing in Copper Valley means solitude and plenty of action.*

Port Valdez is the area highlight of marine fisheries and the only hot spot of Northern Prince William Sound accessible by road. Silver and pink salmon are the main species, both of which yield exceptional fishing during the summer and early fall months. Other species of interest include king salmon, halibut, lingcod, rockfish, and salmon shark. Very lucrative salmon and halibut derbies extend through the summer into fall, providing even more incentive for anglers. Wildlife is abundant.

## Other Productive Fisheries

Besides the main river and marine fisheries, there are several other places to visit that offer good fishing opportunities for at least one or more species of game fish. The vast highland lakes in the northern portion of Copper Valley – Louise, Paxson, and Summit – are known for trophy lake trout (up to 20 pounds or more), grayling, and burbot, while area streams support seasonally excellent grayling opportunities.

However, the southern section of the valley has a quite different angling perspective, with fewer small streams and lakes yet most all harboring populations of salmon, char, and grayling.

There is only one other location in the Valdez area that offers any viable fishing (apart from a couple of stocked lakes). Robe River has decent populations of early-run red salmon, pink salmon, and autumn silver salmon, with hot fishing for Dolly Varden.

*Port Valdez anglers cooperate in successfully hoisting a Labor Day silver salmon to dockside using a modified net specially designed to secure catches from tall heights. Very few road-accessible, shore-based waters in Alaska can compare to the late-summer/early fall silver action in this coastal port.*

## Additional Opportunities

Anglers looking for a little extra adventure to add to their roadside fishing may want to consider a couple of options. One is to fly into a select number of lakes to sample excellent action for lake trout, wild rainbow trout, and grayling. There is even some great fishing available for king and red salmon in a few remote streams. For a really unique experience, consider a trip into the Wrangell Mountains for steelhead trout.

Another option is to do some float fishing. Anglers are dropped off at a lake where they can portage through to a remote stream and spend days to weeks rafting or canoeing through undisturbed wilderness in pursuit of red salmon, rainbow trout, and arctic grayling. For a unique experience, consider a September trip into the Wrangell Mountains and Hanagita River for steelhead trout.

Anglers fishing out of Valdez have great options to add variety to their catch by exploring one of dozens of remote bays, coves, and streams of Prince William Sound that support large stocks of salmon, char, and bottomfish – even sea-run trout. Travel by charter boat is a popular and cost-effective way of fishing the more distant parts of the sound. Aircraft are sometimes used to access locations that are a considerable jaunt from the road system, such as those found on Montague and Hinchinbrook islands.

## Sport Fishing Regulations

The Copper Valley is in the Arctic-Yukon-Kuskokwim & Upper Copper/Upper Susitna River regulations summary booklet as provided by the Alaska Department of Fish & Game (ADF&G), under the "Upper Copper/Upper Susitna River" section. The Valdez area is covered in the Southcentral Alaska regulations summary booklet under the "Prince William Sound" section. Open and closed seasons and areas, legal tackle and gear, bag and possession limits, and fish size restrictions may vary from drainage to drainage and between species. Consult a copy of the regulations before fishing or call the ADF&G regional/field offices directly for information.

**Glennallen:** (907) 822-3309
**Anchorage:** (907) 267-2218

(Courtesy Kingfisher's Perch)

*Copper Valley rivers offer superb opportunities for salmon, such as this trophy king caught off the bank on the Klutina River. Peak time for salmon is mid-June to mid-September.*

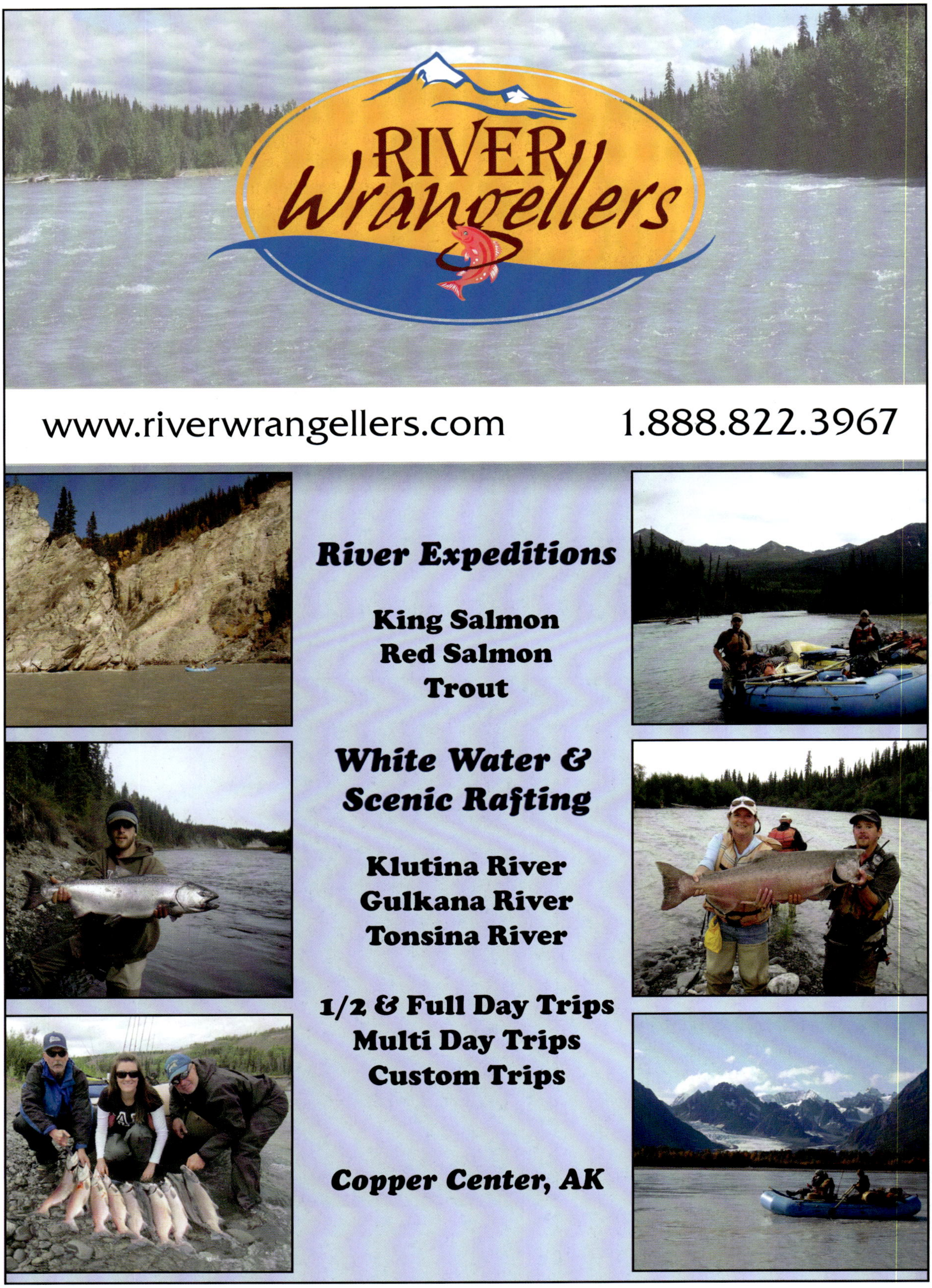

www.riverwrangellers.com 1.888.822.3967

**River Expeditions**

**King Salmon**
**Red Salmon**
**Trout**

**Klutina River**
**Gulkana River**
**Tonsina River**

**1/2 & Full Day Trips**
**Multi Day Trips**
**Custom Trips**

**Copper Center, AK**

Glennallen • Gulkana • Paxson

# Northern Copper

**King Salmon • Red Salmon • Steelhead Trout • Rainbow Trout**
**Lake Trout • Arctic Grayling • Whitefish • Burbot**

*Grayling Streams*

*Float Fishing*

*Canoe Lakes*

*Trout Waters*

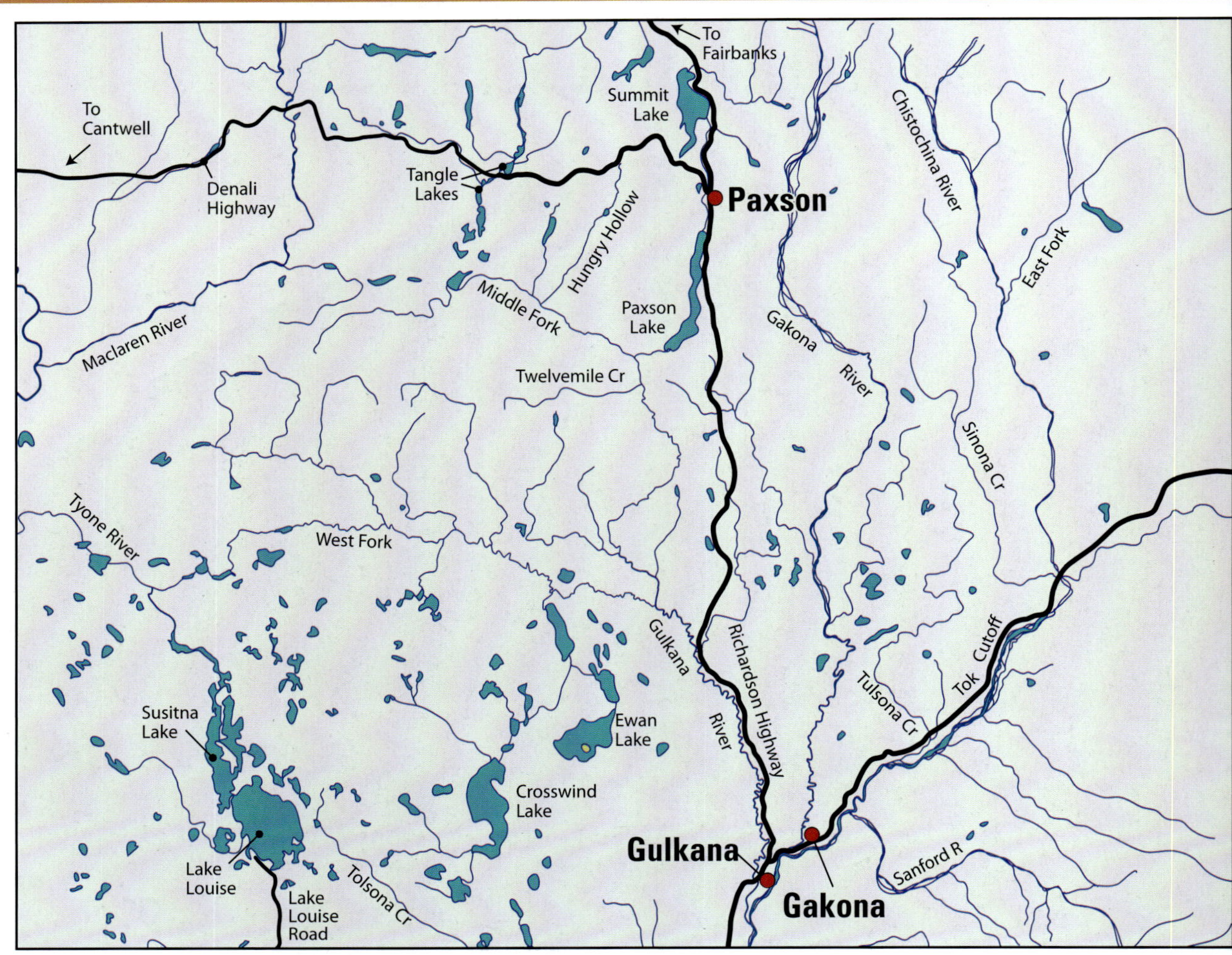


**Area Population Centers:** Glennallen, Gakona, Paxson
**Key Species:** King and Red Salmon, Rainbow and Lake Trout, Arctic Grayling
**Other Species:** Steelhead Trout, Whitefish, and Burbot
**Main Destination/Hot Spot:** Gulkana River
**Other Productive Fisheries:** Louise, Paxson, Summit, and Tangle Lakes; and Upper Copper and Gulkana Area Streams.
**Additional Opportunities:** Middle and West Fork Gulkana River, Middle Fork Gulkana Lakes, Copper and Tanada Lakes, Susitna and Tyone Lakes.

**Summary of Area Fishing:** Carrying a haunting charm of seemingly endless wilderness with very sparse settlements, the upper Copper River basin offers the prospective angler multitude of streams and literally hundreds of lakes in which to explore. In typical Alaska highland fashion, the waters here teem with char and grayling, and salmon and trout are available in many places as well.

For roadside anglers, the Gulkana River drainage specifically is a main source of area fishing opportunities as the Richardson Highway intersects and parallels a great many tributary lakes and creeks with the mainstem Gulkana always being an obvious possibility. Here, anglers can find absolutely tremendous grayling action (some of the best in the state) along with thriving runs of king and red salmon. Despite having swam hundreds of miles by the way of Copper River, these salmon are still in great shape upon arriving in the area and are destined to give a great account of themselves both in sport as well as consumptive qualities. The deeper lakes within this drainage also hold their fair share of lunker lake trout.

But there is also a lesser influence of other important drainages, such as the Susitna and Tazlina rivers, both of which sustain impressive numbers of grayling and lake trout in their lake systems. Although road access is certainly a limiting factor, the Glenn Highway does support a very modest means of reaching at least some of the tributaries.

For those wishing to do some hiking away from the road or launch a canoe or raft will certainly enjoy this area.

Best fishing is from June through September.

# Gulkana River

King
SALMON

Red
SALMON

Steelhead
TROUT

Rainbow
TROUT

Arctic
GRAYLING

**Highlights:** Great roadside hike-in and float-fishing destination, known for its phenomenal grayling opportunities and abundant salmon runs.

**Best Fishing:** Mid-June to early October.

**Regulatory Restrictions:** Moderate.

**Location:** Northern Copper Valley drainage, Gakona area, Richardson Highway, 201 miles northeast of Anchorage, 12 miles north of Glennallen.

**Description:** The Gulkana River is a clearwater drainage, originating from two large lakes, Summit and Paxson lakes in the foothills of the Alaska Range. It then flows south to its terminus at the Copper River near the community of Gulkana. It currently carries the recognition as National Wild & Scenic River. Surrounding land consists of rolling hills and spruce forests, views of 16,200-foot Mount Sanford and 12,000-foot Mount Drum volcanoes looming in the background to the east. There are a multitude of smaller streams and lowland lakes that join the Gulkana along its path, including Summit and Paxson lakes and East Fork to the north and the Middle Fork and West Fork to the west.

With breakup occurring sometime in the first part of April and freezeup not until November, the Gulkana has a fairly long open water season. Snowmelt and turbid water conditions are common in spring, usually lasting from late May into mid-June. The river is also sensitive to heavy rainfall, particularly the West Fork, which can quickly elevate water levels by a foot or two and turn the mainstem Gulkana murky brown. The Gulkana upstream of the Middle Fork confluence is much more placid, running clear the majority of the time despite weather conditions.

There are two sections to the Gulkana River mainstem. The upper section is from the outlet of Paxson Lake to Sourdough, a 50-mile stretch consisting of swift and boulder-strewn water as well as slower, meandering partitions. Canyon Rapids, which has Class III and IV whitewater, must be portaged. After the rapids, the Gulkana mellows out considerably the rest of the distance. Land surrounding the upper section is state and federal owned and is in addition the most popular and scenic.

The lower section is from Sourdough downstream to the Copper River confluence, about a 38-mile stretch of water that flows through primarily private and Native corporate owned land. Numerous BLM trail easements are present. Compared to the upper section, the lower river is much calmer and more predictable in nature, with well defined holes and runs perfect for hike-in fishing, motor boating, and rafting.

It must be noted that land between the Richardson Highway bridge and the river mouth is privately owned and a permit is required for access. Apply in person at the Ahtna, Inc. office in Glennallen, or call (907) 822-3476 for more information. Trail access to lower river and mouth by permission only.

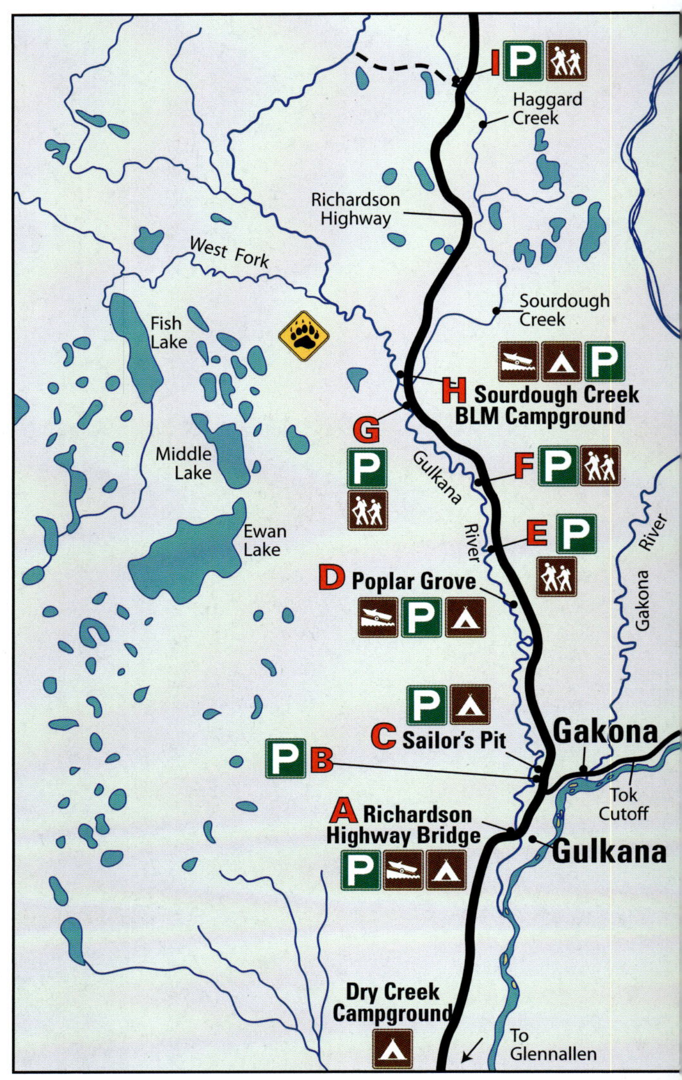


## Lower Gulkana River

**A. Richardson Highway Bridge** – Milepost 126.9. Highway crosses river. Developed parking for all size vehicles and primitive camping. This is a take-out point for floaters having done the upper river, as well as a put-in for those rafting the lower river to the mouth.

**B. Turnout** – Milepost 129.1. Parking. Trail leads 1 ¼ mile west to river.

**C. Sailor's Pit** – Milepost 129.3. West on BLM access road 1.0 mile to river. Parking and campground.

**D. Poplar Grove/Gulkana River Access** – Milepost 136.7. West on gravel road 0.3 mile to river. Parking for all size vehicles, campground, and boat launch. Trails lead upstream and down. Power boaters launch here to access the middle river sections. Floaters go from here to Richardson Highway bridge.

**E. Turnout** – Milepost 139.6. Parking. BLM trail leads ½ mile west to river.

**F. Turnout** – Milepost 141.4. Parking. BLM trail leads 1 mile west to river.

*A scenic view of the Gulkana River parking area on the lower section just downstream of the Richardson Highway bridge near the village of Gulkana. This is a favorite bank fishing spot during the king and red salmon runs. A deep hole is located at the bridge.*

**G. Turnout** – Milepost 146.5. Parking. BLM trail leads 1 mile west to river.
**H. Sourdough Creek BLM Campground** – Milepost 147.6. West on gravel road 0.5 mile to river. Parking for all size vehicles, developed campground, restrooms, picnic area, and boat launch. Power boaters launch here to access the middle river sections. Floaters put in and take out here as well.

## Upper Gulkana River

**I. Haggard Creek Trailhead** – Milepost 160.7. Parking. BLM trail leads 7 miles due west to river (middle fork).
**J. Middle Fork Trailhead** – Milepost 169.4. Parking. BLM trail leads 7 miles due west to river (middle fork).
**K. Paxson Lake BLM Campground** – Milepost 175.0. Parking and camping for all size vehicles, restrooms, and boat launch. This is a launch point for rafters floating the middle fork of Gulkana to access points A-J.
**L. Denali Highway Bridge** – Milepost 185.5. West on Denali Highway 0.2 mile to crossing. Parking. Not recommended for large RVs.
**M. East Fork Gulkana** – Milepost 186.5 -- 191.0. Highway parallels river for 4 1/2 miles. Limited parking. Not recommended for large RVs.
**Note:** Access and fishing information for Paxson and Summit lakes are covered on pages 394 and 395.

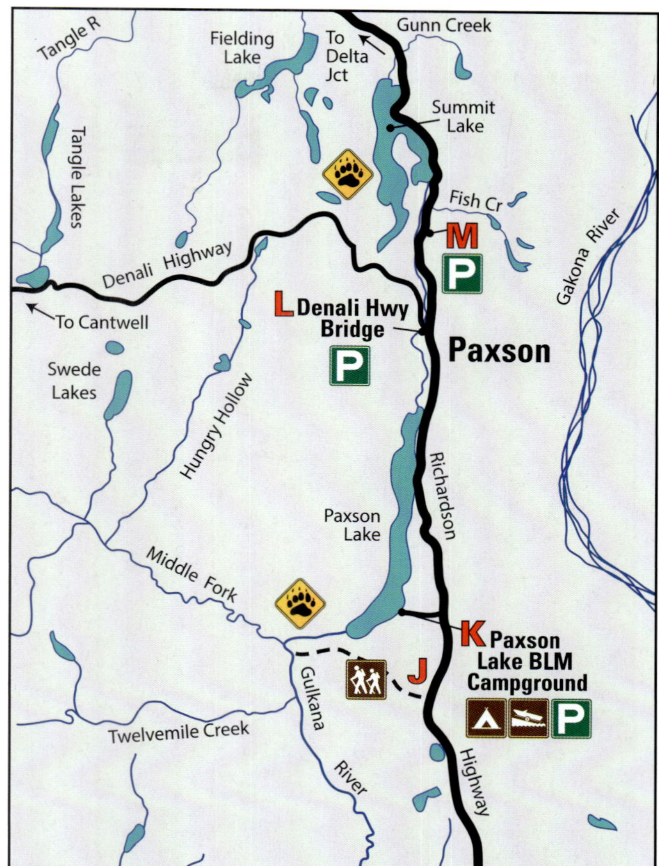

## Rules & Regulations

**Open Season:** January 1 through December 31.
**Open Area:** The entire river is open to fishing throughout the year.
**Legal Gear/Tackle:**
- Downstream of the Richardson Highway bridge to and including river mouth, only unbaited, single-hook, artificial flies are allowed from June 1 through July 31. Only unbaited single-hook, artificial lures may be used from August 1 through May 31.
- Upstream of the Richardson Highway bridge to an ADF&G marker located 7.5 miles upstream of the West Fork confluence, only unbaited, single-hook, artificial lures may be used from July 20 through May 31. Bait and lures with treble hooks are allowed from June 1 through July 19.
- Only unbaited, single-hook, artificial lures may be used year-round in East Fork Gulkana.

**King Salmon**
- Open season is January 1 through July 19 from river mouth to an ADF&G marker located 7.5 miles upstream of the West Fork confluence.
- Bag limit is (1) per day and (1) in possession (20 inches or longer). For kings less than 20 inches (Jacks), the limit is (10).

**All Other Salmon**
- Open all season (see general "Open Season" above).
- Bag limit is (3) per day and (3) in possession (16 inches or longer). For salmon less than 16 inches (Jacks), the limit is (10).
- East Fork Gulkana is closed to salmon fishing all year.

**Rainbow/Steelhead Trout**
- Open all season in all areas of the river.
- Retention of trout is not allowed and fish may not be removed from the water. All fish caught must be released.

**Other Fish**
- Open all season in all areas of the river.
- Arctic grayling bag limit is (5) per day and (5) in possession, of which only (1) may be longer than 14 inches.
- Whitefish has no bag or possession limit, no size limit.
- Burbot bag limit is (5) per day and (5) in possession, no size limit.

KINGFISHER'S PERCH
Gulkana River
Copper River Valley
King
Salmon
Red
Salmon
Rainbows
& Grayling
WWW.ALASKAKINGS.COM
WWW.KLUTINAKINGS.COM
(907)822-5411

## Fishing Gulkana River

**Access:** ★★★
**Scenery:** ★★★★
**Wildlife:** ★★
**Sight Fishing:** ★★★★
**Bank/Wading:** ★★★★
**Boat/Floating:** ★★★★★

**Species:** King and red salmon, rainbow trout, and arctic grayling. Some steelhead trout, whitefish, and burbot present.

**Summary:** The Gulkana River is famed for its healthy runs of king and red salmon, which support one of the largest recreational fisheries in the Copper Valley. Almost equally renowned is the incredibly rich grayling fishery that can easily be described as one of the most productive in Alaska. Both resident and sea-run rainbow trout call Gulkana home with decent fishing available during the summer and fall months.

Kings and reds arrive in the Gulkana roughly at about the same time with fishable numbers of both being present by the second week of June. The entire length of the lower river is ideal for finding schools of fish, with favorite spots for roadside anglers being right around the Richardson Highway bridge. There are a multitude of hot spots farther upstream as well with good opportunities up to Sourdough. The stretch of water at the confluence with the West Fork on the upper Gulkana is highly regarded as one of the top places on the whole river to fish for salmon.

The early-run strain of kings are bound for upper reaches of the drainage with anglers targeting them on the lower and middle river as they first enter the system. The majority of these fish spawn in the mainstem Gulkana below Paxson Lake. For predominantly bright or semi-bright specimens, try early on in the season as the run builds toward a peak but nice salmon can be picked up all season long.

Gulkana sports both an early run and late run of red salmon. The early fish (June-July) are headed for tributary streams and lakes of the upper drainage and are intercepted by anglers along the mainstem river downstream of Paxson Lake. As for the late run (August-September), these salmon are predominantly hatchery fish returning to their release site on the East Fork Gulkana near Summit Lake. As with the early reds, the lower and middle mainstem river is where to target this run.

Rainbow trout are fairly abundant on the upper river but may be caught all along the mainstem from Paxson to the river mouth as well as in the various forks and tributaries of the Gulkana. The section of water right below Canyon Rapids is well-known to produce good fishing and anglers scout this area throughout the summer and fall months as salmon move through and spawn here.

Steelhead trout are a somewhat rare species on the Gulkana, encountered during the spring out migration and in late summer and fall as fish return to spawn in tributaries of Middle Fork Gulkana. A few incidental catches are possible when targeting rainbows and salmon.

Without a doubt it is the arctic grayling that rules much of the Gulkana. An incredibly prolific species here, anglers can expect nothing short of exceptional action. The upper river is notorious for fish-on-every-cast days, the part from Paxson Lake outlet downstream to Sourdough being highly recommended. Very good fishing can also be had from Sourdough to within a few miles of the highway bridge. Downstream from there, fair fishing is the norm. In addition to being numerous, Gulkana's grayling are large with trophy specimens over 20 inches not unusual.

A lesser-fished section of the Gulkana is the East Fork between Summit and Paxson

*Gulkana's rainbow trout population is known as the northernmost on the continent. Expect these unique fish to appear heavily spotted and very aggressive to the fly.*

*(Courtesy Kingfisher's Perch)*

lakes. Different in appearance than the lower portion, it flows crystal clear at a fairly fast clip in spots but slows down and meanders considerably before hitting Paxson. A significant spawning area for red salmon, the East Fork hosts some reliable action for rainbow trout and arctic grayling, yet usually not as fast-paced as what is the norm for the main fork Gulkana below Paxson Lake.

Boating on the Gulkana is a popular option in reaching some of the more productive and remote fishing spots. Particularly floating or rafting the river is good as anglers can cover many miles of water over an extended period of time depending on put-in and take-out points. Day trips are possible but anglers usually spend two to three days on the river in order to experience the Gulkana at its best.

The outlet of Paxson Lake is a favorite launch point, taking out at Sourdough, the Richardson Highway bridge, or any of the other points of access along the river. Anglers utilizing powerboats usually put in at Sourdough and motor miles upstream to favorite holes. The Gulkana has long enjoyed a solid reputation with more beginner floaters as there are very few spots along its course that pose any significant challenges.

## Fish Availability

● = High ● = Moderate ● = Low ● = Closed

| Species | MAY | JUN | JUL | AUG | SEP | OCT | NOV |
|---|---|---|---|---|---|---|---|
| **King Salmon** | Low | Low, Moderate, High, High | High, Moderate, Closed, Closed | Closed, Closed | | | |
| **Red Salmon** | Low | Low, Moderate, High, High | High, Moderate, Low, Low | Moderate, High, High, High | Moderate, Low, Low, Low | Low, Low | |
| **Rainbow Trout** | Low, Low, Low, Low | Moderate, Moderate, High, High | High, High, High, High | High, High, High, High | High, High, High, High | High, Moderate, Moderate, Low | Low, Low |
| **Arctic Grayling** | Moderate, Moderate, Moderate, Moderate | High, High, High, High | High, High, High, High | High, High, High, High | High, High, High, High | High, Moderate, Moderate, Low | Low, Low |
| Angling Pressure | | Low, Moderate, High, High | High, High, Moderate, Moderate | Moderate, Moderate, Moderate, Moderate | Low, Low, Low, Low | Low | |

*(Courtesy Kingfisher's Perch)*

*In order to connect with near chrome and semi-bright kings, targeting these fish early in the season is imperative.*

### King Salmon

**Rating:** ★★½ Good.
**Season:** January 1 through July 19.
**Timing:** May 25 – July 19; peak June 15 – July 10.
**Size:** Average 12 – 30 pounds; up to 60 pounds.
**Tackle:** Spinners, plugs, attractors, flies, and bait.
**Tips:** Salmon roe fished alone or with an attractor is the best way to connect with kings. Search out likely holes and bounce the setup along the bottom. In areas of concentration or shallows permitting anglers to view fish migrating upstream, fly-fishing can be very good using large streamers or attractor flies, spotting and casting to individual fish.

Hot spots for shore anglers include the Richardson Highway bridge and various hike-in and drive-to holes upstream to the Sourdough area. Boaters generally have a much better scope of access with favorite locations including waters above Sourdough, such as the confluence with West Fork.

For those with a permit, the mouth of Gulkana can be absolutely superb as kings gather here prior to moving up the Gulkana and other drainages farther up the Copper River. This is also a great place for chrome specimens and lack the crowds common in the public use areas.

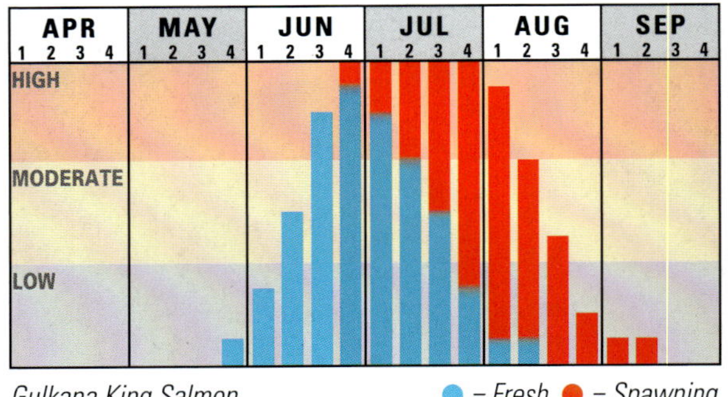

*Gulkana King Salmon* ● = Fresh ● = Spawning

## Red Salmon

**Rating:** ★★★ Good.
**Season:** January 1 through December 31.
**Timing:** May 25 – October 5; peak June 15 – July 10 (early run) and August 5 – 25 (late run).
**Size:** Average 4 – 7 pounds; up to 12 pounds.
**Tackle:** Flies.
**Tips:** Anglers do best on reds by scouting for schools of fish, preferably in places that culminating in moderate to fairly shallow depth with good current flow, focusing the fish in a small area. Small flies are most effective, some even using a colored single bare hook, with darker patterns being preferred.

Fishing can be productive throughout the river, from the outlet of Paxson Lake downstream to the Copper River confluence, yet anglers searching out proper structure in the middle river section generally do best as salmon are more concentrated. Look for good holding water between fast-water stretches. Avoid the long, deep pools which are more conducive in hooking kings.

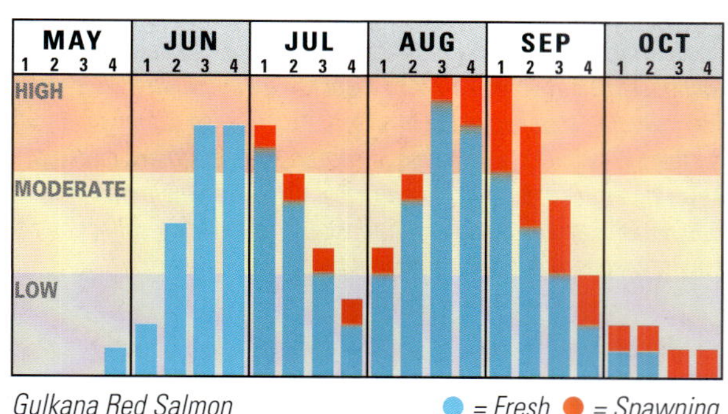


*Gulkana Red Salmon* ● = *Fresh* ● = *Spawning*

*A floater holds up a blushed red salmon, caught on a fly on the middle Gulkana. Spy these fish moving in small schools up the river, pausing momentarily in deeper sections before moving on. Because the Gulkana experiences two separate runs of sockeye, anglers may tie into bright and semi-bright fish throughout the summer months and well into fall.*

*(Courtesy Kingfisher's Perch)*

*Typical autumn view of the lower river near village of Gulkana.*

### Rainbow Trout

**Rating:** ★★★ Good.
**Season:** January 1 through December 31.
**Timing:** April 15 – November 30; peak June 15 – October 5.
**Size:** Average 10 – 20 inches; up to 28 inches (8-10 pounds).
**Tackle:** Spinners and flies.
**Tips:** Nice rainbows, some trophy-sized, can be found on the upper Gulkana between Sourdough and Paxson Lake. Try just above and below the rapids for the best trout action the river has to offer, which can rival some of the more renown waters in Southcentral. Relatively few trout are available near the highway crossing and below.

Forage pattern lures and flies are good prior to July and again in late autumn, egg and flesh imitations become more effective in August and September.

### Arctic Grayling

**Rating:** ★★★★★ Excellent.
**Season:** January 1 through December 31.
**Timing:** April 1 – November 30; peak June 1 – October 5.
**Size:** Average 8 – 16 inches; up to 22 inches (3 pounds).
**Tackle:** Spinners and flies.
**Tips:** The stretch of river from Paxson Lake to Sourdough is prime grayling territory, particularly just downstream of the rapids. Trophy grayling are common from the rapids to the lake, this area being a fall hot spot as well. In spring, anglers can find fast-paced action near clearwater tributaries, such as Sourdough and Poplar Grove creeks.

Forage lures and flies and dry flies work best all season. Some fish also aggressively strike egg patterns in late summer and fall. Rooster tail type spinners perform exceptionally well.

(Courtesy Kingfisher's Perch)

*Gulkana is famous for its incredible grayling fishery. Landing several hundred of these sailfins during a multi-day float is not just possible but very likely. Any insect or fry imitation fly will get hit, including small spinners in sizes 0 to 3. The specimen pictured on the left displays a very unique spotting pattern (black marking covering entire side of fish), with most fish observed in this population, as well as others in Alaska, only having a collection of very few spots right behind the gill plate.*

## Other Gulkana Opportunities

### Gulkana River Float Fishing

The Gulkana makes for a world-class float fishing experience. Not only is it designated a National Wild and Scenic Water but the river size and quality of the stream flow is absolutely perfect for floaters of all levels of experience, from beginner to advanced. This, coupled with the fact that floaters will have the opportunity to sample some of the best grayling and trout action in the state (along with bountiful salmon) in a semi-remote and highly scenic setting, just contributes to the growing popularity of Gulkana as a prime float fishing destination.

There are several ways to go about floating the river depending on length of trip desired and what species are targeted. For the renowned grayling and trout fishery, the upper river (from Paxson Lake) to any of the take-out points in the mid-section is the preferred float. If looking for salmon, the middle river around Sourdough downstream to the highway crossing on the lower river is great and makes for perfect full- or half day trips according to put-in and take-out points. Some anglers may choose to spend several

(Courtesy River Wrangellers)

days on the river and do the whole section from Paxson Lake to the Richardson Highway, thus sampling the whole gamut of fishing opportunities.

The upper river float trip typically begins at the outlet of Paxson Lake, accessed through the Paxson Lake Campground off Richardson Highway. Anglers paddle to the start of the Gulkana and float and fish from there. At this point in the trip, grayling fishing is excellent and even some lake trout may be caught where the river forms at the lake outlet. Red salmon and some rainbows are available too, although these species generally do better where the river current is stronger, such as the canyon or rapids area and below. Expect a few steelhead trout to be present later on in the season (September-October).

This trip is best done in two to three days but can be accomplished overnight depending on take-out point. It, like other river sections, is classified as easy and perfect for beginner floaters.

The middle river float can begin from any one of the Sourdough area access points and usually culminating at the Richardson Highway bridge. This is a great trip if wanting to hook up with salmon. There are a number of long, deep holes and runs in this stretch that harbor schools of kings and reds both, with the majority of fishing targeted towards the former.

For day trippers, this float makes sense as some of the better spots on the river is visited. Again, an easy float.

The last leg, and one that can only be done by permission from Ahtna, Inc., is from the Richardson Highway bridge downstream to the mouth of Gulkana River at the Copper River. This is typically a salmon-only trip but some grayling and a few rainbows may be caught as well. Casting into the confluence area can be exceptional, particularly for kings, and some steelhead are available later on in the season.

Take-out here is by the trail leading to the highway or by arrangement farther downstream on the Copper.

## Middle Fork & West Fork Gulkana

Designated as National Wild and Scenic waters, the Middle Fork and West Fork of Gulkana River present some terrific remote fishing for red salmon in June and July and rainbow trout and arctic grayling from early summer through most of fall. There is also a unique chance of hooking into steelhead trout in this area in September and October. King salmon fishing, however, is prohibited in these drainages.

Anglers typically fly in to headwater lakes of the West Fork or portage in from Tyone River. It is an easy float and a canoe is the way to go. Accessing the Middle Fork is a little more complicated, anglers putting in at Tangle Lakes at the Denali Highway and portaging to Dickey Lake, the headwater of the fork. One may also choose to fly in to the lake. The float here starts off with Class II water, with some Class III, before mellowing out. Inflatable crafts are recommended. Both drainages join with the main Gulkana, taking out at Sourdough or the Richardson Highway bridge.

These trips, including some generous fishing, can be completed in about a week (Middle Fork) to two weeks (West Fork).

(Courtesy River Wrangellers)

*Scene from the mouth of Gulkana River. This is one of the better spots for finding large numbers of bright salmon.*

## West Fork Gulkana Lakes

A cluster of large lakes draining into the lower section of the West Fork Gulkana River contain very healthy populations of fish that are relatively rarely targeted by anglers during the summer and fall months. They are accessed by float plane during the open water season and snow machine and plane on skis in winter. All of the lakes yield great action for lake trout, arctic grayling, and burbot.

Crosswind Lake is the larger of the waters and probably the most visited. It is also the starting point for canoeists traveling to the West Fork Gulkana by the way of Dog Creek. Expect a chance to hook into trophy lake trout (up to 30 pounds). Deep, Fish, and Ewan lakes are another few locations worth trying.

Runs of red salmon are present in these lakes in summer but are generally in spawning condition.

## Salmon Viewing

The upper section of Gulkana River as well as the East Fork Gulkana provide ample observations of migrating and spawning salmon, kings and reds both. The better view point, however, is located near the outlet of Summit Lake where East Fork Gulkana originates. A platform is available next to the large parking lot.

Two runs of reds move into this stretch of the river, with excellent viewing during the early run from late June to late July. The late run is bound for the fish hatchery a ways downstream of the lake and platform and chiefly present from mid-September to mid-October. Hike along highway shoulder by river to see fish.

# Other Productive Fisheries & Additional Opportunities

## LAKE LOUISE

**Fishing:** ★★★ **Scenery:** ★★★
**Accessibility:** ★★ **Solitude:** ★★★

**Location:** Western Copper Valley, Susitna River tributary, 47 miles west of Glennallen, 177 miles northeast of Anchorage.

**Access:** From Milepost 159.8 Glenn Highway, the Lake Louise Road heads north 17.3 miles to a "Y." Left fork, 0.2 mile to access road short distance to lake. Right fork, 0.5 mile to lake.

**Facilities:** Parking, camping, boat rental and launch, lodging, and restrooms available. Other amenities include limited groceries, tackle, and guide services at lodge.

**Species**: Lake trout, arctic grayling, and burbot. The lake also has a large population of whitefish.

**Restrictions:** Salmon fishing prohibited. Size limit on lake trout; must be 24 inches or longer. Consult ADF&G regulations.

**Fishing:** Lake Louise has been a favorite roadside fishing destination since the 60s, known for its trophy lake trout and abundant grayling and burbot. Although the action has cooled somewhat over the years after a fair amount of angling pressure, there are still some big fish to be found and, at the height of the season, catch rates being good. All species are available year-round.

Lakers well over 20 pounds are caught every season and local anglers claim there are fish in Louise that weigh more than 40 pounds. These char respond best to large spoons or plugs trolled in deep water around structure during the summer months, with fish being caught in shallow or mid-depth locations in spring and fall.

Burbot is another sought-after species, especially popular with the ice-fishing crowd. In fact, the state record burbot – just shy of 25 pounds – came from this lake.

(Courtesy Max Root)

Grayling are most responsive during the summer and fall months and may be located in big schools in shallow water near shore and around islands where food sources are abundant. Whitefish, though very plentiful, can be difficult to catch but do strike midges and tiny baits.

Due to the large size of Lake Louise, most successful anglers use boats to reach favorable fishing areas and depth. Casting from shore may be productive for grayling in summer yet it is the fall months that are best for this species as well as lake trout.

**Lake Trout.** Good from boat, fair at best from shore; June and September 1 through November 30; average 3 – 8 pounds. Troll spoons and plugs around islands and in channels, use jigs and bait in winter.

**Arctic Grayling.** Good from boat, fair from shore; June 1 through September 30; average 8 – 14 inches. Try spinners and flies.

**Burbot.** Fair; March through April and November through December; average 3 – 5 pounds. Try jigs and bait.

## UPPER COPPER RIVER STREAMS

**Fishing:** ★★★ **Scenery:** ★★★
**Accessibility:** ★★★ **Solitude:** ★★★★

**Location:** Northeastern Copper Valley drainages, 31 to 92 miles north of Glennallen, 220 to 281 miles northeast of Anchorage.

**Access:** The Tok Cutoff, running between Gakona Junction at Milepost 128.6 Richardson Highway and Tok Junction at Milepost 1422.0 of Alaska Highway, provides direct road access to several waters that are worth checking into if passing through.

*A. Tulsona Creek* – Milepost 17.9. Highway crosses stream. Parking. No established trail but an improvised footpath is present.

*B. Indian River* – Milepost 43.9. Highway crosses river. Parking. Rough, improvised trail leads downstream a ways.

*C. Ahtell Creek* – Milepost 60.8. Highway crosses stream. Parking and primitive camping. No trails.

**Facilities:** Standard parking at turnoffs with some space for large RVs. Lodging, cabins, and RV campgrounds are available in the area.

**Species**: Arctic grayling. A few king and red salmon, Dolly Varden, and whitefish are present.

**Restrictions:** Several drainages in this area are closed to king salmon fishing or have seasonal restrictions. Consult ADF&G regulations.

**Fishing:** There are about a dozen or more waters along this stretch of highway with several of them situated within the Upper Copper River drainage. All of them support at least decent populations of fish, mainly grayling, and quite a few also experience seasonal runs of salmon as well as smaller numbers of char and whitefish.

A few select locations are aptly suited for angling as they run clear, these being Tulsona, Indian, and Ahtell, while other waters perhaps less so because of private property, limited fish populations, or glacial turbidity throughout much of the open-water season.

Those targeting the streams in this area do best hiking away from the road up to a quarter of a mile or more as angling pressure is highest at crossings. Expect the fishing to be quick and easy at times in some holes, especially at dawn and dusk, with good opportunities lasting all summer.

Watch out for grizzly bears at these streams.

**Arctic Grayling.** Good; May 15 – September 30; average 7 – 14 inches. Spinners and flies.

## GULKANA AREA STREAMS

**Fishing:** ★★★ **Scenery:** ★★★
**Accessibility:** ★★★ **Solitude:** ★★★★

**Location:** Central Copper Valley drainage, Gulkana River tributaries, 22 to 45 miles north of Glennallen, 209 to 232 miles northeast of Anchorage.

**Access:** The Richardson Highway provides access to three streams in the Gulkana area that are noteworthy.

*A. Poplar Grove Creek* – Milepost 138.3. Highway crosses stream. Parking. No established trail but a faint foot path is present.

*B. Sourdough Creek* – Milepost 147.6. West on gravel road 0.2 mile to stream crossing. Road parallels stream 0.3 mile to its mouth at Gulkana River. Parking for all size vehicles, camping, and restrooms. No established trail; faint foot path present. Additionally, highway crosses stream at Milepost 147.7. Parking.

*C. Haggard Creek* – Milepost 161.0. Highway crosses stream. Very limited parking. No space for RVs.

*(Courtesy Chris Cox)*

**Facilities:** Parking, camping, and restrooms. Lodging and cabins are available in immediate area.

**Species**: Arctic grayling. A few rainbow trout may be present.

**Restrictions:** There are no specific restrictions governing these waters. Consult ADF&G regulations.

**Fishing:** This trio of clearwater streams are in the Gulkana River drainage and important grayling spawning waters. Although fishing is allowed year-round, the only worthwhile opportunities are during the spring months when hordes of sailfins invade, bound for breeding grounds on the middle and upper reaches of Poplar, Sourdough, and Haggard.

Fish may be present at any time from breakup in mid-April until the snow flies in October, yet the grayling migrations peak during the month of May. Typically few fish remain in the streams after the spawning run has completed, retuning to the Gulkana River to feed for the summer and fall.

Despite the diminutive appearance of these tributaries throughout most of the season, they swell with meltwater in spring, thus prompting thousands of grayling to head upstream. Expect the action to be furious at times, attracting a fair number of anglers.

**Arctic Grayling.** Good to excellent; month of May; average 7 – 14 inches. Try spinners and flies.

## PAXSON LAKE

**Fishing:** ★★★ **Scenery:** ★★★★
**Accessibility:** ★★★ **Solitude:** ★★★

Location: Northern Copper Valley drainage, Gulkana River tributary, 60 miles north of Glennallen, 249 miles northeast of Anchorage.

**Access:** There are two main access points from the Richardson Highway.

*A. Paxson Lake Campground* – Milepost 175.0. West on gravel road next to sign 1.4 miles to a "Y," follow sign short distance to lake. Parking, campground, restrooms, and boat launch.

*B. Paxson Lake Shoreline* – Milepost 179.4—182.5. Highway parallels lake. Numerous turnouts present.

**Facilities:** One developed campground for all size vehicles located at lake. Lodging, gas, and limited grocery and tackle supplies can be found in the community of Paxson.

**Species:** Red salmon, rainbow and lake trout, arctic grayling, and burbot. A few king salmon at lake outlet; big population of whitefish in lake proper.

**Restrictions:** King salmon fishing prohibited. Closed to all salmon fishing from January 1 through July 19. Bait and hook restrictions apply. Consult ADF&G regulations.

**Fishing:** The long and relatively narrow Paxson Lake is another long-time favorite with anglers across Alaska's road system. Known for its productive lake trout and burbot fishing, Paxson draws a fair amount of angling use during the fall and winter months. Ice fishing here is popular and the lake also serves as a starting point for float fishing excursions down the Gulkana River.

The best way to fish this lake is using a boat. Although casting from shore can yield some catches (mainly early and late in the season), boaters consistently hang more and bigger fish by far. Trolling is a proven method, especially effective on lake trout but will catch quite a few rainbows as well. The lakers in Paxson are reputed to reach very large size, up to 30 pounds or more. Boaters may also want to access the inlet stream, East Fork Gulkana River, at the north end of the lake and the lake outlet and the start of mainstem Gulkana River at the south end. Grayling action is always better at the inlet and outlet, particularly towards the beginning and end of the season as fish transition from the lake to summer feeding grounds and back again.

(Courtesy River Wrangellers)

Red salmon are abundant in Paxson and two sizable runs pass through the lake in summer and fall on the way to the East Fork Gulkana and Summit Lake. Fishing for these reds, however, can be difficult and only a small number of fish are taken every season. The early run is currently protected by law.

Anglers having no boat access may do fairly well casting off the bank just after ice-out in late May or early June and prior to freeze-up in October. At these times, grayling migrating through are plentiful while lake trout come into the shallows and aggressively strike properly presented offerings.

Ice fishing can be quite good on Paxson.

**Rainbow Trout.** Fair to good; June 1 – 30 and September 1 – October 15; average 10 – 22 inches. Try the inlet and outlet. Spoons, spinners, plugs, and flies.

**Lake Trout.** Good; June 1 – 30 and Sept. 15 – Nov. 30; average 3 – 10 pounds. Lake inlet, outlet, small bays, and coves are good. Spoons, plugs, flies, and bait.

**Arctic Grayling.** Good to excellent; June 1 – October 15; average 8 – 16 inches. Biggest fish are caught in spring and fall. Try spinners and flies.

**Burbot.** Fair to good; September 15 – April 15; average 2 – 6 pounds. Ice fishing is best. Try jigs and bait.

## SUMMIT LAKE

**Fishing:** ★★★ **Scenery:** ★★★★
**Accessibility:** ★★★★ **Solitude:** ★★★★
**Location:** Northern Copper Valley drainage, Gulkana River tributary, 76 miles north of Glennallen, 265 miles northeast of Anchorage.
**Access:** The Richardson Highway parallels the lake from Milepost 191.0 to 196.0. Pullouts are present.
**Facilities:** Gravel turnouts adjacent to lake, at Milepost 192.2, with parking and boat launch, and Milepost 192.6 with gravel parking. In addition, cabins, B&Bs, and camping are available in the area.
**Species:** Rainbow and lake trout, arctic grayling, and burbot. Red salmon and whitefish are present.
**Restrictions:** King salmon fishing prohibited. Closed to all salmon fishing from January 1 through July 19. Bait and hook restrictions apply. Consult ADF&G regulations.
**Fishing:** Due to the elevation of Summit (over 3,200 feet), the open-water fishing season is relatively short with ice conditions often persisting well into June and freezeup starting in October. Casting from shore is possible and quite rewarding at times (especially right after breakup), yet the most consistent action can be had by using a boat or some form of watercraft to reach deeper water and better structure.

Trout and char are both most active in early summer and fall, grayling being available continuously from breakup until the snow flies. Like Paxson, lake trout in Summit grow to quite significant proportions with catches in the 20- to 25-pound range not unusual. There are some big rainbows to be had as well. Burbot are present year-round and usually encountered in winter when they feed aggressively. Fishing for these freshwater cod is usually a little slower in summer but can still be quite good. Whitefish are abundant but rarely caught.

(Courtesy River Wrangellers)

Red salmon enter the lake but fishing for them is poor. There are two runs in the area, one in June and July and another smaller appearance in August and September.

Decent ice fishing for lake trout and burbot.

**Rainbow Trout.** Fair to good; June 1 – 30 and September 1 – October 15; average 10 – 22 inches. Try near the outlet. Spoons, spinners, plugs, and flies.
**Lake Trout.** Good; June 1 – 30 and September 15 – November 30; average 3 – 10 pounds. Lake inlet and outlet are good. Spoons, plugs, flies, and bait.
**Arctic Grayling.** Good to excellent; June 1 – October 15; average 8 – 16 inches. Spring and fall yield biggest fish. Try spinners and flies.
**Burbot.** Fair to good; September 15 – May 1; average 2 – 6 pounds. Ice fishing is great. Jigs and bait work best.

## TANGLE LAKES & RIVER

**Fishing:** ★★★★ **Scenery:** ★★★★
**Accessibility:** ★★★★ **Solitude:** ★★★
**Location:** Northern Copper Valley drainage, Delta River tributary, 70 miles north of Glennallen, 278 miles northeast of Anchorage.
**Access:** The partially-paved Denali Highway presents the main route of access from the junction with Richardson Highway in the community of Paxson, Milepost 185.5. West on Denali Highway 21.5 miles to Round Tangle Lake on right and the Tangle Lakes area. Continue another 0.1 mile to the Tangle River crossing at Milepost 21.6, followed by Upper Tangle Lake on left at Milepost 21.7.
**Facilities:** Parking, camping, boat launch, and restrooms. Also, lodging is available in the vicinity.
**Species:** Lake trout, arctic grayling, whitefish, and burbot in the lakes; arctic grayling and whitefish in the river.

(Courtesy Carl Jappe)

**Restrictions:** Special lake trout and burbot bag and possession limit restrictions apply. Consult ADF&G regulations.
**Fishing:** Like so many other waters in this area, the Tangle Lakes complex is situated at a relatively high altitude, meaning that spring breakup arrives late, usually around the

first of June, with autumn and frosty nights in full effect by mid-August. Winter conditions come early (mid-September and later). True summer fishing, in this sense, can then be said to only last several weeks, or from about late June to early August, and this is when most anglers zero in on the area to enjoy some truly awesome grayling action for which Tangle Lakes have become known.

The cluster of gin-clear lakes and the short river tying them together are home to species so typical of northern, inland Alaska waters; char, grayling, whitefish, and burbot. Although these lakes do not yield much along the lines of trophies, they are absolutely filled with fish and a reason so many anglers keep coming back here year after year.

Casting from shore can be excellent all season but generally best in June (right after ice-out) and September, such as at the road access points. Even better, if having access to a canoe or kayak, reaching a few of the more remote locations in this system will put anglers on to spectacular fishing, such as the lower reaches of tributaries and where they flow into the lakes. For lake trout, the use of a watercraft is definitely the way to go in order to reach deeper water with structure. A big char here would be in the 10- to 15-pound range. Look for schools of grayling around lake reefs.

**Lake Trout.** Good; June 1 – 30 and August 15 – November 30; average 3 – 5 pounds. Lake reefs and stream inlets and outlets are good. Spoons, plugs, and bait.

**Arctic Grayling.** Excellent; June 15 – September 15; average 7 – 16 inches. Spring and fall yield biggest fish. Try spinners and flies.

**Burbot.** Fair to good; August 15 – May 15; average 2 – 5 pounds. Ice fishing is best. Use jigs and bait.

## ADDITIONAL OPPORTUNITIES

### Float Fishing Rivers & Streams

The northern section of Copper Valley has an abundance of waters that are perfect for rafting trips. Not all are equally endowed as far as fishing goes but they do share the magnificent and largely undisturbed highland scenery that so predominates this part of Alaska.

No matter where a trip originates, anglers can expect to find an abundance of arctic grayling, which is by far the dominant species. However, some waters also yield various salmon runs in season and a few even offer a chance to hook rainbow trout or the ever-elusive steelhead.

While the Gulkana is the king of float fishing destinations in this area, there are other paces to go, such as the Slana and Chistochina rivers that are at least partially road-accessible but may require off-road alternatives to properly fish.

Arranging for remote, fly-out trips, a plethora of waters become available, all featuring wild views with matching fishing. There are several raft fishing specialists in this area that offer excursions into the remotest parts of the valley.

(Courtesy River Wrangellers)

### Copper & Tanada Lakes

These two remote and adjacent lakes at the headwaters of the Copper River are perfect for fly-in excursions. Fish populations are big and healthy, seeing minimal angling activity during the year. Copper and Tanada both have good to excellent fishing for lake trout, arctic grayling, and burbot. The lake trout have a reputation of growing to sizable proportions, up to 25 pounds or more. In addition, landlocked red salmon – Kokanee – are found in small numbers. A modest run of anadromous red salmon also makes the journey into these lakes in summer.

Breakup is in June with freezeup commencing by the first of October, the best times for fast action, but anglers do experience very good catches all season long.

### Susitna & Tyone Lakes

These two sizable waters – Susitna Lake and Tyone Lake – are connected to Lake Louise, all draining into the Susitna River through Tyone River. Access is by boat from Lake Louise Road or float plane; winter travel with snow machine is popular.

Both lakes yield good to excellent fishing for lake trout and arctic grayling in early summer right after ice-out and again in fall leading to freezeup. Trolling or jigging for lakers is a particularly attractive activity here as the fish grow big – up to 30 pounds or more. Ice fishing for burbot is good in early and late winter. Whitefish are also abundant but sometimes difficult to find; try the outlet of Tyone Lake in fall.

## Glennallen • Copper Center

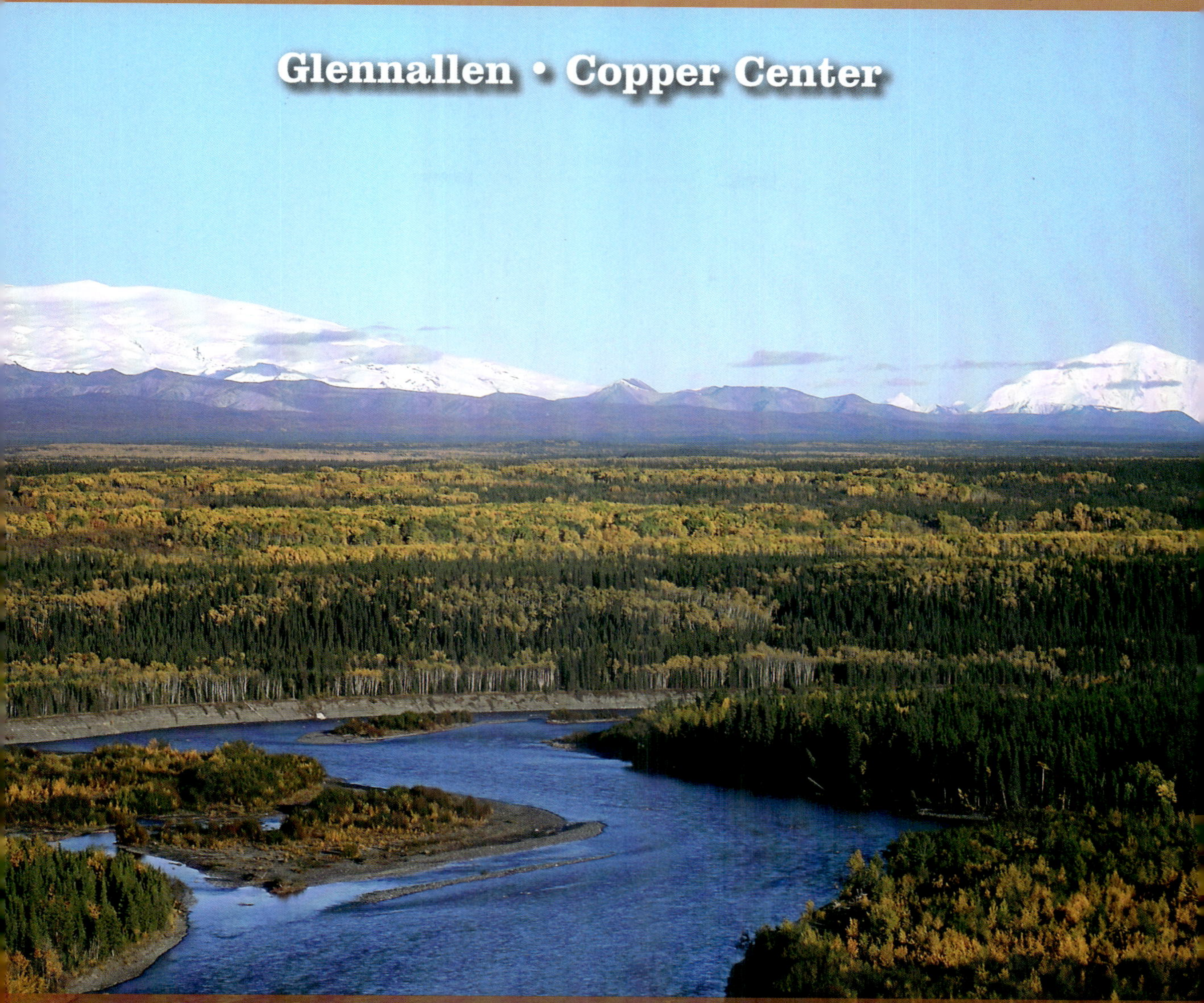

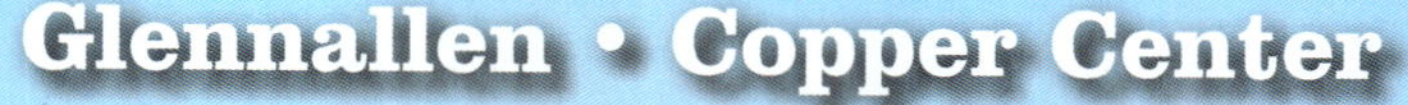

# Southern Copper

**King Salmon • Red Salmon • Silver Salmon • Rainbow Trout**
**Lake Trout • Dolly Varden • Arctic Grayling**

*Scenic Waters*

*Trophy Salmon*

*Lakes of Solitude*

*Raft Fishing*

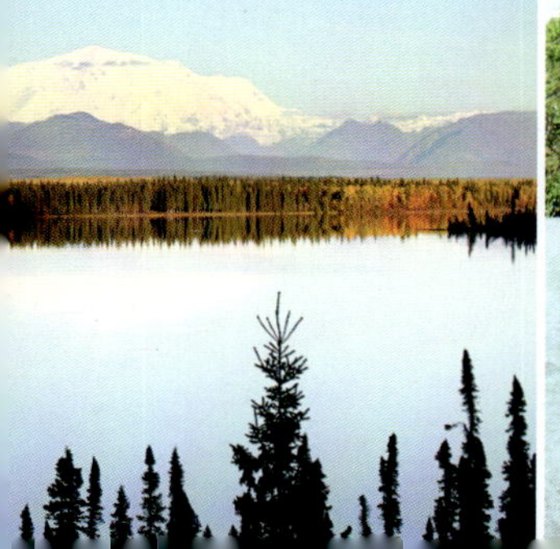

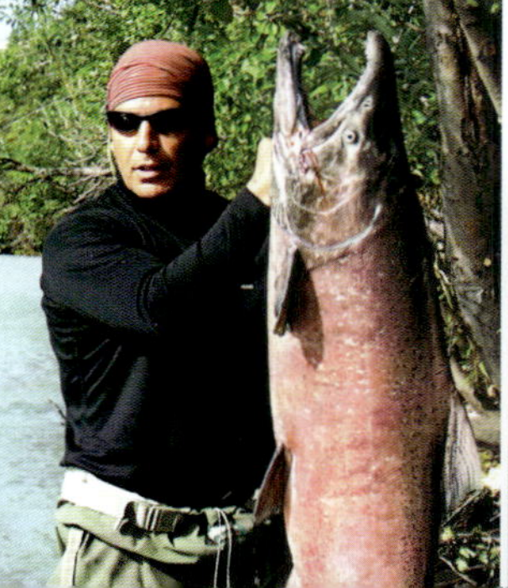

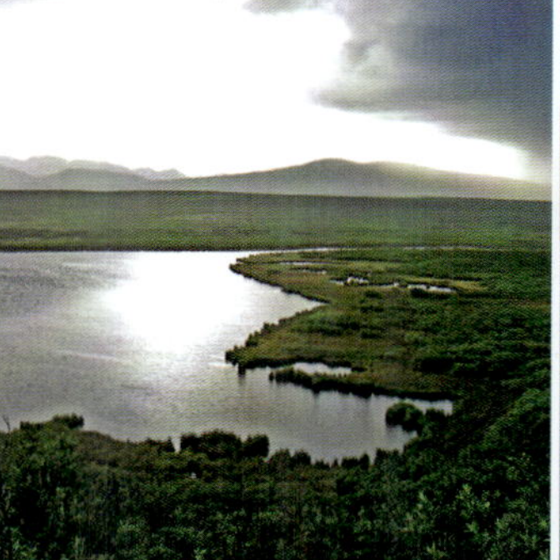

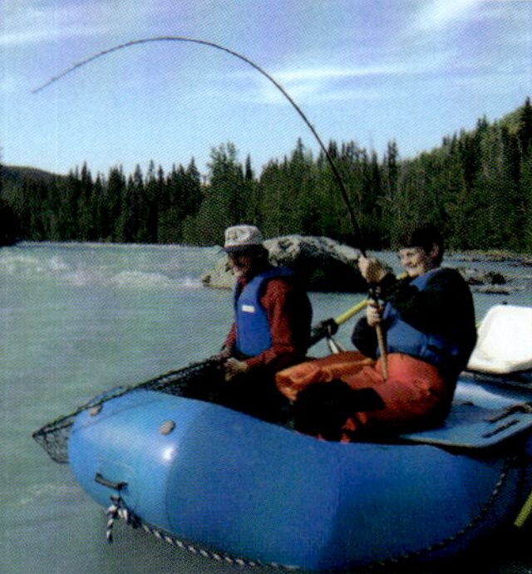

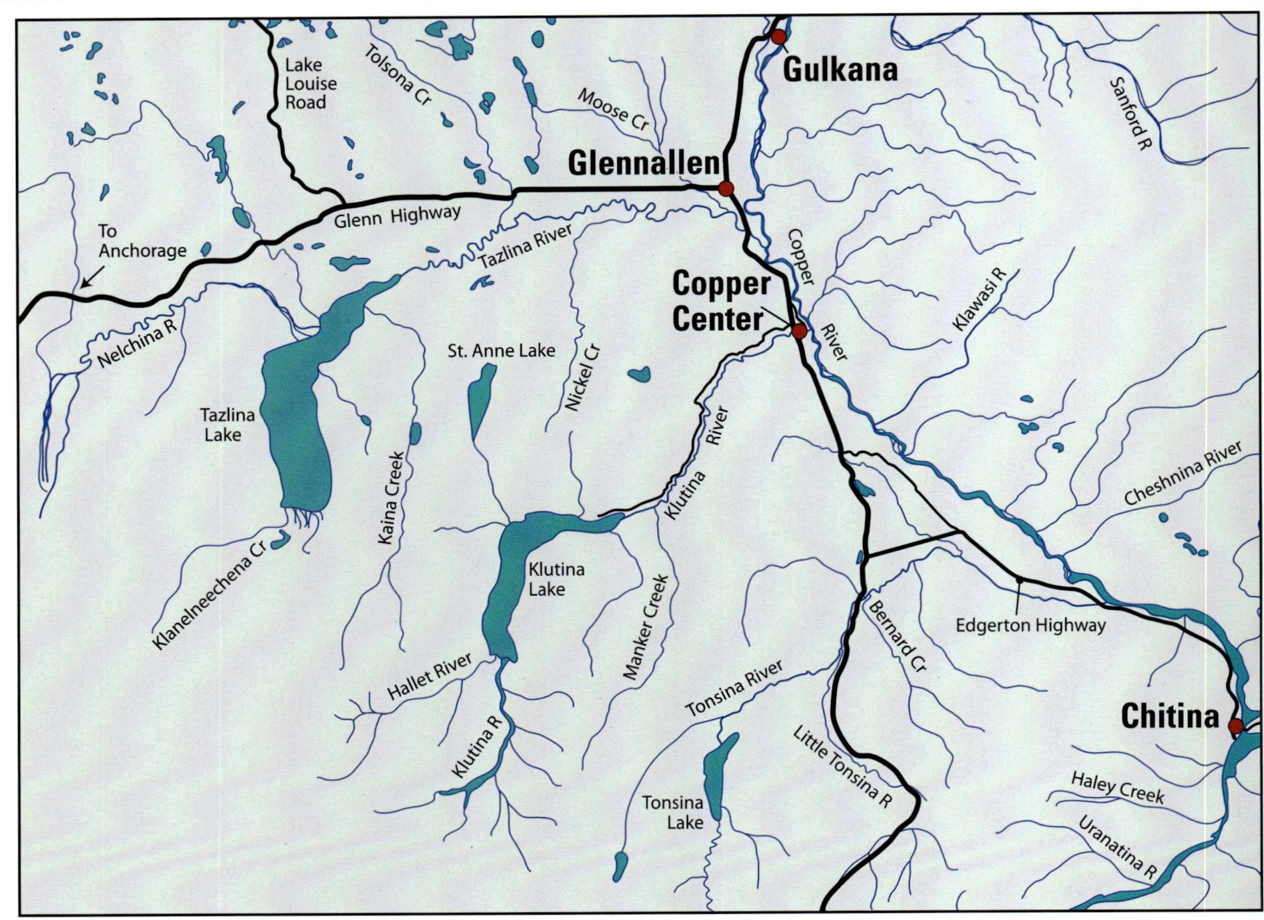


**Area Population Centers:** Glennallen, Copper Center, Chitina

**Key Species:** King, Red, and Silver Salmon, Rainbow Trout, Dolly Varden, and Arctic Grayling

**Other Species:** Steelhead and Lake Trout, Whitefish, and Burbot

**Main Destination/Hot Spot:** Klutina and Tonsina Rivers

**Other Productive Fisheries:** (414); Little Tonsina River, McCarthy and Tazlina Area Lakes, Tolsona and Mendeltna Creeks.

**Additional Opportunities:** Remote Tazlina Streams, and Tebay & Hanagita Rivers.

**Summary of Area Fishing:** Perhaps even more scenic than the northern part of Copper Valley, the southern half is a hotbed for fishing enthusiasts. But unlike the timid, clear, and slow-flowing neighboring drainages to the north, the waters within this area are characterized by rushing glacial rivers and deep lakes with only a smattering of smaller clearwater tributaries accessible from the road. The fishing, however, is nothing short of exceptional, especially for salmon, and the area fast becoming a popular sport fishing destination not just for locals but on a national level.

Without a doubt, it is the Klutina River that drives the center of angling activity here with only very limited number of recognized opportunities elsewhere within the area. Although the state does stock a few lakes with select game species, most waters remain largely unexplored and anglers willing to put in time and effort to scout other river drainages may find some surprisingly good fishing.

From early summer and continuing well into fall, runs of both king, red, and silver salmon penetrate the area, sparking a flurry of action that is rated on par with the best waters anywhere. Yet even with the recent "discovery" of Klutina and surrounding systems, there is still ample room to enjoy great fishing along with solitude, something of an oddity on many other roadside waters of Alaska.

Aside from the spotlight dedicated to salmon, anglers will also find resident species in relatively good numbers, such as Dolly Varden and grayling, with some limited -- but productive -- action for rainbow trout. These are species not targeted to any degree so expect plenty of elbowroom.

Coupled with an excursion to Valdez, this is an area worth exploring.

The months of June into September are best.

# Klutina River

King SALMON

Red SALMON

Rainbow TROUT

Dolly VARDEN

Arctic GRAYLING

**Highlights:** Some of the most intense salmon fishing anywhere, with superb action for red salmon and trophy king salmon. Upper reaches offer nice rainbows and char.

**Best Fishing:** Mid-June to mid-August.

**Regulatory Restrictions:** Liberal.

**Location:** Southern Copper Valley drainage, Copper River tributary, 13 miles south of Glennallen, 202 miles northeast of Anchorage

**Description:** The Klutina River, pouring out of Klutina Lake, is a glacial system, its waters running a silty green that would remind any seasoned Alaskan angler of the famous Kenai River. But one major distinction is the lack of crowds, most of the shoreline and surrounding area void of development of any kind, giving anglers a true feel of being in the wilderness. The only populated area is Copper Center at the Richardson Highway river crossing.

The upper river near Klutina Lake contains a generous amount of slack water along with intermittent current, but as the middle section of the Klutina begins its ascent through the canyon, the river becomes a swift giant. There are still many pools and runs ideal for fishing but experience counts here, especially if trying to negotiate the river using a boat. As a matter of fact, the middle Klutina has some of the most productive angling for salmon in the entire drainage. The river continues to tumble at a fast clip through the lower portion until it hits the Copper River.

As this is a glacial drainage, expect prolonged periods of

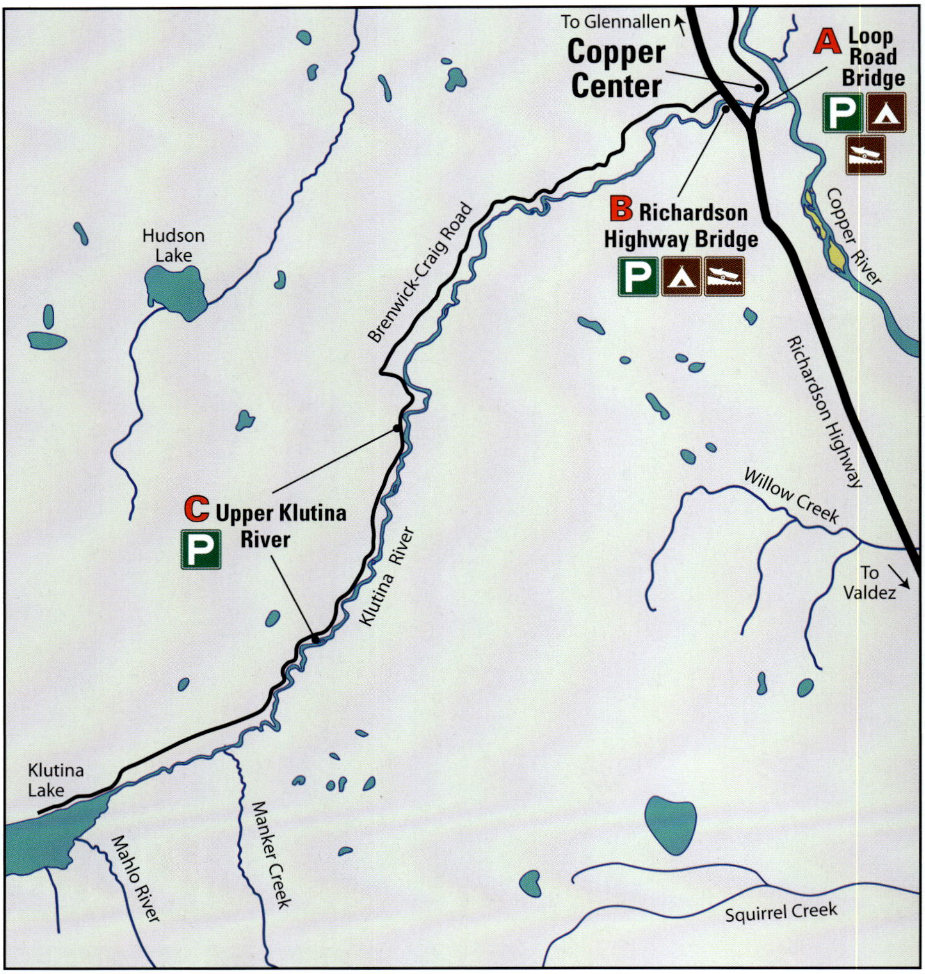

hot weather to affect water conditions through increased snowmelt. Look for periods of mild to cool weather that will optimize water clarity and fishing.

The scenic value of the river is great, particularly the middle and upper areas along the Klutina Lake Road. Wildlife such as moose and bears are abundant.

**Facilities:** Lodging, campground, restrooms, boat launch, guide services, gas, groceries, and tackle available in Copper Center.

**Access:** The Richardson Highway (including Loop Road) crosses the lower river with a side road – Brenwick-Craig (Klutina Lake) Road – providing access to the middle and upper Klutina.

**A. Loop Road Bridge** – Milepost 100.4. East on Loop Road 0.4 mile to the community of Copper Center and the river crossing. Parking for all size vehicles, developed campgrounds, RV parking, restrooms, boat launch, and guide services. Abundance of walking areas along river banks. Improvised trails lead from campgrounds heading up- and downstream. **Note:** Access to confluence of Klutina and Copper rivers is possible by faint trail starting at the south-east side of the bridge. (Park at one of the private campgrounds by permission.) Trail leads 2 1/2 mile to the far lower end of the Klutina River and the river mouth. Crossing shallow river channel may be necessary.

**B. Richardson Highway Bridge** – Milepost 101.4. Highway crosses river. Turnoff southeast of road. Public parking and boat launch at bridge; private river access, campgrounds, restrooms, and guide services available in immediate vicinity. Faint foot paths lead along shoreline.

**C. Upper Klutina River** – Milepost 101.8. West on Brenwick-Craig (Klutina Lake) Road 13.4 miles. Road parallels river more or less next 12.5 miles to outlet of Klutina Lake. Very rough road last few miles; 4WD vehicle recommended. Some parking available; not recommended for large RVs. Improvised foot paths lead from parking areas along river to fishing holes.

To Glennallen
Copper Center
A Loop Road Bridge
B Richardson Highway Bridge
C Upper Klutina River
Hudson Lake
Brenwick-Craig Road
Copper River
Richardson Highway
Willow Creek
To Valdez
Klutina River
Klutina Lake
Mahlo River
Manker Creek
Squirrel Creek

*Overlooking the more remote section of Klutina River along Klutina Lake Road. This area is best fished from boat or hike-in.*

*(Courtesy River Wranglers)*

## Rules & Regulations

**Open Season:** January 1 through December 31.
**Open Area:** The entire river is open to fishing throughout the year.
**Legal Gear/Tackle:** All gear and tackle, including bait, is allowed, including treble hooks.

### King Salmon

- Open season is July 1 through August 10 from river mouth to an ADF&G marker located at Mile 13.0 Klutina Lake Road. Upstream of this marker to Mile 19.2, open season is July 1 through July 31. From this point on to Klutina Lake, open season is July 1 through July 19. Klutina Lake, including all tributaries, are closed to king fishing.
- Bag limit is (1) per day and (1) in possession (20 inches or longer). For kings less than 20 inches (Jacks), the limit is (10). Annual limit is (4).

### All Other Salmon

- Open all season (see general "Open Season" above) from river mouth upstream to an ADF&G marker at Mile 19.2 Klutina Lake Road. From this point on to Klutina Lake, open season is January 1 through July 19.
- Bag limit is (3) per day and (3) in possession (16 inches or longer). For salmon less than 16 inches (Jacks), the limit is (10).

### Rainbow/Steelhead Trout & Dolly Varden

- Open all season (see general "Open Season" above) in all areas of the river.
- Rainbow trout bag limit is (2) per day and (2) in possession, only (1) longer than 20 inches.
- Dolly Varden bag limit is (10) per day and (10) in possession, no size limit.

### Other Fish

- Open all season (see general "Open Season" above) in all areas of the river.
- Arctic grayling bag limit is (5) per day and (5) in possession, no size restrictions.
- Whitefish has no bag or possession limit, no size restrictions.

KINGFISHER'S PERCH
Klutina River
Copper River Valley
King
Salmon
Red
Salmon
Rafting
White Water
WWW.ALASKAKINGS.COM
WWW.KLUTINAKINGS.COM
(907)822-5411
KINGFISHER'S PERCH

## Fishing Klutina River

**Access:** ★★★
**Scenery:** ★★★★★
**Wildlife:** ★★
**Sight Fishing:** ★
**Bank/Wading:** ★★★
**Boat/Floating:** ★★★★

**Species:** King and red salmon, Dolly Varden, and arctic grayling. A few silver salmon and whitefish may be present.
**Summary:** Every season the Klutina experiences huge numbers of salmon, most notably kings and reds, and the river seems aptly suited to provide the very best these runs have to offer. In addition, anglers may find decent populations of resident trout and char. Grayling are not abundant but caught time to time along with an occasional whitefish.

What attracts an increasing number of anglers to the Klutina are the abundant salmon runs. There are two runs each of kings and reds, the June-July fish bound for clearwater tributaries in the system while the later July-August runs are primarily mainstem Klutina salmon. These runs are not always distinct, however, and may overlap to some degree.

King salmon are the top prize on the Klutina. Although fishing for them is currently closed during the early run in June, the late run of July and on into August is recognized as offering great opportunities to catch these trophy-sized fish. Not only should anglers expect to make multiple hookups during an outing but the size of some of these brutes is a pleasant surprise to many. The Klutina strain of kings often top 50 pounds with quite a few 60-pounders mixed in. A rumor of a giant caught here that weighed nearly 90 pounds may be just that but every season there are kings around 70 pounds landed.

(Courtesy Dennis Musgraves)

Besides the impressive physical size of these fish, they are represented in large numbers. Some experienced Klutina anglers even suggest that the river is one of the best waters in Alaska in terms of catch rate.

King fishing on the Klutina can be difficult from shore because of the swift current, leaving anglers who wish to catch a fish to explore areas of the middle and upper reaches of river where holding water is more pronounced and the current perhaps not as strong. Access to a boat is highly advantageous in finding choice locations and there are several guides available running daily trips to some awesome spots on more remote river sections where the current is not as strong and the kings densely concentrated in holes and pools next to shore.

Most roadside anglers visiting the Klutina soon discover the great red salmon fishing available here. And, unlike some prime salmon waters in the state, there is still plenty of elbow room for those willing to walk a little distance away from the road. The first vanguard of reds hit the river in early summer and, like the early run of kings, these fish are bound for spawning grounds in streams flowing into Klutina Lake. The second run appears towards the end of the short summer season and is not nearly as popular with anglers as there are many other species offering good or better fishing this time of year. Also, the run is often smaller than the June run.

(Courtesy Dennis Musgraves)

*Veteran Klutina angler Chris Cox works a section of river for king salmon. Although a few places on the river may see crowds, the majority of the river experiences little angling pressure. For those who elect to hike in from the road a ways or use a boat to reach more remote parts of the river, solitude is very possible.*

A boat is not necessary to catch sockeye and casting from shore typically yield excellent results. The road crossing at Richardson Highway is a popular spot to fish for reds. The water is fast, concentrating fish close to shore, making them very susceptible to the flip-and-drift technique employed on the rivers of Kenai Peninsula.

Other species on the Klutina includes rainbow trout, Dolly Varden, and arctic grayling. The trout and char are more commonly encountered on the middle and upper river near the lake. As this is a salmon spawning area in summer and fall, anglers do well here on fish that may reach 5 to 7 pounds or more; even so, they are not nearly as targeted as the salmon or resident fish of other parts of the road system. As for grayling, the action is rather very much on the slow side compared to other species but can be fairly productive if the water clears somewhat after a period of cool weather, such as in late summer and fall.

With its varying glacial turbidity depending on weather conditions, anglers generally fare better using fluorescent or high-visibility lures and bait. During the fall period, when flows drop and clarity improves, standard lures and colors work just as well as anything else.

## Fish Availability

● = High ● = Moderate ● = Low ● = Closed

| Species | MAY | JUN | JUL | AUG | SEP | OCT | NOV |
|---|---|---|---|---|---|---|---|
| **King Salmon** | Closed | Closed, Closed, Closed, Closed | Moderate, Moderate, High, High | High, Moderate, Closed, Closed | Closed | | |
| **Red Salmon** | Low | Low, Moderate, High, High | High, Moderate, Low, Moderate | High, High, Moderate, Low | Low, Low, Low | | |
| **Rainbow Trout** | Low, Low, Low, Low | Low, Low, Moderate, Moderate | Moderate, Moderate, Moderate, Moderate | Moderate, Moderate, Moderate, Moderate | Moderate, Moderate, Moderate, Moderate | Low, Low, Low, Low | Low, Low, Low, Low |
| **Dolly Varden** | Low, Low, Low, Low | Low, Low, Low, Low | Moderate, Moderate, Moderate, Moderate | Moderate, Moderate, Moderate, Moderate | Moderate, Moderate, Moderate, Moderate | Moderate, Moderate, Low, Low | Moderate, Moderate, Moderate, Moderate |
| **Arctic Grayling** | Low, Low, Low, Low | Moderate, Moderate, Moderate, Moderate | Moderate, Moderate, Moderate, Moderate | Moderate, Moderate, Moderate, Moderate | Moderate, Moderate, Moderate, Moderate | Low, Low, Low, Low | Low, Low, Low, Low |
| Angling Pressure | | Low, Moderate, High, High | High, Moderate, Moderate, Moderate | Moderate, Moderate, Low, Low | Low | | |

*(Courtesy Kingfisher's Perch)*

*Guide and client show off a handsome male chinook, landed from the bank in a remote spot on the middle river. Hooking a fish of this size is not rare on the Klutina, 40- and 50-pound fish being relatively common. Spend a few days on this river and such a trophy could very much become a reality. Battling one of these behemoths from shore is an epic experience.*

## King Salmon

**Rating:** ★★★½ Excellent.
**Season:** July 1 through August 10.
**Timing:** July 1 – August 10; peak July 15 – August 5.
**Size:** Average 20 – 40 pounds; up to 75 pounds.
**Tackle:** Spinners, plugs, attractors, flies, and bait.
**Tips:** Cast-and-drift from shore in spots where slack water meets strong current is ideal for finding and hooking kings. The favorite lure set-up with guides and other Klutina-savvy anglers is an attractor and salmon roe combination fished along the bottom. Fluorescent spinners and gaudy flies are also good, the latter commonly used in fast water areas.

The lower river can be very difficult to land a king salmon due to the swift current, most anglers heading to the middle section or above where the river flow is more manageable and holes defined. A boat is necessary to reach the best locations.

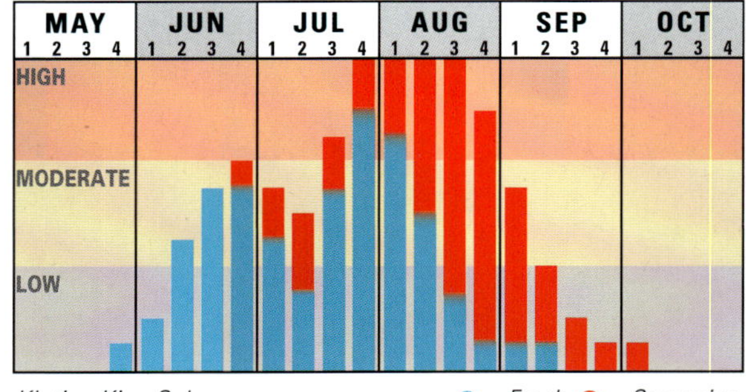


*Klutina King Salmon* ● = Fresh ● = Spawning

*The Klutina is blessed with two large pulses of big, bright sockeye. Flipping flies from the bank is an ideal way of landing one or more reds as they travel upstream within a few yards of the shoreline. The runs typically consist of pulses of fish passing through; one day fishing may be dead slow, the next excellent. Have patience.*

## Red Salmon

**Rating:**  Excellent.
**Season:** January 1 through December 31.
**Timing:** May 25 – September 30; peak June 20 – August 1.
**Size:** Average 5 – 7 pounds; up to 12 pounds.
**Tackle:** Flies.
**Tips:** The lower and middle portions of the Klutina offer the best red action. Fish often migrate close to shore and long casts are not necessary. "Flipping" is the most commonly employed technique. Various fly patterns can be used with success, yet a simple yarn fly in chartreuse or orange is as effective as anything else.

Entire length of middle and upper river fishes good.

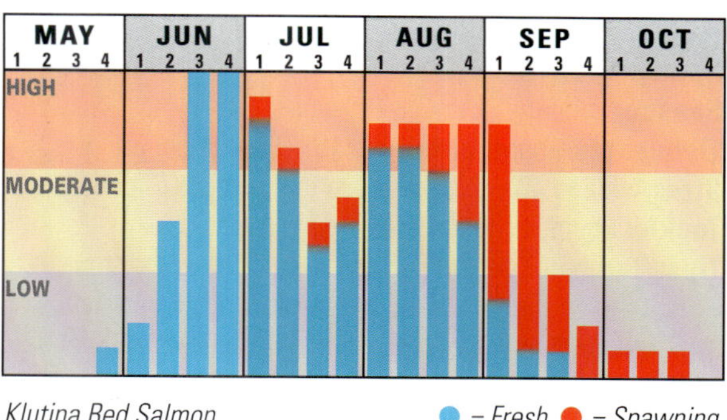


*Klutina Red Salmon* ● = *Fresh* ● = *Spawning*

## Dolly Varden

**Rating:** Fair to good.
**Season:** January 1 through December 31.
**Timing:** Year-round; peak July 1 – October 15.
**Size:** Average 8 – 20 inches; up to 26 inches (7 pounds).
**Tackle:** Spinners, attractors, flies, and bait.
**Tips:** Char can be caught throughout the length of the river but anglers traditionally fare better in the slower current on the upper portion near Klutina Lake. Fishing is productive from mid-summer on, with fall being best to hook large, mature char as they feed on salmon eggs. Use forage imitations lures and flies early in the season, egg and flesh patterns later on.

*Angler Dennis Musgraves attempts to outmaneuver a rampaging 50-plus-pound king from shore, not an easy feat in Klutina's strong current. Finding proper holding structure, utilizing tough and sturdy gear, and applying correct techniques are critical.*

*(Courtesy Dennis Musgraves)*

### Rainbow Trout

**Rating:** ★★ Fair.
**Season:** January 1 through December 31.
**Timing:** Year-round; peak June 15 – September 30.
**Size:** Average 10 – 20 inches; up to 25 inches (6 pounds).
**Tackle:** Spinners, attractors, flies, and bait.
**Tips:** Distributed all through the river, most of the trout caught are on the upper and middle sections where holes, channels, and pools are more pronounced. Flies and beads/corkies in sharper colors are effective, especially when salmon spawn in late summer and fall closer to the lake. Flesh and forage flies may work well in mid- to late autumn when water begins to clear.

### Arctic Grayling

**Rating:** ★½ Poor to fair.
**Season:** January 1 through December 31.
**Timing:** March 15 – Nov. 30; peak June 15 – Sept. 30.
**Size:** Average 8 – 14 inches; up to 20 inches.
**Tackle:** Spinners, attractors, and flies.
**Tips:** Although fish can be caught throughout the river, the majority of catches are made on the upper river, usually by anglers fishing for other species. To properly target grayling on the Klutina, try when water clarity is good, such as late summer and fall, using flashy spinners or colorful beads in orange or pink. Like the resident trout and char, these fish will also feed on salmon eggs.

## Other Klutina Opportunities

### Boat & Float Fishing

Flowing very swift and turbid throughout much of its length, the Klutina is a challenging drainage even to the experienced boater, and a water that should be avoided if novice to river running. However, it is without a doubt the way to go if wanting to get into some of the more remote sections away from the busy road access points. Not only is it a lot less people around but a multitude of choice holding structure can be located where the fishing is nothing short of awesome.

Virtually the whole course of the river is accessible to power boats and rafters, from near the outlet of Klutina Lake all the way downstream to the Copper River confluence and beyond. This makes for a plethora of opportunities for salmon, trout, and char, all of which may be had during a half- to full-day trip as anglers are able to cover a huge variety of water and structure.

Most guides on the Klutina use power boats to shuttle their clients from the highway crossings to the middle and upper reaches of river, yet a few also offer raft trips which is a great way of experiencing the surrounding quiet and peaceful semi-wilderness. Combination trips are available too, using power boats upstream, then floating back downstream using rafts.

A popular method of seeing and fishing the Klutina is to launch a raft on the upper river near Klutina Lake by the way of Klutina Lake (Brenwick-Craig) Road. This is a full-day affair that exposes the floater to the chance of hooking multiple fish species and anglers should bring sufficient gear and tackle to battle anything from 60-pound chinook and fly-happy sockeye to eager rainbows and grayling. The take-out point is either the Richardson Highway bridge or Loop Road bridge in community of Copper Center.

(Courtesy Dennis Musgraves)

No matter the means of utilizing this river, bring a camera as the scenery is absolutely gorgeous and the opportunity to bring home memories of mammoth king salmon very much a possibility.

### Klutina's Trophy Kings

Over the years the Klutina has become renowned as a choice spot for battling kings that regularly top the State of Alaska trophy status mark of 50 pounds. In fact, hit this river at the peak of the chinook run between mid-July and the season closure on August 10 and chances are good to hook into a fish of such proportions.

Casting attractor and bait combinations into any one of the better slots on the middle river will quickly reward anglers with bone-jarring strikes of salmon averaging just about as much as a Kenai River king. While it would be a stretch to speculate that the river may one day yield a record-sized fish, there are enough 60- to 70-pounders in here to at least get the imagination going.

Lack of heavy angling pressure the last several decades means that this genetic strain of Klutina kings is still very pure, meaning anglers have an exceptional opportunity to land a huge fish.

# Tonsina River

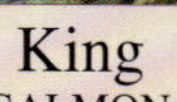
King SALMON

Red SALMON

Silver SALMON

Dolly VARDEN

Arctic GRAYLING

**Highlights:** A true gem of a river, supporting runs of multiple salmon species, char, and grayling in a gorgeous and solitary setting.

**Best Fishing:** Mid-July to Mid-September

**Regulatory Restrictions:** Liberal.

**Location:** Southern Copper Valley drainage, Copper River tributary, 36 miles south of Glennallen, 230 miles northeast of Anchorage.

**Description:** Just a few miles down the highway from Klutina River is the smaller glacial twin – Tonsina. Born out of Tonsina Lake in the Chugach Mountains, this highly turbid river tumbles through a narrow and shallow valley some 60 miles on its course to the vast Copper River. Swift with a distinct greenish-grey color, this rocky-bottomed drainage is one of the last bastions as far as "undiscovered" roadside salmon opportunities is concerned. Apart from a few of the locals that frequent its waters, the Tonsina remains largely obscure to the vast majority of anglers in the Southcentral region.

Nestled between two much more renowned fishing destinations – Port Valdez and Klutina River, the unpretentious Tonsina is a river begging to be fully appreciated by the general angling public. Situated in a supremely gorgeous and highly picturesque area, several salmon species as well as a few resident game fish inhabit Tonsina and its clearwater tributaries. Even though the busy Richardson Highway lends access to some extent, the

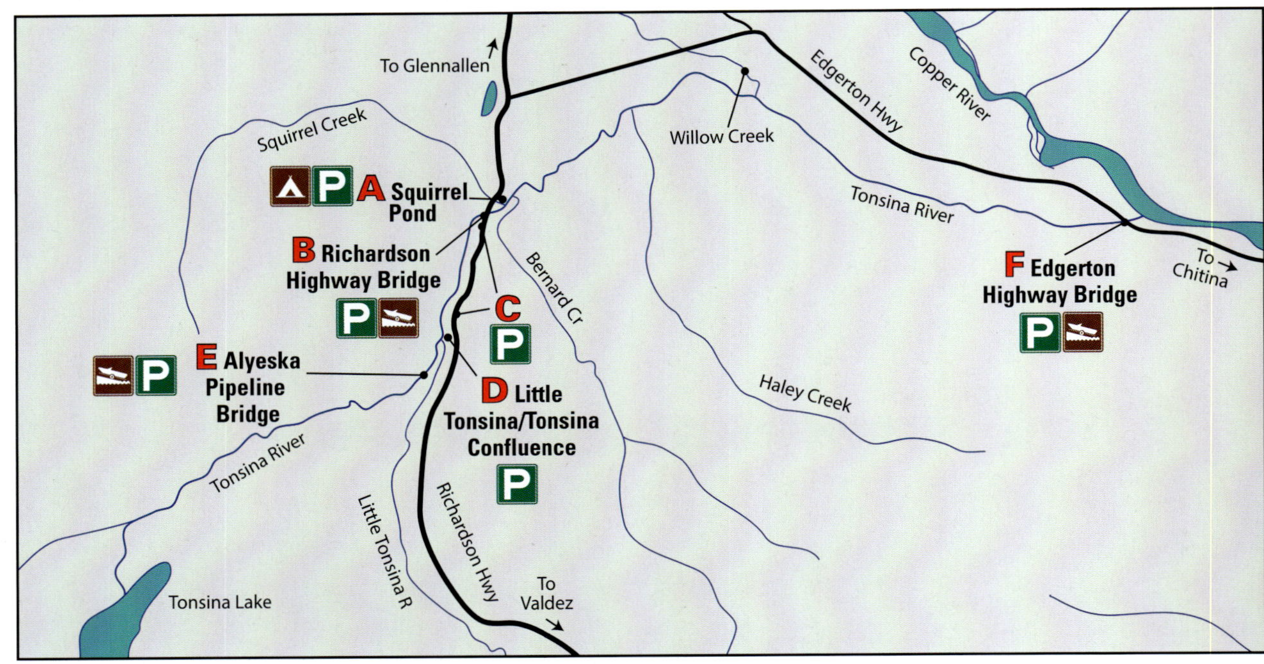


greater portions of the drainage remain remote by most standards with relatively few spots that roadside anglers are able to enjoy. Additionally, there are no developed facilities (trails, campgrounds, boat launches, etc) as is the case with more popular systems to the north, leaving the Tonsina almost solely to the ones with the spirit and adventure in discovering the potentially great but rustic fishing the river harbors.

Running cold and very swift throughout much of its length, the Tonsina is Class III and IV water that demands respect both of those who wander the riverbanks in search of deep holes and pools and of the few that elect to float it. Another word of caution here if bushwhacking along the river: This is grizzly bear country and they are a common sight from mid-summer into fall.

**Facilities:** There are very few facilities or amenities along the Tonsina, with the exception of a full-service lodge located near the river crossing on the Richardson Highway. Lodging, campgrounds, restrooms, guide services, restaurants, gas, groceries, and tackle available in Copper Center several miles to the north.

**Access:** The Richardson Highway crosses the mid-section of the river while Edgerton Highway crosses Tonsina's lower reaches a few miles upstream of the river mouth.

(Courtesy River Wrangellers)

*A view of Greyling Creek where it flows into Tonsina Lake. This remote spot is only reached by float plane but is a place to put in for the exciting journey down Tonsina River to the roadside access points.*

**A. Squirrel Creek State Recreation Site** – Milepost 79.6 Richardson Highway. East short distance to campground with access to Squirrel Pond. Parking for all size vehicles, camping, and restrooms. Improvised trails lead from campground to a section of Tonsina River and the mouth of Squirrel Creek.

**B. Richardson Highway Bridge** – Milepost 79.2 Richardson Highway. Highway crosses river. Limited parking around bridge at pulloffs.

**C. Highway Parallels River** – Milepost 79.2 to 74.0. Richardson Highway runs along the east shore of river more or less for several miles. Limited parking with a few turnouts present; access where river is closest to the road.

**D. Little Tonsina River Confluence** – Milepost 74.5 Richardson Highway. West on gravel road short distance to a "Y," right fork leads 0.5 mile along stream to the mouth at Tonsina River. Some parking for smaller vehicles. Large RVs not recommended.

*Much of the Tonsina is away from the road, requiring a good hike or raft to access. Expect to be fishing in solitude. Some of the holes in this stretch are loaded with kings.*

**E. Alyeska Pipeline Access Bridge** – Milepost 74.5 Richardson Highway. West on gravel road short distance to a "Y," keep to left to end of road by bridge. Some parking available on left before bridge crossing.

**F. Edgerton Highway Bridge** – Milepost 82.6 Richardson Highway. East on Edgerton Highway to Milepost 19.2. Parking available next to bridge for all size vehicles, primitive camping possible.

## Rules & Regulations

**Open Season:** January 1 through December 31.
**Open Area:** The entire river is open to fishing throughout the year.
**Legal Gear/Tackle:** All gear and tackle, including bait, is allowed, including treble hooks.

### King Salmon

- Open season is July 1 through August 10 downstream of Alyeska Pipeline Bridge; and July 1 through July 19 upstream of bridge.
- Tonsina Lake, including all tributaries, are closed to king fishing.
- All waters within a 1/4 mile radius of the mouths of Little Tonsina River and Bernard Creek are closed to king fishing.
- Bag limit is (1) per day and (1) in possession (20 inches or longer). For kings less than 20 inches (Jacks), the limit is (10). Annual limit is (4) kings over 20 inches.

### All Other Salmon

- Open all season (see general "Open Season" above) in all areas of the river.
- Bag limit is (3) per day and (3) in possession (16 inches or longer). For salmon less than 16 inches (Jacks), the limit is (10).

### Rainbow/Steelhead Trout & Dolly Varden

- Open all season (see general "Open Season" above) in all areas of the river.
- Rainbow trout bag limit is (2) per day and (2) in possession, only (1) longer than 20 inches.
- Dolly Varden bag limit is (10) per day and (10) in possession, no size limit.

### Other Fishes

- Open all season (see general "Open Season" above) in all areas of the river.
- Arctic grayling bag limit is (5) per day and (5) in possession, no size limit.
- Whitefish has no bag or possession limit, no size limit.

(Courtesy River Wrangellers)

## Fishing Tonsina River

**Access:** ★★★
**Scenery:** ★★★★★
**Wildlife:** ★★
**Sight Fishing:** ★
**Bank/Wading:** ★★★
**Boat/Floating:** ★★★★

**Species:** King, red, and silver salmon, Dolly Varden, and arctic grayling. A few rainbow trout and whitefish may be present.

**Summary:** For the uninitiated, the Tonsina may at first glance seem somewhat sterile or inhospitable because of the river's strong current, turbid water conditions, lack of developed access, and very few other anglers for company. Yet if taking time to learn the nuances of this river and what it takes to overcome the perceived challenges to connect with the game fish that are present, the Tonsina soon reveals itself as one of the very few ignored roadside drainages that still holds relatively undisturbed runs of the three most sought-after salmon species along with prolific populations of wild resident char and grayling.

There is not an abundance of holding water along the Tonsina so careful scouting is necessary in order to locate spots that afford migratory and resident fish a place of rest; however, when found, these places often see substantial concentrations of all kinds of species. While it is true that the river does not generally present itself kindly towards fly-fishing purists, there are some opportunities at hand still, such as the confluences of clearwater tributaries and sloughs where the fish are better able to see offerings. Of the little angling that does take place, most all of it is by the use of spinning gear and lure-bait combinations, targeting eddies and similar structure.

Visual- and scent-based presentations are the key here. Sharp fluorescent colors function best, especially if fished in conjunction with bait like salmon roe, with orange and chartreuse being top contenders. Additionally, chrome spinners that emit a strong flash will draw attention.

Salmon – mainly kings and silvers – are the main attraction on the Tonsina with mixed success for reds. The latter species tend to be in reasonably good shape upon entering the river with chrome fish common, while many of the kings and silvers show up with at least a slight degree of coloration (some reasonably bright fish will be available still). As there is minimal angling effort on the Tonsina, expect the salmon to be aggressive and genetically robust, with kings frequently topping 40-50 pounds.

There are two runs each of kings and reds, the early tributary components showing in June, overlapping with late-running mainstem fish in July on into August. (The early-arriving kings, take note, are currently protected by law.) The autumn-run silvers present a unique opportunity for the Copper Valley, with majority of fish headed to Little Tonsina River, a clearwater tributary.

Dolly Varden and arctic grayling are caught throughout the summer on into fall with the best fishing occurring at the mouth of tributaries early and late in the season. However, anglers trying their luck around spawning salmon in the mainstem Tonsina will frequently hook char in mid-season as well. Expect an occasional rainbow trout and whitefish to join the fray.

While a boat or raft is perfect in searching out good fishing, anglers should be aware of the abundance of sweepers and submerged rocks and trees.

(Courtesy River Wrangellers)

*Anglers floating or hiking in to various stretches of the Tonsina will find an abundance of solitude, somewhat of a rarity on most roadside waters that are open to king salmon fishing. The Tonsina remains a place that has yet to be fully discovered, making for a perfect destination for those wanting good fishing away from crowds in a semi-remote setting.*

## Fish Availability

● = High ● = Moderate ● = Low ● = Closed

(Dots transcribed as H = High, M = Moderate, L = Low, C = Closed)

| Species | MAY | JUN | JUL | AUG | SEP | OCT | NOV |
|---|---|---|---|---|---|---|---|
| **King Salmon** | C | C C C C | M M H H | H M C C | C | | |
| **Red Salmon** | L | L L M M | L L M H | H H M L | L L L L | | |
| **Silver Salmon** | | | L | L L M M | H H M M | L L L L | L L |
| **Dolly Varden** | L L L L | L L M M | H H H H | H H H H | H H H H | H H M M | L L L L |
| **Arctic Grayling** | L L M M | M M H H | H H H H | H H H H | H H H H | H H M M | L L L L |
| Angling Pressure | | | L L M M | M L L L | L | | |

(Courtesy River Wrangellers)

*Tonsina's kings are large and robust, typically averaging up to 40 pounds. Do not be surprised to hook into trophy kings weighing 50 pounds or more if spending a few days in this area; be prepared for an epic battle in the Tonsina's swift current. Due to the distance traveled, many of these fish show a tint of color, especially toward the latter part of the season (late July-August).*

## King Salmon

**Rating:** ★★★ Good to excellent.
**Season:** July 1 through August 10.
**Timing:** July 1 – August 10; peak July 15 – August 5.
**Size:** Average 20 – 40 pounds; up to 70 pounds.
**Tackle:** Spinners, plugs, attractors, flies, and bait.
**Tips:** The very best bet to hook up with a king on the Tonsina is to use a large corkie/attractor setup with a cluster of salmon roe. Target any slackwater areas, such as eddies, pools, and the mouth of sloughs, or any quiet water at the seam of strong current, letting the setup rest on the bottom or slowly drift with the current. Chrome, size 6 spinners may work too; like bait, retrieve deep and slow.

The confluence of Tonsina and Copper rivers and adjoining waters a ways downstream yield many fish and the best bet for hooking chrome salmon. However, the smaller pools and eddies higher up in the drainage have a way to really concentrate the fish and perfect locations for fast action and multiple hook-ups. Remember, these kings are big and powerful and the river is swift so use strong, sturdy gear and tackle.

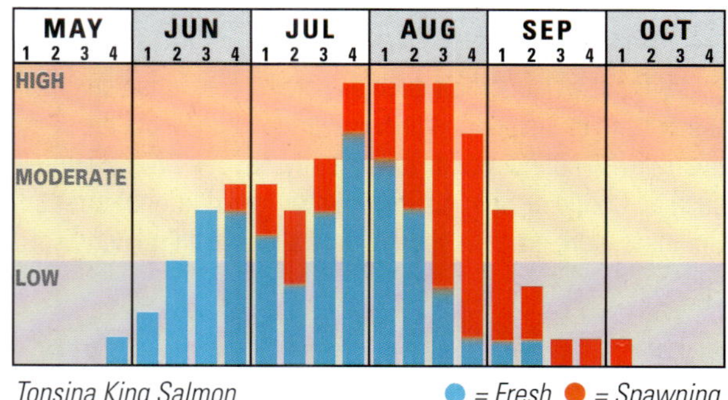


*Tonsina King Salmon* ● = Fresh ● = Spawning

## Red Salmon

**Rating:** ★★ Fair to good.
**Season:** January 1 through December 31.
**Timing:** May 25 – September 30; peak July 25 – August 10.
**Size:** Average 5 – 7 pounds; up to 12 pounds.
**Tackle:** Flies.
**Tips:** Like sockeye fishing in most systems in Southcentral, long casts are not necessary with the most predictable action happening within several yards of the bank as the salmon habitually follow the shoreline to avoid the strong mainstem current. Most anywhere on the river is productive as long as structure matches correct sockeye conditions.

Successful anglers hit the Tonsina at the peak in latter July, scouting out structure that is likely to hold fish as well as provide enough current to work the fly through the mass of salmon. Fly color or pattern is not too important as majority of fish are probably lined. Orange and chartreuse yarn flies make for excellent visual presentations.

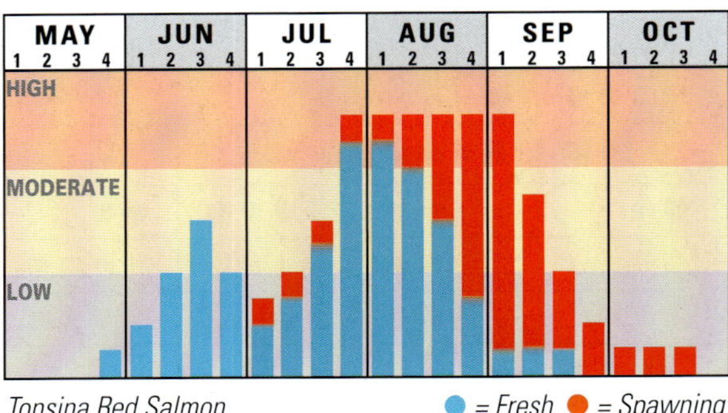


Tonsina Red Salmon ● = Fresh ● = Spawning

## Silver Salmon

**Rating:** ★★½ Good.
**Season:** January 1 through December 31.
**Timing:** August 15 – November 10; peak Sept. 5 – 25.
**Size:** Average 5 – 10 pounds; up to 15 pounds.
**Tackle:** Spinners, attractors, and bait.
**Tips:** Good opportunities are available throughout the lower and middle river sections, from the mouth to the Little Tonsina confluence. Look for concentrations in all holding areas, such as eddies, pools, sloughs, and quiet side channels.

Without a doubt, bait such as salmon roe fished on the bottom or suspended under a strike indicator is the best way to connect with Tonsina silvers. Use an attractor such as Corkie or Spin-N-Glo/Cheater for additional effect. Spinners work great in spots where there is an influence of clear water.

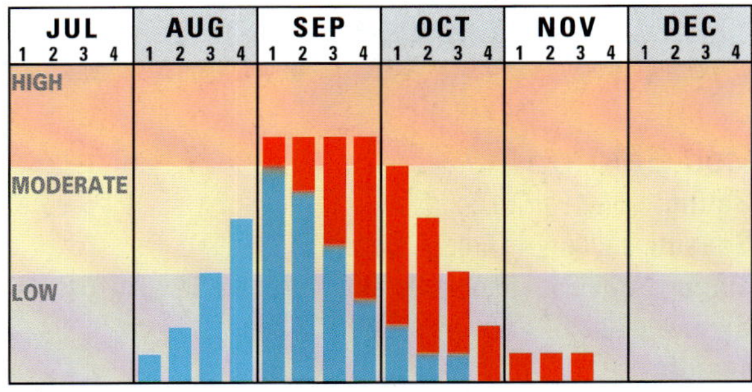


Tonsina Silver Salmon ● = Fresh ● = Spawning

## Dolly Varden

**Rating:** ★★★ Fair to good.
**Season:** January 1 through December 31.
**Timing:** June 1 – November 30; peak July 1 – October 15.
**Size:** Average 8 – 16 inches; up to 25 inches (6 pounds).
**Tackle:** Spinners, attractors, flies, and bait.
**Tips:** The Tonsina can be great for char. Use bait in the mainstem river, in the same spots where salmon are likely to hold. Properly presented flies and lures may draw strikes as well. Action can be exceptional at times in areas such as where clearwater tributaries flow in or spawning salmon are present. Large, fluorescent beads or corkies drifted along the bottom may work.

(Courtesy Ron Ely)

*The Tonsina River drainage is the only roadside water in the Copper Valley that supports a solid run of silver salmon. These are primarily autumn fish, peaking in numbers during the month of September. Target them in small pools and eddies.*

## Arctic Grayling

**Rating:** ★★ Fair.
**Season:** January 1 through December 31.
**Timing:** April 1 – November 30; peak June 15 – October 10.
**Size:** Average 8 – 14 inches; up to 20 inches.
**Tackle:** Spinners, attractors, and flies.
**Tips:** As the mainstem Tonsina is too glacial for productive grayling fishing, anglers do best hitting the mouths of clearwater tributaries. All of the traditional grayling lures and flies should do well.

(Courtesy Eagle Eye Images)

*A most colorful sample of Tonsina Dolly Varden, a typical autumn fish of around 5 pounds that inhaled a gaudy roe imitation fly drifted slowly along the bottom of a hole that also held a school of pre-spawning silvers. Bait is by far most effective but artificials fished in and around the right structure will get strikes.*

*Fishing at the mouth of clearwater streams is a great way to find concentrations of salmon, char, and grayling. This view is from the mouth of Little Tonsina River where it enters the milky mainstem Tonsina, a highly productive spot for silvers among other species. Here, battling a late-season coho that struck an attractor pattern fished at the seam of the two rivers.*

## Other Tonsina Opportunities

### Boat & Float Fishing

The Tonsina is a difficult river to navigate due to a very swift current, numerous braided channels, sweepers and other debris, as well as plenty of Class IV rapids than can make a good day of fishing quickly go sour if not properly prepared. Some stretches are more challenging than others (such as much of the middle and upper river), yet overall this is simply a cold, rocky, glacial drainage that requires very skilled boat handling.

There are several ways in which to access the Tonsina from an angler's viewpoint. One is to launch a powerboat from Copper Center at nearby Klutina River and run downstream to the mouth of Tonsina where it hits the Copper River. Anglers can choose to fish this area (excellent spot for kings and other species) or negotiate up the mainstem Tonsina in search of suitable holding water.

Those wanting to challenge the river on a more intimate (and gutsy) level can opt to float it. Prospective anglers usually launch at one of three access points, these being off the pipeline spur road bridge up at Little Tonsina River, the main Richardson Highway bridge, and the Edgerton Highway bridge. None of these points have developed launch areas. The latter location would require floaters to take out somewhere around the river mouth or below so necessary arrangements must be made to shuttle back to the road system. Expect 1/2- to full-day trips or longer.

(Courtesy River Wrangellers)

Floating the middle river down to the lower reaches will cover some great water, especially for king salmon, with the river being more conducive to fishing.

Another option is to be dropped off (by aircraft) at the outlet of Tonsina Lake and float downstream to any of the above access points for take-out. Expect this leg to be a whitewater adventure with intermittent fishing.

# Other Productive Fisheries & Additional Opportunities

## LITTLE TONSINA RIVER

**Fishing:** ★★★ **Scenery:** ★★★
**Accessibility:** ★★½ **Solitude:** ★★★★★

**Location:** Southern Copper Valley drainage, Tonsina River tributary, 41 miles south of Glennallen, 230 miles northeast of Anchorage.

**Access:** There are three main access points to the Little Tonsina River along the Richardson Highway; two on the upper stream and the third at the confluence with Tonsina River.

*A. Mouth of Little Tonsina* – Milepost 74.5. West on gravel road short distance to a "Y," right fork leads 0.3 miles to confluence area. Parking.

*B. Upper Little Tonsina 1* – Milepost 68.2. Southwest on gravel road 0.5 miles to small parking area. Stream is located beyond hill.

*C. Upper Little Tonsina 2* – Milepost 65.0. Highway crosses stream. Developed parking. Former campground.

**Facilities:** Only parking available.

**Species:** Red and silver salmon, Dolly Varden, and arctic grayling. A small run of king salmon is present in July and some whitefish are available in fall.

**Restrictions:** King salmon fishing prohibited. Consult ADF&G regulations.

**Fishing:** The Little Tonsina is not so much of a river as the name implies but rather a creek. Flowing clear with a slight tannic tint, this small runoff stream is home to several salmon species and native char and grayling. It has the distinction of being the best roadside location in the entire Copper River Valley for silver salmon, with a solid run of these fish infiltrating the Little Tonsina during the month of September. Red salmon often school up at the mouth of the creek in mid-summer but relatively few of these fish actually spawn in this stream. Most are bound for waters farther up the main Tonsina River. Hit the early part of the respective runs for the brightest fish.

Dolly Varden and arctic grayling are seasonally abundant with the mid-summer into fall period being best, although there is some decent spring action for the latter species too.

The mouth of the stream is an obvious hot spot but anglers taking time to scout the Little Tonsina can find good opportunities along most of its length.

**Red Salmon.** Poor to fair; July 10 – 25; average 3 – 6 pounds. Mouth of stream is best. Fish can be difficult to get to bite. Try flies.

**Silver Salmon.** Good; September 10 – 20; average 5 – 10 pounds. Try stream mouth early in the run, higher up later on. Use spinners, flies, and bait.

**Dolly Varden.** Fair; July 20 – October 15; average 8 – 15 inches. Look for char down low early and late in season, upper stream in mid-season. Spinners, flies, bait.

**Arctic Grayling.** Fair to good; September 10 – October 5; average 8 – 14 inches. In summer, try upper access points. In spring and fall, the mouth. Spinners, flies.

## McCARTHY AREA LAKES

**Fishing:** ★★★★ **Scenery:** ★★★½
**Accessibility:** ★★★ **Solitude:** ★★★½

**Location:** Southern Copper Valley drainage, Chitina area, 76-112 miles southeast of Glennallen, 265-301 miles northeast of Anchorage.

**Access:** This small grouping of lakes is situated along the McCarthy Road not far from the community of Chitina. At Milepost 82.6 Richardson Highway, turn east onto Edgerton Highway and follow paved road to Milepost 35.1 and the start of McCarthy Road. The lakes are situated approximately 10 to 11 miles in on this gravel road.

*A. Strelna Lake* – Milepost 10.1 McCarthy Road. Public easement leads north 0.3 mile to lake. Parking. Stocked with landlocked salmon and rainbow trout.

*B. Silver Lake* – Milepost 10.8. Public access site. Parking. Stocked with rainbow trout.

*C. Van Lake* – Milepost 10.8. Turn onto Silver Lake access site. Parking. Trail leads 1 1/4 mile to lake. Stocked with rainbow trout.

*D. Sculpin Lake* – Milepost 11.9. Public access site to south. Parking. Short trail to lake. Stocked with rainbow trout. Dolly Varden also present.

*E. Long Lake* – Milepost 46.0. Public access site at turnout. Parking. Lake contains wild populations of lake trout, Dolly Varden, arctic grayling, and burbot.

**Facilities:** Mainly primitive parking at sites with private fee campground available at Silver Lake.

**Species:** Landlocked silver salmon, rainbow trout, lake trout, Dolly Varden, and burbot.

**Restrictions:** Special restrictions are in effect. Consult ADF&G regulations.

**Fishing:** The relatively small, clearwater lakes in this area host excellent populations of gamefish thanks in great part to state stocking programs. Landlocked silver salmon and rainbow trout are the two most prevalent species. The largest lake (Long) also supports native species, including char and anadromous salmon.

As these lakes are quite remote from the main thoroughfare of the busy Richardson Highway, expect little angling pressure and fishing to be very productive throughout the open water season for most available species. There is a fair amount of traffic coming through, albeit the majority are only visitors heading to the Kennicott Mine at the end of the road. Few people actually stop and fish here.

The prime fishing in this area occurs soon after ice-out in May and first part of June and again in late summer and fall (August-October), with some species also providing great ice fishing opportunities lasting into mid-winter. However, anglers visiting these lakes during the summer months should not be discouraged as the early morning and late evening bites can be exceptional as well. In fact, on overcast days with a light rain, the trout action can be nonstop all day long.

The majority of fishing on these lakes occur with some sort of light watercraft, such as a canoe or kayak, with float tubing being a great option. Yet casting off the bank can provide some decent catches too, especially at dawn and dusk when fish come into the shallows to feed.

While landlocked salmon, rainbow trout, and arctic grayling are typical mainstays of the upper layers of water to the surface, the chars and burbot prefer the deeper, colder parts near bottom and anglers need to plan their methods, techniques, gear, and tackle accordingly for best results.

Long Lake is unique from the other lakes in the McCarthy area in that it is fairly large in size and quite deep. The fish are more of a challenge to locate with some dedicated anglers using trolling equipment for better results. The lake also receives red and silver salmon runs along with a few steelhead trout that spawn in the outlet stream.

The other lakes that contain rainbows often report catches up to several pounds with a few near-trophy class specimens available early and late in the season. These fish can weigh as much as 6 to 8 pounds.

**Landlocked Salmon.** Good to excellent; May 25 – June 15 and August 15 – January 1; average 7 – 12 inches. Try small spoons, spinners, flies, and bait.

**Rainbow Trout.** Good to excellent; May 25 – June 10 and August 15 – January 1; average 8 – 24 inches. Use spinners, flies, and bait.

**Lake Trout.** Fair; August 15 – January 1; average 2 – 5 pounds. Spoons, plugs, jigs, and bait.

**Dolly Varden.** Fair; August 15 – October 15; average 8 – 15 inches. Spinners, flies, and bait.

**Arctic Grayling.** Fair to good; May 25 – September 30; average 8 – 14 inches. Spinners, flies.

**Burbot.** Fair; September 15 – April 15; average 2 – 4 pounds. Fish bait on bottom, jig spoons.

## TOLSONA CREEK

**Fishing:** ★★★ **Scenery:** ★★★
**Accessibility:** ★★★★★ **Solitude:** ★★★★
**Location:** Southern Copper Valley, Tazlina River drainage, 173 miles northeast of Anchorage, 16 miles west of Glennallen.
**Access:** The Glenn Highway provides one main area of access that include two points of fishing access, both located on the middle section of the stream at or near the road crossing.
*A. Glenn Highway Bridge* – Milepost 172.9. Highway crosses stream. Some parking with limited/primitive camping.
*B. Tolsona Creek Campground* – Milepost 173.0. North on gravel road 0.7 mile to private campground and stream. Parking and camping for all size vehicles, RV facilities, restrooms, groceries.
**Facilities:** Services and amenities are very limited in the immediate area, except for at the Tolsona Creek Campground.
**Species:** Rainbow trout and arctic grayling. In some years, small numbers of red salmon spawn here.
**Restrictions:** No species specific regulations in effect. Consult ADF&G for details.
**FIshing:** Flowing tannic stained, Tolsona is a small stream surrounded by dense brush and spruce forest, revealing a wealth of perfect fish holding structure, including long, deep holes, swirling pools, and undercut banks complete with a series of riffles. Largely undisturbed by other anglers, except for some effort around the campground, the Tolsona is the ideal water for those wanting to find complete solitude and good fishing on a water more reminiscent of a true wilderness stream than a roadside destination.

Hiking along Tolsona in either direction will yield very productive fishing for grayling in particular, some of which may stretch to 18 inches or more, along with the bonus opportunity of tangling with a number of rainbow trout. Although usually not very abundant, these trout may in some years present very worthwhile fishing. In spring and early summer, a few trout to several pounds may be present.

With its prowess of consistent opportunity coupled with easy access and very low angling effort, some enthusiasts are returning to this prime fly-fishing stream year after year.

Grizzly bears frequently wander along the stream banks so precautions should be taken. Carry a firearm if going alone away from the road.
**Rainbow Trout.** Fair; May 25 – September 15; average 7 – 15 inches. Small spinners and flies.
**Arctic Grayling.** Good to excellent; May 15 – September 25; average 7 – 15 inches. Small spinners and flies.

## MENDELTNA CREEK

**Fishing:** ★★★ **Scenery:** ★★★
**Accessibility:** ★★★ **Solitude:** ★★★★★
**Location:** Southern Copper Valley, Tazlina River drainage, 153 miles northeast of Anchorage, 32 miles west of Glennallen.
**Access:** The Glenn Highway offers two general points of access to the Mendeltna Creek drainage; one at the main road crossing on the middle stream section, another off Lake Louise Road and the upper portion near Old Man Lake.
*A. Middle Mendeltna* – Milepost 152.8. Highway crosses stream. Parking for all size vehicles, limited/primitive camping, and lodging.
*B. Upper Mendeltna* – Milepost 159.8. North on Lake Louise Road 6.7 miles, left on Oil Well Road 5.5 miles to end of

road at stream. The last couple of miles of this road can be very rough and require a 4-wheel-drive vehicle, especially if road is wet after a good rain. Expect plenty of potholes and mud. Not recommended for large RVs. Limited parking.
**Facilities:** A small campground and private lodge is situated on the banks of the stream at the main road crossing.
**Species:** Rainbow trout and arctic grayling. A run of reds and a few kings and steelhead are present.
**Restrictions:** Salmon fishing prohibited year-round. Open season for grayling is June 1 through March 31; size restrictions are in effect. Consult ADF&G for details.
**Fishing:** In similarity to many other streams in the general Copper Valley region, the Mendeltna is technically a clearwater drainage that is influenced by bog- or marshland waters, hence the slightly iron-stained appearance. It is home to a couple of species of popular game fish, although only the arctic grayling is present in any significant numbers. Other quarries include rainbow and steelhead trout, but they are not targeted to any degree. Salmon run the stream in early and mid-summer.

The Mendletna is a wonderful creek to explore for a few hours to a day or even two, its meandering waters providing plenty of cover for fish to hide, such as undercut banks, deep pools, fallen trees and sweepers, and overhanging brush. Some stretches flow fast, narrow, and rocky with a series of riffles, others slow and wide with plenty of aquatic vegetation. Expect solitude if hiking a short distance away from the access points. Use caution as this is a salmon spawning stream and prime grizzly habitat.

Although the spring spawning run of grayling is protected by law, anglers can still find very good fishing for mostly smaller-sized (7-10 inches) specimens on the upper creek throughout the summer months. The best action, however, comes in fall (mid-September through early October) as the larger, mature grayling head out of the upper drainage lakes and begin the annual migration downstream to over-wintering areas of Tazlina Lake. At this time, big schools of fish typically stack up in some of the holes yielding fish-on-every-cast fun.

Some rainbow trout inhabit Mendeltna as well and are encountered every so often by anglers targeting grayling, especially on the upper stream. Occurrences of steelhead are known in spring and late fall.
**Rainbow Trout.** Fair; May 25 – October 10; average 7 – 15 inches. Small spinners and flies.
**Arctic Grayling.** Good to excellent; June 1 – October 10; average 7 – 15 inches. Small spinners and flies.

## TAZLINA AREA LAKES

**Fishing:** ★★★½ **Scenery:** ★★★
**Accessibility:** ★★★ **Solitude:** ★★★★
**Location:** Southern Copper Valley drainages, 150 miles northeast of Anchorage, 15 to 35 miles west of Glennallen.
**Access:** Glenn Highway is the direct link to a handful of lakes in the Tazlina area that provide very good fishing opportunities within a short distance of the road.
*A. Tolsona Lake* – Milepost 170.5. North on gravel road 0.7 mile to lake. Private lodge with parking for all size vehicles. Arctic grayling.
*B. Mae West Lake* – Milepost 169.3. Paved turnout with parking for all size vehicles. Marked trail leads south 1/4 mile to lake. Arctic grayling.
*C. Kay Lake* – Milepost 168.0. Paved turnout with parking for all size vehicles. Marked trail leads north 3/4 mile to lake. Arctic grayling.
*D. Lost Cabin Lake* – Milepost 165.9. Paved turnout with parking for all size vehicles. Marked trail leads south 3/4 mile to lake. Arctic grayling.
*E. Tex Smith Lake* – Milepost 162.0. Paved turnout with parking for all size vehicles; lake is adjacent to highway. Rainbow trout.
*F. Arizona Lake* – Milepost 155.8. Paved turnout with parking for all size vehicles is located at Milepost 155.6. Marked trail leads south 1/2 mile to lake. Arctic grayling.

*G. Gergie Lake* – Milepost 155.2. Paved turnout with parking for all size vehicles is located at Milepost 155.6. Marked trail leads south 1 1/4 mile to lake. Rainbow trout.
*H. Ryan Lake* – Milepost 149.0. South on dirt road 1/4 mile to lake. Limited parking; not recommended for large RVs. Lodging and cabins available nearby. Rainbow trout.
**Facilities:** Services and amenities are limited in the immediate area, with a few locations offering lodging, camping, cabins, restaurants, and air taxi service.
**Species:** Rainbow trout and arctic grayling.
**Restrictions:** No special regulations in effect. Consult ADF&G for details.

**Fishing:** Although situated in close proximity to a busy highway, the small clearwater lakes of the Tazlina area offer great opportunities to enjoy the scenic beauty of the area while tempting little-fished populations of trout and grayling. Some of these waters are planted regularly, others contain native stocks of fish. What they all have in common, however, is productive fishing in relative solitude.

Anglers can expect to find exceptional action in spring and early summer (May-June) and again in late summer and fall (August-September) when fish are most active. Casting from shore can be good but better fishing is usually the case from a small watercraft or float tube. The lakes only approached by trail tend to yield consistent catches throughout the summer months and may harbor larger-than-average sized fish as well. Trout to 6-8 pounds are possible.

**Rainbow Trout.** Good to excellent; May 20 – September 30; average 8 – 20 inches. Small spinners and flies.

**Arctic Grayling.** Good to excellent; May 20 – September 30; average 7 – 15 inches. Small spinners and flies.

## ADDITIONAL OPPORTUNITIES

### Remote Tazlina Streams

This is a great drainage to explore. Parts of the river is road accessible, such as the far lower end and a few of the tributaries, but the vast majority is remote and only accessible by aircraft or a long powerboat ride.

Flying into Tazlina Lake and working the mouths of clearwater streams flowing into the lake and the upper portion of Tazlina River is an experience not soon forgotten. Kaina Creek produces some good to excellent action for king salmon from late June to mid-July (fish often top 40 pounds) with a good supply of reds present during the month of July as well.

Rainbow trout and arctic grayling abound here and in Durham, Mendeltna, and Tokaina creeks with catch rates frequently described as exceptional throughout the season. Steelhead trout do make it into the Tazlina system and a few of these are reported caught by anglers visiting the area in autumn. The run, however, is very small and catches sporadic at best.

From a roadside perspective, there are somewhat limited opportunities in the Southern Copper Valley region as most of the clearwater tributaries flowing into the Tazlina derive from headwaters in the Northern Copper Valley and are covered in more detail on page 416.

(Courtesy Kingfisher's Perch)

### Tebay & Hanagita Rivers

These two remote clearwater streams situated in the midst of the Wrangell Mountains support good populations of rainbow trout and arctic grayling with added opportunity for red and silver salmon. The adjoining lakes in the system – Tebay, Summit, and Hanagita – also offer fishing for some of these species, as well as lesser numbers of lake trout.

In September and October, a small run of steelhead trout makes its way into the Hanagita drainage with fair sport for those willing to brave inclement weather conditions and the isolation. This is a great adventure destination, especially for fall steelhead. Anglers fly in to these lakes and usually fish the inlet or outlet areas and the next few miles of river just below the lakes. If opting to try this, be prepared to spend a day or two weathered in, this especially the case in late fall (October) and the first snow.

As for salmon, this is one of those few places in the Copper River drainage that offers decent silver salmon fishing. They may be found throughout the drainage but are especially numerous on the lower Tebay River and its mouth. The month of September is best. For reds, targeting the faster water higher up makes sense although access to the more conducive spots can be difficult due to terrain. The run peaks in July.

Special seasonal and size restrictions are in place regarding steelhead/rainbow trout. Consult ADF&G regulations.

Valdez

# Valdez Arm

**King Salmon • Red Salmon • Pink Salmon • Chum Salmon Silver Salmon • Dolly Varden • Pacific Halibut • Lingcod Rockfish • Salmon Shark • Bottomfish**

*Scenic Waters*

*Ocean Fishing*

*Fish Viewing*

*Wildlife*

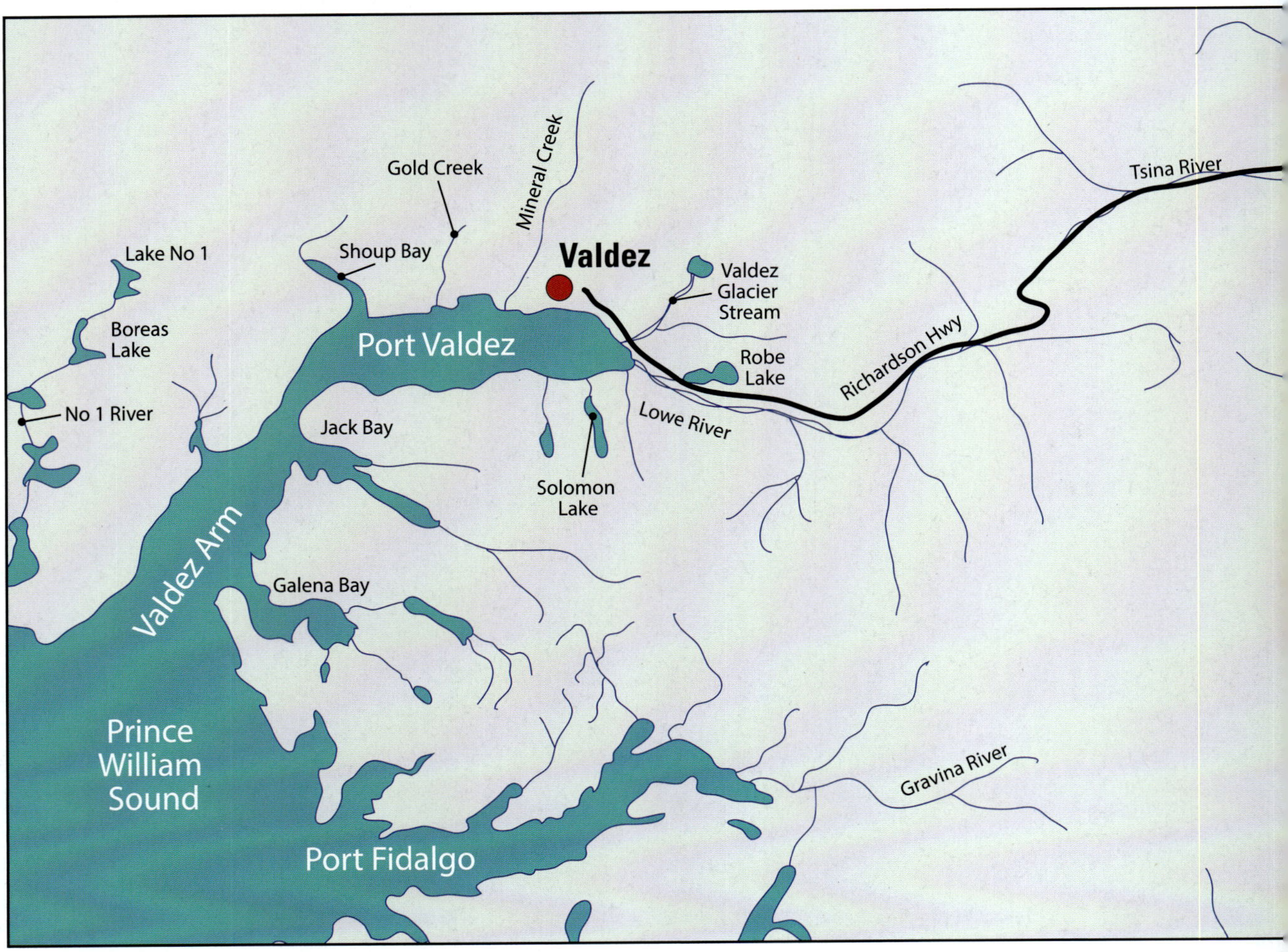

**Area Population Centers:** Valdez.
**Key Species:** King, Pink, Chum, and Silver Salmon, Dolly Varden, Pacific Halibut, Lingcod, and Rockfish.
**Other Species:** Red Salmon, Arctic Grayling, and Salmon Shark.
**Main Destination/Hot Spot:** Port Valdez
**Other Productive Fisheries:** Robe River.
**Additional Opportunities:** Northern Prince William Sound, Wildlife and Salmon Viewing.

**Summary of Area Fishing:** Gifted with tremendous natural beauty, this area of the state is mainly known as a world-class marine fishery for salmon and bottomfish. Although a few lakes and clearwater streams do offer limited sport fishing potential for salmon and resident species, it is the coastal port of Valdez that draws all of the attention. The port is a favorite destination among Alaskans as well as visitors alike not only for its scenic value but the great fishing, further enhanced by the fact that several very lucrative fishing derbies are held here from spring into fall. Recognized mainly as a boat-accessible fishery, Valdez area waters also cater perfectly to roadside bank fishing. In fact, docks and beaches in and around town serve as ideal portals to intercept local salmon runs with even some limited opportunity for sea-run char and bottomfish. Although road access is very scant, essentially only the Richardson Highway leading into the town of Valdez and immediate vicinity roads, this fact does not inhibit anglers at all from enjoying the bounty of available species.

Pink and silver salmon are the main species of interest for roadside anglers but chum salmon are present in good numbers as well. The vast majority of fishing takes place in the port itself and adjoining saltwater since all freshwater in this area is closed to salmon fishing, with the possible exception of Robe River. Some lake-based opportunities do exist for stocked trout and grayling. Robe and Lowe rivers harbor seasonal runs of char, the former location also providing decent angling for red and silver salmon.

The Valdez area is truly a destination of its own but often serves as an extended fishing trip that may include waters of Copper Valley as well. Additionally, do-it-yourself or charter boat marine excursions are extremely popular and perfectly compliment any visit to this area.

# Port Valdez

King
SALMON

Pink
SALMON

Chum
SALMON

Silver
SALMON

Halibut

Rockfish

**Highlights:** Phenomenal action for chrome pink salmon, along with excellent late-season surf-casting opportunities for silvers. Renowned spot for halibut, lingcod, rockfish.

**Best Fishing:** Mid-June to mid-September.

**Regulatory Restrictions:** Very liberal.

**Location:** Northern Prince William Sound, town of Valdez, 305 miles east of Anchorage.

**Description:** Port Valdez, at the head of Valdez Arm, is approximately 15 miles long and four to five miles wide with the town of Valdez situated at the northeast corner of the port. The scenic qualities of the area are exceptional as mountain peaks between 4,000 and 5,000 feet or more surround the port, complete with jagged mountain peaks displaying snow and ice fields, and glacially carved valleys covered with a dense, boreal spruce forest.

As a result of glacial silt entering the port from rivers and streams in the vicinity, water clarity is generally only fair during the warm summer months, the water displaying a greenish or turquoise hue. Oftentimes, however, the water turns grey following a heavy rain or snowmelt due to prolonged periods of sunny, hot weather; yet the fishing typically remains very productive. Anglers are reminded that it is only the upper layers of water that is affected by the film of glacial silt. The water is clear along the bottom.

The port is shallow on the east end where the Lowe River and other area streams dump in, with the water progressively getting deeper beyond Allison Point and the

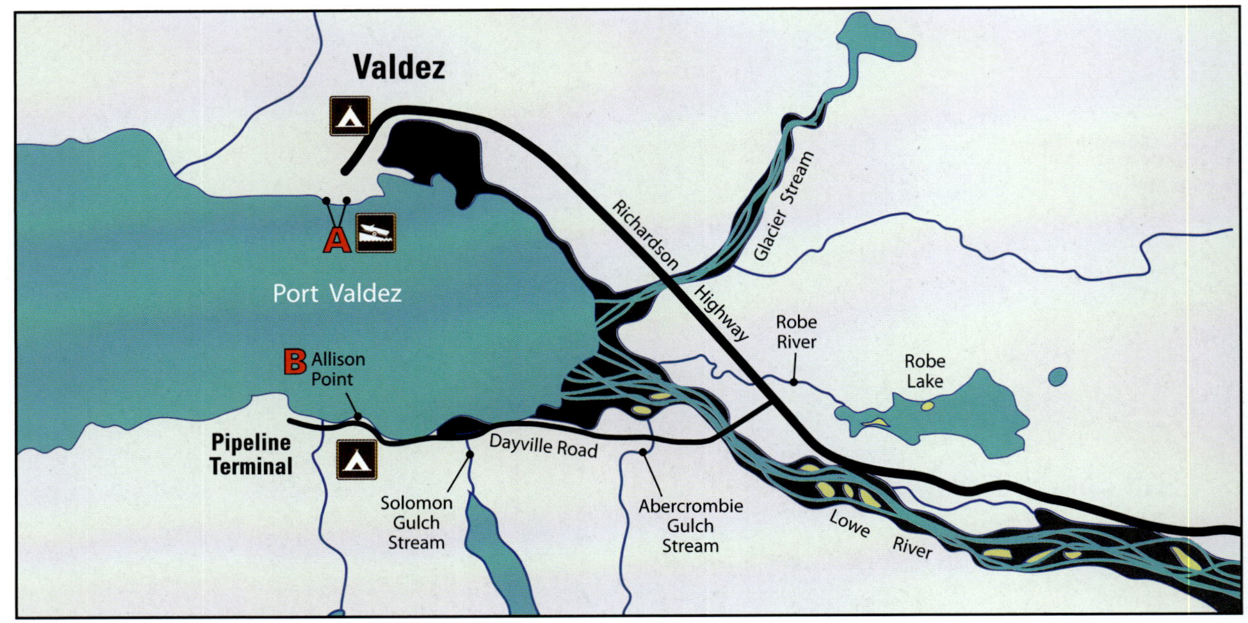


town. Moderate depth of 20 feet or more is the case in front of town, at the city docks. Tides range up to 15 feet.

**Facilities:** The town of Valdez has hotels/motels, lodging, B&Bs, restaurants, gas, tackle shops, groceries, guide services, and RV campgrounds.

**Access:** The Richardson Highway provides road access to the town of Valdez and the port area. Valdez marks the beginning of the highway (Milepost 0).

**A. Valdez Waterfront** – Downtown Valdez. From the end of Richardson Highway, continue on East Egan Drive into town, then left on Fidalgo Drive, right on Hazelet Avenue, and left on Ferry Way to the Valdez Ferry and City Docks. Parking for all size vehicles and boat launch. Anglers can fish from shore within the harbor, the channel connecting the harbor to the port, and cast off the ferry dock or adjoining beaches. All these areas are within easy walking distance from downtown. **Note:** The ferry dock may be inaccessible during brief periods a few times a week whenever the state ferry comes through.

**B. Allison Point** – Milepost 2.8. From the Richardson Highway, turn southwest on Dayville Road and proceed 5.0 miles to point. The road parallels the port starting at mile 2.4 with angler access to entire length waterfront next several miles until Allison Point. Parking for all size vehicles, primitive camping, and restrooms. Abundant space for parking along road, with shoulder parking here being legal. There is primitive camping in this area with restrooms also available.

## Rules & Regulations

**Open Season:** January 1 through December 31.
**Open Area:** The port area is open to fishing throughout the year.
**Legal Gear/Tackle:** All gear and tackle, including bait, is allowed, including treble hooks.

**All Salmon**
• Open all season (see general "Open Season" above) in all areas of the port.
• King salmon bag limit is (2) per day and (4) in possession, no size restrictions. There is no annual limit or recording requirements.
• All other salmon, bag limit is (6) per day and (12) in possession, no size restrictions.

**Dolly Varden**
• Open all season (see general "Open Season" above) in all areas of the port.
• Bag limit is (10) per day and (10) in possession, no size restrictions.

**Pacific Halibut**
• Open to fishing from February 1 through December 31; closed to all fishing during the month of January.
• All areas of the port is open to fishing.
• Bag limit is (2) per day and (4) in possession, no size restrictions.

**Lingcod**
• Open to fishing from July 1 through December 31.
• All areas of the port is open to fishing.
• Bag limit is (2) per day and (4) in possession; must be 35 inches or longer for retention.

**Rockfishes**
• Open all season (see general "Open Season" above) in all areas of the port.
• Bag limit is (4) per day and (8) in possession from May 1 through September 15; and (8) per day and (8) in possession from September 16 through April 30. Other restrictions are in effect.

**Sharks**
• Open all season (see general "Open Season" above) in all areas of the port.
• Bag limit is (1) per day and (1) in possession, no size restrictions.

*Evening view of Valdez Harbor, located right downtown. This is a busy hub for anglers targeting hatchery salmon milling about in the harbor as well as booking charters for guided fishing in Valdez Arm and the northern section of Prince William Sound. It is also a go-to place for sightseers and photographers given its generous scenic qualities, among the best of any roadside port in the state.*

## Fishing Port Valdez

**Access:** ★★★★
**Scenery:** ★★★★★
**Wildlife:** ★★★★
**Sight Fishing:** ★★
**Bank/Wading:** ★★★★
**Boat/Floating:** ★★★★★

**Species:** King, pink, chum, and silver salmon and Dolly Varden. Red salmon and various species of bottomfish also present. Rare catches of halibut.

**Summary:** Port Valdez is the largest recreational fishery in Prince William Sound. The town of Valdez serves as a hub for the local charter boat fleet and roadside anglers are able to experience some phenomenal salmon fishing from area docks and beaches. The port is also Alaska's most popular pink fishery. In fact, Valdez is known as the Pink Salmon Capital of the World with a run of fish numbering in the tens of millions streaming through the port every season. Silver salmon, although not as plentiful as the pinks, draw a large following in late summer and fall. Other species available from the road include king and chum salmon as well as sea-run Dolly Varden.

Roadside anglers converge on Valdez in droves every July in anticipation of the arrival of a most incredible and intense fishery: A 10-25 million strong run of pink salmon. These smallest of salmon have been known to turn the water in some areas almost completely black, with fish-on-every-cast action not only possible but – at the peak of the run – the norm. Light tackle sport is no less than fantastic, both on fly gear and on regular gear. Many anglers, local as well as visiting, make a trip to Valdez during the pink season part of their regular summer activities because of the easy access, intense action, and gorgeous scenery.

A great deal of credit for the exceptionally abundant pink run is due to the Solomon Gulch Hatchery off Dayville Road near Allison Point. Juvenile pink salmon are stocked here, with returning adults literally clogging the stream and adjacent waters.

The Valdez area waters enjoy two runs of chum salmon starting in early summer and continuing into fall. Though fairly abundant, the summer fish (June-July) are headed to various tributaries of the Lowe River while late appearing fish (August-September) are noticeably more numerous and caught consistently through the remainder of the season. They appear most abundant in waters along the town waterfront and are frequently seen spawning in intertidal areas of the port.

Silver salmon enjoy a strong reputation as the number one game fish in town. Starting in late summer and continuing into fall, a run comprising of mostly hatchery salmon move into the port. In recent years, runs have nudged 100,000 silvers, resulting in excellent action for boaters and bank anglers alike. Late in the season it is even possible to sightfish these salmon along area beaches as fish congregate near shore in their search for suitable spawning waters and ducking marauding sea-lions. As with pinks, many of these fish are stocked in Solomon Gulch Creek.

Immature king salmon are available in Port Valdez year-round but are rarely taken by anglers casting from shore. The state initiated a hatchery run of kings some years ago and these fish are now returning to Mineral Creek west of town. Fishing for them, however, is mostly done from boats but

(Courtesy Eagle Eye Images)

*Although the majority of anglers fishing the port use spinning and bait casting gear, fly-fishing for pinks and silvers can be very rewarding in the right spots. Here, angler battles hefty saltwater coho that sucked in a saltwater pattern fly.*

a small number are caught by anglers fishing from the city docks as well.

Red salmon are not taken to any degree except for incidental catches fishing for other species and there is no dedicated fishery targeting them.

Sea-run Dolly Varden are not very plentiful but still provide some level of excitement for anglers using light gear and small lures and flies in the proper locations.

A modest opportunity exists for bottomfish, mainly cod and flounder, with the majority of catches coming from the city docks in front of town. A few small halibut, rockfish, and lingcod are taken on occasion.

Anglers with access to a boat or skiff have increased opportunity for additional species, such as feeder king salmon, halibut, lingcod, rockfish, and salmon shark. All of these sport fish are present in small numbers within the port but more readily caught in waters farther out, such as main Valdez Arm and adjoining bays, inlets, and coves of northern Prince William Sound. Expect superb action in these areas for all species. See "Additional Opportunities" on page 429 for more information.

There are also several fishing derbies held in Valdez every season aimed at pink and silver salmon and halibut.

## Fish Availability

H = High M = Moderate L = Low C = Closed

| Species | | MAY | JUN | JUL | AUG | SEP | OCT |
|---|---|---|---|---|---|---|---|
| **King Salmon** | Shore | L L L L | L M M M | L L L L | L L L L | L L L L | |
| | Boat | L L L L | M M M M | M M M M | M M M M | L L L L | L L L L |
| **Pink Salmon** | Shore | - - - L | L L L M | H H H M | M L L L | L - - - | |
| | Boat | - - L L | L L M H | H H H M | M L L L | | |
| **Chum Salmon** | Shore | | L L L L | M M H M | H M H H | M L L - | |
| | Boat | - - - L | L L L M | M M H H | M M H H | M L L - | |
| **Silver Salmon** | Shore | | | - L L L | L M M H | H M M L | L L L L |
| | Boat | | - - - L | L L L L | M H H H | H M L L | L L - - |
| **Dolly Varden** | Shore | L L L M | M M M M | M M L L | L L L L | | |
| | Boat | L L L L | L L L L | L L L L | L L L L | | |
| **Pacific Halibut** | Shore | L L L L | L L L L | L L L L | L L L L | L L - - | |
| | Boat | L L L L | M M M M | M M M M | M M M M | M M L L | L L L L |
| **Lingcod** | Shore | C C C C | C C C C | L L L L | L L L L | L L L L | |
| | Boat | C C C C | C C C C | M M M M | M M M M | M M M M | L L L L |
| **Rockfish** | Shore | L L L L | L L L L | L L L L | L L L L | L L L L | |
| | Boat | M M M M | M M M M | M M M M | M M M M | M M M M | L L L L |
| **Bottomfish** | Shore | L L L L | M M H H | H H H H | H H H H | H H M M | L L L L |
| | Boat | H H H H | H H H H | H H H H | H H H H | H H H H | M M M M |
| Angling Pressure | Shore | | L L L M | H H H H | H M M H | H M L - | |
| | Boat | L L L L | M M H H | H H H H | H H H H | H M L - | |

## King Salmon

**Rating:** ★½ Poor to fair.

**Season:** January 1 through December 31.

**Timing:** April 15 – August 15; peak June 10 – 20.

**Size:** Average 12 – 25 pounds; up to 45 pounds.

**Tackle:** Spoons, spinners, and bait.

**Tips:** Try chrome lures (especially big spinners) with blue, green, or chartreuse hues. Whole or plug-cut herring fished with a bobber is good. Deep-water spots are best, such as the city docks, but a few kings may be encountered most anywhere within the port, such as off the mouth of clearwater streams.

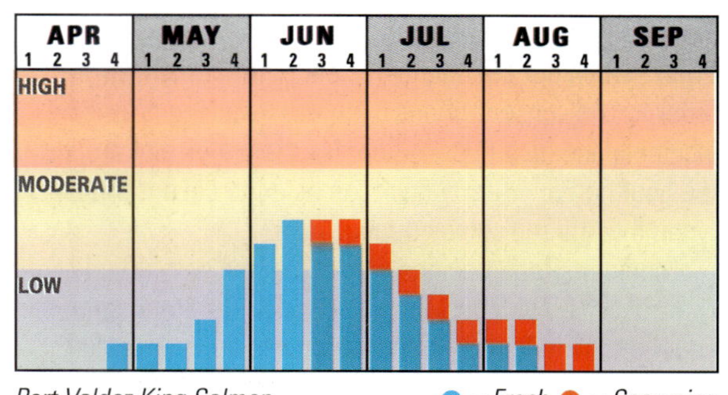


Port Valdez King Salmon

## Pink Salmon

**Rating:** ★★★★★ Excellent.
**Season:** January 1 through December 31.
**Timing:** May 25 – September 5; peak July 1 – 20.
**Size:** Average 3 – 5 pounds, up to 8 pounds.
**Tackle:** Spoons, spinners, flies, and bait.
**Tips:** The most popular color combination lure is chrome and pink, especially when the water is somewhat turbid. Other successful colors include chartreuse, green, blue, red, and orange. If water is very silty, use fluorescent lures. Early in the season, a piece of cut herring fished underneath a bobber is a sure way to hook bright specimens.

Look for multiple fish jumping in order to find a school. The Allison Point area is a hot spot, particularly along the rocky shoreline from the point to the mouth of Solomon Gulch Creek and beyond, but large numbers of salmon may be located throughout the port, such as the town waterfront, including the harbor and city dock.

A great time to look for newly-arriving fish is during an incoming and high tide, yet there is still plenty of action to be had even on low tide at the peak of the run. In some spots, low tides tend to actually concentrate the fish, making for easier catching.

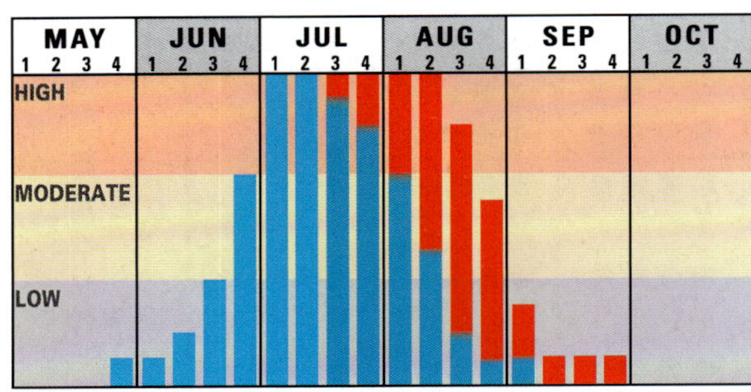


*Port Valdez Pink Salmon* ● = Fresh ● = Spawning

## Chum Salmon

**Rating:** ★★ Fair.
**Season:** January 1 through December 31.
**Timing:** June 1 – September 20; peak July 15 – August 5 (early run) and August 15 – September 5 (late run).
**Size:** Average 6 – 12 pounds, up to 18 pounds.
**Tackle:** Spoons, spinners, flies, and bait.
**Tips:** Search out the mouth of clearwater streams in order to find concentrations of chums, focusing efforts on incoming and high tides; otherwise the waterfront around the boat harbor and city dock can be quite decent fishing when the late run comes through.

Medium-sized lures and flies in chrome with green or chartreuse can be good, fished very slowly at mid-depth to near bottom. In heavily silted water, use fluorescent lure colors or bait. A whole herring rigged with a strike indicator is often a perfect jaw-breaker for finicky chums.

(Courtesy Eagle Eye Images)

*Valdez is the perfect place to go in pursuit of fat, chrome pinks.*

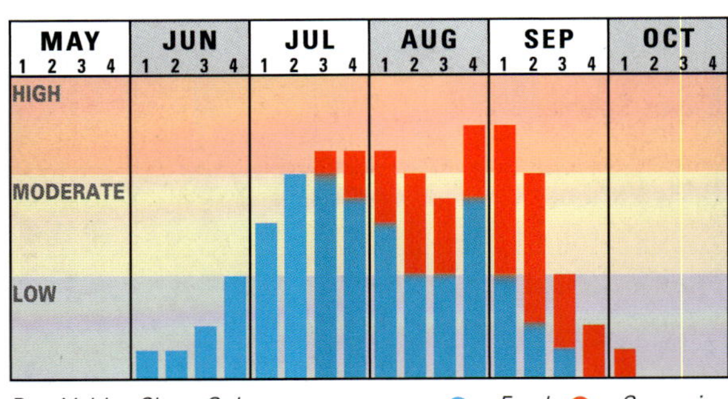


*Port Valdez Chum Salmon* ● = Fresh ● = Spawning

## Silver Salmon

**Rating:** ★★★ Good.
**Season:** January 1 through December 31.
**Timing:** July 5 – November 10; peak August 25 – Sept. 10.
**Size:** Average 6 – 13 pounds, up to 22 pounds.
**Tackle:** Spoons, spinners, flies, and bait.
**Tips:** Use bait such as whole or cut herring with or without a strike indicator, this being the setup of choice for anglers fishing the waterfront near the boat harbor and the city dock. Target water with some depth, some anglers casting from the city dock fishing their bait without a strike indicator right off the bottom.

Within the harbor and along Dayville Road between Solomon Gulch Creek and Allison Point, anglers casting spinners do exceptionally well. Use a size 5 lure with chartreuse, orange, or pink body when water is silty, switching to blue or green when water is clear.

The Allison Point area is a hot spot on incoming and high tides at the height of the run. Fish the point itself just

*Silvers, as with other salmon species in the port, are in their prime here and surf-casting for them can be exceptional. Catching a limit of six fish per day from shore is common at the peak of the run.*

as the tide begins to come in and follow the giant school of salmon through up until high water near the Solomon fish hatchery. Look for fish jumping or breaching surface in order to pinpoint school. This area is also a great spot to flyfish.

Sight fishing for silvers may be possible when fish are close to beach or at the mouth of clearwater creeks or springs, such as the area just south of Allison Point.

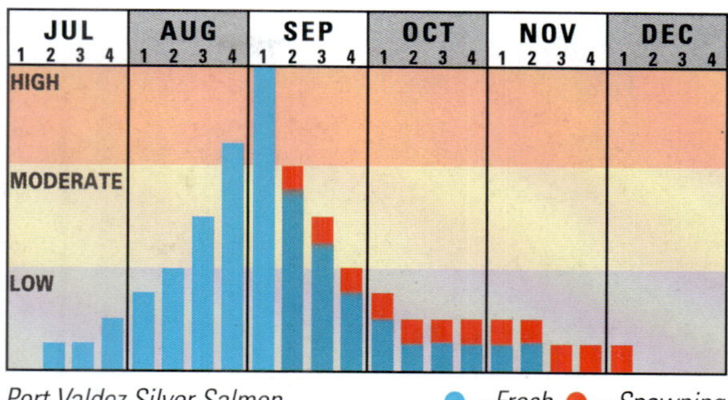


*Port Valdez Silver Salmon* ● = *Fresh* ● = *Spawning*

## Dolly Varden

**Rating:** ★★½ Fair to good.
**Season:** January 1 through December 31.
**Timing:** April 1 – October 5; peak June 1 – July 15.
**Size:** Average 8 – 20 inches, up to 7 pounds.
**Tackle:** Spoons, spinners, flies, and bait.
**Tips:** Small lures and flies resembling baitfish are good. Cast from breakwaters or exposed beach areas on incoming and high tides. Good action can be had at stream mouths, such as Solomon Gulch Creek, where sea-run char can be intercepted in their hunt for juvenile salmon. Starting in mid-summer, some anglers also do well using egg patterns in estuaries where salmon are spawning.

*Anglers surf-casting for Labor Day silvers at Allison Point.*

# Other Productive Fisheries & Additional Opportunities

## ROBE RIVER

**Fishing:** ★★★ **Scenery:** ★★★★★
**Accessibility:** ★★ **Solitude:** ★★★

**Location:** Northern Prince William Sound, 2 miles east of Valdez, 302 miles east of Anchorage.

**Access:** The Richardson Highway provides two main areas of access to the Robe River, one on the lower stream and the confluence with Lowe River, the second at the highway crossing on the middle portion of the stream.

*A. Lower Robe/Mouth* – Milepost 1.5. Southwest on dirt road (by softball field) short distance, turn right 0.5 mile to a "Y," left fork leads 0.4 mile to stream, right fork 0.5 mile to stream mouth. Parking. Not recommended for large RVs. Depending on water levels in the Lowe, hike upstream to confluence area when water is high as it often is in summer and fall.

*B. Richardson Highway Culvert* – Milepost 4.0. Highway crosses stream. Paved parking. Suitable for large RVs space permitting. No established trails but faint footpaths are present.

**Facilities:** None. Some parking available. Town of Valdez has an extensive selection of facilities and other amenities.

**Species:** Red, pink, and silver salmon and Dolly Varden. A few chums and an occasional king present also.

**Restrictions:** Fly-fishing only downstream of the Richardson Highway. Bag limit restrictions on red and silver salmon (1 per day). Consult ADF&G regulations.

**Fishing:** The Robe River is not so much a river as it is a creek. Pouring out of Robe Lake, it is a short, slow-flowing clearwater stream that meanders through a hardwood forest some four miles before emptying into glacial Lowe River. It is a fairly popular early summer and fall fishing spot with locals and receives good runs of several salmon species plus sea-run char.

*(Courtesy Eagle Eye Images)*

The best fishing can be had on the lower stream and the mouth but anglers willing to scout holes farther upstream can do well too. Stretches of the river are also very shallow, perfect for wade fishing and easy crossover.

Salmon are the main target on Robe, starting with early-run reds in May and culminating with the last of the fall silver run in November, making for an extended season of opportunity. Although abundant, the reds do not bite readily due to various reasons, perhaps foremost because of a lack of ideal current flow.

Silvers are available in good numbers throughout the Robe, with small waves of bright salmon moving upstream and easily targeted by anglers, particularly from the road crossing on down. They are the most sought-after species on the river and offer decent to very good action during the height of the autumn season. Some late-run coho destined for spawning areas of mainstem Lowe may be present even until the snow flies and intercepted at the Robe River mouth.

Pinks run very heavy in most years and sometimes inundate the little river completely with their sheer abundance. The best opportunity for fresh or chrome specimens is at the mouth of Robe where it flows into the silty Lowe River.

The chum run here is relatively small and a few fish are taken incidentally to fishing for pinks. Also, a few king salmon do appear in Robe every now and then (June and July), likely the result of stray hatchery fish, and are available for harvest.

Dolly Varden are chiefly present during the spring out-migration from Robe Lake and again in late summer and fall as the char return from sea to feed and spawn in the stream. Large schools of fish are sometimes encountered as they follow the salmon upstream, this being particularly the case in latter July and August when pinks are spawning.

If bushwhacking any distance away from the highway, remember that this is a major salmon spawning stream and bears (both brown and black) are actively feeding here in late summer and fall. Carry protection.

**Red Salmon.** Poor to fair; June 10 – 20; average 4 – 6 pounds. Search stream for schools of fish in areas with some current. Flies.

**Pink Salmon.** Excellent; July 15 – August 1; average 2 – 4 pounds. The best fishing is at mouth of Robe, upper stream is fair to good. Flies.

**Silver Salmon.** Good to excellent; September 5 – 25; average 6 – 12 pounds. Try mouth and deep holes on lower river, fair upstream. Flies.

**Dolly Varden.** Good to excellent; July 20 – November 15; average 8 – 20 inches. Try mouth early in season, upstream in late summer and fall. Flies.

## ADDITIONAL OPPORTUNITIES

*(Courtesy Mark Barnes)*

### Northern Prince William Sound

There is a myriad of fishing opportunities – in both fresh- and saltwater – available from Valdez. The most frequent mode of transportation to known hot spots is by boat, with aircraft landing on beaches near streams and on lakes. Valdez has a significant charter boat fleet offering salmon and bottomfish excursions throughout much of the northern and central portion of Prince William Sound.

Close to town, within Port Valdez, boaters may find excellent fishing for silver and pink salmon (in July/August and July, respectively) at Mineral Creek, Gold Creek, Anderson Bay, and Valdez Narrows, with the latter location also offering some decent fishing for halibut, lingcod, and rockfish. Feeder kings are available from late winter through summer but are not particularly abundant in this area.

Farther out, Valdez Arm is the place to be early on in the salmon season. Sawmill, Jack, and Galena bays are all productive spots for silver salmon in July and August and pink salmon from late June through July. Many of these fish are of hatchery origin and destined for release sites in Valdez, yet some are wild salmon and bound for one of the many smaller streams scattered throughout the arm, including Port Valdez. The various islands and passages in this area also provide fair to good feeder king salmon action year-round with the spring and summer months being tops in terms of catch rate.

Bottomfish are plentiful from spring through fall but perhaps especially so during June and July. Salmon shark are present in July and August and frequently exceed 200 to 300 pounds.

Longer trips to more remote destinations such as Naked Island, Port Fidalgo, Port Gravina, Unakwik Inlet, and the northern sections of Montague and Hinchinbrook islands is possible for those with proper watercraft, such as the guide vessels operating out of Valdez. Some charters specialize in combination trips targeting salmon as well as several species of bottomfish.

Expect legendary halibut, lingcod, and rockfish action with an abundance of prime structure ideal for producing trophy specimens. Halibut in the 300-plus range are always a possibility, as well as lings to 70 pounds or more. Prime months are June through September but fish are available year-round to those braving the off-season weather, which can be very unpredictable at times.

Silver, pink, and chum salmon are in the area from June into September and significant numbers can often be located in bays or coves that are influenced by a clearwater stream. Feeder kings are taken year-round with peak catches from April to August in most areas of the sound.

Salmon sharks are abundant in these parts and usually

found wherever and whenever there are concentrations of salmon present. Often weighing several hundred pounds, they are most prevalent from July into September. A few outfits specialize in shark hunting.

Dolly Varden are locally abundant in many parts of Prince William Sound. Look for them in coves and bays during June and July, and in streams from July into October. Certain streams that support good salmon spawning runs yield spectacular sea-run char action on ultra-light gear. Additionally, the short coastal drainages on Hinchinbrook Island host small but productive populations of cutthroat trout (and salmon).

## Wildlife in and around Valdez

The marine waters, beaches, stream banks, and forest in the Valdez area teems with a surprising variety of animals, from huge sea lions to large coastal brown bears, that are seen on a daily basis during the brief summer and fall months. They make for great viewing at times and can be fairly predictable in terms of when and where they may be observed.

It is without a doubt the presence of fish – especially salmon – that drive these creatures to come right close or even into this community, quite often competing with people in their quest for this protein-rich food supply. In fact, some of these animals are quite brazen about it, pushing their way into locations frequented by anglers to snatch fish off stringers, steal a fighting salmon off a line, or scavenge for scraps. As in all human/wild animal encounters, maintaining a respectful and proper distance is the key to continued safety and enjoyment.

Sea lions and harbor seals are abundant in Port Valdez waters and may be spotted swimming in and around the Valdez small boat harbor and along the shoreline of Dayville Road to Allison Point. From the beginning of July and the arrival of pink salmon to the middle of September and the last of the silver run, dozens of seals can be observed working the briny, some animals even coming within a few yards of unsuspecting anglers.

A couple of the better spots to see them up close is below the fish cleaning station off the Ferry Dock in front of town and at the mouth of Solomon Gulch Creek.

Bears are a special treat around Valdez and may be found anywhere there are salmon, such as spawning streams. The hours of dawn and dusk make for best

*A 1,000-pound sea lion patrols high tide of lower Solomon Gulch Creek right below the hatchery at Dayville Road. This is a great spot to observe these large animals catch their fill of salmon and usually a half-dozen or more may be seen at any one time. Harbor seals may also be present.*

spotting opportunities, yet some animals may venture out at any time during the day.

Black bears are the most common, frequently seen along creeks and sloughs from near city center all around the port to Allison Point and beyond. The fish viewing platform at Crooked Creek and the tidewater lands along Dayville Road are popular places to spot them.

Less common are brown bears. Mainly inhabiting the waterways of Lowe River Valley, a few animals do come close to town and are sighted scouting salmon spawning streams along Dayville Road as well as the beach areas around Allison Point. Anglers in particular should exercise caution in these places, especially during low light hours.

## Salmon Viewing

Most any clearwater stream draining into Port Valdez will have runs of salmon during the summer and fall months. However, there are a couple of spots that do offer great viewing potential.

Crooked Creek: This little tidewater stream at Milepost 0.9 Richardson Highway, only minutes from downtown Valdez, produces surprisingly sizable salmon runs with pinks peaking during the month of August and chums from mid-August into early September. Viewing platform present with interpretive information. A Chugach National Forest Service office is present here as well that has plenty of interesting facts on the salmon life cycle and associated wildlife. Bears usually come here to feed at dawn and dusk.

Solomon Gulch Creek: At mile 4 of Dayville Road next to Allison Point, this semi-glacial stream is the site of hatchery released salmon driving much of the commercial and sport fisheries in the bay area. Pinks can be astoundingly abundant from late July through August and typically blackens stretches of the stream. In latter September on into October, smaller numbers of silvers run the creek. Great spot for close-up photo opportunities of salmon, especially in August. If walking in this area, pay particular attention to bears that commonly roam the waterway as well as the surrounding tidal flats.

Also, the boat harbor in downtown receives a late run of chum salmon, with these fish being abundant along the shoreline through the month of September.

## Fishing in Cordova

For those with a sense of adventure with a little bit more time and money to spend may want to explore the option of extending their journey from Valdez to include a trip to nearby Cordova. Being off the main road system, Cordova is renowned for its great salmon runs and marine fishery.

Access is relatively easy, anglers and other visitors either catching a flight to the typical Alaskan town or, more popularly, hopping on the state-run ferry that spans the eastern portion of Prince William Sound and the North Gulf Coast, connecting the two coastal ports. It is not a daily route so inquiry should be made through the Alaska Marine Highway at www.dot.state.ak.us/amhs/ for latest detailed information, including weekly schedules and pricing policies for bringing vehicles.

Cordova has exceptional natural beauty, sitting on the northern edge of the Pacific Ocean, surrounded by jagged, forest-clad mountains complete with ice fields and glaciers. Although the town is primarily a commercial fishing hub for the Copper River salmon fleet, there are a good number of opportunities for sport fishing on the road system as well.

While surf-casting for salmon and bottomfish may be somewhat limited, a few charters operate out of Cordova that put anglers on to some of the best halibut and feeder king salmon fishing anywhere (peak June to September). The main draw for roadside fishers, however, is Cordova Highway heading out of town. It provides access to several spots featuring good to excellent action for salmon and sea-run trout and char.

Depending on exact location, late May to late July is best for reds, latter July into August for pinks, and mid-August through most of September for silvers. Target Dolly Varden and cutthroat trout in May and again from July to October. There is even a chance to go fish for kings, in June, at a hatchery-release site north of town.

For complete fishing information in and around Cordova, look up the Alaska Department of Fish & Game at www.adfg.alaska.gov/.

*Spawning and dying pink salmon crowd a section of Crooked Creek in early September. The clear and shallow streams of the Valdez area make for perfect salmon viewing locations.*

# Copper Valley & Port Valdez Fishing Derbies and Directory

## FISHING DERBIES

### Valdez Arm

May – September

**Halibut Derby**
**Approximate Dates:** Mid-May to Labor Day weekend.
**Area/Location:** Valdez.
**Prizes/Categories:** Prize for largest king salmon weighed in; also categories in casting expertise.
**Ticket Fees:** Free.
**Note:** Derby is open only to kids younger than 16 years of age.
**Contact Information:** Valdez Fish Derbies, (907) 835-5680; www.valdezfishderbies.com.

July

**Kid's Pink Salmon Derby**
**Approximate Dates:** Mid-May to Labor Day weekend.
**Area/Location:** Valdez.
**Prizes/Categories:** Prize for largest king salmon weighed in; also categories in casting expertise.
**Ticket Fees:** Free.
**Note:** Derby is open to kids younger than 16 years of age.
**Contact Information:** Valdez Fish Derbies, (907) 835-5680; www.valdezfishderbies.com.

July – September

**Silver Salmon Derby**
**Approximate Dates:** Mid-May to Labor Day weekend.
**Area/Location:** Valdez.
**Prizes/Categories:** Prize for largest king salmon weighed in; also categories in casting expertise.
**Ticket Fees:** Free.
**Note:** Derby is open only to kids younger than 16 years of age.
**Contact Information:** Valdez Fish Derbies, (907) 835-5680; www.valdezfishderbies.com.

August

**Women's Silver Salmon Derby**
**Approximate Dates:** Mid-May to Labor Day weekend.
**Area/Location:** Valdez.
**Prizes/Categories:** Prize for largest king salmon weighed in; also categories in casting expertise.
**Ticket Fees:** Free.
**Note:** Derby is open only to kids younger than 16 years of age.
**Contact Information:** Valdez Fish Derbies, (907) 835-5680; www.valdezfishderbies.com.

## FISHING GUIDES & CHARTERS

**Alaska Raft Fishing**
www.alaskaraftfishing.com (907) 255-4601

**Fish Central** *(Valdez)*
www.fishcentral.net (888) 835-5002

**Kingfisher's Perch**
www.alaskakings.com (907) 822-5411

**River Wrangellers**
www.riverwrangellers.com (888) 822-3967

## CAMPGROUNDS & RV PARKS

**Eagle's Rest R.V. Park**
www.eaglesrestrv.com (907) 835-2373

## TACKLE & SPORTING GOODS

**Fish Central** *(Valdez)*
www.fishcentral.net (888) 835-5002

# Copper Valley & Port Valdez Directory

**Valdez Prospector Outfitters** *(Valdez)*
www.prospectoroutfitters.com (800) 795-7372

## AIR TAXI OPERATIONS

**Copper Valley Air Service**
www.majesticadventures.com (866) 570-4200

## FISH PROCESSORS

**Easy Freeze, Inc.** *(Valdez)*
www.easyfreezeinc.com (907) 835-4208

## WATERCRAFT RENTALS

**Fish Central** *(Valdez)*
www.fishcentral.net (888) 835-5002

## GENERAL INFORMATION

**AHTNA, Inc.**
www.ahtna-inc.com (907) 822-3476

**Alaska Department of Fish & Game** *(Glennallen)*
www.sf.adfg.state.ak.us (907) 822-3309

**Chugach National Forest**
www.fs.fed.us/r10/chugach/ (907) 743-9500

**Greater Copper Valley Chamber of Commerce**
www.traveltoalaska.com (907) 822-5555

**Valdez Convention & Visitors Bureau**
www.valdezalaska.org (907) 835-2984

**Valdez Fish Derbies**
www.valdezfishderbies.com (907) 835-5680

**Visitor Information Center and National Parks & Monuments Headquarters** (907) 822-5234

*The tidal flatlands near Allison Point at the head of the port as seen on low tide. Here a commercial fishing vessel waits for the annual but brief silver salmon opener, usually held right after the Labor Day weekend. This is mainly a cost-recovery operation to maintain the Solomon Gulch Fish Hatchery.*

# Appendix & Index

## "COMBAT" FISHING

In many of the better roadside locations it is common to see anglers lining up shoulder-to-shoulder in their quest for salmon. Particularly the king salmon fisheries are crowded yet red and silver salmon draw plenty of attention as well. While the term Combat Fishing implies physical confrontation of some form, such occurrences are relatively rare. A much better expression is Carnival Fishing since people for the most part do get along just fine and the mood more festive than anything else. Many anglers actually prefer to fish in such areas since it brings out camaraderie and friendly competition.

Another reason why not to avoid the more popular fisheries is because of the fish. Where there are a lot of other anglers there are usually a lot of salmon too. Even in such close company it is very possible to experience superb action. Do not be shy in joining in; excellent fishing often awaits.

Discussed here are the finer points of participating in "combat" fishing.

### The Combat Zone

• **Always wear hip-boots or waders.** If every other angler stands in line knee-deep in water, do not proceed to cast behind them while standing on dry land. This is considered very impolite since space is very limited and someone casting from shore will take up the space of two or three people standing in water ten feet out. Also, fishing lines are much more prone to tangle up.

• **Always wear Polaroid glasses.** Flying hooks and sinkers make this a very hazardous area for unprotected eyes. Serious and blinding injuries occur several times every season so do not even think of participating in these fisheries without adequate protection.

• **Always ask permission to join.** When anglers stand elbow-to-elbow and a slot is seemingly open, approach nearby anglers and ask for permission to step in. Often an angler will step out of the line for a minute to land a fish or do some other necessary task. Do not steal another angler's slot. If an angler leaves the area or sits down to take a break, the slot is fair game. Ask the departing angler if the slot is open. Remember, slots are not private property that can be reserved or held indefinitely. Slots are only opportunities.

• **Always use appropriate gear.** Heavier than normal gear is advised under crowded conditions, 20-pound test line being the minimum. If fishing for king salmon, use at least 30-pound test. Do not try to set a new line record on ultra-light gear or attempt to play the fish to complete exhaustion. Most salmon (except kings) hooked in combat zones should be landed within a few minutes at the most. This is not so much a sport fishery as it is a consumptive fishery. Many anglers come here to stock their freezers for the winter.

• **Always yield to anglers with fish on.** An angler battling a fish has the right-of-way over other anglers on the river. Do not cast if a nearby angler has a fish on. Give plenty of space and offer to help by netting the fish.

• **Always alert other anglers.** It is highly recommended to alert surrounding anglers when a fish is hooked. A shout of "Fish On!" or simply "Fish!" will suffice. Communicate with fellow anglers which direction the fish is heading by calling out "Coming down!" or "Coming up!"

*Although crowds may be nearby, it is still very possible to find stretches of river to fish by oneself.*

• **Always break off a snagged fish.** A salmon hooked elsewhere than in the mouth is difficult to control and will take much longer to bring in. Insisting on landing a fouled-hooked fish may not be popular. Cup the reel, hold the pole horizontal, and point the tip towards the fish, and yank straight back. Either the line will break or the hook will come free. Other anglers will often assist in releasing a fish that is illegally hooked.

• **Always cast in rhythm.** If surrounding anglers are making short casts or "flips," do likewise. Making long casts in such a situation will only create line tangles and unhappy neighbors.

• **Always look behind before casting.** Before automatically making that next cast, look behind to see if anyone is in the way. Ignorance of surroundings is not an excuse; prevention of injuries is the key.

And finally: Always show courtesy and respect. Crowded conditions demand patience, understanding, and a sense of humor.

## Avoiding the Crowds

There are many opportunities for a solitary experience, even on some of the more famous salmon "hot spots" on the road system. All it takes is some thorough planning and determination.

The following are some hints and tips to consider in making that fishing trip more peaceful and rewarding.

• **Avoid peak season.** Most all waters have definite peak times of the season when anglers gather, this being when salmon runs are at their height. Try the "shoulder" part of the season, just as the fish are starting to come in or towards the tail end of the runs. There will be less people – and probably less fish – but the action can still be very worthwhile.

• **Hike away from road crossings.** The vast majority of anglers do not bother to walk more than a few hundred yards at most from any road crossing. Oftentimes, hiking upstream or down from the elbow-to-elbow crowds will put an angler into undisturbed waters and eager fish.

• **Fish in September or later.** After Labor Day, the roadside salmon crowds typically evaporate. It is the beginning of autumn and people start thinking about hunting and other activities. This can be the most rewarding time to go fishing in Alaska since late-run silver salmon, trout, char, and grayling are in abundance in many areas.

• **Scout less popular waters.** Research lesser-known drainages in search of solitude and fish. There are a multitude of streams that do not draw the crowds seen on neighboring waters. Reasonably enough, these streams may not have the huge numbers of fish to support a major fishery yet being alone on a hole with dozens of salmon and other species is all it takes to make a successful trip. Do the homework.

*Get away from the road crossings in order to find solitude.*

*(Courtesy River Wrangellers)*

# FISH CARE

## Field Care of Fish

As many anglers fish Alaska waters in a combination of fun, relaxation, and for food purposes, the proper care of a catch is extremely important to ensure quality meat. The following points illustrate the best steps in bringing home a meal.

**Step 1: Kill fish quickly.** After having landed a fish that is to be used as food, kill it right away. Keeping it alive will only promote stress and add acidic values to the flesh. Dispatch fish using a sharp knife, sticking the knife into the neck area.

**Step 2: Bleed the fish.** Immediately after having killed the fish, bleed it by cutting the throat. Hold fish vertically, head down, so blood drains properly. Leaving blood in the meat speeds development of bacteria. Remove gills or fish head as well.

**Step 3: Keep fish in a cool place.** Always keep fish out of the sun. Tie fish to a stringer and leave in the water. If air temperatures permit, wrap fish in a wet burlap bag and keep it in a shaded spot. Do not use plastic garbage bags for fish storage.

**Step 4: Clean the fish.** Remove all entrails, including dark matter along the spine, which is a major promoter of bacterial growth.

**Step 5: Chill fish properly.** Keeping the meat iced down in a cooler will greatly limit the spread of bacteria. Surround fish with ice, including inside body cavity. Be certain to drain water from cooler frequently. Standing water is a major cause of meat spoilage.

**Step 6:** Under no circumstances should a fish be on ice for longer than three days before being frozen. Preferably, freeze fish the same day it was caught or at least the day after.

## Shipping Fish

Anglers wanting to ship fish home or to friends and relatives have two options. First, expedited shipping of seafood products is big business in Alaska and many businesses such as lodges and guide services offer this amenity to their clients. Second, anglers primarily fishing Alaska on their own can purchase packaging material from a retail store, package the fish on their own, and take the fish box to a reputed shipper such as FedEx or UPS for next day delivery.

(Courtesy Shasta Miller)

*Young angler, Spencer, learns how to properly cut salmon fillets from his father, Ronnie Gunter.*

Packaging material normally consists of a sturdy cardboard box with either a heavy wax interior coating or styrofoam to keep fish cold and prevent fluid leaks.

## Transporting Fish

As with shipping fish, there are a few options for transporting. Again, a heavy cardboard box with either a wax coated or styrofoam interior is highly popular and can be purchased in many larger retail stores. One of the best ways to transport fish is by using a sturdy cooler with a locking lid. Make certain to wrap pieces of fish in clear plastic to contain possible fluid leaks.

This latter transportation tool is increasingly popular with anglers, although make sure to tape up cooler sufficiently as to not allow for handles to protrude out.

Do not use dry ice, as this form of cooling agent is not allowed by airlines. Preferably, fish should be frozen although a few pieces of fresh or unfrozen fish can be placed between the other pieces. Mark "Perishable" on outside of box or cooler.

## HIRING A GUIDE

(Courtesy Beverley Bailey)

For many first-timers to Alaska, sorting out all the stream locations with its myriad of species, tackle, gear, regulations, and timing concerns is a formidable task. While it is true that many waters have only very generic rules governing them, others – such as the Kenai River – have extensive and complicated laws that seem overwhelming even for the most die-hard local angler.

It is often recommended that anglers new to Alaska hire a guide for at least a few hours to a day for "hands-on" instruction in how to target one or more species of game fish properly. The few dollars spent on a guide can definitely assist in building a knowledge base that quickly becomes invaluable for the rest of the trip and future excursions as well.

There are several guide outfits advertised throughout this book that are proven in their profession. Make use of them. If in doubt over skills necessary to catch fish in a certain area, consider hiring one of these skilled professionals to gain experience and catch some fish as well. It is worth having a guide familiarize oneself with the fishery before attempting to go it alone.

Ask questions and be willing to listen to the guide. These people practically live on the water throughout the season and many of them reside in area towns and communities with their families year-round. Local guides having spent decades on a particular drainage are a wealth of information concerning fish and their habits, water and weather conditions, identifying trends, proper methods and techniques, and the multitude of details specific to where they work.

Another big factor in hiring a guide is accessibility. If physically challenged by age or other factors impairing the ability to get around easily, fishing from a boat with a guide makes sense. A few boats are even designed to facilitate wheelchair use.

## SPORT FISHING RULES & REGULATIONS

The Alaska Department of Fish & Game (ADF&G), through laws enacted by the Alaska Board of Fisheries (ABOF), publishes several booklets annually, each according to designated statewide regions, describing open and closed seasons and areas, gear and tackle restrictions, bag and possession limits, and many other points to follow in order to protect fish populations from potential harm or over-exploitation.

The Kenai Peninsula, Anchorage Area, Matanuska and Susitna valleys, and Prince William Sound are covered in the Southcentral Alaska Sport Fishing Regulations Summary, while Copper Valley is found in the Region III: Arctic-Yukon-Kuskokwim and Upper Copper/ Susitna River Sport Fishing Regulations Summary.

Due to the ever changing and near unpredictable nature of fishing rules and regulations, they have been practically omitted from this book to prevent the content of becoming prematurely outdated. Furthermore, certain locations have very specific and lengthy restrictions

*Keep an eye out for posted information concerning emergency openings and closures for certain waters and species.*

that would almost require a chapter in itself to list and explain. The information contained within all chapters in this book adheres to current laws; however, any set rule and regulation is, of course, subject to change through "emergency orders" posted by the ADF&G and the ABOF.

In addition, it is entirely the responsibility of the individual angler to have knowledge and be in complete compliance of existing rules and regulations for the water he or she intends to fish. In other words, ignorance is not an excuse. Always consult a current and official copy of the sport fishing regulations before making that first cast. Copies are available in many retail outlets in Anchorage as well as towns and communities along the road. If in doubt or have any questions, contact the nearest ADF&G office. Contact information is listed below.

**ADF&G Division of Sport Fish**
P. O. Box 25526
Juneau, AK 99802-5526
(907) 465-4180
www.sf.adfg.state.ak.us/statewide/sf_home.cfm

## WILDLIFE

Southcentral Alaska has healthy populations of moose, bear, sheep, beaver, wolf, and various kinds of birds, all of which are present to some degree or another along the road system. In fact, many of these animals flourish around the mountains and valleys of several of the fishing locales described in this book. Anglers fishing these waters for any extent of time are quite likely to come across at least one or two large types of animals common in the region – moose and bear. Avoid close encounters, which could promote a life-threatening situation.

- **Bears.** Although usually encountered in more remote areas away from major roads and highways, bears do surprisingly often come into more urban settings, as well as high-use waters. Most numerous along clearwater streams from mid-summer into fall, they are often spotted scouting for salmon in the shallows at dawn and dusk as they forage on fish to fatten up for the long, cold winter ahead.

For information on how to avoid potentially dangerous encounters, see next page.

- **Moose.** Very abundant and frequently seen crossing roads and feeding on water lilies, grass, and leaves near lakes, ponds, and small streams, moose at first appear as quite slow and docile creatures. Do not misjudge them as being less of a potential threat because they are herbivores. Keep a safe distance as moose are able to cover a lot of ground surprisingly fast. There have been a few deadly attacks involving moose so respect is warranted as with any other wild animal.
- **Caribou.** Locally abundant in Southcentral Alaska,

*(Courtesy Beverley Bailey)*

with populations centered around the mountain passes of upper Matanuska Valley and the flatlands near Kenai and Soldotna. While almost the size of moose, negative confrontations are exceedingly rare. Usually not found along salmon streams.
- **Sea Lions.** These large marine mammals may appear very intimidating when observed up close due to their sheer size (up to 1,500 lbs. or more) and somewhat territorial disposition complete with loud guttural noises such as growls and barks. Can be observed in all coastal ports, including tidal areas of rivers and streams.
- **Eagles.** One of the largest wild birds on the continent, eagles are abundant at many roadside locations. Usually most numerous along the coast and can be observed all year long.

Report all aggressive animals to the proper authorities, such as the US Fish & Wildlife Service, Alaska Department of Fish & Game, or local police departments.

## BEAR AWARENESS

The following information and tips need to be understood and heeded when fishing Alaska's waterways. Keep in mind, however, that these are only general recommendations and statements that have proven helpful; bears are still highly unpredictable and their behavior dictates this.

• **Make plenty of noise**. This is the single most important factor in bear country and will alert these animals. Clapping hands, singing, intermittent shouts, talking loudly, and blowing a whistle helps. Bear bells are fine too but remember, like the suggestions above, they are only meant to alert, not necessarily scare away. A very important distinction! A surprised bear can be a dangerous bear.

• **Walk, look, and listen carefully**. On trails along salmon streams especially, do not run. Blind corners and tall vegetation along the trail are places to use increased caution. Slow down the walking pace, eyes scanning sides of trail as well as pathway up front and behind. Listen for noises that are out of the ordinary, and look out for brush or grass suddenly moving; these may be warning signs from a bear for anglers to keep a distance.

• **Day vs. night.** Bears are not known for having sharp vision. This realization is important, particularly if planning to do some low-light or night-time fishing. Even animals that have no apparent interest in people at full daylight may change their behavior drastically once it turns dark in order to compensate for their changed perception of safety and security of themselves and/or their young. Animals may bluff charge or lash out more readily. Also be aware of the fact that bears are usually the most active along salmon streams at dawn and again at dusk.

• **Fish is food.** As with many anglers, bears are on the water to fish in order to eat. Their life depends on being able to catch and consume protein-rich fish – in particular salmon – so they are able to survive the winter. When people catch a lot of fish, bears are at attention, this being particularly the case in locations where a lot of anglers and fish congregate. Bears quickly learn to associate anglers with fish and so the cycle begins. Aft first they manage to steal a meal of salmon on a stringer, then grabbing a fish being landed by an angler, and finally bluff charging someone carrying a fish. It can be a very volatile situation as anglers are always encouraged by officials not to give up their salmon to a bear as to make worse out of a bad habit. If a bear approaches, make sure any fish is kept out of sight and in possession. Retreat to a safe location.

• **Carry protection or deterrents.** These days it is common for anglers to have a canister of pepper spray in their possession. It has shown to be a fairly effective deterrent against charging bears or ones that are simply too curious. If fishing a distance away from the road, bring more than one canister just in case. If spray has been used, move out of the area or to a safe location. If carrying a firearm, positively know how to use it. High-caliber handguns or revolvers may work if a precise shot is placed; better option is a proper rifle. Remember, a wounded bear is the worst possible nightmare.

*Bears squaring off, heads low with ears folded back, is a warning sign that they feel threatened. Keep a distance.*

• **Bring a friend or two.** There is increased safety in numbers, this being especially the case if venturing away from the car a few miles or more or in low-light conditions. Bears are hesitant to approach or charge a group of anglers, although a few individual animals will still test their own courage. Make noise and stand together to show mass and strength.

• **Be aware of surroundings.** Never get too absorbed with fishing or catching fish as not to notice an approaching bear. They are stealthy animals and often able to get within yards of unsuspecting anglers before being noticed. Stay calm.

• **If charged, hold ground.** Do not run from a charging bear. This may be easier said than done. Bears are predators and may see a person fleeing as an invitation to come closer or even prompt physical contact. Back away slowly and talk softly.

• **Get informed and share.** Read materials what exactly to do if attacked and additional precautions that can be taken. There is a slew of material available. Talk to other anglers if they have seen any bears and inform likewise of curious or aggressive animals. Be aware of posted information of recent bear activity and plan accordingly.

## FISHING WITH KIDS

When fishing with kids, safety and security is of utmost importance, which may or may not preclude some locations that qualify as child friendly. "Combat" fishing spots, are not the best places to bring a child as crowds and high activity of flying hooks and sinkers is a problem. Also, rivers are often very swift, deep, and cold with not much footing and could be downright dangerous. It only takes a moment of inattention for disaster to strike.

While most any water can be perceived as being safe for a child as long as he or she is accompanied by one or more responsible adults, there are a certain few specific places that are known to be ideal for kids to practice their newfound angling skills while being surrounded by an environment mostly free of obvious dangers.

*Children are usually fascinated with all things nature but may react differently to fighting, landing, and seeing these creatures up close. The key is repeated exposure in a positive manner, making it fun and not a chore.*

### Top Places

- **Lakes.** Most any lake is safe for kids as there is a lack of current, making these waters much less intimidating. Unless the child is within arms reach and adult is paying attention at all times, a life vest should be worn.
- **Bird Creek** (Seward Highway, page 117). This is a good spot to take kids, but only before the crazed salmon crowds arrive in August. Try around high tide for pinks, chums, and char. Stay off the mud near creek mouth. Beware of tidal movements.
- **Resurrection Creek** (Seward/Hope Highway, page 131). The tidal area of this stream has a great beach where kids can roam and fish. Any time can be good but best near high tide. Mainly pinks, chums, and char in July and August.
- **Resurrection Bay** (Seward Highway, page 179). Good place to let kids catch flounders, cod, and other bottomfish. Plenty of open spaces. For salmon and char, go to stream mouths at Spring and Tonsina creeks and around Lowell Point.
- **Russian River** (Sterling Highway, page 161). Avoid the mouth during peak season where the crowds are and go to the middle river sections. Plenty of reds and trout to practice on. June to September good, August best as water is low and shallow and fish abundant.
- **Kenai River** (Sterling Highway, page 195 and 209). The middle and lower river sections are ideal for kids with beach areas or boardwalks present. Hit the river in August on an even-number year and find millions of pinks. Moose River confluence, Morgan's Landing, the Soldotna Visitor Center, and Cunningham Park are favorite kid locations.
- **Kasilof River** (Sterling Highway, page 221). For youngsters, the lower river section around Crooked Creek Campground is best as the current is normally very slow and there is a large open beach area by the river at the People Hole. Safest and best time is in May and June during king and early red season. Char and steelhead also present.
- **Anchor and Ninilchik Rivers, Deep Creek** (Sterling Highway, pages 251, 235, and 243). These small waters are ideal for youngsters, particularly in July and August when water levels are low. Find pinks, silvers, and char; go to lower stream sections at tidewater. Beware of tidal movements.
- **Dudiak Lagoon** (Sterling Highway, page 267). Little can go wrong here; wide open beach, few snags, and schooling salmon. Go first part of June for kings and again in August for silvers. Some days are designated kids-only days.
- **Kachemak Bay** (Sterling Highway, page 259). Right at the end of the road on Spit Road (Land's End), there is a large beach area by the pilings that is great for first-timers. Tons of bottomfish available mid-May to early September.
- **Eklutna Tailrace** (Glenn/Old Glenn Highways, page 307). Very little to no current makes this spot ideal for youngsters; head upstream to get away from people. August is good time for silvers.
- **Willow, Sheep, and Montana Creeks** (Parks Highway, pages 323, 331, and 337). The mouth of these streams are considered safe with good opportunities in latter July and August for pinks, chums, and silvers. The highway crossings also worthwhile on Willow and Sheep.
- **Port Valdez** (Richardson Highway, page 421). Fishing at the ferry dock in town or Allison Point beach and mouth of Solomon Gulch Creek off Dayville Road can be hot for pinks in July and silvers at the August-September split.

# Creators & Contributors

## GUNNAR PEDERSEN

*AUTHOR*

(Courtesy Eagle Eye Images)

A year-round resident of Anchorage for well over three decades, Gunnar is an avid outdoorsman with a passion for – most notably – fishing but also many other interests such as cross-country skiing, backcountry hiking, wildlife viewing, martial arts, and photography.

Born and raised in Scandinavia, he started his life-long infatuation with nature at an early age, his first cast made from a small rubber raft, targeting perch and walleye on one of Sweden's many lowland lakes. His interest in the activity grew exponentially with the introduction to the incredible marine fisheries of the Norwegian fjords and their myriad of bottomfish and soon carried on to include the finesse of fly-fishing the region's many blue-ribbon salmon and trout streams as well as gorgeous alpine lakes for grayling and char.

Fishing in Alaska soon became a reality, spending a day catching silvers out of Deep Creek on the Kenai Peninsula. More trips were to follow, this time landing a variety of salmon in the tributaries of the Susitna River and catching grayling on the fly at Tangle Lakes.

After moving to Alaska in 1979, interest in fishing peaked. For the next few decades, spring was spent chasing hungry trout and sea-run char and the first returning king salmon, summers dedicated to a plethora of sporting species in both salt and fresh water. Ballistic steelhead and rainbows along with late-run silvers were the focus during the fall months, and the winters meant endless hours outstretched on lake ice peering down a hole in anticipation of a nibble.

However, in addition to the obvious personal rod-and-reel pursuit, Gunnar also made a brief stint as a commercial fisherman in Bristol Bay. Later, he guided anglers from around the world to destinations on the Kenai Peninsula and the west side of Cook Inlet. With varying perceptions of Alaska, its fisheries, and the numerous biological aspects of the multitude of species, an interest blossomed that reached far outside the constraints of simply the angling sport itself.

Decades were spent documenting in exhaustive detail the habits and distribution of sporting species in a wide range of watersheds, which greatly enhanced the overall understanding and appreciation for this incredible resource and the people and animals that interact with it. With this "worldview" of fishing in mind, Gunnar enjoys the rich variety of angling means and methods and does not conform strictly to one specific style of gear, always exploring different techniques and options, be it tricking salmon on a dry fly or surf-casting for halibut.

Having written and published four books and co-authored a fifth, Gunnar has traveled around the whole state and fished many of its waters, focusing mainly on locations, species, and opportunities available along Alaska's highways and byways. He has also authored (but not printed) three other titles that may one day see the light of day. In addition, Gunnar have had several articles published, both in the U.S. as well as in Europe.

## SHAYLA DA SILVA

*PHOTO CONTRIBUTOR*

Born in Brazil to a large family, Shayla attended the college of Elefante Branco where she obtained a degree in accounting. Adventure called and trips to Europe, China and the USA soon followed after graduation. In Europe, Shayla vacationed in Italy, Romania, France, England, and Norway and lived for a time in Rome and Bucharest. Though Brazil lies closer to the equator and Alaska closer to the pole, she was drawn to the adventures of The Last Frontier.

After living in New York and Florida for several years, Shayla ventured north to Alaska and met Gunnar, her future husband, in 1989. Today she holds a teaching degree in Shaolin Kung Fu as well as being a second-degree black belt in Shotokan Karate. Her skills are put into practice by teaching children's Kung Fu classes and studying Karate at the Boys and Girls Club.

When Gunnar took Shayla along to explore nature and sport with rod and reel, she at first wanted nothing to do with fishing. She eventually caught her first fish, a 20-pound king salmon from the Ninilchik River, then cried when it came out of the water. However, her attitude towards the activity soon changed and she became very apt at chasing and hooking all five species of salmon and many other game species, preferring the fly rod to other gear.

Along with an interest in sport fishing came a love for the outdoors in general, in particular photography, and has contributed a good portion of images of scenery, wildlife, fish, and fishing to Gunnar's popular publications.

After having amassed tens of thousands of pictures from her journeys through the state, she launched a new business–Eagle Eye Images & Photography–specializing in outdoor motives.

Besides martial arts, photography, and fishing, Shayla also enjoys walking, jogging, and yoga and continues her education by taking classes at the University of Alaska to achieve her goal of obtaining a Masters degree. Shayla's life philosophy is to gain strength from her faith in God and Jesus Christ, and strives to practice compassion and understanding, respect, loyalty, and love. Shayla truly is an Alaskan from the South.

## ROY & BEVERLEY BAILEY

*PHOTO CONTRIBUTORS*

*(Courtesy Roy & Beverley Bailey)*

Husband and wife Roy and Beverley Bailey, live in a small town in the picturesque Vale of Glamorgan, South Wales (United Kingdom) with their two sons. They first met in 1984 and both being artistic and strongly passionate about nature the two soon became inseparable; Roy frequently painting portraits of birds of prey whilst Beverley particularly enjoyed drawing mammals in graphite.

In Roy's early years he has enjoyed fishing since the age of seven, predominantly surf casting off the varied beaches around his home for cod, pollack and the like and wider a field, including regular boat trips around many of the UK ports, for species including tope and bass. Living near the Bristol Channel where productive and abundant coastal fishing is easily accessible was a key factor whilst Roy's other passion is birds of prey; he was a keen falconer and breeder for some time which led him into a life long passion for wildlife and interest in conservation.

Beverley has always enjoyed wildlife and particularly mammals and with Roy was able to develop a keener interest, extending this into bird watching on hiking and fishing expeditions. It was Roy's keen interest in fishing and Beverley's ambition to observe brown bears in the wild that led them both to only one location possible...

The couple's first trip to Alaska in 2005 resulted in unimaginable success and did not disappoint in providing a range opportunities where so many species were available and where so many techniques in catching them could be adopted, from fly-fishing to surf casting, spinning and boat fishing, with each method providing its own challenges and successes. This was where a double act really made the difference and between them both they were able to utilize their photographic skills both to record each other's achievements and broaden their portfolios. Such experiences include landing a 90-pound skate from shore, observing a juvenile bald eagle catching his fish supper, photographing the belted kingfisher along the riverside whilst landing jumping rainbows and viewing the beluga whales close to shore – the list endless.

Like any successful trip, planning a venture to Alaska demanded a great deal of research and it was at this point that they discovered the extremely useful guides created to assist "The Highway Angler", from author and fisherman Gunnar Pedersen. This became the 'bible' on the journey and not to be without. Each year brings 'unfinished business'; a species of fish not yet caught, a bird on the list not yet seen, friends to return to visit and hence the journey to Alaska has now become an annual event.

## KELSEY GRAY

*DESIGNER*

*(Courtesy John Borland)*

Kelsey is a lifelong Alaskan and has been fishing in Alaska ever since he was old enough to hold a fishing pole. His childhood was spent fishing the Little Susitna River while living in Houston, often with just a twig and whatever line he could find on the beach. He has spent most of his time fishing in Whittier, and can still be seen on the cliffs hoping to spot that next school of ocean fresh reds or silvers. When not climbing he is busy rock climbing and travelling. He is the author of the Alaska Rock Climbing Guide and co-author of the Alaska Bouldering Guide. It is as common to see him on the cliff's on the Seward Highway or Hatcher Pass as it is to find him on the river.

After attending West Anchorage High School he was further educated at Alaska Pacific University and the University of Alaska Anchorage where he has studied art and design in his continuing effort to earn a degree. He has owned several businesses in Anchorage including a photography, graphics, and video business called Azimuth Adventures Photography. His newest business is Azimuth Fitness Studio in Anchorage. Kelsey also currently holds an instructor's degree in Kung Fu, the equivalent to black belt.

When not writing books or finding jobs in video and photography he is usually travelling. He has been to over 49 different countries and more than 30 of the United States, preferring to spend his time in hostels and tents than high-priced hotels. He uses that opportunity for photography and gathers all his pictures on his personal website at:

**Kelsey Gray Photography**
www.kelseygrayphotography.com

## DENNIS MUSGRAVES

*PHOTO CONTRIBUTOR*

(Courtesy Dennis Musgraves)

Dennis started fishing about 20 years ago in Alaska while stationed at Fort Wainwright with the U.S. Army. He moved back up to Alaska with his family upon retiring from the military, knowing that there were too many unfinished angling pursuits in the Great Land.

A true, die-hard Alaskan angler, he spends about 100 days each year on the water, including fresh, salt, and frozen, from the northern reaches of the Arctic Circle to the Southern Capital City of Juneau, and has fished all over the state. The majority of his time fishing is spent in the Susitna and Copper River Valleys. In addition, Dennis really enjoys taking photos and documenting all fishing experiences and relates "it's a great way to share with others and do a little story telling."

Angling achievements include receiving recognition for several outstanding catches by the State of Alaska with honorary Catch & Release trophy fish certificates, including a 20-inch arctic grayling and a 38-inch steelhead trout.

Dennis has been recognized by In-Fisherman Magazine with a Master Angler Award for two regional areas for catches of coho salmon, steelhead trout, and chinook salmon. He is also a member of two International Game Fish Association angling slam clubs, by achieving the requirements for Royal Salmon Slam Club and North Pacific Slam Club.

Dennis currently resides in North Pole with his wife and two daughters, Hannah, Meghan and Kelly respectfully.

## OTHER CONTRIBUTORS

The following individuals and organizations have kindly offered their support by contributing photos/images for use in this book:

Bryan Allen
Jake Askren
Roy & Beverley Bailey
Mark Barnes
Dan Brown
Greg Brush
Chris Cox
Ron Ely
Kelsey Gray
Carl Jappe
Shems Jud
Mike Kersbergen
Mike Larsen
Robert Laskodi
Rene Limeres
Eric & Suzie Mauro
Shasta Miller
Dennis Musgraves
Arild Nielsen
Christian Ornt
Einar Pedersen
Ingrid Pedersen
Jack Rambac
Matt Raye
Max Root
Shayla da Silva
Gary Sinnhuber
Stephen Stidham
Jeff Varvil
Monte Waite
Alaska Clearwater Sportfishing
Alaska Wildland Adventures
Crackerjack Sportfishing
Eagle Eye Images
EZ Limit Guide Service
King of the River
Kingfisher's Perch
Miller's Landing
Mystic Waters Fly Fishing
River Wrangellers

# Advertiser Directory & Index

# Index

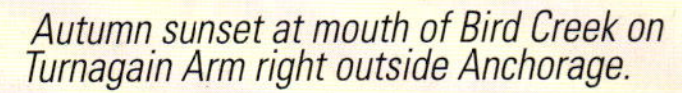
*Autumn sunset at mouth of Bird Creek on Turnagain Arm right outside Anchorage.*